Poetry
for Students

National Advisory Board

for *Poetry* *Students*

Presenting Analysis, Context, and Criticism on Commonly Studied Poetry

Volume 23

Anne Marie Hacht, Project Editor

Foreword by David Kelly

THOMSON

GALE

Detroit • New York • San Francisco • San Diego • New Haven, Conn. • Waterville, Maine • London • Munich

Poetry for Students, Volume 23

Project Editor
Anne Marie Hacht

Editorial
Ira Mark Milne

Rights Acquisition and Management
Edna Hedblad, Lisa Kincade, Ronald Montgomery

Manufacturing
Drew Kalasky

Image Research & Acquisition
Jillean McCommons, Robyn Young

Imaging and Multimedia
Lezlie Light, Mike Logusz

Product Design
Pamela A. E. Galbreath

Vendor Administration
Civie Green

Product Manager
Meggin Condino

For permission to use material from this product, submit your request via Web at http://www.gale-edit.com/permissions, or you may download our Permissions Request form and submit your request by fax or mail to:

Permissions Department
Thomson Gale
27500 Drake Rd.
Farmington Hills, MI 48331-3535
Permissions Hotline:

248-699-8006 or 800-877-4253, ext. 8006
Fax: 248-699-8074 or 800-762-4058

Since this page cannot legibly accommodate all copyright notices, the acknowledgments constitute an extension of the copyright notice.

While every effort has been made to ensure the reliability of the information presented in this publication, Thomson Gale does not guarantee the accuracy of the data contained herein. Thomson Gale accepts no payment for listing; and inclusion in the publication of any organization, agency, institution, publication, service, or individual does not imply endorsement of the editors or publisher. Errors brought to the attention of the publisher and verified to the satisfaction of the publisher will be corrected in future editions.

ISBN 0-7876-6962-8
ISSN 1094-7019

Printed in the United States of America
10 9 8 7 6 5 4 3 2 1

Table of Contents

Guest Foreword
"Just a Few Lines on a Page"
by David J. Kelly ix

Introduction xi

Literary Chronology xv

Acknowledgments xvii

Contributors xix

Allegory
(by Mary Jo Bang) 1
    Author Biography 2
    Poem Text 2
    Poem Summary 3
    Themes 4
    Style 6
    Historical Context 6
    Critical Overview 7
    Criticism 8
    Further Reading 13

All It Takes
(by Carl Phillips) 14
    Author Biography 14
    Poem Text 15
    Poem Summary 15
    Themes 17
    Style 19
    Historical Context 19
    Critical Overview 20
    Criticism 20
    Further Reading 27

The Art of the Novel
(by Natasha Sajé) 28
    Author Biography 28
    Poem Text 29
    Poem Summary 29
    Themes 30
    Style 32
    Historical Context 32
    Critical Overview 33
    Criticism 33
    Further Reading 39

Aurora Leigh
(by Elizabeth Barrett Browning) 40
    Author Biography 41
    Poem Summary 41
    Themes 43
    Style 45
    Historical Context 45
    Critical Overview 47
    Criticism 48
    Further Reading 53

The Crime Was in Granada
(by Antonio Machado) 54
    Author Biography 55
    Poem Text 55
    Poem Summary 56
    Themes 57
    Style 58
    Historical Context 59
    Critical Overview 61
    Criticism 61
    Further Reading 86

An Elementary School Classroom in a Slum
(by Stephen Spender) 87
    Author Biography 87
    Poem Text 88
    Poem Summary 89
    Themes 90
    Style 92
    Historical Context 93
    Critical Overview 94
    Criticism 95
    Further Reading 109

Fiddler Crab
(by Josephine Jacobsen) 110
    Author Biography 111
    Poem Text 111
    Poem Summary 112
    Themes 113
    Style 115

Historical Context 116
Critical Overview 117
Criticism 118
Further Reading 136

It's like This
(by Stephen Dobyns) 137
    Author Biography 138
    Poem Text 138
    Poem Summary 139
    Themes 140
    Style 142
    Historical Context 143
    Critical Overview 145
    Criticism 146
    Further Reading 155

Lake
(by Rosanna Warren) 156
    Author Biography 157
    Poem Text 158
    Poem Summary 158
    Themes 160
    Style 161
    Historical Context 162
    Critical Overview 163
    Criticism 163
    Further Reading 169

Lepidopterology
(by Jesper Svenbro) 170
    Author Biography 171
    Poem Text 171
    Poem Summary 172
    Themes 173
    Style 174
    Historical Context 175
    Critical Overview 176
    Criticism 176
    Further Reading 183

Lost in Translation
(by James Merrill) 184
    Author Biography 185
    Poem Summary 185
    Themes 188
    Style 189
    Historical Context 189
    Critical Overview 191
    Criticism 192
    Further Reading 201

The Nerve
(by Glyn Maxwell) 202
    Author Biography 202

Poem Summary 203
Themes 204
Style 206
Historical Context 207
Critical Overview 208
Criticism 209
Further Reading 220

Pine
(by Kimiko Hahn) 222
Author Biography 223
Poem Text 223
Poem Summary 224
Themes 225
Style 227
Historical Context 228
Critical Overview 229
Criticism 230
Further Reading 238

Practice
(by Ellen Bryant Voigt) 239
Author Biography 239
Poem Text 240
Poem Summary 240
Themes 241
Style 243
Historical Context 244

Critical Overview 244
Criticism 245
Further Reading 255

September
(by Joanne Kyger) 257
Author Biography 257
Poem Text 258
Poem Summary 259
Themes 260
Style 261
Historical Context 261
Critical Overview 263
Criticism 263
Further Reading 267

Song: To Celia
(by Ben Jonson) 269
Author Biography 269
Poem Text 270
Poem Summary 271
Themes 272
Style 273
Historical Context 273
Critical Overview 275
Criticism 276
Further Reading 285

Glossary 287

Cumulative Author/Title Index 307

*Cumulative Nationality/Ethnicity
Index* 315

Subject/Theme Index 321

Cumulative Index of First Lines 327

Cumulative Index of Last Lines 333

Just a Few Lines on a Page

I have often thought that poets have the easiest job in the world. A poem, after all, is just a few lines on a page, usually not even extending margin to margin—how long would that take to write, about five minutes? Maybe ten at the most, if you wanted it to rhyme or have a repeating meter. Why, I could start in the morning and produce a book of poetry by dinnertime. But we all know that it isn't that easy. Anyone can come up with enough words, but the poet's job is about writing the *right* ones. The right words will change lives, making people see the world somewhat differently than they saw it just a few minutes earlier. The right words can make a reader who relies on the dictionary for meanings take a greater responsibility for his or her own personal understanding. A poem that is put on the page correctly can bear any amount of analysis, probing, defining, explaining, and interrogating, and something about it will still feel new the next time you read it.

It would be fine with me if I could talk about poetry without using the word "magical," because that word is overused these days to imply "a really good time," often with a certain sweetness about it, and a lot of poetry is neither of these. But if you stop and think about magic—whether it brings to mind sorcery, witchcraft, or bunnies pulled from top hats—it always seems to involve stretching reality to produce a result greater than the sum of its parts and pulling unexpected results out of thin air. This book provides ample cases where a few simple words conjure up whole worlds. We do not actually travel to different times and different cultures, but the poems get into our minds, they find what little we know about the places they are talking about, and then they make that little bit blossom into a bouquet of someone else's life. Poets make us think we are following simple, specific events, but then they leave ideas in our heads that cannot be found on the printed page. Abracadabra.

Sometimes when you finish a poem it doesn't feel as if it has left any supernatural effect on you, like it did not have any more to say beyond the actual words that it used. This happens to everybody, but most often to inexperienced readers: regardless of what is often said about young people's infinite capacity to be amazed, you have to understand what usually does happen, and what could have happened instead, if you are going to be moved by what someone has accomplished. In those cases in which you finish a poem with a "So what?" attitude, the information provided in *Poetry for Students* comes in handy. Readers can feel assured that the poems included here actually are potent magic, not just because a few (or a hundred or ten thousand) professors of literature say they are: they're significant because they can withstand close inspection and still amaze the very same people who have just finished taking them apart and seeing how they work. Turn them inside out, and they will still be able to come alive, again and again. *Poetry for Students* gives readers of any age good practice in feeling the ways poems relate to both the reality of the time and place the poet lived in and the reality of our emotions. Practice is just another word for being a student. The information given here helps you understand the way to read poetry; what to look for, what to expect.

With all of this in mind, I really don't think I would actually like to have a poet's job at all. There are too many skills involved, including precision, honesty, taste, courage, linguistics, passion, compassion, and the ability to keep all sorts of people entertained at once. And that is just what they do with one hand, while the other hand pulls some sort of trick that most of us will never fully understand. I can't even pack all that I need for a weekend into one suitcase, so what would be my chances of stuffing so much life into a few lines? With all that *Poetry for Students* tells us about each poem, I am impressed that any poet can finish three or four poems a year. Read the inside stories of these poems, and you won't be able to approach any poem in the same way you did before.

David J. Kelly
College of Lake County

Introduction

Purpose of the Book

The purpose of *Poetry for Students* (*PfS*) is to provide readers with a guide to understanding, enjoying, and studying poems by giving them easy access to information about the work. Part of Gale's "For Students" Literature line, *PfS* is specifically designed to meet the curricular needs of high school and undergraduate college students and their teachers, as well as the interests of general readers and researchers considering specific poems. While each volume contains entries on "classic" poems frequently studied in classrooms, there are also entries containing hard-to-find information on contemporary poems, including works by multicultural, international, and women poets.

The information covered in each entry includes an introduction to the poem and the poem's author; the actual poem text (if possible); a poem summary, to help readers unravel and understand the meaning of the poem; analysis of important themes in the poem; and an explanation of important literary techniques and movements as they are demonstrated in the poem.

In addition to this material, which helps the readers analyze the poem itself, students are also provided with important information on the literary and historical background informing each work. This includes a historical context essay, a box comparing the time or place the poem was written to modern Western culture, a critical overview essay, and excerpts from critical essays on the poem. A unique feature of *PfS* is a specially commissioned critical essay on each poem, targeted toward the student reader.

To further aid the student in studying and enjoying each poem, information on media adaptations is provided (if available), as well as reading suggestions for works of fiction and nonfiction on similar themes and topics. Classroom aids include ideas for research papers and lists of critical sources that provide additional material on the poem.

Selection Criteria

The titles for each volume of *PfS* were selected by surveying numerous sources on teaching literature and analyzing course curricula for various school districts. Some of the sources surveyed included: literature anthologies; *Reading Lists for College-Bound Students: The Books Most Recommended by America's Top Colleges*; textbooks on teaching the poem; a College Board survey of poems commonly studied in high schools; and a National Council of Teachers of English (NCTE) survey of poems commonly studied in high schools.

Input was also solicited from our advisory board, as well as educators from various areas. From these discussions, it was determined that each volume should have a mix of "classic" poems (those works commonly taught in literature classes) and contemporary poems for which information is often hard to find. Because of the interest in expanding the canon of literature, an emphasis was also placed on including works by international, multi-cultural, and women poets. Our advisory board members—educational professionals—helped pare down the list for each volume. If a work was not selected for the present volume, it was often noted as a possibility for a future volume. As always, the editor welcomes suggestions for titles to be included in future volumes.

How Each Entry Is Organized

Each entry, or chapter, in *PfS* focuses on one poem. Each entry heading lists the full name of the poem, the author's name, and the date of the poem's publication. The following elements are contained in each entry:

- **Introduction:** a brief overview of the poem which provides information about its first appearance, its literary standing, any controversies surrounding the work, and major conflicts or themes within the work.

- **Author Biography:** this section includes basic facts about the poet's life, and focuses on events and times in the author's life that inspired the poem in question.

- **Poem Text:** when permission has been granted, the poem is reprinted, allowing for quick reference when reading the explication of the following section.

- **Poem Summary:** a description of the major events in the poem. Summaries are broken down with subheads that indicate the lines being discussed.

- **Themes:** a thorough overview of how the major topics, themes, and issues are addressed within the poem. Each theme discussed appears in a separate subhead and is easily accessed through the boldface entries in the Subject/Theme Index.

- **Style:** this section addresses important style elements of the poem, such as form, meter, and rhyme scheme; important literary devices used, such as imagery, foreshadowing, and symbolism; and, if applicable, genres to which the work might have belonged, such as Gothicism or Romanticism. Literary terms are explained within the entry, but can also be found in the Glossary.

- **Historical Context:** this section outlines the social, political, and cultural climate *in which the author lived and the poem was created*. This section may include descriptions of related historical events, pertinent aspects of daily life in the culture, and the artistic and literary sensibilities

of the time in which the work was written. If the poem is a historical work, information regarding the time in which the poem is set is also included. Each section is broken down with helpful subheads.

- **Critical Overview:** this section provides background on the critical reputation of the poem, including bannings or any other public controversies surrounding the work. For older works, this section includes a history of how the poem was first received and how perceptions of it may have changed over the years; for more recent poems, direct quotes from early reviews may also be included.

- **Criticism:** an essay commissioned by *PfS* which specifically deals with the poem and is written specifically for the student audience, as well as excerpts from previously published criticism on the work (if available).

- **Sources:** an alphabetical list of critical material used in compiling the entry, with full bibliographical information.

- **Further Reading:** an alphabetical list of other critical sources which may prove useful for the student. It includes full bibliographical information and a brief annotation.

In addition, each entry contains the following highlighted sections, set apart from the main text as sidebars:

- **Media Adaptations:** if available, a list of audio recordings as well as any film or television adaptations of the poem, including source information.

- **Topics for Further Study:** a list of potential study questions or research topics dealing with the poem. This section includes questions related to other disciplines the student may be studying, such as American history, world history, science, math, government, business, geography, economics, psychology, etc.

- **Compare and Contrast:** an "at-a-glance" comparison of the cultural and historical differences between the author's time and culture and late twentieth century or early twenty-first century Western culture. This box includes pertinent parallels between the major scientific, political, and cultural movements of the time or place the poem was written, the time or place the poem was set (if a historical work), and modern Western culture. Works written after 1990 may not have this box.

- **What Do I Read Next?:** a list of works that might complement the featured poem or serve as a contrast to it. This includes works by the same author and others, works of fiction and nonfiction, and works from various genres, cultures, and eras.

Other Features

PfS includes "Just a Few Lines on a Page," a foreword by David J. Kelly, an adjunct professor of English, College of Lake County, Illinois. This essay provides a straightforward, unpretentious explanation of why poetry should be marveled at and how *Poetry for Students* can help teachers show students how to enrich their own reading experiences.

A Cumulative Author/Title Index lists the authors and titles covered in each volume of the *PfS* series.

A Cumulative Nationality/Ethnicity Index breaks down the authors and titles covered in each volume of the *PfS* series by nationality and ethnicity.

A Subject/Theme Index, specific to each volume, provides easy reference for users who may be studying a particular subject or theme rather than a single work. Significant subjects from events to broad themes are included, and the entries pointing to the specific theme discussions in each entry are indicated in **boldface**.

A Cumulative Index of First Lines (beginning in Vol. 10) provides easy reference for users who may be familiar with the first line of a poem but may not remember the actual title.

A Cumulative Index of Last Lines (beginning in Vol. 10) provides easy reference for users who may be familiar with the last line of a poem but may not remember the actual title.

Each entry may include illustrations, including a photo of the author and other graphics related to the poem.

Citing Poetry for Students

When writing papers, students who quote directly from any volume of *Poetry for Students* may use the following general forms. These examples are based on MLA style; teachers may request that students adhere to a different style, so the following examples may be adapted as needed.

When citing text from *PfS* that is not attributed to a particular author (i.e., the Themes, Style, Historical Context sections, etc.), the following format should be used in the bibliography section:

"Angle of Geese." *Poetry for Students.* Eds. Marie Napierkowski and Mary Ruby. Vol. 2. Detroit: Gale, 1998. 5–7.

When quoting the specially commissioned essay from *PfS* (usually the first piece under the "Criticism" subhead), the following format should be used:

Velie, Alan. Critical Essay on "Angle of Geese." *Poetry for Students.* Eds. Marie Napierkowski and Mary Ruby. Vol. 2. Detroit: Gale, 1998. 7–10.

When quoting a journal or newspaper essay that is reprinted in a volume of *PfS,* the following form may be used:

Luscher, Robert M. "An Emersonian Context of Dickinson's 'The Soul Selects Her Own Society.'" *ESQ: A Journal of American Renaissance* Vol. 30, No. 2 (Second Quarter, 1984), 111–16; excerpted and reprinted in *Poetry for Students*, Vol. 1, eds. Marie Napierkowski and Mary Ruby (Detroit: Gale, 1998), pp. 266–69.

When quoting material reprinted from a book that appears in a volume of *PfS,* the following form may be used:

Mootry, Maria K. "'Tell It Slant': Disguise and Discovery as Revisionist Poetic Discourse in 'The Bean Eaters,'" in *A Life Distilled: Gwendolyn Brooks, Her Poetry and Fiction.* Edited by Maria K. Mootry and Gary Smith. University of Illinois Press, 1987. 177–80, 191; excerpted and reprinted in *Poetry for Students*, Vol. 2, eds. Marie Napierkowski and Mary Ruby (Detroit: Gale, 1998), pp. 22–24.

We Welcome Your Suggestions

The editor of *Poetry for Students* welcomes your comments and ideas. Readers who wish to suggest poems to appear in future volumes, or who have other suggestions, are cordially invited to contact the editor. You may contact the editor via E-mail at: *ForStudentsEditors@thomson.com.* Or write to the editor at:

Editor, *Poetry for Students*
Thomson Gale
27500 Drake Rd.
Farmington Hills, MI 48331–3535

Literary Chronology

1572: Ben Jonson is born sometime between May 1572 and January 1573 in London, England.

1616: Ben Jonson's "Song: To Celia" is published.

1637: Ben Jonson dies.

1806: Elizabeth Barrett Browning is born on March 6.

1857: Elizabeth Barrett Browning's "Aurora Leigh" is published.

1861: Elizabeth Barrett Browning dies on June 29 in Florence, Italy.

1875: Antonio Machado is born on July 26 near Seville, Spain.

1908: Josephine Jacobsen is born on August 19 in Cobourg, Ontario, Canada.

1909: Stephen Spender is born on February 28 in London, England.

1926: James Ingram Merrill is born on March 3 in New York City, New York.

1934: Joanne Kyger is born on November 19 in Vallejo, California.

1936: Antonio Machado's "The Crime Was in Granada" is published.

1939: Antonio Machado dies on February 22 in Collioure, France.

1941: Stephen Dobyns is born on February 19 in Orange, New Jersey.

1943: Ellen Bryant Voigt is born on May 9 in Danville, Virginia.

1944: Jesper Svenbro is born on March 10 in Landskrona, Sweden.

1946: Mary Jo Bang is born in Waynesville, Missouri.

1950: Josephine Jacobsen's "Fiddler Crab" is published.

1953: Rosanna Warren is born July 27 in Fairfield, Connecticut.

1955: Kimiko Hahn is born in Mount Kisco, New York.

1955: Natasha Sajé is born on June 6 in Munich, Germany.

1959: Carl Phillips is born on July 23 in Everett, Washington.

1962: Glyn Maxwell is born in Hertfordshire, England.

1964: Stephen Spender's "An Elementary School Classroom in a Slum" is published.

1974: James Merrill's "Lost in Translation" is published.

1975: Joanne Kyger's "September" is published.

1976: James Merrill's wins the Pulitzer Prize for *Divine Comedies*, the collection containing "Lost in Translation."

1980: Stephen Dobyns's "It's like This" is published.

1995: Stephen Spender dies on July 16 in London, England.

1995: James Merrill dies in Tucson, Arizona.

1999: Jesper Svenbro's "Lepidopterology" is published.

1999: Kimiko Hahn's "Pine" is published.

2002: Ellen Bryant Voigt's "Practice" is published.

2002: Glyn Maxwell's "The Nerve" is published.

2003: Josephine Jacobsen dies on July 9 in Cockeysville, Maryland.

2003: Rosanna Warren's "Lake" is published.

2004: Carl Phillips's "All It Takes" is published.

2004: Mary Jo Bang's "Allegory" is published.

2004: Natasha Sajé's "The Art of the Novel" is published.

Acknowledgments

The editors wish to thank the copyright holders of the excerpted criticism included in this volume and the permissions managers of many book and magazine publishing companies for assisting us in securing reproduction rights. We are also grateful to the staffs of the Detroit Public Library, the Library of Congress, the University of Detroit Mercy Library, Wayne State University Purdy/Kresge Library Complex, and the University of Michigan Libraries for making their resources available to us. Following is a list of the copyright holders who have granted us permission to reproduce material in this volume of *Poetry for Students (PfS)*. Every effort has been made to trace copyright, but if omissions have been made, please let us know.

COPYRIGHTED MATERIALS IN *PfS*, **VOLUME 23, WERE REPRODUCED FROM THE FOLLOWING PERIODICALS:**

The Antioch Review, v. 61, winter, 2003. Copyright © 2003 by the Antioch Review Inc. Reproduced by permission of the Editors.—*Black Issues in Higher Education*, v. 19, April 25, 2002. Reproduced by permission.—*Boulevard*, v. 18, 2003. © Copyright 2003 by Opojaz, Inc. Reproduced by permission.—*Essays in Criticism*, v. 18, January, 1968 for "The Poetry of Ben Jonson," by G. A. E. Parfitt. Copyright © 1968 Oxford University Press. Reproduced by permission of the publisher and the author.—*The Explicator*, v. 59, spring, 2001. Copyright © 2001 by Helen Dwight Reid Educational Foundation. Reproduced with permission of the Helen Dwight Reid Educational Foundation, published by Heldref Publications, 1319 18th Street, NW, Washington, DC 20036-1802.—*Greece & Rome*, v. 11, May, 1942 for "A Song from Philostratos," by J. Gwyn Griffiths. Copyright © 1942 Oxford University Press. Reproduced by permission of the publisher and the Literary Estate of J. Gwyn Griffiths.—*Hispanofila*, v. 117, May, 1996. Reproduced by permission.—*The Hollins Critic*, v. 22, April, 1985. Copyright 1985 by Hollins College. Reproduced by permission.—*Library Journal*, v. 130, January, 2005. Copyright © 2005 by Reed Elsevier, USA. Reprinted by permission of the publisher.—*Modern Language Notes*, v. 113, 1998. Copyright © 1998 The Johns Hopkins University Press. Reproduced by permission.—*The New Criterion*, v. 14, November, 1995 for "Joy and Terror: The Poems of Josephine Jacobsen," by Elizabeth Spires. Copyright © 1995 by The Foundation for Cultural Review. Reproduced by permission of the author./ December, 2003 for "Out on the Lawn," by William Logan. Reproduced by permission of the author.—*New Letters*, summer, 1987 for "The Mystery of Faith: An Interview with Josephine Jacobsen," by Evelyn Prettyman. © copyright 1987 The Curators of the University of Missouri. All rights reserved. Reproduced by permission of the publisher, the Literary Estate of Josephine Jacobsen, and Evelyn Prettyman.—*Ploughshares*, v. 24, winter, 1989–1999 for "An Interview with Stephen Dobyns," by Laure-Anne

Contributors

Bryan Aubrey: Aubrey holds a PhD in English and has published many articles on contemporary poetry. Entry on *September*. Original essays on *The Art of the Novel* and *September*.

Jennifer Bussey: Bussey holds a master's degree in interdisciplinary studies and a bachelor's degree in English literature. She is an independent writer specializing in literature. Entries on *The Art of the Novel* and *Practice*. Original essays on *Allegory*, *The Art of the Novel*, and *Practice*.

Carol Dell'Amico: Dell'Amico is an instructor of English literature and composition. Entry on *The Crime Was in Granada*. Original essay on *The Crime Was in Granada*.

Joyce Hart: Hart is a published author and freelance writer. Entries on *It's like This*, *The Nerve*, and *Pine*. Original essays on *It's like This*, *The Nerve*, *Pine*, and *Practice*.

Neil Heims: Heims is a writer and teacher working in Paris. Original essays on *It's like This* and *Lake*.

Pamela Steed Hill: Hill is the author of a poetry collection, has published widely in literary journals, and is an editor for a university publica-

tions department. Entry on *Lake*. Original essays on *Lake* and *Lepidopterology*.

David Kelly: Kelly is an instructor of creative writing and literature at two colleges in Illinois. Entry on *All It Takes*. Original essays on *All It Takes* and *Lepidopterology*.

Lois Kerschen: Kerschen is a public school administrator and freelance writer. Entry on *Aurora Leigh*. Original essays on *Aurora Leigh* and *Practice*.

Anthony Martinelli: Martinelli is a Seattle-based freelance writer and editor. Entries on *An Elementary School Classroom in a Slum* and *Fiddler Crab*. Original essays on *An Elementary School Classroom in a Slum*, *Fiddler Crab*, and *Pine*.

Wendy Perkins: Perkins is a professor of American and English literature and film. Entries on *Lost in Translation* and *Song: To Celia*. Original essays on *Lost in Translation* and *Song: To Celia*.

Scott Trudell: Trudell is an independent scholar with a bachelor's degree in English literature. Entries on *Allegory* and *Lepidopterology*. Original essays on *Allegory*, *Lepidopterology*, and *Pine*.

Allegory

Mary Jo Bang
2004

Since the publication of *Apology for Want* in 1997, the vivid and distinctive poetry of Mary Jo Bang has been praised by critics and readers alike. Her work is characterized by a light rhythm and a playful tone that draw the reader into her unique world of images and sounds. Bang is also recognized, however, as a subtle, intellectual, and crafty poet who addresses ambitious philosophical themes and maintains careful control over the implications of her varied language.

"Allegory," originally published in the *Paris Review* but included in the 2004 collection *The Eye like a Strange Balloon*, is a superb example of Bang's balance between playful verse and profound themes. Like the other poems in Bang's collection, it is written in the tradition of *ekphrasis*, in which a poem is highly visual or makes close reference to a work of visual art. Interacting with Philip Guston's 1975 painting of the same name, "Allegory" brings Guston's imagery to life in a narrative structure and develops a unique reading of the painting's significance. The poem comments on the position of the artist in society as well as other abstract themes, such as mythology, fate, and identity. Playing with quirky language that climaxes at a point of bleak despair, Bang delights readers at the same time as she provokes them to question how artists interact with reality and how humankind approaches death and destruction.

Mary Jo Bang © Nina Subin

Author Biography

Born in the central Missouri town of Waynesville in 1946, Mary Jo Bang grew up in St. Louis. She went to college at Northwestern University, where she earned a bachelor's degree and then a master's degree in sociology, graduating summa cum laude. Bang also earned a bachelor's degree in photography from the University of Westminster in central London and a master's in creative writing at Columbia University.

Bang's first collection of poetry, the intellectual and allusive *Apology for Want*, was published in 1997 and awarded the Breadloaf Bakeless Prize as well as the Great Lakes Colleges Association New Writers Award. In 2001, Bang went on to publish *The Downstream Extremity of the Isle of Swans*, which won the University of Georgia Press Contemporary Poetry Series Competition. That same year, she published another collection of poetry entitled *Louise in Love*, which received an Alice Fay di Castagnola Award from the Poetry Society of America and is known for its intelligent wordplay. *The Eye like a Strange Balloon*, which includes "Allegory," was published in 2004.

An accomplished editor and professor as well as a poet, Bang has been a poetry editor at the *Boston Review* since 1995. She has received numerous awards and fellowships, including a Pushcart Prize, a Discovery/The Nation Award, a Hodder Fellowship at Princeton University, and a grant from the Guggenheim Foundation. Bang lives in St. Louis, where she is a professor of English at Washington University.

Poem Text

Let us console you.
Music's the answer.
Of couse, we're caught
in this sphere
Where it doesn't much matter   5

whether our song reaches
the ear of Prometheus or not.
He's adamantly chained
to the mountaintop.
Every morning, there's eagle,   10

a beak and a claw on the back.
Such an ache. Somatognosis
is the sixth sense.
What does it feel like
to inch one's way forward?   15

These are the questions.
Dawn on its knees
crawls toward knowledge.
More of us are coming.
All of the adoring.   20

Every day is another broken
tie on a red-leather shoe. A Who-
do-you-wish-to-be?
Tonight we'll be content
with whomever we think we are.   25

The door of the car will click-close
And off we'll go.
In the back is the Jackself
we might have been.
What's the degree of remove   30

between the one at the top
of Pie Mountain
and the tourist motel
at the bottom with its pool
of aqua attitude and blue inflatables?   35

Some vigorous enactment.
Is it three o'clock or twelve fifteen?
Either is only an estimate.
Myth equals fate
plus embellishment.   40

The wheel is set in motion
when our eyes are on the moment.
Later, we drive on four wheels
to the carnival and line up
for a ticket; the air is rife   45

with summer.
The kinesthetic lift of a foot
from the floor

forces itself to be felt.
The actors are standing   50

against a wall and watching
it all unfold. Look,
they say, at the minutiae sutured
to the spine of the climax
when somebody opens the door   55

on the side of despair
and looks out onto death
and destruction.

Poem Summary

Lines 1–7

"Allegory," which is organized into eleven five-line stanzas and a final three-line stanza, begins with the speaker offering to "console" the reader with music. The speaker's use of the pronoun "us" implies that there is a group of artists behind the creative effort, as at the bottom of Guston's painting, which lists "composer," "painter," "sculptor," and "poet" on what appears to be a wave.

In lines 3 through 5, the speaker begins to say that "we" (probably referring, again, to the categories of artists listed in Guston's painting) are "caught in / this sphere" (possibly referring to the earth) where it does not matter whether Prometheus hears their song. This sentence continues over the stanza break between lines 5 and 6, which is an example of *enjambment*, a convention in which a phrase continues from one line of poetry to the next.

Lines 8–15

Lines 8 through 11 explain the predicament of Prometheus, a Titan from classical mythology known as a great friend to humankind. After Prometheus stole fire from the gods and gave it to humans, Zeus punished him by chaining him to a mountain in the Caucasus, where every day an eagle descended and ate out his liver (which would regenerate by night). The speaker alludes to this eagle's biting and clawing into Prometheus's back and how it would ache. Then the speaker claims that "Somatognosis," or the awareness of one's own body, is the "sixth sense." In lines 14 and 15, the speaker asks what it feels like to "inch one's way forward," and it is likely that this line refers to Guston's painting, in which a man seems to be painstakingly moving against a pile of objects that appear to be shoes.

Lines 16–25

The speaker begins the fourth stanza by stating, "these are the questions," although it is not entirely clear what the questions are. The speaker then envisions a metaphor, or a comparison in which one object or idea is substituted for another, in which dawn is someone crawling toward knowledge. If "More of us" refers to the artists mentioned earlier in the poem, the short statements in lines 19 and 20 suggest that poets, composers, sculptors, and painters, described as "the adoring," are also "coming," presumably toward knowledge.

In the fifth stanza, the speaker moves from these thoughts into a meditation on identity. Comparing each day to a broken tie on a red shoe and a "Who- / do-you-wish-to-be," the speaker suggests that each day offers the possibility of tying the shoe in any manner and assuming a variety of roles. It is worth noting, however, that it seems to be the same "red-leather shoe" each day. The speaker then states that "we," which again could refer to the artists of Guston's painting, will be content with whichever identity "we" *think* "we" have, which suggests that the "we" do not know what this identity actually is.

Lines 26–36

In lines 26 through 29, the speaker seems to be describing what will happen "Tonight," when the "we" drive off, carrying the "Jackself / we might have been" in the backseat. These lines are important for a number of reasons, including the suggestion that "we" is literally one or two people, since they are sitting in the front of the car. It is also interesting to note that an alternate identity is included with the "we" in the car, as though the "we" comprises both what it is and what it might have been.

Line 30 begins a somewhat mysterious question that is carried over into the seventh stanza, asking the "degree of remove" between someone or something on top of "Pie Mountain" versus a "tourist motel" below with a "pool / of aqua attitude and blue inflatables." This question does not seem to make much sense until one examines Guston's painting, in which mathematical objects such as a ruler, sphere, cube, triangle, and the digits 5, 4, 3, 2, 1 are grouped in the upper left, somewhat in the distance. In the foreground are a man with a cigarette and, above his face, a strange blue object or creature that may be what the speaker calls an "inflatable."

Line 36 then seems to comment on the previous lines with the statement (which is possibly ironic): "Some vigorous enactment." This implies that the relationship between whoever is on top of

Pie Mountain and whoever is in the tourist motel is an enactment, or an acting out of something. If the statement is ironic (irony occurs when the literal meaning is the direct opposite of the implied meaning), the speaker would be suggesting that the enactment is actually weak and lacking energy.

Lines 37–46

Line 37's question about the time refers to Guston's painting, in which the central male figure's watch has hands of equal length that could be indicating either 3:00 or 12:15. The speaker then says that either time is "only an estimate" and comments that "Myth," which resonates with the title of Bang's poem, is not just "fate" but "embellishment." Since these three lines emphasize that it is difficult to measure or plan time and fate, they highlight Bang's theme of the artist's distance from reality.

In stanza 9, the narrative seems to return to the nighttime car journey mentioned earlier. The "wheel" that is set in motion in line 41 is another reference to Guston's painting, where what seems to be the wheel of a car is in front of the central male figure's face. Together, lines 41 and 42 comment on the inability to see something fixedly while "our eyes are on the moment." In lines 43 through 46, "we" are driving on four wheels, presumably in the car from stanza 6, to a carnival, where "we" line up for a ticket. The air is "rife," or abundant with, summer, although it is apparently still the nighttime.

Lines 47–58

In lines 47 and 48, a foot lifts from the floor in a motion the speaker describes as "kinesthetic," or sensing one's own muscular movements, a concept similar to that of "somatognosis," mentioned earlier. This motion "forces itself to be felt," which perhaps means that the other, somewhat vague beings or identities in the car can feel it. It may also suggest that the driver has taken his or her foot off the pedal and the car is coming to a stop.

The actors mentioned in line 50 may refer to the artists listed at the bottom of Guston's painting, and once again they are portrayed as observers somewhat distanced from reality. They observe "minutiae," or trivial details, that are "sutured," or stitched, to the "spine of the climax." This intriguing description is somewhat vague and abstract, but it may refer to the pile of objects at the lower right of Guston's painting. In any case, the artists are looking at this climax, which is also the climax of the poem itself, when someone opens the car door "on the side of despair / and looks out onto death /

and destruction." The nature of this death and destruction is not specified, nor is it clear why one side of the car faces "despair." Once again, however, Bang is very likely referring to the everyday, but also rather bleak and disturbing pile of objects in Guston's painting, from which the four types of artists are firmly separated.

Themes

Art and the Artist

"Allegory" is closely related to Philip Guston's 1975 painting of the same name, and Bang's commentary directly engages with the central themes of the painting. For example, both works provide a self-conscious commentary on the predicament of the artist, including the artist's relationship to reality and society. Bang produces a somewhat unique perspective on Guston's painting, but she follows his lead in analyzing the dilemma of the visual, literary, and musical artist as he or she attempts to approach the world and create art.

Since it includes a scroll that reads "The Artists" at the top, and what appears to be a wave at the bottom with the words "composer," "painter," "sculptor," and "poet," Guston's painting suggests that the figures in the body of the piece are artists at work. Similarly, Bang suggests that the people represented by the pronouns "we" and "us" may be artists whose function ranges from "consol[ing]," to "adoring," to producing a "vigorous enactment," to looking out "onto death / and destruction." As in Guston's painting, the artist figures seem to be facing powerful and overwhelming obstacles; at the climax of the poem, the "actors," which again seems to refer to artist figures, stand against a wall and look out through a door of despair. Bang may be commenting on the barrier between the real world and the artist, the difficulty in determining the function of art, and the problems of creating successful artwork.

Myth, Fate, and Allegory

"Allegory" contains a reference to classical mythology, a commentary on the connection between myth and fate, and a suggestion (because of the title) that it is an allegory, or a story told in symbols that represent the meaning implied by the narrative. These themes are related because they all refer to the ancient tradition of a work of art that contains a hidden message about the fundamental nature of the world.

Topics For Further Study

- Research the life and artwork of Philip Guston. How would you describe his artistic style? What were his key influences? Why did he shift to practice abstract expressionism, and why did he shift back to figurative painting? What are the differences between abstract expressionist and figurative art, and how are these differences apparent in Guston's work?

- Bang makes reference to the ancient Greek myth of Prometheus in "Allegory." Who was Prometheus, and why was he important? Why do you think the mythology about him has been influential over Western literature? Why do you think Bang refers to him in her poem, and how do you think this reference affects the poem?

- Think of a lesson you would like to teach and then create an allegory for it. Brainstorm until you find the right story and situation to bring across your message. Then tell your allegory to a group of friends or classmates and ask them to describe its message. How did their response compare with your original idea?

- The convention of ekphrasis stretches all of the way back to ancient Greece and Rome, and it was particularly popular in the romantic period. Discuss the relationship between words and images today. When and why does literature become highly visual? What does this say about the work of literature? What are some of the ways a contemporary writer would go about describing artwork, and why would he or she choose to do so?

In the second stanza, Bang makes reference to Prometheus, the titan (a race of immortal gods that preceded Zeus's generation) from ancient Greek mythology known as the benefactor of humankind. This allusion establishes that Bang is interested in connecting her poem to the tradition of classical mythology, and it makes her poem appear to be commenting on timeless philosophical themes. For example, after discussing Prometheus, the speaker makes the abstract claim "These are the questions." Then, in stanza 8, the speaker notes that time in Guston's painting is "only an estimate," which inspires another general and abstract claim: "Myth equals fate / plus embellishment."

Claims such as these are not technically allegorical, since they state precisely the deeper meaning that would be implied by the symbols of a true allegory. The title of the poem seems misleading, therefore, unless it is simply a reference to Guston's painting. However, Bang's poem could be commenting on the very concept of allegory, in the sense that she describes an event or refers to an aspect of Guston's painting and then provides a literal explanation of its allegorical meaning. In fact, in elements of the poem such as the final description of "death / and destruction," Bang seems to be playing with the idea that there is a potential to make a grand or timeless commentary on the world. This is because those looking out at this death and destruction, who presumably represent artists, can see only "the minutiae" connected to the crux of the event instead of its full allegorical significance.

Identity

Another one of Bang's major themes in "Allegory" is her discussion of the notion of identity and selfhood. The idea that "Tonight we'll be content / with whomever we think we are" implies that it is difficult or impossible to discover one's true identity, as does the statement that every day is a "Who-do-you-wish-to-be?" It is likely that Bang's commentary on identity is concentrated on artistic identity, however, since it refers to the main subject of Guston's painting. Indeed, Bang continually emphasizes that the artist has difficulty determining who he is as well as how he fits into the world and creates art. She even seems to refer to artists as "actors" in the tenth stanza, implying that their role as observers of society makes it difficult to determine how they fit into the world.

Style

Ekphrasis

Bang's most important technique in "Allegory" is her use of the convention of ekphrasis, which refers to poetry concerned with the visual, particularly the visual art of painting. Often, an ekphrastic poem will take a work of visual art as its subject and describe or illuminate the visual elements of this work in literary terms. Bang's entire collection *The Eye like a Strange Balloon* is based on ekphrasis, and each of its fifty-two poems takes a work of art as its subject. "Allegory" is based on Philip Guston's painting of the same name, although, as is typical of Bang's use of ekphrasis, the poem does not simply explicate or depict Guston's painting but uses it as a starting point to explore Bang's own themes.

Alliteration

Bang is known for her use of repeated vowel and consonant sounds, particularly the technique of alliteration, which refers to the repetition of initial consonant sounds. The *c* sound in the line "The door of the car will click-close" is an example of this technique, as is the repetition of the *d* sound in the last words of the final four lines of the poem—"despair," "death," and "destruction." In addition to its usefulness as a musical and rhythmical device, alliteration allows Bang to draw attention to certain words and connect their meanings.

Enjambment

Bang frequently makes use of the technique of enjambment, which occurs when the meaning of one line of verse runs over into the next line. In fact, several of Bang's phrases run across stanzas, emphasizing the sense of continuation through a longer visual blank space in the poem. Enjambment can be useful for a variety of reasons, from moving along the action to emphasizing the space, or lack of space, between words in a continuous phrase. In "Allegory," Bang often contrasts a short, end-stopped line, or a line whose meaning does not carry over to the next line, such as "Music's the answer," with the five lines that flow on after it in an example of extended enjambment. Because of this technique, short declarative phrases, such as "All of the adoring," receive more emphasis.

Playfulness and Irony

With its story that is difficult to follow literally and its variety of subtle and ambiguous remarks, "Allegory" can be described as both playful

and ironic. Irony is a device in which language implies the opposite of its literal meaning, and the best example of irony in Bang's poem is the phrase "Some vigorous enactment," since it implies that the enactment is not vigorous at all. Bang's playfulness is evident in the first stanza, when the speaker asks to "Let us console you" with music but goes on to suggest that it does not matter what happens to this music. Here, as in many of the allusions to Guston's painting, it is not entirely clear what the speaker is talking about, and Bang seems to be teasing readers' expectations and challenging their interpretation of the poem and the painting.

Historical Context

Contemporary American Poetry

The contemporary American poetry scene is diverse and varied, and no one movement or poetic school dominates the literary scene. Many poets of the early twenty-first century, however, are influenced either directly or indirectly by the artistic movement of postmodernism, which began in the years following World War II. Known for challenging fixed understandings of reality, postmodern theory suggests that the world is composed of infinite layers of meaning. Psychoanalysts such as Jacques Lacan were among the key early figures to challenge previous standards in psychological, philosophical, and linguistic thought by questioning the commonly held belief that human psychology operates in a structured symbolic universe. In literature, postmodern theory has challenged writers to think about the form and meaning of texts as variable, or not confined to one particular perspective. Many poets have been particularly influenced by the theories of Jacques Derrida, who developed a critical method called "deconstruction," which stresses that texts do not refer to reality but only to other texts.

American poetry since the 1980s, therefore, tends not to take for granted that people experience and remember events in a straightforward manner in which symbols correspond to reality. Some poets have made further advances in the surrealist and abstract impressionist traditions, for example, and these traditions were particularly influential over the avant-garde "New York school" of poetry, which includes intellectual poets such as John Ashbery and Frank O'Hara. Meanwhile, poets such as Billy Collins have attempted to relate the dialect or style of a particular American region or culture, using a direct and conversational voice. Also, the

The Prometheus Fountain at Rockefeller Plaza © Lee Snider/Photo Images/Corbis

poetry scene in the United States since the 1980s has become increasingly interested in voices from a variety of ethnic and cultural backgrounds, especially groups that were marginalized in the past.

Some contemporary American poets have begun to think about history from different, more relativistic perspectives, and some refer to mythology or religion in order to bring out their themes. For example, Louise Glück tends to reinterpret classical mythology as a way to address feminist themes. Other poets, such as Bang, are interested in interacting with diverse artistic, visual, and cultural mediums. Some have stressed the need to reflect advances in computer and film technology in their work, for example, using the convention of fast-forward and rewind to describe a series of events. However, Bang's work in ekphrasis comes from a much longer tradition that stretches back to the classical world. Ekphrasis was particularly popular among romantic poets such as John Keats and Lord Byron, in part because poetry of the romantic era was interested in visionary glimpses of nature and art.

Philip Guston

Born in Canada, Philip Guston (1913–1980) moved to Los Angeles as a child and became friends with his classmate Jackson Pollack, later the leading figure of abstract expressionism in the United States. Guston, largely a self-taught artist, dropped out of the Otis Art Institute in 1930 and began working in the figurative medium, in which painted forms refer to objective, or real, sources. After working on a number of mural projects, Guston began a period of transition to abstract expressionism, a style in which artists express emotional states rather than physical objects, without symbolism or figuration. He became one of America's leading abstract expressionist painters in the 1950s and 1960s, teaching in New York and developing a following, until his style suddenly and dramatically changed back to figurative art in the late 1960s. The symbolic figures he painted during the 1970s, often evoking a bleak and dark side of existence, were controversial and extremely influential over neo-figurative artists. In many of these paintings, including *Allegory* (1975), Guston paints seemingly mundane but representative objects that allow him to engage in symbolism.

Critical Overview

Bang has been an acclaimed poet since the success of her first collection, *Apology for Want*, in 1997. She has a reputation as an intellectual poet who asks major philosophical questions about art and existence, but her lively poetry has a popular appeal as well. *The Eye like a Strange Balloon* was reviewed positively in publications such as *Booklist* and *Publishers Weekly*; in the former, Donna Seaman finds Bang particularly praiseworthy, writing that her fourth collection "is especially commanding in its metaphysical puzzles, tart irony, antic yet adamantly channeled energy, and devil-may-care poise." Michael Scharf, meanwhile, discusses what he considers the collection's central theme in his *Publishers Weekly* review, arguing that Bang's poems "search relentlessly for the meaning of—and the reason for—art in our contemporary world." Although it has received little individual critical attention, "Allegory" is one of the noteworthy poems of the collection, having appeared in the *Paris Review* in the fall of 2004.

Criticism

Scott Trudell

Trudell is an independent scholar with a bachelor's degree in English literature. In the following essay, he highlights the context of Guston's Allegory *and analyzes its significance in order to discuss the aesthetic commentary in Bang's poem of the same name.*

"Allegory" is a coherent, visually compelling poem that, in some ways, stands alone. Bang's vision comes to life because of its own imagery, so it is possible to enjoy the poem without a close familiarity with the Philip Guston painting on which it comments. In fact, Bang's themes tend to explore her own interests instead of the artist's, and she certainly does not simply explain or draw attention to Guston's ideas. "Allegory" very closely and very carefully engages with the painting, however, and to appreciate the deeper resonance of its most important theme—its commentary on art and aesthetics—it is necessary to examine how Bang interprets Guston's work.

Before discussing Bang's particular reading of the painting, it will help to highlight Guston's role in the development of art of the late twentieth century and his self-conscious artistic commentary in *Allegory*. Bang has chosen a painting that makes broad and ambitious claims about the nature of art and engages explicitly with the vehement debate during the 1970s about the direction American art should take. *Allegory* appeared after Guston had

famously and controversially disavowed abstract expressionism, at the height of his return to figurative painting. The work rejects the tenets of abstract expressionism, a movement that centers on the importance of free self-expression that does not refer or allude, symbolically or otherwise, to any external objects or events.

Allegory, a prominent example of the kind of symbolic, representational painting that occupied the final stage of Guston's career, appeared at a point when American artists were breaking away from abstract expressionism, which had been such an important and predominant movement a decade earlier. Andy Warhol, for example, had already established himself as a famous leading figure of pop art, a movement that returns to figurative art and incorporates themes and ideas from mass-produced, mass-media culture. Meanwhile, minimalist artists such as Donald Judd and Sol LeWitt had become popular and influential. Unlike pop art, minimalism was not associated with symbolism, figuration, or representation; on the contrary, it often involved sculpted objects that were abstract and referred only to themselves.

American art in the 1970s, therefore, was in the midst of a debate about what art should be. Few artists were still practicing abstract expressionism, but many artists and critics refused to return to figurative, representational work. Abstract art was seen throughout the years after World War II as a liberating, exciting, pro-American practice that opened up an enormous variety of artistic possibilities. Even the Central Intelligence Agency, eager to denounce the "social realist" art characteristic of totalitarian and Communist regimes such as the Soviet Union, sponsored and promoted abstraction in the arts. As antifigurative movements began to take hold in the 1960s, major American artists' positions in the controversy were closely watched, particularly in New York City, the locus of the debate, where the key artists lived and worked.

Guston had been one of the leading figures in abstract expressionism and a childhood friend of Jackson Pollack, the leading figure of abstract expressionism. A prominent artist living in New York, he was one of the key converts to the movement, involved in its origins in the 1940s. He was also one of its chief exponents in the fifties and sixties. His sudden conversion in the late 1960s to figurative art, therefore, which included cartoonlike figures, ordinary objects, and highly politicized representations, including Ku Klux Klansmen, shocked the art world. Many claimed that Guston was a traitor to the cause of American art, and his return to figuration was extremely influential over other artists of the period.

Allegory is one of the key paintings of Guston's late period, one that is very much a part of the debate between figuration and abstraction. Because it is so overtly symbolic and allusive; because it involves and interacts with language; and because it even claims, with its title, to contain an implicit, secondary meaning, the painting can be considered a landmark in 1970s figurative painting. The "dilemma" of the artists depicted in the work is an aesthetic one: how to interact with the world, how to use the tools at hand for artistic production, how go about the struggle of creating art. The two human figures in the painting are confronted with extremely oppressive obstacles to their artistic goals, and Guston gives the impression that they are making little headway against what appears to be a blue wave or a monster, a wheel, an intimidating pile of metal-soled shoes, and an accusatory red finger from the heavens.

Guston is at his most figuratively clear and direct in this painting, actually including words in his work to establish the significance of his images. The fact that a scroll reading "The Artists" floats above the main body of the work emphasizes that the words "composer," "painter," "sculptor," and "poet" at the bottom are meant to correspond to the figures in the main body. Although there are paintbrushes and other artists' materials in the foreground, the exact artistic medium in which the central human figures are working is unclear; the important thing to recognize is that there is a divide between two different types of art and two different types of artists. While the bodyless head on the left is associated with abstract and mathematical ideas such as a ruler, geometrical shapes in space, and a sequence of five numbers, the head on the right is working with a pile of specific and real objects (mainly, it appears, shoes). One artist, therefore, is working in abstraction, while the other is working in figuration.

The "dilemma" of Guston's *Allegory*, therefore, is closely connected to the artist's own dilemma as he attempted to redefine himself in the 1970s American art scene. A number of conclusions can be drawn from Guston's commentary on abstract versus figurative art. The abstract artist is facing the sky, overwhelmed by what appears to be a kind of blue wave or monster, while the figurative artist seems to be much more in the brunt of the artistic process, his face enmeshed in a wheel.

She seems to be suggesting that, despite Guston's self-conscious exploration of the direction that art should take, artists are at a distance from reality regardless of whether they paint in abstract or in figurative terms."

The latter is holding a length of rope that trails back to the artistic materials in the foreground, and his hair seems to be melting from the imposing red finger from the heavens. This finger suggests that the figurative artist is somehow chosen by God, or that he is burdened by God, or both.

Bang's poem, which centers on self-conscious themes of aesthetics, identity, and myth, is very aware of the debate between abstraction and figuration. She begins with a suggestion that music has a function of consolation but that it does not matter whether this artistic medium engages with the mythological figure of Prometheus. Prometheus, said to be the figure responsible for giving the power of artifice to humankind, is then associated with "Somatognosis," or awareness of his body (and, by extension, awareness of his function as a figurative or representational allusion). The speaker's claims that "it doesn't much matter" whether the work of art is connected to or recognized by its source and its own allusion raises the possibility that allusion/figuration is neither important nor necessary.

Bang proceeds to discuss questions about identity, suggesting that the figure facing up on the left side of Guston's painting is the "Jackself / we might have been," which (if this figure refers to an abstract expressionist) is a slight joke about Guston. The next lines, which probably refer to the scroll that reads "The Artists" ("the one at the top") and the listing of the various types of artists at the "tourist motel / at the bottom," suggest that there is a "degree of remove" between the abstract idea of the artist and the

What Do I Read Next?

- Bang's first collection, *Apology for Want* (1997), established her as a prominent and sophisticated poet able to address intellectual themes while retaining an engaging and playful style.

- Philip Guston's *Late Work* (1998) is an intimate portrait of the artist that focuses on his shift back to figurative painting, written by the renowned poet, and friend of Guston, William Corbett.

- Jill Bialosky's *Subterranean* (2001) is a collection of vivid poetry about grief, motherhood, and desire.

- *The Whitsun Weddings* (1964), by the English poet Philip Larkin, is a collection of masterly verse that ranges in tone from playful to biting and bleak.

- Jonathan Strong's *Secret Words* (1992) is a charming and touching novel about a late bloomer who moves out of her parents' house at age twenty-nine and begins to find her way in the world.

material, functional reality of the artist at work. This comment, as well as the ironic and sarcastic line "some vigorous enactment" and the speaker's comment on the fact that the artist's watch only estimates the time, suggest that both abstraction and figuration are somewhat distanced from the immediate reality.

Bang puts forward this idea even more clearly in the final stanzas of the poem, in which the artists are called "actors" and are reduced to "standing / against a wall and watching / it all unfold." In fact, they are not simply distant from this reality; the artists comment detachedly about the minute, unimportant details connected to the "spine of the climax" rather than the climax itself. Perhaps the key element to recognize about this climax of the poem's aesthetic commentary, however, is that it ceases to draw any distinction between abstraction and figuration. All artists and identities are grouped into the notion of "actors," and none of them seems able to deal with the open door to death and destruction.

It is clear, therefore, that Bang's poem takes Guston very seriously as a painter who is able to bring the viewer into close proximity with the themes of despair, death, destruction. It is also clear from her discussion of identity and artistic creation that Bang engages with the aesthetic debate of the painting. Bang's position on the debate between abstract and figurative art, however, takes a tone that can perhaps best be described as playfully mocking. She seems to be suggesting that, despite Guston's self-conscious exploration of the direction that art should take, artists are at a distance from reality regardless of whether they paint in abstract or in figurative terms. To Bang, the true "dilemma" of Guston's painting, and the true dilemma of the arts, is that there is always a divide between the artist and reality, and abstraction and figuration (like composing, painting, sculpting, and poetry) are simply tools for attacking the same daunting problem.

Source: Scott Trudell, Critical Essay on "Allegory," in *Poetry for Students*, Thomson Gale, 2006.

Jennifer Bussey

Bussey holds a master's degree in interdisciplinary studies and a bachelor's degree in English literature. She is an independent writer specializing in literature. In the following essay, she explores the relationship between mythology and reality in Mary Jo Bang's poem.

Throughout her poem "Allegory," Mary Jo Bang introduces the twin themes of mythology and reality. She sets them beside each other to demonstrate that mythology has no relevance to reality. The poem instead praises experience, preferably personal experience, as the real source of truth and knowledge. Her references to mythology are so readily recognized by the reader that Bang succeeds in making her point that mythology is, and always has been, an enduring element in thought, belief, and culture. By including these references in "Allegory," Bang seems to be challenging them head on and dismantling their past claims to truth.

The first stanza begins the process of defeating mythology by pointing to its meaninglessness in the real world. The speaker comments, "Of course, we're caught / in this sphere" (lines 3 and 4). These lines remind the reader not only that all people have in common their current place in the sphere of this world but also that they are *caught* in it. There is no choice in the matter. It is merely the reality of being here, and it is a common experience shared by people everywhere. The speaker's personal point of view is reflected in her word choice "caught," which gives the reader an initial insight into the speaker's particular experience and personality. While this makes the speaker seem more realistic by giving her a persona, her word choice does not affect the truth of what she is saying.

Finishing the first stanza and moving into the next, the speaker adds, "where it doesn't much matter / whether our song reaches / the ear of Prometheus or not" (lines 5–7). This is an important classical allusion. Prometheus was a character in Greek mythology who stole fire from Zeus to give to the mortals. Some accounts of the story of Prometheus tell us that he had already given the mortals other gifts, including brickwork, medicines, signs to be read in the sky, and art. After Prometheus had tricked Zeus and given mortals fire, however, Zeus punished Prometheus by having him chained to a mountain where an eagle came to gouge at his body and eat his liver. Every night, Prometheus would heal completely, and the eagle would return the next day. It was a horrifying punishment for a kindness done for mortals. In "Allegory," the speaker introduces the image of Prometheus suffering alone high on his mountain to show how useless music on earth is to him in his doomed state. Even if he were real, what good would a song do by reaching him? Bang makes the point that art created on earth is not for the benefit of mythical characters but for that of real people. The first two lines ("Let us console you. / Music's the answer") make very clear that music and, by extension, art in general exist in the earthly world and have the ability to affect people. Music can provide true consolation to a person in emotional need. This is because people think, feel, and have experiences in the real world, not in the world of myths.

In the eighth stanza, the speaker comments directly on mythology, where she states, "Myth equals fate / plus embellishment" (lines 39 and 40). Although fate may or may not be real, the truth is that there is nothing people can do to control or alter it. Because the speaker is developing a theme about truth, the notion of fate seems to be irrelevant. To put it into an equation with embellishment, which is divergence *from* the truth, makes fate even more meaningless. Together, the speaker essentially sums up myth as embellished fate. She understands myth as the creation of people bent on fashioning stories, interest, history, and purpose in their reality. To cast this light on the story of Prometheus, the speaker would likely say that the story was made up as a way for the ancient Greeks to value their ancestors because, after all, some-

> *The speaker rejects mythology as a source of truth or wisdom, but she does not leave the reader wondering where truth can be found. She believes that reality provides truth and meaning and that wisdom is gleaned from experience."*

thing as basic as fire was a divine gift to them, for which someone paid a very high price. This understanding is more exciting than just believing that early people got fire from a lightning storm. To return to the speaker's equation, the myth of Prometheus is simply an embellishment of the fact that early people would inevitably have fire. The myth has no meaning or relevance to reality or truth.

The speaker rejects mythology as a source of truth or wisdom, but she does not leave the reader wondering where truth can be found. She believes that reality provides truth and meaning and that wisdom is gleaned from experience. In the third stanza, the speaker introduces a medical term, "Somatognosis" (line 12). This word refers to a person's sense of his or her body's existence and functioning. Like the story of Prometheus, this word has Greek origins: *somato* means "body," and *gnosis* means "knowledge." This refers to a very concrete form of knowledge; it is knowledge of— and through—a person's bodily existence. Somatognosis is illustrated in the tenth stanza, where the speaker remarks, "The kinesthetic lift of a foot / from the floor / forces itself to be felt" (lines 47–49). This refers to a person's first lifting up on a Ferris wheel and feeling his or her foot leave the ground. It is a very tangible illustration that the reader can easily understand. Because the image is so tangible, the reader almost experiences the lift of the foot as he or she reads the poem. It immediately connects the reader to the truth of that image through physical experience.

At the end of the third stanza, the speaker asks, "What does it feel like / to inch one's way forward?"

(lines 14 and 15), which brings the reader to the idea of experiencing progress. This type of progress is very different from the progress stolen from Mount Olympus by Prometheus; this is progress made and felt through a human body. Also, notice how the speaker says "inch one's way forward," which is progress made on earth, as opposed to "inch one's way upward," which would be progress toward the mountaintop realm of Prometheus. Bang is drawing very sharp lines between the real world and the world of fantasy and mythology. Similarly, the speaker introduces a startling image of a new beginning: "Dawn on its knees / crawls toward knowledge" (lines 17 and 18). Here again, Bang expresses that knowledge is gained by slow and steady movement forward in the real world. Knowledge of the truth is acquired only through experience over time. It requires patience and also willingness to make the slow movements in the right direction.

In developing her theme of myth and reality, Bang utilizes symbolism to give the reader a visual cue. In "Allegory," mountains symbolize the realm of myths, and the bottom of the mountains symbolizes the real world. These mountains give a strong sense of "here" in the real world and "there" in the mythical and unknown realm. In the figure of Prometheus, Bang introduces two mountains that are specific to myths. The mountain to which Prometheus is chained is one, and Mount Olympus is the other. Mount Olympus was the source of the fire Prometheus stole to give to mortals at the bottom of the mountain. Both mountains are fictitious, and both are important to the myth of Prometheus's giving fire to the mortals. This illustration also calls attention to the land at the bottom of the mountain, where the mortals who received fire lived. In the context of this poem, that land represents the realm of truth. The mortals, after all, were no different from real people today. From a historical perspective, those mortals were the ones who created the myths that are rejected in the poem, but the people were as real as the gods they created were not.

Another image of a mountain occurs in the seventh stanza. The speaker asks, "What's the degree of remove / between the one at the top / of Pie Mountain / and the tourist motel / at the bottom with its pool / of aqua attitude and blue inflatables?" The speaker makes a clear delineation between someone at the top of a mountain and ordinary tourists at the bottom of the mountain. She even asks to what extent they are separated, indicating that they are indeed in different realms. Because she gives no specifics about the person at the top of the mountain, or if she is even referring to a person (she uses an indeterminate "one"), the reader immediately relates to the tourists playing in the motel pool. Further, because the tourists are depicted engaged in such a common activity, the reader is able to recall his or her own experiences on similar vacations. This is another way she sets the reader's feet solidly on the ground of truth and experience.

Although Bang makes distinctions between mythology and the real world in "Allegory," she also acknowledges that people have a tendency to create their own personal mythologies, even if they reject classical myths. In the fifth and sixth stanzas, she describes the act of embracing "Who- / do-you-wish-to-be?" She concludes the fifth stanza with the statement, "Tonight we'll be content / with whomever we think we are." In the next stanza, the speaker describes setting off in a car with the person she might have been: "The door of the car will click-close / and off we'll go. / In the back is the Jackself / we might have been." To allow the reader to hear the door closing, Bang very effectively uses alliteration ("car will click-close"), or the repetition of consonants, and onomatopoeia ("click-close"), or the use of words whose sounds suggest their meaning. This makes the reader feel that he or she is also in the car with the speaker and her other self. It brings the poem alive to the reader's senses, so that being in the car seems like something the reader is actually experiencing. According to the way Bang has built the theme of truth in this poem, experience is the litmus test of truth and the path to knowledge. So her decision to make the reader feel that he or she is sitting there in the car is a major cue that something important is about to be revealed in the comfort and privacy of the car.

The speaker returns to the image of the car in the ninth stanza, where the reader finds that their destination was a carnival. What is important to the themes of myth and truth, however, is that Bang ties the two together without contradicting anything else she has claimed about how unrelated the two are. The difference is that with the image of driving her "might have been" self to the carnival, she introduces the notion of a personal mythology. This is why she remarks that people are content with whoever they think they are. That, like the kinesthetic experience of a foot lifting from the ground or playing in a motel swimming pool, is a truthful experience almost any reader has had. A personal mythology may not be any more true than the myth of Prometheus, but the experience of having one rings very true with the reader.

Source: Jennifer Bussey, Critical Essay on "Allegory," in *Poetry for Students*, Thomson Gale, 2006.

E. M. Kaufman

In the following review, Kaufman provides an overview of Bang's intent with her collection and finds "music in Bang's lines."

Bang's fourth collection takes ekphrasis (poetry about works of visual art) to the limit: each of the 52 poems involves a different art object, the last of which is Bang's own "mixed media collage." The work's eclectic nature may worry readers who have watched the film *Mulholland Drive* or seen the paintings of Sigmar Polke and Dorothea Tanning, not to mention Bang's collage. Knowing the artwork would, perhaps, help, but these poems are not tactile explorations of art but rather explorations of the idea of ekphrasis and the relationship between the verbal and the visual. The title poem is an internal rendering of an 1882 charcoal drawing by Odilon Redon, in which a large disembodied eyeball floats upward and away from Earth: "We were going toward nothing / all along. Honing the acoustics, / heralding the instant / shifts, horizontal to vertical?" There is music in Bang's lines, set off by the charming, poetic titles of the paintings: The Tyranny of Everyday Life, The Physical Impossibility of Death in the Mind of Someone Living, and Three Parts of an X. Readers' enjoyment will be determined, in part, by their interest in questions of aesthetic theory: "What harm is there in art? / As long as an image can never bed / the object it represents. / Sex with an effigy. / How much fun could that be? Tsk. Tsk." For academic collections.

Source: E. M. Kaufman, Review of *The Eye Like a Strange Balloon*, in *Library Journal*, Vol. 130, No. 1, January 2005, p. 1.

Publishers Weekly

In the following review, the reviewer notes Bang's "signature quirky pathos and alliterative staccato."

"Art / is the depth of whatever has deepened / an abbreviate existence," writes Bang in this fourth collection, comprising ekphrastic poems that search relentlessly for the meaning of—and the reason for—art in our contemporary world. The book is without sections; instead it operates by proposing its subjects in a somewhat overly direct and thematically oriented first poem titled, "Rock and Roll is Dead, The Novel is Dead. God is Dead, Painting is Dead," which ponders the place of art in the postmodern age. The book proceeds through a series of 52 poems to try to find that place—finding a meager, not entirely satisfying answer in art's resistance to the depredations of time. Each draws upon a different work of art, from sources as various as Willem de Kooning, Cindy Sherman, Picasso and David Lynch. Unlike classical ekphrasis, however, Bang does not attempt to directly describe the work of art, but instead uses the works as springboards for her signature quirky pathos and alliterative staccato: "We are posing. We are poised. / This is where we live. We are ever / but only when ever is all that there is." The collection concludes in a poem drawn from an original artwork by Bang herself. "Here darling, take this," she writes, "and Time gives the mouth a morsel."

Source: Publishers Weekly, Review of *The Eye Like a Strange Balloon*, in *Publishers Weekly*, Vol. 251, No. 42, October 18, 2004, p. 1.

Sources

Bang, Mary Jo, "Allegory," in *The Eye like a Strange Balloon: Poems*, Grove Press, 2004, pp. 55–57; originally published in *Paris Review*, No. 171, Fall 2004, pp. 36–38.

Scharf, Michael, Review of *The Eye like a Strange Balloon*, in *Publishers Weekly*, Vol. 251, No. 42, October 18, 2004, p. 61.

Seaman, Donna, Review of *The Eye like a Strange Balloon*, in *Booklist*, Vol. 101, No. 6, November 15, 2004, p. 547.

Further Reading

Auping, Michael, ed., *Philip Guston: Retrospective*, Thames & Hudson, 2003.

Providing images and analyses of Guston's work throughout his long career, including high-quality reproductions of his paintings, this comprehensive volume will help the reader place Guston's *Allegory* in its artistic context.

Bang, Mary Jo, ed., *Whatever You Desire: A Book of Lesbian Poetry*, Oscars Press, 1990.

The collection of poetry about lesbian themes that Bang edited in 1990 provides a useful background to some of the twentieth-century women authors by whom Bang is influenced.

Heffernan, James A. W., *Museum of Words: The Poetics of Ekphrasis from Homer to Ashbery*, University of Chicago Press, 2004.

In this study of the convention of ekphrasis throughout the history of Western literature, Heffernan pays particular attention to how and why poetic methods of capturing the visual have developed and changed.

Kirby, David, "Give Me Rapture and Bliss," in *New York Times Book Review*, March 4, 2001, p. 23.

Kirby's favorable review of Bang's verse novel *Louise in Love* provides an important example of the critical community's positive reaction to the poet.

All It Takes

Carl Phillips

2004

Carl Phillips, the author of "All It Takes," is one of the fastest-rising stars in the literary world. From his first collection of poems in 1992, *In the Blood*, through his seventh collection, *The Rest of Love*, published in 2004, he has won numerous awards and honors. While it is often lauded for its treatment of the black and gay themes that are central to his identity, Phillips's work is usually deeply imbued with classical allusions and complex imagery that makes his readers see what they know with a new sense of enlightenment.

In "All It Takes" (from the book *The Rest of Love*), Phillips explores the things of the physical world that cannot be directly observed—those things that are knowable only through, as he puts it, "the visible effects by which we know them." The poem moves with ease from observation of common occurrences to reflection on those uncommon events (like the last berries clinging to a dying vine in winter) to suggestions that what we know of the world is nothing more than what the ancient cultures knew when they devised their own mythologies. Although these ideas could steer a less commanding poet into different directions, Phillips stays on course, holding "All It Takes" together as a dreamy meditation on the nature of reality.

Author Biography

Carl Phillips was born on July 23, 1959, in Everett, Washington. As the product of a mixed-race

marriage—his father was a medic in the Air Force and an African American, while his mother, a painter and homemaker, was white—he grew up with the sense of being an outsider. This outsider status was exaggerated by the fact that his family moved constantly in the first ten years of Phillips's life, as his father was assigned to different military bases throughout the United States and Europe. It was while he was living in Zweibrücken, Germany, when he was a young teen, that he first discovered an affinity for languages. He studied Latin and Greek when the family returned to America, showing such proficiency that he majored in those languages at Harvard, graduating with a bachelor's degree in 1981. He wrote some poetry at Harvard and worked on the staff of the *Harvard Advocate*, a literary magazine.

After college, Phillips taught Latin in several high schools throughout the 1980s. He was married for a short while but soon divorced when he came to understand his homosexuality. During this period, he did not write much. His writing was reinvigorated at a poetry workshop that he attended at Castle Hill Center for the Arts in Truro, Massachusetts, in 1990.

Once he started writing, Phillips's output was prodigious and impressive. Within a few months, he had produced the poems that would make up his first poetry collection, *In the Blood*, which won the Samuel French Morse Poetry Prize when it was published in 1992. He then returned to school, earning his master's degree from Boston University, where he studied under the poet Robert Pinsky. His 1995 collection, *Cortége*, was a finalist for the National Book Award and *From the Devotions*, published in 1998, was a finalist for the National Book Critics Circle Award. He has since published poems and poetry collections at a constant rate: *The Rest of Love*, the 2004 collection in which "All It Takes" appears, is his seventh collection and was also a National Book Award finalist. Phillips has been a Guggenheim Fellow and is a member of the American Academy of Arts and Sciences and a 2004 recipient of an award from the American Academy of Arts and Letters. He lives in St. Louis, Missouri, where he is a professor of English and African and Afro-American Studies at Washington University.

Poem Text

Any force—
generosity, sudden updraft.
Fear. Things invisible,

Carl Phillips   Doug Macomber

and the visible effects by which
we know them. Human gesture. Betrayed,   5
betrayed. The dampness of fog as

understandable by how, inside it, form within their
thicket of nowhere left to hide—
that leafless—the winter berries, more than usual,

shine. First always   10
comes the ability to believe, and then the need to.
The ancient Greeks; the Romans after. How they

made of love a wild god; of fidelity—a small,
a tame one. I am no less grateful for
the berries than for the thorns that are   15

meant, I think, to help. As if
sometimes the world really did amount to
a quiet arrangement. Cut flowers. Make

death the one whose eyes are lidless. And
—already—you are leaving. You have   20
crossed the water.

Poem Summary

Lines 1–3

Phillips starts "All It Takes" by reinforcing the title, echoing the meaning of "all" with the poem's first word, "any." While the title of the poem leaves open the suggestion of what might be necessary, the first line narrows the subject of the work down

Media Adaptations

- Phillips and C. D. Wright were recorded reading their poems in the Montpelier Room of the Library of Congress, December 11, 1997. An audiocassette recording of the event is on file at the Library of Congress.

- The Library of Congress also holds another recording of a reading, this one given in 1998 in the Montpelier Room, by Phillips and Carol Muske-Dukes, who were both Witter Bynner Fellows.

- Washington University in St. Louis maintains a website at www.news-info.wustl.edu/sb/page/normal/143.html that gives a thorough overview of Phillips's career and the many honors awarded him.

to a "force," proceeding to define what might be considered to be forces.

The second and third lines suggest phenomena that might be regarded as the kinds of forces the poem is talking about, offering readers a range from positive to negative, aggressive to benign. "Generosity" is, of course, thought to be one of the most selfless of human attributes; "sudden updraft" is a breeze that is beyond the control of an individual; "fear" is one of the most destructive of human emotions. What they all have in common, as pointed out in line 3, is that they cannot be seen by the human eye.

Lines 4–6

In the second stanza, the poem focuses on the ways in which people can understand phenomena that are not directly experienced by the senses. Phillips explains that they have "effects by which we know them." Unlike emotions, gestures can be observed, and the emotions to which those gestures correspond can be understood by interpreting the gestures. At the end of line 5, Phillips uses the word "betrayed" and then employs the same word once again at the start of line 6, to imply that the revealed emotions are reluctant to have their natures exposed by the gestures that reveal them. Repeating the word gives a feeling of sadness to the process, as if the emotions acknowledge the inevitability of the fact that they must be revealed.

The second stanza ends with an image from nature. Fog is sometimes so light that it cannot be seen by the naked eye; still, even when it is not visible, the moisture that it leaves hanging in the air will accumulate on the skin, so that the body can feel what surrounds it more clearly than the eye can see it.

Lines 7–9

Building on the image of fog, the poem moves from the issue of transparency to the feeling of being engulfed. The fog is referred to in line 7 as "it," though the poem does not actually state that the winter berries are "inside it" until two lines later, weaving a complex verbal path that resembles, in its twists and turns, the dense thicket in which the berries grow. A thicket is frequently used as a metaphor for a place so dense that things are hidden from view within it, but line 8 refers to a "thicket of nowhere left to hide": the poem is downplaying the importance of physical distraction, placing emphasis instead on the meaning of the thicket. A person might not be able to see through the thicket, but one knows what is in it, and, in that sense, it hides nothing. The winter berries are an anomaly: while berries and fruit often grow in the summer, on plants nurtured by the photosynthesis of their leaves, these berries are unguarded and cold, seeming to grow from their own force of will.

Lines 10–12

The first word of this stanza, "shine," emphasizes the radiance of the winter berries. Usually such berries on barren branches would be viewed as pitiful objects, abandoned and forgotten, but Phillips uses their isolation to emphasize their individuality, showing how surviving through the winter makes the berries stand out, even in the dense fog and within the center of a thicket.

In lines 10 and 11, Phillips makes a statement about the nature of belief: that it is necessary only after the ability to have faith comes into existence. This contradicts common sense, which would generally hold that the need for belief would create the ability to believe. By reversing this order, the poem puts out a positive, uplifting message: the emphasis on the ability, rather than the need, takes away the sense of desperation. The poem says that belief is not something that has to be found but rather is inherent in consciousness from the very beginning.

The reference to ancient Greeks and Romans in line 12 supports the innate ability to believe, tracing this ability back through the centuries. The poem does not expect readers to just accept this claim, but instead offers proof that ability has preceded need throughout most of recorded history.

Lines 13–15

The Greek goddess of love is Aphrodite, referred to in Roman mythology as Venus. Although her association with beauty might lead people to assume that Aphrodite led a serene life, she was, in fact, a lively participant in the affairs of men and gods. She was, for instance, instrumental in turning the Trojan War into a prolonged and bloody battle: the assembled armies agreed that they would abide by the result of a one-on-one fight between Menelaus, the husband of Helen of Troy, and Paris, her lover, but Aphrodite was so in love with Paris that she removed him and protected him, forcing the battle into a conflict involving thousands of men. There are many other instances in which Aphrodite proved to be an adventurer—the "wild god" mentioned in the poem.

The goddess of fidelity is Hera, the wife of Zeus, the king of the gods. Although she was not necessarily small in stature, as the poem suggests, her exploits were tamer than those of Aphrodite. The most widely known myth about Hera concerns her participation in the judgment of Paris, the event that began the Trojan War: three goddesses (Aphrodite, Hera, and Athena) asked the mortal Paris to judge which of them was fairest, with Aphrodite winning because she bribed Paris with the love of Helen, considered to be the most beautiful of mortal women.

The poem reverses expectations in lines 14 and 15 by stating that the speaker is "no less grateful for the berries than for the thorns": normally, one would consider a person to be vastly more grateful for the berries and to perhaps bring the balance close to even by elevating the position of the thorns, saying, "I am no less grateful for the thorns than for the berries." The way that Phillips puts it, though, makes it seem as if people would expect him to be grateful for the thorns but not the berries.

Lines 16–18

This stanza concerns the balance of nature. The speaker carries over the thought that began on line 15, that the thorns on a bush are probably meant to be helpful, not harmful. The interjection of "I think" in line 16 reminds readers that what the poet is saying is all far from certain in his mind. If thorns

do serve a positive purpose, then there is more order to the world than is apparent from looking at it, just like an invisible fog or a blindingly dense thicket. The "quiet arrangement" mentioned in line 18 supports this idea of an unstated order to the world that one must take on faith, without concrete evidence. It is a balance between violence and beauty, captured by bonding together the words "cut" and "flowers."

Lines 19–21

The poem ends with images of death. Eyes that are lidless are eyes that are always open, on vigilant watch. Death, on the other hand, is usually described as a kind of sleep, most likely because it resembles sleep, in which the body lies still with closed eyes. In this poem, though, the expectations are reversed: the author tells his reader to "make death the one whose eyes are lidless." Thus, he says that death should be the state of constant alertness and that life, by contrast, should be a state of ease and contentment.

In the line before last, the speaker finally mentions another person, a "you." This person is described first as leaving and then as having "crossed the water," a reference to ancient mythology, where the dead were ferried across the river Styx into the underworld when they died. Having already urged thc reader to look at death as a time of awareness, the poem tells the reader that death is not an abstract, future event to be dealt with at some later date; it is already here. The main part of the poem is focused on making readers aware of the unseen things in this world, but the ending lines point in the direction of the ultimate unknowable state, death.

Themes

Invisibility

The main theme of "All It Takes" is the way in which people know truths that do not derive from the direct evidence of their experience. The poem starts off by talking about "things invisible," which are not directly seen but are nonetheless familiar because of their effects. One example from the physical world is an updraft: a wind that has no visible presence but which is evident in snow or leaves or dust swirling in an obvious order. There are also examples of emotions—generosity and fear—that do not have any physical presence in themselves but that set off events that are experienced. People believe in these invisible phenomena without being

Topics for Further Study

- This poem starts out describing how invisible things are revealed through their association with gestures. Write a brief sketch that will convey some human situation without any dialogue. As an observer, try to explain the situation in as much detail as possible.

- Using three-line stanzas, as Phillips does, write an explanation of Einstein's theory of relativity, which explains the connection between invisible energy and visible mass.

- The poem refers to the thorns on a berry bush and makes the observation that they "are / meant, I think, to help." Research the actual theories that botanists have about the development of thorns on different kinds of plants and the functions of the thorns. Make a chart showing the variations in nature.

- Phillips mentions how love and fidelity are explored in Greek and Roman mythology. Choose the mythology of another culture and explain at least two of that culture's myths about either love or fidelity.

---

able to know them directly through the senses because the physical evidence points to the existence of the invisible.

Later in the poem, Phillips talks about things that are just as invisible, love and fidelity. Regarding these emotions, he points out how the ancient Greeks and Romans gave them physical characteristics by personifying them as gods. These gods, with vastly different personalities, could be imagined by artists, and their images could be painted and sculpted, so that people could imagine that they saw love and fidelity before their eyes or at least the characteristics that make such emotions knowable.

In the last stanza, the poem refers to death's having lidless eyes. Given the previous focus on trying to see things that are invisible, this stanza seems to imply that death is a futile search for meaning, while life is enriched by the knowledge that some things just cannot be seen.

Contradiction

Phillips fills this poem with contradictory ideas. The most obvious, of course, is the contrast between things that can be experienced directly by the senses, such as flowers, dampness, and berries, and those that are familiar to the mind but have no real physical presence, like generosity and fear, love and fidelity. There are, however, other, more subtle contradictions woven throughout the poem. The unseen fog, which is recognized only by its accumulated wetness, is contrasted with the thicket, which surrounds like fog but is very tangible. The berries are a contradiction because they are winter berries: most berries need the full warmth of summer to grow. The god of love is contrasted with the god of fidelity, and cut flowers in a vase are contrasted with the uncut flowers that grow out of the ground, in a "quiet arrangement" all over the world.

All of these contradictory notions are used to show that life has room for complexity. It is not a simple world that is being described in "All It Takes," but rather one that can hold truths that are the opposite of other truths. A simple poem might have the strength to examine only a narrow view of life, but this is not a simple poem. It uses few words in short stanzas, but within that compact density, it has room to challenge the imagination and to make readers question their understanding of reality.

Love

In identifying the Greek and Roman manifestations of love as "a wild god," "All It Takes" is not necessarily saying that love itself must be wild, just that its visual representation must be. The main idea of the poem is that abstractions like emotions cannot be known except through the physical manifestations associated with them. Wildness might be necessary to capture the idea of love, but love, like the berries shining in the middle of the thicket, might have a quiet essence that is not necessarily reflected by the wild god but is just pointed toward. This would explain why Phillips provides the contrasting image of a "small, tame" god for fidelity: fidelity is a form of love, but it does not need very much activity to represent it. Readers might think "tame" is somewhat less interesting than "wild" and interpret this passage as Phillips's way of saying that fidelity is less interesting, and therefore less valuable, than love. This would be a mistaken impression that the following line works to dispel. "I am no less grateful for the berries than for the thorns" tells the reader that the berries can also be considered tame, but they are just as much valued as the thorns.

Style

Analogy

Phillips bases his explanation of emotions on analogies to the actions of things in the physical world. An *analogy* draws a comparison between the similarities of two unlike things: one might make the assumption, for example, that a bird will be able to fly because its wings resemble those of other birds who use their wings to fly. In "All It Takes," the fact that a fog that is unseen can still be recognized by the dampness that it creates in one's clothes can help readers understand, by analogy, how emotions can be recognized even though they cannot be seen. Similarly, the characteristics that the Greeks and Romans gave to the emotions of love and fidelity can tell modern readers, by analogy, the prevailing attitude toward those same emotions.

Caesura

A caesura is a pause in the middle of a line of poetry. It is usually used to break up a long poetic line. Writers like Phillips are just as likely to place a caesura in a medium-length line in order to better control the poem's rhythm, especially in a work like "All It Takes," which is not written in a strict metric pattern. In this poem, Phillips uses four punctuation marks for pauses: the comma, the semicolon, the dash, and the period. In a case like line 3 ("Fear. Things invisible,"), he uses the pause to redirect the flow of the argument that he is making by bringing things to a halt with a period and starting a new sentence. Line 5—"we know them. Human gesture. Betrayed,"—starts two new sentences, as the narration stops to comment on the ideas already raised. There are, in fact, numerous spots in this poem where Phillips uses two caesuras in a line: lines 7, 9, 12, 13, 16, 18, and 20 all halt the flow of words twice. The frequent pauses give the poem a thoughtful tone, conveying a narrative voice that is carefully considering the implications of each thing said and is struggling to get the wording of difficult concepts exactly right.

Historical Context

Civil Liberties

In 2004, the year that this poem was first published, American culture was in the process of redefining the distinctions between what is private, "invisible" to the public eye, and what is in the public interest. Things that had once been left invisible were no longer shielded by concepts of "privacy," but were instead opened up to public scrutiny in an attempt to keep ahead of the enemy in the war on terrorism. Two and a half years after the destruction in New York, Washington, and Pennsylvania caused by plane hijackers on September 11, 2001, and a year after the country went to war to overthrow the Baathist regime in Iraq, American law enforcement authorities were vigilant against further terrorist activities enacted against the United States on American soil. Color-coded alerts about the likelihood of terrorist attacks were issued by the Department of Homeland Security, alternating between yellow ("Significant Risk") and orange ("High Risk").

In this climate of caution, many Americans willingly accepted a reassessment of what constituted the public interest. The USA PATRIOT Act, passed by Congress six weeks after the 2001 terrorist attacks, gave the government broad new powers to conduct searches without warrants, to subpoena bank and library records, to track Internet usage, and to monitor the movements of citizens. During the 2004 election year, there was sharp debate about whether these measures, meant to stop terrorism before it had a chance to inflict more damage, were worth the cost in civil liberties. As Phillips examined the ways that the outside world can come to understand what is hidden from view in "All It Takes," the country was in the middle of coming to grips with the fact that previous social norms for what was and what was not private were being redefined.

Marriage

As a writer who has been with the same partner for years and is frequently cited for the homosexual themes explored in his works, Phillips would have certainly been aware of the national debate throughout 2003 and 2004 regarding same-sex marriage. The issue grew in the nation's consciousness after Holland voted to expand the definition of marriage to allow homosexuals to wed. Belgium followed in 2003, and after that came referendums throughout the Canadian provinces, eventually permitting same-sex marriage in most of Canada. In November of 2003, the Supreme Judicial Court of the Commonwealth of Massachusetts ruled that that state's constitution did not allow the state to deny homosexuals the right to marry; marriage licenses for same-sex couples were issued in Massachusetts as of May 17, 2004.

Once same-sex marriage was recognized in one state, the issue was debated throughout the country.

In the city of San Francisco, the mayor ordered city clerks to issue marriage licenses to same-sex couples in February of 2004, only to have the marriages halted the following month by the state supreme court. Several other cities across the country considered the legal responsibility of recognizing same-sex marriages.

One result of this flurry of activity was that it energized the opposition to same-sex marriage. In November of 2004, eleven states voted to pass amendments to limit the definition of marriage to include only one man and one woman, raising the number of states with prohibitions from three before 2004; in addition, thirty-seven states have passed some form of the Defense of Marriage Act to prohibit gay marriages. At a time when gays were struggling for public recognition of their relationships, Phillips, in "All It Takes," focused on the "quiet arrangements" that occur when the visible and the invisible interact.

Critical Overview

Phillips has been considered an important American poet ever since the publication of his first collection of poems, *In the Blood*, in 1992. That book, which won the Morse Poetry Prize, prompted *Publishers Weekly* to describe Phillips as "an unusually accomplished and innovative poet," noting that he had "developed his own painful but luminous method" of examining the world. His reputation has grown since that book, up to and including *The Rest of Love*, the book in which "All It Takes" appears.

In her review of *The Rest of Love* for *Library Journal*, Barbara Hoffert wrote, "As always, Phillips's poems breathe quietude, but despite the wintry tone he seems ready for a reckoning, facing up to a traitorous world . . . and wrestling politely with God. . . . The results are polished and penetrating." Robert Phillips (no relation to the poet) wrote in his review of the book in the *Hudson Review*, "His poetry has been called erotic, yet somehow reserved, reminiscent of the gentlemanliness of older [W. H.] Auden and younger [James] Merrill." He finishes the review by noting, "I would quote, but his best stanzas invariably are run-on, long or complicated, so I'll pass. Just buy the book."

Donna Seaman, the reviewer for *Booklist*, called *The Rest of Love* a "rarified and metaphysical collection, one that features [Phillips's] signature stark landscapes and brooding eroticism." She went on to note that "Phillips' restrained and abstract lyrics are

elegant, enigmatic, and electric, provocative meditations on and enactments of what is 'a human need, / to give to shapelessness / a form.'"

Criticism

David Kelly

Kelly is an instructor of creative writing and literature at two colleges in Illinois. In this essay, he examines the implications of the poem's title.

Phillips's poem "All It Takes" does what good poetry generally aims to do, in that it raises provocative questions that it cannot pretend to answer. The poem does have a point to make, which is something that even a casual reader should be able to sense upon first encountering it, but it does not lay out its case in a direct, linear fashion. The poem makes readers take responsibility for piecing its various elements together: to decide, after thinking it through for a while, which combination of the elements might offer the most meaningful interpretation.

This method of engaging the reader's imagination, of making readers do a significant amount of the work in untangling the complex issues being explored, is what poetry can do best. Some of Phillips's images in "All It Takes" seem to divert from his central themes, and others are situated to yank the poem's train of thought abruptly in a new direction; these are the sorts of difficulties that readers can either reject or choose to absorb. Phillips writes with such reassuring authority, though, that most readers will keep faith and follow the uneven patches into new directions of inquiry. Rather than throwing the poem into confusion, the introduction of new elements serves to show that the issues under discussion are much larger than they may at first seem.

The poem is so complex, in fact, that it would be easy to overlook its most compelling, understated, mystery: that of the title. It has a familiarity, directness, and simplicity that would be more expected of the title of a mediocre coming-of-age comedy at the mall multiplex than in a delicate artwork. Because the phrase "all it takes" is a standard idiom in American English, readers might give in to the impulse to accept it without curiosity. But as a poem title it deserves interrogation: just what is the poem implying actually *is* "all it takes?" What is "it?" What is "all?" Because Phillips develops his poem's ideas in an indirect way, there is no clear answer to any of these questions.

What Do I Read Next?

- By his third volume of poems, *From the Devotions* (2002), Phillips was already recognized as a strong force in American poetry. This volume focuses on the correlation between body and spirit, which was then becoming a major theme in Phllips's work. Particularly representative of his work at the time is the title poem from this collection.

- Phillips explores theories about poetry, nature, and writing in a more linear fashion than he does in his poems with the essay collection *Coin of the Realm: Essays on the Art and Life of Poetry* (2004), published by Graywolf Press.

- The poetry of Brigit Pegeen Kelly has been compared to Phillips's in the way that it combines myth and observation to bring to life a rich spiritual world. Kelly's *The Orchard* (2004) is narrated from the perspective of an observer, describing human emotion and suffering rather than living it.

- One of the most influential books of the twentieth century was Sir James George Frazer's *The Golden Bough* (1888), a study of comparative myths and legends. Although it is more focused on distinctions between "civilized" and "primitive" societies than modern studies find acceptable, Frazer's book is still an influential overview of how civilizations around the world have approached ideas such as love and fidelity. *The Golden Bough* was first published as a two-volume set but was reedited in 1922 to the volume that is still in print.

The most direct answer to the question of what "it" refers to in the title would be to say that it is the "force" mentioned in the poem's first line. Phillips follows this primary idea with a list of variants on the same idea over the course of the first three stanzas: generosity, fear, dampness, and so on. This is, in fact, only a list and does not even pretend to be any sort of explanation. There is not even a verb in the poem until "shine," at the start of stanza 4.

One way of interpreting this pattern would be to think that the items on this three-stanza list do not need a verb because they are all direct objects, all meant to finish off the open-ended statement "All it takes is . . ." What makes this explanation unlikely is that there are quite a few elements listed throughout the first three stanzas. The word "all" is used in the title in the dismissive sense of "simply" or "merely"; this list (force, generosity, updraft, things invisible, dampness) seems a little long to be casually shrugged off. This is so unless the title is meant to be ironic; it is not impossible, but there is nothing else in the poem to indicate an ironic tone.

Moreover, when the poem continues, from the fourth stanza on, it introduces new elements that lead the inquiry into different directions. Readers are left to wonder, as each new element pops up, whether *this* will be "all it takes." Dead center in the poem, in the middle of the middle stanza, there is an idea that sounds as if it should be a likely candidate. Phillips phrases the line about the *ability* to believe preceding the *need* to believe in such a commanding way that it would be difficult to see it as anything but a grand, universal truth. It takes no stretch of the imagination to believe that this idea is placed centrally for a reason: that the rest of the poem is built around it, echoing in both directions. If the ability to believe is "all it takes," then the rest—what comes before and after it—is extra.

While this could easily be the case, it fails to explain many of the poem's intriguing aspects. What, for example, does betrayal have to do with the ability to believe? Clearly, this is an important concept, at least important enough to have the word "betrayed" used twice, mournfully, in the second stanza. Another and similarly perplexing verbal element is the way in which Phillips writes about the thorns on a wintry vine. "I am no less grateful for the berries than for the thorns" implies that readers

> *The image of 'crossing the water' is eternal, and it has a beautifully severe tone, but its very finality and severity are at odds with the lively, unblinking inquiry into the nature of life that has come before."*

might find this unusual, as if the ordinary presumption would be that the speaker should be more grateful for the thorns. But that would not, in fact, be the natural expectation. Both the "thorn" issue and the "betrayed" issue have a negative tone that is not conveyed in the line about having the ability to believe.

The poem makes one more notable detour in its explanation of Greek and Roman gods. Leaving aside the rich implications of the actual gods and their personalities, which it would take a classicist like Phillips to fully appreciate, the poem offers enough to consider just within its words alone. The god of love is said to be wild, the god of fidelity tame. The message, in the context of this particular poem, is that love is the greater mystery and therefore needs more activity of a wider range in order to make itself known. Fidelity, on the other hand, not needing such a showy god to define it, must be more innately familiar.

Focusing on this part of the poem alone, one can at least make a guess at what "it" means in the title: life, or serenity, or perhaps enlightenment. Unfortunately, what is even more obscure is what "it takes": it could take a lot of activity, as love requires, or just a little, like fidelity. Of course, when the title might be interpreted as meaning one thing or its exact opposite, then it does not really have meaning at all.

Whatever this poem's title refers to, it ends with death. It has two things to say about death in the last stanza: one is as enigmatic as anything that comes in the preceding six stanzas and one so commonplace that it feels like the right ending, but for the wrong poem. The directive to "Make / death

the one whose eyes are lidless" is typical of Phillips's poetry, insinuating an issue into the poem as if it has already been the subject of the discussion, though it has not: no "one" or "another" has previously been introduced. In the case of death's being "one," the "other" would have to be life. The poem tells readers to turn the tables, implying that life is normally the one with lidless eyes. The new order of things, prescribed by the poem, is that death should be made to be always vigilant. Therefore, if death's eyes are to become lidless, life is granted eyelids and the ability to close them, to relax its guard now and then.

At last, in a poem of such intensity, some element of acceptance is introduced. This casual acceptance corresponds with the "all" of the title, setting some limit. Life should be relaxed and let its eyes droop, while the advice of the title, telling readers what it takes, is relaxed by the simple "all." In each case, the poem warns to not make things any more complex than they need to be.

Philosophically, then, the poem is ultimately coherent. It deals with the ways actions and emotions become manifest through the physical world; how complex emotions require complex systems—the "wild" gods—to frame them in the mind; and how life should be more than looking for signs, leaving such unblinking vigilance for after death. In its final lines, though, "All It Takes" shifts to addressing its audience in a second-person voice, making a pronouncement of death that is not really a major point of the poem. This adds even more complexity to its meaning than any of the shifts in tone and subject matter that came before.

The phrases "you are leaving" and "you have crossed the water" both imply the finality of death, which is directly referred to at the start of the last stanza. In going from a command about how to treat death ("*make* / death . . .") to the observation that death has already come for the "you," Phillips gives the last line a finality that makes the poem feel complete, but he does so at the expense of what has led up to that point. The image of "crossing the water" is eternal, and it has a beautifully severe tone, but its very finality and severity are at odds with the lively, unblinking inquiry into the nature of life that has come before. It is almost as if the poem, having pondered substantial ideas throughout its seven stanzas, comes to a convenient but inconclusive end by telling readers not to think about all that has been discussed, because it is already too late. In this case, "all it takes" would be resignation, a stoic acceptance of a fate that could not be avoided anyway.

It would be nice if a poem could provide a magic, universal understanding of everything—everything!—and what to do about it. Poems cannot, though: any poem that pretends to explain the whole world in a few stanzas is either terribly naive or cynically insincere. Phillips is neither. With the title "All It Takes," he is being ironic, using the title's simplicity to show off the poem's winding complexity. The main point of this title is to prove its opposite: whatever "it" is, whatever it "takes," no poem will ever be able to tell its readers "all."

Source: David Kelly, Critical Essay on "All It Takes," in *Poetry for Students*, Thomson Gale, 2006.

Christopher Hennessy

In the following essay, Hennessy traces Phillips's life and career as a writer.

Immediately upon entering Carl Phillips's spartan, Cape Cod writing studio—all wood and windows, abutting some forty acres of conservation land—two things catch the eye: an antique horse bridle, worn but handsomely preserved, on the wall, and an old-fashioned stand-up writing desk in the corner. Both objects open windows onto Phillips's writing life and a poetry that is, in his own words, "becoming more about the unsayable, containing more and more questions, and more sentences that end by not ending."

"I'm intrigued by ideas of restraint and release—on the page and with the body," he says, tracing the bridle's collar. It's no surprise that horses, their power, their danger, the gear and vocabulary of riding—all these figure in a complex symbology the poet has developed over the years. As for the stand-up writing desk, it was a surprise birthday gift from Phillips's partner of twelve years, photographer Doug Macomber. The oak desk is literally, and in some ways figuratively, what the poet leans on during composition. "Writing is, for me, a bodily act," he says, "moving the arm, hearing the pen scratch, feeling the paper." Phillips, in fact, is often praised for his intense lyric moments about the body, its needs, wants, and its mortality, yet he also writes about "the invisible things that tie us together—space, desire, the erotic, where the sacred meets with notions of the body."

Phillips is led to poetry by "trying to understand something otherworldly and at the same time something very worldly about oneself," a statement that introduces the notion of paradox lurking behind his life and verse. Take, for example, the fact that Phillips the poet has been critically praised for poems energized by a "trademark phrasal difficulty

> *The book, he hopes, suggests 'that while love and faith may figure in a relationship, they're not sources of our salvation, and shouldn't be expected to be.'*

and oblique half-metaphors [which] remain as beautiful and perplexing as ever," and yet Phillips the man admits he most enjoys that part of his day when he walks his dog—"because it's what's most *un* complicated about life."

Phillips never planned on being a poet at all. Born in 1959 in Everett, Washington, he suspects that his becoming a poet may have had a lot to do with feeling—"being made to feel"—like an outsider from early on, starting with his being the product of a mixed-race marriage: his father is African American, a retired Air Force sergeant from Alabama; his mother, a painter and homemaker, is English-born and white. An instinct to take refuge in a more interior, private space was only strengthened by the transient life of being raised in the military. Every year of his childhood until the age of ten, Phillips's family was uprooted by his father's transfers, leaving little time or incentive for him to form friendships. He found solace in the "portable world" of his favorite books, books usually about secret codes and wildlife. Even today, dividing his time between Cape Cod and St. Louis and calling home "some combination of the two," Phillips carries his world with him: Hopkins, George Herbert, Jarrell, Hayden, and Dickinson are among the staples.

He first discovered the power and mystery inherent in language when he was twelve and beginning to study German during the four years his father was stationed in Zweibrücken. When the family moved back to the States to Falmouth, Massachusetts, Phillips continued studying languages by taking Latin, and then went on to Harvard University, where he earned his A.B. in Greek and Latin—though his intention when he enrolled had been to fulfill a lifelong dream of becoming a veterinarian. "I learned a great deal about surprise, and about opening oneself up to chance." From eating his first bagel to being dumbstruck by Woolf's *To The Lighthouse,* everything at Harvard was about discovery. "I do feel those years have almost everything to do with who I am now," he says. The first person in his family to go on to higher education, Phillips recalls how strange it was to be thrown into a world of wealth and privilege, and of families who had attended schools like Harvard for generations. "For the first two years, I had a job cleaning dorm bathrooms. Walking across Harvard Yard with a bucket in hand and a mop over one shoulder—that's still one of my most vivid memories of my Harvard experience. I wouldn't change it in any way."

While studying the great Latin and Greek poets and playwrights, Phillips was "struck by the immediacy of the emotional content of the work. . . . Reading Sappho or Horace, I didn't feel as if I was reading the work of a people from centuries ago. I saw those writers as companions, whose humanness I recognized; longing, grief, rage, and joy are not emotions which single us out as strangers, but which unify us in our being human." He hopes his verse makes apparent "not the distance between our century and theirs, but the intimacy we share in the arena where body, soul, mind, heart all come together."

As a sophomore, Phillips—who had composed poems here and there in high school—joined the staff of *The Harvard Advocate* literary review and began writing all the more earnestly. "Probably like everyone else, I was discovering Plath's *Ariel,* but getting it all wrong, missing the poetry for the life," he admits, and the poems showed as much. At one point, he applied to a very popular writing course, with competitive admission, taught by Seamus Heaney, but he didn't make the cut, "and rightly so," Phillips asserts. (He would later teach the same Harvard course as a visiting professor.)

After graduating in 1981, Phillips earned a Master's in Latin and Classical Humanities from the University of Massachusetts–Amherst, and began a career teaching Latin in high school. He also married a woman with whom he'd been friends since freshman year at Harvard. And he stopped writing. "It wasn't writer's block—I had no interest in writing, and assumed it had been a passing hobby." But during this time, Phillips was—if only half-aware of the fact himself—trying to come to terms with his homosexuality. When he did return to writing poems, it was, in some ways, "a psychological last-ditch rescue effort." It suddenly made sense, he explains, to turn to the invitation of the blank page, to sort things out "in the private place of the poem."

Perhaps it's no surprise that his motto is, "All art is pain, suffered and outlived," a line from Robert Hayden's "The Tattooed Man." "The things that drive me to write a poem," he adds, "are things that I don't understand about myself, or that I'm afraid to understand, or that I wouldn't dare try to understand in the presence of people who are in my life."

In 1990, with the help of a Massachusetts Artists Fellowship, he enrolled in his first poetry workshop, led by Alan Dugan, at the Castle Hill Center for the Arts in Truro. Dugan insisted the novice poet, again feeling like the uninitiated outsider, be the first to read his work aloud. Dugan's response to his timid reading shocked Phillips: "Well, obviously it's a real poem. Change nothing."

The encouragement meant everything. The young poet produced in a mere six months the poems that would become the bulk of his first book, *In the Blood* (Northeastern, 1992), which won the Samuel French Morse Poetry Prize. The poems were heralded by Rachel Hadas in the book's introduction as "transcendent and terrestrial," composed of "pained contradictions—eros tugging against anger, despair, isolation."

Only weeks before learning he'd won the Morse prize, Phillips met his partner Macomber, who became an essential reader. ("Doug's mind isn't cluttered with poetry jargon and trends. He gives me the only reaction I care about, one from the gut.") Macomber prompted Phillips to pursue an M.A. in poetry at Boston University, even though the admissions deadline had passed. "Doug suggested we call Robert Pinsky, whom I'd never met, and ask if we could drive to his house and hand him a manuscript. It seemed outrageous, and was." But Pinsky—who would serve as Phillips's principal mentor—agreed to look at the work and phoned the next night with a simple message: "Welcome to the workshop."

After BU, Phillips was hired at Washington University in 1993 as a visiting writer-in-residence. Three years later, he was awarded tenure, and he is now a professor of English and of African and Afro-American Studies. His passion for teaching comes through in his voice when he talks about his writing workshops and literature courses, the stimulation of being exposed to the multitude of new voices he encounters every year. He also stresses the necessity of mentoring students in order to keep not just poetry but learning itself alive in the next generation. To that end, he encourages his graduate students to conduct writing workshops in the inner-city schools of St. Louis.

Phillips's second and third books, *Cortège* (Graywolf, 1995) and *From the Devotions* (Graywolf, 1998), were finalists for the National Book Critics Circle Award and the National Book Award, respectively, a remarkable feat for such a young poet. Then, while writing his next book, *Pastoral* (Graywolf, 2000), he stumbled upon a more personal way of writing that "paradoxically also came across as being allegorical," he says, hinting at the attention critics have given to the recurring symbols in the poems. Allegorical or not, the Lambda Literary Award–winning *Pastoral* was received as breathtaking:

> . . . . At this hour of sun, in clubs
> of light, in broad beams failing, I do not
>
> stop it: I love you. Let us finally,
> undaunted, slow, with the slowness that a
> jaded ease engenders, together
>
> step into
> —this house, this sun: city of trumpets,
> noteless now; of tracks whose end is here.

His fifth book, *The Tether* (Farrar, Straus and Giroux, 2001), "was written during a period of crisis about the inability to distinguish between art and life—or the temptation to blur the distinction, as a means of explaining questionable behavior," he says. One critic reviewing the book, which Phillips believes is most markedly different from his other work, praised him for "some of the most formally accomplished first-person poems of male desire and relationships of his generation." While Phillips regards *The Tether* as "so much about thrashing at the limitations in a relationship with another person or with something like God," his most recent book, *Rock Harbor* (FSG, 2002), "though not a book of compromise, has a more anchored quality of the mind." The book, he hopes, suggests "that while love and faith may figure in a relationship, they're not sources of our salvation, and shouldn't be expected to be."

The publication of three critically praised books in three consecutive years has solidified his reputation as a prolific and vital force in American poetry, the work garnering the prestigious Kingsley Tufts Poetry Award and fellowships from the Guggenheim Foundation and the Library of Congress, as well as an Award in Literature from the American Academy of Arts and Letters, who cited Phillips as a "poet of restless imagination—part mythical, part mystical—and an artist of generous instincts and rare authority."

He shows little sign of slowing down. This year, Oxford University Press will publish his translation of Sophocles's *Philoctetes*. Next year,

Coin of the Realm, a collection of his essays, and *The Rest of Love,* his seventh book of poetry, will appear—the works rooted, as always, in personal experience, serving as testimony against the "prevailing age of cool irony where we deny we even have woundable feelings."

Source: Christopher Hennessy, "About Carl Phillips," in *Ploughshares*, Vol. 29, No. 1, Spring 2003, pp. 199–204.

Kendra Hamilton

In the following essay, Hamilton provides background on Phillips's academic and literary endeavors in the wake of his becoming only the second African American poet to win the high-profile Kingsley Tufts Poetry award.

Carl Phillips has become only the second African American poet to win the Kingsley Tufts Poetry Award, a highly coveted prize that carries with it a career's worth of prestige—and a $100,000 check.

Phillips says the reality of following in the footsteps of Yusef Komunyakaa—the first African American poet to win the prize in 1994—is just beginning to sink in.

"Some people have asked how I'm planning to spend it (the money), but quite frankly I haven't gotten that far," says Phillips during a break from his weeklong residency at the University of Virginia's Creative Writing Program. "I'm still having my Sally Field moment, reveling in the fact that they 'really do like me.' But I guess what it means is that I can now believe that people really do find my work of importance."

He admits that some might argue that's a message that should have gotten across by now. Phillips' very first book of poetry, *In the Blood,* won the Samuel French Morse Poetry Prize in 1992, while his second, *Cortege,* was a finalist for both the 1995 National Book Critics Circle Award and the Lambda Literary Award for gay-themed poetry. He's won fellowships to support his writing from the Witter Bynner and Guggenheim foundations, among others. And now, with the Kingsley Tufts Award for his fifth book, *The Tether,* Phillips currently is the toast of the poetry world.

Although being recognized for your work is most people's dream, Phillips says he did not have childhood aspirations of becoming a poet. "I wanted to be a veterinarian, and I thought that I would—all through my high school years," Phillips says.

During his undergraduate years at Harvard, however, that dream died on the vine as Phillips

> *Although being recognized for your work is most people's dream, Phillips says he did not have childhood aspirations of becoming a poet."*

discovered the academic subjects he loved in high school—calculus, biology, and so on—were suddenly downright dull to him. Instead, he fell in love with classical poetry, particularly the work of Sappho, and decided to major in Greek and Latin instead.

That choice parlayed itself into a career teaching Latin at the high school level for nearly eight years. Indeed, Phillips says, becoming a poet was something that likely would not have happened but for a series of coincidences.

"I guess in around '88 or '89, when I would have been about 29 or 30, I started writing. And I don't think I would have ever seen it as anything more than a hobby," Phillips explains, had he not taken a class with someone from the Poets in the Schools program. The poet thought Phillips' work showed promise and advised him to apply for an upcoming state grant. Phillips followed his advice— and won $10,000 on his first try.

The rest, as Phillips describes it, was "a whirlwind." The grant allowed him to take a workshop to hone his writing skills—and the workshop leader was Alan Dugan, a Yale Younger Poet and winner of the National Book Award and Pulitzer Prize, among other numerous honors. Dugan quickly became a believer in Phillips' work, advising him to collect his poems into a book and start trying to win one of the many prestigious first-book prizes, which are the surest way to recognition for a young writer's work.

Phillips followed Dugan's advice, though he also continued making more traditional plans for his life—such as entering a doctoral program at Harvard in classical philology. Then came the news that changed his life: He heard his book, *In the Blood,* had won the Morse Prize for publication of a first

book. "And it really made me question whether I belonged in a Ph.D. program," Phillips recalls.

Quickly, he shifted gears, leaving Harvard to enter Boston University's creative writing program, then basking in the glory of Derek Walcott's Nobel Prize for Literature in 1992. Robert Pinsky, soon to be named the nation's Poet Laureate, became a mentor, working closely with Phillips on his manuscript and advising him on his job search.

Phillips ended up taking a visiting professorship at Washington University in St. Louis. In his second year there—just as he had accepted another visiting professorship at Harvard—Phillips learned that his second book, *Cortege,* had been nominated for the National Book Critics Circle Award. That, apparently, was all the administration at Washington University needed to hear: They rushed to offer the young poet tenure. And the rest, as they say, is history.

Sometimes Phillips simply shakes his head in wonder at the turn his life has taken. "I hadn't planned on being a professor, let alone a professor of poetry," Phillips says.

Like many other successful African American poets, Phillips has found that the academy is an ivory tower both figuratively and literally.

Phillips says there are only five other tenured faculty members in his school's arts and sciences division. "Yes, five when I arrived—one died, and they hired another," he says. But while others might see that as a reason to leave, Phillips says it just makes him work harder at being "an effective presence" at the school.

"I think I've been able to have a good deal of influence over, for example, the courses that are taught in the English department. I know that African American poetry had not been taught before I arrived. I teach it now, and so do several other faculty members," he says.

In addition, Phillips has incorporated a service-learning unit into the writing program, requiring his mostly White students to teach poetry in inner-city St. Louis schools.

"It's, shall we say, a new experience for most of them, one that allows them to see what it feels like to be a minority for a change," Phillips says. "And I have to say, from the point of view of the graduate students teaching in the program, they love doing it—they all come out of the experience transformed."

Phillips doesn't think the experience he's currently basking in—that of being the toast of the poetry world—is one that will transform him. The glow of the moment, he says, "is passing very quickly because this is, ultimately, about the work and *Tether* is now old work. It's time to get on to the new."

Source: Kendra Hamilton, "The Current Toast of the Poetry World," in *Black Issues in Higher Education*, Vol. 19, No. 5, April 25, 2002, pp. 26–27.

Sources

Hoffert, Barbara, Review of *The Rest of Love*, in *Library Journal*, Vol. 128, No. 18, November 1, 2003, p. 87.

Phillips, Carl, *The Rest of Love*, Farrar, Straus and Giroux, 2004, p. 21.

Phillips, Robert, "Light and Dark," in *Hudson Review*, Vol. 57, No. 3, Autumn 2004, pp. 519–22.

Review of *In the Blood*, in *Publishers Weekly*, Vol. 239, No. 46, October 19, 1992, p. 72.

Seaman, Donna, "New Works by African American Poets," in *Booklist*, Vol. 100, No. 12, February 15, 2004, p. 1026.

Further Reading

Blacker, Mary Rose, *Flora Domestica: A History of British Flower Arranging, 1500–1930*, Harry N. Abrams, 2000.
When Phillips uses the metaphor of an arrangement of cut flowers, he implies a broad history of domestic floral arrangement. Unlike the many books about the subject that focus on advice, Blacker, who was with Britain's National Trust for thirty years, uses the subject of handling flowers as a basis for sociological study.

Daniélou, Alain, *Gods of Love and Ecstasy: The Traditions of Shiva and Dionysus*, Inner Traditions International, 1992.
There are several gods that can qualify as the "love" god mentioned in this poem. Daniélou's book examines the concept of a god of love across Western and Indian traditions.

Hilfrich, Karen, "Symbolic Changes: An Interview with Carl Phillips," in *Lambda Book Report*, Vol. 6, No. 9, April 1998, p. 15.
This interview, conducted when Phillips had been publishing poetry for just a few years, is noteworthy in the way the conversation veers from artistic theory to personal information to thoughts on the state of poetry in general.

Rich, Adrienne, "Format and Form," in *After New Formalism: Poets on Form, Narrative and Tradition*, Storyline Press, 1999, pp. 1–7.
Rich, one of the most respected of contemporary American poets, examines the general concept of form, as opposed to free verse. Readers who are interested in Phillips's mix of the casual and the structured should take note.

The Art of the Novel

Natasha Sajé

2004

Natasha Sajé's "The Art of the Novel" appears in her 2004 collection *Bend*. The poem's speaker is an intellectual literary critic with a longstanding love of literature who ultimately chooses not to allow literature to influence her personal romantic aspirations. In twelve free-verse couplets, she discusses love themes from novels, and she lists many of the heroines of classic fiction. Because she finds too much tragedy, turmoil, and unrequited love in literature, she chooses to bid farewell to the heroines and to novels in general. She decides instead to forge her own path in life.

The poem meditates on love, independence, self-assurance, and the appropriate place of fiction in real life. Sajé peers into the mind of a speaker who has come to a crossroad in her life and who chooses risk over familiarity. Despite having spent so much of her life immersed in the world of literature, she finds herself with a clearheaded view of the world around her, and she chooses to engage that world instead of retreating into the familiar but fictional literary world.

Author Biography

Natasha Sajé was born June 6, 1955, to Josef Sajé and Hiltrud Klima in Munich, Germany. She moved with her family to the United States in 1957 and spent her childhood and young adulthood in New York and New Jersey. Sajé earned her bachelor's

degree from the University of Virginia in 1976, graduating with honors in English. In 1980, she completed her master's degree at Johns Hopkins University, and in 1995, she earned her doctorate in English from the University of Maryland.

Sajé's first poetry collection, *Red under the Skin*, was published in 1994. In 1993, the work had been chosen over nine hundred other manuscripts to receive the Agnes Lynch Starrett Poetry Prize; it was later also awarded the Towson State Prize in literature. Additional honors for her poetry include the 1993 Academy of American Poets Prize, the 1998 Robert Winner Award from the Poetry Society of America, and the 2002 Campbell Corner Poetry Prize. In 2004, Sajé completed her second poetry collection, *Bend*, which includes "The Art of the Novel."

Sajé's poems and articles have appeared in such journals as *Ploughshares, Shenandoah*, the *Writer's Chronicle, Legacy: A Journal of American Women Writers*, the *Henry James Review, Essays in Literature*, and *Dalhousie Review*. She was the Bannister writer in residence at Sweetbriar College in 1995 and was a poet in residence for the Maryland State Arts Council from 1989 to 1998. Sajé has also been an associate professor of English at Westminster College in Salt Lake City, Utah, where she has also served as the Weeks Poetry Series administrator. In addition, she has taught in the Vermont College Master of Fine Arts in Writing Program.

Natasha Sajé   David Baddley

Poem Text

In 1790 a woman could die by falling
for her guardian who happens to be a priest

or a man who is penniless. *A Simple Story.*
Ruined. As if a woman were a building and love

centuries of bad weather. *A mirror carried on a*   5
    highway,
said Stendhal, and in the case of Emma Bovary

or Lily Bart, a highway to hell, with me riding
    shotgun.
Did I like the relentless bleakness because Emma's
    not

me, or because she could be me? Years spent in a
    haze
of fiction, living through characters, writing about   10
    them,

looking for loopholes in cloth woven tight.
Perhaps nothing's changed, love is still fatal,

except today she starts her own company.
But I've had it with this form of desire, this

Continuous dream: I can't read in the past tense,   15
Those surprising but inevitable endings. So
    farewell, Tess,

Moll, and Clarissa; Miss Bennett and Miss Milner;
Isabel and Scarlett. And for the record, novel,

I abandon you—you who are, Lukács said,
the epic of a world abandoned by God,   20

you who made my world bigger and kept me on
    the beltway,
life transformed into destiny. My odometer's
    clicked

past the point of counting. I now prefer footpaths,
    or no paths,
and thickly wooded country; the moon.

Poem Summary

Lines 1–5

"The Art of the Novel" opens with a reference to the story line of Elizabeth Inchbald's *A Simple Story*, with the comment that back in 1790, "a woman could die by falling" in love with a forbidden man. A specific reference to the title of Inchbald's book follows, with the text "A Simple Story." In lines 4 and 5, a single word, "Ruined," is set apart with a period from the speaker's comparison of a woman to a building and of love to "centuries of bad weather." These images reflect the speaker's view of love as something that slowly batters and erodes an otherwise strong and stable woman. Sajé continues with the image "*A mirror carried on a highway*," referring to the French author Henri Stendhal's own description of his novel *The Red and the Black*.

Lines 6–7

The speaker now mentions two tragic heroines: Emma Bovary of Gustave Flaubert's *Madame Bovary* and Lily Bart of Edith Wharton's *House of Mirth*. Stendhal's "highway" becomes a "highway to hell, with me riding shotgun." The speaker thus feels that she has suffered through the heartbreak felt by Emma and Lily as she read these novels and emotionally invested herself in their outcomes.

Lines 8–11

In lines 8 and 9, the speaker admits that she was drawn to the tragedy of *Madame Bovary* but wonders if it was because she herself was not in Emma's predicament or because she felt as though Emma "could be me." This is an important moment in the poem, in which the speaker pauses from her reflection on literature to focus for a moment on her own life. This self-reflection leads her to remember that she has spent years concentrating on fiction, years "spent in a haze." By living through fictional characters, writing about them, and providing critical analysis of the stories in which they appear ("looking for loopholes in cloth woven tight"), she has failed to engage the real world that is all around her.

Lines 12–20

The idea that the modern world is no different from the world portrayed in classic literature is introduced briefly in lines 12 and 13. The speaker realizes that love in her world can still be fatal, but now strong women, like the fictional heroines she has admired, can start their own companies. Line 14 denotes a turn in the poem, with the speaker's declaration "But I've had it with this form of desire, this / continuous dream." At this moment, she decides that living her life immersed in stories about fictional people from long ago is not a healthy approach to life. One by one, she bids farewell to seven tragic heroines and their broken hearts. She then bids farewell to novels in general, but she cannot completely let go of her years of formal training. As she releases herself from the hold of fiction, she quotes Georg Lukács, a Russian critic who said, "The novel

is the epic of a world abandoned by God." This statement alludes to the idea that the concept of rejecting fiction is not new to the world, but it is a new consideration in the speaker's own life.

Lines 21–24

As the poem closes, the speaker acknowledges that novels have broadened her horizons but have also kept her on the "beltway," which means that she could go where a novel took her but that she could not stray from the book's path. This reference also reminds the reader of the previous Stendhal quote about a highway. When the speaker says, "My odometer's clicked / past the point of counting," she realizes that the metaphorical car she has been driving on the beltway/highway has been driven for too long. She decides that it is time to get out and forge her own path in the real world—a risky endeavor for the speaker, who is accustomed to the safety of being guided through fiction. Now, however, she is ready to be her own guide and to engage the real world.

Themes

Fiction versus Real Life

In "The Art of the Novel," Sajé depicts a woman whose life has centered on classic novels and their heroines. The speaker clearly loves literature and has given it an important place in her life. She writes that the plots have unfolded "with me riding shotgun" and that novels have "made my world bigger." These images are indicative of a person who has allowed classic fiction to be a very real part of her life and who has permitted herself to be deeply influenced by what she reads. The speaker not only loves literature as a pastime, she has also made a career of writing about it. Presumably, she is a literary critic or a scholar, based on the lines "Years spent in a haze / of fiction, living through characters, writing about them, / looking for loopholes in cloth woven tight." She seems to have spent many years closely reading well-crafted novels, writing about them and their characters as she scrutinized the text.

As the poem progresses, the speaker comes to a point where she makes a life-changing decision to set fiction aside in favor of experiencing the real world firsthand. In lines 14 and 15, she writes, "But I've had it with this form of desire, this / continuous dream: I can't read in the past tense," which reveals her choice to live in the present. At the end

Topics For Further Study

- "The Art of the Novel" uses a lot of imagery—an eroding building, a mirror, a highway, numerous fictional characters, woods, and more. Create a multimedia presentation pairing images with the text of the poem. You may choose to do a PowerPoint presentation, for example, or create a sequence with video-editing software. The presentation should reflect not only the images of the poem but also the tone and emotional landscape of the speaker.

- Choose one of the heroines named in the poem and write an essay relating the heroine's story to that of the poem's speaker. Look for similarities and differences between the heroine and the speaker and for compelling reasons why the poem's speaker has mentioned the character you chose.

- Choose five people you know who enjoy reading fiction. Interview them about their personal histories with regard to reading and books, what reading means to them, and how their reading habits affect their lives. Summarize each interview and then see what conclusions you can draw about the ways people internalize the fiction they read. Present your findings in an article written for high-school English teachers.

- Read Robert Frost's poem "The Road Not Taken." Pretend that you are a speaker who has been asked to talk to a class of graduating English majors and that you have decided to use both Frost's poem and Sajé's poem to encourage these students to take risks after graduation. Prepare your speech, along with any visuals or handouts you want to incorporate, and deliver your presentation to your English class.

---

of the poem, the speaker essentially gets out of the car in which she has been riding shotgun so she can pursue "footpaths, or no paths." She likens reading fiction to being on a highway or beltway; these are well-traveled, basically safe paths. They take passengers to faraway destinations, but they also confine passengers to the highway itself. The speaker opts to venture off on her own, onto slower, more personalized paths. It is a choice much like the one Robert Frost makes in "The Road Not Taken," in which he chooses "the [path] less traveled by." For the speaker in "The Art of the Novel," the choice is a risky one because she has always found adventure, love, relationships, and human experience within the safe pages of books. The place of fiction in her life thus changes from being the very framework of her experience to being merely a part of her knowledge base.

Role of Women

In the opening statements of "The Art of the Novel," women seem fragile and vulnerable to the consequences of their emotions. Sajé tells the reader

that in 1790 a woman could actually die just from falling in love with the wrong man. This is a startling opening that makes the reader wonder if the speaker will elaborate on how fragile women are or will continue to explain how women today are much stronger. In line 3, Sajé clarifies that her opening statement is, in fact, a brief plot summary of *A Simple Story*, a novel by Elizabeth Inchbald. As the poem continues, the speaker makes clear that she does not see women as helpless victims but rather as people who make choices for themselves. Not all of these choices are good and healthy, however, as evidenced by the mention of such tragic characters as Emma Bovary, Lily Bart, and Scarlett O'Hara. Line 9 reveals that the speaker sees in these tragic characters the frightening possibility of her own potential. The line also reveals that the speaker is a woman who does not yet know herself very well.

In lines 12 and 13, the speaker contrasts the restrictive societies of the past with contemporary society. While in the past women were subject to the pain of heartache with few ways to take control, contemporary women have opportunities to wield power, such as starting their own businesses. Sajé writes, "Perhaps nothing's changed, love is still fatal, / except today she starts her own company." The remark that "love is still fatal" is almost parenthetical; the speaker is saying that although women have more outlets than they did in the past, they are still vulnerable to the pitfalls of love.

More subtly, the speaker herself has made a career that women in the past did not have. She is a literary scholar who writes intellectually about great works of fiction, whereas in the past women were not even expected to read or to have opinions about intellectual matters. Because the speaker is so well versed in stories of women of the past, she understands that she lives in a cultural reality different from those of many of the heroines from classic fiction.

Style

Apostrophe

For the first fifteen lines of the poem, the speaker seems to be talking to an anonymous confidant. At the end of line 16, the speaker reveals the audience being addressed in the poem. She is talking to fiction itself, in the forms of characters and the novel genre. After lamenting the heartache of numerous novels and expressing her own emotional stake in them, she directly addresses the heroines of those novels. She bids farewell to Tess (from Thomas Hardy's *Tess of the D'Urbervilles*), Moll (from Daniel Defoe's *Moll Flanders*), Clarissa (from Samuel Richardson's *Clarissa*), and four others. She then turns her attention to the real villain, in lines 18 and 19: "And for the record, novel, / I abandon you." This marks a turning point in the poem and in the poet's life. She has reached a crossroad where she must decide whether to continue living the lives already written in classic novels or close her books and get out in the world. Sajé effectively communicates the drama and importance of this moment by using apostrophe, direct address to an inanimate object, a concept, or a nonexistent person. Because the speaker addresses the novel, a nonliving thing that cannot respond to her, the reader understands that the speaker is really talking to herself in a symbolic way. By using numerous other literary devices throughout the poem (including allusion, simile, metaphor, symbolism, assonance, alliteration, and oxymoron), the

speaker shows that she knows how to "talk" to works of literature in their own unique language.

Couplet Structure

"The Art of the Novel" is written in twelve free-verse couplets. Couplets are two lines of poetry with the same rhyme and meter, usually expressing a self-contained thought. However, the couplets in this poem do not express self-contained thoughts, with the text in each couplet extending into the next couplet to finish the thought. While the couplets give the poem a visually ordered appearance, the content does not support this impression. Given that the poem is about the speaker's lifelong love of literature, Sajé seems to reinforce the speaker's personality by using traditional poetic form as a default. The reader senses that the speaker is expressing herself in a natural, flowing way but is somehow obligated by her training to structure the poem in a traditional form. The tension between the content and the form reflects the transition the speaker is preparing to make from relying on her knowledge of literature to relying on herself. The poem may appear to comply with convention, but it is actually a very personal expression of the speaker's decision to change the direction of her life.

Historical Context

Modern Reading Habits

In 2002, the Census Bureau conducted a survey to determine the cultural habits of Americans of all ages, races, and income levels. More than seventeen thousand Americans were surveyed, making it among the most comprehensive surveys of its kind ever conducted. In the reading section, participants were asked if they had read any novels, poems, short stories, or plays in the prior twelve months. The survey was called the Survey of Public Participation in the Arts, and it was done at the urging of the National Endowment of the Arts (NEA). The NEA compiled the findings on reading habits into a publication called *Reading at Risk: A Survey of Literary Reading in America*. When the NEA chairman, Dana Gioia, summarized the findings at a news conference at the New York Public Library held July 8, 2004, he said that the report indicated a crisis and a breakdown in adult advanced literacy.

The cause of Gioia's deep concern is that the survey reports a significant decline in literary reading across age groups. On average, the decline from 1982 to 2002 indicated 10 percent fewer literary readers, a figure that reflects a loss of 20 million potential readers. Even more troubling is that the decline is trending downward. A major concern is that the trends identified by the survey have indirect effects on society and on culture in general. Literary readers, for example, tend to be more interested in and supportive of other cultural activities and events, including volunteering.

Although the decline in literary reading was observed across demographic groups, the sharpest decline was among young adults. In fact, some estimates predict that literary reading as a leisure-time activity in this age group will be obsolete within fifty years. Comparing genders, the survey found that although literary reading has declined for both men and women, the rate for women is slower. This means that women generally read more literary materials than men do. As for genres, readers preferred novels and short stories, which were read by 45 percent of readers. Poetry was read by 12 percent, and plays were read by only 4 percent. The number of people trying their hand at creative writing, however, actually increased by 30 percent.

Critical Overview

Critics describe Sajé's poetry as appealing to both the senses and the mind. They often find her poetry to be clear, well paced, and descriptive. Her award-winning debut collection, *Red under the Skin*, was embraced by reviewers upon its release in 1994. Angela Sorby in the *Chicago Review*, for example, declares it "a substantial collection, written in a voice that is consistent without being predictable." Sorby later adds, "Even in her moments of weakness, this poet commands respect, because she never strains for false epiphanies or connections."

In 2004, Sajé's second poetry collection, *Bend*, was published. Literary commentators note how skillfully Sajé presents topics as wide ranging as food and great literary figures. Some critics express surprise at her references to such writers as Cotton Mather, Mary Shelley, Marcel Proust, and Gertrude Stein. In the *Women's Review of Books*, Alison Hawthorne Deming describes *Bend* as a "finely prepared feast of pleasures, body and mind dancing through the house of her imagination. Words and images, their tumbling forward through the mind, are as delicious to this poet as a blueberry crisp."

Criticism

Jennifer Bussey

Bussey holds a master's degree in interdisciplinary studies and a bachelor's degree in English literature. She is an independent writer specializing in literature. In the following essay, she examines each literary allusion made in Sajé's poem as a way to explore new levels of meaning.

Sajé's second poetry collection, *Bend*, includes the poem "The Art of the Novel." In this poem, a literary scholar describes her relationship with literature and the fictional heroines of classic novels. The relationships are described in terms that reflect a very personal connection to these characters and their stories, but the speaker ultimately turns away from them so that she can see what story life has in store for her. Because the speaker's life has been so steeped in literature, it is not surprising that she introduces numerous literary allusions throughout the poem. It is also not surprising that these allusions contain valuable information about the speaker and her mindset in the moment of making her decision to seek her own path rather than to continue following fictional ones. A speaker as well read as this one can easily call up any number of characters, stories, or comments by literary critics, but she chooses the specific references used in the poem. Why these and not others? A careful reader should not assume that the choices the speaker makes about her literary allusions are random but instead that they provide important insight into the meaning of the poem. By examining them individually, readers find that the speaker will come into sharper focus, opening up a new level to the reading of the poem and to the speaker's brave decision at the end.

The poem opens with the statement that in 1790, a woman could die by making foolish or unfortunate choices in love. The third line reveals that the speaker is briefly summarizing the plot of Elizabeth Inchbald's *A Simple Story*. What is revealing about the speaker, however, is that the way she presents the story initially suggests that she is relating historical information, as opposed to a bit of fiction. The speaker states the information as fact, indicating that her immersion in classic fiction has blurred the lines somewhat between fantasy and reality. This connection to literature is carried all the way to the end of the poem, even when the speaker decides to turn away from literature to face the real world. Rather than closing a book and stepping outside, she takes the time to bid farewell to seven

> *A careful reader should not assume that the choices the speaker makes about her literary allusions are random but instead that they provide important insight into the meaning of the poem.*"

fictional heroines and to the novel genre itself. This shows a person who feels an intensely close bond to the fiction that she loves but who realizes that the hold it has on her is not healthy. As she works through these feelings, she revisits other heroines and calls up comments made by literary theorists. Each of these references holds significance to the speaker's decision, so it is worthwhile to consider them one at a time.

The first allusion, as noted, is to *A Simple Story*. The protagonist in *A Simple Story* is Miss Milner (mentioned again in line 17 of the poem), who boldly admits her love for her guardian, a Catholic priest. Miss Milner challenges social conventions about what is appropriate for women and finds that she is unhappy when the man she loves is released from his religious vows to marry her. Her rebellious nature prevents her from being peacefully submissive to her husband's strong moral leadership in their home. Miss Milner is a flawed character who is unable to find joy even when she gets what she thinks she wants. Her story is ultimately tragic because she takes enormous risks to win the man she loves, only to find her marriage unsuitable for her unconventional personality. This character likely appeals to the speaker in "The Art of the Novel" because Miss Milner is independent and outspoken and believes in love. Miss Milner is also a woman who thinks that she knows herself but is actually unsure of what she needs to lead a contented and satisfying life. These are qualities to which the poem's speaker can relate, having resided so long in the world of fiction that she is unsure what would bring true love and happiness into her life.

The next allusion is to a statement made by the French author Henri Stendhal in his novel *The Red and the Black*. In the book, he describes the novel as a mirror passing over a main road, sometimes reflecting both the blue sky above and sometimes reflecting the mud below. This allusion accomplishes two things, one directly and one indirectly. The direct contribution to the poem is in the quote itself. Sajé cites only the first sentence from this quote, but her speaker certainly knows the rest of the passage. This quote introduces the idea of the role fiction plays in our lives. According to Stendhal, fiction accompanies people on their life journeys but is nothing more than a reflection of what already exists in the real world. As the quote explains, sometimes the reflection is beautiful, uplifting, and affirmative, but at other times it is harsh, realistic, and ugly. These ideas relate directly to "The Art of the Novel," because the poem's speaker is struggling to put fiction back in its proper place and to stop substituting it for reality. The indirect contribution this allusion makes to the poem is in knowing its source. The poem implicitly states that the quote is from *The Red and the Black*, but identifying it provides additional insight into the speaker. The novel is about a young man named Julien Sorel, who strives to overcome his humble beginnings to ascend to greater wealth and influence. Like Miss Milner in *A Simple Story*, however, Sorel never really achieves happiness, because he, too, is flawed. For all his ambition and greed, his own romanticism and the political climate of France at the time of the novel prevent him from getting everything he thinks he wants. Again, this reflects back on the poem's speaker herself.

The poem's speaker remarks that the highway mentioned by Stendhal is a "highway to hell" for Emma Bovary and for Lily Bart. Emma Bovary is the main character of Gustave Flaubert's *Madame Bovary*. She marries an aging doctor so she can leave her father's farm, but she finds married life to be extremely disappointing and unromantic. She does not love or respect her husband, so she seeks exciting romance in affairs with other men. Her story is tragic because she spends so much money traveling to see her lover and buying him gifts that she commits suicide to avoid the repercussions of her inability to pay her mounting debt. Sajé introduces Madame Bovary because Bovary is a classic tragic figure whose misguided quest for love and romance bring nothing but misery and hopelessness.

The other literary character mentioned in lines 6 and 7 of "The Art of the Novel" is Lily Bart from

What Do I Read Next?

- Robin Behn's *The Practice of Poetry: Writing Exercises from Poets Who Teach* (1992) is a portable, self-contained work that aspiring poets may use to gain insight and guidance from numerous writing teachers. The book contains ninety exercises, along with essays to help the reader hone his or her craft.

- In *Brave Dames and Wimpettes: What Women Are Really Doing on Page and Screen* (1999), the author Susan Isaacs lines up female characters like Jo March (from Louisa May Alcott's *Little Women*), Elizabeth Bennett (from Jane Austen's *Pride and Prejudice*), and the actress Katherine Hepburn (who played Jo March on-screen) to illustrate what makes a woman truly strong and independent. She contrasts this type of woman with characters such as Gustave Flaubert's Madame Bovary and the television character Ally McBeal, who are termed "wimpettes." By drawing from past and modern literature, film, and television, Isaacs provides a cultural image of womanhood.

- Kimberley Reynolds and Nicola Humble provide an overview of literary heroines in *Victorian Heroines: Representations of Femininity in Nineteenth-Century Literature and Art* (1993). They show how female protagonists in this period are unique and how they influenced later heroines in fiction.

- Sajé's *Red under the Skin* (1994) is her debut poetry collection. This volume won the Agnes Lynch Starrett Poetry Prize, and critics found that it showed great promise.

Edith Wharton's *The House of Mirth*, which is set in turn-of-the-century New York. Lily wants all the power, prestige, and luxury of the upper class but is not willing to bend to the social rules that accompany such a lifestyle. Her rebellious nature eventually costs her her social standing and her chance to live in leisure. Lily is similar to Miss Milner, who is also more committed to being herself than to being what society expects her to be; in both cases, this fidelity to self comes at a high price. Sajé's speaker is sympathetic toward these characters, calling them "ruined" and on a "highway to hell." It is not clear whether the poem's speaker admires the spirit of these characters or if she is just moved by their dire fates. It is clear that she is fixating on heroines whose lives were tragic and lonely.

In line 16, the speaker begins a list of seven female protagonists from major works of classic literature. Her rapid-fire delivery of the names signals an increase in the pace of the speaker's intentions to put them behind her and move on to the real world. The reader, however, should pause to consider briefly why the speaker is thinking of these seven women at this important moment in her life. The first heroine is Tess from Thomas Hardy's *Tess of the D'Urbervilles*. Tess endures extreme trials in her life as she struggles to care for her family, make a good marriage, and release herself from the grasp of an immoral and conniving man. In the end, she commits murder to free herself from him and is arrested and put to death for her crime. Tess is driven by the knowledge that a good life is available to her if she can only escape from her circumstances.

Then there is the title character from Daniel Defoe's *Moll Flanders*, set in England. Moll's story is tragedy turned to triumph. Orphaned when her criminal mother dies, Moll struggles in her early years, only to find herself a widow several times over. When she is no longer young enough to find a suitable husband, she resorts to theft and is caught. Her sentence is to be sent to Virginia in the United States, and she persuades another man to accompany her and to be her husband. Together, they grow a successful tobacco plantation and are able to return to England under assumed names.

The next heroine is Clarissa, who appears in a novel of the same name written by Samuel Richardson. Clarissa is another heroine who refuses to submit to the will of her family and her society by agreeing to a loveless marriage. When she runs away with a man she finds attractive, she finds that his motives are vengeful and cruel. Although she eventually dies alone, she never compromises her convictions. Clarissa is yet another heroine who is strong and resolute but who pays dearly for her insistence on doing things her own way.

"Miss Bennett" refers to the character Elizabeth Bennett from Jane Austen's *Pride and Prejudice*. Elizabeth is a self-confident young woman who refuses to be impressed by the men her society believes should impress her. She is spirited, proud, cynical, and outspoken, and in the end she finds love in a most unexpected man. In her story, happiness in love comes to her in spite of herself.

After mentioning Miss Bennett, the speaker bids farewell to Miss Milner, whose story was introduced at the beginning of the poem. The next heroine is Isabel from Henry James's *The Portrait of a Lady*. When Isabel arrives in England from America, she surprises everyone by rejecting suitable marriage proposals and instead marrying a man of no social standing or wealth. The more she gets to know of him, however, the more she realizes that he is manipulative and feels more disdain than love for her. Despite opportunities to escape and seek a better life, Isabel is committed to being a good wife.

The final heroine in the speaker's list is Scarlett O'Hara from Margaret Mitchell's *Gone with the Wind*. Scarlett is another woman who makes foolish choices in love. Her fixation on one man renders her incapable of finding happiness with any other man, and her strong but doting husband eventually abandons her.

What is striking about these heroines, taken collectively, is that none of them finds happiness easily. Either they arrive at happiness by experiencing a difficult series of events, or they end up unhappy, tragically heartbroken, alone, or dead. These are stories from which the speaker in "The Art of the Novel" might learn, but they are not stories she should embrace as being everything the world has to offer. In the poem, the speaker seems to come to a point where she suspects that these are enduring characters and novels *because* they are so tragic and flawed, not because they represent what is normal in the real world. The speaker's decision to put them all behind her is a decision of empowerment and hope. Although there is a great deal of risk involved, the risk is worth taking because staying immersed in the lives of these women, with all their suffering, denies her a chance to do better. When, at the end of the poem, the speaker effectively steps out of her car with its exhausted odometer, she is stepping out of the world of fiction. The highway she leaves behind is the limitations of the genre, which, however expansive and exciting, cannot really compare with the opportunities offered by the world. Realizing this, the speaker seeks the settings opposite the highway—"footpaths, or no paths, / and thickly wooded country, the moon."

Source: Jennifer Bussey, Critical Essay on "The Art of the Novel," in *Poetry for Students*, Thomson Gale, 2006.

Bryan Aubrey

Aubrey holds a PhD in English and has published many articles on contemporary poetry. In the following essay, Aubrey discusses the literary allusions in Sajé's poem.

Sajé is an engaging young poet who does unusual and unexpected things in her poems. Like "The Art of the Novel," many of the poems in her collection *Bend* contain literary or philosophical allusions that add extra layers of meaning or are simply used playfully by the poet. In "Marcel at the Station House," for example, Sajé imagines the French novelist Marcel Proust being questioned by the police about a crime he did not commit and giving some delightfully oblique, Proust-like answers. "Seven Types of Ambiguity" is a reference to a well-known—at least to students of literature—book of that title written in 1930 by the literary critic William Empson. The title of the poem is no more than a wink to those in the know, since the poem itself makes no reference to the book. "The Art of the Novel" is remarkable in terms of its allusions, since in a poem of only twenty-four lines, Sajé manages to pack in a total of twelve literary references.

The female speaker of the poem sounds rather like a graduate student in comparative literature, or perhaps a former graduate student, who has read everything put in front of her during graduate school as far as the novel and the theory of the novel are concerned. For many years, she has deeply loved this literary genre, identifying strongly with literary heroines and being drawn completely into their worlds as if they were her own. But now, having studied the novel and books about the novel and also having written about them—graduate school papers, perhaps—she has had enough. She declares that despite all she owes to novels ("you who made my world bigger"), she is never going to read another novel again—and that's final!

The poem is therefore at once a tribute to the power of novels to captivate and enthrall the reader and a decisive farewell to a literary genre that, as far as the speaker is concerned, has outlived its usefulness. She is clearly exasperated by the fate often meted out to the heroines of mostly eighteenth- and nineteenth-century novels. Her first three examples, which set the tone for the poem as a whole, allude to female characters whose lives end tragically. She gives pride of place to *A Simple Story*, by Elizabeth Inchbald, who published this minor novel in England in 1791. The heroine, the beautiful and vivacious Miss Milner (who is named in line 17 of "The Art of the Novel") falls passionately in love with her guardian, a Catholic priest named Dorriforth. She regards this as a "fatal attraction" and a "sacrilegious love" and at first tries to hide it. In the meantime, Dorriforth inherits the title of Lord Elmwood and leaves the priesthood. When the truth of Miss Milner's love for him comes out, he falls in love with her, and they marry.

For four years they are happy, but then Lord Elmwood goes away for several years on business in the West Indies. Miss Milner, now Lady Elmwood, is distressed at his absence and has an affair with one of her former suitors. When her husband returns unexpectedly, she flees, guilt-stricken and in disgrace. Thereafter she lives a life of seclusion, devoid of all comforts, permanently estranged from her now vengeful husband. After a long decline, she dies, still young, "ruined," as the speaker in "The Art of the Novel" puts it, by her own recklessness and impatience. However, it is clear that the speaker has some argument with the word "ruin" as applied to women who, for one reason or another, lose their good names in society: "Ruined. As if a woman were a building and love / centuries of bad weather."

The next literary character mentioned by the speaker of the poem might also be considered "ruined." Lily Bart is the protagonist of Edith Wharton's novel *The House of Mirth* (1905). She is an attractive, unmarried woman of twenty-nine, who is financially ruined by her addiction to gambling at high-society parties. She never achieves her goal of marrying a wealthy man; instead, she ends up being shunned by upper-class society after false rumors are spread that she has had an extramarital affair. Lily then plunges down in social class. She

> *Whereas life comes to us incomplete, its final outcomes always unknown, the novel presents life as destiny, a realized thing, leaving us to reflect on its significance and meaning."*

takes jobs as a secretary and then as a milliner and lives in a boarding house. Although she just manages to pay off her debts, she is lonely and depressed, and one day she takes an overdose of sleeping medicine that kills her.

Emma Bovary, the protagonist of Gustave Flaubert's famous novel *Madame Bovary* (1857), is an even greater tragic heroine. Emma is a romantic young woman whose marriage to an unintelligent and tedious country doctor so disappoints her that she looks for love elsewhere. But after having two sordid and unsatisfactory affairs, her life goes into a downward spiral of despair, and she eventually commits suicide by swallowing arsenic. Emma indeed travels a "highway to hell," as the speaker of the poem characterizes it.

Why then do so many people enjoy reading this and other, similar novels? What is it about the "relentless bleakness" (the speaker's words again) that draws the reader in? Why did the speaker so much enjoy "riding shotgun" with these female characters on their harrowing highways to hell?

First, it should be pointed out that anyone who has ever read a good novel knows how easy it is to lose oneself in the fictional world that the author has created. This is particularly true in the case of novels that adhere to the principles of realism, in which the author tries to present life as it really is. As William James put it in his influential essay "The Art of Fiction" (the title "The Art of the Novel" may well be an allusion to this essay), "the air of reality . . . seems to me to be the supreme virtue of a novel—the merit on which all its other merits . . . helplessly and submissively depend." Even though realism is, in fact, an artfully created illusion, the reader is willingly drawn into the illusion. It is as if we are temporarily living in the world of the novel, which seems to represent life so faithfully. Moreover, as the Russian critic M. M. Bakhtin pointed out, this imaginative escape can be taken to an extreme, in which case "we might substitute for our own life an obsessive reading of novels, or dreams based on novelistic models" (quoted by Jeremy Hawthorn in *Studying the Novel: An Introduction*). Bakhtin's comment puts in mind the "Years spent in a haze / of fiction, living through characters," which is how the speaker of "The Art of the Novel" describes the period in which novels gripped her attention with such intensity.

Curiously, Emma Bovary in Flaubert's novel goes through a rather similar experience. She identifies so strongly with fictional models that she uses them to justify her own life. This happens when she feels guilty at having taken a lover and deceived her husband.

> Then she recalled the heroines of the books that she had read, and the lyric legion of these adulterous women began to sing in her memory with the voice of sisters that charmed her. She became herself, as it were, an actual part of these imaginings, and realised the love-dream of her youth as she saw herself in this type of amorous women whom she had so envied.

Thus Emma, herself a fictional character, testifies to the power of fiction to fill the imagination and (as Bakhtin says) blur distinctions between real and fictional life, so strong is her need to identify with her chosen models.

With this in mind, return to the question of why the speaker of "The Art of the Novel" (or any reader) so much enjoyed accompanying Miss Milner, Lily, and Emma on their fatal journeys. She herself addresses the point in the form of a question: "Did I like the relentless bleakness because Emma's not / me, or because she could be me?"

The way the question is posed puts in mind Aristotle's famous statement, in his *Poetics*, that the pleasure experienced by the audience at a tragic play is due to the release of two emotions, pity and fear. The audience feels pity because it watches the sufferings of someone else, the hero, whose misfortunes are greater than he deserves (this is the "not / me" element in the poem's quoted lines). The second emotion, fear, arises from the realization that the character is much like ourselves and the same could happen to us ("she could be me"). Although Aristotle's comments, which have been much interpreted, were intended to apply to the drama, a similar process of empathic identification may well operate for the reader of a tragic novel and produce the same kind of pleasure.

The speaker of "The Art of the Novel" hints at a second reason why the novel, which since the nineteenth century has been by far the most popular literary form, fascinated her for so long. The relevant phrase occurs at the end of the following lines: "you who made my world bigger and kept me on the beltway, / life transformed into destiny."

A novel may be said to transform life into destiny in the sense that it imposes order and direction on the chaos and uncertainty of life. It creates a pattern of cause and effect, a pattern that in life is not always possible to discern. In a novel, the fates of the characters acquire a kind of inevitability, unlike the unknowableness of life. In life, the inner lives of others (and perhaps even our own) can never be fully understood, but a novelist like Flaubert can provide unerring insight into the smallest fluctuations of Emma Bovary's mind and emotions. Whereas life comes to us incomplete, its final outcomes always unknown, the novel presents life as destiny, a realized thing, leaving us to reflect on its significance and meaning.

The speaker of "The Art of the Novel" does her own reflection on the novels she has in mind when she quotes the influential Russian literary critic Georg Lukács, who wrote in his book *The Theory of the Novel* (first published in 1920) that the novel is "the epic of a world that has been abandoned by God." Lukács meant that the novel rose to prominence after the age of epic and romance, at a time when belief in the Christian God and a beneficent Providence were on the wane. As the world became in a sense meaningless, "man became lonely and could find meaning and substance only in his own soul, whose home was nowhere." The quotation is an apt comment on the tragic novels to which the speaker alludes.

Finally, the question arises, What has replaced the novel in the speaker's affection? The answer is contained in the final lines of the poem, "I now prefer footpaths, or no paths, / and thickly wooded country, the moon." In changing the metaphor from highways to footpaths, or no paths at all, she suggests that she is now satisfied by things less grand than the novel. She no longer feels drawn to a long prose narrative that tells a human story from hopeful beginnings to tragic ends. Instead, she prefers, perhaps, the alternative path of poetry, of sensory images plucked from the onrushing tide of life—not stories, but moments.

Source: Bryan Aubrey, Critical Essay on "The Art of the Novel," in *Poetry for Students*, Thomson Gale, 2006.

Sources

Allison, Alexander W., Herbert Barrows, Caesar R. Blake, Arthur J. Carr, Arthur M. Eastman, and Hubert M. English, Jr., eds., "Robert Frost," in *The Norton Anthology of Poetry*, 3d ed., W. W. Norton, 1983, p. 913.

Aristotle, "On Poetics," in *The Works of Aristotle*, Vol. 2, Encyclopaedia Britannica, 1952, pp. 677-99.

Deming, Alison Hawthorne, "Walking on Rough Water," in *Women's Review of Books*, July 2004, pp. 18–19.

Flaubert, Gustave, *Madame Bovary*, translated by Eleanor Marx-Aveling, Dent, 1966, p. 134.

Hawthorn, Jeremy, *Studying the Novel: An Introduction*, 2d ed., Edward Arnold, 1992, p. 2.

Inchbald, Mrs., *A Simple Story*, edited and with an introduction by J. M. S. Tompkins, Oxford University Press, 1967, pp. 79, 87.

James, Henry, "The Art of Fiction," in *The Norton Anthology of American Literature*, 2d ed., Vol. 2, W. W. Norton, 1985, p. 437.

Lukács, Georg, *The Theory of the Novel*, translated from the German by Anna Bostock, M.I.T. Press, 1971, pp. 88, 103.

Sajé, Natasha, *Bend*, Tupelo Press, 2004, pp. 37, 48, 60.

Sorby, Angela, Review of *Red under the Skin*, in *Chicago Review*, Vol. 41, No. 1, January 1995, pp. 97–98.

Wharton, Edith, *The House of Mirth*, New American Library, rpt. ed., 2000.

Further Reading

Burt, Daniel S., *Novel 100: A Ranking of the Greatest Novels of All Time*, Checkmark, 2003.

> Burt undertakes the task of choosing and ranking the top one hundred novels in literary history. This book is meant to appeal to lovers of literature and to newcomers looking for an overview of classic fiction.

Ellmann, Richard, and Robert O'Clair, *Modern Poems: A Norton Introduction*, W. W. Norton, 1989.

> One of the most respected publishers of literary anthologies offers this collection of works by 119 poets, along with essays about the poets and about reading poetry. The styles and perspectives of the poets are wide ranging, giving the reader a good grasp of modern poetry.

McKeon, Michael, *Theory of the Novel: A Historical Approach*, Johns Hopkins University Press, 2001.

> McKeon has compiled essays on various topics related to the novel and its place in history. The essays include important theoretical texts and essays by major literary critics and scholars.

Stendhal, Henri, *The Red and the Black*, Penguin Books, 2002.

> This novel introduces Julien Sorel, considered to be one of the greatest characters in European literature. Driven by greed and hypocrisy, Sorel tries to ascend to the top of his society, only to bring about his own failure in the end.

Aurora Leigh

Elizabeth Barrett Browning

1857

As early as 1844, Elizabeth Barrett wrote Robert Browning that she was thinking about writing a novel in verse form on modern themes. Several years later, she began work on *Aurora Leigh* (1857), which turned into one of the longest poems in the English language in its number of lines. Browning thought it her most mature work, and it turned out to be her biggest commercial success. *Aurora Leigh* deals with some of the major social problems of her age, particularly the difficulty of being a professional woman. There is a frank treatment in the story of the "fallen woman" in an effort to show an unwed mother as a victim and not necessarily someone to be condemned, as was the Victorian practice. The poem also reveals a distrust of socialist theory, in that Browning feared that communist-style communities would exclude artists and poets.

Aurora Leigh elicited much praise from the public and other poets, but professional reviewers found it coarse, vulgar, and highly flawed. Even those who admired the work found deficiencies and inconsistencies, while those who decried the book admitted that the attempt showed genius. Undeniably, *Aurora Leigh* was one of the most avant-garde publications of its day. A progressive thinker, Browning was also definite about her morality and the joy that romantic love had brought to her. Thus, this largely autobiographical poem does not discuss prostitution lightly, and the liberated poet decides in the end that the pursuit of one's art cannot bring to a woman's life the satisfaction found in an

enduring, loving marriage. Modern readers of Browning are more familiar with her romantic poetry, particularly *Sonnets from the Portuguese*, her love lyrics to her husband. However, as evidenced by a 1996 Norton publication of *Aurora Leigh*, edited by Margaret Reynolds, feminist scholarship has resurrected interest in this verse novel and promoted a new appreciation of the talent and intellect of Browning.

Author Biography

The oldest of Edward Moulton Barrett and Mary Graham Clarke's twelve children, Elizabeth Barrett was born on March 6, 1806. Part Creole, her family had derived great wealth from Jamaican sugar plantations for two hundred years but went to England to live the life of gentry at Hope End estate in Herefordshire. Educated at home, Barrett became an expert in several languages and the ancient classics. At age fourteen, she contracted a lung illness that lasted all her life and, at fifteen, suffered a spinal injury that contributed to chronically ill health. In 1828, her mother died, and then, in 1832, the family fortune declined, causing the Barretts to move to the coastal town of Sidmouth for three years before settling in London. In 1838, she returned to the coast to recuperate from a serious illness. There, Barrett's favorite brother, Edward, drowned, sending her back to London and into a five-year decline as a recluse and invalid.

Nonetheless, she continued a writing career that she had begun at age twelve. Her first collection of poetry was published in 1826, and a translation of *Prometheus Bound*, by the Greek dramatist Aeschylus, came out in 1833. Her reputation as a poet grew throughout the 1830s. When she published another collection in 1844, international celebrity and a prolific correspondence with the poet Robert Browning resulted. Barrett's tyrannical father did not want any of his children to marry, so she eloped with Browning in 1846, moving immediately to Italy, where her health improved. Her father never spoke to her again. A son, Robert Wieland, nicknamed Pen, was born in 1849. *Sonnets from the Portuguese*, which she wrote for Robert before their marriage, was published in 1850 and has become probably the most widely known book of English love lyrics. Elizabeth Browning's intense interest in Italian politics, as well as social concerns about slavery, child labor, and other injustices, are reflected in later works. In 1857, she published a

Elizabeth Barrett Browning   © Corbis-Bettmann

controversial and groundbreaking verse novel, *Aurora Leigh*, that addressed professional roles for women. Considered the greatest female poet of her time, Browning died in Florence on June 29, 1861. Her place of esteem in literature waned after the Victorian period but has been revived by feminist scholarship.

Poem Summary

First Book

As a personal narrative, *Aurora Leigh* begins when the central character is born in Italy to an English father and Tuscan mother. When Aurora Leigh's mother dies, the grieving father withdraws to a mountain cottage, where he educates Aurora in the classics amid the wonders of nature. However, when she is only thirteen, her father dies, and she is taken away from her beloved nurse and sent to England to live with a coldhearted maiden aunt who had not approved of Aurora's mother. There, Aurora is submitted to a conventional female education. Her only comforts are her father's books; her cousin, Romney Leigh; and Romney's friend, the painter Vincent Carrington, who talks of Italy.

Media Adaptations

- *Aurora Leigh: Authoritative Text, Backgrounds and Contexts, Criticism* (1994) is available on audiocassette, edited by Margaret Reynolds and produced by HarperCollins Publishers.

Second Book

The expectation is that Aurora will marry Romney, heir to the family estates, and he proposes to her when she is twenty years old. Romney thinks that Aurora should join him in his work for social reform, but she believes that she has a right to her own vocational fulfillment and does not want to be just his helper. He scoffs at her artistic ambitions, thinking them of little value compared with his noble endeavors. Dismayed by his attitude, Aurora rejects Romney's proposal. Angered by this refusal, her Aunt Marjory disinherits her and dies shortly thereafter. Aurora heads to London nonetheless, determined to begin a new life and maintain her independence.

Third Book

Aurora loses touch with Romney over the seven years that she pursues her career as a writer in London. With only three hundred pounds a year on which to support herself and little income to be had from writing poetry, she works days as a prose writer and spends only evenings on poetry until her verse gains sufficient reputation to provide a living. Lady Waldemar, a wealthy widow, visits Aurora to tell her that Romney is going to marry Marian Erle, a lower-class woman he has rescued from her deathbed. He has found Marian a job as a seamstress and now wants to marry her in a socialist gesture to equalize the classes. Lady Waldemar wants Aurora to stop the wedding, but Aurora refuses to interfere. Instead, Aurora seeks out Marian. She hears Marian's story about the abusive parents who eventually abandoned her, leaving her to wander alone and ill until a stranger took her to a hospital, where she met Romney, who was making a charitable visit.

Fourth Book

Marian tells Aurora how, a year after first meeting Romney at the hospital, she encounters Romney again when Lucy, a fellow seamstress, dies. Romney proposes marriage to her with the idea that she will help him in working to bring rich and poor together. Marian adores Romney for his kindness, but when he happens by, he explains to Aurora that although he is fond of Marian, he is marrying her primarily to make a social statement. He thinks his love of humanity is better than romantic love. Aurora thinks he is hopelessly unrealistic and living in the abstract, but she wishes the couple well. She goes to the wedding, where, on the groom's side of the church, Romney's high-society friends are gossiping unkindly about the marriage. On the bride's side are seated many of the destitute people who are aided by Romney's projects. However, Marian does not show up. Instead, she sends a note explaining that Lady Waldemar has convinced her that the marriage would be a mistake and that she could not make Romney happy. When the indigent wedding guests hear of the cancellation, they riot. Aurora faints and is carried away by Lord Howe, a friend of Romney's. As Romney fruitlessly tries to find Marian, he relies on Aurora as a confidante, and they reconcile as friends but continue to disagree about each other's life choices.

Fifth Book

This book opens two years later. There is an extended description of a party at Lord Howe's and several hundred lines dedicated to the art of poetic composition. Aurora expresses her rebellion against established literary conventions and decides that poetry must change with the times, not only in content but also in form. She remarks that women artists are often too dependent on a single person, be it a friend or a lover, and are at a disadvantage as artists because of their emotional nature. There is also an admission of loneliness for the woman poet who forgoes real love to write about love. In addition, she is critical of the quality of the drama of her era and recommends that writers look to the stage of the soul instead—that is, practice the intense subjectivity characteristic of poetry. Aurora has heard that Romney has converted his estate into almshouses, that Lady Waldemar is his most active partner in charity, and that he plans to marry her, unaware that her efforts are an insincere ploy to win him. Aurora has an unpleasant encounter with Lady Waldemar at Lord Howe's. Depressed and disheartened, Aurora decides to avoid the wedding and try to find solace in Italy.

Sixth Book

Aurora leaves England and passes through Paris, where she happens to see Marian with a baby. Aurora follows Marian and learns about the misfortune that has befallen her. She was supposed to go to Australia, but the man that Lady Waldemar sent to help Marian get away took her to Paris instead and sold her to a brothel, where she was drugged and raped. Driven nearly to madness by the realization of her circumstances, Marian had escaped but endures many struggles to survive.

Seventh Book

Marian tells Aurora about finding refuge with a miller's wife, only to be kicked out when it is discovered that Marian is pregnant. She has been working for a seamstress, but Aurora persuades Marian to come with her to Italy. Aurora wants to write Romney, but she thinks he has already married Lady Waldemar, and she does not want to hurt him with the news of what his wife did to Marian. Instead, Aurora writes to Lord Howe to ask him to tell Romney that she has found Marian and is caring for her. Then Aurora writes a scathing letter to Lady Waldemar, tempering it with a promise not to seek vengeance if Lady Waldemar takes good care of Romney. As Aurora and Marian settle into life in Italy, Aurora begins to think that Romney was right in stating that neither art nor a woman could fully comprehend universal truth or capture the meaning of life's experiences. Aurora then hears from Vince Carrington, a painter and friend to Romney, that her new book is doing well and that Lady Waldemar has nursed Romney through an illness.

Eighth Book

Just before Romney appears on her terrace, Aurora experiences a strange reverie about the city of Florence that is dreamy and sexy. Aurora and Romney have a long conversation in which they each admit their mistakes and faults, but Aurora still holds back on her feelings because she thinks Romney is married. Romney tells Aurora that the people he tried to help turned on him and burned down his estate. He is discouraged by the failure of his social reforms, and, after reading Aurora's book, he is more understanding of her endeavors. Aurora is about to send him away when she finally learns that he never married.

Ninth Book

The news that Romney did not marry Lady Waldemar is verified by a stinging letter that he brings to Aurora from Lady Waldemar. Romney still feels obligated to Marian and once again offers to marry her. However, Marian declares that she must devote her life only to her child and makes plans to leave, to live on her own. With this turn of events, Romney and Aurora are freed to admit their love for each other. Aurora says that they gave God too small a part in their plans. She also realizes that she should have first sought fulfillment as a woman, and then her art would have grown from that strong base. Aurora and Romney agree to marry and work together for the good of humankind.

Themes

Woman as Artist

Browning was committed to writing as a woman, so her main character in *Aurora Leigh* has the same intensity of purpose. Furthermore, the emphasis is on the right of a woman to work as an artist. Aurora rejects Romney's proposal because he sees her role in marriage as a partner in his work, with no room for a career of her own. Romney also belittles Aurora's work as unimportant compared with his endeavors, so Browning makes sure that Romney fails in his socialist endeavors while Aurora succeeds as a writer and communicator. Thus, the reader is left with the impression that perhaps a poet can indeed have more influence than philanthropist reformers on changes in society.

It is important to the message of the story that Aurora is successful as a poet. In Victorian times, Browning and other female writers complained about the gender prejudice evidenced by critics. They wanted to be judged as authors, not as women. They did not want their works to be dismissed out of hand just for being written by a woman. To avoid the problem, a number of female authors used male pseudonyms, for example, Mary Ann Evans writing under the name of George Eliot. Browning refused to resort to this tactic to get an impartial reading. Instead, she insisted, through her own perseverance as a writer and through the character of Aurora Leigh, that women could and should be accepted, even successful, as poets.

The Proper Subject Matter of Poetry

In the mid-eighteenth century, literary debate often focused on the proper subject matter for poetry. Intrinsic to this debate was the relationship of poetry to current affairs. While some writers called for a poetic representation of the times, others, such as the noted critic and poet Matthew Arnold,

Topics For Further Study

- Browning was an avid reader of the French and English novelists of her day. Make an annotated list of these novelists and their works, providing the most notable information in terms of their influence, themes, and popularity.

- Robert Browning was, of course, an important influence on his wife's life and works. Write a brief biography of Robert Browning, including mention of his major works, a comparison with his wife's career and commitment to women's issues, and an analysis of the artistic relationship of the couple.

- Browning has become of interest to modern feminists. What questions were being addressed about the role of women in Victorian England? What were the feminist influences on Browning?

- Browning was very well read in the classics. Compare the importance of ancient Greek and Latin literature in Victorian education with that of today.

- The Barrett family fortune came from Jamaican sugar plantations. Research the history and economic impact of such Caribbean plantations during the 1700s and 1800s and write a summary of your findings.

---

declared that contemporary concerns were unsuitable for poetry. It was thought that poetry should concern itself only with lofty ideals and representations of pastoral beauty and love. Browning came down decidedly on the side of those who believed that current affairs were appropriate to poetry. *Aurora Leigh* is her most notable effort that takes this position, since it discusses issues of importance to Victorian society, such as the "woman question," the problems of prostitution and poverty, and the value of socialist reform.

Love or Art

The moral to the story of *Aurora Leigh* is that without love the rewards of fame and success are insufficient. The entire story line is a journey for Aurora and Romney to this conclusion. Romney learns that he cannot save the world by himself; further, he will do better in his work if he first gets his own life right and has love to support him. Aurora realizes that she, too, should have based her life on love and that she would have been an even better poet because of it. As partners, fortified by the strength and confidence that comes with love, Aurora and Romney have a fulfilling and fruitful future ahead of them.

The Fallen Woman

Victorians placed so much value on purity and virtue for women that a failure to adhere to these ideals received severe disapproval. Scandal could result from just a hint of impropriety. Hypocritically, at the same time that Victorians preached about the sanctity of marriage and the home, prostitution became a major social problem. Part of the cause for this situation was the lack of good employment opportunities. There was a surplus of women in the population, leaving many women unmarried but without jobs to occupy and support them. What jobs were available involved such poor working conditions that some women preferred prostitution to the harsh life in the mines and factories. Browning addresses this situation in *Aurora Leigh*, not only through what Aurora says but also through the characters of Rose Bell and Marian Erle. Rose's story was a brief one told by Marian about a delightful, motherless little girl she knew who could not escape her poverty and grew up to be a prostitute. This sad story set up the later events that happened to Marian. Even though Marian was virtuous, she became the victim of circumstances. Although she did not become a prostitute, she did become an unwed mother. Such a woman would have been ostracized by Victorian society, and Browning wanted to show how unjust that judgment could be. Consequently, Browning makes Marian as good and noble as she could be, to evoke sympathy from the readers and persuade them to consider a kinder, more understanding approach to women placed in compromised positions.

Style

Kunstlerroman

This specialized form of the bildungsroman, a novel form that addresses psychological and moral growth, concerns itself with the development of a writer or other artist. In this case, the protagonist reaches maturity upon achieving mastery of his or her craft. Thus, graduating from apprenticeship not only ends the formative stage of life but also establishes the destiny that the hero has sought. Marcel Proust's *Remembrance of Things Past*, James Joyce's *Portrait of the Artist as a Young Man*, and Thomas Mann's *Doctor Faustus* are examples of this subtype. The most likely influence on Browning's choice to write a *kunstlerroman* was the poet William Wordsworth's lengthy autobiographical poem *The Prelude*, published in 1850. The story lines and themes are very similar, including criticism of radical social reform and the conclusion that poetry can be a force for goodness in the lives of individuals. However, Wordsworth's hero worries that he feels too much, whereas Aurora recognizes a need for human love.

The Female Bildungsroman

When the protagonist of a bildungsroman is a female, the genre takes on an extra dimension. The protagonist encounters not only the usual problems of growing up but also the unique problems of growing up female in a male-dominated world. As a woman trying to make it as a professional, Aurora encounters these problems head on. Early examples of the female bildungsroman followed the traditional expectation that a woman would see marriage as her fulfillment upon reaching maturity. In a sense, that is true of Aurora, but Browning's conclusion is more like later novels that portrayed women as accepting marriage not just for social advancement or exposure to the world but also as the culmination of the mutual growth that occurs in a loving relationship. While a male protagonist in a bildungsroman might meet his pivotal crisis in the course of his professional career, the female protagonist's turning point traditionally results from a romantic entanglement. Her voyage of discovery is much more internal, or psychological, than that of her male counterpart, who has more opportunities for interaction with the public world. Although Aurora does not lack for involvement in the public world, it is true that her conflict is more psychological and internal than just professional.

Blank Verse

Blank verse is poetry written in an unrhymed meter, particularly iambic pentameter, which is a line of poetry containing five accented syllables and ten syllables in all; the result is poetry that has the sound of the natural rhythms of English speech. Blank verse should be read in sentences; line breaks are determined by the meter, so the narrative has a strong pull from line to line. Blank verse originated in Italy in the sixteenth century and became very popular in Renaissance literature, because it sounded like classical poetry. It became the standard in poetic drama for such writers as Christopher Marlowe and William Shakespeare. John Milton used blank verse for *Paradise Lost* in 1667. In the next century, blank verse was used for a number of important works by Wordsworth, Percy Bysshe Shelley, and John Keats. It was a natural choice, then, for Browning to write *Aurora Leigh* in blank verse, since it was the medium for many admired long works and the best fit for the innovation of the verse novel. In the twentieth century, the use of blank verse was continued by poets of the caliber of William Butler Yeats, Ezra Pound, Robert Frost, and Wallace Stevens.

Allusions

One of the most frequently used literary devices in *Aurora Leigh* is the allusion. As a reference to a person or event outside the story, the allusion serves as a shortcut to a connection with the reader's knowledge base. The point is to avoid lengthy explanations of an idea. However, for the modern reader, the abundance of allusions to classical literature and the Bible in *Aurora Leigh* are more of a hindrance than a help. Browning was an expert in mythology and a devout reader of the Bible; therefore, it was natural for her to include this knowledge in her writings. However, her familiarity with ancient Greek and Roman literature is so much more extensive than the average reader's that her allusions become obscure and make the reading more difficult. Footnoted editions of *Aurora Leigh* often devote half of a page just to explaining the multitude of allusions in the text. Nonetheless, the allusions in *Aurora Leigh* bring a richness to the work that is an education in itself.

Historical Context

Victorian Poetry

The Romantic movement was dominated by poets, but the Victorian age is better known for its novels. Still, poetry was an important and popular form

Compare & Contrast

- **1856:** For the first time, during the Crimean War, the government allows women to provide nursing services in combat. Florence Nightingale and thirty-eight other women care for sick and wounded soldiers and promote sanitary practices and record keeping in hospitals and in the field. Nightingale made nursing a respectable profession and opened up a new employment avenue for women.

  Today: Almost all modern nursing systems and techniques can be traced back to Florence Nightingale. Her promotion of data and statistical evidence has led to the use of patient medical histories, calculation of mortality rates, and an organized method of medical and surgical education. While nursing is no longer a job solely for women, the role of women in medicine has expanded enormously because of their entry into nursing.

- **1856:** The synthetic dye industry begins when an eighteen-year-old chemistry student, William Henry Perkin, accidentally discovers purplish mauveine while working with aniline and quinine. The next year, he and his father open the first synthetic dye factory.

  Today: Natural dyes have been almost completely phased out, as more than seven thousand different color-providing substances have been found for commercial use. Synthetic dyes are no longer used just for textiles but also in paints, inks, plastics, rubber, and cosmetics.

- **1856:** The Steinway Piano Company, founded in 1853 in New York City, builds its first grand piano and will obtain the first patent for a concert grand in 1875.

  Today: Making more than five thousand pianos each year, Steinway is a highly prestigious brand name and the instrument of choice for most of the world's concert pianists.

- **1856:** During the Crimean War, Henry Bessemer invents a more powerful artillery shell, but the cast-iron cannons are not strong enough to deal with it, so Bessemer then develops an improved iron-smelting process capable of producing large quantities of ingots of superior quality that can be used for making cannons.

  Today: The Bessemer steelmaking process that is still used is an extension and refinement of the one developed in 1856 and is the dominant steel-manufacturing technology for mass-producing steel inexpensively.

---

of literature for the educated public, and some of England's best-known poets come from this time period. Browning's reputation was growing as a poet in the 1830s, while that of her friend Alfred Tennyson was being established as that of the greatest poet of the era. A successor to Keats and Shelley, Tennyson at first lent his remarkable lyric talent to highly subjective verse. Then he turned to the public issues of the day and introduced two new poetic techniques. One is that of the dramatic monologue, also developed by Robert Browning, and the other is the English idyll, which combines glimpses of the contemporary scene with a casual debate. Later in his career, Tennyson built long poems out of short ones, such as *In Memoriam*, an elegy that is shaped by 133 individual lyrics. Tennyson was named poet laureate of England in 1850. Robert Browning contrasted Tennyson's style with more stark and colloquial poetry. Browning's dramatic monologues engage the reader in the thought process of an unconventional character and require active participation in the sense of personal discovery and morality. Another notable Victorian poet is Matthew Arnold, whose lyric talent blended with the dark philosophical attitude of the times. Arnold, too, experimented with a process he called "the dialogue of the mind with itself." Later in his career, however, he became better known for his literary criticism.

Nineteenth-Century Feminism

The "woman question" was an important topic of debate in Victorian England. Gender inequality in politics meant that women could not vote or hold office. Women's suffrage was advocated already in the 1840s but did not become law until 1918. Economically, married women had to give control of their property to their husbands until the Married Women's Property Acts of 1870–1908. The first college for women was not established until 1848, but by the end of the Victorian era, women could get degrees at twelve colleges, though not at Oxford or Cambridge. The Industrial Revolution brought thousands of lower-class women to the cities for factory jobs and showed the need for a changed attitude about women's work. Unfortunately, when reform of working conditions for poor women finally came, the argument was not for equality but that women were too frail to withstand the sixteen-hour day and other hardships. In the meantime, the reaction of Victorian society was to put further emphasis on the importance of the woman's role in the home.

An immensely popular poem by Coventry Patmore, *The Angel in the House*, published in 1856, stressed the value of a woman's purity and selflessness. Women's enshrinement in the home became an entombment for many. Browning, Charlotte Brontë, Florence Nightingale, and others complained that middle-class and upper-class women were taught such trivial skills that they had almost nothing important to do. *Aurora Leigh* pointed out the constriction placed on the female mind by the traditional education in homemaking. The only respectable employment was that of a governess, until utter boredom and the example of successful novelists like the Brontë sisters, Jane Austen, and George Sand provoked women to rebel in the late Victorian period and demand a wider variety of opportunities.

Critical Overview

Perhaps the best summary of the critical reaction to *Aurora Leigh* is the following quote from William Edmondstoune Aytoun, the famous literary critic for *Blackwood's Edinburgh Magazine*: "With all its faults, this is a remarkable poem; strong in energy, rich in thought, abundant in beauty." Aytoun had blasted the poem as "fantastic, unnatural, exaggerated" and had found the character of Aurora to be unattractive, some of the language coarse and revolting, and the images often bewilderingly intensified. Nonetheless, writing in 1857, he felt that *Aurora Leigh* sustained Browning's high reputation.

Similarly, W. C. Roscoe, a contemporary of Aytoun's, wrote in the *National Review* that Browning "has produced a work which, in completeness of form and artistic execution, falls far short of many of her previous efforts; but which in matter far surpasses the best of them." Roscoe thought the poem excessively long with superfluous detail and remarked that the characters were "vague hazy embodiments given to certain contrasted sets of ideas." Another contemporary, Henry Fothergill Chorley, commented that he could write page after page about "the huge mistake of the plan, the disdain of selectness in its details." On the other hand, he could also write multiple pages about "the high thoughts, the deep feelings, the fantastic images showered over the tale with the authority of a prophetess, the grace of a muse, the prodigality of a queen."

A later critic, examining the work of the greater Victorian poets, wrote in 1892 for *The Victorian Age of English Literature*: "The remarkable thing in [*Aurora Leigh*] is its energy and strong poetical vitality, the rush and spring of life" of its narrative, which, however, was "not sufficient for the fervour and power of utterance." Not long after, in the early twentieth century, changes in taste and critical emphasis led to a devaluation of Browning's work. Her irregular meters and half rhymes did not suit a new insistence on technical correctness. Besides, cultural expectations assumed that no great poetry could contain womanly topics. On the other hand, Browning's relationship with her husband was the stuff of romance and the appropriate realm of a woman, so she was idealized as the loving companion of her husband, the great poet Robert Browning. Her own talents were thereby dismissed.

Toward the end of the twentieth century, however, the growth of women's studies led to a reexamination of *Aurora Leigh* from a feminist perspective. This reevaluation has led to a new appreciation of the innovative techniques and messages contained in the poem. In 1986, Dorothy Mermin declared in the *Victorian Newsletter* that *Aurora Leigh* "goes farther than any other poem or novel of the Victorian period towards transcending the limits imposed on literature by gender." In her analysis of *Aurora Leigh* for the *Review of English Studies*, Catherine Maxwell comments on the "many allusions and intertextual influences." Maxwell also points to the "poem's intelligent self-consciousness, its images of visual art, especially portraiture, and its metaphors of reading and writing."

Regardless of the critic or the century, the innovative uniqueness of *Aurora Leigh* provides a challenge. Although she was writing in 1980, Kathleen Hickok probably speaks for every reader when she says in the *International Journal of Women's Studies*, "In *Aurora Leigh*, Barrett Browning departed from the feminine traditions of the century with sufficient force to impress many, alarm some, and startle nearly all of her readers." As with all new inventions, there are flaws and missteps in *Aurora Leigh*. Nonetheless, the consensus is that this verse novel was a bold step for a poet, a grand experiment, and a remarkable achievement.

Criticism

Lois Kerschen

Kerschen is a school district administrator and freelance writer. In this essay, she examines the influences that affected Browning's themes about women in Aurora Leigh *and the allusions in the poem that indicate these influences.*

In 1822, when Elizabeth Barrett was only sixteen, she started an essay, under the original title of "An Essay on Women," that she never finished but whose subject matter found its way into many of her other works. Thus, it is apparent that women's issues were a lifelong cause for Browning that culminated in the publication of *Aurora Leigh*, a story about the woman as an artist. In the unfinished teenage essay, Browning argues that women's poetry was being suppressed by the dominance of poetic forms and subject matter that were male oriented. Consequently, *Aurora Leigh* is an experiment in a new poetic form, the verse novel, and has as its subject matter those things that were issues of the day for Victorian women.

One of Browning's closest friends was the poet Alfred Tennyson. His 1846 long, blank-verse poem *The Princess* addressed the role of women, but his story was a fantasy. While Browning was disappointed by the manner of presentation of the ideas, Kerry McSweeney points out, in her introduction to a 1993 edition of *Aurora Leigh*, that Browning "could hardly have failed to notice that *The Princess* explores the relation of sexual love, marriage, and the nurturing of children to the intellectual and vocational aspirations of nineteenth-century women."

Perhaps his example helped inspire Browning to explore these same topics in a work of her own.

Role models were scarce for Browning, who once complained in a letter, "I look everywhere for grandmothers and see none." However, there were a few women writers to whom she could look for example. She highly regarded the poetry of Joanna Baillie (1762–1851) and gleaned ideas about the special gifts and problems of female poets from two significant poets of the next generation, Felicia Hemans (1793–1835) and Letitia Elizabeth Landon (1802–1838). In terms of writing a novel, Browning found help in many contemporary works, such as Madame de Stael's *Corinne* (1807), which portrays a modern woman. Aurora borrows much from the story of Corinne, who had an Italian mother and an English father, lives in Italy as a child, is taken to England when orphaned, is raised to follow social conventions but decides to be an artist, and returns to Italy to pine for a man who has married someone else. George Sand's novels were favorites of Browning's. Sand's *Consuelo* was a female odyssey in which the main character insists on liberty as an artist. Browning did not like the novels of Jane Austen, but she did admire Charlotte Brontë and possibly patterned Romney after the hero in *Villette* and after Rochester in *Jane Eyre*, who is blind at the end of the novel.

Besides these literary influences, Browning was, of course, aware of the attitudes about women in her day, and she was involved in discussions about changes in the social, political, and economic positions of women. Consequently, *Aurora Leigh* is filled with allusions to the attitudes about and the problems for women of her culture. For example, Aurora says that her father, she knows, loved her, "but still with heavier brains, / And wills more consciously responsible, / And not as wisely, since less foolishly." The "heavier brains" phrase alludes to anatomy studies that noticed that men tend to have brains that weigh more than women's. This fact is not surprising, given the relative difference in average body weight. The difference was taken to mean, however, that the male possessed a higher intellect than the female.

Aurora describes her Aunt Marjory, saying, "She had lived / A sort of cage-bird life, born in a cage, / Accounting that to leap from perch to perch / Was act and joy enough for any bird." The reference is to Mary Wollstonecraft's *Vindication of the Rights of Women* (1792), in which she describes women as a feathered race confined in cages with nothing to do but to plume themselves. The image

What Do I Read Next?

- Browning's best-known work today is probably *Sonnets from the Portuguese* (1850). These are forty-four interlocking love poems that she wrote for her husband. The sonnets are available in many editions, one of which was published in 1997 with twenty-two other Browning works.

- Christina Rossetti, another Victorian poet, was influenced by Browning. Her work, collected in *The Complete Poems* (2001), shows a wide range of subject matter and verse form.

- *Middlemarch* (1872), by Mary Ann Evans under the pen name of George Eliot, is about a fictional English provincial town in the 1830s and the individuals who shape the community. It is considered one of the best novels of all time.

- *Lady Audley's Secret* (1887), written by Mary Elizabeth Braddon, was a bestselling sensationalist novel in Victorian England that mocked the typical heroine of the times and the respectability of the middle class.

- The poetry of Robert Browning, which later exceeded his wife's in reputation, is available in numerous editions, including *Robert Browning's Poetry: Authoritative Texts, Criticism* (1980).

- A close friend of Robert and Elizabeth Barrett Browning was their fellow poet Alfred Tennyson, whose fame continues today. A collection of his poetry can be found in *Tennyson's Poetry: Authoritative Texts, Context, Criticism* (1999).

---

of the caged bird is a distinctly female metaphor in literature of the nineteenth century. In describing the type of instruction that her aunt provided, Aurora says that she read books on womanhood that portrayed English women to be "models to the universe," "comprehending husband's talk / When not too deep," but who otherwise "keep quiet by the fire," "their angelic reach / Of virtue chiefly used to sit and darn." Numerous books on moral and practical advice for women were published in the 1830s and 1840s, particularly those of Sarah Stickney Ellis, whose twelve editions of didactic instructions created, Browning says, "model-women of the most abominable virtue."

In the Second Book, when Romney says, "Among our female authors we make room / For this fair writer, and congratulate / The country that produces in these times / Such women, competent to . . . spell," he is being used to parody the condescending reviews that Browning's poetry sometimes received from male critics. Later, Romney says that he "took / The woman to be nobler than the man," expressing a common Victorian supposition that in a woman was placed an elevated sense of moral and spiritual values. Conveniently, this

belief fed into the double standard that men could misbehave and be excused because they were men but that misbehavior in a woman was reprehensible.

Aurora herself repeats one of the platitudes of sexual difference that was commonly accepted as truth in her times. In the Fifth Book she says, "We women are too apt to look to one," that is, the notion that a woman could be inspired only by the personal and the sentimental. This concept appears also in Aurora's argument with Romney in the Second Book, reappears in the Sixth Book, and is discussed again in her revised debate with Romney in the Eighth and Ninth Books. In addition, love was assumed to be a woman's whole concern, but just a part of a man's life. Browning refers to this belief in Vince Carrington's letter to Aurora, announcing his intent to marry Kate Ward, when he says, "Most women . . . counting love Life's only serious business." These notions added fuel to the opinion that female poets could write only about sentimental and domestic matters, whereas men wrote about loftier aims. Browning has Lady Waldemar express this criticism in her letter in the Ninth Book when she says, "A woman who does better than to love, / I hate; she will do nothing very

> *One of the few occupations open to Victorian women was that of a seamstress, yet they were so poorly paid and work was so scarce because of the overabundance of women in the trade that many seamstresses turned to prostitution as an income supplement."*

well: / Male poets are preferable, straining less / And teaching more."

While the whole verse novel is concerned with the position of a woman as a professional, it is not until the Fifth Book that Browning actually uses the phrase "the Woman's question." This public debate involved the issues of employment, education, property rights, voting, and equality in marriage, all of which were supported by Browning. A specific instance is alluded to in the Third Book with the lines "As ready for outrageous ends and acts / As any distressed sempstress." One of the few occupations open to Victorian women was that of a seamstress, yet they were so poorly paid and work was so scarce because of the overabundance of women in the trade that many seamstresses turned to prostitution as an income supplement. The situation was so common that just being a seamstress called one's virtue into question. An example of the desperation of women is given in the character of Rose Bell, Marian's sweet childhood friend who becomes a prostitute. In another reference to the problem of prostitution, in the Eighth Book, Browning mentions the huge numbers of women engaged in the illicit profession in London: "With eighty thousand women in one smile, / Who only smile at night beneath the gas."

Prostitutes often committed suicide because of their situation, however. Since they worked the docks, it was convenient for them to jump to their deaths in the river, be it the Thames in London or the Seine in Paris. Browning refers to this practice in the Seventh Book when Marian says, "I might sleep well beneath the heavy Seine, / Like others of my sort." Since decent people were not supposed to talk about prostitutes, Browning was highly criticized for making this occupation such a prominent topic in *Aurora Leigh*. Browning even dared to include in Marian's story references to "the stews," which were brothels, and to "the poor street-walker."

Another common expression referred to the "charming woman," as referenced in the Fifth Book. This type of woman was the kind that men did not want to marry because she had too strong a personality, was political, and was perhaps even forward in her speech and actions. Victorian sensibilities were such that the line in the Fifth Book "catch / Upon the burning lava of a song / The full-veined, heaving, double-breasted Age" was shocking. This juxtaposition of images of lava and a woman's breast in the same simile was too radical for the critics, but it was just the type of writing that Browning wanted to introduce into literature.

Browning intended for *Aurora Leigh* to be bold and shocking. As Margaret Reynolds notes in her preface to the 1996 Norton edition of *Aurora Leigh*, what appeals to the modern reader is that Aurora "is bold, she is brave, she is independent and liberated and, above all, she gets everything she wants in the end." Reynolds added that *Aurora Leigh* spoke to the anxieties of the nineteenth-century woman concerning the "exclusions and prohibitions that hedged about their aspirations" and "said things would be all right." Venturing into the forbidden territory of those subjects debated in the "Woman's question" was a way for Browning to challenge society through poetry and, in the process, to defend the claims for women's poetry. The book had a big impact when it was published, and it is worthy of study yet today.

Source: Lois Kerschen, Critical Essay on *Aurora Leigh*, in *Poetry for Students*, Thomson Gale, 2006.

Margaret Reynolds

In the following preface to the 1996 Norton critical edition of Aurora Leigh, *Reynolds describes the influence* Aurora Leigh *has had on legions of admirers.*

At the heart of *Aurora Leigh* there is a book. It's the book that Aurora sits down to write when she begins her story (1.1–9). It's the new and brave book that she attempts in the center of the poem (5.351–357). It's the manuscript book that she leaves with her publisher before setting out for Italy (5.1212–1213 and 5.1261–1266). It's the book that

Romney reads and that makes him realize, ten years too late, that Aurora really is a poet (8.261–262 and 8.278–297).

This imagined book is the pattern for *Aurora Leigh* itself. The real verse-novel published by Elizabeth Barrett Browning at the end of 1856 mirrors the made-up poem written by the fictional Aurora. Both books tell the story of a woman poet that is, and is not, her own story. Both books aspire to a new poetic form, both deal with the topical questions of the day, both appear in England while the author travels to Italy. So much is true of both Aurora's book and Barrett Browning's. The part that Barrett Browning had to make up, because it hadn't yet happened, is the story of what became of the book that is and is not *Aurora Leigh.*

Fantasizing about the reception of her own book, Barrett Browning tells us how the critics admired Aurora's book, how they exclaimed over this unlooked-for triumph from a woman, how they accorded Aurora respect and fame (7.551–571). In the event, it didn't work out quite like this for *Aurora Leigh.* Some reviewers were amazed because the work was so big and bold; some deemed it cumbersome and excessive. But they all agreed that it was important for two reasons. First, it tackled with enthusiasm the pressing contemporary issues of socialism and the position of women. Second, it outlined the model for the successful working woman poet. Readers from Queen Victoria to the art critic John Ruskin, from the historian Thomas Carlyle to the poet Christina Rossetti found *Aurora Leigh* riveting because of its politics; because of its passionate defense of individual, as opposed to collective, enterprise; because of its eager championing of the "fallen" woman and the single mother. The book had a huge success with a wide general public. The first edition sold out in a fortnight, and it was reprinted five times before Elizabeth Barrett Browning's death in 1861. By the end of the nineteenth century it had been reprinted more than twenty times in Britain and nearly as often in the United States. It became one of the books that everyone knew and read. Oscar Wilde loved it, the poet Algernon Charles Swinburne wrote a gushing preface for it, the novelist Rudyard Kipling borrowed the plot for *The Light That Failed* (1890), and, in America, the feminist activist Susan B. Anthony presented her treasured copy to the Library of Congress in 1902 and wrote on the flyleaf:

> This book was carried in my satchel for years and read & re-read. The noble words of Elizabeth Barrett ... sink deep into my heart. I have always cherished it above all other books. I now present it to the

She is bold, she is brave, she is independent and liberated and, above all, she gets everything she wants in the end."

> Congressional Library Washington D.C. With the hope that Women may more & more be like "Aurora Leigh".

This one aspect of Barrett Browning's feminist politics remained urgent and relevant throughout the nineteenth century: how was the writing woman to make her life? and where could she look for a role-model? This, too, Barrett Browning wrote into her imagined version of what happened to Aurora's book. When Vincent Carrington writes to tell Aurora of the book's success, he also tells her how she has acquired a disciple in the person of his young fiancée, Kate Ward. Vincent paints Kate's portrait, but she insists on appearing in an old cloak just like one that Aurora herself had worn. Kate insists too upon being represented holding a copy of Aurora's book, and in using Aurora's arguments to quarrel with her future husband:

> She has your books by heart more than my words
> And quotes you up against me.... (7.603–604)

Barrett Browning's imagined Kate Ward was only the first of any number of real writing and thinking women who made Aurora, and Barrett Browning herself, their special heroines. George Eliot was one of these. She reviewed *Aurora Leigh* when it was first published and admired it deeply. She borrowed images from the novel-poem for *The Mill on the Floss* and *Middlemarch,* and in her verse-drama about an artist/opera singer, *Armgart* (1871), she too quoted arguments derived from Barrett Browning. But it was the women poets of the latter nineteenth century who formed Aurora's most dedicated band of acolytes. Dora Greenwell wrote two love sonnets to the older poet; the activist Bessie Rayner Parkes wrote her a hesitant dedication ("Indeed I should not dare—but that this love, / Long nursed, demands expression, and alone / Speaks by love's dear strength—to approach near you / In words so weak and poor beside your own"; the Irish poet Emily Hickey adapted the verse-novel form in her poem *Michael Villiers: Idealist* (1891) to mix public questions about colonial domination and personal questions of individual development; Katherine Bradley and Edith Cooper, who together wrote the extraordinary poems published under the name Michael Field, used pseudonyms—"Isla" and "Arran Leigh"—that reflected their admiration, and they traveled to Italy to stay with Elizabeth's son, Pen Browning, and to commune with the spirit of their predecessor; and the Modernist poet Charlotte Mew, whose taut controlled work is so different from Barrett Browning's extravagance, nevertheless reworked many of her subjects and managed, to some extent, to live the independent working life imagined for the woman poet in *Aurora Leigh.*

The verse-novel form of Barrett Browning's work had many poetic successors, but it was the model of Aurora's independent life that made the fictional heroine so precious to the writers and scholars that came afterwards. One young disciple, Kate Field, really did have a picture of herself painted, in the manner of Kate Ward, as an homage to *Aurora Leigh.* In the portrait, which she commissioned from Elihu Vedder, she is shown in half profile, wearing classical drapery and posed against the skyline of Florence. Field donated the picture to the Boston Art Gallery, and though the original is now lost, a version of the portrait appears on the cover of this Norton Critical Edition of *Aurora Leigh.* The icon once would have been recognized by thousands of young intellectual women. At Wellesley College in Massachusetts, for instance, at the end of the nineteenth century, stained glass windows representing scenes from Barrett Browning's work were installed for the edification of the women educated there. These windows too have gone, destroyed by fire.

And for a time in the twentieth century *Aurora Leigh* itself also disappeared. It's a curious critical history. After nearly half a century of being read, discussed, and revered, *Aurora Leigh* came off the bookshelves, and Barrett Browning, that stalwart of women's independence, dwindled into the sofa-dwelling invalid portrayed in Rudolph Besier's well-known play *The Barretts of Wimpole Street* (1930). It's hard to say why it happened, but happen it certainly did. Perhaps the lush hagiography coming from Browning critics such as Lilian Whiting was too much for the new and lean Modernist sensibility. Certainly, as the extract included in this Norton Critical Edition from Marjory Bald makes plain, Barrett Browning seemed too strident, too self-conscious, too angry, to appear sympathetic to the cooler, more refined, version of early-twentieth-century feminism. Even Virginia Woolf—who, after

all, was born a Victorian and knew the ubiquitous influence of Barrett Browning in her own youth—found *Aurora Leigh,* with all its many good points, too long, too heavy, too dated, too roundly upholstered with facts and dates and times and arguments. So that was that. Elizabeth Barrett Browning became an odd little aside in the life of her much-greater-poet-husband, and there was no more *Aurora Leigh.*

And then. And then in the 1960s . . . feminism happened. It took a while, of course, to percolate into literary studies, but when it did, it was *Aurora Leigh* that became the heroine-text. First Ellen Moers took it up in her astonishingly forward-thinking book *Literary Women* (1977). In *Aurora Leigh* she found all the metaphors (the caged bird, the need to stride out, the improvisatrice, Italy as mother-country) that were important to women writers of the nineteenth century and that have become topics for numerous theses since. Then Cora Kaplan reprinted *Aurora Leigh* with the radical Women's Press in Britain. And in the States, Sandra Gilbert and Susan Gubar restored this neglected text to the canon of nineteenth century women's writing by including it in their monumental book *The Madwoman in the Attic.* In the 1980s and 1990s *Aurora Leigh* has become the central text of nineteenth-century women's writing in academic circles; it competes with Christina Rossetti's ever-popular *Goblin Market* for first place as the most written-on text of Victorian women's poetry. In Britain it has even found its way out to a more general audience. In the early 1980s a stage version by Michelene Wandor appeared at the National Theatre and was broadcast by the BBC's Radio 3. More recently, an audiotape of the poem has been published, with the well-known actress Diana Quick reading the part of Aurora. I see no plans yet for a Hollywood movie, but who knows?

The reasons for Aurora's current popularity are clear, and curiously they are exactly the same reasons that made her popular in the nineteenth century. She is bold, she is brave, she is independent and liberated and, above all, she gets everything she wants in the end. In the nineteenth century *Aurora Leigh* told contemporary readers a great deal about their own time. Today the poem can still tell us a great deal about that time. In that sense *Aurora Leigh* is a historical document more than a poem. But it's also a significant literary document and, as such, it works both for then and for now. In the nineteenth century, women writers were only just beginning to come to terms with the exclusions and prohibitions that hedged about their aspirations.

Aurora Leigh spoke to those anxieties and said things would be all right. In the late twentieth century, when we are only just beginning to understand the subtle history of women's invisibility in literature, *Aurora Leigh* helps to explain how it happened in a particular place and time.

At the heart of *Aurora Leigh* there is a book. When Aurora starts to write that book she knows that her work is necessary for herself, and for others—writing women into a literary history that had left them out:

> Of writing many books there is no end;
> And I who have written much in prose and verse
> For others' uses will write now for mine. . .
> (1.1–3)

This is why Aurora's book is important. And because Aurora's book and Barrett Browning's book are one and the same thing, *Aurora Leigh* is important. *Aurora Leigh* may not figure in Harold Bloom's canon, for he privileges the aesthetic, and charts only the cultures and the texts that have made Western civilization the way it is. But *Aurora Leigh* makes the canon for a new culture. For women are a civilization still in the making. A country without history, without art. A country making its laws, its myths, its histories. *Aurora Leigh* is one of those myths. When its uses are no longer so urgent, it will fade into history. But until then *Aurora Leigh* speaks to us, because it is empowering, because it is encouraging and cheerful, because it is necessary.

Source: Margaret Reynolds, Preface, in *Aurora Leigh*, edited by Margaret Reynolds, Norton, 1996, pp. vii–xi.

Sources

Arnold, Matthew, *The Poems of Matthew Arnold, 1840–1867*, Oxford University Press, 1913, p. 1.

Aytoun, William Edmondstoune, "Mrs. Barrett Browning—*Aurora Leigh*," in *Blackwood's Edinburgh Magazine*, Vol. 81, No. 495, January 1857, pp. 23–41.

Browning, Elizabeth Barrett, *Aurora Leigh*, edited by Margaret Reynolds, W. W. Norton, 1996, pp. 7, 10, 14, 18–19, 46, 51, 86, 143, 150, 162, 174, 218, 232, 265, 289.

Chorley, Henry Fothergill, Review of *Aurora Leigh*, in *Athenaeum*, No. 1517, November 22, 1856, pp. 1425–27.

Hickok, Kathleen K., "New, Yet Orthodox: Female Characters in *Aurora Leigh*," in *International Journal of Women's Studies*, Vol. 3, No. 5, September/October 1980, pp. 479–89.

Maxwell, Catherine, "*Aurora Leigh*," in *Review of English Studies*, Vol. 45, No. 180, November 1994, pp. 586–87.

McSweeney, Kerry, ed., "Introduction," in *Aurora Leigh*, Oxford University Press, 1993, p. xvi.

Mermin, Dorothy, "Genre and Gender in *Aurora Leigh*," in *Victorian Newsletter*, No. 69, Spring 1986, pp. 7–11.

Oliphant, Mrs., "Of the Greater Victorian Poets," in *The Victorian Age of English Literature*, Vol. 1, Lovell, Coryell, 1982, pp. 203–46.

Roscoe, W. C., "*Aurora Leigh*," in *National Review*, Vol. 4, No. 8, April 1857, pp. 239–67.

Further Reading

Bristow, Joseph, ed., *The Cambridge Companion to Victorian Poetry*, Cambridge University Press, 2000.
> Containing a detailed chronology of the period, this book provides a good overview of the poets of the period, their culture and interests, and the critical interpretations they have received over the years.

Bloom, Harold, ed., *Elizabeth Barrett Browning*, Chelsea House Publishers, 2002.
> Bloom's book is a collection of expert modern criticism concerning the works of Elizabeth Barrett Browning, with a helpful introduction and bibliography.

Gilbert, Sandra M., and Susan Gubar, *The Madwoman in the Attic: The Woman Writer and the Nineteenth-Century Literary Imagination*, Yale University Press, 2000.
> This groundbreaking book of feminist criticism is an important study of women writers in the Victorian era that provides a different perspective for critiquing these authors and their messages and motivations.

Leighton, Angela, *Elizabeth Barrett Browning*, Indiana University Press, 1986.
> This book assesses all the recurring themes of Browning's life and works in light of feminist theory, particularly the poet's relationship with her father and family and the difficulty a woman poet has in dispossessing herself from her masters and her own past.

Radley, Virginia, *Elizabeth Barrett Browning*, Twayne Publishers, 1972.
> One of the best known of Browning's biographies, this book actually presents only a short life history, followed by a series of analyses of her works in chronological order. Radley provides extensive notes and a bibliography.

Stone, Marjorie, *Elizabeth Barrett Browning*, St. Martin's Press, 1995.
> An authority on Victorian and gender studies, Stone applies gender and genre ideologies to the works of Browning and reestablishes their value and impact for the modern reader.

Stott, Rebecca, and Simon Avery, *Elizabeth Barrett Browning*, Longman, 2003.
> Not just a biographical survey, this book also contains criticism of the poet's works and comments on her influence in literature. Myths are dispelled about her reclusiveness, and her intellect and innovations are emphasized.

The Crime Was in Granada

Antonio Machado

1936

Antonio Machado's poem "The Crime Was in Granada" is about a real historical event, the murder of the Spanish writer Federico García Lorca on July 18, 1936. Lorca was killed at the onset of the Spanish Civil War (1936–1937); it was a murder almost certainly politically motivated in part. The poem was first published in memory of Lorca in the newspaper *Ayuda* on October 17, 1936.

Lorca is said to have been killed by supporters of General Francisco Franco, who were intent on eliminating influential artists and other figures who did not support the general in his attempt to take over Spain. Others suggest that a personal vendetta was involved and that Lorca's support of those opposing Franco was only part of what instigated his murder. Either way, this killing was a shameful assassination of a great literary figure whose involvement in politics was minimal, despite his political convictions; this shame is a major theme in Machado's poem. That is, by emphasizing so strongly that Lorca was killed in his own hometown (he was born in 1898 just outside Granada, in Fuente Vaqueros, and his family moved to Granada in 1909), Machado suggests the degree to which Lorca's death was a terrible betrayal of fundamental decencies.

As a mature and powerful poem, "The Crime Was in Granada" is a respected work of Machado's. Most broader collections of Machado's poems, such as the *Selected Poems*, translated by Alan S. Trueblood, include the poem, and most larger libraries own a copy of Trueblood's translations.

Author Biography

The poet Antonio Machado was born on July 26, 1875, on his family's estate near Seville, Spain. His father and grandfather were scholarly men, and Machado would go on to teach as well. Machado began his schooling in Seville, but his family moved to Madrid, Spain's capital city, when he was eight years old. There, he began attending the Institución Libre de Enseñanza (Free Institute of Teaching). This school was known for its progressive curriculum and for one instructor in particular, Giner de los Rios. De los Rios was a great influence on many of Machado's contemporaries, who, like Machado, went on to play prominent roles in the artistic and political life of Spain. Some of these figures have come to be known as the Generation of '98; most scholars associate Machado with this group. This generation of artists and thinkers attempted to revitalize Spanish cultural and political life.

After graduating from high school, Machado and his brother, Manuel, with whom he was close, went to Paris to work for a publisher. As they had in Madrid, in Paris they participated in the artistic and intellectual life of the city. Machado appreciated the heady pace of their bohemian life in Paris less than his brother did, and soon he was back in Madrid. There, he studied for a teaching certificate, as the early death of his father had reduced the family's finances, making it necessary for him to secure steady employment.

Machado's first teaching post was in the area of Spain called Soría. In Soría, in 1909, Machado met and married a young woman, Leonor Izquierdo. The couple spent time in Paris, where Machado began studying philosophy, a lifelong interest. In fact, Machado would go on to pursue a university degree in philosophy. The completion of this degree, along with his growing reputation as a poet, led to better teaching positions. The marriage did not last long, however, as Leonor contracted tuberculosis and died just three years after they married.

Machado's first published poems appeared in 1901 in a Madrid literary periodical called *Electra*. His first volume of poetry, *Soledades*, was published in 1903. Machado is known as an exacting writer who would destroy those writings with which he was not completely happy. He published four volumes of poetry as well as diverse other writings in his lifetime.

Throughout his life, Machado had close associations, or acquaintanceships, with other Spanish artists and intellectuals, including Federico García Lorca, whose death is recounted in "The Crime Was in Granada" (1936). Lorca was an internationally known literary figure by the time of his death, which was but one terrible event among many that so demoralized Spaniards during the civil war the country suffered from 1936 to 1939.

Machado died on February 22, 1939, in Collioure, France, where he and a number of others had fled, to escape capture and persecution by General Francisco Franco's forces. Machado's health had been failing for some time, and this difficult passage across the Pyrenees into southern France proved to be too much for the poet's fragile constitution.

Poem Text

I *The Crime*

He was seen, surrounded by rifles,
moving down a long street
and out to the country
in the chill before dawn, with the stars still out.
They killed Federico   5
at the first glint of daylight.
The band of assassins
shrank from his glance.
They all closed their eyes,
muttering: "See if God helps you now!"   10
Federico fell,
lead in his stomach, blood on his face.
And Granada was the scene of the crime.
Think of it—poor Granada—, his Granada . . .

II *The Poet and Death*

He was seen with her, walking alone,   15
unafraid of her scythe.
Sunlight caught tower after tower,
hammers pounded on anvils,
on anvil after anvil in the forges.
Federico was speaking,   20
playing up to Death. She was listening.
"The clack of your fleshless palms
was heard in my verse just yesterday, friend;
you put ice in my song, you gave my tragedy
the cutting edge of your silver scythe;   25
so I'll sing to you now of your missing flesh,
your empty eyes,
your wind-snatched hair,
those red lips of yours that knew kisses once . . .
Now, as always, gypsy, my own death,   30
how good being alone with you,
in these breezes of Granada, my Granada!"

III
He was seen walking . . .
Friends, carve a monument
out of dream stone   35

for the poet in the Alhambra,
over a fountain where the grieving water
Shall say forever:
The crime was in Granada, his Granada.

Poem Summary

I

The first part of Machado's poem "The Crime Was in Granada" is called "The Crime," and it describes, or imagines, the assassination of Lorca. The first line of the poem says that Lorca "was seen, surrounded by rifles." By saying that the writer is "seen," Machado reinforces his idea that what occurred was a hideous "crime," since Lorca's having been seen in this context is akin to a crime having been *witnessed*. Notably, also, this first line declines to humanize Lorca's murderers—they amount to no more than the "rifles" they are carrying: "He was seen, surrounded by rifles."

In the next three lines, the setting of Lorca's journey to his death is imagined and described: he is escorted outside of the city ("down a long street"), into the surrounding countryside, in the "chill before dawn, with the stars still out." This simple description of Lorca's last walk manages to conjure a sense of a vast universe—cold, impartial, and uninvolved—so that Lorca's death strikes the reader as a terribly sad and lonely affair, lending a somber, mournful mood to the poem.

The next two lines are ironic in effect, as Lorca is killed "at the first glint of daylight." That is, the sun's rising would seem to be an occasion for joy, being somehow a rebirth—the signaling of a new day. Yet this is the moment Lorca is killed, the moment that a death, and not a birth, occurs. Thus, there is the sense here that nature does not concern itself with or coincide with the wishes of humans. Still, in the following two lines, Lorca is elevated above his "assassins," even if he has not been elevated above nature. This is so because the structure of the four lines, even in the original Spanish, encourages the reader to equate the sun's first rays with Lorca's look, from which his murderers shrink:

They killed Federico
at the first glint of daylight.
The band of assassins
shrank from his glance.

The next line of the poem furthers this effect, as, in writing that the assassins "closed their eyes" as they shot, the idea of Lorca's visage, which is

like a ray of the sun, underscores the murderers' moral puniness and blindness.

Lorca's death is next bluntly, simply described: "lead in his stomach, blood on his face." This simplicity, in its starkness, conveys the brutality of the writer's murder. The first part of the poem ends with an exclamation that Granada was "the scene of the crime," as if to say that no place would ever want to be known as the place that hosted such a shameful and horrible event. Certainly, in writing "poor Granada," Machado expresses his sympathy for the pain and shame Granadinos must feel.

II

The second section of the poem is called "The Poet and Death." In this section, Machado imagines Lorca in conversation with Death. Death is personified as an old woman. So, in place of Lorca's being seen walking down a "long street," in this section he is "seen with her [Death]," "unafraid of her scythe." This indication of the poet's bravery in the face of death continues what is begun in the poem's first part, namely, Machado's paying homage to his fellow writer. Indeed, Machado writes that Lorca is "playing up to Death"; that is, he is in some way courting her and entertaining her. The suggestion is that Lorca is equal to Death—he is a man so extraordinary that a force as powerful as Death would be inclined to pass the time with him. To be sure, Death, says the poet, is "listening" to Lorca.

In the next lines' description of sunlight striking off towers and "hammers" pounding on "anvils," Machado conjures a tense, apocalyptic mood, commemorating the terribleness of the event. This reference to the "forges" where this ironwork is taking place also calls to mind strange, otherworldly places, places from which Death might emerge to make a claim. In the following lines, in which Machado imagines Lorca's conversation with Death, he calls to mind Lorca's own astonishing writing, often so full of elemental and startling imagery:

"The clack of your fleshless palms
was heard in my verse just yesterday, friend;
you put ice in my song, you gave my tragedy
the cutting edge of your silver scythe;

More specifically, Machado is calling to mind the series of rural tragedy plays that Lorca most recently had been working on before he was killed: *Blood Wedding*, *Yerma*, and *The House of Bernarda Alba*. In these lines and the immediately following lines of section II, Machado also emphasizes, again,

Lorca's equality with Death, as Machado has Lorca calling Death "friend." The poet develops, in this part of the poem, the idea that Death and Lorca were always intimate—that Lorca was in some sense always in love with Death and even welcomes his death now that it has arrived. Hence, the following erotic flourish and Lorca's happiness at being finally alone with Death:

> those red lips of yours that knew kisses once . . .
> Now, as always, gypsy, my own death,
> how good being alone with you,
> in these breezes of Granada, my Granada!"

Section II's closing reference to Granada manages to convey, as do the references to the city in section I, a sense of general blame, as Lorca's loving evocation of his native city seems somewhat undeserved, considering that its inhabitants were unable to protect him.

III

Section III of Machado's poem is untitled, as if to suggest the poet's exhaustion at the contemplation of such a terrible event; words to describe the subject of his writing finally elude him. Indeed, in repeating the first section's opening, which then trails off with an ellipsis, this sense of tired exhaustion is underscored: "He was seen walking. . . ." The poet's exhaustion also undoubtedly pertains to the exhaustion of Spaniards in general, as both the armies of Franco and the opposition had already, by the time of the full-scale inception of the civil war, committed numerous acts of terrible brutality.

The second line of section III follows a blank space on the page, as if to conjure once again the crime—but a crime the poet, in his exhaustion, again cannot bring himself to describe further. This blank space on the page also signifies Lorca's death—his absence. The poem ends with a lament and an exhortation:

> Friends, carve a monument
> out of dream stone
> for the poet in the Alhambra,
> over a fountain where the grieving water
> shall say forever:
> The crime was in Granada, his Granada.

This shortest section of "The Crime Was in Granada" achieves a number of goals. First, it maintains that Lorca must be memorialized with a monument. Second, it insists on Lorca's greatness by proposing that a monument be placed in the Alhambra, an ancient, grand fortress and palace that is Granada's greatest edifice. Third, it suggests that this monument not only will memorialize Lorca but

also will remind the world forever of the terribleness of the "crime" committed against him. Indeed, the crime is such an awful one that the Alhambra's fountain, personified like Death, will flow with "grieving water," crying "forever." Last, the closing of the poem reiterates Machado's sense that Spaniards, and Granadinos in particular, should feel shame for what happened to Lorca: he was betrayed and killed in the very town in which he grew up.

Themes

Betrayal

A civil war means that a nation is divided, that a country is at war within itself. Sometimes, these wars take place between obviously different groups within a nation, but not always. The Spanish Civil War was one of the latter wars. It divided friends from friends and family members from family members. As Spaniards picked their sides in the conflict, long-standing friendships came to an end, siblings broke forever with siblings, and parents were sundered from children. Further, some people involved in the war were ruthless in their tactics, acting as spies, informing on former acquaintances, and so forth. In short, Spaniards on both sides felt that they were subject to terrible betrayals, not to mention that each side felt that the other was betraying the future of Spain itself. In repeating so often that Lorca was killed in his own hometown, Machado conveys the idea that Lorca was betrayed by his own—and so he sounds the note of betrayal that was so prevalent a feeling in Spain at the time.

Shame

Machado's repetition that Lorca was killed in his hometown purveys the idea that Granadinos should feel shame for what happened. Somehow, the citizens of Granada should have prevented the murder of their talented son. Beyond this, Machado includes the theme of shame in his poem because of his particular political convictions. That is, he viewed with dismay the prospect of the triumph of General Francisco Franco's fascist forces. After all, as a fascist, Franco was associated with Germany's Adolf Hitler and Italy's Benito Mussolini; he was aiming to control Spain with an iron hand, squashing the democracy that preceded him. Thus, for Machado, those Spaniards who were supporting Franco should especially feel shame, for they were contributing to the cause of a leader who would halt the forward movement of Spain's political and cultural life.

Topics For Further Study

- Research the aspirations, motivations, and beliefs of Spain's Generation of '98, with which Machado is associated.

- Research Federico García Lorca within the context of the Generation of '27, of which he was a part. What beliefs, concerns, and goals united this group of artists?

- Research the Abraham Lincoln Brigade. Why did U.S. citizens decide to volunteer to fight in the Spanish Civil War? Why would they volunteer to give their lives in another country? How large was the brigade? How does it compare with other international brigades? What was at stake in this war in their view?

- Ernest Hemingway, the American writer, was a war correspondent in Spain during the Spanish Civil War. Examine his war writings and explain his attitude toward the events he was witnessing. Or read and report on his fiction novel *For Whom the Bell Tolls*, which takes place during the Spanish Civil War.

- General Francisco Franco received substantial aid from Adolf Hitler's Germany and Benito Mussolini's Italy. Research the circumstances of this fascist web of power in Europe during the 1930s. What, exactly, is fascism?

- What are the roots of flamenco, the dance and music associated with Spain's gypsies?

Brutality

The Spanish Civil War was a bloody war, known not only for brutal assassinations such as Lorca's but for other atrocities as well. One well-known atrocity was the destruction in a bombing raid of an entire town, Guernica, along with a great number of its civilian inhabitants. One of the most famous of the well-known Spanish painter Pablo Picasso's works is a stark black-and-white painting depicting this atrocity, called *Guernica*, after the town. Like Picasso's stark painterly style in this painting, so Machado's stark poetic style and word choice in "The Crime Was in Granada" conveys the brutality of the event being described. The poet calls Lorca's assassination a "crime," so that we understand that a "murder" was committed, and he describes the dead Lorca vividly and bluntly, as a body with "lead in his stomach, blood on his face."

Style

Imagery

Poetic images are generally understood to be elements within a poem that create a sensory impression in the reader's mind, whether that impression is visual, aural, or dependent on another sense. Thus, the opening image in "The Crime Was in Granada" is of a long, empty street. Less obvious images in Machado's poem, however, are its sound images. For example, in section II, Machado describes "hammers pound[ing] on anvils" and the "clack" of Death's "fleshless palms." The load and heavy sound of hammers on iron, as much as the sharp crack of bone against bone, bring to mind the shots of the rifles that killed Lorca. The hammers on the anvils and the clack of Death's palms also evoke the staccato clapping that accompanies performances of flamenco music and dance, not to mention that one type of flamenco song is said to have grown out of the singing of forge workers. Flamenco music (and dancing) is an art form of Spain's gypsy population, most of whom reside in Spain's southern region of Andalusia. Granada, Lorca's hometown, is in Andalusia, and Lorca often celebrated the culture and art of Spain's gypsies in his work.

Elegy

"The Crime Was in Granada" is a type of poem known as an elegy, a poem written in memory of someone who has died. Rules and conventions of elegy writing have differed over time, and the tone and approach taken in an elegy depend on whether the person being elegized was close to the writer or a more distant public figure. In cases where the person being memorialized was close to the poet, the tone of the elegy might be quite sorrowful throughout. In other cases, expressions of sorrow might be more restrained, with the poet concentrating on honoring his or her subject. Machado's elegy, on the whole, is quite restrained emotionally. His drive in the first part of the poem is to memorialize Lorca as one casualty of war among many, as the description of Lorca's assassination brings to mind any number of assassinations that took place during the Spanish Civil War. The second part of "The Crime Was in Granada" is similarly restrained, as Machado here is primarily interested in paying homage to Lorca as a brave man and a brilliant artist. Essentially, Machado waits until the final part of his elegy to convey his deep sorrow over Lorca's death.

Personification

In personification a poet invests something not human with human qualities. For example, a poet might refer to thunder as "the sky's bellow," thus endowing the sky with a human "voice." Or a poet might call a fly "an irritating busybody," giving an insect another type of human attribute. Machado employs personification in his poem when he describes Death as an old woman and invests the fountain's water with human emotion (the waters of the fountain are "grieving").

Diction

Diction refers to word choice—a poet's decision about precisely which words he or she is going to use. Will a baby in a poem "cry," or will it "screech?" If it screeches, how will this choice of word affect the overall tone and meaning of the poem? An extremely important word in Machado's poem is "crime." To commit a crime means to break the law, yet what of law in times of war? Are not civilians killed every day in war zones, with no one ever having to pay the price? When is a civilian death in wartime not a reasonable casualty and instead, as Machado says of Lorca's death, a crime, a murder? When do persons other than soldiers become fair targets in times of war? Answers to these questions depend upon how the civilian is killed and what kind of war is being fought. In the case of Lorca, Machado's word choice is sadly apt and to the point. Lorca, no matter his political convictions, was not a justified target for assassination, and so he was, in effect, murdered in the first days of the Spanish Civil War. By including the word

"crime" in his title and by referring to the scene of Lorca's death as "the scene of the crime," Machado's poem points to the brutal truth of what happened on July 18, 1936.

Translation

There are always difficulties involved when writing about a poem that has been translated into another language. Has the translator chosen the right words? What does a reader do with different translators' versions of a poem if the versions differ considerably? Are these differences of word choice, or are they perhaps differences in how entire lines or sets of lines are arranged grammatically and spatially? Ultimately, a translator must make many difficult decisions, some of which might change the nature of a poem significantly. For example, it may be impossible for a translator to present a poem's original rhymes or rhyme scheme, for there may be no way to create rhymes out of the words that the second language calls for in order to translate the meaning of a poem reasonably accurately.

Readers of translated poetry, in short, must be aware of the fact that they are reading a translation, as this will determine, to a certain extent, what they can discuss about a poem. More specifically, English-language readers of "The Crime Was in Granada" must remember that the poem was originally written in Spanish, so that, first, there are elements and effects in the original that are not present in the translation, and, second, there are quite possibly meanings and effects conveyed by the translation that are not in the original.

Historical Context

The Spanish Civil War (1936–1939) and the Abraham Lincoln Brigade

Like so many European nations, Spain began vigorous attempts to modernize and democratize its governmental institutions beginning in the nineteenth century. Still, the course of these changes was never smooth, with the result that Spain was suffering great political instability in the early part of the twentieth century. Conservative, even dictatorial, elements vied with democratic-socialist elements, with no side ever gaining a firm purchase. On the eve of the civil war, a progressive democratic government was in place, but contesting its legitimacy was a coalition of conservative groups, which included fascist elements, the Catholic

Compare & Contrast

- **1930s:** In their attempt to modernize their governmental bodies, the Spanish have banished their royal family. The last acting king, Alfonso XIII, resides in Portugal in exile, refusing to give up his claim to the throne.

  Today: Despite its status as a democracy, Spain, like England, has a royal family whose ceremonial presence serves as a national symbol of unity. The current popular king, Juan Carlos I, is the grandson of Alfonso XIII.

- **1930s:** Spanish society suffers a period of profound political instability that eventually erupts in the brutal Civil War of 1936–1939. This war's conclusion brings Spain under the rule of the dictator General Francisco Franco.

  Today: Spain is a parliamentary democracy like all other European nations and is a part of the European Union.

- **1930s:** Antifascist sympathizers the world over congregate in Spain to fight against the forces of General Francisco Franco. Those who traveled from the United States to fight against Franco are known as the Abraham Lincoln Brigade, and their fight is known as the Good Fight.

  Today: Spain's latest elected government, headed by Prime Minister José Zapatero, bands with other European nations to contest the U.S. invasion of Iraq.

- **1930s:** Spanish artists such as Federico García Lorca and Pablo Picasso are internationally known as vital innovators in the arts.

  Today: The most internationally prominent Spanish artists are those who work in film, such as director Pedro Almodóvar.

- **1930s:** Spain is economically hampered by a lack of industrial development.

  Today: Thanks to a period of steady growth in all sectors beginning in the 1940s, Spanish citizens enjoy a standard of living equal to that of citizens in other so-called First World nations.

Church, the army, and other groups. The Civil War officially began with an uprising in Morocco of army forces under the leadership of General Francisco Franco, a fascist sympathizer who would go on to receive aid from other fascist European leaders, Germany's Adolf Hitler and Italy's Benito Mussolini, most notably.

As the rise of fascism in Germany and Italy suggests, Europe, in general, at that time was undergoing vast political upheavals. Indeed, like the United States, these countries were suffering economic depressions and other problems. As Franco began his war in Spain, the rest of the world looked on anxiously. To the watching world, the war in Spain augured what was almost certainly going to happen in Europe—a war between progressive and dictatorial elements. This European war was called World War II (1939–1945).

The war in Spain was also a cause for anxiety because, from the point of view of the United States, England, and other solidly democratic nations, the worst thing that could happen in Spain was for Franco to triumph. This would signal the strength of fascist currents in Europe. The forces that opposed Franco were called the Republicans, as they were for a democratic republic instead of the dictatorship Franco had in mind.

Because people thought that the Spanish Civil War reflected the larger struggle in continental Europe at the time, many felt that they had to travel to Spain to fight for the Republican cause. The Republican armies consequently were truly international, with American fighters gathered together in the Abraham Lincoln Brigade. As it turns out, Franco's forces won, but not without the valiant efforts of the Republicans and their supporters.

The Generation of '98

Machado is considered to be a member of what is known as the Generation of '98 (1898) in Spain. This group of artists and other public figures were united by their belief that Spain was ripe for refreshing new directions in the arts, politics, and society in general. Prominent members of this group besides Machado were, to name but a few, Miguel de Unamuno, Pío Baroja, Ramón del Valle-Inclán, and the writer known simply as Azorín. Most especially, this generation was eager for Spain to open itself up more vigorously to new ideas originating beyond its own borders, to the goal of Spain's becoming a more thoroughly modern nation in values and customs.

Federico García Lorca and the Generation of '27

A new, younger generation of artists followed the Generation of '98, establishing new standards of artistic expression. However, like their predecessors, they were vigilant in avoiding stylistics in any way reminiscent of nineteenth-century currents. One new trend that some of this later generation, including Lorca, embraced was surrealism. Surrealist artworks employ dream imagery and logic in their work, the sort of odd, startling images and juxtapositions of images that are characteristic of dreams. A strong surrealistic current is evident, for example, in Lorca's book of sequential poems titled *Gypsy Ballads*. Lorca remains most well known as a poet and a playwright.

Critical Overview

English-language (Anglophone) studies of "The Crime Was in Granada," considered on its own, are rare. Instead, most Anglophone criticism tends to be general estimations of Machado's work (his career as a poet), explorations of a group of poems (for example, a particular collected volume of poems), or examinations of some aspect of his work running throughout his career (for instance, the significance of fountains in his verse).

In terms of general estimations of Machado's poetic career, the criticism can be divided into two phases, according to Alan S. Trueblood. As Trueblood writes in "Antonio Machado and the Lyric of Ideas" (in *Letter and Spirit in Hispanic Writers: Renaissance to Civil War*), early critics of Machado were "disconcerted" by certain "changes of direction in successive stages of his career." That is,

some earlier critics had widely admired his first verse publications and then felt that changes in his later work signaled a waning of his vitality as a writer. However, with hindsight, these successive stages in Machado's career have come to be seen as the reasonable development of a writer whose sense of what he wished to accomplish changed over time.

Despite these changes in Machado's verse over time, certain poetic elements remain fairly consistent. For example, Machado often employs images of fountains and roads in his poems, as in "The Crime Was in Granada." Machado's sense of the evocativeness of fountains derives from his southern Spanish provenance, as fountains in courtyards are common features in southern Spanish buildings, including Machado's own childhood home.

Criticism

Carol Dell'Amico

Dell'Amico is an instructor of English literature and composition. In this essay, she considers Machado's poem about Federico García Lorca within the context of the characteristic elements of Machado's and Lorca's work.

Within a few years of the first publication of "The Crime Was in Granada," Machado had died. As a poem written near the end of his life, it contains many elements typical of many other poems he wrote. Yet the way in which Machado incorporates typical qualities of Federico García Lorca's works, as a way of paying homage to his fellow writer, distinguishes this poem.

One of the tenets of Spain's Generation of '98, with which Machado is associated, was that the art of the new twentieth century should reflect the modernism of the era. For Machado, this meant ridding his poetry of typical nineteenth-century flourishes (adorned language) and syntactical (grammatical) complexities. The modernism of his prose, in other words, is seen in his plain choice of words and straightforward sentence constructions: there are few rare words to be found in Machado's poetry and few lines that require a reader to read many lines before understanding their meaning within some larger, lengthy, and complex sentiment. This simplicity of diction and expression is especially evident in the first section of "The Crime Was in Granada"; indeed, portions of this first section are particularly stark in their simplicity and

> *The way in which many southern Spanish artists like Lorca (and Machado) began incorporating flamenco traditions in their art was fairly revolutionary, as the gypsy population in Spain—along with their art—had been disdained by the general population and elites for a very long time.*"

straightforwardness, as is seen in the description of the killing itself:

Federico fell,
lead in his stomach, blood on his face.
And Granada was the scene of the crime.

Machado's decision to write an especially blunt description of Lorca's assassination can be attributed not only to his modern poetic method but also to his sense that one of the poem's purposes was to document an atrocity that should not in any way be romanticized. The means of Lorca's death should strike the reader as a brutality and nothing else.

Section I of "The Crime Was in Granada" is in other ways reminiscent of Machado's work as a whole. For example, its initial description of the country landscape in which Lorca is killed attests to the importance of landscape in general in Machado's writing. As Willis Barnstone has written in *Six Masters of the Spanish Sonnet*, "clear geographical images" are highly characteristic of Machado's art. As Barnstone also points out, the Spanish poet is an "introspective and landscape-oriented" writer, a writer in whose poems "landscape, or the open-eyed dream of it, does all." Landscape, he says, "is thing and symbol." Of course, since "The Crime Was in Granada" is primarily designed to be a poem written in honor of Lorca, it is not a poem in any way dominated by a focus on landscape. Nevertheless, the opening

description of Granada's outskirts, where Lorca was killed, is both "thing and symbol" in the poem. It is "thing" because it is a simple description of how Machado imagines the scene on the morning of Lorca's death. It is "symbol" as well, because the description of the scene conveys ideas:

He was seen, surrounded by rifles,
moving down a long street
and out to the country
in the chill before dawn, with the stars still out.
They killed Federico
at the first glint of daylight.

At the same time, Machado's description of the scene is factual in the sense that Lorca was apprehended just before dawn and killed soon after. Machado's emphasis on the cold of the early morning hours appropriately conveys the cold and terrible nature of the writer's murder. Moreover, instead of being a symbol of warmth, the first rays of the sun in the poem are yet one more cruel detail, as Alan Trueblood's choice of the word "glint" as a translation for these first rays conveys. That is, "glint" calls to mind a sharp brilliance, a cutting ray that suggests the bullets that pierce Lorca's flesh. The cold, cutting universe of the first section of "The Crime Was in Granada" communicates, in short, the cruelty and loneliness of Lorca's tragic death.

Section II of "The Crime Was in Granada," the poem's longest section, is Machado's homage to Lorca. It is his homage in one important respect: Machado takes great pains to evoke much of what is characteristic of Lorca's own writing and artistic concerns. For example, Lorca is known for his interest in the art of Spain's gypsy population, which is largely southern Spanish in provenance, as gypsy territory stretches from South Asia through southern Europe and into the north of Africa. This population is known for its vital music and dance traditions, which in Spain developed into what is known as flamenco. Flamenco songs take on many subjects, such as love, death, and the beauty of nature. Sometimes gypsy entertainments feature only singers, backup singers, and guitar players. At other times, a dancer or group of dancers will accompany the song. In either case, a certain staccato rhythm often predominates. This is so because flamenco dancers (both men and women) stamp their feet as they dance on wooden floors, the female dancers play castanets (small wooden clappers held in the hands), guitar players occasionally rap on their guitars, and even onlookers clap a sharp accompaniment.

Machado calls to mind flamenco song and dance in his inclusion of the sound image of "hammers"

What Do I Read Next?

- The expansive collection of Machado's poems in *Selected Poems* (1982), translated by Alan S. Trueblood, offers an excellent view of his breadth and development as a poet. This volume is also attractive for its inclusion of the original Spanish text of the poems alongside the English translations.

- *Solitudes, Galleries, and Other Poems* (1987), translated by Richard L. Predmore, is Machado's second published collection of verse. Reading a collection of a poet's poems as he or she wanted them to be collected in a single volume—as opposed to reading a collection of a poet's poems from many different volumes compiled by an editor—is a necessary exercise for students of a poet's work. The original Spanish-language text of Machado's poems is included in this book.

- *Poet in New York and Other Poems* (1940), translated by Rolfe Humphries, is a collection of poems by the young Federico García Lorca about his time in New York City and other places in the northeastern United States in 1929–1930.

- The plays *Blood Wedding, Yerma*, and *The House of Bernarda Alba* are Federico García Lorca's three brilliant rural tragedies. They are published singly and together, with one compilation having an introduction by the poet's brother, Francisco. This collection is titled *III Tragedies: Blood Wedding, Yerma, Bernarda Alba* (1947), translated by Richard L. O'Connell and James Graham-Luján.

- *Our Fight: Writings by Veterans of the Abraham Lincoln Brigade, Spain, 1936–1939* (1987) is a compilation of writings by members of the brigade of American citizens who fought against General Francisco Franco's fascist forces during the Spanish Civil War. The collection is edited by Alvah Cecil Bessie and Albert Prago.

---

pounding on "anvils," "on anvil after anvil in the forges." This mention of forges reminds Machado's readers of how flamenco song flourished in the forges of Granada and other southern Spanish towns. There are many forges in these towns, mainly because the architecture of the south utilizes ironwork extensively: heavy wooden doors are adorned with iron details, houses are fitted with strong iron balconies, windows are faced with decorative iron bars, and so forth. Many gypsies worked and continue to work in these forges, singing to the rhythm of the iron-headed hammers striking the iron anvils.

The way in which many southern Spanish artists like Lorca (and Machado) began incorporating flamenco traditions in their art was fairly revolutionary, as the gypsy population in Spain—along with their art—had been disdained by the general population and elites for a very long time. To many Spaniards, gypsies seemed, and even continue to seem, an impoverished, rough group, stuff merely for tourists to think that they are witnessing the "real" Spain. A better picture of gypsies is that they have entirely different values from those of the Spanish mainstream, unique ideas about what makes life worth living and how life should be lived. The gypsy population guards its own traditions and culture jealously, making little attempt to join the mainstream. Thus, Lorca's and others' acceptance of this fact, along with their embrace of gypsy traditions, was a gesture that insisted on the greatness of these traditions as well as any population's right to be a part of the Spanish nation without necessarily conforming to the values and customs of the mainstream.

Machado's own respectful attitude toward gypsy culture undoubtedly derives from his father, who was a serious scholar of these and other southern popular traditions. (Machado's family, like Lorca's, hails from the south, from the southern Spanish city of Seville. Like Granada, Seville has a large and flourishing gypsy population and set of traditions.) More to the point in terms of Lorca and gypsy arts, he is known for a very beautiful sequence of poems called the *Gypsy Ballads*, which, like the series of three rural tragedy plays Lorca had just completed before his death (*Blood Wedding*, *Yerma*, and *The House of Bernarda Alba*), draw extensively on gypsy styles and themes. In this context, we find Machado's notion in "The Crime Was in Granada" that Lorca imagines Death as an old "gypsy" woman. Here, Machado reminds the reader of how flamenco song-poetry contains so many brilliant evocations of the inevitability and grandeur of death, a fact that underwrites the lucid tragedy of Lorca's last superb plays:

> "The clack of your fleshless palms
> was heard in my verse just yesterday, friend;
> you put ice in my song, you gave my tragedy
> the cutting edge of your silver scythe;

Section III of Machado's poem to Lorca again emphasizes many of these same ideas. That is, Machado stresses the idea that Lorca—like Machado himself—was a southern poet interested in all of the diverse traditions of southern Spain. This is seen in Machado's call for a tomb for the poet in the Alhambra, Granada's greatest structure, and his mention of a fountain in this regard. The Alhambra is a structure that calls to mind all of Spain's history and southern Spanish history in particular. It evokes southern Spanish history in the sense that it was originally built as a Moorish palace by Moorish rulers during their occupation of southern Spain. It was one of the Moors' most beautiful buildings, containing much of what classic Moorish architecture is known for: towers, decorative tiles, and courtyards with pools and fountains. Thus, one significant aspect of the Moorish heritage in southern Spain is found in the typical characteristics of the region's architecture—the tiled courtyards and the lovely fountains, for example. Once the Moors were expelled from Spain in the fifteenth century, the Alhambra was inhabited by Spanish nobles, who added to the structure and its gardens.

Since the Alhambra has twenty-three towers on its primary outer walls, Machado says in section II that "Sunlight caught tower after tower"; he means here that, as Lorca was escorted out of Granada, the first rays of the sun were highlighting the tops of these towers. In stating that Lorca merits a tomb or memorial in the stunning Alhambra, Machado is saying that Lorca deserves a great honor. Equally important, he reminds the reader that Lorca embraced all of southern Spanish history; unlike others, he did not attempt to forget the Moorish past and heritage—to which, indeed, gypsy traditions can be connected, thanks to the gypsies' association with northern Africa.

Source: Carol Dell'Amico, Critical Essay on "The Crime Was in Granada," in *Poetry for Students*, Thomson Gale, 2006.

Salvador J. Fajardo

In the following essay, Fajardo examines Machado's war sonnets—their sequence and "how they reflect Machado's own evolution in the context of the [Spanish] Civil War."

Antonio Machado wrote his nine war sonnets in 1938. They appeared together in the June 1938 issue (no. XIX) of *Hora de España*. On the whole the sonnets have not elicited particular interest, and when they have done so, their reception has been generally negative. In his book on poetry of commitment, Lechner dismisses them as not particularly interesting; Sánchez Barbudo in *La poesía de Antonio Machado* finds in them a "tono de énfasis declamatorio," while Lázaro Carreter, in his article "[e]l último Machado" says that Machado's poetry is not well suited to the demands of his "ímpetu político y bélico" (119–134). Generally speaking, these views highlight a series of problems related as much to our critical deficiencies as they are to the intrinsic interest of the poetry. Actually, we still tend to approach committed poetry with the same instruments that we apply to traditional lyrical expression, and our expectations also remain the same.

This difficult problem needs to be addressed with imagination and acumen, so as to lay to rest some of the hackneyed ideas that are regularly served up whenever we deal with committed poetry, or committed literature in general. In most cases—and I include Lechner and García de la Concha in my caveat—readers of committed poetry fail properly to contextualize the texts they address. As well, neither commitment to a cause, nor the demands of historical circumstance necessarily reduce the significance or impact of poetic communication. And perhaps it is this latter aspect of the poetry that one ought to focus on: communication First, what the poet is communicating and wether he does so effectively; second, with respect to the poet's own trajectory (that is to say, viewing the poetry as an expression of the speaker's condition at the time) what does it express? In this manner we can distinguish in committed poetry, and in Machado's sonnets, their role as action in a context, and action from a context. For one thing, communication as a whole can be viewed as an action; in this sense, communication "is not a neutral vehicle for the conveyance of messages, but rather an inherently political practice that constitutes the site of the struggle over what defines knowledge in our society." Certainly this applies to Machado's sonnets and to their role in conveying what defined knowledge for the poet during the Civil War.

In my approach to the sonnets I want to look at their disposition as a sequence, and seek to show how they reflect Machado's own evolution in the context of the Civil War. To my mind, the sequence expresses the sundering of the poet's self by the conflictive reality around him, as well as an effort to achieve a workable subjectivity overall, through a development that seeks to join his post-symbolist and engagé agencies. Students of Machado have located as early as the 1907 edition of *Soledades, galerías y otros poemas* the beginning of his transition away from symbolist/solipsistic individualism and toward the "yo fundamental" concerned with a collective task. In this latter position poetry becomes communicative action engaged in what Cerezo Galán describes as an "acto poético de conciencia," oriented toward "la búsqueda de una palabra esencial, que pueda convertirse en un vínculo común" (573). This concern will predispose the poet favorably toward socialist ideas which would respond to those "gotas de sangre jacobina" that he always felt he had. For Machado, human beings define themselves in dialogue, in contact with the "other." And this contact, or outward disposition, encompasses as well a relationship to the material world: "Mi sentimiento ante el mundo exterior, que aquí llamo paisaje, no surge sin una atmósfera cordial. Mi sentimiento no es, en suma, exclusivamente mío, sino más bien *nuestro*. Sin salir de mí mismo, noto que en mi sentir vibran otros sentires y que mi corazón canta siempre en coro aunque su voz sea para mí la voz mejor timbrada" (*Los complementarious* 41–42 & II, 102).

I see these views as an evolution away from Kant's radical notion of human freedom and toward an organic, expressivistic position such as that proposed by Gadamer or Charles Taylor. In fact, Machado's cordial understanding is quite in tune with Gadamer's notion that understanding transcends the distinction between subject and object. And because, following Heidegger, *Dasein* involves both a relationship to others and to past and future, Gadamer says: "Understanding is not to be thought of so much as an action of one's subjectivity, but of the placing oneself within a process of tradition, in which past and present are constantly fused (Gadamer, *Truth and Method* 258).

As well, neither commitment to a cause, nor the demands of historical circumstance necessarily reduce the significance or impact of poetic communication."

Charles Taylor argues that this hermeneutic tradition harks back to the romantic philosophy of language developed by Herder and Humboldt and continued, somewhat modified, by Heidegger (and, thereafter, Gadamer). For Taylor this involves the doctrine of expressivism, according to which language implies three aspects: first, "through language we can bring to explicit awareness what we formerly had only an implicit sense of"; second, "language enables us to put things in public space"; third, it "provides the medium through which some of our most important concerns, the characteristically human concerns, can impinge on us all." Language in general, Taylor says, is "a pattern of activity, by which we can express/realize a certain way of being in the world, that of reflective awareness, but a pattern which can only be deployed against a background which we can never fully dominate, and yet a background that we are never fully dominated by, because we are constantly reshaping it" (Taylor, quoted by Callinicos, 98).

In this context, a reading of Machado's war sonnets shows them functioning:

1. as communicative action (putting things in public space);

2. as an exploration of human concerns in the context of the Civil War;

3. as an explicitation of Machado's trajectory from a personal to a public space and a realization thereby of his own split agency. This realization also relates to Gadamer's notion of understanding within a tradition.

It should be noted, first of all, that from 1936 to 1939 Machado was devoting most of his waning energies to the prose pieces that he regularly produced for *Hora de España* and *La Vanguardia*—by and large in his "Juan de Mairena" voice—, and for some public occasions when he was asked to speak. The upheaval of the war and his failing health were not propitious to the writing of poetry, and with his brother Manuel, on the other side, there was no question of writing any drama. Upon his removal to Valencia in November '36, however, Machado, impelled by outrage at the indiscriminate bombardment of Madrid, and by admiration at the courageous defense of the capital by its inhabitants, seems to regain some energy. In an interview for *La Vanguardia* in Valencia (November 27, 1936) he begins: "La guerra está en contra de la Cultura, pues destruye todos los valores espirituales. . . . Y es el pueblo quien defiende el espíritu de la cultura. . . . Ante esta contienda, el intelectual no puede inhibirse. Su mundo está en peligro. Ha de combatir, ser un miliciano" (*Antonio Machado. Poeta en el exilio* 258–59). This is the claim that he is putting forth about himself: he will be a "miliciano," combatting with his own weapons—words and ideas.

During the period proper when the sonnets are composed (from March 1938 on), Machado had begun to write political pieces for *La Vanguardia*. By writing the sonnets he was relying on his considerable "symbolic capital," to borrow Pierre Bourdieu's phrase. Machado was fully aware of the problems of writing verse under such circumstances; thus, when he sent the first four sonnets to Juan José Domenchina, editor of the Republic's "Servicio español de información," he says: "Le envío esos cuatro sonetos de circunstancias que quisieran estar a la altura de las circunstancias. Creo que dentro del molde barroco del soneto, contienen alguna emoción que no suelen tener los sonetos" (Whiston 150).

As communicative action, the sonnets represent Machado's "armas de combate." They are the most effective weapons that he could forge because they tap powerfully his "symbolic capital":

1. as poetry—and, of course, Machado's prestige was still very much the poet's;

2. as sonnets proper, because the genre is the most highly structured and demanding, the most clearly "poetic" form available.

This very form requires of the reader a meditative, reflective pause, a self-distancing from circumstance, parallel to that of the poet upon their composition. The striking contrast between the chosen form—which is like an invitation to meditative dialogue—and the circumstances in which the form is cast into the public forum, makes their functioning as action more patent, reminding the reader that the values the sonnets incorporate are theirs, that the Republic defends them. These values are the background to the conflict; they cannot be sensed, realized, unless one pauses and reflects. At the structural level this is the communicative action that the sonnets perform. This outward tension is matched by an inward within the sonnets proper: the clash between their form and their subject. For while the form tends generally toward a resolution through the logic of meditation—1. situation, 2. complication, 3. resolution—the subject, the multiple sunderings of the war, seems not liable to such containment. Yet the form holds and functions with great effectiveness, just as the values espoused by the Republic, by the people, should supersede the sunderings of the conflict.

It is my contention, as I mentioned earlier, that the sonnets constitute a structured whole and should be read as such. On the one hand sonnet V divides the sequence into two parts, I to IV, and VI to IX. Across these two parts individual sonnets echo one another as VI to II, VII to III, VIII to IV, and IX to I. The dual structure of the group shows a development from the general symbolic (or representative) in I to IV, to the specific circumstantial, in VI to IX. Sonnet V represents, and inscribes, the sundering of past and present, of friend and foe, of National and Republican spaces, of personal and public spheres and spaces as well. This sonnet also addresses the inner sundering of the poet between his post-symbolist and his committed voice, in the sense that his post-symbolist expressivism, while it realized the need for cordial understanding, had not fully integrated it or put it into practice. This the war will bring about. At the same time the sequence as a whole seeks to contain within its general disposition the development of the poet's voice, and to show it as a necessary evolution required by the needs of the conflict and the poet's assumption of his public responsibility as another "miliciano," one with intellectual weapons.

In his excellent book on Machado's war writings James Whiston does a reading of the poems in which he seeks to counteract the oft-expressed negative views I mentioned above. His interest is to uncover in these poems the poetic values to which Machado had accustomed his readers. On the whole I agree with Whiston, but my interest lies elsewhere. While I cannot go here into the analytic details of the sonnets, I do want to show how they conform to the pattern that I just suggested by looking at the main thrust of each piece. Also, I am less concerned in seeing what the sonnets *are* than seeing what they *do*. In fact I am convinced that, generally speaking, we would gain much if we looked at committed poetry less as expression and more as performance.

Each one of the sonnets seeks to overcome some sort of division, or conflict. The first, harking back to perennial values of resurgence and birth, contextualizes the war immediately under the aegis of a Spring which is "[m]ás fuerte que la guerra." Against the background of the telluric forces of nature, violence and death are aleatory. The menace from above, "el ominoso trimotor," can only be momentary, its rumbling overcome by the "agrio son de tu rabel florido." In contrast sonnet IX, "A Lister," appears to deal with specifically partisan concerns. Yet, though at this concrete level, there is a confrontation between a particular occasion and its background, where communication—in this case a letter—renews in the poet, some hope in the future. Lister's letter against the background of the war is like the "rabel florido" of the Spring against the sound of menacing airplanes. In the last two lines the poet specifically relates his own endeavor to that of the soldier: "Si mi pluma valiera tu pistola / de capitán, contento moriría." It is easy to think of the sonnet exclusively as a propaganda piece—though even in this sense it works rather well. But seen as the concluding installment in a development, and relating it to the first, the sonnet to Lister supports and confirms the implicit concerns of the collection: both the soldier and the poet are "milicianos" in a war that defends lasting human values, a "lucha santa sobre el campo ibero." As the final installment in the series the sonnet also marks the point of arrival for Machado, and inscribes the trajectory between his agency as poet and his agency as poet/"miliciano." The fusion, however, is not complete. The last two lines quote a voice, and stand out against the rest of the sonnet. The citation suggests a more active level of communication, a concrete situating of the piece in a public context, as if the meditative thrust of the sonnet as form were superseded by the requirements of public action. Also, the concluding distich's condition as quote authorizes their somewhat emphatic tone. Retroactively the sonnet, and its conclusion, accomplish for the sequence its performative role as a public statement that defines the poet's participation in the conflict.

In sonnet II the poet reconnects with his personal poetic past through imagery and direct reference: "perfil zancudo . . . de la cigüeña," "vuelo de ballesta," "campo empedernido," "Soria pura," "alto Duero," and "rojo Romancero," the latter being a reference to the Alvargonzález sequence. Like the surge of Spring in I this memory is contrasted with the war, again represented as the threat of an airplane and seen as a tragic re-enactment of the Alvargonzález violence: "¿o es, otra vez, Caín, sobre el planeta, / bajo tus alas, moscardón guerrero?" Again the poet actively puts his symbolic capital into play, engaging his entire poetic past in the present conflict. In sonnet VI the general threat of the airplane has gained specificity—"Alguien vendió la piedra de los lares / al pesado teutón, al hambre mora, / y al ítalo las puertas de los mares"—, rumbling against the emotion—laden memories of the poet's Sevillian childhood, the personalized, intimate remembrance of the man, as well as of the poet.

Sonnet III is a celebration of Valencian work and fecundity. The war is only implicitly referred to in the contrast between past and present: "feliz quiero cantarte como eras." Sonnet VII, on the other hand, emphasizes the enemy's destruction of such riches:

> Manes del odio y de la cobardía
> cortan la leña de tus encinares,
> pisan la baya de oro en tus lagares,
> muelen el grano que tu suelo cría.

Poetry as communicative action in a time of conflict also seeks to do this. The Republic's defense of cultural values is then itself a "poetic" endeavor.

Sonnet IV stands sharply against the overall meditative tone of III. It focuses on the immediacy of death, individualizing the impact of the war through the death of a child and the mother's sorrow: "¿Duermes, o dulce flor de sangre mía? / El cristal del balcón repiquetea. /—¡Oh, fría, fría, fría, fría, fría!" Sonnet VIII recontextualizes IV in terms of the war. Spain is now the mother, confronted by her traitorous son (the sonnet's epigraph, "A otro conde don Julián" presumably refers to Franco). The accusation is now quite specific but is not described in terms of politics, rather as a betrayal of nurturing which transcends ideology, just as in sonnet IV the death of the child and the mother's sorrow transcend any partisanship.

Sonnet V is in many ways the keystone to the sequence. Its topic is the very division that it marks within the sequence between Machado's two agencies, his poetic past and his engaged present. These two components of the poet's self figure in the multiple sunderings addressed in the sonnet: the sentimental past, represented by Guiomar, sundered from the writing present by the war's "tajo fuerte," is also a poetic and a political prehistory to the conflict. The disjunction is also rendered in terms of space (Atlantic/Mediterranean) and as the cropping of a possible intimate future: "la flor imposible de la rama / que ha sentido del hacha el corte frío." The sonnet marks both a division and a transition. It divides the sequence of sonnets, as I mentioned above, between the first that inveigh against the war in general human terms, and the last four, where specific responsibilities are explored in a notably committed voice: on these terms, the poet embodies his country's sundering. The sonnet is transitional in the sense that it formally holds together the sequence and contributes to its overall thrust or development in terms of the personal history of the poet's voice toward political agency, a voice impelled by the requirements of the transformed public space into which it is thrown.

In this sense the division the sonnet incorporates foregrounds the new conditioning of this poetry as active, engaged communication, as communicative action. The sonnet sequence explicates Machado's own trajectory from general expressivism to commitment, and recontextualizes his poetry at this moment, as required by circumstance but also as rooted in his own evolution. In fact, with a more trenchant voice, the same concerns are transmitted here that sustained Machado's meditations on Castile, and inspired the prescient tragedy of "La tierra de Alvargonzález."

The particular structuration of the nine sonnets as a whole composes both a sundering and a communicative action, in terms of the poet's own vital trajectory, as well as in terms of his country's immediate past and present. Also, the sonnets' communicative intent wants to mold the readers' own response as a communication between past and present moments that does not forget but engages their difference. The reader of Machado would note the particular use made by the poet of his poetic prehistory as a *selected* past from his anguished present, as the past from which his present has evolved. They form different moments of the same being, seen from a present of conflict. Thus do the sonnets' communicative action seek to reconstruct personal and political sunderings as moments and spaces (the war zones) of a communicating whole: the struggle separates and identifies, for it leads us to search, in our own past and among our opponents, for the possibility of communication in conflict.

Source: Salvador J. Fajardo, "Machado's War Sonnets: The Sundered Self," in *Nuevas perspectivas sobre el 98*, edited by John P. Gabriele, Iberoamericana-Vervuert, 1999, pp. 63–71.

Elizabeth Scarlett

In the following essay, Scarlett examines the image and purpose of fountains in Machado's poetry, including its role as a "feminine counterdiscourse" to "the poet's masculine discourse of solitude."

Readers of Antonio Machado's poetry have often selected the road as his most central image, a metaphor for life as a journey with no fixed destination (Zardoya 340). A close second, it has been suggested, is running water in a variety of forms (Ribbans 26). Water in motion conveys well Machado's conception of poetry as "la palabra esencial en el tiempo." The river and the ocean, representing the course of an individual life and the collective destiny of death, are permanent metaphors in Hispanic poetry thanks to Manrique, a debt that Machado acknowledges openly. The multiple meanings of *fuente* have a similarly rich history in Spanish poetry, especially in the divine wellsprings of mysticism: Juan de la Cruz's "fonte que mana y corre, aunque es de noche" and Teresa de Jesús's inner fountains build upon a Biblical tradition of the fountain as source of life and goodness, and hence, of divinity. Symbolist and *modernista* fountains are an intervening influence to which Machado also responds: they tend to pour out nostalgia musically against a motionless or silent background. Having absorbed these images, Machado develops his own set of associations for the fountain. I hope to clarify how this image contributes to the meaning of poems in which it appears, and to draw attention to a particular motivation that makes Machado's fountains uniquely conspicuous in his early poetry. This is his employment of the fountain as articulate water that offers a feminine counterdiscourse in opposition to the poet's masculine discourse of solitude.

Criticism of Machado has noted the capacity for speech enjoyed by the fountain in *Soledades* (1899–1907). As Zubiría asserts, "Ciertamente, las fuentes de Machado son manaderos de melancolía, y lo que cantan la tristeza de los amores perdidos, o el dolor de la existencia" (38). Alonso has suggested that the fountain embodies femininity in the fluidity of its water and masculinity in the stone construction that holds the water in place (147). Both Zubiría and Lapesa view the fountain represented in Machado's early poetry as the most vital and significant one. While fountains also appear in *Campos de Castilla* (1907–17), *Nuevas canciones* (1917–30), and the *Cancionero apócrifo* (1924–36), it is with decreasing frequency and prominence.

The fountain is mentioned in twenty-two of the ninety-five poems contained in the expanded edition of *Soledades*. In contrast, the 152 poetic texts that compose *Campos de Castilla* include only three mentions, and only five of the 217 poems or poetic fragments of *Nuevas canciones* are graced with fountains.

The difference is more than one of quantity. The fountains of post *Soledades* volumes are usually more conventional; they are not gifted with the eloquence of earlier examples. They often blend in with the rest of the landscape. In a few instances they are distant echoes of the vocal fountains from before, but their clarity has diminished with repetition. This study will focus above all on the more significant fountains in Machado's first complete volume of poetry. Further examination of fountain imagery in *Soledades* shows that it substitutes for a suppressed part of the poetic self; the philosophical Other of the Noventayochistas aligns itself through the fountain with the otherness of repressed memories, silenced voices, and half-forgotten scenes and sentiments. In the network of associations that grows from one poem to the next, a feminine Other comes to speak through the dripping, laughing, or bubbling fountain. The poet assigns the gender that he is not (female) to the voice that reminds him of when he does not possess: love, or the past. This lost element varies from poem to poem. The use of gender is in keeping with the dichotomies of male/female, subject/object, civilization/nature, mind/body, day/night, and life/death that Beauvoir discerned at the foundation of patriarchal culture. The first term in each is the more familiar, comfortable, identifiable, rational, or controllable one from the point of view of patriarchy, or culture that takes the male subject as its center. The feminine that signals absence in opposition to the poet's presence, and past to his present, is found not only in his use of fountains but in a series of other images developed throughout *Soledades:* the phantoms, mysterious hands, and voices that guide him along the galleries of the soul.

While I seek to privilege the fountain as feminine voice springing from the poet's consciousness, this seme or sub-meaning of the image is connected to and bolstered by other semes that I will illustrate as well. Kristeva describes how the branching out of meanings and connotations from the symbol is one of the chief ways in which "art seems to bypass complacency and, without simply turning mourning into mania, secure for the artist and the connoisseur a sublimatory hold over the lost Thing." The fountain, through the multiplicity

> *The fountain may speak as a teasing sister or it may evoke the memory of maternal nurture. The feminine Other exists outside of the constraints of time but lacks the mobility of the male subject."*

of its associations, thus goes beyond the mere description of the lost Thing; naming alone does not help to transcend suffering. Along with prosody and identification with an all-forgiving ideal, the polyvalence of the sign and symbol ensures that the poetic artifice will stand on its own outside of the writer's psyche to make transitory beauty or the lost object of love more permanent. This polyvalence "unsettles naming and, by building up a plurality of connotations around the sign, affords the subject a chance to imagine the nonmeaning, or the true meaning, of the Thing" (97). Just as many of Kristeva's examples have to do with mourning for lost maternal love, we shall notice a strong maternal coloring of the memories brought to mind by the articulate fountain in Machado.

In this way, we find that the fountain as reminder of maternal nurture is closely related the fountain as projection of a feminine counterdiscourse. This in turn is connected to the fountain of the childhood home and of nostalgia for that period, which for Machado necessarily entails a sense of the centrality of the fountain in Andalusian architecture and urban planning. The Andalusian fountain, reminiscent of the fountain as oasis in Islamic architecture, carries the added connotation of the harem fountain, which is activated by means of a few poems that engage in Hispano-Moorish orientalism. These timeless fountains are found alongside the fountain that keeps time, the Bergsonian water clock (*clepsidra*). The *noria,* or water wheel, signifies the drudgery that seems to govern human existence, and it heralds the poet's later concern for the socially oppressed. Another fountain that reminds the poet of mortality is the stagnant pool he situates in cemetery landscapes. This in turn is balanced in other poems by his reworking of the mystical fountain or source of eternal life in a way that incorporates existential anguish and doubt. We shall also find the fountain as reservoir of a nearly lost oral culture, entoning ancient rhymes and legends, and with an erotic shading, as a setting for chance romantic encounters. The provincial fountain that spouts monotonously contrasts with the fountain that represents the faculty of poetic creation and source of inspiration. This metapoetic fountain speaks in a feminine mode, turning the image into a concrete muse and bringing us full circle to the fountain as feminine Other normally repressed within the male subject's consciousness.

The flexibility of the image does not dilute its potency, but rather causes a chain of associations to be built, so that for the careful reader all fountains are present in each instance. Riffaterre incited a new appreciation of the importance of semes, semantic units that cluster to form sememes and underlie surface meanings in a series of poems, and Bousoño applied this to Machadian studies in his observation of bisemic image chains: those sequences of images in which a single seme, not necessarily the most obvious one, rises to the surface in each image because of the influence of others in the chain. At the same time, however, the multiplicity of associations in such images produces a continental deferral of ultimate meaning in such a way that the latter can never be concisely defined. Sesé noted that Machado's constant visualization of thought resulted in a criss-cross between mental and physical realities that was at bottom undecidable: "Parece como si el poets dudara entre los paisajes exteriores y la región secreta del alma. Se confunden a menudo, y siempre mantienen íntimas correspondencias" (58). Hence, I will clarify as many correspondences for the fountain as possible, as well as their interrelations, but I will not claim to have singled out the ultimate meaning of the image in the Machadian poetic universe.

The most autonomous of all his fountains is the one that awaits the poet behind the rusty gate of an old park in "Fue una clara tarde, triste y soñolienta" (VI). Here the author turns the fountain jet into something akin to Luis de León's vocal river in "Profecía del Tajo." At the end of the latter text, the river itself rears its head to spout ominous predictions of the Muslim Conquest at King Roderigo, prophecies that ring true in the light of ensuing history. "Fue una clara tarde" also endows a current of water with speech in an Iberian tradition that may date as far back as prehistoric river worship in areas settled by Celts. In contrast to the sibylline Tajo, however, Machado's fountain is a more private voice, and the subject about which it discourses is the poet's past compared to his recollection of it. Along with the narrator, we have unlocked a garden of things past: instead of future doom, as in Luis de León, the spirit that inhabits the fountain conjures up forgotten gloom from youthful days. As part of the masculine/feminine tension in the poem, the fountain cheerfully but insistently offers up these remembrances of unhappiness to the poet, who walks away in a manner resembling defeat.

The animism that imbues the fountain with life makes it a mirror reflection of the narrator, who engages in dialogue with it. But like the reverse symmetry of the mirror, the fountain reflects the opposite of what the poet would like to believe about his past. There is no recovery of lost happiness to be hoped for, since even that happiness is an illusion invented by the poet. The lighthearted mood of this interlocutor also strikes a contrast with the melancholic male subject. The attribution of a feminine gender to the fountain ("hermana la fuente") makes the opposition of this voice to the poet's complete, and hints at another source of solace besides deceptive nostalgia. Since the singing and rhyming fountain can be seen as a generator of verse and hence a poet in her own right, then writing itself is the genuine solace that reveals the falsity of the nostalgia in which the poet is submerged. In this way, the fountain as feminine counterdiscourse combines with the fountain as muse and as metapoetic commentator in this poem. The poet's most explicit desire (recovery of past happiness) may be denied, but this second source of pleasure is offered in its stead by the feminine Other or sister fountain.

After the fourth verse, which introduces the fountain that sounds or rings, the image emerges again in the tenth, where it can be heard singing couplets of bubbles. The inanimate object is not only given a subjectivity; it assumes the role of poet parallel to the author, who at the same time creates the verses sung by the water. The play of mirrors becomes clearer when the dialogue between lyric voice and Other begins, and the poet and fountain address each other as brother and sister:

> La fuente cantaba: ¿Te recuerda, hermano
> un sueño lejano mi canto presente?
> ***
> —No sé qué me dice to copla riente
> de ensueños lejanos, hermana la fuente. (431)

The symmetry of this mirror reflection is upset by discrepancy between the two memories. While the poet expects to hear a happy, forgotten story of the madness of love, the fountain goads his memory to convince him that the sorrow he feels in the present is the way he felt then as well:

—Yo no sé leyendas de antigua alegría,
sino historias viejas de melancholía.

Fue una clara tarde del lento verano. . . .
Tú venías solo con tu pena, hermano;
tus labios besaron mi linfa serena,
y en la clara tarde, dijeron tu pena.

Dijeron tu pena tus labios que ardían;
la sed que ahora tienen entonces tenían. (432)

At this point the poet bids the fountain goodbye forever, as the bitterness of recognition is harder to bear than his own melancholy. Sesé notes, in addition to the *modernista* preciosity of the word "linfa" for water, how the fountain represents here, as it does elsewhere in Machado, "la parte de su alma o de su espíritu en que se alían la lucidez y la ansiedad" (145); he appears to no longer wish to acknowledge this part of himself that has crossed over into the element of water (141). The reaction of the poet's inner state to the elements of the outside world is similar to the nearly chemical reaction in "Crear fiestas" (XXVIII), in which party revelers perceive a chillingly mortal affinity between their flesh and the dampness of the earth. In the latter poem, Ortega detected a trace of the pre-Socratic philosopher Anaxagoras, who held that some elements that compose each substance are shared by every other substance in the world, creating a mutual understanding and sympathy among all things, as well as all beings: "Así, en el hombre hay agua, tierra, fuego y aire e infinitas otras materias" (351). The water of the fountain brings out a lucidity and longing already present but dormant in the narrator of "Fue una clara tarde," in the form of a feminine spirit held in check by a solitary and nomadic male point of view. When the narrator leaves behind the feminine voice he cannot bear to hear, he leaves behind the solace of the waters that assuaged his thirst in that earlier time. Given the gender of the fountain, it would not be overextending the image to see in the "linfa" once kissed by the poet a faint reference to the sustenance of mother's milk. Upon leaving this life-giving source of solace behind, he finds himself alone amidst "el silencio de la tarde muerta." While this maternal aspect of the fountain is secondary here to the more accessible submeanings of feminine-voiced Other, muse, and metapoetic commentator, we shall find it closer to the surface in other texts.

The feminine voice of Machado's poetics privileges changelessness and cohesion. In effect, the fountain's outpouring of monotony negates the passage of time; time passes and the world changes only in the eyes of the male subject. The afternoon of the poet's visit is identical, for the fountain, to the distant afternoon to which they both refer with differing meanings. The dialogue between poet and fountain acknowledges the multiplicity of voices with which Machado writes. At least one of those voices, although not the one more closely identified with the author, is concerned with what remains the same. The more recognizably human and masculine voice is the one that wanders through the world, is affected by the passage of time, and would silence the fountain's perfect recall. When the feminine Other dispels the male narrator's unfounded nostalgia, she must be suppressed, but this results in the silence and sense of death that seal the poem. The male subject may find solitude preferable to the maddening loquacity of this nonstop truthteller. Still, there is no denying who is right, and when the poet uses his key to lock the nagging presence out of his consciousness, the sense of closure is not at all complete. Sister-fountain leaks out of confinement in the garden and into a score of other poems in *Soledades,* often washing off the debris that had covered half-buried truths. This runs parallel to the semiotic impulse itself that seeks through the overgrowth of associations of the poetic image to compensate for loss or absence of the object of love.

The next most memorable fountain in Machado displays traits of femininity that together make of it a feminine Other, but it has less of a speaking part and is less autonomous in role. "El limonero lánguido suspende" (VII) brings out the passive side of the fountain as recipient and reservoir (a secondary aspect in "Fue una clara tarde"). In contrast to the talkative Other of sister fountain, this is more of a nurturing mother who is not altogether present, harmonizing with the overall tone of pleasant nostalgia troubled by a note of uncertainty in this text. Lapesa found that there are only a few constants in Machado's use of water imagery: the opposition of thirst to quenching water and the representation of the flow of time and therefore of life (394). "El limonero lánguido" has a fountain that is not only vital flow but source of life, bringing out the denotation of *fuente* that is more of a figurative sense in English. The poet feels warm and in familiar surroundings; he sees golden fruit dreaming at the bottom of a crystaline fountain basin, and remembers sinking his hands in to grasp the enchanted fruit as a child, the same fruit he now sees at the bottom. The maternal presence is felt through semes that achieve prominence in image chains: the warmth of the afternoon, the rustle of a gown, a virginal fragrance that is absent, and another, delicious fragrance that is present in memory. The latter emanates from his mother's potted plants, repeating the original image of uterine containment found in the fountain basin. Unlike the womb, however, the fountain basin makes its fruit clearer and more visible ("la fuente limpia . . . los frutos de oro") than the fruit that remains outside of its reach on the dusty branch. If sister fountain was the feminine Other of "Fue una clara tarde," mother fountain inhabits "El limonero lánguido suspende" just as powerfully though less tangibly. Both images elucidate past and forgotten feelings for the male narrator. Mother fountain does not speak directly to the poet; hence the air is pervaded by traces of her rather than her actual presence:

En el ambiente de la tarde flota
ese aroma de ausencia,
que dice al alma luminosa: nunca,
y al corazón: espera. (433)

It may be useless to await the return of the lost Thing, but the fountain enables the poet to remember when possession of it was still possible:

Que tú me viste hundir mis manos puras
en el agua serena,
para alcanzar los frutos encantados
que hoy en el fondo de la fuente sueñan. . . . (433)

Not only the site of poetic genesis, the fountain as transparent womb makes it possible to break the water in reverse and return to some semblance of the harmony of the mother-child bond. Even if the lost Thing cannot be regained and perhaps was never possessed in the first place, invoking it through the fountain leads to the comforting recognition that time has not changed the serenity, plenitude, and purity of stored maternal memory.

Several other motivations probably add to the vividness of these two fountains. The Machado family rented a dwelling for several years during Antonio's early childhood in the Palacio de las Dueñas in Sevilla: the rooms let out onto an exemplary Andalusian patio replete with fountain and plants. The esthetic sensibility developed by the adult poet shapes the childhood memory of idealized maternal love into an archetype of lost paradise, as Herrero has affirmed regarding "El limonero lánguido suspende": the fountain is artistry itself working to perfect and poeticize the otherwise murky raw materials of reminiscence (567). One step removed from the feelings that inspired the poem, artistry in the form of the fountain can also cascade with laughter over the poet's suffering, as it does in "Fue una clara tarde." We see the connection between the fountain, blissful closeness to the mother; and poetic craft even more clearly in "Si yo fuera un poeta" (LXVII), in which the poet wishes he could appropriate the fountain's voice to write a poem dedicated to his beloved. The imagined fountain-voiced poem would express how much she reminds him of the happiness he felt when viewing the world from his mother's arms.

Criticism has also discerned an influential intertextual relation between these two poems and Verlaine's "Après trois ans," from *Poèmes saturniens.* Similar associations arise here among the memory, an enclosed city park, a fountain, and a statue. The fountain sounds as an inarticulate voice of continuity, although the ending of the poem subverts the changelessness with images of decay: "Nothing has changed. I have seen it all again. . . . The spurt of water still makes its silvery murmur." Machado clearly activates the potentiality of this intertext by making the fountain a living form of otherness, and assigning it to an enclosed corner of his own consciousness. His is the fountain of the Andalusian inner patio rather than that of the Parisian city street. Not only was there was no way for Verlaine to lock the door behind him when leaving; his park fountain is less charged with remembrances of the childhood home. This may partially account for the way that his barely articulate fountain does not quite metamorphose into the feminine Other of Machado's poetry.

As part of an Andalusia family home, the fountain also bears strong connections to oasis elements in Hispano-Arabic architecture. Where Verlaine evokes harem scenes from more of an external, Orientalist perspective, Machado need only invoke the multicultural heritage that existed in his childhood environment. The Arabic echoes in Machado's fountains are heard clearly in "Era una mañana y abril sonreía" (XLIII). The poet opens his windows at dawn and the fragrance of an orchard wafts inside:

Como sonreía la rosa mañana
al sol del oriente abrí mi ventana;
y en mi triste alcoba penetró el oriente
en canto de alondras, en risa de fuente
y en suave perfume de flora temprana. (458)

At the conclusion of the poem, we find once again that the poet does not share in the fountain's laughter; in fact, here he feels mocked by it. He asks whether all this refreshing beauty means that happiness is approaching his house, and the morning itself responds, "la alegría . . . pasó por tu puerta. Dos veces no pasa." While it is true that the East is where the sun rises and hence the only logical point on the compass to be addressed in a poem about the morning, other elements enhance the connection between the East and Hispano-Arabic Orientalism. There is something of the Generalife in this fragrant garden that invades the poet's room from the East. The uncollected but contemporaneous "Cenit" (S. III) has a talking "Oriental" fountain that warns the poet to listen carefully so that he will remember its refreshing laughter "en los tristes jardines de Occidente" (743). Once again there is the temporal dimension of the East as morning and the West as afternoon or dusk, but the relation between the fountain and Hispano-Moorish architecture is still unmistakable. This fountain also verbalizes the connection between its symbolism and that of the other most prominent image, the road: "Yo soy la eterna risa del camino." The Eastern or Hispano- Arabic association is strengthened by other poems with Andalusian referents. In "Fantasía de una noche de abril" (LII), the poet wanders, led more by the wine he has imbibed than by his own sense of direction, down disorienting Moorish streets in a city that is either Sevilla or Granada (he is not sure himself). Eventually he is drawn to a beautiful woman held captive behind a window grate, and he woos her with assurances that he possesses "la copla más suave, más dulce y más sabia / que evoca las claras estrellas de Arabia / y aromas de un moro jardín andaluz." Of course, this scene turns out to be a dream from which the poet awakens, only to find,

Ya muerta la luna, mi sueño volvía
por la retorcida, moruna calleja.
El sol en Oriente reía
su risa más vieja. (467)

Thanks to the network of associations among these texts with "Eastern" influences, we see that the Moorish presence can inhabit either the fountain or the sun, and that it casts an omniscient glance, not unlike that of an ironic bystander, on the melancholy of the speaking subject. The cultural Other within Spain, the often denied persistence of Islamic elements in a culture supposedly returned to Christian homogeneity centuries ago, is another voice that haunts the recesses of Machado's consciousness and speaks through the fountain. Whether feminized or Islamicized, the image maintains strong ties to the Andalucía of Machado's youth, contrary to the claim that his writing soon became thoroughly Castilianized to the exclusion of Southern elements (Peers 30). In fact, two poems burlesque or bemoan the false adoption of Southern signifiers by Castilians. On passing by a florist shop in "A un naranjo y a un limonero" (LIII), he sympathizes with a potted orange tree and lemon tree, both sadly out-of-place in the capital: "¿quién os trajo a esta castellana tierra . . . hijos de los campos de la tierra mía?" (467). The poetic voice strikes an unusual note of personal animosity in "Jardín" (LI), apparently provoked by the sight of pretentious Andalusin kitsch. As usual, however, the fountain has the last laugh:

¡Malhaya tu jardín! . . . Hoy me parece
la obra de un peluquero,
con esa pobre palmerilla enana,
y ese cuadro de mirtos recortados. . . .
y el naranjito en su tonel. . . . El agua
de la fuente de piedra
no cesa de reír sobre la concha blanca. (464)

Thus the Hispano-Arabic fountain is linked to the feminine Other that speaks through other fountains. Both are examples of cultural Others that cannot be wholly suppressed and find an outlet equated with timelessness and distance (at times, ironic distance) from the male subject. The Hispano-Arabic fountain is also embedded in the theme of the captive woman who may at any time beckon to the male wanderer from her home or harem. The Islamicized fountain, like the feminine one, is to be found in a garden or oasis that hints at a lost paradise. Its pleasing musicality or transparency gives voice to what had previously been hidden, denied, or forgotten.

The fountain as wellspring of divinity may seem a very different symbol; its literary antecedents are distinct and profound. However, it shares an element with the female-voiced fountain because of the cultural connection between femininity and spirituality, which had become more pronounced by the end of the nineteenth century. Male and female spheres of activity had become polarized: the male was the public and secular one, while the female sphere was to be devoted not only to the home but to the cultivation of the soul. As Western culture became more markedly secular in the century leading up to Machado's writing, the spiritual turned into a form of cultural otherness that receded from the center of patriarchy and hence became aligned with the feminine. It makes sense, then, that Machado's restless spiritual quest should take the form of fountain imagery for his relation of the fountain to the feminine as well as for the traditional alliance in scripture and other religious writings between the fountain and spirituality.

"Anoche cuando dormía" (LIX) exhibits a clear intertextual dialogue with mystical uses of fountain imagery by both Santa Teresa de Jesús and

San Juan de la Cruz; they in turn find their roots in the Bible. McDermott calls attention to the enigmatic tone of this intertextuality: "The absence of the hidden or dead God/Christ is made more poignant by the echoes of the ghost voices of the religious and mystic poets of the past" (4). In a deconstructionist study, Cardwell traces the enigma to the impossibility of anchoring oneself to any sort of metaphysics by means of the artistic word, since words produce meaning only by difference or deferral and not by direct correspondence (33). Whether the cause of the poet's uncertainty is linguistic or not, the fountain is again the vehicle for the otherness repressed within himself, and signifies a desire for what has been lost or what was never possessed:

> Anoche cuando dormía
> soñé, ¡bendita ilusión!,
> que una fontana fluía
> dentro de mi corazón.
> Di, ¿por qué acequia escondida,
> agua, vienes hasta mí,
> manantial de nueva vida
> en donde nunca bebí? (471)

Unlike the feminized and Islamicized fountains, the divine wellspring strikes the speaker as unfamiliar, and he admits never having tasted of it. Along with the beehive, the sun, and the Godhead that follow, it is defined as an illusion, one fervently to be hoped for but definitely out of waking grasp. Still, the quest is so imperative that the poet appears willing to pursue it no matter how dim the prospect of success. The modern poet (unlike some of his postmodern readers) has not resigned himself to the schism between signifiers and significance; he would rather peer into the abyss that they have created and await any new images that might materialize from it. What separates Machado's fountain from the mystical font of San Juan de la Cruz, in addition to the former's less tangible existence, is that it is a more complex image, tied in with the associations that have arisen in one text after another. San Juan's nocturnal font, like much of his imagery, has the raw semiotic pulsation of the sacred and the erotic intermingled. Machado writes already with the self-conscious excess and entanglements of modernity. The *abulia noventayochista* of his poetic temperament robs him of the drive to transform the fountain into a gushing forth of the sensual and the divine.

Elsewhere in *Soledades* we are likely to see the fountain that pours out sheer provincial monotony ("En medio de la plaza y sobre tosca piedra" [XCIV]), or one that symbolizes an extinguished love

("¿Mi amor? . . . ¿Recuerdas, dime?" [XXXIII]), an eerie twilight ("El sol es un globo de fuego" [XXIV]) or death itself ("Las ascuas de un crepúsculo morado" [XXXII]). In the uncollected "La fuente" (S. I), Machado meditates self-consciously about what the image means to him. The conclusion emphasizes rumination and stagnation, and the poet's wish to lose himself in the fountain water:

> Hay amores extraños en la historia
> de mi largo camino sin amores,
> y el mayor es la fuente,
> cuyo dolor anubla mis dolores,
> cuyo lánguido espejo sonriente
> me desarma de brumas y rencores
> ***
> Y en ti soñar y meditar querría
> libre ya del rencor y la tristeza,
> hasta sentir, sobre la piedra fría,
> que se cubre de musgo mi cabeza. (742)

The loss of self in the fountain implies more of a death drive than an erotic fusion of self and world. There is no avoiding the thanatopsis in some of Machado's duskier and more decayed fountains. Water stagnating in marble basins, symbolizing life-giving force held captive, is present in several of these darker poems (Albornoz 9). While this may stand in contrast to the mother fountain and divine wellspring, finding the feminine associated with death is actually the complement in patriarchy to the feminine as cradle of mankind. As Beauvoir noted, the origin and the end of man's existence are often intermingled in the significance assigned the feminine by a male-centered worldview. The funerary fountain, no longer the metapoetic voice of creativity, is conspicuously silent in "Hoy buscarás en vano" (LXIX):

> Está la fuente muda,
> y está marchito el huerto.
> Hoy sólo quedan lágrimas
> para llorar. No hay que llorar, ¡silencio! (478)

The fountain as funerary architecture is one extreme along the spectrum in which the image works as a keeper of time, a Bergsonian *durée* clock that detains the minutes at will, while vitality seems to rush out of the prematurely aged poet. He equates his spent youth with the shedding of tears, which he relates in turn to the dripping of a fountain ("Coplas mundanas" [XCV]). More explicitly, he introduces the clepsydra or water clock in "Daba el reloj las doce" (XXI), and something of this temporal dimension lies latent in every Machado fountain. In this text silence speaks paradoxically to the anxious poet to calm his fear of death: his hour has not yet come, and when it does he will not see the last drop fall from the water clock. Instead, he will merely wake up refreshed one day on the opposite shore. Thus the sea as symbol of death, a debt he acknowledges to Manrique ("Nuestras vidas son los ríos" [LVIII]), fits into the semiotics of water as the fountain does. When the two appear together, the seme of mortality rises to the surface in both, and the fountain's role as keeper of time whose existence is unaffected by time (a condition shared by sister fountain) is foremost.

Running water is ideally suited to encode the passage of time as Machado conceives of it. His adherence to Bergsonian philosophy has a profound influence on his poetics, as several critics have explained. For Bergson, only intuition could capture the deepest truths of life in their perpetual process of transpiring or becoming. Machado adopted this intuition as the sense that offers us "una 'íntima revelación de la vida' y asigna a la lírica la misión paralela de captar la existencia y el tiempo en su perpetuo fluir" (Cano Ballesta 80). Therefore the fountain merits a privileged place as literary symbol, because it opposes the coursing spiritual essence of water to the petrified spirit of the material world, the marble or stone that shapes and is sculpted by the current ("Los árboles conservan" [XC]). The fountain as measure of the flow of time can also be adapted to measure the expending of energy, as occurs in "La noria" (XLVI), in which a mule with blinders turns the water wheel interminably and in time to the water's couplets. The Bergsonian idea of duration is emphasized in this workaday fountain by the never-ending circle the mule must trudge around it. The text also contains a spark of the poet's incipient concern for the oppressed in the face of indifference. Here it is divine indifference, but later this develops into the indifference of other social classes toward the oppressed. God the divine poet seems to have set the water wheel in motion ingeniously, but takes no further interest in it.

As mentioned before, Kristeva lists prosody and the polyvalent sign as two of the three most important techniques for making the poetic artifice transcend mourning for the lost Thing and achieve a sense of permanence. Certainly, poetic form and polysemia not only function in each poem of *Soledades,* but each influences the other in such a fundamental way that it is hard to distinguish which one is primary. Observing some of the pairings of prosody and type of fountain is therefore instructive. Most of the more ironic or somber examples we have been examining emanate from hendecasyllabic forms (although the hexasyllables of "La noria" and the octosyllables of "Anoche cuando dormía" are exceptions). If we turn to the lively *cuarletas* of "Yo escucho los cantos" (VIII), a different facet of the image arises. Here, rhythmic hexasyllables that imitate children's jingles combine with the theme of childhood lore as perpetuator of a collective unconscious that repeats vague stories of vivid sadness. A parallel is developed between the children singing poorly remembered ballads and the fountain telling its own unintelligible story over and over, in apparent solidarity with human emotion:

> Jugando, a la sombra
> de una plaza vieja,
> los niños cantaban. . . .

> La fuente de piedra
> vertía su eterno
> cristal de leyenda. (434)

Thus the singsong rhythms of "Yo escucho los cantos" accompany or create the formation of yet another identity: the fountain as voice of childhood and hence of a half-vanished oral culture. Like that of the feminine Other, this voice seems to reside in the recesses of the male subject's consciousness. It is also associated with what is changeless and cohesive in human existence and so lies outside of the domain of time. The connection to Machado's poetics is as evident as it is in "El limonero lánguido suspende," for here the fountain represents pure feelings devoid of surrounding circumstance or anecdote (Ribbans 26). The fountain water washes away the sediment of fact so that only truth (the emotion to be conveyed) remains. The form itself, with its many truncated verses, staccato rhythms, and echoing rhymes, blends the prosodic qualities of children's voices with those of gurgling water. Similarly, in "¡Verdes jardinillos!" (XIX), the fountain in hexasyllabic form is more dynamic than in longer verse forms: a place where chance encounters with young women, who are usually confined to their homes and domestic tasks, may take place. The algae on this buoyant fountain join other images of fertility on an early autumn afternoon. Nostalgia for the past ways of men and women, inhabiting largely segregated spaces and mingling only at certain approved spots, motivates this poem. It includes a sidelong glance at the communal fountain as a public place affording relative freedom to women whose movements were otherwise circumscribed.

Despite the variety of significances to which the fountain is attached, I hope to have demonstrated in a comprehensive way that there are a few constants that link the image from one text to another. These interrelated associative meanings had not hitherto been thoroughly studied, but understanding of them enhances interpretation of *Soledades*. They include the fountain as feminine counterdiscourse in dialogue with the male subject, calling his attention to what lies hidden in the recesses of his mind. The male discourse of wandering, dreamy solitude in *Soledades* is contrasted with a feminine counterdiscourse that not only provides company but emphasizes commonalities that link the poet to the rest of humanity, not the least of which are time, mortality, a hoped-for divinity, the mother / child bond, and the communication made possible by poetry as the purest and most transparent form of language.

In this role, the fountain may speak as a teasing sister or it may evoke the memory of maternal nurture. The feminine Other exists outside of the constraints of time but lacks the mobility of the male subject. From what is known about ego formation thanks to theorists like Kristeva, I believe that the image evolved out of the internalization of an idealized memory of the mother, which was then projected outward in the process of visualization of thought for which Machado is well known. The fountain of the childhood home is also associated with the Andalusian fountain with pronounced Hispano-Arabic connotations; on a collective level this fountain brings a cultural Other into the mainstream of consciousness. The Eastern fountain is an ironic onlooker and laughing companion along the roads of life. The fountain unites the feminine with the spiritual in the image of the divine wellspring, a less concrete artifice that can only be dreamed or imagined. The funerary fountain is related to the dripping water clock, the first symbolizing entropy or stagnation and the second Bergsonian flow of time. We have seen how the fountain aligned with the origin of life (the maternal body) is not far in terms of cultural logic from the fountain signifying death. The fountain that speaks with the voice of children incites awareness of an Other, like the feminine one, that has been internalized but is normally repressed. In giving voice to what the male subject usually perceives as inaccessible, these fountains broaden the range of essential emotions that the poet may reveal in his writing. For this reason, the fountain symbolizes the poetic craft itself in many poems, and engages the narrator in metapoetic dialogue that hints at writing as the key to solace for the subject immersed in suffering and loneliness.

Source: Elizabeth Scarlett, "Antonio Machado's Fountains: Archeology of an Image," in *Modern Language Notes*, Vol. 113, 1998, pp. 305–23.

Susan J. Joly

In the following essay, Joly employs the theories of Freud and Jung to explore the role that dream, imagination, and the unconscious play in Machado's poetry and one's understanding of it.

Marcel Brion, speaking about the dream in the poetry of Novalis [the pen name of the German poet Friedrich Leopold (1772–1801), who influenced later exponents of European romanticism] said, "El sueño se mueve en dimensiones diferentes; es contemplación mística, intuición profética y revelación de verdades sublimes que no podrían ser enunciadas ni comunicadas en estado de vigilia" (Cerezo 27). ["Vigilia" refers here to a state of complete consciousness.] The same statement could easily apply to Machado's poems. Within them, contemplation, intuition (which Jung incidentally has called "perception via the unconscious" (*Archetypes and the Collective Unconscious* 282) and the revelation of the unconscious provide the depth for which his verse is known.

Indeed, fundamental to the prevalent element of mystery in Machado's works is the dream, into whose depths the poet journeys, eager to tap the knowledge hidden within. Many of Machado's poems can be traced back to this basic dreamlike quality, explaining why he has been called the "poeta en sueños." Note, for example, the oneiric quality of the approaching twilight in the following verses: "Blancos fantasmas lares / van encendiendo estrellas. / Abre el balcón. La hora / de una ilusión se acerca. . . . La tarde se ha dormido / y las campanas sueñan" (Alvar 105).

In this paper I will examine the dream within Machado's verse, first by defining the dream in accordance with the poet's own vision of it. I will then justify my reasons for using psychoanalytical theories of analysis, referring to the two thinkers most famous for their views on dream interpretation. After giving a background on these theories, I will justify my own approach, as it relates to the dream within Machado's poetry. In addition to studying the role of the dream, I will also focus on the role the imagination plays (with its related element of fantasy) in the revelation of the poet's unconscious.

Dreams

It is essential that one note from the outset the nature of the dream to which Machado refers. Rather than being merely the action of a passive sleeper, the poet's dream is usually, instead, that of an awake, reflective, vigilant person, as illustrated in the following selections from *Proverbios y cantares* (in Alvar's edition): "Despertad, cantores; / acaben los ecos, / empiecen las voces" (XXIX 293). "Si vivir es bueno, / es mejor soñar, y mejor que todo / madre, despertar" (CLXI 303). "Tras el vivir y el soñar, / está lo que más importa: / despertar" (LIII 298). "Tres palabras suenan / al fin de tres sueños / y las tres desvelan" (437).

Christopher Caudwell, in *Illusion and Reality*, differentiates the dream from the daydream, saying that the daydream contains more reality and more possibility. It also lacks "the wild extravagances or abrupt transitions of the dream" (209). Moreover, Caudwell continues, in the daydream man adapts himself to reality rather than the other way around, as in the dream (209).

Carl Cobb defines Machado's dream as a purposeful daydream or "state of intense reverie" (49), often involving the faculty of memory. He states that "for Machado, to be 'en sueños' is a mental state the poet pursued and achieved in his most inspirational waking hours" (49). Machado himself believed that the dream of sleep has never produced anything of significance. For him, "los poemas de nuestra vigilia, aun los menos logrados, son más originales y más bellos y, a las veces, más disparatados que los de nuestros sueños" (*Obras, poesia y prosa* 394). Whether occurring during actual hours of sleep or during the waking hours as in a reverie, the dream is, notwithstanding, one of the most important ways to learn about the unconscious processes. Hence psychoanalytic theories regarding the dream may be used as a tool toward better comprehension of the poet's verses containing reverie.

Although this study involves a psychoanalytical perspective, one cannot say that Machado himself intentionally approaches his dreams from a psychological vantage point. However, this being said, it does not follow that the reader cannot utilize psychoanalytical studies on the dream in order to achieve an original and different interpretation of Machado's dreams, as well as of his "modus operandi." These theories may also help answer the question: "What else could this dream represent that the poet may not have openly stated or admitted?"

Of course, one cannot discuss the dream from a psychological point of view without mentioning the two psychoanalysts renowned for their theories on the dream—Jung and Freud. Although both agreed on several points regarding dream interpretation, it is their differences of opinion which remain prominent. Both believe there is an area of the psyche in which elements are stored, hidden from

Although many choose to ignore their innermost anguish, preferring to lead a life of frivolity and shallowness, Machado sees this as self-deception."

the conscious. Thoughts or wishes which may be repressed are then manifested through symbols and images. As Jung says in *Man and His Symbols*, "Thus far, nobody can say anything against Freud's theory of repression and wish fulfillment as apparent causes of dream symbolism" (27). Where Jung disagrees is in the content of the repression. Freud believed the cause of the repression lay in sexual trauma. Jung told Freud of numerous cases of neurosis in his practice in which motives other than sexuality were the prime influence. To Jung's chagrin, Freud continued to find sexuality as the only cause.

Another salient point of difference is Jung's rejection of Freud's dream-interpretation method known as "*free association*"—whereby the patient is allowed to discuss anything that enters his/her mind, in order to bring to light those repressed elements. Freud views the dream mostly as a means of determining one's "*complexes,*" that is, "repressed emotional themes that can cause constant psychological disturbances or even, in many cases, the symptoms of a neurosis" (*Man and His Symbols* 27). Jung, however, believes that the complexes could be determined just as well by other means, i.e. contemplation of a crystal ball, an abstract painting, an inkblot test, or even during seemingly trivial conversation. Jung determined, therefore, that the dream must have some deeper significance than Freud had attributed to it.

According to Jung, the problem with Freud's method is that the dream is not given the importance it merits. In fact, instead of confronting the dream's contents, attempts are made to escape them. With Freud's free association, the dream for its own sake becomes subordinate to complexes, thus leading one away from the much more significant content of the dream. In Jung's *The Symbolic Life* he says of Freud's method:

> I no longer followed associations that led far afield and away from the manifest dream-statement. I concentrated rather on the actual dream-text as the thing which was intended by the unconscious, and I began to circumambulate the dream itself, never letting it out of my sight, or as one turns an unknown object round and round in one's hands to absorb every detail of it. . . . It is chiefly and above all fear of the unexpected and unknown that makes people eager to use free association as a means of escape. (190, 192)

With regard to Machado's use of the dream, I find a Jungian approach to be more plausible than a Freudian one for several reasons. The first reason for the Jungian approach stems from his belief that a dream is not necessarily reducible to negative components. Surely the unconscious contains more than elements of sexual repression or fantasy, more than resentments, or harmful aggressions and instincts. Gregory Zilboorg in *Sigmund Freud: His Exploration of the Mind of Man* says of Freud's concept of the unconscious: "It is a repository of volcanic forces and dammed-up, twisted psychological energies" (20). These forces are primarily seen as negative, harmful or unhealthy ones.

Jung, in *The Spirit in Man, Art, and Literature,* contends that Freud almost *wants* to see the weakness in everyone, the flaw, "the unadmitted wish, the hidden resentment, the secret, illegitimate fulfillment of a wish distorted by the 'censor'" (45–6). Jung finds that by concentrating only on the weak spots, individuation and healing are prevented. In Freud, the unconscious is not treated as a potentially salubrious mechanism but rather as something which hinders one's psychological well-being: "Every position is undermined by a psychological critique that reduces everything to its unfavourable or ambiguous elements, or at least makes one suspect that such elements exist" (45–6).

Jung's unconscious, in contrast, involves much more than destructive instinctual energies, extending itself to include all perceptions, intuitions, thoughts, deductions and inductions. It not only contains the past, such as distant memories, but also that which is new and original.

Obviously, the matter of creativity, hardly a destructive force, is relevant and inherent to the study of any poet. The dream can thus also become a source of positive inspiration for poetry, and give fresh ideas and insights to other aspects of life. An example of the latter is found in organic chemistry, in which Friedrich Kekulé's (1829–1896) dream (described in the *Encyclopaedia Britannica*) of the serpent grabbing its tail led him to the discovery of the cyclic nature of aromatic compounds such as benzene (748–49). This chemist's belief in the power of the vigilant dream, or daydream, parallels Machado's. Kekulé comments: "Let us learn to dream, gentlemen; then perhaps we shall find the truth. But let us be aware of publishing our dreams till they have been tested by the waking understanding" (Pine 6).

A second reason for favoring Jung is the mentioned attempt of Freud to escape or reduce the actual dream images to habitual complexes instead of utilizing these symbols, in Jung's terms, "to know and understand the psychic life-process of an individual's whole personality" (*Man and His Symbols* 28–29). A key word here is "whole," since, as mentioned numerous times, balance between the unconscious and conscious is of utmost importance in joining the fragments of the personality. Jung finds Freud to be one-sided in his view of the unconscious, calling him "blind toward the paradox and ambiguity of the contents of the unconscious" (*Memories, Dreams, Reflections* 152). Everything in the unconscious consists of two parts; thus Freud only deals with one half of the whole.

For Jung, central to dream analysis is what William James terms "the fringe of consciousness," which Jung defines as "the almost invisible roots of conscious contents, i.e., their subliminal aspects" (*The Symbolic Life* 209). This "fringe" acts as an intermediary between the conscious and unconscious, closing the gap between them. A chasm that is too wide may result in neurosis or "lead to an artificial life far removed from healthy instincts, nature, and truth" (209). Jung then believes that dreams are a manner of re-establishing balance between the conscious and unconscious, as in the individuation process. Machado's vigilant dream likewise is a balance between the conscious and unconscious, its contents rising from the unconscious although the dreamer is aware, awake and vigilant.

Thus Jung's method of dream analysis, because of its direct confrontation with topics clearly contained within the dream, entails an undeviating, more inquisitive approach to the unknown than free association can offer. This Jungian approach is quite relevant to a study of Machado, since it is in fact the new or unknown side of his inner being which the poet *himself* confronts. He is in search of truth which will bring about wholeness and well-being and it is this desire of his that I wish to explore.

Machado's use of the dream is significant for several reasons. One is the role the dream plays in allowing the individual to explore the mysteries of the universe, a world which Machado describes saying, "Una neblina opaca confunde toda cosa" (Alvar 413).

Another role of the dream is to allow one to explore the hidden mysteries lying within one's self, in order to yield inner or self-knowledge. Just as the analyst examines the dreams of the analysand, Machado, too, achieves self-knowledge upon descent into a cryptic world. Jung says each male individual must encounter his anima (the female element in the male psyche linking him to the unconscious); the anima may manifest itself symbolically through a man's dream in the form of an "initiator and guardian," such as the Indian *guru* guiding man to an inner world (*Man and His Symbols* 196). The illuminating anima is suggested in poem LXIV of "Galerías," in which a female figure invites the poet to explore the soul:

> Era la buena voz, la voz querida.
> —Dime: ¿vendrás conmigo a ver el alma? . . .
> Llegó a mi corazón una caricia.
> . . . .Y avancé en mi sueño
> por una larga, escueta galería,
> sintiendo el roce de la veste pura
> y el palpitar suave de la mano amiga.
> (Alvar 134)

In another poem Machado, addressing himself to what seems to be the image of a guide in his dream, finds illusive mysteries and contradictions he cannot comprehend:

> Arde en tus ojos un misterio, virgen
> esquiva y compañera.
> No sé si es odio o es amor la lumbre
> inagotable de tu aljaba negra.
> Conmigo irás mientras proyecte sombra
> mi cuerpo. . . .
> —¿Eres la sed o el agua en mi camino?
> Dime, virgen esquiva y compañera. (XXIX 107)

He does not know whether to fear her or welcome her. This ambiguous quality of the anima is emphasized by Jung.

The truth contained in the dream is just waiting to spring forth: "Es una flor que quiere echar su aroma al viento" ("Galerías" LXI 132). But the act of facing the unknown often entails some fear, what anthropologists call "misoneism." The modern poet echoes the fear experienced by primitive man when faced with shocking novelty: "he visto en el prufundo / espejo de mis sueños / que una verdad divina / temblando está de miedo" ("Galerías" LXI 132). In poem LXIII of "Galerías" the devil / angel of his dream urges him to explore the "honda cripta del alma" (134): "¿Vendrás conmigo?—No, jamás; las tumbas / y los muertos me espantan" (134). This

figure seems closer to the Jungian shadow than to the anima figure; the psychoanalyst discusses mankind's insecurity in confronting the "formidable" shadow. The shadow seems threatening since it represents that which has been rejected or ignored by the conscious self, or ego. (Unlike the anima, the shadow is personified in the dream by someone of the same sex as the dreamer.)

However, the shadow is not frightening merely because it may represent the unfavorable elements of the personality. Also contained within the shadow are creative impulses and other positive qualities, according to Jung. Thus the shadow need not necessarily contain *solely* the negative aspects of the personality, just as the ego (or conscious self) does not possess purely positive traits. Jung believes, however, that many parts of the shadow which may be helpful to the personality become like demons when they are repressed. The ego is not then superior to the shadow but rather the shadow and ego are interdependent, much as thought and feeling are connected. Jung uses the phrase "the battle for deliverance" to describe the continual conflict between the shadow and the ego. This idea is important to Machado's dream in that one witnesses a journey into the poet's inner being, but not without a certain amount of pain or apprehension.

The dream in Machado's work can also be partially understood as an image of the soul-searching *viajero,* or traveler, agonized by a sense of "El viajero," in which the poet (or traveler) prepares to dream during the lazy afternoon hours when even nature reclines:

> En el ambiente de la tarde flota
> ese aroma de ausencia,
> . . . .
> Sí, te recuerdo, tarde alegre y clara,
> . . . .
> . . . .cuando me traías
> el buen perfume de la hierbabuena,
> y de la buena albahaca,
> que tenía mi madre en sus macetas.
> (Alvar 92)

The traveler wanders through the paths of his dreams, with Machado characterizing the *viajero* as having "caminos," "senderos," "parques," "criptas," and "escaleras":

> Sobre la tierra amarga,
> caminos tiene el sueño
> laberínticos, sendas tortuosas,
> parques en flor y en sombra y en silencio;
> criptas hondas, escalas sobre estrellas;
> retablos de esperanzas y recuerdos. (XXII 104)

"El sueño" and "el camino" (the latter image lending a sort of active nature to the dream) are once again linked: "Yo voy soñando caminos / de la tarde. ¡Las colinas / doradas, los verdes pinos, / las polvorientas encinas! . . . / ¿Adónde el camino irá?" (95). Thus begins the traveler's quest for that which is he lacking, be it love or the recapturing of a happier past, as will later be illustrated.

This archetype of the traveler, seeking to fill a void and learning to distance himself, has yet another function. Jolande Jacobi, a member of Jung's "Zurich circle," notes that the process of individuation is often depicted in terms of a "voyage of discovery," as in John Bunyan's *Pilgrim's Progress* and Dante's *Divina Commedia* (*Man and His Symbols* 277). Certainly this is true for the traveler in Machado's poems, who learns to discern inner secrets and the voice of his unconscious.

For his bravery in confronting the mysterious, the traveler resembles a character in a myth much discussed by Jung—the myth of the hero. Typically, in this myth the hero must battle the monster or dragon. In psychological terms, the ego fights against the shadow, personified by the monster. Joseph L. Henderson in *Man and His Symbols* says, "The hero . . . must realize that the shadow exists and that he can draw strength from it . . . before the ego can triumph, it must master and assimilate the shadow" (121–22). In Machado's case also, the feared "monster" is the shadow, the unknown, or the unconscious. Nevertheless, the poet proceeds traveling through his dream, pursuing self-knowledge. Thus the poet = the traveler = the dreamer. All three embark on a journey towards the discovery of mystery, of the hidden or secret; all are set apart because of their desire to explore these secrets, despite any misgivings they may have. As Machado writes in "Coplas elegíacas": "Ay del noble peregrino / que se para a meditar, / después de largo camino / en el horror de llegar!" (Alvar 113)

Poem LXIII of "Galerías" is a good example of a Jungian combat between monster and hero. Machado's horrific images parallel the potential "demons" of his irrational nature: "Y avancé en mi sueño / cegado por la roja luminaria./ Y en la cripta sentí sonar cadenas, / y rebullir de fieras enjauladas" (134). Once again the struggle with the shadow is suggested in the image of the dreamer, bravely dueling within the depths of the crypt.

In Machado's poetry the dreams, or journeys into one's unconscious depths, usually occur during the afternoon, twilight, or night hours. For example, in the following poem note the equating of an afternoon of solitude with a time for reflective soul-searching: "Recuerdo que una tarde de soledad y hastío / ¡o tarde como tantas!, el alma mía era" (XLIX "Elegía de un madrigal" 122). In poem LXX of "Galerías" Machado writes: "Tú sabes las secretas galerías / del alma, los caminos de los sueños, / y la tarde tranquila" (137).

In poem VII of "El viajero" once again afternoon becomes synonymous with a time for reverie, when the traveler yearns to enter his unconscious state, in search of memories or illusions: "Es una tarde clara, / . . . / y estoy solo, en el patio silencioso, / buscando una ilusión cándida y vieja: / alguna sombra sobre el blanco muro, / algún recuerdo . . ." (92). The poet later reflects on this distant afternoon when he was able to achieve his goals of soul-searching: "Que tú me viste hundir mis manos puras / en el agua serena, para alcanzar los frutos encantados / que hoy en el fondo de la fuente sueñan . . ." (93).

The afternoon reverie may then also be a time for nostalgia, as in LXXIV. During the tranquility of the hour, the poet desires to return to the days of his youth: "para ser joven, para haberlo sido / cuando Dios quiso, para / tener algunas alegrías . . . lejos, / y poder dulcemente recordarlas" (138–39). In poem V Machado walks during the summer sunset, comparing the redness of the sky to the nostalgia of a lost love: "Roja nostalgia el corazón sentía, / sueños bermejos, que en el alma brotan / de lo inmenso inconsciente, / cual de región caótico y sombría" (396).

In "La tarde en el jardín" the garden is the scene for the recapturing of lost time. The mood is somber as "las fuentes melancólicas cantaban" (399). Along the garden's still paths, a thousand dreams from ages gone by are resuscitated and the soul is made eternal. Finally in poem VII a March afternoon has an "aroma de ausencia" floating about it, "que evoca los fantasmas / de las fragancias virgenes y muertas" (92). Youth, with its innocence, has passed.

Other poems occur during the tenebrous hours following "la tarde." Facing and conquering one's doubts and fears has its rewards and is sometimes expressed in symbolic terms of light and darkness. Such chiaroscuro may be seen in those poems having a twilight or night setting. Jung notes that a dark scene often indicates a dimming of the conscious, a time when the inner self emerges (*Man and His Symbols* 215), as exemplified in poem XXXVII of "Del camino." Here, as in other poems, one even witnesses a familiarity between dreamer and night, the night customarily lending ear to the dreamer's cries like an old friend: "Yo me asomo a las almas cuando lloran y escucho su hondo rezo" (Alvar 110).

Joseph Campbell, whose writings seem to reflect some of Jung's philosophy, believes that the deeper one goes into the dark abyss, the closer one comes to achieving tranquility and salvation. He says: "The black moment is the moment when the real message of transformation is going to come. At the darkest moment comes the light" (*The Power of Myth* 46). Machado similarly speaks of darkness, followed by a light deep within:

> Yo he visto mi alma en sueños,
> como un estrecho y largo
> corredor tenebroso,
> de fondo iluminado. . . .
> Acaso mi alma tenga
> risueña luz de campo,
> y sus aromas lleguen
> de allá, del fondo claro. . . .
> (Alvar 406)

Another example of chiaroscuro occurs in poem LXIII of "Galerías," in which darkness and light battle in the symbolic forms of an angel and a devil: "Y era el demonio de mi sueño, el ángel / más hermoso. Brillaban / como aceros los ojos victoriosos, / y las sangrientas llamas / de su antorcha alumbraron / la honda cripta del alma" (133–34). Once again, from the darkness comes light, a voice of salvation, resulting in a new understanding and truth. Initial fear leads to an inner serenity.

Indeed, Machado frequently evokes a simultaneously peaceful yet haunting dream world in which the unconscious flows freely, leaving behind ambiguous forms which must be confronted and deciphered. For instance, in poem XCIV's depiction of a man preparing to enter the dark recesses of his unconscious state, Machado describes a *plaza* containing a fountain. A tall cypress tree casts its shadow ("la mancha de su ramaje yerto") on the garden; in southern Europe, cypress trees often are planted around cemeteries. There is a peaceful atmosphere as the afternoon hours cast their own shadow. However, the dream itself does not appear to be equally tranquil and serene, as nightmarish images such as skulls emerge and the soul is likened to an "alma en pena:"

> La tarde está cayendo frente a los caserones
> de la ancha plaza, en sueños. Relucen las vidrieras
> con ecos mortecinos de sol. En los balcones
> hay formas que parecen confusas calaveras.
> La calma es infinita en la desierta plaza,
> donde pasea el alma su traza de alma en pena.
> El agua brota y brota en la marmórea taza.
> En todo el aire en sombra no más que el agua
> suena.
> (Alvar 148)

One may view the continually flowing water symbolically as the unconscious, unbridled in its movement. There is a sense of quiet, of mystery and peace in its melodic stream but this water, nevertheless, also evokes a painful element. The shadow cast by the cypress on the garden together with the dying rays of sun creates an aura of impending darkness. The soul then enters into a dream state, in which confusing images surface. Confusion and fright are again the vital elements often inherent in confronting one's shadow.

Pertinent to a discussion of the ever-present dream in Machado's verse are Jung's comprehensive studies on the nature and significance of dreams. He divides them into two types: 1) the *personal* and 2) the *archetypal-mythic* containing images which survive, almost unconsciously, from generation to generation. Following Jung, we may interpret Machado's poetry, either through the personal unconscious, or through association with myth / archetypes—myth being society's dream.

Of the personal sort are those poems dealing with Machado's own nostalgia, pain, and with lost love or youth. Also included are those poems expressing hopes or wishes, like those in which the poet searches for a new recipient of his love or the rebirth of an old one. A source of much of his grief is the death of his wife Leonor. Prior to 1907 the timid Machado had not yet experienced any romantic relationships with women. Then during his employment as a professor of French at a school in Soria, he met Leonor Izquierdo in the boarding-house where he was living.

Two years later, in July 1909, they were married, he 35 and she 16. In 1911 Machado received a fellowship to study in Paris, where, among other things, he attended various lectures by Henri Bergson. All was bliss during this happy and satisfying period of his life, until Leonor began hemorrhaging from tuberculosis. She was put in the hospital for a month but showed few signs of recovery, prompting Antonio to return to Soria with her. He stopped writing completely, dedicating himself to caring for her. Tragically, in spite of all efforts, Leonor never returned to health and died on August 1, 1912.

This experience left Machado unable to deal with Soria and all its cherished memories. Therefore he moved to the southern town of Baeza only eight days later. His pain and nostalgia are expressed in the following lines in which he bids farewell to Soria: "Adiós, campos de Soria, / . . . / Adiós, ya con vosotros / quedó la flor más dulce de la tierra. / Ya no puedo cantaros, / no os canta ya mi corazón, os reza . . ." (Alvar 411).

For a year Machado's mother came from Madrid to look after the practically incapacitated Antonio. The touching, inspirational words that he wrote to Juan Ramón Jiménez during this time prompts the reader to lament along with the poet:

> Cuando perdí a mi mujer, pensé pegarme un tiro. El éxito de mi libro me salvó, y no por vanidad ¡bien lo sabe Dios! sino porque pensé, que si había en mí una fuerza útil, no tenía derecho de aniquilarla. Hoy quiero trabajar, humildemente, es cierto, pero con eficacia, con verdad. (*Obras, poesía y prosa* 904)

One can witness the death of the poet's spirit upon Leonor's death in the 1913 poem "A Xavier Valcarce;" here Machado admits to his friend that he has lost "la voz que tuve antaño" (Alvar 252). He continues dejectedly: "No sé, Valcarce, mas cantar no puedo; / se ha dormido la voz en mi garganta" (253).

Several poems refer directly to Leonor's death, while others are more subtle. In poem CXIX of *Campos de Castilla* Machado laments: "Señor, ya me arrancaste lo que yo más quería. / Oye otra vez, Dios mío, mi corazón clamar. / Tu voluntad se hizo, Señor, contra la mía. / Señor, ya estamos solos mi corazón y el mar" (212). In poem CXXIII of the same collection he says:

> Una noche de verano
> —estaba abierto el balcón
> y la puerta de mi casa—
> la muerte en mi casa entró.
> Se fue acercando a su lecho
> —ni siquiera me miró—,
> con unos dedos muy finos,
> algo muy tenue rompió.
> . . . .
> ¡Ay, lo que la muerte ha roto
> era un hilo entre los dos! (213–14)

This is the background for Machado's frequent nostalgic reveries of a happier time, when all of nature seemed to share in his joy.

Unfulfilled wishes of having Leonor with him once again emerge in dreams, such as in poem CXXIV of *Campos de Castilla*. Here, amidst the green plain of April, new life and vitality abound:

> y piensa el alma en una mariposa,
> atlas del mundo, y sueña.
> Con el ciruelo en flor y el campo verde,
> . . . .
> con este dulce soplo
> que triunfa de la muerte y de la piedra. (214)

In poem CXXII the poet dreams that Leonor is leading him along a white path, amidst images of rebirth and rejuvenation, and a general feeling of hope. He envisions them hand in hand, her voice sweetly ringing in his ear: "como una campana nueva, / como una campana virgen / de un alba de primavera. / ¡Eran tu voz y tu mano, / en sueños, tan verdaderas! . . . / Vive, esperanza" (213).

Thus Machado's dream, seen on the personal level, mixes nostalgic reminiscences of Leonor with the hope that he will one day see her again. In fact, the above examples of hopes and distant memories seem to fit the poet's own description of the dream, which consists of "caminos laberínticos," winding paths, hidden places, etc.: "retablos de esperanzas y recuerdos / Figurillas que pasan y sonríen /—juguetes melancólicos de viejo—; / imágenes amigas, / a la vuelta florida del sendero, / y quimera rosadas / que hacen camino . . . lejos . . ." (XXII 104). In an interview with Pascual Pla y Beltrán in August of 1937, Machado described his verses as "experiencias latentes, . . . precisamente por lo que tienen de testimonios de momentos que fueron, de sombras del pasado, nos llevan fatalmente a la elegía" (Gullón and Phillips 45).

Indeed, many of his poems could be described as laments, mournful remembrances of things or people gone forever. Some memories involve Machado's youth or childhood, such as in "Las moscas." Even flies are capable of evoking recollections of his infancy: memories of them landing on his young head, flying through the rooms of his family's house and through his schoolroom. He addresses them as if they were his long-lost friends: "Moscas de todas las horas, / de infancia y adolescencia, de mi juventud dorada; / . . . / vosotras, amigas viejas, / me evocáis todas las cosas" (Alvar 122).

In "Acaso" Machado recalls the innocence and happiness of childhood, symbolized in the poem by a fairy who takes him to "la alegre fiesta / que en la plaza ardía" (134). She tenderly kisses his forehead and the poet reflects on the vitality and beauty of his life as a child when all seemed to fall at his feet: "Todos los rosales / daban sus aromas, / todos los amores / amor entreabría" (135). In poem LXXXV the poet stops to meditate on his youth, somewhat wasted without love: "Bajo ese almendro florido, / todo cargado de flor /—recordé—, yo he maldecido / mi juventud sin amor" (143).

Memories of a happy time generally serve as a contrast to Machado's present pathos. In each line of the following poem, for example, past and present are juxtaposed, timeworn objects of the present acting as a shocking reminder of the contrast between "ayer" and "hoy":

> ¡Tocados de otros días,
> mustios encajes y marchitas sedas;

salterios arrumbados,
rincones de las salas polvorientas:

. . . .

cartas que amarillean;
libracos no leídos
que guardan grises florecitas secas;
romanticismos muertos,
cursilerías viejas,
cosas de ayer que sois el alma, y cantos
y cuentos de la abuela! . . . . (137–38)

The wind, too, in poem LXVIII brings a message of death saying that all the flowers of the garden where the poet once retreated have died. The petals have now withered and the fountains are weeping, melancholy like the poet (136–37). Poem LXIX once again contains a withered garden and Machado's hopes have turned to tears (137). In "El poeta," he addresses his soul in these lines which adequately summarize the poet's despair: "¡Alma, que en vano quisiste ser más joven cada día, / arranca tu flor, la humilde flor de la melancolía!" (101).

Such are the repressed memories of Machado's personal unconscious with which he has come to terms and reconciled himself. Although many choose to ignore their innermost anguish, preferring to lead a life of frivolity and shallowness, Machado sees this as self-deception. Only through confrontation with the unconscious can one attain the rewards of self-knowledge. The dream is one way in which Machado makes known his inner secrets.

In addition to the personal unconscious, the collective unconscious also manifests itself in Machado's "sueño," encompassing all that which lies outside of the dreamer's personal experience. It is composed of archetypes reflecting collective experience, those psychic contents which have been acquired from primitive man. For example, a dream of mythic or archetypal content is suggested by the following lines from poem XXXVII, when the night declares to the dreamer: "pero en las hondas bóvedas del alma / no sé si el llanto es una voz o un eco" (110). The night is uncertain whether the dreamer's cry belongs to the dreamer himself or whether it is merely an echo of his ancestors' or of society's similar cry. The echo, therefore, becomes a symbol for the timeless, collective unconscious, thus linking past and present.

The dreamer / poet, in turn, asks the night whether or not his tears are in fact his own. Maybe they are merely artistic recreations of his ancestors' cries, as suggested by the word "histrión." The word can mean either an actor in the theater or an affected person, both of whom purposefully pretend something, with hopes of making an impression on others.

In the case of a poet, he or she may be expressing collective feelings or ideas, rather than merely personal ones, in order to evoke a specific feeling or action from the reader.

¡ . . . .

dime, si sabes vieja amada, dime
si son mías las lágrimas que vierto!
Me respondió la noche:
Jamás me revelaste tu secreto.
Yo nunca supe, amado,
si eras tú ese fantasma de tu sueño,
ni averigüé si era su voz de la tuya,
o era la voz de un histrión grotesco.
(Alvar 110)

The collective or mythic unconscious is again visible, in this same dialogue between dreamer and "la fuente," in poem VI of *Soledades*. (Notice the images remarkably similar to those of poem XCIV mentioned earlier, such as a sleepy afternoon, an ivy-covered wall, a continually-flowing fountain, and the marble onto which the water gushes.) Once more, the water of the fountain may be seen as a symbol for the flowing of the unconscious (as was described in poem XCIV earlier); as the metaphorical water flows, the dreamer gradually drifts deeper into his inner self. He is aware that the contents of his inner whisperings are nothing new, merely archetypal, an echo of yesteryear. Thus today's message has its roots in an era long ago, modern man's voice once again a mere reverberation of his ancestors'.

Fue una clara tarde, triste y soñolienta
tarde de verano. La hiedra asomaba
al muro del parque, negra y polvorienta. . . .
La fuente sonaba.

. . . .

En el solitario parque, la sonora
copla borbollante del agua cantora
me guió a la fuente. La fuente vertía
sobre el blanco mármol su monotonía
La fuente cantaba: ¿Te recuerda, hermano,
un sueño lejano mi canto presente?
Fue una tarde lenta del lento verano.
Respondí a la fuente:
No recuerdo, hermana,
mas sé que tu copla presente es lejana.
(Alvar 91)

Interestingly, the word *copla* is a type of popular song, that is, a song of the people. Thus personal "property" has given way here to collective property, and the poet does not always express purely literal occurrences of what he has experienced. It is not likely that Machado literally spent an afternoon in dialogue with a fountain. Instead, one may presume that the fountain is a symbol; in order to discover the commonly shared experience(s) suggested by the symbol we must interpret it. For instance, Machado's fountain might be viewed as the unconscious vessel, with the song being its contents.

The whole notion of the traveler on a journey, often a night journey, is an archetype of the individuation process. The shadow and anima mentioned earlier are further archetypes, elements of a mythical nature. The hero, too, is an ancient myth seen in Machado's verse as the poet who battles with his own self. The list of archetypes could go on but are beyond the scope of this paper.

The Imagination

Related to the dream is Machado's use of the imagination which, once again, he defines as a vigilant dream or reverie. In chapter XIV of *Juan de Mairena* he writes that only in moments of idleness should a poet interpret dreams (the passive dreams of sleep, that is), finding in them elements to use in poetry (Belitt 31). He continues saying that the oneiroscope has produced nothing of importance, relegating the passive dream to an inferior position in comparison with vigilance (31). One should dream while awake, via the imagination—the daydream or meditation:

> Los poemas de nuestra vigilia, aun los menos logra-
> dos, son más originales y más bellos y, a las veces,
> más disparatados que los de nuestros sueños. Os lo
> dice quien pasó muchos años de su vida pensando lo
> contrario. Pero de sabios es mudar de consejo.
> (*Obras, poesía y prosa* 394)

Instead, it is essential to have one's eyes wide open in order to see things *as* they are, more open to see them *other* than what they are and, finally, even more open to see them *better* than they really are (394). "Yo os aconsejo la visión vigilante, porque vuestra misión es ver e imaginar despiertos, y que no pidáis al sueño sino reposo" (394).

Through acknowledgement of the imagination, one can explore the unconscious while in a vigilant state—a "vigilant vision." Regarding Machado's fusion of the conscious and unconscious aspects of the vigilant dream, Gullón says: "el ver en sueños es un ver imaginario, un ver con la zona del cerebro que permanece en vela mientras las demás descansan" (70).

Art, likewise, may simultaneously entail the unconscious and conscious as when the artist utilizes elements of a rational world, but by mixing them in unlikely combinations produces an irrational one. German art historian Herbert Kühn has differentiated two types of art works: the "sensory" and the "imaginative." The "sensory" involves a rational, direct imitation of the person, object, nature

or universe, while the "imaginative" is a more irrational portrayal of the subject. In order to interpret this imaginative quality, so much a part of modern art, one must utilize the intellect, or rational mind to some extent (*Man and His Symbols* 246). For example, in Marc Chagall's painting "Time is a River without Banks," real images are used such as a fish, violin, clock and a pair of lovers. However, it is the mixture of these elements within the painting that creates the work's visual oddities. One sees a fish, perched on top of a clock, and playing the violin.

The irrational nature of much modern painting can be explained by the existence of what Jung calls the "subliminal aspects" of the conscious, or the "fringe of conciousness" discussed earlier. Once again, these terms represent those parts of the consciousness which have entered the unconscious. Jung states:

> Our conscious impressions, in fact, quickly assume
> an element of unconscious meaning that is psychi-
> cally significant for us, though we are not consciously
> aware of the existence of this subliminal meaning or
> of the way in which it both extends and confuses the
> conventional meaning. (*Man and His Symbols* 40)

Machado's dream via the imagination, while containing commonplace objects, also demands attention because of the deep-rooted, unconscious meaning behind the objects. This is the subliminal aspect of the surface or conscious meaning. Therefore, it is necessary to be somewhat vigilant in order to interpret these metaphorical representations of reality.

At the beginning of this paper, I stated that I wished to explore how the poet reveals his private, inner nature, his intimate experience, his own truth. A relevant question is then how does the imagination reveal Machado's inner truth, if the very word itself suggests that which is fiction, that which is not real? Are many of his writings merely the fictitious products of literary and creative games or do they accurately reflect the psyche of the poet? Basically the question becomes "what is fact and what is fiction"?

While it is true that one meaning of the phrase "product of the imagination" comprises that which is nonexistent or, at least, has not yet been experienced, this definition is incomplete. The imagination may also be the most adequate expression of the author's most implicit reality, masked though it may be. As Leon Edel points out in "Literature and Biography," unconscious art may reveal more truth about its creator than a conscious, detailed study of the author's life or an author's own conscious self-study (65). Such is the case in Eugene O'Neill's *Desire Under the Elms,* whose autobiographical elements were confirmed by O'Neill's second wife. However, interestingly enough, these same elements did not appear in the dramatist's autobiographical play *Long Day's Journey into Night,* leading Edel to affirm:

> I suspect that many autobiographies are less 'autobiographical' and candid than they pretend. They project a preferred self-image and often unconsciously (though sometimes deliberately) alter or omit parts of experience which we can discover reflected with great accuracy in the imagined creations. A work of art may thus be found to contain truths—and direct facts—which a biographer can hardly ignore. (65)

Through psychoanalysis, art can be seen as an instrument for viewing the writer's thoughts and truths which might otherwise go unsaid.

In the case of Machado, the imagination often has to do with love, or, better still, the absence of it. One clear example of Machado's use of imagination occurs in relation to the intriguing story of Guiomar. Such was the name he gave to a woman of his affection years after the death of his wife. He began to write love letters to a mysterious lady in Madrid, many of which have been collected and published in Concha Espina's *De Antonio Machado a su grande y secreto amor.* Although many thought Guiomar was merely imaginary, this belief was disproven when, in 1929, Machado wrote a letter to Unamuno saying, "A few days ago I sent to you with our *Juan de Mañara* the book *Huerto Cerrado* of Pilar Valderrama. This lady, whom I met in Segovia . . ." (Cobb 37). Pilar was in fact a poet who, though her poetry was generally unpopular, had much impressed Machado; in 1930 he expressed this admiration in an article. It is believed that they met around 1926 at the latest (37), during Machado's time as a professor in Segovia. He made several trips to see her in Madrid but the relationship was not meant to be. He mentions "la barrera que ha puesto la suerte entre nosotros" (108). Guiomar was married and never fully reciprocated his attentions.

In this hopeless situation, all he could do was dream and imagine, and imagine he did, as witnessed in a letter to Guiomar. In it he says love for him is almost like a mere game of the imagination, reality being of secondary importance: "Pienso yo que los amores, aun los más 'realistas,' se dan en tres cuartas partes en el retablo de nuestra imaginación" (Zubiría 138). He even confesses that he preferred to dream about her from afar in Segovia rather than to remain in Madrid with her.

In *De un cancionero apócrifo* Machado includes several poems concerning his love for

Guiomar, such as his "Canciones a Guiomar," where he appears to have imagined her existing in a timeless world of illusion: "En un jardín te he soñado, / alto, Guiomar, sobre el río / jardín de un tiempo cerrado / con verjas de hierro frío" (Cobb 119). One can then conclude that he did not merely dream up or create an imaginary Guiomar, but rather that she exists in an imaginary world, where nothing can disturb it. Time has ceased and the world is protected by iron gratings. Nothing can intrude on their secret love. The existence of the love is not imagined, only the nature of the love, when a relationship was not meant to be.

Guiomar once wrote Machado a letter expressing jealousy, upon discovering that he had met with another woman. He responds, assuring her of his profound love and insisting that Guiomar (or his "diosa" as he often called her) is not imaginary:

> A ti y a nadie más que a ti, en todos los sentidos—¡todos!—del amor, puedo yo querer. El secreto es sencillamente que yo no he tenido más amor que éste. Mis otros amores sólo han sido sueños, a través de los cuales vislumbraba yo la mujer real, la diosa. (Cobb 110)

Here we see how the poet distinguishes between the unreal woman of his dreams and the very real Guiomar of his imagination. Thus through the imagination, Machado ultimately arrives at the truth. Similarly, by observing the imagined world where time stands still and nothing can harm the two lovers, one may deduce the actual nature of Machado's reality—the preoccupation with his brief temporal existence.

Thus the dream, as well as the imagination, and their link with the memory and soul-searching, are a fusion of the conscious and unconscious. Both allow for the revelation of the unconscious in that they act as a bridge between the two parts of the psyche. Although many choose to ignore their innermost anguish, preferring to lead a life of frivolity and shallowness, Machado sees this as self-deception. Only through confrontation with the unconscious can one attain the rewards of self-knowledge.

Source: Susan J. Joly, "The Dream and the Imagination in Antonio Machado's Poetry," in *Hispanofila*, Vol. 117, May 1996, pp. 25–43.

Sources

Barnstone, Willis, *Six Masters of the Spanish Sonnet*, Southern Illinois University Press, 1993, pp. 104, 107.

Machado, Antonio, *Selected Poems*, translated and with an introduction by Alan S. Trueblood, Harvard University Press, 1982, pp. 262–65.

Trueblood, Alan S., "Antonio Machado and the Lyric of Ideas," in *Letter and Spirit in Hispanic Writers: Renaissance to Civil War*, Tamesis Books Limited, 1986, p. 255.

Further Reading

Beevor, Antony, *The Spanish Civil War*, Penguin Books, 2001.
  This is a thorough and up-to-date history of the Spanish Civil War.

Cobb, Carl W., *Antonio Machado*, Twayne Publishers, 1971.
  This biography of Machado is an excellent introduction to the writer's life and works.

Edwards, Gwynne, *Flamenco!*, Thames and Hudson, 2000.
  With its many vibrant photographs by Ken Haas, this visually exciting book is an entertaining and informative introduction to the art and history of flamenco song and dance.

Shaw, Donald Leslie, *The Generation of 1898 in Spain*, Barnes and Noble, 1975.
  This book explores the concerns and motivations of the figures who are known as the Generation of '98, of which Machado is one.

Schreiner, Claus, ed., *Flamenco: Gypsy Dance and Music from Andalusia*, Amadeus Press, 1996.
  This is an excellent sourcebook for students interested in learning about flamenco, as its collection of essays (by different authors) addresses all aspects of the art form.

An Elementary School Classroom in a Slum

Stephen Spender

1964

"An Elementary School Classroom in a Slum" was first published in 1964 in Stephen Spender's *Selected Poems*. The poem has since appeared in several collections, including *Collected Poems 1928–1985*, published in 1985. "An Elementary School Classroom in a Slum" is perhaps the best example of Spender's political voice resonating throughout a poem. In this poem, Spender expresses his ideological positions on government, economics, and education. The students in this classroom are underprivileged and malnourished. The capitalistic government is supposed to supply equal opportunity for education, but the classroom in the slum offers little hope for change or progress for its lower-class students. This poem, written during the time of the Civil Rights movement in the United States, is fitting both in its commentary about race issues in American education and as a Socialist proclamation against capitalism and social injustice in general. Although Spender was British, his extreme left-leaning political ideologies were in response to the global question concerning social injustice. His poem does not explicitly name any country, location, race, or citizenship. Spender's intent was to shed light on social injustices worldwide; regardless of Spender's own ethnicity, the hotbed of this global struggle was the American Civil Rights movement.

Author Biography

Stephen Spender was born on February 28, 1909, in London. The son of a journalist, he grew up

Stephen Spender © Jerry Bauer

steeped in the art of writing. Spender was educated at University College, Oxford, but left the university without taking a degree. His life as a poet and writer began in the 1920s while he was at Oxford, where he surrounded himself with respected writers, such as W. H. Auden, Christopher Isherwood, Cecil Day Lewis, and Louis MacNeice. Spender was also closely associated with the literary giants Virginia Woolf and T. S. Eliot. In fact, the two are often referred to as Spender's surrogate parents.

Spender took a particularly keen interest in politics and was a self-proclaimed socialist and pacifist. His early poetry was often inspired and fueled by social protest. In 1937, he served for a short time in the International Brigades, an international force of volunteers dedicated to protecting the Spanish Republic during the Spanish Civil War. Spender explored the experiences of the war in *Poems for Spain* (1939), which he edited with John Lehmann, and in *Ruins and Visions* (1942), a collection of his own poems spanning the years 1934 to 1942.

Although Spender was associated with the Socialist and Communist movements, he eventually became disillusioned with their ideologies. He expressed much of his dissent and frustration with the politics of the 1930s and 1940s through his poetry and essays

as well as in his autobiography, *World within World* (1951), which delves into his political beliefs, social frustrations, and much-hidden homosexuality.

In 1936, Spender married Agnes Marie Pearn, from whom he was later divorced. In 1941, he married the pianist Natasha Litvin; they had two children. He enlisted in the London Fire Service during World War II. After the war, Spender joined UNESCO (United Nations Educational, Scientific and Cultural Organization) as a cultural emissary. He coedited two magazines, *Horizon* (published from 1939 to 1941) and, later, *Encounter* (published from 1953 through 1966). He also worked for the Congress of Cultural Freedom, International PEN, and the British Council. Spender's poem "An Elementary School Classroom in a Slum" first appeared in 1964 in his *Selected Poems*.

Spender was a prolific writer, authoring and editing many books. Besides poetry, he published several plays, novels, and short stories and many nonfiction works. His books of poetry include *Poems of Dedication* (1946), *The Edge of Being* (1949), *The Generous Days* (1969), and *Dolphins* (1994). His nonfiction works include *The Creative Element* (1953), *The Struggle of the Modern* (1963), and *Love-Hate Relationships* (1974). In 1970, Spender became a professor of English at University College in London, a post he held for seven years. He was awarded the Queen's Gold Medal for Poetry in 1973, and in 1983 he was knighted.

Although Spender is rarely heralded as one of the greatest poets of the twentieth century, his work is well respected. The bulk of his acclaim can be credited to his passionate, charming, and insightful work concerned with politics, education, and the rights of all human beings. From his early break into the literary scene until his death on July 16, 1995, in London, Spender pursued literary recognition amidst colleagues who far exceeded him in their own abilities; his achievements were thus dwarfed by the greatness of the company he kept.

Poem Text

Far far from gusty waves these children's faces.
Like rootless weeds, the hair torn round their
    pallor:
The tall girl with her weighed-down head. The
    paper-
seeming boy, with rat's eyes. The stunted, unlucky
    heir

Of twisted bones, reciting a father's gnarled
    disease,   5
His lesson, from his desk. At back of the dim class
One unnoted, sweet and young. His eyes live in a
    dream
Of squirrel's game, in tree room, other than this.

On sour cream walls, donations. Shakespeare's
    head,
Cloudless at dawn, civilized dome riding all cities.   10
Belled, flowery, Tyrolese valley. Open-handed map
Awarding the world its world. And yet, for these
Children, these windows, not this map, their world,
Where all their future's painted with a fog,
A narrow street sealed in with a lead sky   15
Far far from rivers, capes, and stars of words.

Surely, Shakespeare is wicked, the map a bad
    example,
With ships and sun and love tempting them to
    steal—
For lives that slyly turn in their cramped holes
From fog to endless night? On their slag heap,   20
    these children
Wear skins peeped through by bones and
    spectacles of steel
With mended glass, like bottle bits on stones.
All of their time and space are foggy slum.
So blot their maps with slums as big as doom.

Unless, governor, inspector, visitor,   25
This map becomes their window and these
    windows
That shut upon their lives like catacombs,
Break O break open till they break the town
And show the children to green fields, and make
    their world
Run azure on gold sands, and let their tongues   30
Run naked into books the white and green leaves
    open
History theirs whose languages is the sun.

Poem Summary

Stanza 1

The opening stanza of "An Elementary School Classroom in a Slum" provides a clear, dreary depiction of the students in the classroom. The first child is a "tall girl with [a] weighed-down head." This girl is physically and emotionally exhausted, as if all life has been dredged from her body and sapped from her mind. Her classmates are in no better condition. "The paper- / seeming boy, with rat's eyes" is paper-thin and weak. His eyes are defensive and scared, like a scavenger, a rat. His prospect for survival, let alone success, is bleak. Another student, "the stunted, unlucky heir / Of twisted bones," is the victim of a genetic disorder. Spender writes that the boy has inherited his "father's gnarled disease"; he has been left disfigured, trapped in a physically challenged body.

Media Adaptations

- Two audiocassettes of Stephen Spender's poetry are available: *Poetry of Stephen Spender* (1964), published by Audio-Forum, and *Stephen Spender Selected Poems* (1994), published by Spoken Arts.

Spender then describes the boy "at back of the dim class," stating, "His eyes live in a dream." This last student represents both a glimmer of wary hope and a shiver of mental damnation. It is unclear whether he is dreaming of a life he may achieve or has lost his mind to the "squirrel's game." This vague distinction between these two conflicting interpretations exposes all the students' futures: there is little or no expectation that they will succeed, and the best they can hope for is to keep their sanity and not fall victim to a faux reality. Beneath it all, the boy's dreaming eyes may harbor an honest desire for true success. This last boy, "unnoted, sweet and young," may understand his position in society and see the sadness of his fellow students. With this understanding, he may represent hope for social change, instead of merely being an individual who has lost his mind.

Stanza 2

In the second stanza, Spender describes the classroom and its contents. The classroom is full of "donations." The children are from the lowest class; they are the children of proletarians. The classroom is constructed through donations of others' capital. All that the students possess comes from their oppressors, the bourgeoisie. The upper class, which holds these children in their place, also offers them their only tools to escape. The maps, books, and "Shakespeare's head" that give the students hope of something outside their dreary existences are gifts from the very hands that clamp them down in their economic and social position.

Spender writes,

    . . . for these
    Children, these windows, not this map, their world,

Where all their future's painted with a fog,
A narrow street sealed in with a lead sky
Far far from rivers, capes, and stars of words.

The "donations" may give a glimpse of some world to the students, but not of their world. The students do not perceive their world as like the one depicted in the classroom's "donations." It is not the "belled, flowery, Tyrolese valley" but instead a foggy, "narrow street sealed in with a lead sky." Their future is bleak, unknown, and dreary. The children in "An Elementary School Classroom in a Slum" are trapped by their social and economic status as children of proletarians.

Stanza 3

In the third stanza, Spender responds cynically to the reality of the students' futures. He calls Shakespeare "wicked" and the map a "bad example." He writes that the stories from the books of "ships and sun and love" are "tempting them [the students] to steal." The world presented by the bourgeoisie to the students in "An Elementary School Classroom in a Slum" is intended to lure them and drag them into a life of crime. Spender's cynicism is a commentary on the upper class and their circumventing tactics in the effort to hold a firm grip on lower-class citizens. By exposing the students to the beauties of the world, the bourgeoisie appear to be assisting the proletarians' children, instilling in them hope for something better. However, Spender sees the bourgeoisie's "donations" as something far more evil. His cynical view of the "donations" is that they were given not to infuse the students with hope but rather to force them to commit crime and thus be branded as thieves. As such, the bourgeoisie are readily empowered to oppress the lower class for no other reason than to protect their own families, assets, and futures from the lawbreaking hands of the proletariat.

Although Spender voices cynicism, he does not lose sight of the true victims of the injustice of the class struggle: the children. In this stanza, he continues to describe the children "on their slag heap." He returns to their thin, malnourished bodies, stating that they "wear skins peeped through by bones." They also wear "spectacles of steel / With mended glass, like bottle bits on stones." Spender is making a resounding humanist statement about the treatment of children in this poem. It appears that he is more sickened by humanity's disregard for the children than by the social and economic framework that has doomed these children to the slums.

Stanza 4

In the final stanza, Spender comes full circle. He replaces cynicism with hope, a plea for a new manifesto for the children. He is petitioning "governor, inspector, visitor" to transform the sour temptation of the bourgeoisie's donations into a reality. He begs for a change that will "break O break open" the "windows / That shut upon their lives like catacombs" and free the children from the constraints of their position in society. Spender asks that the children be shown—directly, not through "donations"—"green fields" and "gold sands."

Spender further hopes that the children will be able to "let their tongues / Run naked into books the white and green leaves open." The "white and green leaves" could be seen to represent money, bourgeoisie donations that supply the books the children use. However, with this statement, Spender is asking for a pragmatic alteration in the practical application of "donations." Given the current bourgeoisie scheme to oppress the proletariat through donations, the students either are locked in their social position or are led into a world of crime through temptation. Spender is claiming that if students are truly allowed free exploration—naked tongues running freely through donated books—then their education and their "language" will become the "sun" burning away the "fog" that has sealed their fates and doomed them to "An Elementary School Classroom in a Slum."

Themes

Poverty

The theme of poverty is principal to the poem "An Elementary School Classroom in a Slum." Spender creates a crisp image of children in poverty through his descriptions of dire situations and malnourished students, revealing a sad, hidden segment of society that was prevalent throughout the world. He is not commenting directly on any particular nation in his poem; instead, he exposes the widespread neglect of children of all nationalities, races, and ethnicities. It is poverty that has caused the students in "An Elementary School Classroom in a Slum" to be "weighed-down," "paper-seeming," diseased, and "twisted." Spender believes this poverty is created through the oppressive power of capitalism.

This poem was written during the American Civil Rights movement, and although Spender was British, the injustice that occurred in the United

Topics For Further Study

- Stephen Spender used his poetry to express his political ideology and to voice his support of Marxist ideals. Write a poem expressing your personal political ideology, or, if you prefer, write a poem from the standpoint of a political theorist, such as John Locke, Alexis de Tocqueville, or Niccolò Machiavelli.

- Spender uses an allegory to present the struggle between the proletariat and the bourgeoisie. Other writers and thinkers have used allegories to convey complex social struggles and concepts. Compare and contrast Spender's allegory to another. You might choose, for example, Plato's "Allegory of the Cave" in the *The Republic* or George Orwell's *Animal Farm*.

- Research Karl Marx and write a short paper on his role as an educated proletarian. Was Marx a wealthy man? How did he support himself? What was his relationship to the capitalist society he

so wished to overturn? Make sure that your paper addresses Marx's forced position within a capitalist society and that you examine how he interacted with a social structure he despised.

- "An Elementary School Classroom in a Slum," though it is heavy with Communist allusions, still focuses primarily on education. Examine the modern education system and try to pinpoint similarities and differences between it and the system about which Spender wrote. Do you think there is still a difference in the quality of education offered at wealthy schools as opposed to that offered at poor schools? Has the current government reformed the education system to change society's intervention in the classroom, or has everything remained the same? Support your answers with research. Identify changes that you can recognize and explore ways to improve the modern education system.

States was a global issue that affected the entire world, especially close English-speaking allies like Britain. Spender was affected by the struggles for equality in the United States because of his staunch dedication to social and political reforms. Although this poem was written during this time of oppressive racial injustice in America, Spender does not directly focus on a select group of underprivileged children, based on race, religion, or creed. Instead, he hones the content of his poem and remarks about the social injustice imposed upon all children, making it much more difficult to ignore. When the spotlight is cast upon a select group of individuals, certain members of particular groups are able to shrug their shoulders or cast a doubtful eye at the authenticity of the group's plight. However, when the spotlight is cast upon children writ large, no one can turn a blind eye. Regardless of their upbringing, history, race, or ethnicity, children are innocent beings dependent on the helping hands of humanity. Without aid, children are effectively left to die, and adults who do not help are left with an undeniable sense

of guilt and worthlessness. Spender cultivates these emotions in his poem and uses them to his advantage, delivering a powerful message about poverty, its effect on children, and the oppressive power of money.

Communism and Education

Karl Marx firmly states in *The Communist Manifesto* that education is "social, and determined by the social conditions under which you educate, by the intervention of society, direct or indirect, by means of schools." Spender thoroughly supports this statement in "An Elementary School Classroom in a Slum" and asks for a complete subversion of the dominant social model with regard to its direct and indirect intervention in schools. Although this poem may not be perceived wholly as a Communist poem, a keen dissection of its parts clearly reveals a Marxist solution to the educational crisis caused by poverty.

Spender does not appreciate the "donations" given to the children, because he sees them as an indirect intervention of capitalistic society in schools. These donations are not given for the good of the children's education but for the sole purpose of keeping them in position as lower-class citizens. This end is achieved in that the donations project a world outside the slum that is seemingly unattainable and thus press the children into lives of unfulfilled dreams or of crime—the delusional last resort for gaining wealth and escaping the slum. Spender asks for a pragmatic shift in the way these donations are given and used—a Communist approach—in which money empowers the children to truly explore books, maps, the world, and themselves. In other words, it would give them the chance to pursue education without the pretense of temptation or a future of unfulfilled aspirations.

This changed use of "donations" is a Communist attitude to education. "An Elementary School Classroom in a Slum" pictures the children as proletarians and the donors as bourgeoisie. Spender does not wish to remove education from society, but he aspires to transform it into an institution managed by a Communist, not a capitalist, society, where all children are given the opportunity to excel, with no favoritism given to their social starting point. This change demands a proletariat revolution, shifting the social tides, because Spender, like Marx, still believes that education is social and that the only society that should be intervening in education is a Communist one.

Knowledge and Revolution

Knowledge and its effect on revolution is a key theme in "An Elementary School Classroom in a Slum." As shown earlier, this poem strongly embraces Communism and its ability to transform education and uproot poverty, yet Spender's undying embrace of education stands above everything else as the most empowering and most important influence on the future of humanity. For Spender, the children's minds possess the power of the sun and the ability to clear the fog from the bleak future. As he puts it, "History theirs whose language is the sun." These children, empowered by a substantial, honest education, can achieve a mental prowess that will free them from futures "painted with a fog." With knowledge, the children can change the future. They can raise their educated arms in revolt and overturn the oppression that desperately tries to keep them in place.

Spender has placed himself in a bind with these proclamations. Although it may be true that knowledge is empowerment, empowerment is the only hope for change, and change is predicated on

revolution, it still appears that education cannot change without a new society. A vicious circle presents itself. Education is social, and the capitalist society intervening in education does not benefit proletarians. Thus, education benefits only the bourgeoisie. In order to change this dominant paradigm, proletarians must become educated, but with the bourgeoisie controlling society, the ability to become educated is difficult, if not impossible, for them. This, of course, leads into a much larger discussion of a worker revolution and the institution of Marxism in society, to overturn the dominant, capitalistic paradigm. Spender does not provide an answer to the struggle between proletarians and bourgeoisie, Communist and capitalist, in his poem. His theme of knowledge and revolution in "An Elementary School Classroom in a Slum" is intended to shed light on the power of education and the necessity to reform the way society delivers knowledge to all people, regardless of social or economic position.

Style

Allegory

Allegory is a literary technique that employs characters as representations of ideas that are used to convey a message or to teach a lesson. Spender uses the classroom and the children in his poem as an allegory about the struggle between proletarians and bourgeoisie. The children in "An Elementary School Classroom in a Slum" are clearly underprivileged, lower-class proletarians. The classroom donors are wealthy, upper-class bourgeoisie. Without directly using either term—proletarian or bourgeoisie—Spender weaves a descriptive, allegoric vignette about capitalism and its dependence on an oppressed working class. He vividly depicts the hardships and struggles of proletarians through his descriptions of the tired girl with her "weigheddown" head, the paper-thin boy, and the "unlucky heir" of "gnarled disease." The exhausted students are equivalent to the oppressed working class. The children of this class are doomed to inherit their parents' diseased position in society.

Although the future holds little promise of fortune for the children or the proletariat they represent, Spender sees a glimmer of hope in education. The students represent the working class, but they also hold the answer to a changed society. If the students can achieve an education, then they may be empowered to topple the bourgeoisie hold over society. Spender writes, "Break O break open till they break the town," offering hope that education will break open the minds of the children. Once their minds are free, empowered with learning, Spender believes that they will have the power to change the social hierarchy. He effectively uses such imagery to explore poverty, education, and the Communist-capitalist struggle.

The Unidentified Narrator

When reading "An Elementary School Classroom in a Slum," it is difficult to pinpoint the identity of the narrator. It may be deduced that there is no narrator and that the entire construct is built wholly around Spender and his desire to examine and pontificate on politics and its effect on education. Other readings of the poem have led educators to believe that the narrator is a teacher. Spender delivers the crux of his message on poverty and education through the use of this unidentified narrator, a narrator who, in the vagueness of his identity, appeals to a wide variety of people in society. He focuses on imagery that describes the children and the classroom, that is upsetting to the reader, and that fuels a desire for change.

Historical Context

Poverty as Social Injustice

When Spender wrote "An Elementary School Classroom in a Slum," the world was in the midst of major cultural and political change. In 1954, in the landmark case of *Brown v. the Board of Education of Topeka*, the Supreme Court ruled that segregation in the schools was unconstitutional. In 1955, Rosa Parks refused to give up her seat at the front of a bus to a white passenger, inciting a bus boycott by the African American community that ultimately led to desegregation on buses in 1956. Beginning in 1960, student sit-ins and other nonviolent protests became a popular and effective way of desegregating lunch counters, parks, swimming pools, libraries, and the like. In 1963, Martin Luther King Jr. delivered his "I Have a Dream" speech, and President John F. Kennedy was assassinated. The year Spender's poem was published, President Lyndon Johnson signed into law the Civil Rights Act of 1964, which prohibited discrimination of all kinds based on race, color, religion, or national origin. This legislation was unprecedented.

Behind these major historical events, countless lives were changed or ended during this tumultuous time. The late 1950s and early 1960s unearthed an America that had been kept hidden for centuries. Although slavery had been abolished, African Americans were dying every year at the hands of racists. Equality was a seemingly futile hope not only in America but also across the globe. Poverty was rampant among African Americans, especially in the South. They were often undereducated and perpetually oppressed by white southerners bent on thwarting and hampering African American progress.

When the injustice of society's oppression is revealed, it is usually forced to end. Sometimes, however, such injustice takes new forms. For example, after Abraham Lincoln abolished slavery, the oppressive conditions of slavery were converted into racial segregation and the denial of civil rights to African Americans. American society in the South had exploited African Americans as slaves and reaped economic benefits; after Reconstruction, society subjugated them once more, this time as an underprivileged working class without civil or human rights. During the 1960s, the Civil Rights movement—led by Martin Luther King Jr., Malcolm X, John F. Kennedy, and Robert Kennedy—struggled to free African Americans from segregation and discrimination. With civil rights, though, came another type of oppression: widespread poverty that affected African Americans in particular. The new social imbalance was touted as a struggle between rich and poor rather than as a racial issue. The U.S. economy still had its underprivileged working class, and the oppressors were off the hook because the so-called oppressed now had civil and human rights. The oppressed people's low place in society was said to stem from their own lack of ambition or intelligence. Poverty as a tool for social subjugation became extremely powerful, far more so than blatant racism.

Spender recognized this power. As a professed Socialist during the 1920s and 1930s, he was well aware of the oppressive power of capital. Much of his work conveyed the heavy politically charged ideologies of Communist and Marxist thought. The shifting perception of oppression from the 1950s into the 1960s fueled Spender's political commentary. In "An Elementary School Classroom in a Slum," he focuses on the power that capitalism holds over the children in the slums, rather than on race. Although some readers may assume that the students in the poem are African American, Spender was far more concerned with the economic and social implications of the new face of oppression than he was with its possible racial implications. Spender was first and foremost a leftist and

Compare & Contrast

- **1960s:** Communist countries are considered the greatest threat to the United States and the free world, with Vietnam, Cuba, and the USSR at the helm.

  Today: Although Communist countries like Vietnam and China still exist, most are looked upon favorably as allies and trading partners. Now so-called rogue states, or regimes that sponsor terror or are thought to be developing nuclear weapons—such as Iran, North Korea, and Syria—are viewed as threats to the Western world.

- **1960s:** Socialism is frowned upon as a vile offspring of Communist ideologies. Capitalism is the driving force behind which democracy accelerates throughout the world.

  Today: Although capitalism is still a driving force, socialism is far more widely accepted, with many developed countries in the Western world offering socialized medicine and adequate welfare for the needy.

- **1960s:** The American Civil Rights movement to end segregation and discrimination in public accommodations, employment, and education is in full swing, focusing on equal rights and protections for blacks. Three Civil Rights Acts are enacted during this decade.

  Today: Related civil liberties movements have spurred change for women and the disabled and have begun to make inroads in rights for gays. Massachusetts has become the first state to allow gays to marry, with Vermont and Connecticut legalizing civil unions between gays. Some believe, however, that the USA Patriot Act, enacted to combat terrorism, threatens civil liberties in the name of national security.

- **1960s:** The annual salary of a minimum-wage worker is equal to the U.S. federal poverty line for a family of three.

  Today: The annual salary of a minimum-wage worker is 30 percent below the U.S. federal poverty line for a family of three.

---

a Socialist. His writing was influenced by global injustice and during the years before he wrote "An Elementary School Classroom in a Slum," there was no greater social injustice than lack of civil rights in the United States. His exploration of the social change occurring in the 1950s and 1960s reflects the turbulence not only of this era in American history but also of this era in global history.

Critical Overview

There is not much written about Spender's work as a poet and even less about his individual poems. In fact, much of the critical response to Spender's poetry is negative or tepid at best in its praise. David R. Slavitt writes in *Boulevard* of attending a lecture given by Spender at Yale in 1955, stating, "He

was also, I thought then and still think, a dismally bad poet." This is the familiar and resounding opinion of but one of Spender's critics. His greatest literary achievement is his autobiography, *World within World*. No matter how poorly received his poetry may have been by his contemporaries and critics, the bulk of what is written about Spender's life and, in particular, about his autobiography, is heavy with critical praise.

Written in 1951, *World within World* explores Spender's bisexual lifestyle. It is unusual in its frankness. Spender, who always went to bat for the oppressed and underprivileged, puts his own life and sexuality on the table, examining the civil and human hardships of a nonheterosexual person in the sexually repressed 1950s. Richard Freadman writes in *The Ethics in Literature*, "*World within World* is a powerful and nuanced call for renewal, a call which imagines some of the processes of renewal that ethical beings now need to undergo." Spender's autobiography as well as his poem "An Elementary School Classroom in a Slum" show his dedication to equality and understanding among humans. Although Spender may not be seen as one of the greatest English poets of the twentieth century, he is recognized as a humanist and a political activist with a keen eye for social commentary.

> " *Spender's description of each student is a comment on the exploitation of the proletariat.*"

Criticism

Anthony Martinelli

Martinelli is a Seattle-based freelance writer and editor. In this essay, Martinelli examines how Spender's poem delivers a Marxist message about Communism, education, and the need for social revolution.

Spender's poem "An Elementary School Classroom in a Slum" is an excellent example of his lifelong dedication to the pursuit of social change and human equality. During the earliest stages of his writing career in the 1920s and 1930s, Spender was a pacifist and Socialist. He was so stirred to action by the proletarian struggle that he joined the International Brigades—an international force of volunteer soldiers organized by the French Communist Party leader Maurice Thorez and the Soviet leader Joseph Stalin. Clearly, Spender was an advocate for the working class and an avid supporter of sociopolitical reform. His poetry was a reflection of his support of social reform. Even as he aged, Spender continued to fight for social change and equality for all of humankind. Although he became less of a vocal supporter of Communism, these ideals were still at the foundation of his writing and his political ideology. In the turbulent decade of the 1960s, Spender wrote "An Elementary School Classroom in a Slum," a vivid, didactic poem calling for a Communist social reform that mirrors the writings of Karl Marx and Frederick Engels in their penultimate work *The Communist Manifesto*.

In 1848, Karl Marx and Frederick Engels wrote *The Communist Manifesto* as the platform of the Communist League, a workingmen's association. It was unavoidably formed as a secret society, because any organized uprising of the working class in Europe would result in a dramatic change both politically and socially for the ruling class. However secret the Communist League may have hoped to remain, by 1850 *The Communist Manifesto* was quickly translated into most European languages and the work became the doctrine of the proletarians, the exploited, working class, as they struggled for emancipation from the bourgeoisie, the exploiting, ruling class. Escape from this social hierarchy proved very difficult. In fact, neither Marx nor Engels saw the realization of the goals of their manifesto, yet it continues to fuel social revolutionaries across the globe.

The fundamental proposition that forms the nucleus of *The Communist Manifesto* states that every historical generation, since the dissolution of primitive society in exchange for political society and individual ownership of property, is built upon a socioeconomic structure that necessitates a struggle between two classes, the proletariat and the bourgeoisie. In order to emancipate the proletariat, Marx and Engels contend that society at large must be freed from exploitation, oppression, class distinctions, and class struggles. Looking back to the shift from primitive to political society, the ownership of property is the fuel that powers the machine that oppresses and exploits proletarians. Marx writes, "Communists everywhere support every revolutionary movement against the existing social and political order of things. In all these movements they bring to the front, as the leading question in each case, the property question." This is the base struggle for which the proletariat must fight: the dissolution of private ownership.

If dissolution of private property is key to the emancipation of the proletariat, then there is no peaceful resolution to the class struggle. The bourgeoisie will certainly not relinquish ownership of their capital and private land, and thus the proletariat must subvert and overturn the dominant social paradigm with a forcible revolution. Marx writes

> The Communists disdain to conceal their views and aims. They openly declare that their ends can be attained only by the forcible overthrow of all existing

What Do I Read Next?

- *Letters to Christopher: Stephen Spender's Letters to Christopher Isherwood, 1929–1939* (1980), edited by Lee Bartlett, is a collection of letters Spender sent to his great friend the poet Christopher Isherwood during their early years as writers and political activists.

- *World within World* (1951; reissued in 2001) is Spender's autobiography. The book explores his life, his friendships, and his unspoken bisexuality.

- W. H. Auden's *Selected Poems* (1989), edited by Edward Mendelson, provides the original versions of many of Auden's poems, which he revised later in his career as his ideologies matured. Auden and Spender met in their twenties and maintained their friendship throughout their lives.

- *The Berlin Stories* (1946) combines Christopher Isherwood's two finest novels, *The Last of Mr. Norris* and *Goodbye to Berlin*, in one volume. These stories of exile, which meld Isherwood's real life with an imaginary life, formed the basis for the Broadway musical *Cabaret*.

---

social conditions. Let the ruling classes tremble at the Communist revolution. The proletarians have nothing to lose but their chains. They have a world to win.

Workingmen of all countries, unite!

This is, effectively, the proletariat's war cry. *The Communist Manifesto* was much more than a political theorist document; it truly incited action among the working class, igniting and fueling revolution, uprising, and social reform. Marx was before all else a revolutionist. His life mission was to overthrow capitalistic society and emancipate humanity from the constraints of a social construct founded upon the perpetual struggle between exploited and exploiting classes. This was the goal of *The Communist Manifesto* and the purpose of Marx's life.

Marx's message in *The Communist Manifesto* continued to resonate throughout Europe and Russia in the 1920s and 1930s, and it had a great impact on the foundation of Spender's writing, activism, and political ideology. Although Spender agreed with Marx's message and with the proletarian struggle, the way in which he explored Marxism and Communism changed as he aged. By 1964, when Spender wrote "An Elementary School Classroom in a Slum," his political ideology had altered focus. Although he was still opposed to capitalist society, Spender seemed more concerned about human equality than about the forcible emancipation and

social revolution for which he had fought in the 1930s. The poem reveals this altered perception.

"An Elementary School Classroom in a Slum" is written in four stanzas. The first stanza looks at the students in the classroom. The first student, a "tall girl with [a] weighed-down head," is both mentally and physically exhausted. The next, a "paper- / seeming boy, with rat's eyes" is malnourished and terrified of the world. The third student is an "unlucky heir / Of twisted bones," carrying a genetic disorder, his "father's gnarled disease." The last is an "unnoted, sweet and young" boy with "eyes [that] live in a dream." Spender's description of each student is a comment on the exploitation of the proletariat.

Like the tall girl, the working class is overworked, exhausted, and sapped of any energy that may be used to turn against the ruling class. The bourgeoisie struggle to keep proletarians weak, malnourished, and frightened, again to keep their energy level too low to revolt. The third boy speaks to the lack of adequate health care for proletarians, another means of oppressing uprising. The last boy, however, seems to represent a sign of hope. Spender writes that the boy dreams of a place "other than this," showing that the proletarian class has not lost sight of an end to oppression. If there were no hope for equality, then the last boy would have nothing to fuel his dreams of a place outside the classroom in the slum. Spender uses the first stanza to paint a picture of the proletarians' plight and their hope for social equality.

In the second stanza, Spender brings in the distant, yet invasive role of the bourgeoisie in the proletariat's classroom. He writes of books, maps, a bust of Shakespeare, and other classroom items that are all "donations." These items show the students a world outside the slum, an existence that is "belled, flowery," and beautiful like the "Tyrolese valley." However, this world is as fantastic as an imaginary, alien world. The world the children see is "painted with a fog. / A narrow street sealed in with a lead sky"; this is their existence. Anything beyond this world is pure fantasy.

In the next stanza, Spender writes that the donations are "wicked" and "a bad example" that tempts the students "to steal." Spender suggests that the bourgeois donors of these classroom gifts intend to use the donations to hold the proletarians in place. The donations do not help advance the children's education; they simply show the students in "An Elementary School Classroom in a Slum" a glimpse of a beautiful world outside of what they have come to accept as reality. However, this beautiful outside world is wholly unattainable because of their position as the exploited working class.

Spender seems to be pounding his fist, proclaiming that the donations leave only two options for the students in the classroom: resist the donors' temptation and live moral lives with unfulfilled dreams or give in to temptation and resort to a life of crime with the hope of gaining enough capital to break the chains of exploitation and escape the working class. Neither option is adequate, as one forces the students to remain in the "fog" as proletarians and the other compels them to exchange their proletarian life in the "fog" for one of an "endless night" as bourgeois thieves.

In the final stanza, Spender makes a plea for change. He begs the "governor, inspector, visitor" to help the students. Spender is calling for a change in the way in which donations are given and used and, thus, in the way in which society intervenes in education. He writes, "show the children to green fields, and make their world / Run azure on gold sands, and let their tongues / Run naked into books the white and green leaves open." Spender is asking society to change for the benefit of the children. He is not directly calling for a working-class revolution as Marx did; instead, he is asking that the donations, that is, the money, be used to empower the students to freely explore the books they have been given. His message is that all students, regardless of social class, should be given the opportunity to "Run naked into books" without suffering fear, malnourishment, exhaustion, or disease. Spender is asking for a change to benefit all students; although this change might mandate a change in society, his concern is education and children, not necessarily the proletariat revolution.

Marx states in *The Communist Manifesto* that education is "social, and determined by the social conditions under which you educate, by the intervention of society, direct or indirect, by means of schools." Therefore, neither Marx nor Spender hopes to remove society from education—as both see education as inherently social—but both hope to change the way society intervenes in education. Without a new approach to education, Spender would say not only that there is no hope for proletarian children but also that there is no hope for children in general. Here, too, we see Spender's new emphasis on a fresh vision for bringing about human equality.

Spender does not simply posit a different way of looking at the same struggle. In this poem, he takes us away from the struggle of the proletarians against the bourgeoisie and reminds us that behind this adult struggle are the children of all classes. Suddenly, the political revolution for equality takes a backseat to the general oppression of children. Regardless of social class, adults undeniably have a responsibility for the care of children. Spender uses this position to forward the Communist agenda and, at the same time, to shed light on the inequalities affecting poverty-stricken, underprivileged children. "An Elementary School Classroom in a Slum" seems to demand a social change for the benefit of all children—not only proletarians—and delivers a strong, Marxist message about Communism, education, and the need for social change.

Source: Anthony Martinelli, Critical Essay on "An Elementary School Classroom in a Slum," in *Poetry for Students*, Thomson Gale, 2006.

David R. Slavitt

In the following essay, Slavitt recounts a poetic incident at Yale during lectures given by Spender and Robert Frost.

The day I remember with greatest clarity of my four years as a Yale undergraduate was the one on which Stephen Spender and then Robert Frost appeared and I saw that poetry wasn't just a literary genre but, literally, a blood sport.

> *Sometimes I'm Frost. More often, I'm Spender, out there in the night bleeding, and hearing the line and the laughter of undergraduates, sharper than any glass shards."*

Spender had come two or three years before to read poems, so this time, when he offered Norman Holmes Pearson the choice of a reading or a lecture, Pearson suggested that, for variety's sake, the lecture might be agreeable. Spender said he would be happy to deliver it.

Happy, though, turned out not to be quite the right word. The trouble was that Cleanth Brooks introduced Spender. Cleanth, a short, courtly Southerner with thick eyeglasses and steel-gray hair, initiated the proceedings with a typically graceful few words from the stage of the large lecture hall in S.S.S. (Sterling Sheffield Strathcona Hall), and then sat down on an armchair at the side of the stage. Spender—not yet Sir Stephen, for this was 1955, I think—shambled to the lectern, drew a sheaf of folded pages from jacket pocket, and commenced to talk, the burden of his message being that we should never trust any critic who was not, himself, a poet. Ostensibly, he was attacking F. R. Leavis, but it was malapropos here, because Cleanth, on the stage with him, motionless, as if he were trying somehow to disappear into the crewel work of the large chair on which he sat, was a critic who was not, himself a poet. (Or, even worse, he'd published a couple of poems as a young man but then decided to give it up.)

It was an uncomfortable forty-five minutes, and, to make it even worse, there was a page missing from Spender's lecture—which mattered perhaps less than he thought, and for which, as I later learned, there was a glorious precedent. Dame Edith Sitwell—Litt. D., Litt. D., Litt. D, her letterhead proclaimed, because she had three of them—had two lecture fees, a thousand dollars and the bargain rate of five hundred, for which she would do every other page of the thousand dollar lecture,

giving a flavor of her style but with some of the intricacy of the argument withheld. This, anyway, was the word I'd heard in the Elizabethan Club.

Spender's missing page, however, had no such assertive elegance. Tall, gangly, and awkward, he was rather like one of those bowler-hatted twits in Monty Python routines. He was also, I thought then and still think, a dismally bad poet. The one Spender line we all knew was the opening of his best known poem, "I think continually of those who were truly great." There are two adverbs in it, a sure sign that we are being told what to feel rather than given something that might legitimately arouse our feelings. It is, quite unintentionally, a funny line, because it invites the reader to supply at that point the names of Auden, Louis MacNeice, and Day Lewis, with whom Spender was always associated and of whose greatness he might well have been thinking often if not continually.

He was trendy in ways that seem dated now and nearly quaint. He was anti-Georgian, and showed his modernity with aggressively urban and industrial images, so that he could say, with a perfectly straight face, addressing a beloved that he "turned away, / Thinking, if these were tricklings through a dam, / I must have love enough to run a factory on, / Or give a city power, or drive a train."

I'm not being hideously unfair. I seem not to have a volume of Spender's poetry on my shelves, and those lines are from the *Oxford Book of 20th Century English Verse, Chosen by Philip Larkin,* presumably because the five poems Larkin included were the best that Spender had produced.

Spender's strengths and weaknesses as a poet had little to do with the argument he was making, but it now strikes me that Auden has written somewhere that practicing poets are unreliable critics, preferring what they can learn from, or can steal, to those qualities that an impartial reader might value. Still, even then, in the lecture hall, while I didn't have that counter-argument to what Spender was proposing to us, I remember being unconvinced. I was also puzzled about why there needed to be any *a priori* judgment of any kind about what kind of critic was better than what other kind. Why couldn't we just decide, on a case by case basis, whose insights were shrewd, or useful, or entertaining, or provocative? In any event, Dr. Leavis's influence was not high on my list of intellectual problems. And, like everyone else in the room, I was uncomfortable for Cleanth's sake.

That evening, Frost was appearing in Pierson College. He was a fellow of the college and came by every year. He would do a reading, meet with a few of the literary students in the living room of the master's residence, and then spend the night in the Pierson guest quarters. It was an elaborately honed performance. He knew what he was doing, having done it so many times before. Frost, after all, more or less invented the college poetry reading and by then he was making a substantial part of his living from these gigs. The common room was quite full, and *le tout* New Haven was there—Pearson, Brooks, Spender, faculty members from other residential colleges, and of course members of Pierson College.

Frost's guise was the old codger, hard of hearing, except when he wanted to be, rambling, almost aimlessly, but with a sharpness that this pose made all the more startling. I remember that on two or three visits he read, "Provide, Provide," or, to use the term he preferred, he *said* that poem to us. And the ending was not quite what he had on the page:

> Some have relied on what they knew,
> Others on being simply true.
> What worked for them might work for you.
>
> No memory of having starred
> Atones for later disregard,
> Or keeps the end from being hard.
>
> Better to go down dignified
> With boughten friendship at your side
> Than none at all. Provide, provide!

He paused a moment, and then added, mischievously, "Or somebody else will provide for you," and when that got the small, uncomfortable chuckle it was supposed to get, topped that with the next line. "And how would you like that?"

These must have begun as spontaneous remarks, almost inadvertent filler, a part of the patter a poetry reading requires because no audience can supply for very long that kind of heightened attention poetry requires. It would be exhausting. And Frost was a skillful enough performer to know that he had to let us relax a little, recoup, and regather our wits and emotions. But this taunting of conventional liberalism had become a part of the routine, reliable and habitual. The throwaway lines have all but joined the poem itself. They are part of the pose that allows or even demands the "boughten," which is defiantly folksy. The implied claim is that this is hard-won country wisdom. (It may, indeed, have been hard won, but there was nothing of the rube in Frost.)

He did his maundering, offering his familiar remarks about free verse, and then, more generally, about freedom to and freedom from, which are quite different. And then, as if the thought had just that minute occurred to him but hadn't been prompted by anything so vulgar as an actual occasion, something or someone out there in the external world, he threw in a line that wasn't familiar: "You know, there are a lot of fifthrate poets who, without their social conscience, might be third rate."

It ran right by me, and by many of my classmates, I have no doubt. But Spender was smart enough to know that he'd been insulted. Perhaps Pearson and Brooks and some of the others had sneaked glances at him, or maybe not sneaked but looked, candidly, to see how he'd behave now that the afternoon's shoe was on the other foot. Nobody smiled. But that was because nobody had to. It was nice, and deft, and done with. Or it could have been, if Spender had been inclined to tough it out. But he was, as I've suggested, very tall, and he felt conspicuous. And he decided that perhaps the best thing for him to do was to withdraw.

It wasn't an altogether catastrophic plan, but he was also clumsy as some tall Brits are. And he hadn't noticed that if he was going to try to leave through the French doors, it was essential to look down and see where the electrical cord went from the outlet to the lamp beside the grand piano. Not having watched exactly where he was putting his feet, he tripped over the wire, and fell through the glass doors and onto the flagstones outside, with a shattering of glass and, actually, blood from his cut hands.

A painful business, and we were worried. Heads turned toward the door and the fallen figure out there who lay stretched out on the flagstones. And Frost?

He waited until the first moment of excitement had passed, asked, "What was that?" and then answered his own question: "Nothing important, I'm sure."

What was I to make of all this? It is generally known that Frost could be . . . frosty. I can't remember who it was who told me about some editor inviting him to be part of an anthology of America's Hundred Greatest Poets, and his declining with the quip that is probably true—"America hasn't had a hundred great poets." Spender's fall and his bloodied hands weren't Frost's responsibility but the result of the British poet's own clumsiness. Frost's oblique and incidental insult was a kind of twitting that seems perfectly appropriate in the light of Spender's own performance, a few hours earlier. Poetic justice, call it. All I can imagine Frost would have reasonably expected would have been Spender having to sit there in discomfort for a couple of minutes, which was less than what Brooks had had to suffer up on the stage.

All that is true enough, but beside the point, I think, which was something quite different and much more important: Frost thought of himself as a better poet than Spender. And therefore, Spender was an annoyance, even an affront.

We spend our lives at this, working hard, demanding of ourselves a standard of excellence that we can only occasionally meet. We have our moments—and months—of doubt and even despair, and we worry that we will never be able to write another poem again. Or that the poems we have written weren't as good as we'd wanted, and we've been kidding ourselves, wasting our time in a delusional and pathetic enterprise. We learn to be tough with ourselves, even brutal. And that brutality is a part of our aspiration, is allied somewhere to the best that is in us.

Sometimes, it comes out and shows itself, as it did that evening. Frost was being brutal to poor Spender, but nowhere near as brutal as he would habitually be to himself.

"I think continually of those who were truly great"?

Trip him. Throw him through that French door and out onto the patio.

No, maybe not that. But to ride him a little, to make a remark that might cause him an instant's distress? I can see that.

And the remark afterward, the really cruel one, about "Nothing important, I'm sure," isn't just Frost speaking. It's poetry, itself.

It's a phrase that goes through my head a lot, almost half a century later. Sometimes I'm Frost. More often, I'm Spender, out there in the night bleeding, and hearing the line and the laughter of undergraduates, sharper than any glass shards.

Source: David R. Slavitt, "Poetic Justice," in *Boulevard*, Vol. 18, No. 2 and 3, Spring 2003, pp. 93–97.

Brian Finney

In the following essay, Finney surveys various autobiographies of "sexual minorities" before analyzing Spender's World Within World, *which he praises for its "greater frankness."*

I

Why focus this essay on the autobiographies of members of sexual minorities? What I wanted to write about was the modern autobiographer's tendency to portray the self in the light of his or

her sexual history. How has the genre been affected by the admission into its spectrum of that most private of human activities, sex? For the most part, however, autobiographers have not seen in their sexual behaviour the key to their identity, the search for which is a central obsession with writers of this century. Although reticence about disclosing intimate details of both their own lives and those of their sexual partners has undoubtedly played its part, most autobiographers, because they belong to the heterosexual majority, tend to treat their sexual lives as something they hold in common with most of their readers rather than as clues to the uniqueness they seek to identify within themselves. Even the few heterosexual autobiographers who have given special prominence to their sexual identity, such as Frank Harris, feel compelled to dramatise and exaggerate their sexual encounters so as to demonstrate the uniqueness of their own experiences. Harris's sexual gymnastics reveal more about his neurotic need (a leftover from childhood) to excel in his father's eyes in whatever he turns his mind to than about the inner workings of his psyche. In fact his sexual feats occupy a relatively small portion of *My Life and Love,* and this is true of most heterosexuals' autobiographies which, like H.G. Wells's for example, attempt to include their sexual history as a prominent element.

So it is not surprising to find that only in the autobiographies of members of sexual minority groups is sexuality seen as a key to their sense of identity. Members of a repressed minority group, they find that the social ostracism which accompanies their sexual tastes produces in them an acute crisis of identity. In fact this crisis places them in a situation which is very similar to that experienced by numerous earlier autobiographers, the situation of the outsiders, of the socially ostracised who are compelled to reject the culture and beliefs of the majority in order to justify their lives. One immediately thinks of all those religious confessions written by protestant sectarians during the seventeenth and eighteenth centuries with their appeal to an inner light by means of which they justify themselves in face of their rejection by the bulk of their fellow Christians. Many of the most celebrated autobiographies are written by individuals who see themselves as outsiders—in religion, in the advancement of scientific knowledge, in the world of politics, or in the literary spectrum. The confessions of religious converts merge with those of famous criminals in their writers' desire to reconcile their own pattern of existence with the expected norm. Almost invariably the reader is treated both as confessor and as representative of the social norm. As Michel Leiris points out in his earliest volume of autobiography, "every confession contains a desire to be absolved." But this desire is at odds with the outsider's need to assert his own sense of identity, one which places him in conflict with the reader whose absolution he seeks. Rousseau's *Confessions* is a brilliant attempt to reconcile these conflicting needs. But he is sufficiently attentive to the genre to appreciate the impossibility of such a reconciliation and adroitly changes the object of his confession from the society of his own day (which he despairs of winning over) to a revolutionary society of the future from which he would win absolution because he would no longer be an outcast from it.

So the tradition of the outsider's autobiography naturally places its writer in the position of either a social outcast or a social revolutionary, and frequently both. To assert one's socially unacceptable sense of individual identity normally involves adopting a radical stance towards the society of one's day even while one is seeking to win its approval. It is the paradoxical nature of this predicament which I want to explore in this essay. Most of the autobiographies discussed here display a structural ambiguity which reflects their ambivalent relationship to the heterosexual majority. The situation is further complicated by the mixed if not muddled attitudes adopted by the majority towards the "deviants" in its midst. For instance the majority, which has a tendency to scoff at the findings of psychoanalysis in most cases, tends to accept its diagnosis of sexual deviancy, whereas almost all those to be considered here reject the theories of the childhood origins of their pattern of behaviour offered by Havelock Ellis, Kraft-Ebbing, Freud and his successors. The genre itself imposes strains on its practitioners because of its tendency to reveal more than they intended and because it encourages self-criticism on the part of the writer. One modern British autobiographer who is a bisexual has, in my opinion, responded to these generic characteristics by exploiting them rather than by trying to evade them. This is Stephen Spender in his autobiography. *World Within World* (1951). For this reason I have devoted the latter portion of this essay, after a survey of a number of other "sexual" autobiographies, to a more detailed, if still highly selective, consideration of this work. Like Rousseau he confronts the paradox of his situation head-on and makes of the conflicts inherent in that paradox the substance and form of his outstanding autobiography.

> *In Spender's case the desire to confess stems largely from his wish to win literary recognition from the 'normal' world, while his need to explore hetero- and homosexual forms of relationship places him not in a sub- but a supra-culture."*

II

It is possible to discern among the autobiographies of outsiders a recurrent pattern which reflects the outcast's need to win some form of social acceptance without abandoning his or her restless search for individual identity. Consider for a moment the autobiographies of black writers living in a predominantly white society. I am thinking of writers like Malcolm X, Richard Wright, Ezekiel Mphahlele or Maya Angelou. A very similar pattern of behaviour can be discerned in all of them. As members of an oppressed minority their early reactions are likely to include fantasies about finding themselves members of the dominant majority and bouts of self-accusation and guilt at their failure to earn acceptance from the white majority. Both traits betray a fundamental need to belong to the dominant social grouping so as to allay their latent feelings of childhood anxiety. Failure to achieve this and the threat this failure poses to their whole sense of identity lends them to seek a sense of belonging from within their minority group, usually by raising its (and therefore their) status in their eyes to one at least equal to that of the larger group which is responsible for their crisis in identity. A moment arrives when they do finally achieve a sense of their collective identity as blacks among blacks who are proud of their kind. Maya Angelou, for instance, has this experience on her high school graduation day when the senior black graduate turns his back on the platform with its hypocritical white politician and leads the year's class in an impromptu rendering of the black national anthem. This realisation of a collective identity appears to be an essential preliminary to the continuing search for individual identity. A sense of belonging to a wider social grouping releases the individual from a feeling of rootlessness and a consequent lack of normal self-esteem.

A similar pattern can be traced in the autobiographies of members of sexual minority groups. Jan Morris, a transsexual who felt him/herself from early childhood to be a woman born in a man's body, echoes, in her autobiography, *Conundrum* (1974), the feelings of her fellow exiles that her sense of disquiet came from her lack of any sense of identity which coincided with the identity conferred on her by society: "I was not to others what I was to myself." This condition she sees as the exact opposite to the dictionary definition of identity which she quotes—"the condition or fact that a person or thing is itself and is not something else." In his autobiography, *The Naked Civil Servant* (1968), Quentin Crisp, a homosexual, describes how he found himself in a similar predicament as a child, torn between his sexual fantasy that he was a woman, and the fact that he was biologically a boy. The fantasy is similar to that of the black child imagining that he or she is really white. In Crisp's case he took the fantasy to unusual lengths in his late teens by declaring his feminine proclivities in the form of nail-varnish, lipstick and what he calls "effeminate" dress. "By this process," he argues, "I managed to shift homosexuality from being a burden to being a cause. The weight lifted and some of the guilt evaporated." Crisp goes on to find his own kind in the Black Cat, a drab Soho café where flamboyant homosexuals would meet over tea to argue how homosexuality had been a source of national culture: "The great names of history from Shakespeare onward were fingered over and over like beads on a rosary" (30). Here at last was a group of men—like some minority religious sect—united by their desire to be feminine and by the persecution they suffered as a consequence of this innate desire. Yet even after meeting them his sense of group identity is extremely tenuous. He describes the group in the Black Cat as "pseudo-women in search of pseudo-men." And he points to a paradox underlying their sense of identity. Homosexuals of this kind "set out to win the love of a 'real' man. If they succeed they fail. A man who 'goes with' other men is not what they call a real man" (62).

It is worth recalling here the difference between sex and gender. Sex refers to the biological distinction between "male" and "female," while gender is a psychological and cultural distinction between "masculine" and "feminine." The last two terms may be applicable quite independently of biological sex. Gender identity can be the product of social conditioning and can refer to the sense an individual has of him- or herself as belonging to one sexual group or the other. It is ironical that psychoanalysts like Robert Stoller, John Money, and John and Joan Hampson, who did much of the pioneering work on problems of gender identity, also subscribe to the view that transsexualism and homosexuality are gender "disorders." They argue that male transsexuals and homosexuals have identified with their mothers far more closely than so-called "normal" men. It is claimed that transsexuals' sense of gender is wholly unseparated from that of their mothers, which is consequently directed to other men.

This explanation finds little corroboration in the autobiographies of transsexuals or homosexuals. Christopher Isherwood, for example, in his autobiography of the nineteen thirties, *Christopher and His Kind* (1976), maintains that his homosexuality was an assertion of defiance against his mother and society at large: "*My* will is to live according to my nature, and to find a place where I can be what I am." He sees his homosexuality as a conscious choice adopted not out of any unconscious identification with his mother but out of his need to remove himself from her domination. Of course one can argue that this interpretation is mere self-delusion, since few people care to believe that they are the unthinking products of sonic abnormality in their childhood development. Nevertheless Isherwood's account of his childhood in *Kathleen and Frank* (1971) contains little evidence to suggest that he was unduly identified with his mother during the first eleven years of his life. He saw more of the servants than of her.

Isherwood, the adult autobiographer, is patently concerned to construct his own myth around his sexual identity and shows impatience with psychoanalytical diagnoses of his condition. In the opening chapter of *Christopher and His Kind* Isherwood cheerfully quotes the Jungian psychoanalyst, John Layard, whom he met in Berlin, and who claimed, according to Isherwood, "that *anything* one invents about oneself is part of one's personal myth and therefore true" (4). Fur Isherwood, as for most autobiographers, the writing of this autobiography constituted an additional stage in his life-long endeavour to make his life conform to the myth or myths which had helped him to make sense of it. He has described an early draft of *Christopher and*

His Kind as "an attempt, influenced by Jung, to explore one's personal sexual mythology and identify one's sexual archetypes." His own dream lover is a foreigner and, unlike him, from the working class. In uniting with embodiments of this sexual archetype Isherwood achieved some kind of solidarity against the English upper-class culture from which he came and from which he desperately wanted to detach himself. By becoming homosexual he could at a stroke outlaw himself from his family, class and country. Homosexuality gave him an identity he could accept—that of the rebel, the wandering exile, the social outcast whose sense of freedom came from his rejection by the majority culture. It is interesting that Quentin Crisp also talks of the way homosexuals (by which he means those with a feminine sense of gender) "clutch with both hands at the myth of the great dark man." This masculine lover, however, in Crisp's case proves constantly elusive and is a source of life-long disappointment. Crisp and his compeers achieve a dubious kind of negative collective identity in their shared experience of perpetual frustration. Crisp's sexual archetype represents the shadow of Isherwood's conscious and positive projection. But both need an ideal male lover around whom they can construct a counterculture within which they can achieve a sense of their identity.

One of the most subtle and readable autobiographies in which a homosexual identity plays a key role is Elizabeth Wilson's *Mirror Writing* (1982). Early on in the book she displays many of the fantasies and suffers much of the guilt to be found in black autobiographies. Her early years as a teenager and young adult are marked by a series of poses she adopts which contrive to hide her lesbian nature behind the fashionable androgyny of the sixties. "Both trendy dolly and pretty boy," her aim became that of a generation—"to fuse, narcissistically, the glamour of the sexual object with the glamour of the sexual predator." In her striped trouser suit and huge-brimmed yellow Biba hat, she felt part of the majority culture, accepted as what she appeared to be. But behind this pose lay ambiguity and confusion, she realises in her retrospective review of the multiple mirror images she had adopted in the course of her life. Again and again she is confronted by reflections of past selves which simultaneously display and screen her inner self. Mirrors frequently form key images in women's autobiographies. While the traditional male artist uses the mirror for self-portraiture, women find themselves painting their faces in the looking-glass to conform to a male-formulated image of femininity

which deprives them of their own sense of identity. Elizabeth Wilson recalls one reflected image after another which she adopted in her desperate search for a socially acceptable identity. But her homosexuality constantly undermined her acceptance by others, especially as she was not prepared to settle for either traditional gender role in her lesbian relationships:

> My place was with the girlfriends and the wives—or was it? Yet I didn't belong with the men. So I often felt threatened by a kind of social extinction. I was a nothingness, neither masculine nor feminine. (90)

So acute was this feeling of negation that she tried reverting to heterosexuality. When the man cast in the role of her saviour rejected her she turned to psychoanalysis. But this concentration on individual identity failed to meet her needs at the time. This was partly because she could not subscribe to the Freudian concept of an unchanging identity and partly because she still lacked any sense of collective identity without which her various personal masks failed to find acceptance outside herself. Then in 1971 she participated in the formation of the Gay Liberation Front. This movement combined political revolt, sexual protest and a rejection of the psychoanalytical treatment of homosexuality as a perversity. "I was no longer a Fairy Carabosse," she recalls with relief (123). The first taste of sexual solidarity soon evaporated as the women found it necessary to detach themselves from the male gays and re-group under the Women's Movement. Nevertheless Gay Liberation at its height was the time, she claims, "when my lesbian identity achieved a kind of unitary coherence because it fused my socialism and my sexual politics" (129–30). Thereafter she felt free to abandon her three-year course of analysis and to pursue her quest for individual identity along lines of her own choosing.

The gender issue, she realises, had merely been an imposition from without. Her "most authentic self," she writes, "was not particularly a gendered self at all" (142). But what is that inner self? The "soul"? The author of her own autobiography? The observing self that can only be observed in the course of its observations? She calls it "the threshold between private interiors—worlds of fantasy—and the public domain where we became performers" (152). This begs as many questions as it answers. As if she recognised this, Elizabeth Wilson ends the book not with a definition but with an image of individual identity as a process, a continual becoming which can therefore only be discerned by retrospective reflection, by a leap into a room of mirrors which reflect back the leaper's image into infinity. Like so many autobiographers before her she feels compelled to resort to the indirection of symbolism when confronted with the enigma of her identity. That leap with which the book ends is as much an act of faith as any form of religious belief, just as the ungendered self could easily be taken as a description of the traditional concept of the soul.

At one point in her autobiography Elizabeth Wilson rather surprisingly claims that lesbianism was meant to give her "a transcendent identity that would melt masculinity and femininity together in some new and potent sense of self that improved upon both" (144). This search for wholeness in the face of an externally imposed gender is characteristic of most autobiographies written by members of sexual minority groups. Heterosexual couples have, to this way of thinking, simply succumbed to the sexual conditioning of their society and settled for half their full range of potentialities, This common rationalisation stems from that sense of nothingness which Elizabeth Wilson experienced when she was feeling imprisoned by the expectations of a gender role which she could not accept. Jan Morris had a similar experience in early adult life: "If I could not be myself, my subconscious seemed to be saying, then I would not be." Out of this sensation grew her mystical belief in the integrity of a self that transcended the limitations of the two genders. She represents the conundrum of her life as a quest for unity by the soul. In wishing to be transplanted as a boy into a female body she claims that she "was aiming at a more divine condition, an inner reconciliation" (18), and cites the ancients' belief that there was "something holy in a being that transcended the sexes" (23–4). The book ends with a prayer that one day she might transcend both her earlier life as a man and her later life as a woman.

Yet behind her spiritual desire to go beyond the gender differences which have made of her life one long ambiguity one can trace her original boyish adoration of womankind in preference to the male sex. This preference (or prejudice) no doubt originated in the mother's wish that her son had been a daughter and in the boy's unconscious desire to fulfil her wish so as to win her unreserved love. Her sexual bias repeatedly surfaces, as in her comparison between the repugnance she felt for the male world of the successful career on which she turned her back when still living as a man and her cultivation of the "impotent" but "real" world of women. Seen in this light, her opposing myth of transcending differences of gender appears to be answering her longing to win approval from her

society for her transsexuality. Her reticence about her relations with her parents and her refusal to probe into the original circumstances from which her obsession with changing sex arose point to her use of the genre for self-justification. André Manrois has observed that even "the severest autobiography remains a piece of special pleading." In *Conundrum* Jan Morris is far from severe on herself. In "Introductory" she goes so far as to admit that she is "disinclined to self-analysis." This is necessarily a disability in the field of autobiography.

Is this what accounts for the feeling of dissatisfaction with which the book leaves one? On the other hand is it possible for any transsexual who has gone through the complete surgical change of sex to allow him- or herself to examine his or her psycho-sexual history without bias? There is a strong probability that the psychological investment is too great to allow radical questioning of such a powerful obsession. Yet by its nature autobiography is self-referential and cannot help providing evidence of the writer's evasions and blindnesses. To assert, as Jan Morris does, that her compulsion to think of herself from early childhood as a woman was "sui generis" suggests an underlying fear of what she might find if she were to delve into the murkier depths of her sexual identity. To do this would entail asking such awkward questions as, why was it that only after her sex change did she allow herself to see men as desirable? Instead she offers a kind of pseudo-mysticism in which she becomes in her own eyes "a figure of fable or allegory" (15).

In *A Man's Tale,* the autobiography of John Pepper, a transvestite, *Conundrum* is dismissed with the comment: "how sad, he'd merely switched one half-personality for another." Not that Pepper himself didn't spend much of his life switching roles alternately from one gender to the other. But he was never prepared to settle for either in isolation. He resented from childhood the gender conditioning to which he was subjected, likening it to an amputation, but of the psyche. In reaction he found himself at the age of six or seven trying on his mother's underwear. As a young man, like most transvestites, he lived out what appears to have been a healthy heterosexual sex-life. But he found that his affairs with the opposite sex only led to what he calls "emotional imperialism" (34). In seeking in the other for the missing feminine half in himself he simultaneously found himself trying to chain her to him so as to maintain the sense of wholeness she gave him. "However," he points out, "imprisoned people couldn't ever be whole; they'd have to keep trying to escape to find their wholeness. Thus the proverbial war of the sexes" (33).

To reach this insight took him years of what he terms "pairings of cripples" (75). Meantime he compensated himself for the limitations of the masculine role he felt forced to play by continuing to spend periods of time dressed as a woman. On joining the Beaumont Society for transvestites he invented a feminine persona for himself whom he named Angela Summerfields. As in the case of Jan Morris, Pepper cites the ancients' view that—in this case—transvestism is a sign of divine endowment. To him it felt far more than a mere matter of dressing up in women's clothes. The act gave him a sense of god-like androgyny. When, for instance, he went out dancing as a man he simultaneously felt like "the whirling goddess"; it was as if, like a hermaphrodite he had fused sexually into his own flesh (37). Psychoanalysts would probably identify this sensation as retarded sexuality of the narcissistic kind. Pepper's frequent use of imagery drawn from the pantheon of the classical gods reveals what it was about transvestism that appealed to him—the sensation it gave him of having transcended the limitations of his gender conditioning.

It is therefore not that surprising that he finally turned to Tibetan Buddhism for a spiritual answer to his needs. For, "seeking to fuse the dynamic opposites of all creation, the male and female . . . was what the transcendental rites of the East were all about" (112). Buddhism incidentally offered him that sense of belonging to a like-minded group which has played so important a part in the autobiographies of other members of social minority groups. The effect of Buddhist teaching on Pepper was to give him a completely different understanding of what heterosexual love could become. With his latest female lover "the revived male" in him was able "to be more aware than ever of her Eve-ish charms, while the female alongside could know what it was like to *be* her" (137). This androgynous state of mind caused Angela, the transvestite, to start fading away. It appears that she was finally exorcised by the writing of the autobiography itself. Pepper concludes the book celebrating the "psychic unity" he realises he had been seeking all his life, a unity he considers indistinguishable from "a state of gracefulness" or "the completeness that precedes all creation" (137). It is for the reader to decide whether the autobiography represents a radical critique of the gender roles that the majority of us play out unthinkingly or whether it is another example of retrospective rationalisation. When, for instance, Pepper, dressed as a woman, says to himself, "If only my father could see me now," one cannot help speculating how far he was attempting to rival or alternatively to identify with his mother. Is *A Man's Tale* yet another example of an elaborate edifice constructed by an adult unwilling to face the source of his identity crisis in an arrested stage of childhood sexuality? And if this is so, is it another instance of art born out of repression? If this is the case then it is also true that this particular genre exposes more than others the sublimation involved.

Classical psychoanalytical theory sees all the sexual stances considered here as arrested stages of normal child development, defence mechanisms which enable "deviants" to enact sexual impulses which the neurotic represses. But they still represent arrested development at an infantile stage of sexuality. Members of sexual minorities, on the other hand, judging from the testimony in their autobiographies, are convinced that their unusual sexual proclivities are inborn or, as Isherwood would have it, self-chosen. The heterosexual majority mostly prefers to accept the explanations of Freud and his followers on this question and to see sexual minorities as unnatural, childish and therefore at best to be pitied and tolerated with condescension. Perhaps this ready acceptance of psychoanalytical theory by the prejudiced majority partly explains why most members of sexual minorities refuse to confront the application of that theory to the origins and circumstances surrounding their own sexual identity. Most of them mention the theory only to dismiss it with derision. Even Quentin Crisp, who admits in humorous fashion how he and his parents had constructed the classic Oedipal triangle "for all the world as if we had read the right books on psychology," immediately distances himself from the Freudian explanation by asserting that he soon came to require of his mother "not love so much as unconditional obedience." These autobiographies are partly the twentieth century inheritors of the tradition of the apology, the justification of a life, of which the greatest English example is Newman's *Apologia Pro Vita Sua*. But they normally combine self-justification with the urgent modern search for a sense of identity. The tradition of the apology encourages them to seek the sympathy and approval of the heterosexual majority who read their autobiographies, while the urge towards discovering their identity drives them to assert the culture of the minority groups they join as a defence against that same majority. The two traditions pull them in opposite directions, while neither encourages them to examine with any rigour the psychological roots of their sexuality.

III

An exception to most of these generalisations is Stephen Spender's *World Within World* (1951). This remarkable autobiography is not confined to a search for sexual identity alone. Poetry and politics play equally prominent parts. But his exploration of bisexuality features prominently. As a practitioner of autobiography he takes himself extremely seriously, describing himself as "an autobiographer restlessly searching for forms in which to express stages of my development." He also appears to be unusually honest about himself, and is quite prepared to expose himself to ridicule. His account of his childhood and parents is highly revealing, perhaps more so than he was aware of, and provides the reader with ample evidence on which to draw his or her own conclusions about the origins of his sexual conduct. The book, as he explains, begins, revolves around and ends with his childhood, so that its form reflects a belief that the key to his adult identity lies in his earlier years.

Spender's brief description of his parents comes within the opening pages and offers a pattern which, he proceeds to show, determined his subsequent development either positively or as a model against which to react. Often his reaction was a complicated mixture of positive and negative attitudes which, however self-contradictory, he courageously reveals in the hope that out of such mixed material a harmony might emerge. His autobiography, then, is genuinely exploratory in its search for a meaning that he will not allow himself to reach by over-simplification. A good example of this is his highly ambivalent relationship to his father. In the opening section he portrays his father as a man imbued with an abstract mind whose sense of unreality terrified the young Stephen. By turning everyday schoolboy tasks into such weighty issues as the Battle of Life, Honour or Duty, he implanted in his son a desire for the ideal at the expense of the real. Much of Spender's early adult sex life was the product of both of his parents' fear of discovering some shameful depravity in their son. In reaction to their fear that he might turn out to be some moral outcast he spent his early adult life taking various outcasts for lovers.

Spender warns his readers that his portrait of his father may be oversimplified by the fury of adolescence since his father died when he was seventeen. But in fact no such simplified response emerges from the book taken as a whole. When Spender was twelve his mother died and his father remarked to his headmaster how untouched his son

was by this event because of his youth. Spender recalls longing for his father to die so that he could demonstrate his grief to him as his father watched him from the grave. This complex fantasy can be interpreted either as the son harbouring a death-wish for his judgemental father or alternatively as an indication of his need to win his father's approval even at the expense of losing the flesh-and-blood reality. There is plenty of evidence to show that the father continued to make his ghostly presence felt in the years that followed. Spender's thirst for publicity is a straight reproduction of his father's own thirst for fame either for himself or for his son. It was his father who first implanted in him the seed of poetry when he was nine years old. Clearly the son is closely identified with a figure he ostensibly turned against in his late teens and this creates a fascinating tension within him between the ideal and the real, admiration and contempt. Christopher Isherwood, in reviewing *World Within World,* acutely observed the way in which the young son's fascinated hatred for his father became indistinguishable with the passing of time from love.

Spender's paradoxical relationship to his father re-surfaces in the paternal role he assumed in his homosexual affairs with Walter and Jimmy Younger. In Walter's case he saw his lover's faults as projections of his own guilt, a guilt which originally had been implanted in him by his father. Walter was the moral outcast his father had so dreaded discovering in his son. By taking Walter as his lover Spender was simultaneously rebelling against the memory of his father and yet internalising his father's disapproval to such an extent that he felt compelled to treat the outcast's failings as his own. His longer account of his more committed affair with Jimmy Younger reveals the way in which he cast Jimmy in the role of himself as a boy by playing out the role his father had performed in his earlier life. As he writes, "Jimmy had really become the son whom I attempted to console, but of whom I was the maddening father." It is as if he casts his male lovers in the role of outcast sons in order to confront the father in himself with the moral depravity he so feared—not just confront him with it but have him understand and forgive it. This desire to turn his internalised father into the good and lovable parent would square with classical Freudian theory which would expect him in his homosexual phases to identify with his mother's erotic feelings for the father. He also claims to have played out a paternal role in his first disastrous marriage with Inez. But the scenario between them is entirely different in that she became, according to him, a substitute daughter to him rather than an embodiment of his earlier self.

Clearly his mother, of whom he remembers less, also played a key role in his unusual childhood. A semi-invalid, with a tragic perception of life, she was given to violent fluctuations of mood. In the course of describing the way in which she habitually put him down, Spender implicitly indicates the extent to which he nevertheless identified with her: "She recognised in me someone as hypersensitive as herself and snubbed me accordingly, being, like many sensitive people, unable to resist wounding those as vulnerable as herself, in revenge for wounds she suffered from the seemingly invulnerable." When he meets Elizabeth, who becomes his lover, the first thing he notices about her before they have even spoken to each other is her resemblance to photographs of his mother taken before he could remember her: "In her appearance there was a look of her having suffered at some time." Subsequently he sees in her suffering "something which after all I could console." This is a very different way of relating to a lover than the entangled web of guilt and blame he spun around his relationships with the male lovers in his life. It is as if he wants to replay his brief early years with his mother and this time win her whole-hearted love by consoling her for all the hurts she received from the harsh outside world.

His affair with Elizabeth ran side by side with his continuing relationship with Jimmy who was completely dependent on Spender at this time. Spender recalls his own deep-seated ambivalence during this period of his life, his constitutional inability to choose between his two lovers of opposite sexes. He appears to blame himself for this lack of decisiveness and the guilt that ensued. This is at odds with a declaration he makes earlier in the book in favour of bisexuality. There he asks whether people should feel forced to choose between homosexuality and heterosexuality. This was never felt necessary, he argues, in the past, for instance in Shakespeare's time. He is even-handed in his condemnation of the artificiality of such a choice, denouncing the homosexual chauvinism which he undoubtedly met among friends such as Auden with as much vigour as he scorns conventional heterosexuality. He also offers a definition of "normal" that is at variance with the psychoanalytic understanding of normality: "what is 'normal' for the individual is simply to conform with his own nature." What he means by his own nature is something he sets out to uncover in the course of the autobiography. It is complex, not simple, bi- rather than uni-sexual, and often self-contradictory.

The presence of self-contradiction in the book suggests that Spender is attempting a more honest portrait of his own vacillations and changes in direction than is usual. He is prepared to abandon narrative consistency where his own past inconsistencies come into conflict with it. One of the most glaring inconsistencies in the book is that between his early championing of bisexuality and his later evaluation of the relative rewards that hetero- and homosexual relationships have to offer. Ostensibly he argues that each type of relationship has a mutually exclusive set of properties. Relationships between men express a need for self-identification, one in which their work, ideas, play and physical beauty correspond with each other. Relationships between opposite sexes, on the other hand, according to Spender express the need to relate to all that is opposite and different from the self. It seems more than likely that Spender was indebted to D.H. Lawrence for his concept of woman as "otherness," the unknown. This concept, however, leads him, as it did Lawrence, into a negative definition of homosexual relationships, since men reach "a static situation where everything that is possible to be known between two people is known." On looking back at both types of relationship he decides that homosexual relationships are inherently destructive because they reach a point of stasis which prevents further development of the self. This seems a dubious conclusion. What he means by self-identification appears to be some form of total projection onto the male other. But surely the male other can be no more "knowable" than the opposite sex? Indeed at one point in the book he explicitly states that there is "something withdrawn, inaccessible and unexplained" about the motives of others of both sexes about whom he attempted to write "in the spirit of . . . exploring the unknown."

His generalisations are evidently based on his own particular experience and are more interesting if taken as insights into his unique history than as observations about the nature of homo- and heterosexual love in the abstract. It becomes apparent in the course of the book that he unquestioningly accepts traditional gender roles and does not cast his male lovers into either stereotyped part. With women he bases his relationships on the difference in gender and uses the women in his life to play out the unexplored feminine side of his personality. That is why they come to represent for him "the wholeness of a life outside" him, the missing otherness which is "unknown" because unexplored in himself. He asserts that each kind of sexual relationship met needs in him which the other could not hope to do. Nevertheless he comes down in favour of his heterosexual relationships based on the difference between the two sexes because he found them "the most enduring."

Even this definition of heterosexual relationships is at odds with the description he gives of his two marriages. The first marriage to Inez was a failure, he concludes, not because they failed to offer one another otherness, but because their love, he writes, "was not of a kind which made us feel as though we were always one person. We were never completely together." His second successful marriage to Natasha was founded, he explains enigmatically, on "the research for a unity which was ourselves belonging to one another." What is one to make of this chain of contradictions running all the way through the autobiography? Is it that Spender feels free to write what he believes while generalising but under the need to compromise when writing about individuals such as his second wife who were still alive when he was writing the book? After all, compromise for the sake of the living is an inherent characteristic of the genre. Or is it a conscious cultivation of subjectivity? Does he feel more comfortable with the contradictions experienced in the course of his life exposed for all to detect in the narrative of that life? Alternatively are these contradictions a reflection of that opposition between the real and the ideal which was implanted in him as a child? Ideally he would like to feel that both kinds of relationship contribute to a more integrated sense of identity than either does on its own. But in reality he appears to have found more fulfilment in his long-standing hererosexual marriage to Natasha which has survived to the present day.

Another motive also plays a part in the drama of his conflicting loyalties towards rival points of view. As a writer he shows latent fear of becoming alienated from the heterosexual majority by the exclusivity that the homosexual sub-culture tends to construct around itself. "For the artist to feel cut off from this warm flow of the normal general life, is to cut himself off from what absorbs other people, perhaps also to place himself too much in the company of those who feel cut off in the same way." In the same passage he argues that homosexuals really ought to do their best to adjust themselves "to the generally held concept of the normal." This definition of the normal is in conflict with the definition previously cited, as he acknowledges. Does this need to contradict himself so blatantly indicate a further division of loyalties? Did his ambition as a writer induce him to adopt a partial stance towards genuine bisexuality? Just as Isherwood constructed a myth of romantic homosexual love to meet his need to break with family and country, so Spender appears to have constructed his theory about the superiority of heterosexuality to homosexuality to satisfy his desire to make his name as a poet in the heterosexual world.

My exclusive concentration on Spender's search for a sexual identity could be misleading. Equally important to him is the search for his identity as a writer. *World Within World* does not just describe this search; it enacts it. Towards the end of the book he defines what he understands by poetic form—"the struggle of certain living material to achieve itself within a pattern." If life is a struggle to achieve a form of wholeness called "identity," then the narrative of his life mirrors this struggle. He argues that the "refusal of a poet to sacrifice what he means to a perfectly correct rhyme . . . can more powerfully suggest the rhyme than correctness would." In the same way his refusal to sacrifice the contradictory nature of his experience of life is able to suggest the wholeness or form he is seeking in his life and in his autobiography without bending the facts of his life to achieve it. In terms of sexual identity he is searching for an integration of the different senses of self that different kinds of sexual relationship can offer him. The search is what is important, even if the particular compromise he has reached is partial.

Whatever confusion he shows is the result of daring to experience more than most people do and then sharing his experience and his confusion with the reading public. His struggle to find his sexual identity interacts with his struggle to achieve literary form within the autobiography which itself constitutes a further stage in his search for identity. His confusions and contradictions contribute to a self-portrait which partly depends for its effect on the humour with which he depicts his own conflicting nature. The humour which he employs in the book is not simply a literary strategy but a reflection of an attitude towards life. In his review of the book Isherwood shrewdly claimed that Spender's comic exaggeration of the clownish, self-mocking elements in his own character was a way of protecting himself from becoming the fool his father made of himself in public appearances. At the same time it prevents him from taking himself and his sexual search too seriously. One recalls, for instance, the comic scene in which an overladen Moroccan donkey reminded him of the way he had lumbered Jimmy Younger with "loads of ideas, of music, of literature, of politics." No one in the book is more the object of satire than himself. Yet the comic element never prevents Spender from offering penetrating analyses of characters or situations. V.S. Pritchett, himself a master of comic autobiography, called the book "sincere farce." It is this combination of seemingly opposed elements that allows Spender to admit self-contradiction within his struggle to find form. Ultimately it is as much his skilful employment of the formal elements in the autobiography as its unusually honest exposure of his emotional and sexual experiences that is responsible for its high repute within the genre.

IV

It has already been shown how autobiographies concerned with sexual identity seem generally to be constructed around two contradictory needs—the need for self-justification in the eyes of the heterosexual majority, and the need to establish an identity of kind which inevitably revolves championing the minority group in the face of the majority. Many of the contradictions that I have identified in *World Within World* stem from this clash of sub-genres. The desire of the apologist to confess and win absolution conflicts with the longing to belong to a social group of similarly inclined individuals. In Spender's case the desire to confess stems largely from his wish to win literary recognition from the "normal" world, while his need to explore hetero- and homosexual forms of relationship places him not in a sub- but a supra-culture. What distinguishes Spender's contribution to the genre is the greater frankness with which he traces these conflicting sets of needs back to their origins in his childhood scenario. His need for praise, like his need to embrace the sexual outcast, can both be traced back to his parents, the father in particular. By revolving his autobiography around his childhood Spender provides us with primary evidence (however much he has shaped it for his own purposes) from which we can judge for ourselves the extent to which classical psychoanalytical explanations of sexual "deviation" appear valid. Most of the other examples examined in this sub-genre withhold the evidence needed to make such a judgement. Because autobiography by its nature is self-referential, omissions as glaring as these only serve to expose the partiality and defensiveness of the majority of autobiographers in search of a sexual identity. They provide fascinating insights into the by-ways of human sexual behaviour and the myths that are constructed around them. But ultimately they tend to evade the issue of normality, abnormality and their origins, and leave in the reader a sense of disappointment that they have failed to rise to the full potential of the exacting genre they have been using.

Source: Brian Finney, "Sexual Identity in Modern British Autobiography," in *Prose Studies*, Vol. 8, No. 2, September 1985, pp. 29–44.

Sources

Freadman, Richard, "Ethics, Autobiography and the Will: Stephen Spender's *World within World*," in *The Ethics in Literature*, edited by Andrew Hadfield, Dominic Rainsford, and Tim Woods, Macmillan Press, 1999, p. 35.

Marx, Karl, and Engels, Frederick, *The Communist Manifesto*, International Publishers, 1948, pp. 27, 44.

Slavitt, David R., "Poetic Justice," in *Boulevard*, Vol. 18, No. 2 and 3, Spring 2003, p. 94.

Spender, Stephen, "An Elementary School Classroom in a Slum," in *Collected Poems 1928–1985*, Faber and Faber, 1985, pp. 46–47.

Further Reading

Huntington, Samuel P., *The Clash of Civilizations and the Remaking of World Order*, Simon and Schuster, 1998.
    Huntington analyzes world politics after the fall of Communism. Much of what was at the heart of Marxist revolutionary theory still remains, with an increasing threat of violence arising from renewed conflicts between countries and cultures that base their traditions on religious faith and dogma.

Marx, Karl, *Capital: A Critique of Political Economy*, Vol. 1, Penguin Classics, 1992.
    Capital, an influential book considered by many to be Marx's greatest work, details the faults of the capitalist system and is based on Marx's thirty-year study of capitalism in England, the most advanced industrial society of Marx's day.

Richardson, R. Dan, *Comintern Army: The International Brigades and the Spanish Civil War*, University Press of Kentucky, 1982.
    Richardson explores the history of the International Brigades, the volunteer army that fought on the side of the Spanish Republic during the Spanish Civil War. He contends that the brigade was an instrument of the Soviet Communists. Spender served for a short time in 1937 as a member of this brigade.

Sutherland, John, *Stephen Spender: A Literary Life*, Oxford University Press, 2005.
    Sutherland uses information gleaned from Spender's private papers to create this insightful biography of Spender's life and the literary society in which he was immersed.

Fiddler Crab

Josephine Jacobsen

1950

"Fiddler Crab" was, according to the chronological sections in Josephine Jacobsen's collection of poetry *In the Crevice of Time: New and Collected Poems* (1995), written between 1950 and 1965. Unfortunately, no exact date is available for the poem's original publication. In fact, since this collection is subtitled *New and Collected Poems*, the poem may have been written between 1950 and 1965 but not published before its inclusion in this collection.

"Fiddler Crab" is a good example of a primary theme that runs through Jacobsen's entire body of work. In this poem, Jacobsen explores the connectivity between all living things and God through her observation of a fiddler crab on the beach. This poem conveys religious principles through a narrative storyline. Her decision to deliver her beliefs in this fashion is intentional and, in fact, makes the poem timeless.

Regardless of when it was written or published, "Fiddler Crab" resonates with Jacobsen's religious exploration and understanding. Where other poems may reflect on society, Jacobsen's poetry reflects upon God and the exploration of the human soul. With this at the helm of Jacobsen's thought, her poetry is written without a social reference. Her work is far too personal to be tied to anything but her own search for truth and understanding. Jacobsen was a self-proclaimed devout Catholic, and although her work is rich spiritually, it is rarely preachy. Her message is warm, clever, and devout. With her massive, far-reaching collection of work, Jacobsen is

heralded as one of the finest, most respectable poets of the twentieth century.

Author Biography

Josephine Jacobsen was born August 19, 1908, in Cobourg, Ontario, Canada. Soon after her birth, Jacobsen's family moved from Canada to New York. The Jacobsens then moved to Baltimore, Maryland, when Josephine was fourteen years old. She was educated by private tutors at Roland Park Country School and graduated in 1926.

Jacobsen was renowned as a poet, short-story writer, and critic. She served as the Consultant in Poetry to the Library of Congress from 1971 to 1973 (a position that has since been renamed Poet Laureate Consultant in Poetry) and as honorary consultant in American letters from 1973 to 1979. In addition to these duties, Jacobsen was the vice president of the Poetry Society of America in 1978 and 1979. Jacobsen was also a member of both the literature panel for the National Endowment of the Arts and the poetry committee of Folger Library from 1979 to 1983.

Somehow, amidst all these remarkable responsibilities, Jacobsen was able to write numerous collections, including, but not limited to, *The Instant of Knowing: Lectures on Criticism, and Occasional Prose* (1997); *What Goes without Saying: Collected Short Stories* (1996); *In the Crevice of Time: New and Collected Poems* (1995), a collection spanning nearly sixty years of writing; *The Chinese Insomniacs* (1981); and *The Shade-Seller: New and Selected Poems* (1974). Her extraordinary writing career spanned an astounding eight decades, with her first poem published in a children's magazine at the age of ten.

In the Crevice of Time: New and Collected Poems is Jacobsen's most expansive collection of poetry. The book is broken into five sections, each section covering a portion of Jacobsen's life as a poet. The second section of the collection spans the years 1950–1965 and includes the poem "Fiddler Crab." This poem is a timeless work that is an excellent example of Jacobsen's thinking and writing. In this poem, Jacobsen explores religion and God, concluding that the universe and all creatures are tied together by the struggle for survival. This theme features in the bulk of Jacobsen's writing and interviews, acting as a personal mantra about her understanding of her own life, all life, and God.

Josephine Jacobsen   Erlend Jacobsen

Jacobsen's clear, resounding voice and her exploration of the spiritual world garnered her great praise. In 1988, she won the L. Marshal Award for the best book of poetry. She was awarded the Shelley Memorial Award for lifetime service to literature in 1993 and was inducted into the American Academy of Arts and Letters in 1994. Additionally, the Poetry Society of America gave her its highest honor—the Robert Frost Medal for Lifetime Achievement in Poetry—in 1997. Jacobsen's awards and honors also include a Doctor of Humane Letters from Goucher College, the College of Notre Dame in Maryland, Towson State University, and Johns Hopkins University. Jacobsen died July 9, 2003, in Cockeysville, Maryland, at the age of ninety-four.

Poem Text

The fiddler crab fiddles, glides and dithers,
dithers and glides, veers; the stilt-eyes
pop, the legs prance, the body glides, stops,
the front legs paw the air like a stallion,
at a fast angle he veers fast, glides, stops,   5
dithers, paws.

The water is five shades of blue. On the rocks
of the reefridge the foam yelps leaping, the big
    rock

here is glutted with breathers under their clamped
    clasp,
scarab shapes and tiny white and black whorls.   10
The lacy wink lapses, behind it the black lustre
lapses and dulls.

I saw the fiddler crab veer, glide, prance,
dither and paw, in elliptical rushes
skirt the white curve and flatten on the black   15
shine. He veered in a gliding rush
and up to piled sand and into a trembling hole
where grains fell past him.

I imitated him with my five fingers, but not well.
Nothing else moved on the sand. He came out.   20
My hand cast a shadow. He raised a notch and ran
in tippity panicky glide to the wave's wink.
Each entirely alone on his beach; but who
is the god of the crabs?

On the balcony over the rocks two hours later   25
The Spanish-Chinese boy brought him to show.
His stilted eyes popped over three broken legs
but he ran with the rest of them over the edge
and died on the point of the drop down
twenty feet.   30

So it is simple: he can be hurt
and then he can die. In all his motions
and marine manoeuvres it was easy to miss
on the sand how I should know him and he me
and what subject matter we have in common.   35
It is our god.

Poem Summary

Stanza 1

In the opening stanza of "Fiddler Crab," Jacobsen describes the fiddler crab as it moves through its routine on the beach. The prehistoric beast "veers," "glides," and "dithers." It repeats its motions endlessly, over and over, as if it is completing its necessary tasks. With this descriptive stanza, Jacobsen intends to draw similarities between the fiddler crab and other organisms. She compares the crab to a horse, stating the crab's "front legs paw the air like a stallion." However, the crab relates to more than just a stallion. The crustacean's activities are similar to those of human beings. Both organisms go through their regular routines. Whether it is a human being moving and shifting through society or a crab veering and dithering about on the beach, both organisms are living their lives just as they believe they should.

Jacobsen also alludes to the crab's power to observe, stating, "the stilt-eyes / pop," as if to imply that the crab is observing his surroundings and assessing his next move. This gives the crab human traits, grouping the organisms together into an expansive, undefined category.

Stanza 2

In the second stanza, Jacobsen portrays the crab's world: the rocky beach and the shifting tide. The water on the beach moves over the rocks, and "foam yelps leaping." The big rocks are "glutted with breathers under their clamped clasp." Jacobsen is describing the rocks covered with barnacles and other shellfish, holding desperately to the rocks as the waves wash over them, creating frothy, turbulent waters. She alludes to the waves as a "lacy wink" that "lapses and dulls."

The waves on the beach move unhindered over the rocks and the sand. The rocks and the sand compose the society in which the crab exists. The waves represent time as it "lapses and dulls" society, crashing over and over again against the rocky beach. Like the waves, time can move fast or slowly, be disruptive or benign. Yet no matter how time *washes* over one and changes one's life for better or worse, time itself is completely amoral. The impact of time is easy to see—people age, the sun rises and sets, the seasons pass—what goes unanswered is why time does what it does. Jacobsen's answer is linked to the concept of amorality. Time is amoral because it works beyond any moral code. Time passed before there were human beings, and time will continue to pass after the end of human beings; thus it is set apart from that which would be considered right or wrong, moral or immoral. It is without an ethical code, because it exists outside the realm of moral judgment. Hence, the crab is affected by time similarly to a human being precisely because time makes no distinction between the crab and a human being.

Generally, a person is not disturbed when someone kills a crab. Most people, however, are disturbed when a human being kills a fellow human being. Time makes no such distinction. The morality of these two actions is outside the scope of time, as are all forms of morality. With these lines, the fiddler crab becomes just as dramatically affected by time as humankind, binding the organisms together at a level beyond, yet still anchored in, the physical world.

Stanza 3

In the third stanza, Jacobsen enters the poem as a first-person voice. She witnesses and observes the crab's plight and struggle against the tide. She writes, "I saw the fiddler crab veer, glide, prance, / dither and paw, in elliptical rushes / skirt the white curve and flatten on the black / shine." The crab is battling against the elements, trying its best to survive and live well as the tide rushes forward. Jacobsen is empathizing with the crab from the common ground that all organisms must battle the elements of the world and struggle against them for survival. The crab rushes into a "trembling hole" to avoid the crushing surf. Jacobsen would argue that all creatures must, at some point, seek a safe haven from the uncontrollable tempests or face the only other alternative: death. With this, Jacobsen indirectly frames *life* as the struggle for survival that occurs between a creature's birth and its death.

Stanza 4

In the fourth stanza, Jacobsen reveals that she is standing on the beach with the crab. This draws her directly into the crab's world, intricately tying Jacobsen to this particular fiddler crab. The two suddenly are not of separate worlds; they are simply affected by different elements, in different ways, within the same world. She writes, "I imitated him with my five fingers, but not well." The crab is much better at being a crab than Jacobsen is. However, when the crab comes out of his hole, he runs in a "tippity panicky glide to the wave's wink," showing that Jacobsen is much better at being a human than the crab is, because Jacobsen does not have to run or hide from the wave's power. Last, Jacobsen writes, "Each entirely alone on his beach; but who / is the god of the crabs?" Although Jacobsen has identified that she and the crab coexist in the same world and that both creatures' lives are defined by their individual struggles for survival in the world, Jacobsen questions what god has created the crab's world.

Stanza 5

In this fifth stanza, Jacobsen returns to strict observation and gives a short narrative about the crab's final moments. She writes,

> The Spanish-Chinese boy brought him to show.
> His stilted eyes popped over three broken legs
> but he ran with the rest of them over the edge
> and died on the point of the drop down
> twenty feet.

Jacobsen tells the story of the boy and of the crab plunging to its death. The crab struggled to free himself from the boy. After freeing himself, the crab tried to run for safety, plunging to his death twenty feet below. This moment in conjunction with the crab's birth frames the crab's life and ends its struggle against the elements of the world.

Stanza 6

In the final stanza, Jacobsen sees the simplicity of existence in the crab's death. She writes, "So it is simple: he can be hurt / and then he can die." After all her observations and conclusions about the differences and similarities between herself and the crab, Jacobsen ends with a base understanding of life as pain and the struggle against death. Although it may take on different forms—for example, for the crab it was the surf and the Spanish-Chinese boy, whereas it may be an earthquake or cancer for a human being—all creatures face the same essential challenge for survival. If this is accepted as true, then, as Jacobsen professes at the end of "Fiddler Crab," the "subject matter we [all] have in common . . . is our god."

Themes

The Levels of Time

In Jacobsen's poem "Fiddler Crab," time is a principal theme. Time plays a tricky role in the lives of most humans. Frequently, time seems to pass at differing rates. Sometimes it flies by, and at other moments it creeps. When a person looks back on events from the past, some of them seem as if they happened only yesterday, while others seem as if they happened to a different person, in a different life. Oddly, these feelings may not be hinged to events chronologically. In fact, more often than not, the variable feeling of the passage of time is intricately tied to the suffering of the individual. For example, in Jacobsen's own life, she recalled a wonderful day spent with her husband some twenty years in the past, which seemed to have just taken place. But when she recollected her grandson's death—a painful event that occurred long after the wonderful day spent with her husband—she told Evelyn Prettyman in an interview for *New Letters*, "I remember when I went back to our summer house the summer after our grandson's death . . . it seemed to me that there were hundreds of years between that summer and the summer before." This level of time is a pervasive theme in "Fiddler Crab" and in all of Jacobsen's work.

In the poem, it is fair to assume that time is similar to the tide and the waves. This is metaphoric on several levels. First, time seems to happen in irregular intervals. The waves represent the strange, unpredictable moments in time. The tide, like minutes, hours, days, and weeks, can be predicted and plotted. However, the moments—the waves—still

Topics For Further Study

- In "Fiddler Crab," Jacobsen draws a connection between herself as a human being and the fiddler crab she observes on a beach. Her poem intricately ties humanity to all living things through shared suffering, struggle, and death. This commonality leads Jacobsen to assume that all living things share the same god. Research Native American beliefs and the ways in which their observations connect humans to animals. How do the beliefs of Native Americans mirror or oppose Jacobsen's understanding?

- Select an animal that you feel mimics your life and write a poem describing the animal, its movements and activities in the world, and its relation to you. Beyond simple observation of the animal, try to draw similarities between the animal and your physical manifestation as well as any connectivity you might detect about the animal's essence and your own being. On the other hand, if you find no connectivity between your being and the animal's or if you do not believe in the

concept of a soul in general or that either you or the animal has a soul, express this opinion through your poem.

- Jacobsen was a devout Catholic, and although her work is not heavily religious, it does carry a clear spiritual message. What other stories or poems have you read that also carry a spiritual message? Select one other story or poem and try to draw a link between the work and a particular religion or spiritual path.

- Jacobsen began writing poetry and fiction at the age of ten. Her work was always heavily influenced by her Catholic upbringing, and her devotion to Catholicism did not waver. Select another poet from the twentieth century with a large corpus of work spanning many decades and choose a variety of poems from his or her expansive collection. Do you notice a change in the feeling or motive of the work as the poet ages? Explain your selected poet's transformation, or lack thereof, in a short essay.

---

remain an unpredictable mystery. Just as time clearly passes from today to tomorrow, so do the tides shift from high to low, but from moment to moment the waves that hit the shore are like the mysterious instances that cause humans to feel a strange relationship to time and its passing. These mysterious instances happen in the present. The effects that follow are unpredictable. When an event happens, a moment passes, a person does not know its effect until it is over and the person has reflected upon it. In the poem, most of the waves that the crab struggles against are nothing remarkable and so have little impact on his life. But the one wave that washes him into the boy's hands, or off to sea, or into a fertile feeding ground will have a profound effect on his life, though he is unaware of this impact until that particular, mysterious instance has passed.

From a different perspective, time frames existence. For Jacobsen, life is a struggle for survival,

with a beginning and an end. At birth a creature comes into being and effectively starts surviving, starts living; at death the creature stops surviving, stops living. This simplistic understanding of time is applicable across the board to the lives of all creatures. That there is a beginning and an ending to life is true for all creatures, human or not. Since Jacobsen believes that the gift of life is given by God, all life, human or not, comes from God. Without time framing life, it would be difficult for Jacobsen to reach the conclusion that life is the same for all creatures and that God is the same for all creatures.

These analyses of time, no matter how interesting, come from a human dissection of something eternal. They cannot be wholly explained with common intellectual analysis. Jacobsen often delves into these profound questions in her poetry. In this case, she accepts that she will never be able to fully understand the impact of time because, effectively, they lead to questions about God. For Jacobsen, the unanswered questions about God are satisfied by her faith in the Catholic Church. Faith and religion fill the holes left by her human dissection of time and the unanswerable questions about God. Without her leap of faith, these questions would remain unsatisfied.

Life as Survival

In "Fiddler Crab," Jacobsen observes a crab's existence and, in doing so, defines life as the struggle for survival against the elements of the world. The crab must battle the never-ending pounding of the surf. The crab "fiddles, glides and dithers / dithers and glides, veers" in a ceaseless dance to continue living. Later, Jacobsen notes that the fiddler crab, "veered in a gliding rush / and up to piled sand and into a trembling hole / where grains fell past him." The crab not only dances about, dodging the surf, but also must take shelter in holes and "skirt the white curve [of the wave] and flatten on the black shine." The crab's existence on the rocky beach is nothing but a moment-to-moment struggle for survival against the constant, aggressive assault from an amoral force: the surf. As if this daily routine were not enough, the crab must also survive other elements: other creatures.

In the poem, "two hours later," after Jacobsen has stopped observing the fiddler crab, a Spanish-Chinese boy has captured the fiddler crab. The crab, battling for survival against the waves, may never have seen the approaching boy. When Jacobsen returns to the scene, the boy has the crab on a balcony; the crustacean now has "three broken legs / but he ran with the rest of them over the edge / and died on the point of the drop down / twenty feet." The crab's life and struggle for survival were framed by his birth and his death, a twenty-foot fall. Here again the observation of the crab's complex struggle—the constant fiddling, gliding, and dithering—is reduced to a simple, frank existence: birth and death. Everything that passed between was just surviving, just life.

The Commonality of God

The two themes of time and life as survival come to an apex with a simple understanding of life as that which occurs between birth and death. The time between these two events is a painful struggle to stay alive. In "Fiddler Crab," Jacobsen observes that she and the crab share this plight. She writes, "So it is simple: he can be hurt / and then he can die." Just like the crab, Jacobsen could be hurt and,

just like the crab, someday she will lose her struggle for survival and die. This is a difficult conclusion to reach, because Jacobsen and the fiddler crab look so dissimilar and live so differently. A human and a fiddler crab: What could they possibly have in common? Strangely enough, the answer, for Jacobsen, is of immense proportions. She concludes in her poem "Fiddler Crab" that "it was easy to miss / on the sand how I should know him and he me / and what subject matter we have in common. / It is our god." Laying all characteristics aside that separate and distinguish Jacobsen from the fiddler crab—and all humans from all fiddler crabs or any one creature from another—there is beneath these differences a struggle for survival. This struggle is life, and this life is given by a creator to the creatures. For Jacobsen, that creator is God. Hence, if creatures struggle for a common survival that defines their lives, then that life must also come from a common god. Therefore, Jacobsen would argue, all creatures have in common the god that gives them life.

Style

Narrative Poetry

Narrative poetry is generally a nondramatic style of poetry in which the author tells a story. In "Fiddler Crab," Jacobsen tells a story about the life of a fiddler crab on a beach. The construction of the narrative is simple. Jacobsen witnesses the crab's activities and motion on the beach, battling the surf. She describes the beauty of the water, the rocks, and the frothing waves. Jacobsen brings herself into the narrative, imitating the crab with her hand and casting a shadow across the beach. In addition, Jacobsen introduces another character—the Spanish-Chinese boy—who is ultimately responsible for the crab's demise. Although Jacobsen uses the poem to deliver a message about life and God, "Fiddler Crab" is still an example of narrative poetry.

Personification

In "Fiddler Crab," the crab takes on human qualities, showing the similarities between Jacobsen and the crab. The crab's "body glides" and "dithers" like that of a dancer or a boxer. The creature observes and reacts to life, and Jacobsen refers to the crab in a friendly way, calling the creature "he" and "him." The crab's human qualities lead Jacobsen to believe that they share a common struggle, which in turn suggests to Jacobsen that they share a common god. Without some catalyst to

Compare & Contrast

- **1950s:** The U.S. presidency term is restricted to eight years.

  Today: The U.S. presidency is still restricted to eight years, but there are discussions about removing the requirement that an individual must be born a U.S. citizen in order to run for president.

- **1950s:** It is reported that lung cancer is linked directly to smoking. However, tobacco companies continue to produce and sell cigarettes without any repercussions.

  Today: Millions of people still smoke cigarettes, even though the habit has been linked directly to many diseases. However, tobacco companies are increasingly held responsible for producing and selling dangerous products to consumers.

- **1950s:** James Watson and Francis Crick decipher the structure of DNA, opening an entirely new field of biological study: genetics.

  Today: DNA is at the forefront of scientific exploration into genetic disease, stem-cell research, and cloning. Religious and scientific communities are at odds with one another as the struggle between God and science continues.

- **1950s:** Racial segregation in American schools is declared unconstitutional.

  Today: Although racial segregation is still unconstitutional, the American education system continues to suffer under the division of wealth, with students from wealthy neighborhoods receiving a better education than students from poor neighborhoods.

---

draw a connection between the crab and Jacobsen, there would be no way the poet could effectively deliver the message of a common, life-giving god.

The Effects of Irregular Rhythm

Although the poem is narrative in style and tells the story of the fiddler crab, it also irregularly changes rhythm, instilling different emotions in the reader. The first three stanzas are frantic and frenetic as the crab eludes the waves, whereas the last three are slow and introspective. Even though the crab's struggle for survival wanes and eventually ends in the last three stanzas, the rhythm of the poem does not reflect sadness. Instead it presents the crab's death rather in a matter-of-fact way, bolstering Jacobsen's analysis of life rather than focusing on the dramatic, painful demise of the crab.

Historical Context

Spirituality and Catholicism

Jacobsen's "Fiddler Crab" is set in an indeterminate time and a nonspecific place. The poem has no direct relationship to any moment in history for

two reasons. First, a primary theme of the poem is time and its levels. To adequately address the questions of the levels of time (for example, eternity), framing life between birth and death, a sense of proportion, and so forth, the poem cannot be fixed to or affected by any one relative moment. In order for Jacobsen's observations and commentary on time to maintain a sense of timelessness, she must question the nature of time outside any reference to history and chronology. Although "Fiddler Crab" was written sometime between 1950 and 1965, no particular date is given or referenced in the poem.

Second, Jacobsen avoids any reference to a particular time or place because the poem is also a personal exploration of faith. Jacobsen is a self-proclaimed devout Catholic, and her personal spiritual journey is long and introspective. Her body of work clearly outlines how she feels about human life as a struggle for survival. Religion, or faith, is present in much of her writings, and she works from simple facts. These simple facts are free of the convulsions of history, free of varied perspectives of particular moments. For example, in "Fiddler Crab" she concludes, even through rigorous analysis of

A male fiddler crab on the beach © Joe McDonald/Corbis

time and life, that for all living creatures life is a struggle for survival. From this very simple fact, Jacobsen assumes, in the context of her faith, that life is given by God—not just human life, but all life. This solves the problem of multiple gods, because there is no need for a Crab God and a Human God if life is defined the same for all creatures. There is a difficulty with this model, in that it does not introduce an ethic. Yet an ethic is unnecessary at this basic level. Ethics are formed by human and social interests. Hence, this type of spirituality cannot be seen through a political, social, or historical lens. Not only is it a religious analysis of life, it is also an individualistic analysis of life.

Jacobsen is inexplicably tied to the physical world because she believes that the spirit is encased in physical bodies, whether it is a human or a fiddler crab. However, her exploration of the world and her pursuit of God and personal spirituality must exist wholly outside the time-bound constraints of historical, political, and social ideologies. Otherwise, the mysteries of faith and religion become a point of reference for viewing these ideologies rather than the goal of the exploration.

Critical Overview

Given that Jacobsen is considered a contemporary poet, there has been a surprisingly substantial amount of criticism written about her work. On the other hand, it might be fair to say that very little has been written about her body of work that spans eight decades. Regardless, Nancy Sullivan's praise in the *Hollins Critic* summarizes Jacobsen's greatness, stating, "The energy and quality of Josephine Jacobsen's work in poetry, fiction, and criticism, as well as her public service on behalf of poetry, are remarkable." Jacobsen is easily one of the twentieth-century's greatest poets, writers, lecturers, and critics. Her work is highly spiritual, yet not preachy or overtly in support of a religious doctrine. Although she was a devout Catholic, her poems explore her individual pursuit of spirituality, her personal interpretations of the word of God, and her never-ending search for answers to the mysteries of life and faith.

The collection that contains "Fiddler Crab" may be Jacobsen's greatest achievement. This work, *In the Crevice of Time: New and Collected Poems*, spans sixty years of Jacobsen's poetic productivity. The chronological organization of her

What Do I Read Next?

- *What Goes without Saying: Collected Stories by Josephine Jacobsen* (2000) comprises thirty short stories, all previously published. These stories take the reader to exotic lands and are of the highest literary merit.

- *The Instant of Knowing: Lectures, Criticism, and Occasional Prose* (1997) features two lectures delivered at the Library of Congress during Jacobsen's term as Consultant in Poetry.

- *Adios, Mr. Moxley: Thirteen Stories* (1986) is a collection of short stories that explores the highs and lows of love and life.

- *Spinach Days* (2003), by Robert Phillips, is a short collection of poetry. Phillips's work is inspired by Jacobsen, and this book presents poems in his various, innovative styles and poetic forms, including haiku, long narratives, short lyrics, and free verse.

work unfolds Jacobsen's deeply personal journey of spiritual exploration, personal growth, physical aging, and deepening understanding. Elizabeth Spires writes in the *New Criterion*:

> To read *In the Crevice of Time: New and Collected Poems* is akin to watching some frightening or wondrous natural process, say a tree or flower blooming, captured in time-lapse photography—from the first stirrings of a germinal impulse to the rapid movement into individuality, maturity, and inevitable denouement. It's a disturbingly compressed tale of birth, change, growth, and oblivion.

Spires's summarization of *In the Crevice of Time: New and Collected Poems* is also a clear summarization of Jacobsen's life, her work, and her pursuit of life's mysteries. Though she gained great acclaim and recognition, Jacobsen's greatest contribution may be her effect on individual lives. Her writing was so deeply personal that it seemed to open the door for other critics, poets, writers, and lecturers to embark on their own explorations. Although Jacobsen should rightly be remembered for her awards, honors, achievements, and work, the world should not forget her paramount desire to solve life's greatest mysteries.

Criticism

Anthony Martinelli

Martinelli is a Seattle-based freelance writer and editor. In this essay, he examines how Jacobsen uses the poetic narrative to tell a story about the life of a fiddler crab and then from the story makes the claim that all life comes from one god.

The poem "Fiddler Crab" appears in Jacobsen's expansive collection *In the Crevice of Time: New and Collected Poems*, published in 1995. The work is a short narrative poem telling the story of a fiddler crab's life and death. It is nondramatic, but this does not detract from its complexity. "Fiddler Crab" is an excellent example of how narrative poetry can, in fact, deliver a complex message. Beyond this, "Fiddler Crab" can be better understood as a benchmark example of Jacobsen's entire body of work. Throughout her eight-decade-long career, Jacobsen delivered nothing short of profound, rich, spiritual work, and "Fiddler Crab" is no exception. In this poem, Jacobsen tells the story of a fiddler crab: the crab's struggle for survival and ultimately his demise. Beneath the surface of the narrative, the poem questions and defines existence, compares the lives of all creatures, and uses the story of the fiddler crab to deduce that all life is created and given by one god.

In the opening stanza, Jacobsen begins to construct her narrative poem. The crab is observed as "he veers fast, glides, stops, / dithers, paws." The creature is simply moving about, almost going through a routine. There is almost no discussion of the fiddler crab's crablike features, that is, no remarks about the crab's claws, shell, chitinous burrs, and so forth. Jacobsen avoids this description with intent. She intends to draw parallels between the fiddler crab's existence and her own. The most important aspect of the first stanza is what it *does not* do; namely, it does not demand a distinct separation between fiddler crabs and humans.

In the second stanza, Jacobsen describes the crab's setting. Her rich, lyrical images paint a vivid picture of water that is "five shades of blue" and a rocky beach covered with "scarab shapes and tiny white and black whorls." She also comments on the waves, remarking that the "lacy wink lapses, behind it the black lustre / lapses and dulls." The waves are these lacy winks, and the reference to lapsing is not arbitrary. From a narrative poetic standpoint, this stanza describes the poem's setting, but Jacobsen, with her ever-complex intentions, is making a greater comment about time. The waves are winks because they represent moments in time. Jacobsen's verb choice—"lapses"—is connected to the passage of time. Each wave that crashes to the shore is a wink, an instant in time. Collectively, these instants make up history, and this is time lapsing, or gliding along. All the waves that have crashed against the shore represent all the history of the world, while all those that have yet to break represent the unknown future. The individual wink that occurs is nothing more than the fleeting moment that marks existence—life—between what has passed and what has yet to become.

Jacobsen's comment on time is integral to the third stanza, where she brings together the crab and its interaction with the waves. In this stanza, Jacobsen herself enters the narrative poem as a character—the observer. This, too, is not unintentional. From a narrative poetic standpoint, this stanza describes the crab dodging, attempting to "skirt the white curve" by "flatten[ing] on the black shine." The fiddler crab is trying in desperation to avoid the rushing waves, and when he is caught by the frothing waters, he holds on to the shiny black rocks for dear life. At one point the crab even has to escape into a "trembling hole" as he fights for survival against the surf. Again Jacobsen is making a greater comment about the crab's battle against time. For Jacobsen, life is defined by the struggle for survival. All the physical, living moments that occur between the crab's birth and death are nothing more than a collective struggle against time. Just as the crab strains against the constant, ever-breaking waves, so does the crab struggle against each wink of time, not knowing which one will be the last contribution to the lapse of time that constructs his individual history.

In the next stanza, Jacobsen makes her personal connection to the crab more obvious, bringing it to

> *The most important aspect of the first stanza is what it does not do; namely, it does not demand a distinct separation between fiddler crabs and humans."*

the forefront by mimicking his movements. She writes, "I imitated him with my five fingers, but not well." Here, Jacobsen points out that she and the crab are physically different creatures and that she is, in fact, poor at being a crab. She watches the crab come out of a hole in the sand, witnessing again his "tippity panicky glide to the wave's wink." This moment—this wink in time—is shared by the fiddler crab and Jacobsen. They have shared a moment together in their individual struggles for survival. She further binds herself to the creature in the last two lines of the stanza, writing, "Each entirely alone on this beach; but who / is the god of the crabs?" The question at the end of the stanza is difficult to answer. Through their shared wink in time, Jacobsen realizes that both her life and the crab's are defined by a singular common element: the struggle for survival. Although the wink in time they shared—the breaking wave—did not threaten Jacobsen's existence, it was still a moment in common. The struggle for survival differs subjectively from creature to creature and, for that matter, from individual to individual. However, through this moment shared with the crab, Jacobsen suddenly understands that all creatures—not just all humans—define their existence through their struggles for survival, creating a sticky problem in terms of the existence of divine beings.

Jacobsen believes in one god as presented by the Catholic Church. She accepts, as a presupposition, that this singular god has given life to humankind. From this perspective, Jacobsen struggles to define the life that has been bestowed upon her by God. The spiritual journey to define existence is rich throughout her work, and "Fiddler Crab" is certainly no exception; still, what results in this stanza clearly creates a predicament. God has given life to Jacobsen. Jacobsen's spiritual exploration of her life has led her to the conclusion that life is defined by the struggle for survival. Surviving the winks, the moments, through the passage of time defines Jacobsen's existence. In "Fiddler Crab," Jacobsen supports this claim in a poetic narrative about the fiddler crab. However, the poem's narrative defines the fiddler crab's life in a fashion identical to her own life, as a fight for survival: given Jacobsen's belief that God gave her life, she asks, with respect to this companion creature, "who / is the god of the crabs?" Jacobsen knows that something must have given the crab life and that that something must be a god. Thus, the answer to this sticky question alludes to the existence of more than one god, that is, Jacobsen's Catholic God and the "god of the crabs."

In the fifth stanza, Jacobsen returns to her narrative, almost leaving the predicament of the fourth stanza and the question of multiple gods. In these lines, Jacobsen tidies up the fiddler crab's existence with his death. She writes

The Spanish-Chinese boy brought him to show.
His stilted eyes popped over three broken legs
but he ran with the rest of them over the edge
and died on the point of the drop down
twenty feet.

In a straightforward manner, Jacobsen describes the end of the crab's struggle for survival and, with it, the end of his life. This stanza is intentionally linked to the physicality of the crab, which is an important concept for Jacobsen. In an interview with Evelyn Prettyman in *New Letters*, Jacobsen states, "I believe in the explicable tangle of body and spirit; the spirit is encased in the physical. If you're going to know God you've got to know him in physical terms." Although this stanza is not overly dramatic, it does comment directly on the crab's physical body, remarking on his "broken legs" and "stilted eyes." The death of the crab is the end of him in physical terms, leaving only the exploration of his spirit and, thus, his connection to God.

With the death of the crab comes Jacobsen's revelation about God. It is as if with the death of the crab's physical body the question of his spirit becomes easily understood. Jacobsen writes, "So it is simple: he can be hurt / and then he can die." Like a human being, the crab's life is defined by the struggle for survival, the power to withstand the pain of life until the end. More important, in this stanza Jacobsen highlights the connectivity of herself with the crab and all living things, but she overlooks something in the predicament she reached in the fourth stanza. It is true that the crab and Jacobsen both define their lives by their struggle for survival, and it is also true that they are different both as species—a crustacean and a human—and as separate individuals—Jacobsen and fiddler crab. However, Jacobsen failed in the fourth stanza in her understanding of the definition of life. Jacobsen and the crab are not tied together by their common definition of life as a struggle for survival. The struggle for survival is life, and it is what ties all of existence together. God did not give a different life to Jacobsen, to the fiddler crab, and to this or that individual; God created all of life. All that is alive is from God and of God; the individual understanding of this life, that is, the crab's individual struggle against the surf or a human's individual struggle against illness, is subjective. Jacobsen concedes this point in her interview with Prettyman, stating, "We're even united with the whole of the animal kingdom by the fact that they can suffer, and fear and be hurt."

In the last lines of "Fiddler Crab," Jacobsen writes

. . . In all his motions
and marine manoeuvres it was easy to miss
on the sand how I should know him and he me
and what subject matter we have in common.
It is our god.

With this, the subjective differences and similarities that Jacobsen observes between herself and the crab in the first five stanzas are reduced to that which defines their physical existences and their individual, physical struggles for survival. Although the moments of survival collectively define their individual histories, it is what lies beneath that is the true definition of life. That life is created by and bestowed upon all living things by a single, solitary god.

Source: Anthony Martinelli, Critical Essay on "Fiddler Crab," in *Poetry for Students*, Thomson Gale, 2006.

Elizabeth Spires

In the following review, Spires discusses the major themes of Jacobsen's poetry as captured in In the Crevice of Time.

Art is long and life is short. Or is it the other way around? On the evidence of *In the Crevice of Time: New and Collected Poems,* a 258-page volume that spans sixty years of poetic productivity, both art and life have been long and rewarding for Josephine Jacobsen.

The collected poems of a greatly gifted poet may not offer the suspense of a well-plotted novel, but there is still a certain drama in seeing the arc of a life's work fitted between the covers of one book. To read *In the Crevice of Time* is akin to watching some frightening or wondrous natural process, say a tree or flower blooming, captured in time-lapse photography—from the first stirrings of a germinal impulse to the rapid movement into individuality, maturity, and inevitable denouement. It's a disturbingly compressed tale of birth, change, growth, and oblivion. So it is with Josephine Jacobsen, who, at eighty-seven, has probably been writing longer than any other American poet living today, and who continues to write poems of extraordinary force and passion. Like the aging, prescient figure in "Hourglass," a recent poem, "She perfectly understands the calendar / and the sun's passage. But she grips the leash / and leans on the air that is hers and here."

Unlike many of her poetic contemporaries, Jacobsen has not pursued a particularly "literary" life. She was born in 1908, part of a generation that included Lowell, Bishop, Berryman, and Roethke. Her formal education ended with her graduation from high school; it had been decided early on by her mother (Jacobsen's father had died when she was five) that she would not go to college. In the spirit of the time, she married early and had a child. Her first four books, *Let Each Man Remember* (1940), *For the Unlost* (1946), *The Human Climate* (1953), and *The Animal Inside* (1966), published by smaller presses outside the circle of New York, did not establish her as a major poet of her generation, although by all rights they should have. She did not teach, nor was she deeply involved with the literary world until she was named Consultant in Poetry to the Library of Congress in 1971, when she was sixty-three. For the most part, her writing was done "on the side," in brief intense spurts during isolated months at Yaddo and MacDowell, and during winter stays in the Caribbean, a locale to which she has always felt attracted because of its "wonderful sense of strangeness . . . which was totally other." With the publication of *The Shade-Seller*, in 1974, and *The Chinese Insomniacs*, in 1981, Jacobsen became better known, although even today she is still a "poet's poet." Despite receiving various awards and honors in the past decade, she has often been overlooked, especially when major anthologies have been compiled.

Having said all that, and now having *In the Crevice of Time* in hand, does it matter? Of the 169 poems included here, several dozen are perfect and irreplaceable, far more than the precious half a dozen Randall Jarrell spoke of in his famous remark about poets spending their lives standing out in fields waiting for lightning to strike. A necessarily incomplete list of some of her best work would

> *The overriding thematic preoccupation of her poetry, from first to last, is impermanence and loss."*

include, I think, "The Three Children," "My Uncle a Child," "Instances of Communication," "Poems for My Cousin," "The Starfish," "The Enemy of the Herds, the Lion," "The Birds," "Colloquy," "Daughter to Archeologist," "In the Crevice of Time," "The Mexican Peacock," "Treaty," "The Chanterelles," "The Shade-Seller," "Pondicherry Blues," "Notes toward Time," "The Sisters," "The Chosen," "Winter's Tale," "The Woods," "The Limbo Dancer," "Tears," "First Woman," "Reading on the Beach," and "Hourglass." *In the Crevice of Time* is a selection of only about two thirds of the approximately 250 poems included in her eight books, and any reader familiar with all of Jacobsen's work might easily add another dozen to the two dozen or so just mentioned.

Throughout her career, she has persistently chosen to write poems of an unnervingly pure lyric intensity. (About her early years she has written, "I had an unidentified craving for the lyrical.") She is a formal poet with the ability, when she wants to and the poem demands it, to be "free." She has, unfashionably, always been clear in her refusal to use personal, intimate experience in a direct or explicit way in her poems. What one observes in Jacobsen's poetry is experience worked into the very fabric of the poem, in its tone and stance, rather than experience overtly disclosed. In a memoir she explained, "If there is little trace in this account of . . . things which are darker, of pain and loss, it is never because these things were nonexistent, but because they are *in the very texture of writing* where they belong" (italics mine).

A Josephine Jacobsen poem will not come alive for the reader until this subtle texture is both intellectually processed and viscerally felt, the way meaning in spoken conversation is understood as much through a subtle tone of voice, a shift in inflection, as by simple denotation. Readers desirous of an explicit topical poem (which many readers seem to be these days) will go away from Jacobsen dissatisfied because her concerns are not so easily categorized. She is part traveler ("Born travelers must and will have terra incognita"), part archeologist ("We breathe through our future. / Remember me is the message"), and part seer ("I know all about what is / happening in this city at just / this moment; every last grain of dark I conceive").

In the Crevice of Time is arranged chronologically, beginning in 1935 and continuing up to 1994. Initially, Jacobsen moves through a period of literary influence, trying out various modes and styles, both romantic and modern. About her early models and influences, she said once, "If I have cause for gratitude, let it be to Robert Service, Rudyard Kipling; to Dante Gabriel Rossetti; to Keats, Yeats, and Donne." Here is Yeats in "Fergus and the Druid":

> I see my life go drifting like a river
> From change to change; I have been many things—
> A green drop in the surge, a gleam of light
> Upon a sword, a fir tree on a hill,
> An old slave grinding at a heavy quern,
> A king sitting upon a chair of gold. . . .

And here is the young Jacobsen in "Winter Castle":

> I am many-minded, diverse-shaped:
> I am the horses, hay-warmed in the stalls,
> The snow-snagged spruces, and the starving hare
> Coursing the slopes of snow.

Other early poems, such as "For Any Member of the Security Police" or "'It's a Cold Night,' Said Coney to Coney," show Jacobsen assimilating the influence of Auden. Much of her early work is characterized by a tight reining in of the subject matter, by an ironic or distanced treatment, and by the imposition of formal constraints, where lines are carefully counted out and fitted into set forms.

At around the age of forty, when many poets privately wonder, "What now?," Jacobsen stepped out from the shadow of influence and the confinement of closed forms to begin writing the poems that are most hers. Working outside of any poetic circle, she said of the process, "I was forced . . . to develop a sense of my own intention." And her intention, from almost the beginning, seemed to be to write a poetry in which "the experience, wherever found, is the experience of being taken out of oneself, simultaneous with an inner penetration to unity. In that respect, the aesthetic experience is similar to the religious experience, and vice versa."

The overriding thematic preoccupation of her poetry, from first to last, is impermanence and loss.

Chief among the many questions that her poems seek to answer are these three: What is the difference between the animal and the human? How do humans know and communicate with one another? And, how shall we be reconciled to the fact of death? In "Notes toward Time," Jacobsen reflects that "the schizoid heart tells / what is alive, by its dying." An early poem, "Spring, Says the Child," connects the child's (and poet's?) acquisition of language to the onset of consciousness, with its fateful recognition that all things die:

> There are words too ancient to be said by the lips
> of a child—
> Too old, too old for a child's soft reckoning—
> Ancient, terrible words, to a race unreconciled:
> *Death, spring. . . .*
>
> The composite heart of man knows their awful
> age—
> They are frightening words to hear on a child's
> quick tongue.
> They overshadow, with their centuries' heritage,
> The tenderly young.
>
> *Death,* says the child, *spring,* says the child, and
> *heaven. . . .*
> This is flesh against stone, warm hope against salt
> sea—
> This is all things soft, young, ignorant; this is even
> Mortality.

Here, as in so much of her poetry, Jacobsen presents human existence as having a disturbing double aspect: a precarious, desperate balancing of life and death forces, one light, one dark, one hopeful, one unassailably grim. The formal arrangement of the poem, with the abruptly cut-off fourth line of each stanza, heavily emphasizes the words *death, spring, tenderly young,* and *mortality,* the words almost a précis of the poem's argument. But even as Jacobsen acknowledges the fact of death, she also perceives nature's recurring cycles and promise, both cruel and hopeful. In the texture of the poem, one intuits a certain timeless knowledge: that the law of life is barbaric.

The concerns articulated in "Spring, Says the Child" have occupied and preoccupied Jacobsen for a lifetime. If we are "a race unreconciled," then where can we look for consolation? In "Instances of Communication," one of Jacobsen's most masterly poems, the poet traveler posits one answer:

> Almost nothing concerns me but communication.
> How strange: Up the Orinoco, once, far
> up the Orinoco after jungle miles, great flower-
> heads
> looping the treecrests, log-crocodiles, crocodile-
> logs, bob-haired
> Indians naked in praus: a small, hot, town and in
> an upper dining-room

plashed at by a fountain, cooled by fans, guardian
of a menu the size of a baby,
speaking six languages, with seven capital cities
behind his eyes, a headwaiter,
a man, who said without hope, *"And when does
your ship sail?"* And no one
said to him, *"What are you doing here?"*

In the hall of the inn at Mont Serrat I came out of
my room and
"Stand back, stand back!" cried the criada in her
softest Spanish, *"the bride—*
the bride is coming!" out of her room, down the
hall, down to the steps
on her way to the church, to the groom. She was
pale, and dark; she clouded
the carpet with the mist of her train, she moved by
me but turned and bent and caught
my fingerbones seeing me like fate, watching the
three of her, the old, tall, childhood girl,
the darkly seen half-a-thing, and the white bride
lost on the point of love, and *"Buenas,
o buenas tardes!"* she called into my ear, she
crushed my fingers and laughed with panic
into my widened eyes and went proudly on whis-
pering
over the hall runner.

I drove five madwomen down a roaring redhot
turnpike in a July
noon; the one behind me had a fur ragged coat
gathered about her in that furnace;
she reached in the horrid insides of a purse and offered me a chocolate, liquid
and appalling. *"Look! Look! A bird!"* I cried and
flung it over the side
and munched my empty jaws as she turned back,
and cried: *"How good!"*
And while the others hummed and cursed, and
watched simply, suddenly she put
her lips—behind me—to my ear and soft as liquid
chocolate came purling
the obscene abuse. *"Hush, hush, Laura, hush,"*
said the nurse; *"the nice lady
likes you!"* Laura did not believe so, and went on
softly, slowly, lovingly,
with O such a misery of hate.

Underlying the deliberately difficult, rapid syntax
of the first three stanzas is a sense of isolation and
panic, madness and terror, in which the characters
speak different languages, both literally and
metaphorically. Throughout the poem, the narrator
feels the press of other people's identities. She sees
but cannot rescue the hopeless waiter from his remote exile; their conversation is limited by the
empty language of social convention and by cultural boundaries. Likewise, she sees the Spanish
bride in a mystical, transfigured state, but the girl's
"o buenas tardes!" fails to adequately express the
gravity of her wedding day, when her girlhood
identity and innocence will be forfeited. And in the
third stanza the narrator and nurse must suffer the

obscenities of the madwoman Laura. All three
vignettes contain disturbing examples of failed
speech, and yet, playing against this, each also contains an example of the narrator's uncanny ability
to fathom the interior of the people she observes.
It is a Keatsian moment where the poet becomes a
nerve-like receptor to the lives around her and finds
herself in helpless, knowing communion with them.

In the final stanza, Jacobsen shifts from these
painful, disturbing scenes of human communication to a sacramental communion:

> In frosty Philadelphia the freighter lay and loaded
> in the Sunday ice.
> The great cranes swung, the huge nets grabbed and
> everything echoed from cold:
> docks, warehouses, freightrails, ships' prows;
> everything clicked and echoed;
> but it was possible to go down the long cold docks
> over the strange dark street under
> the dim sky into a cold great warehouse Sunday
> still, up still cold stairs, along
> a dark dim cold thin hall through a brown door into
> a small square room with lit
> peaky candles and kneeling take—cool, slick, thin,
> little larger than a quarter—
> God's blood and body charged with its speech.

Stanzas three and four are striking in their juxtapositions: we are led from the hot hell of the turnpike to the cold heaven of the "great warehouse,"
from the image of the obscene chocolate offered
by Laura, an unwanted communion, to the Eu-
charistic host, a divine communion. In receiving
the sacrament of Holy Communion, the speaker is
in the grip of something powerfully symbolic, literally in communion with a wordless, mystical language, the antithesis of the obscene speech in
stanza three. It is an epiphanal moment that takes
us back to Jacobsen's remark that "the aesthetic experience is similar to the religious experience, and
vice versa." For Jacobsen, faith and imagination are
closely connected, not exclusive of each other, the
physical world a place of potential symbol and
metaphor, a place where divine speech—the speech
of poetry and prayer—can exist. In "Instances of
Communication," the world of imaginative experience and the world of religious experience bril-
liantly intersect and momentarily become one.

If religious faith is one form of consolation in
a time-bound world, one path to epiphany, even
more so for Jacobsen is art. In "The Interrupted,"
a poem about art and antiquity, she writes, "These
[statues] escape from their maker's limit to rejoice
us with hope." In the title poem of *In the Crevice
of Time,* she describes the moment when a "hunter-
priest" made the first cave painting, "his art an act

of faith, his grave / an act of art: for all, / for all, a celebration and a burial." It is a recurring theme in Jacobsen's work. Art, for Jacobsen, connects us to the timeless and eternal, as in "The Enemy of the Herds, the Lion," a poem about a memento mori, a "decorated boxlid, ca. 2500 B.C., which was found in the grave of the Lady Shub-ad at Ur." The poet describes the image on the box as "a lion-sheep without division," predator and victim "tranced and ardent in the act of taking / utter enough to be love." She asks, "What / word did her box-beasts mean?" and considers various answers:

> Possi-
> bilities; the chic symbols
> of the day, on a fashionable jewel-toy,
> the owner modishly ignorant; or, corrupt,
> an added pulse to lust.
>
> Or:
> mocking, or wise, remembrance
> of innocent murder innocent death,
> the coupled ambiguous desire,
> at dinner, at dressing, at music.
>
> Or,
> best, and why not? of her meeting
> all quiet terror, surmounted by joy,
> to go to her grave with her; a pure
> mastery older than Ur.

Again, Jacobsen presents the twinned, inseparable aspects of human existence, its joy and terror, in her juxtaposition of life and death, death and art. (The phrase comes up again in "The Clock" where she writes, "In joy and terror / I move in time where / nothing points to error.") Hunter and hunted, death and life, are, in the poem's phrase, "without division." This idea of "terror, surmounted by joy," infuses much of Jacobsen's work and is absolutely central to understanding what she is about as a poet.

Although there are many Josephine Jacobsen poems that delight and entertain, she is, in her greatest poems, capable of staring death in the eye and drawing its wrenching lineaments down to the last wrinkle. This two-mindedness—in which she is both in the moment and yet also self-consciously aware of time's rapid passage—is perfectly embodied in "The Chanterelles," a poem about mushroom-gatherers. Even as they cook their find "in cream and Neufchâtel / and onions, to devour it together close to the first flames," they are also aware that more deadly, poisonous mushrooms, "some single, breastbone white; others the color of dust, the color of rain," grow among the chanterelles in the dark fairy-tale wood. It is the experience of a happy picnicker in a sunlit field watching, out of the corner of her eye, a dark cloud approaching.

The recent poems that make up the last section of *In the Crevice of Time* are some of Jacobsen's very best. There is an open, direct, colloquial quality to them, and a remarkable sense of self-disclosure. Guises and disguises (Dickinson's "slant truth") are abandoned, poetic pretense dropped. In "Calling Collect," she implores someone on the other end of a telephone line, "For the love / / of God let me hear your voice locate me. / Over distance, long, it is saying my name. / I speak to you," an address as much, perhaps, to her readers as to a personal beloved. Running through these poems is an intense desire to connect. One has only to scan the titles to see that time and death are very much on Jacobsen's mind: "Next Summer," "Survivor's Ballad," "The Chosen," "The Night Watchman," "Winter's Tale," "We Pray Most Earnestly," "You Can Take It with You," "The Blue-Eyed Exterminator," "The Thing about Crows," "The Shrivers," "Loss of Sounds," "Hourglass."

In "First Woman," the narrator observes a bleak winter landscape that mirrors her own ravaged spirit. The poem is a desperate interrogation of self, the poet reaching far back into the deep past to address the skeletal remains of "Lucy" (so named by archeologists), the earliest known woman:

> Do animals expect spring?
> Ground hard as rancor,
> wind colder than malice.
> Do they think that will change?
>
> Sky no color and low;
> grass is no color, and trees
> jerk in the bitter gust.
> In this air nothing flies.
>
> Do they believe it will change,
> grass be soft and lustrous,
> rigid earth crack
> from the push of petals,
>
> sky retreat into blue,
> the red wide rose breathe
> summer, and the butterfly
> err on sweet air?
>
> First woman, Lucy, or another,
> did you know it all waited
> somewhere to come back?
> On the first stripped, iron day
>
> did you believe that?
> On this merciless morning
> I wake, first woman,
> with what belief?

The vocabulary of "First Woman" speaks for the naked condition of the spirit and the violent elements that would destroy it: *rancor, malice, bitter, stripped, iron, merciless.* There is an immense projection of emotion outward onto the landscape, the poem nothing less than a harrowing self-portrait, a poem of brutal "inner weather." One of the most remarkable aspects of "First Woman" is the way Jacobsen pushes the possibilities of the lyric, so often centered in one moment, to encompass past, present, and future: the deep past of Lucy's original knowledge, the bitter present, and the hoped-for future with spring's "push of petals" and summer's "red wide rose." It is a poem poised on the brink of an abyss, a "crevice of time," but through a supreme act of will, the poet resists giving in to despair. In "First Woman" Jacobsen has gone full circle, from the first intimations of knowledge in her early poem "Spring, Says the Child" to the hardest and harshest recognitions imaginable, earned only through age and experience. It is one of the most successful contemporary lyrics I can think of.

Isn't it for this kind of truth-telling, this way of seeing that penetrates to the very core and marrow, that we read poetry? It seems no accident that a deliberately sibylline countenance floats on the cover on *In the Crevice of Time,* bringing to mind the Sibyl's proverbial words to Aeneas: "Yield not to disasters, but press onward the more bravely." In a long life of writing, Josephine Jacobsen has.

Source: Elizabeth Spires, "Joy and Terror: The Poems of Josephine Jacobsen," in *New Criterion*, Vol. 14, No. 3, November 1995, pp. 28–33.

Josephine Jacobsen and Evelyn Prettyman

In the following interview, Jacobsen discusses her background and life and how her experiences have shaped her poetry.

[*New Letters*]: *In your writing, your world is a world of pain, usually because someone else is hurt. How early did that awareness begin?*

[*Josephine Jacobsen*]: That touches on very tender points. . . . My mother was an unhappy person. She had a young husband who was killed tragically in an accident. Personally, she was passionate and intense, either depressed or elated; she had great shifts. She had no ability to handle finances, she was unprepared for it. For us, it was boom or bust.

My brother was humorous and talented; he was a good writer, a fine sculptor and a professional actor. But he had all kinds of serious emotional problems. Eventually he had a series of crackups.

Mother was always worried about finances or her son; her life never had any kind of serenity. I was devoted to both my mother and my brother,

> *Everyone should be outraged by pain, but if you once accept the mystery of it, that it has some significance that you'll never understand, then it can be purifying; it activates sympathy."*

and I was aware very soon that I was living with people I loved who were not happy people. I felt responsible. I thought there ought to be something I could do.

It's interesting that you say that your mother and brother always felt in peril, and yet I find you a person who is challenged, even healthily thrilled by danger.

Don't you think that you're either terribly tough or you go under? If you're under tremendous strain as a child, it just tips; you sink, or if you stay on top you develop certain resources in yourself that have got to be called on.

In your poems, you have even equated danger with beauty and joy.

Well, there's the challenge of the ball being in your court. And there's the blissful feeling of serenity when it's out of your hands, what a patient feels going into the operating room, or one can feel just before an automobile accident. And of course there's the physical exhilaration. Our oldest grandson, Ricky, was a racing driver. Then, ironically, he was killed by a truck, run down on a Boston street.

You also equate beauty with pain.

Everyone should be outraged by pain, but if you once accept the mystery of it, that it has some significance that you'll never understand, then it can be purifying; it activates sympathy. It has been associated with rites of purification. If you do come through pain, for you there is a beauty.

Then your childhood was unhappy?

No, I felt that I was loved by my mother and brother. I had a variety of friends; although as soon as I made friends anywhere, we moved away. Mother had the wonderful ability when things were going well to enjoy life, to dress up and look beautiful. She was a person of great charm. So it was never a dreary or loveless atmosphere. There was usually warmth and gaiety, and a certain amount of grace; and then everything would fall in pieces.

What books did you read?

My mother read an enormous amount to me. She read Dickens, *Lorna Doone, Jane Eyre, The Cloister and the Hearth,* among many, many others.

I also grew up on fairy tales. My mother read me fairy tales until I could read them, and then I read *The Red Fairy Book, The Green Fairy Book, The Blue Fairy Book,* Hans Andersen, Grimm, Oscar Wilde. Although I had kind of a weird life, looking back, I don't even know much to regret. Perhaps one regret: I have wished passionately that I had been to college or that I had had the opportunity to decide if I wanted to go. Mother, who was from North Carolina, had that Southern conception that college was a refuge for girls who were having problems, who didn't have a young man on the scene. It was years later, when I had begun to realize that my life might develop along the lines of writing, that I thought, "My God, someone should have told me. I should have gone to college." At times it just lacerates me to think of, oh, if I'd had that experience, the friendships, the contacts, the launching. But then I question that, and I have never made up my mind to this day whether it was a good or a bad thing that I didn't go. Maybe my whole career would have been different. But I concentrated entirely on poetry. That was my life line; it was the only thing I had left. It was my only intellectual contact. It was a fairly rough track for a while.

What did you do between high school and marriage? Did you write poetry?

I had met my husband-to-be by then; and the year I fell in love, I wrote a lot of poetry. That's the poetry that's in *Let Each Man Remember.*

"Winter Castle?"

Yes, exactly. That was the first solid effort at professional poetry that I ever made, and Harriet Monroe took a couple of those for *Poetry.* I just dropped them in the mailbox. I subscribed to *Poetry,* and I thought I'd like to send something in, and I thought, "This is ridiculous, but what can they do to me?" She took two or three sonnets from "Winter Castle." And she used quite a lot of my poetry from then on. That's one thing I'm very proud of, that every single editor of *Poetry* has used my poems.

From what else would you say your happiness has come?

My work. My husband. And the family relationship has always been lucky. We happen to have a son, Erlend, with whom we are extraordinarily congenial. And our daughter-in-law. We had one grandchild, the oldest, to whom we were especially close: Ricky, the one who was killed in that random accident.

Tell me again about the trip you, your husband and Ricky took to Africa.

It was one of the high points of my life, but it was a very simple thing, and I don't want to exaggerate it. When Ricky was a small child we had gone together to see *Born Free.* Oh, several times. And he had said he'd give anything to go and see the animals; and I, in that lighthearted, adult, irresponsible way that one does, said, "Well, tell you what, Ricky, some day we will all go to Africa together." And he believed this implicitly, as you do when you're seven or eight. And almost immediately afterward, I got an attack of devastating guilt, and I thought this is exactly the thing that people do to children all the time—they lie to them. So the first moment I got the job at the Library of Congress, the first thing I thought was that we could make this thing come true.

So it was real. We got to Kilimanjaro on New Year's Eve, camping right at the foot of the mountain; and it was, of course, covered with clouds. You couldn't even see the snows on the top. And everybody said it's almost never in a clear sky. You can look at pictures of it, but you're not going to see the summit.

So we all had a New Year's Eve party, and we were exhausted and went to bed about ten o'clock. We were fast asleep, and all of sudden we heard this pounding on the door. We got up and went to the door, and it was Ricky in a tremendous state of excitement, in his pajamas with a blanket around his shoulders. He said, "Get a blanket, get a blanket! Come out!" We came out—it was about five minutes of midnight, which was the weird thing—and every cloud had cleared away. The sky was absolutely crystal clear, and there was this moon blazing right on the snows right up at the top. We stayed there looking at it for maybe ten minutes, so that we were there before and after the beginning of the year.

There are so many sources of joy. When I get these awful fits of desolation, I feel guilty.

Was your trip to Africa the beginning of your interest in animals? They're in so much of your writing.

I've always had this animal fascination. I've always been drawn to this mysterious kingdom. Animals have been great mythical figures. You go back in the Bible or in any great literature and you see mythical figures of the lion, and the serpent, the dragon and the scorpion, very potent images. And I think fairy tales had a lot to do with my feelings. There's this huge mysterious world—of which we're such a small, messy, crossed-up part—that is going on without us all the time. For me there's something liberating in that.

Wild animals live their separate lives. They don't know anything about humans; they've never seen them; they don't care about humans. Monkeys are almost a lower human, whereas when you see an elephant or a leopard, a tiger or an antelope, you don't feel that they have tried to become human and failed; you feel they belong to a whole different order.

I think we've lost the sense of mystery and wonder in the world. I think of my grandchildren, and I worry about what is going to be left for them on this marvelous planet. We've turned everything into what can be utilized. We've put up oil derricks to get oil out of the earth, we've cut down the game preserves so that agriculture can go ahead. Gradually we're eliminating all the unconquered, beautiful parts of the planet, all the frontiers.

Tell me how you see fire; it's such a strong image in your poems.

I'm fascinated by the mysterious levels of fire. I build a little fire and warm myself at my hearth, and then I see these devastating forest fires that sweep through thousands of acres and tower up to the sky. I strike a match and it's light, it's fire, a little thing that I can get for a few cents and blow out. And fire went so far back. The hunters used to build fires at night to keep the wolves away, and then there were the sacred fires built on Walpurgis Night, and then we brought the fire inside, the civilized fires. It has been a sacred thing always, in some form.

But not always benign, in your poems, by any means.

No, no, by no means. Absolutely not. Nothing ever is always the same. That's what is so confusing and compelling about life to me. I never see anything in a simple way.

Tell me how you see shadows.

A shadow is a fascinating statement because you can see a man's shadow, for instance, on bright green grass, and you know exactly what it is. It's a man. You can see how tall he is, you can see the shape of his head, his hands and his body, and yet every particular is withheld from you. I mean you don't know the color of his eyes or the expression of his eyes. It's almost as if shadows were the simplest image of almost anything, the thing reduced to its primitive self, the first signal.

And there's something mysterious to me about the way it follows you, and that every single person has this primitive notice, without any details that will modify or explain it. It's like the spirit of someone about which you really know nothing.

Quite a few of your poems deal with the different levels of time.

Time has been almost an obsession with me. I'm conscious of the fact that our ideas of time are so warped. I think we lose the sense of proportion. The proportion is so strange. Two people loving or living in a house, and their voices and their actions, and then you think, ah, that happened 20 years ago. On the other hand, I remember when I went back to our summer house the summer after our grandson's death. I kept finding theater stubs from when we'd gone to the summer theater, or a particular recipe I'd written out because he'd liked it, and it seemed to me that there were hundreds of years between that summer and the summer before. I felt that I couldn't have lived through so much so long.

Archeology and paleontology have always fascinated me. They give me a sense of how far back things reach. My father was an amateur archeologist. He was tremendously interested in it, he did some work in it in Egypt. He translated scarab inscriptions, and he knew hieroglyphics.

But you were only five when he died.

I often wonder if interests don't sometimes run biologically in a family. However, I probably began consciously to think about these things when I read *The Golden Bough,* in my 20s. *The Animal Inside* is just filled with the influence of that book. From then on, I began to be drawn to traces of things. I am always fascinated by cities. I think most people are; look at Atlantis, it's a romantic thing in most people's mind. And I try to remember how much closer Genghis Kahn is to me today than he was to the period when the equus horse developed.

Religion, or faith, is present in some of your work. Tell me about your early poem, "The Faithful."

The great term in the Mass is "the mystery of faith," and what I'm trying to say is, isn't it really marvelous that people know that these things are going to happen to them, night, winter, death, burial, and they still believe. How *can* men live through life and see how it goes, see that everything that is beautiful dies, that everything that is good goes away, that everyone they love is vulnerable, and still say that they know that they are going to rise from the grave, they know that all is going to be well. How can they?

Is it fair to say that for you the answer to these mysteries lies somewhere in the inscrutability of whatever we mean by the divine?

Yes, yes. I think the whole basis of the thing is probably that the inability to comprehend God sets up a tremendous sense of contradiction. I assume that the inability to comprehend God is universal, and I don't care who tells me that they do comprehend Him, I don't believe it. I have a poem about an optimist who says you can't look at anything in nature without believing in God, by which he means that you can't look at flowers or butterflies; he does not mean you can't look at sharks or hyenas.

It's like your poem about Christmas. . . .

Yes, "Bush Christmas Eve." That's one of my half-dozen favorite poems that I've ever written, because it more or less postulates all my confusion and the fact that I'm not willing to accept the people who say God is obvious because He created kittens. I say, He also created the praying mantis and the animal that stings something and takes it away and eats it piecemeal. You don't try to falsify that.

I don't see in your writing that you go much further than wonder at these contradictions.

I wonder. . . . It is in me, and I'm wondering why it isn't more reflected in the poems. I think that the tension I have with people who see God's beneficence in the world all the time has kept this confidence out of my work. I do believe in a design, but I would hate to take the case for it in court.

I think I want never to forget that there is a terrible price you pay for believing; that you have to submit your intellect, and the testimony of your senses and your experience, to faith. In other words, you make a great sacrifice when you say, I believe in a design; I believe in an ultimately good and great God. You're making a statement that can be made to ignore all the suffering and all the horror of which life is so often so largely composed.

So if you did say that you believed in a design, you'd also have to say so much more.

Yes, that's what I'm trying to say exactly: that God says, as in my poem "Mr. McMirty," "Don't forget, I am who I am. Don't try to explain this or you'll fall flat on your face."

So, what is your religion?

I come back to the very simple facts. The Eucharist in the Catholic church is the center of my whole belief, because I believe in the inexplicable tangle of body and spirit; the spirit is encased in the physical. If you're going to know God you've got to know Him in physical terms. A lot of people think that the symbols of the Church are so childish, so crude: feeding on the body and blood of Christ, multiplying the fishes; but when they drop that out and get talking about spiritual things, they lose me.

I don't care if you're a philosopher or a king, you've got these things that are going to happen to you; You're going to be born; if you're cut, you're going to bleed; we're all united by this physical presence. And we're even united with the whole animal kingdom by the fact that they can suffer, and fear and be hurt.

Death and pain: In your poems, those are the common denominators that connect us with the human afflicted, including the urban isolates, the urban lost.

I think there's a terrific amount of condescension that creeps into poems about the unfortunate, always as if they were somebody else, as if they were Martians, and they're not; they're just like us. That's what "Deaf-Mutes at the Ballgame" finally says: Inside of us sits his own deaf-mute, fingerless. There's something there at the bottom of all of us that we can't tell anybody because it cannot be put into words. So we are all isolated in that sense. There are these dropouts constantly in the human race, people always getting lost, people whom life completely passes by, especially in the big cities. I just wrote a poem, it isn't even finished yet, about Potter's Field. The sad thing is also that people tend to be overlooked, to get lost, in quite different circumstances, as they become a chore to be with. We tend to cooperate in this isolation by gradually saying to ourselves, "Goodness, I haven't seen so-and-so in a couple of years," but we haven't really tried to find them.

Your poem, "They Never Were Found," about urban isolates, is an illustration of how we are all connected. But there is no explicit statement of connection in that poem. It just describes the lost. What did you mean?

Well, I think of it perhaps as going through a jungle and seeing a path going off in what looks like a very deserted direction, but there is a little sign indicating that something is there. I'd like to tell you something, and I doubt if this has any bearing. My own best friends don't know it, not because I've tried to conceal it but because it's almost meaningless to me. Everybody says, do you have any brothers, do you have any sisters; and I say I had a brother. . . . I also had a half sister . . . whom I saw for 15 minutes in my life. She was 30 years older than I. I'm telling you this because I'm wondering if it had anything to do, subliminally, with this feeling. I must say it meant so little in my life except as a sort of shadowy, beautiful thing about my father. When he was a very young doctor, he attended to a woman, a widow, who was 20 years older than he was, and this woman had a retarded child who was dying. She was never going to get beyond nine years old and maybe she was 12 or 13. In any case the child died of scarlet fever. My father had come very close to the mother; he admired very much the way she handled herself, and he had great sympathy for her. He was a young man, and they married. This was his first wife; my mother was his second wife. A second child was born, and she was supposed to have had brain fever, but actually the same thing occurred; there was an arrest in development when she was a small child. Well, the mother died, and my father was left with this teenaged daughter, to whom he was very, very devoted; and he made up his mind that he was going to keep her with him, hoping that an attempt to lead a normal life might possibly make some sort of improvement. Well, obviously, it didn't; and it became more and more difficult for her. As she tried more and more to come up to her age, it became more tragic for her. All my father's family grew up in Italy, my father was brought up in Italy; and he knew of some nuns in Bologna who were lovely, gentle people, and he sent Elsa for holidays with them every year. She became the pet of the convent. I mean, she was the kind of person who could go out and gather bouquets of flowers and bring them in, decorate the altar, be very proud of that, have a plot of garden, learn to sew, learn to sew beautifully.

You only met her for 15 minutes?

This was so many years before I was born. Finally it became obvious that this was the one place where she was really not under pressure, where she was happy. So father made an arrangement for her to live there. He visited her regularly every month, and he would take her away for a day or two.

When she was about 30 years old, my father met my mother, who was a widow with a son from her first marriage, and they fell in love and got married. Father went back every year of his life, twice

a year, to spend time in this little village and be with Elsa Louise. To me she was just a name. As a child, I knew she existed. I had a friendly feeling, in fact I had a little picture taken of her, with curls. And she was to me like somebody in a story. Finally when I was 19 years old, my mother and I went over to Italy and Mother wanted to have a conversation with Elsa Louise with nobody else in the room. She was infinitely relieved because Elsa was obviously very happy in an infantile way. Then I was called in and for about 15 minutes we sat there, and they said, "This is your sister, Josephine," and we kissed each other. She died—oh heavens, I guess when I was 26 or 27—so my entire contact with her was when I was 19 with no way to communicate except to say a few friendly things.

What role does your religion play in your feelings about human communication and suffering?

It seems to me that the Christian religion is overwhelmingly right for me, because I cannot conceive of any religion sheltering me that didn't acknowledge *in* its God a degree of human suffering, and, indeed, failure.

That is why the moment on the cross when Christ is supposed to have said, "My God, my God, why have You forsaken me?" is the most important thing that has been said in all the testaments. In other words, they always say that Christ experienced all the sorrow and suffering of being a human being, but if He didn't lose that sense of His own omnipotence, then He didn't experience everything. To me this is something that is priceless. I feel that all my poems have a religious background, in the sense that they spring out of that view of life, yet very few of them deal explicitly with religion, very few.

I'd like you to explain something you once said about the changes in your style of writing. You said that you started out writing rhymed, lyric poetry, and that you changed to a rougher, looser style, and that now you write a more terse, compact form. And you've said that you write according to what the poem demands, which I take to mean according to what you want to say. What has changed about what you want to say?

It's a very interesting question. There's no intention, no theory involved. I deal with each poem according to my own aesthetic impulse of the moment. I started out with rather musical, rhymed poetry, and then I began to feel constrained, to feel that the purely lyric, 19th-century terms didn't seem to express the tangled life that was happening around me.

In that case, the first stimulus to change your poetic style was primarily a change in your aesthetics rather than an actual change in your personal life. What was it that moved you from the looser style to a more compact one?

As I get older and life gets more complex and more confusing, the expression of it has to get simple. You can't be diverse and wander; you have to take the gist, the seed, the one vital core. My recent poems deal with big issues, maybe inadequately, but big issues. One is about the way body and mind work together. Another, grim poem is about someone who misses a midnight train and gets to Pennsylvania station at 1:30 a.m. and sees this great terminal where most people are milling about, busy, motivated to get somewhere; and old ladies are lying down outside the toilet downstairs—poems concerned with the vital, less and less with the peripheral. When you get to the end of your life, you've got to make decisions about what is important.

A young person looks out at the world and thinks there are five hundred thousand things I can do, and this should be different; but at the end of your life, you ask what shall I save, what are the one or two things that matter?

About technique: You said, mostly in reference to your fiction, that one of the great challenges is how to make your theme clear. There is a sort of inexpensive way in which a writer suppresses all those things that go against the point he's making, so that he's left with a straightforward impact. But you said that for you, you must infuse into the story instead something that is more like real life, contradictions and irrelevancies, against which your theme has to sustain itself.

I believe somebody else said it, it's too good. Did I really say it?

Yes. Do you find that somewhat true about your poetic style, too?

Yes, I do, absolutely. I have no interest in a poem that just makes a flat statement and has no counter current, because nothing in life goes smoothly from start to finish. I just had this impressed on me recently, because I met for the first time in my life a military-career man, with whom I had absolutely no opinion in common, not one single one; but he was a perfectly lovely man. His basic premises were all different from mine, but he was good, kind, gentle, obviously sincere. I wish I could have known him longer. And that's what I think life is like. I get terribly impatient with stories that don't leave something that you can't resolve, a ragged edge.

But the poems, diffuseness and contradictions in poems. . . .

I'm much more conscious of what I'm doing in stories; it's a funny thing, in a poem I'm much more at sea on a sea shell. That's one reason I find writing prose such a relief.

Because you know more where you're going?

It's so much easier. Because I can have fun. I develop the characters, and I say it would happen just this way. It's really—I don't want to say escape, because that means escape-writing, which I don't like—but it's much less tearing apart than poetry is.

You've written that writing poems is dangerous. There are many ways you could mean that. How do you mean it?

Just what we've been talking about. You're starting out on a journey in which you don't really know your destination. The chances are that it's not going to come off, that you're never going to get this nebulous, mysterious thing into language at all.

Whereas if you're a professional short-story writer, if you can't get it into language there's something wrong. You may have to work and go back and do it over two or three times, but you've got the material; you've got the language. You ought to be able to get the material into the language.

Do you think what a writer tries to capture in a story is less precious than what he tries for in a poem?

You know, I think I secretly do feel that. I don't want to admit it because I think the short story is a great form, a terribly difficult form. I prefer it to the novel. But in my heart, to me there is nothing that compares to poetry. Because I don't have any confidence that I can do it until I've done it. There's much more to lose here, you see. I never have any confidence until the poem is over that I can capture that beast in the net. It's like a delicate operation. Under certain conditions, you can't go that far in because you get to an organ that is a life source. I feel that with poetry you get closer to that organ; I feel that you're getting as deep as it's possible.

Source: Josephine Jacobsen and Evelyn Prettyman, "The Mystery of Faith: An Interview with Josephine Jacobsen," in *New Letters*, Summer 1987, pp. 41–56.

Nancy Sullivan

In the following essay, Sullivan discusses a range of Jacobsen's poetry to "suggest the scope and radiance of [her] achievement as well as its power."

The energy and quality of Josephine Jacobsen's work in poetry, fiction, and criticism, as well as her public service on behalf of poetry, are remarkable. She has dedicated years of her long life and enduring talent both to her own writing and to the cause of literature. Josephine Jacobsen has always demanded a high standard of excellence of herself and has rejoiced in discovering the skill and insights of other writers. She is a "woman of letters" in the purest and best sense; and the range of her work, particularly in poetry, is singular and wonderful. I trust that my discussion of a few representative works will suggest the scope and radiance of Josephine Jacobsen's achievement as well as its power.

To speak of power in connection with poetry is to conjure up images of the poetry Mafia, cultural politics, and various other questionable arenas which by definition seem antithetical to the genre. Josephine Jacobsen's concerns are certainly not with poetry hustling; they are with the intrinsic nature of the poem itself. In a poem called "The Poem Itself" she clarifies the issue:

> From the ripe silence it exploded silently.
> When the bright debris subsided
> it was there.
>
> Invisible, inaudible; only
> the inky shapes betrayed it.
> Betrayed, is the word.
>
> Thence it moved into squalor,
> a royal virgin in a brothel,
> improbably whole.
>
> It had its followers, pimps, even
> its lovers. The man responsible
> died, eventually.
>
> When the dust of his brain left the bones
> the bond snapped. It escaped to itself.
> It no longer answered.
>
> On the shelf, by the clock's tick, in the black
> stacks of midnight: it is. A moon
> to all its tides.

Here the pure poem escapes to speak of and for itself. It *is*. Pure energy. In a lecture called "The Instant of Knowing" delivered in Washington in 1973 while Josephine Jacobsen was Poetry Consultant to the Library of Congress, she commented that one must not "veer from the core of the job. . . . As I see it, the cause, the purpose, and the end of the position of Consultant in Poetry is poetry itself, as poetry is the poet's own job. . . . The center of everything is the poem. Nothing is important in comparison to that. Anything which in some valid way is not directly connected with that current of energy which is the poem is dispensable."

A poem need not have power as its overt subject in order to concern itself with that issue. The

"current of energy which is the poem" conspires with and enhances whatever subject it ignites. This is certainly true in "The Poem Itself," and as additional examples I might have cited any number of poems from *The Animal Inside* such as "Deaf-Mutes at the Ballgame" or "Yellow" or even earlier poems which reflect her theory of poetry as energy and, therefore, as a vehicle of power. In an essay called "From Anne to Marianne: Some Women in American Poetry," delivered as a lecture at the Library of Congress on May 1, 1972, Jacobsen writes about women in terms of power and powerlessness, "Power is related to energy, and poetry is energy." This theory is a constant motif throughout Josephine Jacobsen's poetic canon.

In one of the "new" poems in *The Shade-Seller, New and Selected Poems* called "Gentle Reader" Jacobsen's subject is her response to reading a genuine poet, "A poet, dangerous and steep," as opposed to a versifier or "a hot-shot ethic-monger." Jacobsen recognizes the real thing in an instant, in a blast of light and comprehension. The short poem ends with this stanza:

> O God, it peels me, juices me like a press;
> this poetry drinks me, eats me, gut and marrow
> until I exist in its jester's sorrow,
> until my juices feed a savage sight
> that runs along the lines, bright
> as beasts' eyes. The rubble splays to dust:
> city, book, bed, leaving my ear's lust
> saying like Molly, yes, yes, yes O yes.

Josephine Jacobsen's theory of poetry as energy, as power, is here realized and made incarnate in the brightness of "the beasts' eyes" and "the ear's lust." The poet *knows* that she has encountered the real thing. As Jacobsen remarks in her lecture, "The Instant of Knowing," "Poetry is energy, and it is poetic energy which is the source of that instant of knowing that the poet tries to name. The test for the true poetic energy which rouses Barth's sleeping dragon is, it seems to me, the only universal test which can be applied to poetry." In this poem, both the articulation of the theory in such radiant language and the theory itself miraculously fuse, and that, says Josephine Jacobsen, is what poetry is all about.

In an intricate poem called "Language as an Escape from the Discrete" from Jacobsen's 1981 collection, *The Chinese Insomniacs,* an arc is constructed from the insect world where two wasps mate (or fight) to a cat who puts "its furred illiterate / paw on my page" and who, like the poet, drinks milk and will inevitably experience one breath which will be final. The fourth stanza introduces a human element in the person of a questioning child, and the arc is completed in stanza five by the adult who

in love, says hush; says, whatever
word can serve, it is not here.
All the terrible silences listen always; and hear
between breaths a gulf we know is evil.
It is the silence that built the tower of Babel.

The darker side of the poet's ongoing search for the radiant center is thus energized by this exploration of the frustrating side of the medium of language. The poet gropes and grapples and finally turns the inarticulate into an advantage: all silence is not golden. Babel with all of its ensuing conflicts was inevitable and necessary.

In a more recent poem, "The Motion," not yet collected into a volume of poems, Josephine Jacobsen examines the hush of the moment of change. What is transition? When and how does the geranium's bud burst into full flower? Time and the seasons move forward yet "turn over / without stir or whisper." The energy crouches unseen, a flicker. Note the beautiful closure of "The Motion."

If I could see it happen, I could
know when all tides tip; low luck
shifts; and when loss is ready. When
you are saying goodbye to someone you think
you'll see next week. And don't ever.

These lines, in their wisdom and scope, are beyond comment as the mysterious, stoppered aspects of natural forces beckon Jacobsen into truth's fathomless mysteries. How unlike the "power of Nothingness" as interpreted by Genet and examined by Jacobsen in her book on Ionesco and Genet.

Josephine Jacobsen often writes poems one must characterize as "narrative" in that they are animated by some progression or action that culminates in a resolution. The characters in these narrative poems are people we come to care very much about such as Mr. Mahoney in "Mr. Mahoney" or Father O'Hare

and Mrs. Pondicherry in "Pondicherry Blues" or Mrs. Mobey in "Spread of Mrs. Mobey's Lawn," all poems in Josephine Jacobsen's most recent collection *The Chinese Insomniacs.* Another poem in this volume called "The Fiction Writer" reveals not only her commitment to the storyteller's art but her ability to evoke its mysteries:

Last night in a dream
or vision or barrier broken
strange people came to me.
I recognized them.

Some I had made, I thought.
Still they were strange—fuller, somehow—
with distinct objects ahead of their steps.

Others who looked at me invitingly,
but threateningly too,
I had not seen.
Familiar though they were.

In his arms, in hers,
each carried a secret.
All were self-lit, like fish
from deepest water.

Nothing told me then
if I were bench or dock.
Only *cousin, cousin, cousin*
said my blood, circling.

Her observations on reading submissions for NEA poetry fellowships in 1981 inspired her candid remarks in an essay, "Like Hunger and Thirst," published in *TriQuarterly* in 1984. Attempting to catch the flavor and to categorize the manuscripts of the 873 entrants in that competition, she reports that the most frequently recurring subject matter dealt with the father-son relationship and with sexual experiences. The former subject, she reports, was discussed somewhat nostalgically and elegiacally, while the latter was generally treated with disappointment, "bewildered resentment," or "a sort of acid regret." Despite some good poems, the submissions were marred, she says, by a great deal of mediocrity, triviality, and plain badness. It is a distasteful business to define these traits: they have a tendency toward contagion. Jacobsen observes, "as we swim desperately in the tide of mediocrity, like Alice in her pool of tears, I can think of no lifeline so hardy as hostility to the trivial." In her view, triviality does not have to do with subject matter, form, language, or technical tricks; it is quite simply an absence, "an awful little void where the life of the seed should pulse."

In this essay she recites the difficulties facing the contemporary poet—outworn language, the disappearance of shared convictions and assumptions, the paucity of readers amid the abundance of writers. The very business surrounding poetry stands in the way of the poem: "the heavy processes of submission, of publication, of reviewers; the supercargo of grants and residencies, prizes and honors. Sometimes it is difficult, in the turmoil of appendages, to keep steadily in mind that solitary, dangerous encounter with the thing itself—that lonely meeting that can never be predicted or totally defined, and from which all authentic poetry, whether most minor or most major, arises."

As a striking example of authentic poetry, she cites two lines which she once discovered in a 19th century New Hampshire cemetery, carved on a leaning gravestone: "It is a fearful thing to love / what death can touch." For years she searched, unsuccesfully, for the source of that quotation. Indeed, neither this idea nor these individual words provide the key to the magic: it is the balance, "the cadence, the sequence of words, the action of the first line, the heavy fall of the last line's four monosyllables which call out the response." All the technical effects of a poem, Jacobsen believes, must fuse in its language. Dishonesty, triviality, sententiousness, tiredness are first betrayed by the words themselves. The necessity of following such advice remains paramount throughout her work, particularly in the most recent.

When a poet plays Scrabble, the game, since it involves words, becomes the chanciest game of chance and its goal not merely to score but to examine the nature, the ambiguities, and the mysteries of language. Or so it seems in the first section, "A Game of Scrabble," of Josephine Jacobsen's poem *A Dream of Games* published in November 1984 in *Poetry.*

As are many of her short stories, "A Game of Scrabble" is set on a tropical island: "Beyond the balcony the sea / flees in long quivers. . . . Below, slick and lovely, the frangipani / boughs, black as snakes and bare, spring / into pink at the top. . . ." The three players contemplate the Scrabble board grasping for words that spell out secret, often unintentional messages:

> The tall child makes *gory,* doubled.
> The smooth tiles spell
> relationships, accidents.
> . . . . *eath,* . . . *eath,* Fingering
> a *d,* one pauses there. A *d*
> would do; *br* would be better.

An ominous atmosphere pervades the poem, suggesting sinister events which never materialize but which hover over the game board. The poet is more aware of it than are the other two players. The poet wins the game or, rather, her words, as in a poem, win. Once again, she has chosen well and made a new order out of the chaos of vocabulary.

In "Bridge of Knaves," the second section of the poem, the game shifts from Scrabble to bridge and the poet examines the characteristics of the Jacks or Knaves of Clubs, Diamonds, Hearts, and Spades. They are a mercurial quartet bent on the slippery pursuits of the game. The poet endows each with a separate background and personality. The Knave of Clubs claims "deep chairs, deep rugs, / hot andirons, snow beyond glass; exclusions;" He is "the ancient heir." The glittering Knave of Diamonds swaggers while the Knave of Hearts claims variety as his lure. The last Knave, the Spade, is viewed suspiciously by the other three:

> Three Knaves know how absurd
> is the fourth's eminence.
> Spade must be the dealer's
> irony; yokel, upraised:
>
> the root's, the earthworm's visitor,
> the flower's clownish uncle.
> But in cardboard, one-eyed and natty,
> in the end, he says, depend on me.

The regal cast in this section of *A Dream of Games* assumes surreal and animated postures as do the figures in dreams. The poet, the "dealer", has won all the "tricks" in this game of guises.

In section III, "A Dream of Games," Jacobsen explains that "The game is dreamed for the rules." The game here is ostensibly a ballgame, but this final section is an amalgam of the various games and gamesters that concern the poet throughout *A Dream of Games.* The poet, posing both as shill and participant, wins the game by default. The poem, a game of catch, is the ultimate power arena where contests for fabulous stakes are won or lost.

> The game is dreamed for the rules.
> Monte Alban's old rule dreamed
> that ball-court from which the loser died.
> Chaos, soft idiot, is close
>
> as breath. But the games appear,
> celestial in order; contracts we make
> with light: the winner humbled,
> the loser connected with his law.

In a recent interview (I interviewed Josephine Jacobsen on tape on October 15, 1984. The full text of this interview will appear in a forthcoming issue of *13th Moon,* a journal edited by Marilyn Hacker.) she told me that she thought of herself as a poet who writes short stories, never as a short story writer who writes poetry. She considers herself by profession a poet. She did not, as a matter of fact, begin to publish fiction regularly until she was in her late fifties, although she had written a great deal of fiction at a much earlier age. At that time, her agent couldn't place the stories in viable magazines, and she believed "short stories just aren't for me," although she never stopped wanting to write them. When Jacobsen became more established as a poet, she decided that it didn't really matter whether her stories got published or not; she wanted to write more of them, and she did. Almost all of these "second-wave" stories have been published and several of them have been reprinted in O'Henry anthologies honoring the best stories published in periodicals of a given year.

Josephine Jacobsen's short stories are classic examples of the genre. Something happens in them; people change; development occurs. This is also true in her numerous narrative poems. Jacobsen dislikes stories with tidy endings, the climactic sentence. Her stories are open-ended as she indicated in our interview:

> I'm desperately conscious when I'm writing a story that the human beings of whom I'm writing have had a long history before they've come into my story and, except in the case of death, they are going to go on having a history after the story.... And in all the stories the reader is left with a choice; in other words, in story after story after story the denouement completes that particular part of the plot but it leaves wide open the subsequent action of the characters.... In stories I don't care for, I frequently get the feeling that these people have never existed until they stepped on the page and that they are going to be dropped like paper figures the minute it is over. And life not being like that, I think one of the fascinations of fiction is that if you have created real people, you have created a possible future for them and that this is something that the story ought to be powerful enough to make you speculate about.

Most of Josephine Jacobsen's best stories are concerned with her belief that human beings when given power all too often misuse that power. The themes of these stories, and of many of her poems, are political in the cosmic rather than the literal sense. Sometimes the accoutrements of the powers struggling involve a conflict between blacks and whites in her native Baltimore or on tropical islands where blacks are in the majority rather than in the minority, at least in numbers; sometimes the power struggle revolves around the oppression of the young by the old or vice-versa. Among her newer stories, "Sunday Morning," "The Squirrels of Summer," and "Protection," for example, explore these conflicts. While the settings and situations in the individual stories vary considerably, the theme is a constant.

In one of Josephine Jacobsen's best known stories, "A Walk with Raschid," one finds a classic Jacobsen situation. The setting is exotic: Fez, Morocco. The happiness of the recently married heroine, Tracy Gantry, is threatened by the invisible presence of Oliver, son of her husband James Gantry's previous marriage. This lurking presence is mirrored in the character Raschid, a small ten-year-old Arab boy, a child as dark as Gantry's own son is fair and who is the same age as the absent Oliver Gantry. The tight plot which encircles the story revolves around a walk with Raschid as guide, which never takes place, but in the end provides the impetus for speculation as to the future of all of the characters, and especially about the lasting power of James Gantry's second marriage to Tracy.

James Gantry experiences an instant rapport with Raschid when he arranges for the boy to take him and a somewhat reluctant Tracy on a guided tour of the town on their last day in Fez, instead of their going to visit a film director who is an acquaintance of a restless, aimless couple they've met at the hotel. Tracy is less enthusiastic about the arrangement not merely because she wishes to meet the director but because, as we surmise later, she recognizes James's paternal attraction to the boy Raschid, who reminds him, in a perverse way, of Oliver, who is her chief rival for James's love. Secretly, Tracy pays off Raschid before he can take them anywhere. Reacting to this demeaning bribe, he kicks her. The story is beautifully crafted; at its conclusion we are forced to speculate about the future of the Gantry marriage.

A darker strain becomes more apparent in many of Jacobsen's stories published since the volume *A Walk with Raschid.* In a recent long story with an island setting, which has a peculiar similarity to "A Walk with Raschid," and which is called "The Mango Community," (recently published in *The Ontario Review* and soon to be reprinted in the O'Henry anthology of *Best Stories of 1984*), an unmarried American couple, Jane Megan, a painter, and Henry Sewell, a writer, along with Dan Megan, Jane's fifteen-year old son by a previous marriage, are discovered by the reader living on the island of Ste. Cecile where they've come for an indeterminate stay. The surface conflict is both political and racial on this island where one's color determines one's destiny. The Vice-Consul urges the Americans to leave before the growing political tension erupts into a malignant violence. Their next-door neighbors, the Montroses, are native blacks; the Montroses' son, Alexis, and Dan play cricket together and come to symbolize much that is latent in the rest of the story and in the culture. Jane, as mother, is obsessed with the notion that Dan might be shot, arrested, or otherwise hurt. As it turns out, it is Alexis who is "hurt" in a most awful manner: paralyzed for life as the result of the brutality of the local police and thus never again able to aspire to his dream of becoming a professional cricket player, a profession that would buy his way out of the poverty that is the lot of his people on this their native island.

Alexis's accident is partially the result of happenstance and of Henry Sewell's pseudo-liberal political leanings, which tempted young Dan to join him on a political march. Without his parents' knowledge or permission, Alexis also joins them. Jane discovers the tragic result of the march when she returns from what had been a very rejuvenating painting session.

The Montroses respond to the assault on their son with spartan rage. Mr. Montrose snarls at Jane, "You go to hell. . . . Evil, evil, evil. All of you. Go home—if you have one." Jane and Dan do go home. Henry Sewell remains on the island to try to "fix things." The double doors close on the story leaving the essential questions unanswered but exposed and discussed. The questions posed are more interesting than any possible answers might be. Will Jane and Henry meet again, marry, make a good life together with Dan? Have the circumstances over which they had little control made or broken them? The reader is left to speculate on the futures of these three characters as well as the nationals left on Ste. Cecile. All of these fictional people have a life beyond the events in the story, as is true in all of Jacobsen's best stories.

A close examination of the wide spectrum of Josephine Jacobsen's short stories reveals a great variety of characters and situations as well as a diversity of settings, but all of them enlighten the reader through a similar integrity of vision. Her carefully plotted, meticulously written stories reveal a conscious awareness of the dark vein running through human endeavors. There are no "happy endings" in the traditional sense, only pockets of knowledge which will guide their readers towards a more sensitive and informed view of their own responses to them. Jacobsen's stories are harbingers of quiet, sometimes dark, but always reliable wisdom.

In her early life, Josephine Jacobsen confesses to having been stage struck. As she explained in her interview with me: "I had one of those beautiful, clear convictions one has when one is 15 or 16 or 17 that it was quite possible to meld two of the most demanding professions in the world, and I seriously thought I could be a full-time poet and a full-time actress." At 15 she began 5 years of acting with the Vagabonds, at the Baltimore Civic Theatre, an exciting and talented group with an ambitious schedule. She has certainly used her early theatrical training well. She is a frequent lecturer and a particularly intelligent public reader of her own work. Reflecting on her brief but intense theatrical career, she said, "I think that having a certain amount of poise on a stage and the necessity of communicating, the necessity of being heard, and above all of creating a rapport between the audience and the poet is, after all, the basic thing an actor has to do: to bring something alive. It's something the audience and the actor do together and something that the audience and the poet do together."

Although she has not written a play, she collaborated with William R. Mueller (Professor of English at Goucher College) on two volumes of innovative dramatic criticism: *The Testament of Samuel Beckett* (Hill and Wang, 1964) and *Ionesco and Genet: Playwrights of Silence* (Hill and Wang, 1968). At the time of their publication, both books were in the vanguard in dealing with their subjects; both remain fresh and incisive. They are intended for the intelligent general reader, and they focus on the dramatists thematically, while discussing their plays individually.

The uniqueness of the critics' study of Beckett lies in their initial classification of Beckett as a poet. The choice of this vantage point is fortuitous; it allows them to move rapidly past technique directly to language and intention. They view Beckett's canon as the "internal autobiography" of one man, a twentieth century Everyman with a "mirthless howl," a laugh that is not a laugh. They examine the procession of brooding central characters (Celia, Vladimir, Estragon, Hamm, Clov, Winnie, Krapp, Molloy) the combination of tragic clowns and rebellious poets, caught in a "communion of suffering." Each of these characters is, as the critics indicate, "like one of those pen strokes of a Picasso drawing in which a single pure line defines the expression of an entire human personality." Beyond the individual clowns, the riddling and repetitious language, the dictated soliloquies, the general atmosphere of "intimidating simplicity" of Beckett's landscape, they point out how cohesive his work finally is, how faithful he remains to his individual vision. The stark economy of his message is sharply outlined in their humane critical study.

The two critics construct their second book with Beckett as the foundational figure and attempt to define the common themes of Beckett, Ionesco, and

Genet: alienation, suffering humanity, God's silence, the difficulty of communicating in language and emotions. They suggest as a perfect trilogy, as portraying the dilemma of modern man, one work by each playwright: *Waiting for Godot, The Killer,* and *The Balcony.* But the harmony and cohesion displayed in the Beckett study is not really possible here. Ionesco's plays are more difficult to classify than Beckett's; they seem to contain more diffuse action, a proliferation of characters and places in constant motion, and, of course, a continuing obsession with an inexplicably lost paradise. The two critics are most successful when discussing the paradox of Ionesco's language: his struggles to renew and refresh language despite his contradictory belief that it is nearly hopelessly worn out. "It is like cleaning a room or nourishing a body or breathing: it can never be finished until the room or the life is closed."

Genet's elaborate images and action are even more dazzling and diffuse. Wisely, the critics concentrate on his plays, using the fiction and autobiography as a sort of "seed ground." They return to the classification of the playwright as poet and to Genet's identification of poetry with power. "Power, the fascination of power, its adoration, the means whereby it can be procured and the manner in which it can be enjoyed, maintained, and protected, this is Genet's central concern." They discuss Genet's interest in ritual and the sacred and the prevalence of certain "creators of poetry" in his work—dancers, blacks, boxers, prostitutes and soldiers. They note the progression in his plays of the varieties of power, culminating in *The Screens* in a quintessential and indestructible power: absolute "ugliness, beauty's absence, that ugliness which is in reality the hole at the center of all," the power of Nothingness.

Throughout her fortunately long and energetic literary career, Josephine Jacobsen's work has shown persistent and humane power. The clarity of her vision and the competence of her technique, even the selection of central themes, have been consistent in her prose and poetry. These elements are evident in her earliest work. The title poem of her first collection *Let Each Man Remember* (Kaleidograph Press, 1940) describes various reactions to stress. The cogent metaphor is selected from one recurring trauma of daily living—how people get up to face a new day. It is a situation which is not less terrifying for its commonality.

> It is indisputable that some turn solemn or savage,
> While others have found it serves them best to be glib,
> When they inwardly lean and listen, listen for

> courage,
> That bitter and curious thing beneath the rib.

In the more than 45 years since writing those lines, Jacobsen has listened well to courage, "That bitter and curious thing beneath the rib."

Source: Nancy Sullivan, "Power as Virtue: The Achievement of Josephine Jacobsen," in *Hollins Critic*, Vol. 22, No. 2, April 1985, pp. 1—10.

Sources

Jacobsen, Josephine, "Fiddler Crab," in *In the Crevice of Time: New and Collected Poems*, Johns Hopkins University Press, 1985, pp. 37–38.

Prettyman, Evelyn, "The Mystery of Faith: An Interview with Josephine Jacobsen," in *New Letters*, Vol. 53, No. 4, Summer 1987, pp. 47, 49, 50.

Spires, Elizabeth, "Joy & Terror: The Poems of Josephine Jacobsen," in *New Criterion*, Vol. 14, No. 3, November 1995, p. 28.

Sullivan, Nancy, "Power as Virtue: The Achievement of Josephine Jacobsen," in *Hollins Critic*, Vol. 22, No. 2, April 1985, p. 1.

Further Reading

Beck, Edward L., *God Underneath: Spiritual Memoirs of a Catholic Priest*, Image, 2002.
    This collection of short stories takes an innovative approach to religion and spirituality. Father Beck's vignettes are touching and hilarious but deeply esoteric. The book brings together preaching and storytelling to deliver a profound, yet entertaining message.

Bokenkotter, Thomas, *A Concise History of the Catholic Church*, Doubleday, 2003.
    This critically acclaimed history covers the most important events that have shaped Catholicism over the past two thousand years. It is a useful reference book and one of the best-selling religious histories of the past two decades.

Craig, David, and McCann, Janet, eds., *Place of Passage: Contemporary Catholic Poetry*, Story Line Press, 2000.
    This is a diverse and intriguing collection of modern poems on Catholic themes arranged around the Christian calendar. Selections include writings from Thomas Merton, Robert Fitzgerald, and Annie Dillard.

Martin, James, ed., *Awake My Soul: Contemporary Catholics on Traditional Devotions*, Loyal Press, 2004.
    In this book, Martin has collected essays focusing on devotion and the contemporary believer. The book includes works by some of today's most prominent Catholic writers, including Ron Hansen, Emilie Griffin, Joan Chittister, and Eric Stoltz, as they celebrate traditional Catholic devotions through vignettes and essays.

It's like This

Stephen Dobyns
1980

"It's like This," originally published in 1980 (and collected in 1994 in *Velocities: New and Selected Poems, 1966–1992*), is a not-so-pleasant look into the not-so-inspiring life of some undefined everyman. Even if it is taken on a metaphoric level, the outlook as espoused by Stephen Dobyns's poem is not good. There is existential angst lingering here, to which almost everyone can relate at various times in a lifetime—those moments when everything seems to be going wrong or, worse yet, when nothing seems to be happening or, even worse than that—as in this poem—when something is going on but it is difficult to express it and no one else seems to care.

"It's like This" is a philosophical poem that might have been written to frighten people into waking up from the stupor that a modern, mechanized existence can induce. It is not clear if the nondescript protagonist of this poem even knows who he is. Instead, he seems to be trying to become what he thinks other people want him to be. His only solace appears to come at nighttime, when he sinks into the nothingness of sleep.

Dobyns's poems have been studied and applauded by literary critics, other poets, and scholars. He is an award-winning writer, whose language and style are down to earth and whose subject matter is easily understood. He is a philosopher and writer, but his topics are not hidden behind abstract thoughts. "It's like This," for example, can be read by anyone and from whatever philosophical stance, and it can be used as a meditation. As Dobyns

Stephen Dobyns   University of Pennsylvania Library

often does, in this poem he opens his soul and invites his readers to take a peek inside. It is as if he is saying, through this poem: This is how one man's life is going. Then, after one reads the poem, it seems that Dobyns might be encouraging other people to ask themselves: How is my life going in comparison?

Author Biography

Stephen Dobyns is an award-winning poet and the author of several mystery novels and one collection of short stories and another of essays. Critics tend to say that his writing leans toward the dark side, but most also admit that Dobyns has an incisive wit and sense of humor. He is known for writing about everyday events in the lives of everyday people in an everyday vernacular. It has also been said that he tackles his material with courage, which, in the end, produces writing that moves his audience.

Dobyns was born in Orange, New Jersey, on February 19, 1941. His father was a minister. He attended Shimer College in Illinois, later transferring to Wayne State University in Detroit, where he graduated with a bachelor's degree in 1964. Three years later, Dobyns earned a master of fine arts degree from the University of Iowa. After gaining his master's, he taught for a short while but changed his career focus in 1971 when he became a reporter for the *Detroit News*. Throughout the years, he has been a visiting teacher at several colleges, such as Boston University, the University of Iowa, the University of New Hampshire, Goddard College, and Warren Wilson College; he has also been a professor of creative writing at Syracuse University. For most of his life, however, his attention has always been centered on writing.

Poetry is his main love, Dobyns has stated in various interviews. *Concurring Beasts* (1972) was his first published collection of poems, and it was the 1972 Lamont Poetry Selection of the Academy of American Poets. Other works that have earned awards are *Black Dog, Red Dog* (1984), which was a winner in the National Poetry Series, and *Cemetery Nights* (1987), which won a Melville Cane Award. Dobyns has twelve poetry collections to his name, including *Mystery, So Long* (2005). Before being collected in book form, many of Dobyns's poems are often first published in prestigious literary magazines and journals, such as the *American Poetry Review*, *Poetry*, *Ploughshares*, the *New Yorker*, *Antaeus*, *Iowa Review*, *Paris Review*, *Gettysburg Review*, and the *Virginia Quarterly Review*. Since most of his poetry lacks a traditional form, his poems fall into the categories of free verse and narrative poetry. Dobyns has been referred to as one of the best narrative poets in the United States.

In fiction writing, Dobyns is even more prolific, with twenty books to his credit. His mystery novels, with the recurring character Charlie Bradshaw, come under the series title of the *Saratoga* stories. Detective Bradshaw has been described as having visible flaws, which means that he is more human than many other stereotypical fictional detectives. The stories are set in Saratoga Springs, New York, where the racetrack typically serves as background. Dobyns's latest mystery in this series is *Saratoga Strongbox*, published in 1998.

Dobyns's other novels include *Church of the Dead Girls* (1997) and *Boy in the Water* (1998). In 2000, he published his first collection of short stories, *Eating Naked*.

Poem Text

Each morning the man rises from bed because the
    invisible
    cord leading from his neck to someplace in the
    dark,

the cord that makes him always dissatisfied,
has been wound tighter and tighter until he
    wakes.

He greets his family, looking for himself in their   5
    eyes,
but instead he sees shorter or taller men, men
    with
different degrees of anger or love, the kind of
    men
that people who hardly know him often mistake
for him, leaving a movie or running to catch a
    bus.

He has a job that he goes to. It could be at a bank   10
or a library or turning a piece of flat land
into a ditch. All day something that refuses to
show itself hovers at the corner of his eye,
like a name he is trying to remember, like
expecting a touch on the shoulder, as if   15
    someone
were about to embrace him, a woman in a blue
    dress
whom he has never met, would never meet
    again.
And it seems the purpose of each day's labor
is simply to bring this mystery to focus. He can
almost describe it, as if it were a figure at the   20
    edge
of a burning field with smoke swirling around it
like white curtains shot full of wind and light.

When he returns home, he studies the eyes of his
    family to see
what person he should be that evening. He
    wants to say:
All day I have been listening, all day I have felt   25
I stood on the brink of something amazing.
But he says nothing, and his family walks
    around him
as if he were a stick leaning against a wall.

Late in the evening the cord around his neck draws
    him to bed.
He is consoled by the coolness of sheets,   30
    pressure
of blankets. He turns to the wall, and as water
drains from a sink so his daily mind slips from
    him.
Then sleep rises before him like a woman in a
    blue dress,
and darkness puts its arms around him,
    embracing him.
Be true to me, it says, each night you belong to   35
    me more,
until at last I lift you up and wrap you within
    me.

Poem Summary

Stanzas 1 and 2

"It's like This" begins by introducing what the speaker of this poem refers to as "the man." He "rises from bed" and begins his day, not of his own free will but by a cord that is wound around his neck and is pulled "tighter and tighter" until the man is disturbed enough by it that he awakens. The speaker makes no comment concerning how the man feels about this situation. He does not mention any anxiety or frustration or anger. The man in the poem merely seems to accept the cord's existence as something he has to tolerate without complaint, as if it is a part of him.

In the second stanza, the man "greets his family," but there is no sense of his acknowledging them or of their acknowledging him. The speaker mentions the family only in relationship to the man's "looking for himself in their eyes." This man, it seems, does not have an identity of his own. He looks into the eyes of his family to find himself. Although he might not know who he is, he does know what he is not. The speaker states that the man cannot find himself in his family's eyes when he looks into them. Instead, he sees men who are shorter or taller than he is. The man also has a sense of his own inner life, because when he looks into the eyes of the members of his family, he also sees "men with / different degrees of anger or love." Of course, he would not recognize this if he were not in touch with his own emotions.

This is an ordinary man who does ordinary things, like waking and sleeping, going to movies, and catching a bus. But he is not ordinary in other ways. People try to define him, but the speaker points out that these people never quite get it right. They do not know him, no matter how much they think they do. This is evident when the man states that all he sees when he looks into the eyes of other people is "the kind of men / that people who hardly know him often mistake / for him." In other words, all he sees are stereotypes of himself. No one knows his inner self. It is not clear whether the man knows himself much better than his family or friends know him. If he did, why would he be looking for himself in someone else's eyes? Or is it that he is looking for himself in their eyes to discover whether they know him? Maybe he does know himself but just cannot find his definition of himself in the people around him.

Stanza 3

The third stanza starts off with a concrete statement: "He has a job." But quickly following this comment is an abstraction. The concrete job that this man has "could be at a bank," the speaker states. This puts the definition of the man back into fuzzy territory and becomes a reflection of the first two stanzas, leaving the reader to question: Does this man have a job or not? Does he know himself or not? Another possibility is that the speaker is merely offering all the options of this man, to give the impression that the speaker is not talking about one man but about a philosophical everyman. In other words, the speaker might be meaning to say, *This could be any man, one who might have a job working at a bank or in a library or digging a ditch.*

The speaker then goes on to offer something very mysterious about this man. This man, whoever he is and wherever he works and whether or not he is a concrete someone or an abstract everyone, has a not-so-clear vision. It "hovers at the corner of his eye." This man does not really see it, but he senses it is there, "like a name he is trying to remember." The speaker further describes this thing that the man cannot quite bring into focus. He uses different senses to grasp it. If it is a name he cannot remember, then it is something intangible. If it is "a touch on the shoulder," then it relates to a sensual experience. If it is "as if someone were about to embrace him," it is not only sensual but could even be joyful, especially if it was "a woman in a blue dress." This at first arouses a sense of pleasure. Blue is the color of the sky and could represent openness. But then the speaker adds that this woman is someone the man "has never met." That throws the reader back into ambiguity again. The woman is a stranger wanting to offer a hug, and this could be pleasant, or it could be threatening. Next, the speaker adds another phrase that turns the feeling in yet another direction. Not only is this woman a stranger, she is also someone the man will "never meet again." This adds mystery to the equation and heightens the sensuality; it also infuses the stanza with a sense of isolation and loneliness.

The speaker then informs the reader that the kind of vision the man is experiencing, this thing that is just out of focus, is the whole purpose of the man's "labor." Bringing the fuzzy image into focus is the whole meaning of the day and the man's effort. But the man never seems to grasp the thing fully. "He can almost describe it," but that is as close as he gets. It is as difficult to seize, the speaker states, as "a burning field with smoke swirling around it."

Stanzas 4 and 5

In the fourth stanza, the man returns home from his day on the job. Again he "studies the eyes of his family." He does this to see if he should change or has changed. Who, he wonders as he stares into their eyes, should he be tonight? He wants to tell his family that he made a discovery that day, that he felt as if he were standing "on the brink of something amazing." But he does not say this. He cannot say this,

perhaps because it would make no sense to them or perhaps because it makes no sense to him. He cannot tell them, because he has not fully understood it himself. Because he does not say anything, they look at him as if he were nothing. They walk "around him / as if he were a stick leaning against a wall." He is inanimate to them, dead, useless.

Then, as darkness falls again, the same cord that appeared in the first stanza reappears in the last stanza. The cord is still wrapped around his neck and now "draws him to bed." This time an emotion is mentioned, but it is not what readers might have expected. Instead of being angry about being forced into bed by a cord wrapped around his neck, the man is "consoled." He likes the "coolness of sheets, pressure / of blankets." This coolness runs in opposition to the heat of the "burning field" that the man imagined when he was attempting to understand that "something," that vision that had eluded him earlier in the day. But it is the coolness that comforts him. The man goes to bed and turns not to his wife but rather to "the wall." He is alone in his own world, separated from his family and the world. Instead of embracing his wife, he stares at a blank wall. "And as water / drains from a sink so his daily mind slips from him." His experiences of the day wash away. Seemingly, no residue of the past remains. His memories no longer cling to him.

Sleep comes to him "like a woman in a blue dress." This could imply that his sleep is also a stranger. His sleep might be pleasant, or it might not. The implications of relating his sleep to the strange woman are not clear, but the poem seems to indicate that even his sleep does not belong to him. It will come like a stranger and leave like a stranger. The speaker personalizes the darkness, however. It "puts its arms around him, embracing him," much like the woman had, except that the darkness talks to him. "Be true to me, it says, each night you belong to me more." It is the darkness that wants the man, more so than the woman or the man's family. Darkness appears to know the man better than anyone knows him. The darkness is the only place that the man finds comfort. "I lift you up and wrap you within me," the darkness tells him, much as a lover might say.

Themes

Hopelessness

That the man in Dobyns's poem "It's like This" is comforted by the darkness and that the speaker of the poem likens the same darkness to a

*Topics
For Further
Study*

- Go online and gather as much information as you can so you have an understanding of the basic beliefs of existentialism. Then write a paper on how Dobyns's poem might have been influenced by this philosophy, pointing out specific issues he raises that are reflected in this philosophy.

- Research the current clinical responses to depression. What kinds of therapy are being used? What are the different types of depression, and whom do they affect? Are there differences in the statistical details between the genders? Does age or ethnicity or environment (where someone lives) make a difference? Write a paper about your findings.

- Write a poem that is an extended metaphor. Choose a concept you want to portray and then

create an image that will convey the message you want to offer to your audience. You may make your images as surreal as you want, but be sure that the images you create are consistent with your message. For instance, if your subject is a dark one, keep the images dark. If the subject is a joyful one, make sure your metaphor expresses that feeling.

- Chose five people and ask them to read Dobyns's poem. Give them time to digest the meaning of the poem and then ask them either to tell you or to write an essay about this poem's subject. Next, write a paper about your findings, discussing the similarities in the five people's interpretations. Also compare their evaluations with your own understanding of the poem.

---

sensual embrace create a sense of hopelessness in this poem. If darkness is the only thing that soothes this man, he is forever lost in an unreal world where there is no light. If there is light in his dreams, it is only his imagination playing tricks on him, just as the darkness pretends to be a lover. A soul in darkness is not a positive image. It does not translate as someone who is inspired.

Another indicator of hopelessness is that the man goes out each day and tries to focus on what appears to be something that cannot be put into focus. Throughout his day, the man runs into situations that would totally frustrate most people. No one seems to know who he really is, his family treats him like a nobody, his job is an ambiguous vocation, and the only person who pays much attention to him is a woman whom he will never see again. Moreover, the man is jerked around by a rope that is tightly wrapped around his neck. It yanks him out of his sleep and stays wrapped around his neck all day, waiting for the night so it can jerk him to bed. It seems that the only place the man finds comfort is in the darkness and in his sleep, but, still, that same rope will not allow him to remain there. As

soon as the man falls into a deep sleep, the rope wrenches him out of his dreams again.

Isolation

It is not clear whether the man truly knows or understands who he is, but it is stated definitively that no one around him knows him. It is hard to tell if the man is searching into their eyes to find out how much they can see of him or if he is looking to them to tell him who he is. It is obvious, however, that the man is alone. His family sees him as someone he himself does not recognize. His friends see him as someone he is not. The only person or thing that attempts to embrace him is a stranger and a personification of the darkness. The man is not just a stick to his family but also a stick that they have leaned against the wall. He is of no use to them. When he tries to tell them who he is and what he has experienced, he cannot find the language to convey his messages. He is confined to his own world. Finally, when he goes to bed, the only place where he finds any sense of belonging, he turns his body toward a wall. It is as if he were a blank, a nothing that is self-enclosed. He lives in a world in which he has no essence. The thing that he tries to focus on is fuzzy and ambiguous, and it is very much like him. He is isolated because he has no language with which to communicate; he has no image that anyone can grasp. He cannot be named.

Death

Beneath the surface of Dobyns's poem is a sense of death. Death is the darkness that soothes the man in this poem. Life, on the other hand, is the rope around his neck. But a rope around the neck implies death by hanging. Even in the concept of life there is death. Life is a completely baffling experience for the man; he cannot grasp its meaning. He has difficulties playing out its games. Everything about life appears absurd or foreign to him. He tries his best but always comes up short, as if he did not exist. The closest he comes to making contact with life is with a stranger who will shortly disappear. The darkness is the only place where the man feels any comfort. That darkness, which can be interpreted as death, wants to embrace him and pull him up and wrap itself around him until the man is within the darkness forever. It would be difficult to interpret this passage as meaning anything less than that the man wants to die.

Existence

What is existence? this poem seems to be asking. Is it one's identity? If so, what does that mean? What is identity if everyone sees a person as someone that he or she is not? Should one conform to what others think, even if those definitions do not in any way match one's self-definition? Why do those definitions differ so widely?

These are a few of the basic questions about existence that this poem seems to be asking. Is existence language? What happens when one tries to speak but becomes so frustrated in trying to explain oneself that nothing comes out? Try as one might to grasp the meaning of life, it is always somewhere out of reach. The closest the man in the poem comes to touching something real in this life is a chance meeting with a stranger who will shortly leave. The man in this poem tries many different ways to relate to existence or to understand it, but it constantly eludes him. It becomes, in the end, not much more than waking up in a world in which no one knows him and no one really cares. Even if he did figure it all out, darkness (death) will eventually call him, and everything or anything that he has claimed as his existence will be washed, like water, down the drain.

Style

Sound

Dobyns has stated that one of the effects that he enjoys in writing poetry is the sound of the words that come together—not only the words, he has said, but even the sound of the individual syllables, consonants, and vowels. With this in mind, readers might want to pay attention to the sound of this poem. For example, in the first line, the words "morning" and "man" both begin with the letter *m*. The words "bed" and "because" both begin with the letter *b*. This is alliteration, the repetition of the same initial consonant in a string of words. The poet purposely creates a specific sound to which he is drawn. There is also the repetition of the word "cord" in the second and third lines, another purposeful act of writing, which adds emphasis to that word. Then, too, there is the repetition of the word "tighter" in the last line of the first stanza.

In the next stanza, there is more alliteration. Three words begin with the letter *h* in the first line: "he," "him," and "himself." The word "men" is repeated in the second line. In the third line of the second stanza, the phrase "different degrees" is another example of alliteration, as is the phrase "smoke swirling" in the second to last line in stanza 3. In the second line of the fifth stanza is the phrase "consoled by the coolness." In the fifth stanza, there is a long series of the sound of *s*. It begins with the same phrase, "consoled by the coolness," and then continues to the next line with the words "blankets," "turns," and "as" in the next line. This is not technically an example of alliteration, because the similar sound does not appear at the beginning of each word; the sound nevertheless continues to be heard in close succession. The *s* sound builds up even more strongly in the next few lines: "drains from a sink so his daily mind slips," followed by "sleep rises" and "dress." Finally we have the phrase "darkness puts its arms" and the word "embracing" at the end of the third to last line, which carries the same *s* sound with a soft *c*.

The reader can also pay attention to sound by listening for rhyming. Although there are no lines ending in rhyme in this poem, there are phrases that have unexpected rhyming sounds. Such is the phrase "family to see," with the final *y* in "family" rhyming with the word "see" in the first line of the fourth stanza. This rhyme continues into the next line, where one finds "what person he should be," with "he" and "be" rhyming. More examples of the sound of *e* are also found twice in the word "evening" and once more in the word "he" that follows. Another rhyme begins at the end of that line with the word "say" and continues into the next line with the word "day," which is repeated farther into that same line. A sort of "false" rhyming appears in the last two lines of stanza 4 with the words "walks" and "wall" in the following line.

Metaphor

Metaphors are often used in literary writing. Using metaphor, the author presents the reader with a comparison between two things that at first appear to be dissimilar. In Dobyns's poem, the metaphor is extended, making up the construction of the entire poem. In other words, this poem is not really about a man who has a cord around his neck. It is not really about some man looking into the eyes of his family and having them look at him as if he were a stick. Dobyns is striving to relate a deeper meaning beneath the surface of the words of this poem. He uses the images, such as the woman in the blue dress or "something that refuses to / show itself hover[ing] at the corner of his eye," to try to put an abstract concept into an image that is more concrete. For example, in this poem Dobyns may be attempting to explain his philosophy about life. Instead of talking in esoteric terminology—words designed to be understood by only a few people—he creates a generic man who lives in a very strange world, to give his readers a model upon which they can build an image. In this way, Dobyns is building a bridge, so to speak, so his ideas can connect with his readers' understanding. If nothing else, readers can walk away with a feeling, if not a full comprehension of what Dobyns is talking about. The extended metaphor exudes a feeling of frustration and depression, a sense that existence on this earth is not a very easy concept to grasp. The poet has done this by telling a metaphoric story about a man with a cord wrapped around his neck.

Historical Context

The 1980s

Dobyns's poem "It's like This" was published in 1980, the beginning of a decade that would force Americans to witness many optimistic but also numerous equally desperate events, things that could make one feel depressed, as the man in Dobyns's poem does. It was around this time that the human immunodeficiency virus, or HIV, first showed up in the United States, spreading fast, before many people understood what it was and what caused it. At the same time, people suffering from depression started using the medication Prozac. The 1980s also saw interesting positive developments. For instance, compact discs (CDs) were created, and tapes were fading out of use. Then, too, computers were beginning to be used more and more at home, instead of just at work.

Television went through major transitions at this time as well. The Cable News Network (CNN) began broadcasting news twenty-four hours a day, which was unheard of in earlier years. Previously, most people had watched a half hour to an hour of news a day at most. Another now-popular television station, Music Television, or MTV, began broadcasting. This music station grew so popular that it soon became necessary for most musical performers not only to know how to read music and play an instrument but also to learn how to project themselves in videos. MTV would eventually affect the film industry, influencing directors to make full-length movies out of short, quick shots, similar to the MTV music video setup. Another new network, Fox, was born during this decade, as was Oprah Winfrey's television show. The first hand-held video system, Game Boy, now found in many American households, was developed in the 1980s.

The decade began with a deranged fan's tragic and fatal shooting in 1980 of the British rock star John Lennon, formerly of the Beatles. In 1981 in Great Britain, Prince Charles married Lady Diana Spencer in what seemed to be a fairy-tale wedding. Their union was not based on romance, but that did not stop the world from falling in love with the British princess. The later 1980s saw the dismantling of two icons of World War II, the Berlin Wall and the Soviet Union, bringing the hope of a united world.

Modernism

There are hints of the modernist influence in Dobyns's poetry. Although it is hard to define modernism in relation to poetry, in general, modernism represents a movement away from formalized vocabulary and themes to a more relaxed stance, one in which everyday objects and events are the topics and everyday language more closely related to normal speech is used. Whereas it once was a poet's custom to use gods or kings and queens as elevated models upon which to meditate in order to create a poem, in the past hundred years more personalized subjects have been explored, especially such personal topics as marital problems and depression.

Compare & Contrast

- **1980s:** Mount Saint Helens volcano erupts, causing loss of life and sending up thick black clouds of ash that darken the skies in the Pacific Northwest. This is the largest volcanic explosion ever in the United States.

  Today: A tidal wave sweeps over wide-ranging coastlines from Indonesia to Africa, killing hundreds of thousands of people. The earthquake that sets off the tsunami is so strong that it causes the earth to wobble on its axis and permanently shifts various geographical formations, including islands off the coast of Sumatra.

- **1980s:** The spacecraft *Columbia* makes its first trip into space in 1981. Five years later the space shuttle *Challenger* explodes on liftoff from the Kennedy Space Center. Seven astronauts die.

  Today: The *Columbia* explodes before its scheduled landing in Florida. Seven crew members are killed.

- **1980s:** War erupts when Iraq invades Iran in an attempt to control waterways that the two countries share.

  Today: War erupts between the United States and Iraq, when the United States accuses Iraq of developing weapons of mass destruction.

- **1980s:** Attempted assassinations of Pope John Paul II and President Ronald Reagan occur. Anwar Sadat, president of Egypt, and the Iranian president, Mohammed Ali Raji, are killed.

  Today: Thousands of people all over the world, including many civilians, are murdered by terrorists. Several contractors and journalists, including the American journalist Daniel Pearl, are kidnapped and beheaded or shot in the Middle East.

Some poets who emphasize the personal realm are referred to as "confessional" poets because they reveal their inner secrets to the public and often explore social ills as well as personal philosophies about life. There is less reliance, if any at all, on rhyme in these modern verses.

Existentialism

Besides the modernistic traits of Dobyns's writing, there is also an element of existentialist thought running through his poetry. The existentialism demonstrated in the myth of Sisyphus comes close to reflecting the underlying tone of Dobyns's poem. In this myth, Sisyphus is ordered by the gods to repeatedly roll a huge boulder up a hill and, once at the top, to let it roll back down again. Sisyphus is condemned to repeat this process over and over again. According to some existentialists, life, much like the one described in the myth, can be meaningless. Despair, as defined by some existentialists, is the feeling humans experience when they realize that nothing in this life is definite. This existence (hence the name *existentialists*) is all that humans have. There is no afterlife, no god, no reward. Human beings direct their own reality and have full freedom to choose what their lives will be like. The emphasis, in this philosophy, is to make the most of one's earthly existence, since it is all there is. Sometimes associated with this philosophy is an overall sense of gloom due to feelings of isolation, alienation, and depression. Without a belief in a god who judges good and bad or a belief in an afterlife, one might feel quite alone. Often, writers who are influenced by existential thought express these types of emotions in their work. A strong consciousness of death also influences those who believe in this philosophy.

The concept of existential thought was taken from the writings of such philosophers as Martin Heidegger, Karl Jaspers, Søren Kierkegaard, Friedrich

Nietzsche, and Jean-Paul Sartre. The ideas that were put forth by these men were later exemplified in the writings of many playwrights and authors; among the most famous were Samuel Beckett, Albert Camus, Simone de Beauvoir, Fyodor Dostoyevsky, Henrik Ibsen, Eugène Ionesco, and Franz Kafka, whose works were mainly published in the first half of the twentieth century.

Then, in the 1950s and 1960s, Jack Kerouac and the Beat poets adopted existentialist themes. Even though there is rarely a modern writer who is specifically referred to as an existentialist, literary critics often point out existential elements in the works of those who are categorized as postmodern poets.

Rainer Maria Rilke

In an interview in the literary magazine *Ploughshares* a few years ago, Dobyns praised the poet Rainer Maria Rilke (1875–1926) as one of the few poets whose writing most thoroughly exemplified great art. Rilke is remembered as one of Germany's greatest poets. His poems continue to be widely published, but one of his most read books is his *Letters to a Young Poet* (1929), in which he advises a new writer to seek his teacher not in some school but rather within himself. Rilke was much involved in his poetry with finding spirituality. In the course of his relationship with the sculptor Auguste Rodin, Rilke's writing took on a sharp focus on objects. He wrote what some have called "thing-poems." Things are definite, Rilke is known to have explained, and poems must be even more definite than things. His *Sonnets to Orpheus* (1922) took a turn toward the abstract, however, as they contemplated the union of life and death. He believed that artists came closest to creating a bridge between life and death through acts of creativity. He spent his later years encouraging other artists to express themselves and to search for a higher degree of reality.

Critical Overview

Dobyns's poem "It's like This" was published in the collection *Velocities*, which the *Booklist* reviewer Donna Seaman describes as a book that "takes us on a journey into territories both mythical and commonplace." *Velocities* contains material from eight previous volumes of poetry plus several new and previously unpublished poems. As Seaman points out, the title of this collection is significant because most of the poems are about movement of one sort or another. Seaman compares this movement to that of water, "which can move at many speeds and fill any space."

In an article called "Story Tellers," published in the *American Poetry Review*, Louise Glück, a poet herself, analyzes Dobyns's poetry and also describes it in terms of motion, saying that his poems take "a rapid downward trajectory." She goes on to state that Dobyns's poetry overall is "apocalyptic" and continues with the statement that his "poems are fierce, impatient, judgemental, wildly funny." Glück comments that because Dobyns writes in so many different genres and is so prolific, some poetry critics overlook his work. Just because he is prolific, she argues, does not necessarily mean that his writing stays on the surface. Glück sees it differently: "The manifold examples of Dobyns's mastery continue to appear with stubborn frequency under various numbers in the Dewey decimal system." If Dobyns's work is not read in the classroom as some other great contemporary poets' works are read, Glück says, it is probably because his poetry is often "too entertaining, too well written."

Dobyns's subjects are often about depression or depressed people. This is the case in his tenth collection of poetry, *Pallbearers Envying the One Who Rides*, which many reviewers praise for the skill in writing but find the poems to be depressing. In a review for *Poetry*, for instance, the critic John Taylor says that "the poet pokes fun at everything, including love and virility." But Taylor goes on to describe these poems as "absorbing" and writes that Dobyns is a "very skilled and profoundly concerned poet." A critic for the *Virginia Quarterly Review*, a literary magazine that has published many of Dobyns's poems, also finds his work to be depressing. However, this reviewer puts it a different way, saying that Dobyns "is darkly funny and provocative as ever." In the end, though, this same reviewer suggests that the readers who might fully appreciate Dobyns's poetry might be those who are likewise "depressed."

Dobyns's tone and the themes that are found in his poetry often carry over to his works of fiction. In a review written for *Booklist*, the critic Bill Ott describes Dobyns's novel *The Church of Dead Girls* as "an unusually thoughtful psychological thriller." Ott points out that, even in his fiction, Dobyns "combines both his poetic and popular sides." Also referring to his fiction, Mary G. Szczesiul, writing for the *Library Journal*, recommends Dobyns's collection of short stories, *Eating Naked*, praising the writer's ability to write in a "natural, compelling, and convincing voice about ordinary people and people on the edge." Michele Leber, reviewing Dobyns's collection of

What Do I Read Next?

- Dobyns is often called not merely a prolific writer but also one who can handle many different writing forms. In his book *Best Words, Best Order* (2003), Dobyns discusses poetry in the form of essays. In this collection, he writes about the basic elements of poetry, such as tone, pacing, metaphor, and voice. He also provides his insights on other poets' work, including that of Rilke and Anton Chekhov.

- Dobyns's first collection of short stories, *Eating Naked: Stories* (2001), has been referred to as profound and funny, as Dobyns tries to capture the idiosyncrasies of modern life.

- In yet another genre, Dobyns published a novel called *The Church of Dead Girls* (2001). On its surface this is a mystery story, but underneath, Dobyns writes about more than just the death of three girls. He includes the disintegration of a whole community.

- Dobyns's tenth collection of poetry, one that gained a lot of critical attention, is the book *Pallbearers Envying the One Who Rides* (1999). Dobyns has said that the poems in this collection revolve around one character he calls "Heart." The first half of the collection is easier to read but offers suggestions on how to read the second half. This is a collection of philosophical poems that become more complex and abstract as one reads through them.

- Frederick Seidel has written a book of poems, *Going Fast* (2000), that has been praised for its ability to capture contemporary life in a cinematic image. Seidel is also a screenwriter, so it comes naturally to him. This is his sixth collection, and many of the poems focus on people living in New York, Milan, Tahiti, and Paris.

- Henri Cole has earned a lot of praise for his sixth collection, called *Middle Earth* (2003). Many of the poems collected here deal with the death of the poet's father. The poems are lyrical and passionate and tinged with the author's visit to Japan in search of his childhood.

- In an attempt to capture a more comprehensible image of the present, Dan Beachy-Quick has written poems that focus on historic figures as they encounter a different, seemingly more simple present moment. This collection is *North True South Bright* (2003). By looking back, Beachy-Quick tries to delineate the complexities of the current age.

- Reviewers have found the poems in Lucie Brock-Broido's *Trouble in Mind* (2004) to be dark but beautiful and often compare her writing to Emily Dickenson's.

---

short stories for *Booklist*, remarks that in taking on the genre of short fiction, Dobyns "allows a show of ingenuity, even exuberance." Leber liked the collection and praised Dobyns, calling this work an "accomplishment by a multitalented writer."

Criticism

Joyce Hart

Hart is a published author and freelance writer. In the following essay, Hart probes Dobyns's poem in search of the essence of life.

From the very first words, Dobyns's poem "It's like This" is a commentary about life. It might take reading the entire poem to make readers realize that even the title of this poem indicates this fact. The title works as an announcer, calling the attention of its audience: Ladies and gentlemen, what you are about to hear is my take on what life is all about. The body of the poem supplies the text.

What, then, is the philosophy of this poem, or the essence of life? The answers are hidden behind every stanza, line, and sometimes even individual words. The clues are not that hard to find. For instance, the first two words of the poem provide a very important hint. They set the mood of the poem even before the reader is certain of the subject matter and theme. Dobyns's poem begins with the words "Each morning." These two words, as simple as they seem at first, bring the myth of Sisyphus to mind. This is the story of the man who must roll a huge boulder up a hill only to watch it roll back down, knowing that he must descend the hill and perform the task over and over again. "Each morning" implies the same drudgery, for the speaker in this poem must perform the same tasks over and over again. Each morning he rises and faces the same situation. As readers will soon find out, that situation is bleak.

Next, readers learn that the man rises out of his bed each morning solely because he has a cord around his neck. The cord is invisible, so no one sees it, but its pressure upon the man's neck is real. The source of the cord is "someplace in the dark," and the response of the man to the cord's pulling him out of bed and into the day is dissatisfaction. He is "always dissatisfied" by the rope because it forces him to awake. It brings the man out of the darkness into the light, and the man does not like the light. The following stanzas of the poem explain why.

The man reluctantly rises out of bed to face the day. He "greets his family," the people who should be the closest to him, sharing the majority of his life's experience, his emotions, and his reflections with them. But the first thing the man does is to look for "himself in their eyes." What does he find? He discovers that there are men in there, but they are nothing like him. Or, at best, these male images that his family holds of him are stereotypes that do not fit *his* description either physically or emotionally. They all have "different degrees of anger or love" than the man believes that he has. There is ambiguity here, however. It is not clear whether the man's family does not know him well or rather that the man does not recognize their images as himself. In other words, has the man hidden his true identity from them? Has his family not taken the time to get to know him? Or is the man so unaware of himself that the image he sees of himself through their eyes appears so distorted that he does not recognize himself? Does he think he is better than that image? Or has he not put in the time and affection that is required for his family to see him as he wishes they would see him? This part of the poem will remain a mystery. All that readers know for sure is that, according to the man, the image that he has of himself and the image that his family has of him do not match. For whatever

> *Only in the dark, only in his nighttime wanderings that bring him closer and closer to death, does he find peace."*

reason this has come about, the outcome is not comforting. It pushes the man away from his family, creating a barrier between them. The family is living with one set of concepts, while the man is living with another. There are no bridges connecting the man to his family; a chasm lies between them. They are virtual strangers to one another. This man's family looks at him like "people who hardly know him," mistaking him for someone else.

In the third stanza, the man leaves his family and wanders out into the social world, where he fares not much better. He has some nondescript job, possibly "turning a piece of flat land / into a ditch," and the only thing that provides any sense of a spark in his life is a vague "something that refuses to / show itself." This is as close as the man in this poem comes to experiencing joy. This is the only part of life that excites him, but the excitement is frustrating. This "something" always remains fuzzy and out of reach. No matter how hard the man tries to fully engage with it, no matter how much he fantasizes about it, he never fully realizes it. This image of the man trying to grasp this "something" is another attempt to connect with life. He has trouble dealing with his family, which represents his more personal relationship with life. But even on a less intimate level, the man still cannot find a way to join the common experience of humankind. No matter where he turns, he finds himself locked in a personal closet, alone and terribly out of touch. He appears to want to be a part, however. There is an element of searching in the man. He may not know what he is searching for or how to find it, but he longs for an embrace. He wants to be recognized. When this "something" that the man cannot fully grasp is mentioned, it is described "as if someone / were about to embrace him, a woman in a blue dress." The same woman is mentioned later in the poem, also embracing him, and it is one of the few places in the poem where a sense of a positive emotion is expressed. As readers will find later, however, it is a positive reaction to something that in itself may not be construed as positive.

So far, the vision of this man's take on life is rather despairing. He is reluctantly awakened, must face his family with little to show for the effort, and then go out into a world, which he cannot quite define. So he returns home. At home he once again checks out his family, hoping to determine from them who he should be. Maybe things have changed. He wants to communicate with them. He wants to express something positive, something inspired. He wants to share with them, but he does not have the language to do so. He cannot bridge the gap. The reason is that he does not even know how to talk to himself. How can he describe his life experience if he cannot quite put his finger on what life is to him? And so his family dismisses him. He is nothing to them, totally useless, and so they ignore him.

The most intimate thing in this man's life, in this whole poem, is the cord wrapped around his neck. It is always with him and is the only thing that touches him. But what is it? And what do its actions represent? Earlier, the cord was described as being invisible and attached to the darkness at one end. With these descriptions, the cord could represent something spiritual. The cord could be like an umbilical cord, attaching the man to the unknown, to someplace where he was before he was born. It could represent the soul, for instance. But the actions of the cord are strange. The cord tightens around the man's neck and squeezes it until the man is forced to awaken in the morning. Although this is stimulating in a way, prompting the man to open his eyes and confront the day, it is not a pleasant image. A cord tightening around someone's neck is a symbol of death. The cord's having its origins in darkness also links the cord to death. To most readers, the cord would suggest a negative image, but, strangely, it is to the darkness that the man in this poem appears to most want to go. In effect, the cord, for this man, might be something positive.

To stress this point, the final stanza of the poem is the most rewarding for the man. It is here that he leaves behind his family and the world. "He turns to the wall, and as water / drains from a sink so his daily mind slips from him." He completely forgets about everything to do with life. And that is when the darkness beckons to him, "like a woman in a blue dress." It is here in his bed where he is "consoled." This is the only place in his life that gives him any semblance of pleasure, other than the fleeting encounter with that vague "something" that constantly eludes him in his waking life.

He is cuddled by the darkness and soothed. It is the darkness, not life, that embraces him. It is the darkness that talks to him. No one else in this poem has said a word to him. "Be true to me," the darkness says, as if the darkness were a lover. The reason the man must remain true to the darkness is that one day the darkness will reclaim him. "Each night," the darkness tells him (reflecting the words "each day" at the beginning of the poem, when the man awakens), "you belong to me more." This implies that each day the man belongs to the day (to life) a little less. And with the last line, the darkness reminds the man that death is the man's final home: "until at last I lift you up and wrap you within me."

It is in the light that the man finds dissatisfaction. He does not want to be awakened to the day. He feels alienated to what he finds in his day. He is out of focus and pushed aside there. No one knows him, and he might not even know himself in the light. Only in the dark, only in his nighttime wanderings that bring him closer and closer to death, does he find peace. Life is a struggle and a challenge, whereas darkness (which implies death) is as sensual and as comforting as a lover.

Source: Joyce Hart, Critical Essay on "It's like This," in *Poetry for Students*, Thomson Gale, 2006.

Neil Heims

Heims is a writer and teacher working in Paris. In the following essay, Heims argues that Dobyns presents an everyman for whom the lure of death is stronger than his attachment to the routines of his life.

The opening stanza of "It's like This" alerts the reader to the central theme of the poem, a struggle—which goes on inside "the man" himself—between life and death. This struggle is repeated throughout the poem, represented in a series of images and situations that outline the contours of "the man's" daily life. What is ironic about the conflict as it is presented in the poem is that the conditions of life frustrate the man and that death, as it unfolds and is fully revealed in the last stanza, is the only gratifying element in his life. Life itself offers no pleasure, but death is alluring. Within the framework of a profound crisis of the spirit, Dobyns constructs a critique of the daily life that the poem suggests most people lead, by identifying the central figure generically as "the man" rather than as a particular person.

"Each morning the man," who is the victim-hero of the poem, wakes up choked. Wound tightly round his neck is an "invisible / cord leading from his neck to someplace in the dark." As the poem begins, there are two unknowns: the nature of the invisible cord and the dark place. As the poem unfolds, those unknowns are revealed, and the violent tension between them, which is stated in the first stanza and described and developed in the following stanzas, is resolved.

Dobyns, a novelist as well as a poet, is a storyteller. In his poetry he follows the precept of the American poet William Carlos Williams that there are no ideas except in *things*. Dobyns moves the reader away from the metaphorically vague world created by the imagery of the first stanza and fills the second stanza with concrete images of routine domestic situations. But the images arise from within the consciousness of the man. He greets his family and looks for himself in their eyes. He does not find himself there. He sees himself reflected back as someone else, as a man he might be mistaken for. He finds only other people's vague impressions of him. This feedback serves to make his sense of himself lack firmness or clarity. Dobyns is describing alienation and isolation, but not as abstract events—and he does not use abstract language. Through the concrete presentation of the man's conscious awareness of other people's perceptions of him, and because of his search for himself in them rather than in himself, Dobyns shows that the man conveys very little of himself to others and, in fact, has very little real existence either in their consciousness of him or in himself.

The sequence of the poem follows the sequence of the events of the man's day. Dobyns's account of his day traces the course of his encounter with the conflicting forces of life and death. After rising and greeting his family, he goes to work. What the work is does not matter. It could be any of a number of jobs, just as he could be any of a number of men. What is important about his job, whether he works in a bank, a library, or a construction site, is that it holds no interest for him. What does attract his attention is something that is not there: "All day something that refuses to / show itself hovers at the corner of his eye." It presses against him with a mental and a physical presence, "like a name he is trying to remember, like / expecting a touch on the shoulder." In the context of the rejection and alienation the poem has shown, the man experiences the hint of a wished-for presence, something that will give him a sense of his own existence. The vague sensation taunting him is "as if someone / were about to embrace him." And then the image is no longer vague. It is no

> *The woman is the emblem of something he is approaching, something he is trying to see and to know, something that can truly define him.*"

longer "someone" but "a woman in a blue dress / whom he has never met."

Even this apparently specific image is a chimera, an illusion, a representation of a vague and desperate longing: it is the image of a woman "he has never met" and "would never meet again." It becomes both clear and impenetrable, however, when she transforms into a guide who can lead him, the image suggests, beyond a veil: "a figure at the edge / of a burning field with smoke swirling around it / like white curtains shot full of wind and light." Light or dark, all is blank. The woman is the emblem of something he is approaching, something he is trying to see and to know, something that can truly define him. The man does not know it, but the reader begins to sense, and the end of the poem will confirm, that the darkness to which the cord pulls him is what he vaguely perceives in the woman. Because he has not seen it or felt it clearly yet, he thinks he is seeking something hidden in life. He is mistaken. It is something outside life that is hinted at by the darkness. "It seems the purpose of each day's labor / is simply to bring this mystery to focus," the man thinks. Paradoxically, the emptiness and purposelessness of his life sharpen his sense of the dark mystery of his life and propel him toward it. The frustration and barrenness of his life make the darkness of death clearer to him and more alluring.

Each day brings no real breakthrough. Day's end brings the man no closer to a revelation but only back to his family and the way things were in the morning. As he had been "looking for himself in their eyes" then, now, "When he returns home, he studies the eyes of his family to see / what person he should be that evening." His experience at home is marked by the same unfulfilled longing and denial that everything else about him has suggested. He cannot communicate. "He wants to say," Dobyns writes, not "he said." The man continues to live in a world where the inside of his mind sharply splits off from the world, where what he wants and what he does bear no relation to each other. Those who perceive him never realize what he has experienced.

Even to himself, what the man has to say is vague: "All day I have been listening, all day I have felt / I stood on the brink of something amazing." Even to himself he can describe his experience only as standing "on the brink of something amazing." But what that "something amazing" is, he cannot articulate. "He says nothing." Without the power to "say," to create and to assert himself by expressing himself, the man indeed is like what his family takes him for, "a stick leaning against a wall," which they walk around. The images of the man and of his family's behavior toward him jointly suggest the low point in his hopeless and empty life, so devoid of meaning or contact.

In the context of his despair, the last stanza rises in the poem almost like a happy ending. "The cord around his neck," which the reader has learned is the man's life itself and which, we were told in the first stanza, "makes him always dissatisfied," now does not. It "draws him to bed," where, for the first time in the poem, the man experiences something that is not dissatisfying, vague, or alienated from himself. "He is consoled by the coolness of sheets, pressure / of blankets." The image is tangible and familiar. Dobyns follows it with another sharp image that clearly shows the condition the man has entered: "his daily mind slips from him" the way "water / drains from a sink." It is an image of cleansing and emptying. It signifies release and relief, as if the water stands for his life as well as for his "daily mind" and draining represents the unclogging of life.

The images that follow confirm the suggestion of death. The man "turns to the wall," something solid, and "sleep rises before him like a woman in a blue dress." The mysterious and vague woman who had haunted him during the day returns fully defined as sleep. Sleep and "darkness" are equated. The sensation represented equally by sleep, darkness, and the woman "puts its arms around him, embracing him." The darkness speaks to him, too, and its words represent the first instance in the poem when the split between outer and inner forces is healed and the man experiences unity. "Be true to me," the darkness, which is the woman in the blue dress, says. "Each night you belong to me

more, / until at last I lift you up and wrap you within me." Death is the mystery he is drawn to, the lover who beckons to him, who, ironically, by leading him into the nonexistence of death, will lead him out of the nonexistence of his life. Only death can see him as he really is, satisfy him, and accept him completely, just as he is—unlike anyone or anything else in his life.

Source: Neil Heims, Critical Essay on "It's like This," in *Poetry for Students*, Thomson Gale, 2006.

Stephen Dobyns and Laure-Anne Bosselaar

In the following interview, Dobyns expounds on his philosophy of writing and poetry, the function of music and noise in his poetry, and his influences.

Stephen Dobyns is the author of nine books of poetry, including *Concurring Beasts, Griffon, The Balthus Poems, Cemetery Nights, Body Traffic, Velocities,* and *Common Carnage.* He is also the author of a collection of essays on poetry, *Best Words, Best Order,* and nineteen novels, ten of which comprise a very popular series of detective books, known as the Charlie Bradshaw mysteries, set in Saratoga Springs, New York. He began his writing career as a police reporter in Detroit.

[LAURE-ANNE BOSSELAAR]: In his book of essays Orphan Factory, *Charles Simic ends one of his essays by saying: "It makes absolutely no difference whether gods and devils exist or not; the secret ambition of every true poem is to ask about them, even as it acknowledges their absence." What do you think about that?*

[STEPHEN DOBYNS]: Well, I think you're always asking about them. One of the functions of poetry is to create a cosmology, to map out the dimensions of what we imagine reality to be, and what, then, may be beyond that. We're always dealing with our existential isolation and trying to decrease that isolation. So that by mapping out that greater area, there's always the attempt to people it. And when one tries to people it with something larger than human, some kind of spiritual or deific creature, then one's not only peopling it, but attempting to create a reason for being as well. It becomes part of our constant endeavor, identifying the reason for populating a cosmos. That's one of the reasons one writes. But the basic reason is to try to erase the isolation.

Camus once told his students: "Writing is a man's trade, not God-given inspiration." In a recent interview in The Connecticut Review, *Richard*

Eberhard said: "I believe in inspiration, which is not a popular concept these days." In your essay "Writing the Reader's Life," you say: "The act of inspiration is, I think, the sudden apprehension or grasping of metaphor." Can you extrapolate about that?

Any piece of writing is a metaphor which, at one level, stands for or represents the writer's relation to what he or she imagines the world to be. By relation I mean emotional, spiritual, intellectual, physical. So you hit upon something that you can use as metaphor; for instance, a liar is like an egg in midair—that metaphor that W. S. Merwin uses. To hit upon the idea of the egg in midair may lead to the realization that one can use this to present an idea of the liar, what it is to lie. All art is metaphor. Even Anna Karenina obviously is metaphor. So as I say, that aspect of intuition is to hit upon something that will function as metaphor. But it may not be an idea, it may be a sound or it may be just a wriggling in the brain. One writes something to find out why one's writing it, and one pursues it. And in that search, often the metaphor evolves. I don't believe in inspiration as something that comes from the other. I think all that comes from within the self. But there are different aspects of the self, the conscious self and unconscious self. Sometimes that act of inspiration seems to be a joining of that conscious and unconscious self. There's suddenly a kind of traffic between those two places, because the metaphor that one suddenly understands has to have some kind of psychological relation to the person who's having it. It's not an arbitrary grasping. It's something with some personal, psychological, spiritual, emotional meaning.

Right, right—but then art is the consequence of grasping the metaphor. It is the discovery of how and why one has grasped that metaphor.

In part. I mean, art becomes something made. And what makes it art is the nature of that end product—that there is something within it which corresponds to our definition of art.

I know that music has a very big importance in your life, and that you like many kinds of music: classical, jazz, rock-and-roll. You often listen to music when you write. How does it help your writing?

It orders the silence, it orders the chaos. I don't write all the time to music, but sometimes I do. And otherwise, it's often playing. And it can be mixtures, as you say, of classical or jazz or South American. I don't listen to that much rock-and-roll anymore; I find the lyrics too tiresome. I also listen to music for the rhythms, that there is much in the rhythms that I try and use in the poems. So

> *One writes something to find out why one's writing it, and one pursues it. And in that search, often the metaphor evolves. I don't believe in inspiration as something that comes from the other."*

there's also that aspect of listening in order to steal, if I hear something that I think works well, or that I might be able to use. And I'm sure that in some ways I use it for completely middlebrow reasons, almost as Muzak. But beyond that there's that general sense that it orders the silence around me. It gives structure to it. And it gives me a constant example of art, of a kind of metaphor which is being presented through the medium of sound.

Which brings me to noise. In our many conversations about poetry, you often mention liking the noise in certain poems. What exactly do you mean by noise?

Most simply, it's rhythm; and then on top of the rhythm there's the relationship between stressed and unstressed syllables; and on top of that there's the sound of different consonants, the relationships between different consonants; and then beyond that there's the relationship of vowels; beyond that there's the relationship of pitch. And so you have those different aspects of sound, which you try and weave into some kind of a pattern, something which may not even seem to be a pattern. But often the poem will begin with a particular sound that works as a kind of tonic note that I keep up through the poem, and sometimes I'll switch to another pattern, or sometimes keep the same pattern all the way through, which can be no more but a simple *t* sound. The noise aspect of it becomes one of the things that I like best about it. And also that the noise can have some metaphoric relation to the content, and can point to a greater kind of cacophony in the world, a greater kind of chaos in the world, so that while the content can be fairly mellow, the noise in the background can be the opposite, can seem nearly out of control. That becomes something else that I like: the sense of the poem in its noise as being almost out of control, seeming to be out of control, yet never out of control.

What directed, what influenced the noise in "Freight Cars"? I hear it in the first two lines: "Once, taking a train into Chicago / from the west I saw a message / scrawled on a wall in the railway yard." There's an emphasis on the assonances.

Well, the first noise is the "Once/west" rhyme, and then using as you say the "wall," all those noises: "scrawl," "rail." In the making of the poem was the desire to create a series of noises, relationships between those noises, that would have some metaphoric relation to the subject matter, and which would be almost cacophonous, in that what the poem then deals with is the lost, a world populated by people who are wandering and wandering. And that all our rationalizations, all our statements of what we're doing and what we're worth and what we're meaning to do, etc., etc., are just so many bits of color imposed on that basic idea of wandering, wandering. And what becomes most important obviously in the poem is the relationships between people, and that those relationships become sacrificed to these ideas of ambition or desire or—

[Quoting a line in "Freight Cars."] "Imagining some destination for oneself. . . ."

Exactly. *[Quoting another line.]* "Some place to make all the rest all right."

Yeats, who I know you admire, once said: "Great art chills us at first by its coldness, or its strangeness, by what seems capricious; and yet it is from these qualities it has authority, as though it had fed on locusts and wild honey." I love that quote, and find it particularly appropriate to your poetry. Who for you wrote or writes "great art" today? In fiction or poetry? And could you briefly explain why those authors are important to your work?

I don't know if anyone alive now writes great art. I expect that they do; I don't have the objectivity to judge it or to look at it that way. I was struck the other night listening to C. K. Williams read how marvelous those poems were, and how completely they made a shape—his poem "Ice," for instance. There are people that I like: Thomas Lux's poems, I admire greatly; Simic's poems, I admire, and some of Mary Oliver; Ellen Bryant Voigt, Louise Glück, and a few others. But when I think of that quote and who it brings to mind, it has to be people like Rilke. Perhaps Baudelaire, perhaps Neruda. But Rilke comes closest to personifying those words for me.

Given the strength of that remark by Yeats, I think, Who is this true of? There are a few Yeats poems, there are a few of Philip Larkin's poems, a couple of Auden poems. . . . I can't think of any Lowell poems, I can't think of anyone in those other generations. There are certainly poems that I love by Roethke and Berryman and Lowell and Bishop, but none that do that kind of work on my interior, as is suggested by that quote. That's something that I see in Rilke more than anyone else.

And in fiction? Chekhov?

I suppose Chekhov. I admire him certainly more than anyone else. Possibly some Faulkner, but I'm not even sure of that. A book I read recently that I felt was powerful in that way was Thomas Mann's *Doctor Faustus.* It had that kind of strength. Other writers that I like—Kundera, I think is a marvelous writer. Also Cormac McCarthy, also William Trevor. But of those three, William Trevor is the one that I admire the most . . . what he's able to do. Yes. I don't know if there's anyone in poetry who can do anything comparable to what Trevor can do in prose.

Often, when I ask you what poetry you're reading, you're reading either South American or East European poets. You seem to prefer them to many contemporary American poets. Why?

I really despise American popular culture, and so its appearance in contemporary fiction or poetry becomes sufficient reason for me not to read it. It's one of the reasons I also don't see many American films. It seems to be a culture driven by a frenzy of appetite, that has no empathy, no sympathy, no roots, no direction. It's just a matter of filling its belly as quickly as possible. There's other kinds of writing—I mean, I used to read mystery novels, Chandler and Simenon. There are the high peaks that one reads for and then there are the low peaks that one reads for, and obviously there are far more low peaks than high peaks. But Thomas Mann's novels, certainly, I would see as high peaks. Dostoyevsky, all the Russians, seemingly. Otherwise I can't think of any contemporaries except for the ones I've mentioned. And the Poles, there are five or six great postwar Polish poets, beginning with Zbigniew Herbert.

To go back to your own poems, and to the "sudden apprehension or grasping of metaphor"—what sudden apprehension or grasping of metaphor occurred when you wrote a poem as wild as "The General and the Tango Singer" in Cemetery Nights, *or more importantly the Cézanne sonnets in* Body Traffic?

"The General and the Tango Singer" is for me much more of a political poem, with these two definitions of art being argued at the expense of the world around them. What is going to triumph in the world? Is it going to be this definition of art or that definition of art? Well, basically, by that kind of ignorance what will triumph in the world is the fire which obviously destroys the restaurant and will destroy other things as well. That is one of the poems that I wrote when I was living in Santiago, Chile, and it was certainly affected by living under a dictatorship, with a curfew, with constant evidence of living in a police state. That's what the General represents, that aspect of it. As for the Cézanne sonnets, I think more and more I was seeing Cézanne as someone who I wished I could emulate. I don't mean necessarily in his ability or his skill, but his concentration on the work to the exclusion of all else. It would seem that he had every reason to stop painting, because he was surrounded by people who told him how bad it was, from all the critics who were writing, from many contemporary painters of his time, from his best friend, Zola, from his wife and son—everyone. And he was very crude, his table manners were awful, he was clumsy in his speech, he was very shy, yet he continued to work, with a single-mindedness that really approached madness, considering how determined it was. And even the fact that he died in the midst of working. He was working on one of those last landscapes, and it rained. He was in his sixties, he caught cold, and was dead three days later. He'd stayed out in the rain trying to finish what he was doing. I admired that steady-mindedness in the face of all else. The world becomes a tremendous distraction. It's hard not to pay attention to it, to be caught up in ideas of success, ideas of publication, ideas that people are patting one's head. "People like my poems, they don't like my poems," or bulls— like that. Ideally I should just have the poems themselves, as Cézanne seemed to have the painting. I'm not saying that would result in better poems—there clearly have been poets, painters, and musicians who have worked with that same steadiness of purpose whose work never amounted to anything at all. What I admire is that ability to work without interruption.

And is the sonnet form of the Cézanne poems appearing in groups throughout Body Traffic *a kind of willed structure and homage? A metaphor within the metaphor?*

Just to the degree of linking it to the history of art, of linking it to the tradition, that art is something ongoing, that has a past, a present, and ideally will have a future; to write those poems in an established form, yet also taking liberties with that form.

Which you did.

It seemed to make the homage more significant to me.

About discipline: do you have a strict writing discipline? When do you write the poems, when do you write fiction, or journalism, or the mystery novels? How do you go from one to the other?

It goes back and forth—if I'm caught up in an idea for a poem or for a series of poems then I work on those, and the fiction gets pushed off a little bit. When I'm busily revising the poems, then I'm also able to work on the fiction. When I finish a larger novel, then I'll often do a mystery novel right after that. The fiction creates an order in my life that I find useful. If I only wrote poems, then I feel my life would be far more disorderly. But the practice of fiction requires a plan, it requires doing something every morning, working on it every day, maintaining that schedule, following an outline. And that makes my life more orderly than it might otherwise be. If I could write poems far more at will and have it come at any time, then I suppose I would do more of that and less of the fiction. But I also write fiction for economic reasons: it pays the bills. And I have very mixed feelings about that, really. I sometimes wonder what kind of writing I would do if I didn't need that money. It's a distraction rather than a burden. I love writing fiction as well.

When will your next book of poetry come out? What is its title?

The next book's scheduled to come out from Penguin in the fall of '99, and it's called *Pallbearers Envying the One Who Rides*. It's a group of sixty poems which is split in the middle by a long other poem called "Oh, Immobility, Death's Vast Associate." The sixty poems are all about one character, who I call Heart. Ideally, one learns how to read the poems, and so the first thirty poems show one how to read the later poems, which are far more complex in their arguments, in their meditations, in their language, in their syntax, in their sound. I suppose to some degree we don't see the character from early life until late in life, but the development of that character follows some kind of chronology. The poems that conclude the book are more concerned with the end of life, and the poems that begin the book are more concerned with those emotional relationships which we value in the middle of our lives.

Who is Heart? You?

Heart is not me. He's not a persona for me. He has many childlike and absurd aspects—in that way, he's closer to the [Christian] Morgenstern poems, which are poems that I've read for a long time, and which were one of the influences for the series. He's also somewhat like Henry, but Henry's far more sophisticated in the Berryman poems. As is Mr. Cogito, far more sophisticated in the [Zbigniew] Herbert poems. So they're closer to the Morgenstern, although Morgenstern's poems are mostly comic. These poems of mine often use the comic to move to a much more serious conclusion.

To go back to the body of your poetry: in Concurring Beasts *you were very much influenced by, or aware of, the Vietnam War and the Democratic Convention in Chicago. When you wrote* Griffon *you were a journalist for* The Detroit News—*so again, one feels the influence of the outside world. Some poems in* Body Traffic, *the new poems in* Velocities, *and some poems in* Common Carnage *have to do with Chile. There is a political attentiveness present, but not constantly so, in your work. Some of your books have no autobiographical poems— like* The Balthus Poems, *for example. In* Body Traffic *one feels you are completely engaged with the autobiographical. I feel this movement of looking out, looking in, looking out. Is that willed?*

All my poems are autobiographical; all my poems are political. Sometimes they're more obviously autobiographical, and use the first-person pronoun. Anything I write about—if I write about a chair, and talk about nothing but the chair—I'm still writing an autobiographical poem. There's just no way for a human being to not do that. At the same time, if I'm writing about an event which I believe happened, then there's no way that I can write precisely or realistically or truly about that event. All autobiography really becomes a form of fiction, because I'm seeing it through a filter that's so subjective that its relation to what actually happened may be impossibly distant. As for the political, there's always that question behind every work of art: how does one live? Sometimes that's focused very clearly on the events within the society, and sometimes it's more internalized. But the very nature of that question—how does one live?— obviously has its political dimension. So those become constant concerns. One of the attempts of art, ironically, is to use the subjective to try and be free of the subjective, to break loose of the self by using

something which is totally of the self. In dealing with the question of how does one live, one is attempting to grasp some larger sense of the political, some larger sense of the society, and be able to identify oneself as a participant, as a member within that society. That becomes very tenuous, especially if you're arguing from a position of existential isolation, where you're wondering, Do I really exist at all? To what degree am I a figment even to myself?

But I have pretty much the same themes all through my books, and basically from one book to another, I'm choosing to deal with those themes slightly differently; I feel that I've found a new access, or a new way of writing about those themes, or I feel that my command of the language has become more precise. All of it, I think, is trying to get through the mirror to the other side, to the so-called real. And that just may be a case of self-delusion. Yeats says that we write about the same themes all our lives. When I first read that in his autobiography at the age of twenty-two, it seemed preposterous. Now at fifty-seven, I think it's true. And I could find poems that I've written again and again and again. They may be similarities that nobody else would recognize, but they're recognizable to me. One seeks paradigms, new ways of doing something, and when a paradigm is discovered, then usually that can result in a new body of poems. It may be that that body of poems constitutes a whole book. In this new book, *Pallbearers Envying the One Who Rides,* that whole book is controlled by the new paradigm. That was also I think true of *Cemetery Nights* and *Body Traffic.* That can be very exciting, because you feel that you have this huge thing in front of you and you're trying to map out all its dimensions. And the writing of the poem is the mapping of those dimensions. And you do it until every scrap is gone. Then it's over, and you sit there half out of breath and half impatient for some new paradigms to take its place.

How important is friendship for you?

I find it the thing that really sustains—yet I suspect that I also have great doubts about it. One has been betrayed in one's life, or has betrayed others, and so one sees the fragility of friendship. Yet if the enemy is really existential isolation, if the enemy is the solipsistic, then friendship is one of the only tools, or one of the strongest tools one has to defeat that enemy, and so it has to be constantly nurtured.

But isn't there also the constant fear of losing that friendship? And the temptation of preferring isolation to the pain of that loss—be it through death or disloyalty?

I think that's a danger. The people I know who have chosen to be single, who have chosen to have not friends but acquaintances, all veer into eccentricity, and are unable to judge themselves accurately. They're unable to judge their work, they're unable to judge the right and wrong of any situation in their lives. It's not simply a matter of becoming self-indulgent. They no longer are able to see themselves in relation to the world. We need friendships for many things, but one of the reasons we need friendships is to keep us sane, because without them we veer off.

But when a dear friend dies—an essential friend, someone who has been integral to your life like your friend the Spanish painter José Berruezo— what happens then?

Then there's a great vacancy in one's life. One's reaction to any death is partly a selfish reaction: How can this person have deserted me? How can this person have removed himself or herself from my life? Didn't they know I needed them? That's very difficult. I think the tendency then is to close down, and not let any person get that close. But that's even more destructive. One has to remain vulnerable to pain. If you're going to be an artist, you have to remain vulnerable to pain. If you become completely self-sufficient, completely impervious, then you can't make anything that anyone's going to ever care about. [*Long silence.*] I mean, all that you're finally left with is wit.

Yes . . . and books. But they don't talk back.

No. They don't talk back.

Source: Stephen Dobyns and Laure-Anne Bosselaar, "An Interview with Stephen Dobyns," in *Ploughshares*, Vol. 24, No. 4, Winter 1998– 1999, pp. 64–73.

Sources

Bosselaar, Laure-Anne, "An Interview with Stephen Dobyns," in *Ploughshares*, Winter 1998–1999, pp. 64–73.

Dobyns, Stephen, "It's like This," in *Velocities: New and Selected Poems, 1966–1992*, Viking, 1994, pp. 100–101.

Glück, Louise, "Story Tellers," in *American Poetry Review*, Vol. 26, No. 4, July/August 1997, pp. 9–12.

Leber, Michele, Review of *Eating Naked*, in *Booklist*, Vol. 96, No. 15, April 1, 2000, p. 1432.

Ott, Bill, Review of *The Church of Dead Girls*, in *Booklist*, Vol. 94, No. 16, April 15, 1998, pp. 1368–69.

Review of *Pallbearers Envying the One Who Rides*, in *Virginia Quarterly Review*, Vol. 76, No. 2, Summer 2000, p. 70.

Seaman, Donna, Review of *Velocities*, in *Booklist*, Vol. 90, No. 9, January 1, 1994, p. 801.

Szczesiul, Mary G., Review of *Eating Naked*, in *Library Journal*, Vol. 125, No. 6, April 1, 2000, pp. 133–34.

Taylor, John, Review of *Pallbearers Envying the One Who Rides*, in *Poetry*, Vol. 177, No. 3, January 2001, pp. 273–75.

Further Reading

Friebert, Stuart, and David Young, eds., *Longman Anthology of Contemporary Poetry*, Pearson's Education, 1989.
A highly praised collection of some of the best poetry of the twentieth century. Included in this anthology are well-written introductions to each poet and his or her work.

Gibbons, Reginald, *The Poet's Work: 29 Poets on the Origin and Practice of Their Art*, University of Chicago Press, 1989.
Reading poetry provides one kind of satisfaction, but the depth of how one reads poetry can sometimes be enhanced by understanding the process that a poet goes through to create the poetic lyrics. This book offers readers a look into that process.

Hugo, Richard, *The Triggering Town: Lectures and Essays on Poetry and Writing*, W. W. Norton, 1992.
This has been called one of the freshest collections of essays ever written on poetry. Using humor and good sense, Hugo claims that while he may not be able to teach everyone to write, he can teach them how he writes; perhaps that example will be enough to send readers off on the exciting journey of becoming an author. He also states that one will learn the most not from someone else's writing but from one's own.

Kowit, Steve, *In the Palm of Your Hand: A Poet's Portable Workshop*, Tilbury House Publishers, 1995.
Kowit's style of demonstrating how to write poetry comes with a lot of praise from reviewers, who found his "show, don't tell" approach to writing easy to follow and enriching. If you want to get a jump start on writing, this might be a good place to start.

Lake

Rosanna Warren
2003

Rosanna Warren's poem "Lake" appears in her collection *Departure*, published in 2003. As the title suggests, the overall theme of this collection is one of parting ways—whether through intended separation, a relationship breakup, a slow sinking into dementia, or death. Several poems in the book were inspired by the mental illness and eventual death of Warren's mother, and several others focus on the strains of marriage and the difficulties of remaining in love. Regardless of the subject, however, most of the poems, including "Lake," are underlined with messages of farewell and exit.

"Lake" is a twenty-six-line, one-sentence work, heavily dependent on the use of water as a metaphor. A metaphor is a figure of speech that expresses an idea through the image of another object. That is, metaphors help explain thoughts or feelings by comparing them to something else, often something physical. In this poem, the speaker uses the touch and motion of water in a lake to describe the need for comfort in a time of sorrow. The water's gentle movement is like a caress to the person standing in it, but having to leave it and go back to the shore symbolizes the person's acknowledgment that temporary comfort must be abandoned in order to face the reality of sadness and loss.

"Lake" is a relatively brief but powerful poem whose plain language and clear imagery disguise the significance of its theme. It is at once simple and striking—a testament, perhaps, to Warren's

ability to communicate a complex message with moving clarity.

A note about the line breaks in the poem: although some may consider the words "would be withdrawn" (in line 10) to be simply a continuation of line 9, which is too long to stretch across the allowed width of the page, the short phrases on the right margin of the rest of the poem appear to be significant enough to stand on their own. Their placement on the right side of the page is reason enough to consider them separately, but their content, too, merits a closer look. As such, this entry discusses "Lake" as a twenty-six-line poem rather than as an eighteen-line poem.

A copy of the poem is also available at the *Slate* online magazine website at http://slate.msn .com/?id=2073776, where it was posted a year before *Departure* was published. Note, however, that the line breaks appear differently on the website than they do in the published book.

Rosanna Warren   Mark Richards

Author Biography

Rosanna Warren was born July 27, 1953, in Fairfield, Connecticut. She is the daughter of two noted authors. Her father, Robert Penn Warren, won the Pulitzer Prize for both his fiction and his poetry, and her mother, Eleanor Clark, who published novels and works of nonfiction, won a National Book Award in 1965. Not surprisingly, Warren grew up in a home in which poems and stories were read aloud and books and journals were as common as many youngsters find televisions and computers today.

Warren's literary parents influenced her own desire to be a writer, and they were also able to provide her with an education that went well beyond the walls of typical grammar and high schools. When she was twelve, Warren studied French writers, such as LaFontaine, at a school in the south of France, and as a teenager, she fell in love with such Latin poets as Horace and Virgil. She eventually attended the Accademia delle Belle Arti in Rome and, later, Skowhegan School of Painting and Sculpture in Maine.

In 1975, Warren studied at the New York Studio School and then entered Yale University, graduating summa cum laude and earning a bachelor's degree in 1976. In 1980, she received her master's degree from the Writing Seminars at Johns Hopkins University. She accepted her first teaching position at Vanderbilt University in 1981. The following year, she served as a visiting professor at Boston University, where she eventually accepted a permanent position as assistant professor of English and modern foreign languages. In 2004, she received the Metcalf Award for excellence in teaching at Boston University and has served as the Emma Ann MacLachlan Metcalf Professor in Humanities as well as a professor of English and French. In 1999, she was elected a chancellor of the Academy of American Poets.

Warren's first collection of poems, *Snow Day*, was published in 1981. Subsequent volumes include *Each Leaf Shines Separate* (1984), *Stained Glass* (1993)—winner of the Lamont Poetry Prize from the Academy of American Poets—and *Departure* (2003), which includes the poem, "Lake." Warren has also edited or coedited collections of other poets' works and was a cotranslator of *Euripides: Suppliant Women* (1995). She is at work on a literary biography of the early-twentieth-century French poet and painter Max Jacob.

Besides the Lamont Poetry Prize, Warren has received a Pushcart Prize, the Award of Merit in poetry, the Witter Bynner Prize from the American Academy of Arts and Letters, and the Ingram Merrill Foundation Award. She is also the recipient of fellowships from the Guggenheim Foundation, and, in 2000, she was the *New York Times* Resident in Literature at the American Academy in Rome.

Poem Text

You stood thigh-deep in water and green light
        glanced
off your hip hollows and stomach which is where
        the pilot light
flickers in ancient statues of Dionysus,
and for a moment as you strode deeper it seemed
        as if
this water might rinse away the heaviness   5
of your own seasons and of illness not your own: it
        was a caress
cool and faithless, it lapped against your waist,
it took you in its arms and you gave yourself, a
        little,
only a little, knowing how soon and how lightly
        that touch
        would be withdrawn,   10
how soon you would be standing again on the
        rootwebbed
        shore, drying, restored
to the weights and measures, pulses, aches and
        scars you
        know by heart,
the cranky shoulder, cramping heel tendons, bad   15
        knees, bad
        dreams
you would recognize in the dark, anywhere, as
        your own;
and you knew, too, how those you cannot heal
        would remain
        unhealed
though you reach for them, kiss them on the   20
        forehead, and
        they stare back out of the drift;
and you knew the mountains would continue their
        slow,
        degrading shuffle to the sea
until continental plates shifted in their sleep, and
        this whole
        lake was swallowed   25
in earth's gasp, ocean's yawn.

Poem Summary

Line 1

The first line of "Lake" introduces an ambiguous "you" as its subject, and this individual is addressed throughout the poem. It is worth considering the actual identity of "you," because poets often use this second-person pronoun in various and interesting ways. Sometimes there is a detail or a description within the work that identifies—or

even names—the "you." At other times, "you" can refer to the audience in general, drawing readers themselves into the poem by seeming to speak directly to them. Still other poets use "you" to mean the speaker him- or herself. That is, "you" really means "I," but referring to oneself in the second person allows a *distance*—or a chance to examine a situation more objectively—that the first person does not afford. Which is the case in "Lake"?

The short answer is that we do not know. But Warren is noted as an autobiographical poet, so this "you" could be someone in her personal life: her mother, whose illness and death were the basis for several poems in *Departure*, or her husband, since this poem falls within the so-called marriage section of *Departure*. Another viable option is that "you" is "I," whether referring to a generic speaker or to Warren herself. After considerable analysis, the bottom line is still the same: who "you" is does not affect the overall tone or message of the poem. It is simply a noteworthy subject that adds a little intrigue to the work. In this first line, then, the subject is standing in a lake, water up to the thighs, and "green light"—the lake's reflection—appears to bounce off his or her skin.

Line 2

The second line helps to further define the body of the person in the water, with the "hip hollows and stomach" reflecting the sunlight on the lake. But a different type of light is also mentioned in this line, one that seems out of place in a natural environment. A "pilot light" is a small jet of gas kept alight to ignite a gas burner, such as in a furnace or on a kitchen range. It is generally a blue flame, which plays off the green light mentioned in the previous line.

Line 3

This line introduces yet another odd allusion, or reference, this time to an ancient Greek god, most commonly known as the god of wine. Dionysus is also associated with all the effects that accompany drunkenness—from laughter, sexual arousal, and relaxation to forgetfulness, sickness, and violence. His correlation to sexual pleasure is called out in the poem in references to the body's midsection. The pilot light that flickers there in "ancient statues" is a metaphor for the constant desire that burns within a human being, regardless of his or her situation.

Lines 4–5

In these lines, the speaker watches the subject walk farther out into the lake. The vision of this deeper submergence makes the speaker think that the "water might rinse away" the pressing weight of something that troubles the subject. Note, however, that the thought lasts only "for a moment," suggesting that optimism is short-lived and that, in reality, the water cannot rinse away anyone's problems.

Line 6

Line 6 identifies the causes of the "heaviness" that the subject apparently endures. First, it is the weight "of your own seasons," meaning not only the person's age but perhaps also the toll that years of distressing experiences have taken on the body. Second, it is the burden "of illnesses not your own." This phrase introduces the real crux of the poem: a loved one in "your" life is seriously ill, and "you" can do nothing about it. The lake, however, offers a momentary "caress" of comfort for the person standing in it.

Lines 7–8

These lines suggest the deceptiveness of the water's soothing touch. It is described as "cool and faithless," implying that unlike most caresses, this one does not evoke warmth and promise. It does, however, lap "against your waist" and take the subject "in its arms," and the subject, in turn, gives in to the enticement—but note that it is only "a little." It is as though the subject understands how easy it is to be deceived by something that feels so comforting.

Lines 9–10

The first words of line 9 reemphasize the slightness with which the subject responds to the water's caress, and the remainder of the line, along with line 10, explains the reluctance to give too much. The subject knows "how soon and how lightly" the tender touch of the lake will "be withdrawn," so there is no reason to get used to its consolation. There is a deep sense of pessimism and foreboding evident in these words, and one cannot help but think something worse is about to come.

Lines 11–12

These lines pick up on the notion of "how soon" the subject will lose the solace of the water when he or she returns to the shore, which is knotted with tree roots. Line 12 portrays the common scene of a bather drying off after a dip, but it concludes with a misleading connotation. The word "restored" is generally a positive term, implying various good qualities or actions—renewal, healing, regained strength, and so forth—but readers

Media Adaptations

need only scan the next line to know that the restoration here is not necessarily welcomed.

Lines 13–16

These four lines primarily convey the *physical* aspects of what is restored to the subject. The "weights and measures" refer to the difference between a body partially submerged in water and one standing on dry land. A person, of course, feels much lighter in water and will lose balance with increased depth. Many of the remaining images reflect pain in one form or another: "aches and scars," "cranky shoulder, cramping heel tendons, bad knees." All these references point to the irony of the word "restored" in line 12. The end of line 15 and the one-word line 16 also present an interesting twist. As noted, all the qualities that return to the subject on shore are physical thus far. But the final one brings back the poem's somber tone: "bad / dreams."

Line 17

Line 17 continues the allusion to the subject's dreams, employing an almost playful depiction with "you would recognize in the dark . . . as your own." Dreams, or nightmares, obviously happen when one is asleep, when the mind is "dark." It is also interesting to note specifically the words "your own," which seem directly connected to the same two words used twice in line 6.

Lines 18–19

The connection between the earlier part of the poem and this later part is further advanced in lines 18 and 19. The sentiment implied in "of illnesses not your own" is echoed in "how those you cannot heal would remain / unhealed." Once again, the end of one line is cautiously hopeful until the next line contradicts it. Loved ones who are ill will not remain in a good way—they will only remain unhealed.

Lines 20–21

In these lines, the speaker describes the sorrowful and futile attempts of someone trying to reach out and comfort the sick. Even though "you" lovingly "kiss them on the forehead," the subject gets no warm response. Instead, "they stare back out of the drift," as though completely preoccupied with their own dismal, consuming thoughts. Note the use of third-person plural to refer, presumably, to only one person with whom the subject is concerned. The vagueness and ambiguity of "them" and "they" provide no identity for the ill person and serve only to retain a curious distance between the speaker, the "you," and those who are unhealed.

Lines 22–23

These lines introduce the metaphor that brings the poem to a funereal, bleak end. The terminally ill are compared to mountains that inevitably "continue their slow, / degrading shuffle to the sea." Words such as "slow" and "shuffle" connote age or sickness or both, and the word "degrading" suggests the debilitating effects of disease on both the body and the mind.

Lines 24–26

The final three lines enhance the metaphor, bringing the poem back around to the depiction of the natural environment with which it began. But nature is now an ominous force—like disease—that human beings can neither stop nor guide. This sense of helplessness is compared to a simple lake "swallowed / in earth's gasp" when geological plates shift and rearrange both ocean floors and land masses. In the end, the poem's subject is resigned to the fact that the ill will soon be swallowed as well and, like an earthquake, nothing can prevent it from happening.

Themes

Terminal Illness

Although a specific disease is never identified in the poem, a major theme of "Lake" is the grief and resignation that naturally accompany serious illness, especially when it is terminal. Words such as "heaviness," "faithless," and "withdrawn" all

point to a somber mindset, and the phrase "those you cannot heal would remain / unhealed" clearly implies that there is no recovery expected. Warren uses a water motif—a thematic or metaphoric element that recurs throughout a work—to portray both faint hope and final abandonment in the process of dealing with incurable sickness. In the beginning, the subject walks deeper into the lake in a halfhearted effort to "rinse away" emotional pain. Toward the middle of the poem, the "you" is back on the shore, drying off, while a loved one simply stares "back out of the drift," apparently lost in melancholy thoughts. In the end, mountains crumble to the sea, and the lake is "swallowed" by the ocean—a powerful act of nature, not to be denied, like death.

While "Lake" concludes on an obviously sad note, its overall sorrowful tone is evident long before, when the idea of illness is introduced. Even the futile attempt to alleviate grief with the water's caress seems mournful. The "you" is unable to enjoy a moment of solace because he or she knows the moment will soon be gone and there will be only dry, "rootwebbed" land to stand on. This pictorial description is simply a poetic way of saying that you cannot enjoy a moment of life, because the death of one you love is just around the corner. Essentially, the mere presence of terminal illness is a heavy weight on the shoulders of all it touches. In this poem, the identities of those touched are vague at best, but the heaviness of disease is unmistakable.

Disease and Human Perspective

If the most prominent theme in "Lake" is terminal illness, human perspective on the subject is an important companion theme. But the twist in this poem is that the perspective is not that of the person who is ill but of someone who must bear the burden of having a loved one who is ill. That is, the "you" whose thoughts and actions dominate the work is not sick. Rather, it is an ambiguous figure who is dying and who is portrayed only in the brief, vague terms of sitting on the shore with a blank stare on his or her face.

Warren explores this theme with such grace and subtlety that it is almost unnoticeable on first reading. The poem makes no dramatic announcement about perspective, and it is quite easy to assume that the viewpoint of the sick will be given equal consideration to that of the healthy. But that is not the case. The first word of "Lake" establishes the subject of the work, and in line 6, the speaker

Topics For Further Study

- In the past ten to fifteen years, several notable people have announced that they have been diagnosed with Alzheimer's disease. Present to your class the reason(s) that you believe famous people make their diagnoses public and what effect the disclosure has on other people with Alzheimer's, on medical professionals who research and treat the disease, and on American society in general. Invite classmates to offer their own opinions as well.

- Warren is noted for her allusions to figures from Greek and Roman mythology as well as to actual writers and artists from the ancient world. Write an essay on why she might find these metaphorical references so attractive, and give your opinion on whether they strengthen or

weaken her otherwise contemporary style and themes.

- Write a personal essay on where you might turn for comfort or for a momentary distraction from stress and sorrow if a loved one in your life were diagnosed with an incurable disease. Would it be an actual place, another person, a hobby, or any one thing in particular?

- Write a poem in which line breaks play as important a role as the subject or theme. Then write a brief synopsis of the process. Is it difficult to place such emphasis on line breaks? Does the construction itself get in the way of just saying what you want to say? Explain why or why not.

---

makes clear that the illnesses are "not your own." Whose, then, are they?

Not until line 18 is anyone else mentioned and then only as an unknown "those." Note, however, that the "you" is consistently paired with the ambiguous third-person reference: "those you cannot heal," "you reach for them, [you] kiss them on the forehead." Even though the one suffering from illness is now brought into the picture, it is still the perspective of the subject "you" that is important. The heaviness described in the poem is that of the subject, not of the ill person, and it is "you" who bears the weight of loss and sorrow and gloom. The subject is portrayed in detail, both emotionally and physically, and from these descriptions one can both see the subject and feel what he or she is going through. The mountain-and-sea metaphor that rounds out the poem compares a progressing disease to a "slow / degrading shuffle to the sea" while it also indicates the hopeless mindset of the subject who imagines the scene in the first place. That is, line 22 makes it clear that "you knew" that the illness "would continue," and, from the subject's perspective, the end of the loved one's life will be like a lake swallowed up by an immense ocean—an ocean indifferent to grief, as it manages only a "yawn."

Style

Contemporary Free Verse

In the late nineteenth century, French poets such as Arthur Rimbaud and Jules Laforgue started a literary revolt against the long-established rules of what makes a poem a poem, which at the time were believed to be strict adherence to specific patterns of rhyme and meter. The *vers libre* (free verse) movement called for a relaxation of poetic restrictions, allowing the poet to compose in a more natural voice using common language to express familiar themes. Contemporary free verse simply refers to the progression of original free verse in the twentieth and twenty-first centuries toward even fewer restrictions, especially with regard to content and language usage. Contemporary free verse poets do not shy away from subjects that are sexual, violent, or controversial in nature, and descriptions are usually presented in a plain, conversational manner.

Metaphor and Allusion

In "Lake," the language is predominantly straightforward and unadorned, with a splash of metaphor here and there to add intrigue. For instance, there is a lengthy description of the subject standing in waist-high water and then coming to shore to dry off the "cranky shoulder, cramping heel tendons, [and] bad knees." These solely physical aspects are set against a more highbrow and obscure allusion to "ancient statues of Dionysus" as well as to the highly imagistic metaphor that concludes the poem. Adding allusions to creative works is an effective way to make an idea or description more easily understood by referencing something familiar. At the end of the poem, for instance, Warren alludes to the actual shifting of earth's continental plates and the resulting degradation of land and water to describe how disease "shifts" human bodies and minds and ultimately "degrades" them. Regardless of the content, however, the language is primarily simple and conversational, with no rhyme or metrical patterns.

Line Breaks and Margins

The most noticeable aspect of this poem's construction begins with line 9 and runs through to the finish at line 26. In typical poems, the second part of a line break is indented with one tab, or a few letter spaces, from the left margin. The first and second parts are often considered one line that is simply too long to fit in the allowed page width. But here the indents are wide enough to push the second parts of line breaks to the right margin of the page, not only making them stand out but also warranting their consideration as separate lines instead of continuations of previous lines. The effect is beneficial. It serves to call attention to important ironies and concepts in the work. For example, the phrase "bad knees" leads directly—and surprisingly—into "bad / dreams"; "would remain" drops immediately into "unhealed." Lines 25 and 26 are both very short and produce their own interesting effect on the page. The phrase "lake was swallowed," set against the right margin, flows into "in earth's gasp, ocean's yawn," set against the left margin. Visually, the lines appear with a clear gap between them, creating their own "yawn" on the page.

Historical Context

Dementia

Warren does not specify any year or even a decade in which "Lake" takes place, nor is any particular region or state identified. The place is insignificant, but readers may make a careful, and educated, assumption about the time period. This poem is probably inspired by the author's awareness of her mother's deteriorating mental faculties due to dementia, which some critical accounts suggest accompanied the despondency and melancholy that Eleanor Clark sank into after Robert Penn Warren's death in 1989. Clark died in 1996. Given these facts and suggestions, it is safe to consider the time frame for "Lake" as the early to mid-1990s; its composition time may be the same or a few years later.

By the end of the twentieth century, great strides had been made in studying various types of dementia, particularly Alzheimer's after the former president Ronald Reagan was diagnosed with the disease in 1994. Ironically, the increased number of older people suffering from these mental ailments is commonly credited to the fact that humans are living longer. In general, dementia is a progressive brain dysfunction that leads to an increasing restriction of daily activities. A slow destruction of nerve cells in the brain causes the victim to lose the ability to function normally and to communicate thoughts and feelings effectively. Typical symptoms include forgetfulness, difficulties performing familiar activities, language problems, impaired judgment, and problems with abstract thinking.

Although data on the frequency of dementia have been more closely studied in recent years, there is no indication that the illness occurs any more or less often than in the past, when not as much attention was afforded it. In general, statistics show that its frequency increases with age, with about 2 percent of people age sixty-five to seventy suffering from it, 5 percent of those age seventy-five to eighty, and 20 percent of those age eighty-five to ninety. Nearly one in three persons over the age of ninety is a victim.

In the 1990s and into the early twenty-first century, treatment for the various types of dementia included a combination of physical, emotional, and mental activities. Thinking and memory training as well as physical therapy and anti-dementia or other types of drugs combine to help slow down the progression of this mentally debilitating disease. As yet, there is no cure. Warren's acknowledgment of this unfortunate fact is made clear in her declaration that "those you cannot heal would remain / unhealed."

Tsunamis

It is perhaps apt to mention the startling coincidence of the metaphor that concludes "Lake" and the devastating natural disaster that happened fourteen months after *Departure* was published. Warren ends the work with "until continental plates shifted in their sleep, and this whole / lake was swallowed

/ in earth's gasp, ocean's yawn." These lines describe poetically, and nearly perfectly, the natural phenomenon known as a tsunami.

Obviously, Warren was not making geological predictions and had no idea of what was to come the following year, but anyone reading this poem today may be ominously reminded of the terrible event that struck on December 26, 2004. On this date, the biggest earthquake in forty years occurred between the Australian and Eurasian plates in the Indian Ocean. The quake caused the seafloor to rupture along the fault line, triggering a tsunami that spread thousands of miles over a seven-hour period. A tsunami is not actually a single wave, but a series of waves that can travel across the ocean at speeds of more than five hundred miles an hour. In the deep ocean, hundreds of miles can separate wave crests. As a tsunami enters the shallows of coastlines in its path, its velocity slows, but its height increases. A tsunami that is just a few feet or yards high from trough to crest can suddenly rise to heights of over a hundred and fifty feet as it hits the shore, destroying land, buildings, and, of course, life.

The December 26 tsunami originated in the Indian Ocean just north of Simeulue Island, off the western coast of northern Sumatra, Indonesia. The resulting wave destroyed shorelines along Indonesia, Sri Lanka, South India, Thailand, the east coast of Africa, and other countries. The death toll in early 2005 stood at over 283,000 people, but with more bodies still being discovered on a daily basis—and given that many of those who were swept out to sea will never be found—an accurate figure on loss of life may never be known. This tragedy has left survivors who know all too well what it is like to be "swallowed / in earth's gasp, ocean's yawn."

Critical Overview

The overall critical response to Warren's poetry—and to *Departure*, in particular—has been mixed. Critics seem to want to praise her work (and many do), but many cannot defer from registering a common complaint: she is too academic. Still, Warren's four poetry collections have been generally well received, despite a few jibes scattered throughout the reviews.

In his column for *Poetry* magazine, the poet and critic David Orr points out that *Departure* is obviously the work of someone well versed in both classical literature and art. He notes that readers are subjected to a string of allusions, such as to "the *Iliad*, the *Aeneid*, Wilfred Owen, Georg Trakl," and more than half dozen others. Orr takes a humorous shot at Warren, saying, "So if you're looking for poems about corn dogs and the J. Geils Band, get ready for disappointment." Orr continues with an offhanded compliment, however, noting that "most of the work in *Departure* takes up the volatile subjects of love and death (particularly the death of the poet's mother), with the former pieces generally being more successful than the latter."

The reviewer Judy Clarence, writing for *Library Journal*, notes, as Orr did, that the obscure allusions in some of the poems may make the poems "inaccessible" to some readers, but she also calls Warren "one of today's outstanding American poets" and describes the poems in *Departure* as "thoroughly grounded and stunningly written explorations of death, the passage of time, loss, and impermanence." Echoing this praise, a book critic for *Publishers Weekly* describes the poems as "long and masterfully elaborate sentences and unrhymed stanzas" and includes "Lake" among the poems that "display insight and hidden discipline."

Criticism

Pamela Steed Hill

Hill is the author of a poetry collection, has published widely in literary journals, and is an editor for a university publications department. In the following essay, she examines the poem's reference to Dionysus as an odd, yet poignant allusion in a work that offers no obvious reason for its inclusion.

On its own, "Lake" is an obscure poem in regard to defining its persona and the relationship between the speaker and subject or the subject and the mysterious "they." But when the poem is considered among the others in *Departure*, readers can make intelligent guesses about its source of inspiration—the poet is the speaker, the speaker is the subject, and the "they" is the speaker's ailing mother suffering from incurable dementia. Or are they?

In the end, the truth about specific identities makes little difference. What is noteworthy, however, is the intriguing one-time allusion to Dionysus, a famous Greek god, that seems to have nothing whatsoever to do with the subject, tone, theme, and style of the poem.

"Lake" is undoubtedly a work about the desperation, grief, and final resignation of someone

What Do I Read Next?

- In a *Boston Review* article (Vol. 29, October–November 2004) titled "Not Your Father's Formalism," the critic Rafael Campo offers interesting commentary on contemporary poets writing in formal verse. Campo contends that poets like Warren are not quite as strict as the formalists of long ago, but neither are they as loose as many contemporary experimental writers. Campo addresses Warren's *Departure* as well as new volumes by Marilyn Hacker and Mimi Khalvati.

- When Warren's mother, Eleanor Clark, was diagnosed with macular degeneration, she reacted with shock and despair. But she also used her permanently impaired eyesight as inspiration for *Eyes, etc.: A Memoir* (1977). Clark's near-blindness and later decline into dementia were the source for several poems in *Departure*, and this autobiographical book by Clark is a stirring account of the brave and determined battles she waged in later life.

- Deborah Digges, a poet and a contemporary of Warren, recently published *Trapeze* (2004). Her work is similar to Warren's in style and in substance—highbrow at times but also somber in addressing familiar themes. In this volume, several poems focus on loved ones who are dealing with loss and death, while others describe the rural New England landscape, with its woods, gardens, and barns.

- Margaret Lay-Dopyera offers a sometimes sad, sometimes funny, always intense account of what it is like to live with parents suffering from Alzheimer's and Parkinson's diseases in *Until the Trees Are Bare: Losing One's Parents to Dementia* (2002). Like Warren, Lay-Dopyera experienced firsthand the heartbreak, anguish, and exasperation of watching a parent (both, in Lay-Dopyera's case) lose the capacity to think, reason, and remember.

---

dealing with the pending death of a loved one. Twenty-four of its twenty-six lines are dedicated to the description of the subject's futile attempt to escape pain—both emotional and physical—and the mournful acknowledgment that reaching out, touching, and kissing the one who is ill will not save him or her from a "slow, / degrading shuffle to the sea."

But then there are lines 2 and 3. Like the well-known "sore thumb," these two lines stand out with their strange and sudden departure from the seemingly straightforward running motif of the poem. What is the point of this quirky allusion? Why is it mentioned only once? To make sense of this imagery from mythology that appears early on in "Lake," readers need to understand who Dionysus is and what possible connection he may have to a poem about sorrow, death, and desperate longing.

Most commonly, Dionysus—and his Roman counterpart, Bacchus—is known as the god of wine, but that is only the beginning. A supreme being whose claim to fame is a popular drink must

have some "baggage" to rule over as well. For Dionysus, it is all the associations, both good and bad, that come along with being drunk—from giddy happiness, relaxation, and sexual arousal to anger, depression, self-doubt, and violence. Dionysus is the god of all these.

What many abbreviated accounts of Dionysus's role in mythology fail to mention is that he is also noted as the archetype of dying and resurrecting in the Greek world. Even though there are a variety of scenarios detailing his birth and early life, one common thread that runs among them is that Dionysus "dies" several times or is transformed into a different being, such as a snake or other animal. Each time, however, he returns to life, a vital and powerful god.

Many scholarly studies in Greek mythology concentrate more on this "dying and renewing" aspect of Dionysus than on his noted drinking and reveling. And it is likely this same aspect that underlies Warren's inclusion of an allusion to the motley god in "Lake." Themes of illness and death are evident in the poem, but "the pilot light / [that] flickers in ancient statues of Dionysus" adds a subtle, yet important dimension to the subject's and/or speaker's demeanor regarding the loss of a loved one.

For the first half of "Lake," the "you" is portrayed in water, and there is a clear desire for what he or she would like the water to do: "rinse away the heaviness" that weighs on the subject's mind. But the speaker has already likened the subject to Dionysus, with the "green light" shining off "your hip hollows and stomach" like the pilot light in statues of the ancient god. This comparison implies that "you" is also going through a process of dying and resurrecting. While the subject is not the one who is ill, the grief that he or she experiences is a kind of death—a killing of the spirit, so to speak. But if the subject is like Dionysus, a rebirth or renewal will follow the demise.

Does this, then, suggest that the poem is not as bleak or pessimistic as a less-detailed reading would imply? Is there actually something positive about the speaker's or subject's approach to such a difficult time? Not likely. Logistics alone indicate otherwise, with the reference to Dionysus being extremely brief and the clear statement on "how soon and how lightly that touch / would be withdrawn" closing the door on any hope for recovery. And if this line closes the door, the poem's ending nails it shut.

After the subject emerges from the water, "Lake" takes a downward spiral to the bottom of hopelessness and resignation. The speaker's statements about what the subject accepts as reality are straightforward and unyielding: "you knew, too, how those you cannot heal would remain / unhealed," "you knew the mountains would continue their slow, / degrading shuffle to the sea." The subject does not merely believe—the subject knows.

The only thing left to ponder, then, is whether this doleful abandonment applies across the board for the subject—that is, regarding the sick loved one, as well as him- or herself and life in general— or if the Dionysus allusion suggests the possibility of renewal, at least for the "you." Since Warren is noted for (or accused of, in some cases) being a bit erudite and inaccessible in her poetry, it may stand to reason that this cryptic, short-lived reference to a Greek god is included simply as a brainteaser. Its brevity makes it easy to dismiss as mere poetic fluff, but it is unlikely that a highly academic, cultivated poet like Warren would throw something in as fluff. A brainteaser is another matter.

> " *The reader is forced to delve a little deeper into the 'pilot light' metaphor and ask what it has to do with Dionysus and what Dionysus has to do with a person standing in a lake trying to escape the emotional turmoil of depression, grief, and death.*"

Anyone who knows a bit of biographical information about Warrren knows that she is well versed in the classics, that she has years of experience studying and living in Europe, and that her work does not shy away from grandiose allusions— from classical writers and mythology to French poets and Italian painters. Whether readers actually appreciate the effort is sometimes doubtful, but it is safe to assume that Warren's intent is sincere. In "Lake," Dionysus must serve a purpose. For those who read the poem seriously and carefully, he definitely causes readers to stop and *think*.

The contention here is that *that* is his purpose. Readers not at all familiar with Dionysus have quite a bit of research to do, but even those who can readily name him as the god of wine and good times must be puzzled by his presence in a poem whose subject and tone are just the opposite. The reader is forced to delve a little deeper into the "pilot light" metaphor and ask what it has to do with Dionysus and what Dionysus has to do with a person standing in a lake trying to escape the emotional turmoil of depression, grief, and death. Finding the answer may not be easy, but then the brain would not get much of a workout if it were.

In the end, the allusion to Dionysus has no bearing on the overall meaning and subject of the poem. Read it through and simply omit the phrase "which is where the pilot light / flickers in ancient statues of Dionysus." The meaning does not change, nor does the tone or any of the themes.

> *The process of poetic transformation activates the essential process of connection that joins together the person and the world in an unstrained unity, even in the face of the great terrors of nature, such as passion, catastrophe, and mortality, which threaten continuously to overwhelm us with their unrelenting power."*

Even the syntax remains coherent. The inclusion of this reference, then, is arbitrary, but it is there nonetheless. Maybe it signifies that the subject will "live again" after the loved one is gone or maybe it even implies that the sick will be resurrected in one form or another, but neither of these possibilities is certain. What is certain is that an odd allusion usually generates curiosity and curiosity makes people think. If for no other reason, the poet is probably satisfied with that.

Source: Pamela Steed Hill, Critical Essay on "Lake," in *Poetry for Students*, Thomson Gale, 2006.

Neil Heims

Heims is a writer and teacher working in Paris. In this essay, he argues that the poet's perception and the world she perceives determine each other and that the poem derives its energy from this interaction.

Whatever else it may be, a poem is an act of transformation. By means of a poem, a poet's consciousness and experience become part of the world, and parts of the world become aspects of the poet's consciousness and experience. This dizzying interchange, this delicate interaction, creates the potential stored in the poem, which is released as the energy of poetry when the poem is read or recited.

Words turn into things, and things turn into words. The tangible objects of the world represent the intangible sensations—thoughts and feelings—of the poet, and the intangible sensations of the poet—those thoughts and feelings—render the tangible objects of the world meaningful and even symbolic, that is, representative of things they commonly, in themselves, are not. The process of poetic transformation activates the essential process of connection that joins together the person and the world in an unstrained unity, even in the face of the great terrors of nature, such as passion, catastrophe, and mortality, which threaten continuously to overwhelm us with their unrelenting power.

A connection as fundamental as the connection between any person and the world is the connection that we have to ourselves. It is a connection that is continually broken and repaired by consciousness. Because of consciousness, each of us is divided into our own subject perceiving ourselves (and even perceiving ourselves perceiving) and our own object perceived. Yet it is through this split, through conscious perception, that we know ourselves, become whole, and know the world in which we find ourselves.

Rosanna Warren's poem "Lake" is a meditation, a wide-awake, trancelike contemplation of her own experience of herself through her experience of nature. She stands momentarily at a still center of a world that is anything but still. In "Lake" the poet—divided between the speaker and the "you" to whom she speaks—encounters her own painful, apparently incurable anguish, and her own division, in her several sorts of encounters. The poem describes an encounter with nature: "You stood thigh-deep in water." Warren gives her thoughts about nature and about culture ("ancient statues of Dionysus"), her own burdens ("the heaviness of your own seasons / and of illnesses not your own"), and the relation between herself and nature as that relationship is formed by her consciousness of nature, by her personification of it ("it [the lake water] lapped against your waist, / it took you in its arms").

In the poem Warren transforms the simple act of slowly stepping into a lake into an encounter with what the Greeks would call her *moira*, meaning her portion, the substance and the conditions of her life, including those aspects of being and feeling (with regard to the contents of her life) that define and delineate her.

Fire and water meet and represent the two forces that encounter each other in the first two lines of the poem—the glancing comfort of the reflection of the lapping water and the flickering frenzy of Dionysian fire. The poet feels the power that both exercise upon her as she steps into the lake, "thigh-deep in water." The lake water that embraces her up to the thighs as she enters it reflects itself as glancing "green light" on her "hip hollows and stomach" and introduces us to the first moment of transformation, which is accomplished by means of the process of mental association. The glancing light of the water becomes a flickering Dionysian fire, a disturbing frenzy beyond our rational control, as a natural event reminds her of how the ancient Greeks represented the power of one of their gods in a work of art. The part of her body that is illuminated is "where the pilot light / flickers in ancient statues of Dionysus." The soothing, but fleeting caress of water and the unsteadiness of passionate energy encounter each other in the image. Flame and water meet at the center of her body and the center of her consciousness. Torment and comfort approach each other in the struggle between what is real and what is desired.

In this encounter, we begin to learn the situation of the poet. Trouble burns inside her. She hopes for something soothing from without, from outside herself. She catalogues her pain: "the heaviness / of your own seasons and of illnesses not your own," "the weights and measures, pulses, aches and scars you / know by heart, / the cranky shoulder, cramping heel tendons, bad knees, bad / dreams." Against this trouble, she personifies the water as a consoling lover, a tender comforter with the power to "rinse away the heaviness." But the water's "caress" is "cool and faithless." It is not enduring: "it lapped against your waist, / it took you in its arms," but "how lightly that touch / would be withdrawn." This touch of this water will not extinguish that Dionysian fire piloting the poet's anguish. In consequence, when "it [the water] took you in its arms . . . you gave yourself, a little, / only a little, knowing how soon and how lightly that touch / would be withdrawn."

From the fluid medium of short-lived solace, the poet returns to the firmer territory of her own life, "standing again on the rootwebbed / shore." The shore is solid ground, not flowing and disappearing, but it is "rootwebbed." Her trouble is the ground under her feet, the history upon which she stands, and by means of it she identifies herself. This, her real condition, is her problem and her solace. It is more permanently solacing in her acceptance of it—this tangled foundation of what is, that which supports and grounds her—than the fleeting caresses of water. Warren expresses its power

through the economy that is peculiar and particular to successful poetry, in this case, by the single placement of a word that by that placement carries two meanings, which contradict each other and therefore coexist.

The word "restored," which ends the line "how soon you would be standing again on the rootwebbed / shore, drying, restored" if the line is read end-stopped, that is, if the reader pauses at the end of the line, takes on a positive character. It suggests being brought back to life, being brought up to capacity, being "restored," becoming whole, an intransitive quality of the thing itself, something about the poet. But even though the line ends with that word and therefore permits us to stop momentarily as we read, there is no punctuation, and we must continue and let the sense slide over the side of the line into the next line, a poetic device called "enjambment." This is what we get: "how soon you would be standing again on the rootwebbed / shore, drying, restored / to the weights and measures, pulses, aches and scars you know by heart." The glancing possibility of comfort slips away like water to be replaced by the solidities of "weights and measures, pulses, aches and scars." She is not her own but is given over, "restored," *to* the actualities of her life.

The simultaneous representation of opposite realities achieved by the contrasting meanings united in the word "restored" governs the tone of the rest of the poem, which, although it is full of anguish, even despair, and death violence, has a mournful tone of calm acceptance. The content is grim. Warren speaks of "how those you cannot heal would remain / unhealed / though you reach for them, kiss them on the forehead, and / they stare back out of the drift." Here is a tender presentation of caretaking, but the caretaking brings neither solace nor connection. Rather than a last or a lasting communion with a departing beloved, such attentions signify hopelessness. The poet realizes the inevitability of pure death, of departure itself.

But the poet pictures death only as the plight of matter. "Lake," which begins with the poet's conscious confrontation with energy, with the lapping of water and the flickering of fire, concludes with images of heavy and decaying lifeless matter: "the mountains would continue their slow, / degrading shuffle to the sea / until continental plates shifted in their sleep." The end of what is tangible is slow, monumental, cataclysmic, indifferent, and eerily peaceful. The gently erotic and short-lived consolation of lapping water that figures in the first

> *In her own poems, Warren uses all the right devices—similes, metaphors, allusions, lists—in a slightly mechanical way.*"

lines of the poem is transformed into the strange solace of an overwhelming and all-encompassing flood in the last lines.

What remains after matter's destruction is the energy into which it has returned, which has consumed it: "this whole / lake was swallowed / in earth's gasp, ocean's yawn." And these overwhelming forces, "earth's gasp, ocean's yawn," are encompassed in the poet's consciousness and expressed in her words through the transformations accomplished by her art, which puts them under her poetic sovereignty, inside the domain of her poem, subject to her imagination for their existence.

Source: Neil Heims, Critical Essay on "Lake," in *Poetry for Students*, Thomson Gale, 2006.

William Logan

In the following review excerpt, Logan asserts that Warren "does what a lot of other poets do, often a little better, sometimes a little worse."

Rosanna Warren has a warm, classical sensibility (if she has a chip on her shoulder, it's a chip of Greek marble), and some of her poems are an atlas of Greek temples, a phone book of Greek gods. Though *Departure* is her fourth book, her imagination is not highly distinctive—she does what a lot of other poets do, often a little better, sometimes a little worse. There's a poem contemplating a Hellenistic head, poems about her dying mother, poems about gardening or a story by Colette or a landscape seen from a plane, even a poem that almost makes Boston a classical ruin (in a book that invokes the *Iliad*, it's amusing to come across the lines "By beer bottles, over smeared / Trojans").

Warren has the disadvantage of being the daughter of two once well-known writers—when she mentions her father, it's hard not to think, "But

that's Robert Penn Warren." When her mother is ill, you're tempted to cry, "But of course. Eleanor Clark." Warren never drops names, but then she doesn't have to. The children of writers must be aware that in their work biography intrudes more dramatically than for poets whose parents are anonymous.

The poems about her mother's last years ought to be among the most appealing; yet, however carefully coddled, however dryly observed, they seem merely dutiful. Not dutiful toward her mother—dutiful toward poetry.

> Your purpled, parchment forearm
> lodges an IV needle and valve;
> your chest sprouts EKG wires;
> your counts and pulses swarm
> in tendrils over your head
> on a gemmed screen; oxygen,
> heart rate, lung power, temp
> root you to the bed—
> Magna Mater, querulous, frail,
> turned numerological vine. . . .

With that sudden nod toward grandiloquence, all the heart seeps out of the poem. The description is good as such descriptions are, but with nothing stirring in the phrases—it's life worked up into art; yet, while the strangeness of life has gone, the intensity of art has not arrived.

The most curious work here is a series of translations from the notebooks of a young French poet, Anne Verveine, who disappeared while hitchhiking in Uzbekistan. The poems themselves are stale and unprofitable—they seem, like so many translations, just the translator wearing a different suit of clothes. At times the Frenchwoman sounds more like Warren than Warren. This would be unremarkable, if Verveine were not completely imaginary. Having admitted as much in the notes, Warren oddly tricks her out with a dry biography ("She lived obscurely in Paris, avoiding literary society and working as a typographer") and then smartly packs her off to her death.

It's hard to know what to make of this convoluted business. W. D. Snodgrass published a book of poems under the pseudonym S. S. Gardons (a cheerful anagram), making his alter ego a gasstation attendant. The British poet Christopher Reid, twenty years ago, published translations of an imaginary Eastern European poet named Katerina Brac—some readers were convinced she was real. In recent decades, there have been examples enough of literary imposture, authors winning awards by impersonating an Australian aborigine or a Jew who survived the Holocaust. Warren's "translations" give no special insight into Paris or the lives of young women. It's strange to have gone to so much trouble.

In her own poems, Warren uses all the right devices—similes, metaphors, allusions, lists—in a slightly mechanical way. Her favorite method of construction is a violent turn or peripeteia, but such swervings often seem nervousness, not nerve. What salvages this book of intelligent, well-meaning poems, most of them conventional as cottage cheese, are one or two that rise from some dark source even the poet seems unsure about:

> For six days, full-throated, they praised
> the light with speckled tongues and blare
> of silence by the porch stair:
> honor guard with blazons and trumpets raised
> still heralding the steps of those
> who have not for years walked here
> but who once, pausing, chose
>
> this slope for a throng of lilies:
> and hacked with mattock, pitching stones
> and clods aside to tamp dense
> clumps of bog-soil for new roots to seize.
> So lilies tongued the brassy air.

This has the intensity missing elsewhere—the densities required by rhyme seem partly responsible. Whatever ritual the poet incanted, however she prepared for description so coolly rehearsed and a transcendence effortlessly reached some lines later, she ought to do it again and again.

Source: William Logan, "Out on the Lawn," in *New Criterion*, December 2003, pp. 85–87.

Sources

Clarence, Judy, Review of *Departure*, in *Library Journal*, Vol. 128, No. 16, October 1, 2003, p. 80.

Orr, David, "Eight Takes," in *Poetry*, Vol. 184, No. 4, August 2004, pp. 305–16.

Review of *Departure*, in *Publishers Weekly*, Vol. 250, No. 43, October 27, 2003, pp. 60–61.

Warren, Rosanna, *Departure*, W. W. Norton, 2003, p. 111.

Further Reading

Clark, Eleanor, *The Oysters of Locmariaquer*, 1965, reprint, Ecco Press, 1998.

> This travelogue earned Warren's mother, Eleanor Clark, a National Book Award in 1965. It explores life in the town of Locmariaquer in Brittany, a region in southern France where Warren spent part of her childhood. Clark focuses on the lives of the people who cultivate the famous Belon oysters that come from this region as well as the history of the area.

Simic, Charles, "Difference in Similarity," in *New York Review of Books*, Vol. 51, No. 4, March 11, 2004, pp. 21–23.

> In this review, the poet and critic Simic addresses the wide variety of style and content found in contemporary American poetry. Claiming "it is no longer easy to stick labels on poets," he focuses on three new collections in particular, including *Departure*.

Warren, Robert Penn, *The Collected Poems of Robert Penn Warren*, Louisiana State University Press, 1998.

> This lengthy, comprehensive collection of Warren's father's poetry, edited by John Burt, is worth perusing, even if readers do not make it through all 800-plus pages. Robert Penn Warren's influence on his daughter's writing is unmistakable, and many poems in this collection give evidence of that.

Warren, Rosanna, *Stained Glass*, W. W. Norton, 1993.

> *Stained Glass* is Warren's most acclaimed volume of poetry to date, and it is interesting to compare its poems to those in *Departure*, published ten years later. *Stained Glass* won the Lamont Poetry Prize from the Academy of American Poets.

Lepidopterology

Jesper Svenbro

1999

Jesper Svenbro has been one of the leading poets in his native Sweden since he published his second collection of poetry in 1979. His poems are evocative and engaging, rich with allusions ranging from classical mythology to the landscape of Scandinavia to poets such as the ancient Greek Sappho and the modernist T. S. Eliot. An accomplished classical scholar who lives and works in Paris, Svenbro addresses philosophical, psychological, linguistic, and political themes in such a way that they are accessible to the average student but are also provocative for the most learned readers.

Svenbro made his debut in the English language with poems such as "Lepidopterology," which was originally published in the fall 1999 issue of *Chicago Review* and is also included in *Three-toed Gull* (2003), Svenbro's first poetry collection translated into English. With its extended comparison of the human psyche to the various stages of the butterfly's life cycle, "Lepidopterology" is a vivid poem that profoundly explores psychology, language, and science. Dramatizing what Svenbro in the poem calls "the seemingly insoluble conflict between dream and reality," "Lepidopterology" depicts the caterpillar's process of ceasing to eat and beginning to spin its cocoon—which Svenbro characterizes as an act of "total resignation"—as well as the butterfly's emergence from its pupa. These rich metaphors compare the butterfly's flight to the miracle of human psychology as well as the ability of a poem to burst outside the confines of language.

Author Biography

Jesper Svenbro was born on March 10, 1944, in Landskrona, a small town in southern Sweden. His father, a highly respected clergyman, died when Svenbro was a child, and memories of this experience appear in the poet's later work. Svenbro began reading the classics when he was young, and he also enjoyed hiking in Lapland when he was a teenager. He studied for a short time at Yale University and then at the École pratique in Paris. He later earned his doctorate in classics from Lund University, the largest university in Scandinavia. In 1977, he moved to Paris to work for the Centre national de la recherche scientifique, a prominent French public research organization.

After publishing his first volume of poetry in 1966, at age twenty-two, Svenbro concentrated largely on his career as a classical scholar, waiting thirteen years before publishing another collection of poems in 1979. He has since published another seven volumes of poetry, and his poems have been translated into many languages. "Lepidopterology" was translated into English and published in the *Chicago Review* in 1999. It later appeared in the first book-length English-language publication of his poetry, *Three-toed Gull*, published in 2003. Allusions in Svenbro's poetry have ranged from the poets Sappho and T. S. Eliot to artistic and cultural figures that include the French mime Marcel Marceau and elements of Svenbro's personal life, such as a notebook his father kept during World War II.

Svenbro is a successful poet in Sweden, where he has won many awards. In addition to his poetry, he has published two collections of essays in Swedish. He has also translated Greek, Italian, and French poetry into Swedish and has published numerous articles. An internationally renowned classicist, Svenbro has published three scholarly works about ancient Greek literature and culture.

Jesper Svenbro   Cato Lein

Poem Text

For a long time the butterfly held a prominent
    place in psychology
because of its caterpillar phase, its difficult
    sloughing,
and especially because of it pupa stage
which is a period of total paralysis of the will:
fascinated, people studied the frustrated dreams of   5
    the caterpillar,
such high-soaring dreams which corresponded so
    badly

to its ungainly earthbound body; observed
how the seemingly insoluble conflict between
    dream and reality
ended at last in total resignation
as the creature stopped eating, spun a shroud   10
    around its body,
and prepared to die. But in the deepest winter,
in the dried-out condition which is also that of
    taxonomy
when the pupa might have been classified
and placed in a showcase in some windless
    museum,
something unexpected, something totally   15
    unforeseen occurred
which gives us the right to believe in the
    impossible.
Georg Stiernhielm brandished his pencil, wrote
    "The Silk-Worm,"
and thus became the founder of lepidopterology on
    Swedish soil.
But in his poem psychology took a great step
    forward,
left the pupa stage, and established itself as a full-   20
    fledged science:
psykhé really means "butterfly," as you told me,
and warily it crept from its cocoon, its prehistory,
spread its wings and committed itself without fear
    to the wind.
So the poem is only the shroud left on the ground
where its miserable crumpled heap is only a   25
    measure
of victory announced by the butterfly's wings

now ablaze in the sun when it finally flies out of
    language
affirming its brilliant and dizzying love.

Poem Summary

Lines 1–4

"Lepidopterology" begins by stating that the butterfly was an important creature "in psychology," which seems to mean the science of psychology but also suggests the human mind in general. The word *lepidopterology* simply means the study of lepidoptera, which is the order of insects comprising butterflies and moths. The idea that the butterfly has played an important role in the development of human psychology, and the implication that its process of transformation is a metaphor for the mind, will continue to be important throughout the poem. Since the first line begins "For a long time" and is in the past tense, however, Svenbro implies either that the butterfly no longer holds its prominent place in psychology or that its prominence has nothing to do with its caterpillar and pupa stages.

Line 2 suggests that it was because of the butterfly's caterpillar phase and its "difficult sloughing" (which refers to the process of shedding the protective covering of the pupa) that it held a prominent place in human psychology. In lines 3 and 4, however, the speaker places particular emphasis on the pupa stage as the reason that the butterfly used to be important to psychology. During this stage, the caterpillar surrounds itself for one to two weeks in a protective covering that hangs from a branch and allows the pupa to undergo an internal metamorphosis, during which it develops its adult organs. The speaker describes this phase as involving a "total paralysis of the will," which is an example of the literary device of personification, because it attributes human characteristics to an insect.

Lines 5–16

Lines 5 and 6 describe people's fascination with the pupa stage, because of the "frustrated" and "high-soaring" dreams of the caterpillar. Again, the speaker is associating caterpillars with the human experience of dreaming and is engaging in personification. Also, since it is impossible to have studied a caterpillar's dreams, there is the suggestion that caterpillars are being used as metaphors for humans or the human mind. In any case, the people who are studying the caterpillar's dreams notice how they are at odds with its "ungainly," or awkward and unwieldy, body.

Beginning with the last word of line 7 and running through the middle of line 11, the speaker describes the caterpillar dreaming of something greater than its reality; eating no more food; making its "shroud" (which refers to the garment wrapped around a dead human body); and preparing to die. This description implicitly compares the human "conflict between dream and reality" with a caterpillar's process of ceasing to eat and its creation of a membranous shell to protect it during the pupa stage, as though the caterpillar has given up on life because it was unable to realize any of its dreams.

The middle of line 11 signals a shift in the poem, since it is the end of the first sentence and it opens with the word "But." Skipping to the end of the pupa stage, lines 11–14 describe the "dried-out condition" of the former caterpillar as similar to taxonomy, the process of scientific classification of a species and its mounting in a museum showcase. The speaker then says that something "unexpected" and "totally unforeseen" occurred, which allows people "to believe in the impossible" and, presumably, in dreams. It is interesting to note, however, that the reader both expects and foresees the transformation of the caterpillar into a butterfly, which suggests that there is something else that will unexpectedly give people the right to believe in dreams.

Lines 17–23

The turning point of "Lepidopterology" comes in line 17, with the introduction of Georg Stiernhielm (1598–1672), a late–Renaissance writer and scholar known as the father of Swedish poetry. Writing that Stiernhielm's poem "The Silk-Worm" established him as the founder of Swedish lepidopterology, the speaker suggests that this poem is the unexpected and dramatic event described in lines 15 and 16. Then, in lines 19 and 20, the speaker says that psychology "took a great step forward" in Stiernhielm's poem, by turning into a butterfly and establishing itself as a science. It is important to note that the speaker begins line 19 with the word "But," as though to suggest that the taxonomical science of studying butterflies is somehow opposed to the "full-fledged science" of psychology.

In line 21, the speaker states that "you," which may refer to Stiernhielm, told the speaker that "*psykhé*"—Swedish for the "mind" or the "psyche"—"really means 'butterfly.'" This is a curious way of phrasing the idea that the human mind is like the life cycle of a butterfly, and it seems to come from Stiernhielm's poem. The speaker then goes on to say that "you" said the butterfly (and the human psyche) crept out of its cocoon, or prehistory, and began to fly fearlessly in the wind. Svenbro's use of the word "prehistory" to describe the cocoon reinforces the idea that the butterfly's life cycle represents not just an individual human mind but also the evolution of the human mind in general.

Lines 24–28

Continuing the conceit, or extended comparison, that a poem is like the human psyche/butterfly life cycle, the speaker states that the poem, like the cocoon, is the burial shroud from line 10. Discarded in a miserable heap on the ground, this cocoon is "only a measure" of the triumph of dreams "announced" and represented by the butterfly's flight. The butterfly has flown out of the language of this poem to be "ablaze in the sun," and its flight displays and verifies its "brilliant and dizzying love."

These final four lines are important for a number of reasons, perhaps primarily because they achieve the very effect that they describe: the butterfly seems to fly out of the poem "Lepidopterology" to affirm something greater than the language used to describe it. The choice of words in these lines is also interesting; the word "victory" in line 26 stands out, for example, and may suggest that the butterfly and the poem are victorious over the frustrating realities that plagued the caterpillar early in the poem. The last phrase, "brilliant and dizzying love," is also an important turn, and it is likely that Svenbro is associating the triumphant and victorious dreams represented by the successful poem and the flying butterfly with the phenomenon of human love.

Themes

Psychology

One of Svenbro's most important themes in "Lepidopterology" is psychology, beginning with the speaker's comparison of the butterfly's earthbound stages of development to the psyche and continuing through the last lines about the psyche/butterfly escaping the confines of language. Svenbro uses the butterfly in its various stages of development as a metaphor for the human condition, treating the pupa stage, for example, as an illustration of the universal psychological desire to live and dream beyond the confines of "earthbound" existence. Similarly, the butterfly's emergence from its

cocoon is compared to the human capacity to forge ideas, achievements, and self-consciousness emerging from mundane reality.

Svenbro's examination of psychology is not just a commentary on the human mind itself but also a view of the scientific discipline of psychology. In fact, sometimes it is difficult to distinguish whether the poet is discussing the historical development of the human mind or the history of the scientific study of the mind. Svenbro's use of lepidopterology, which means the scientific study of moths and butterflies, along with his references to taxonomy (the science of categorization and classification) imply that human psychology can be rather like the classification of animals. When he discusses the emergence of psychology as a "full-fledged science," however, the poet distinguishes the endeavor from taxonomical science, which involves placing dead butterflies and pupae in museum showcases.

One interpretation of this commentary on psychology is that Svenbro is praising the developments in human arts and sciences, such as the Renaissance poet Georg Stiernhielm's innovations in poetry, which fostered humankind's ability to think of psychology outside its constraints of reality and "frustrated dreams." The poet envisions this triumph in terms of a "victory" over the strictly rationalistic science represented by the "windless museum." Svenbro may be suggesting that the European Renaissance of the fourteenth through seventeenth centuries opened up possibilities far beyond methodical scientific process and allowed people "to believe in the impossible," or to recognize meanings above and beyond the quantifiable.

Literary Aesthetics and Science

Beginning with the reference in line 17 to Georg Stiernhielm, Svenbro expands his commentary to the subjects of literature and philosophy of art, or aesthetics. The poem associates Stiernhielm's poem "The Silk-Worm," and poetry in general, with psychology, implying that innovations in literature allow a glimpse of the true and wondrous nature of the mind. Svenbro establishes this idea by dramatizing a butterfly's emergence from its cocoon alongside his description of the "great step forward" of Stiernhielm's poem, as if the butterfly were coming to life out of the words of "The Silk-Worm."

By separating the poem's first half, with its references to taxonomy, from the references to poetry in the second half, Svenbro suggests that the power of great literature is greater than that of scientific

Topics For Further Study

- Svenbro is an accomplished classicist in Paris. How does scholarly work influence poems such as "Lepidopterology?" Read a section from one of Svenbro's articles or scholarly books, such as *The Craft of Zeus: Myths of Weaving and Fabric* (1996), in order to form your answer.

- Research the history of lepidopterology. Who are the key historical lepidopterologists? How have they advanced the goal of this scientific branch? How have attitudes toward lepidopterology changed over time? What work is currently being done in lepidopterology?

- Poetry has played a unique and prominent role in Swedish history and culture. Research this tradition and Svenbro's place within it. How does Svenbro incorporate Swedish identity into his poetry? What is his relationship with the other poets of his generation? How does "Lepidopterology" evoke Swedish history and culture?

- Research the development of the science of psychology in Western civilization. Describe some of the most important periods in the history of psychology. Who were the key psychologists in the Renaissance and in the twentieth century, and why were they important? When has the butterfly been used as a symbol or metaphor for human psychology and why? Discuss how the history of psychology relates to Svenbro's poem.

---

classification. While taxonomic classification results in a butterfly pupa's being placed inside a showcase, poetry allows the "*psykhé*" the "victory" of its full expression. The poem implies, therefore, that science has its limitations and, in fact, becomes "full-fledged" only when it is given the linguistic power to transcend literal language. This is why the butterfly flies "out of language" and the literal words are a dead burial "shroud" that merely points the way toward the true meaning of an object or living thing.

Dreams and Reality

In line 8, Svenbro refers to "the seemingly insoluble conflict between dream and reality," and he expands on this idea throughout the poem. He goes on to suggest, for example, that there is a connection between dreams and reality that can be affirmed by the "great step forward" of poetry's insight into the human psyche. The poem seems to imply that it is necessary and important to achieve a connection to dreams and that it is the function of psychology and poetry to bring people closer to what is characterized by "brilliant and dizzying love," unconfined by language. Svenbro's allusion to Stiernhielm's poem "The Silk-Worm" reinforces this idea, because the silkworm was a common motif in Stiernhielm's time, representing love's restorative power.

Style

Personification

Throughout "Lepidopterology," Svenbro describes the butterfly and its transformation process as if it were a human. "Frustrated dreams," "paralysis of the will," and "brilliant and dizzying love" are aspects of human, not animal, psychology, and their inclusion in the speaker's description of butterflies requires readers to suspend disbelief and imagine that butterflies think and feel as humans do. This method of envisioning a butterfly as a creature with a human mind is an example of the literary device of personification, in which human characteristics are associated with an animal, idea, or object. Personification is a key tool in Svenbro's poem, because it allows him to make insights about human psychology in a much more vivid manner than would be possible with a literal description of the "conflict between dream and reality" in a person's mind.

Conceit

The technique of personification, described earlier, makes it possible for Svenbro to establish his poem's central "conceit," or elaborate and extended metaphor. (A metaphor is a comparison in which one object or idea is substituted for another.) The conceit of "Lepidopterology" is that the butterfly serves as a metaphor for the human mind. Thus, instead of ceasing to eat and spinning a shroud around its body because it is ready to transform into a butterfly, the caterpillar does these things because it is totally resigned to the "insoluble conflict between dream and reality." Svenbro extends the logic of this conceit to compare the similarities between the ways in which psychology views and treats the human mind and the caterpillar's "dried-out" pupa. The conceit continues throughout the poem until the butterfly in flight serves as a metaphor for the "brilliant and dizzying love" of the human mind. It is through this conceit that Svenbro is able to comment on his primary themes—the nature of the mind and the development of psychology.

Historical Context

Contemporary Sweden

Known for its model of public-private partnership, Sweden has one of the most advanced welfare systems and highest standards of living in the world. The taxation rate is very high in exchange for excellent social services, including universal health care and education. Although the Swedish economy experienced some setbacks during the 1990s, it is growing quickly, and the rate of unemployment is low.

Swedish politics were dominated in the late 1990s by the country's relationship to the European Union. One of three European Union countries to reject a common currency, Sweden continues its history of retaining a degree of independence from European and international politics. Sweden maintains its long-standing foreign policy of neutrality and declines to become a member of the North Atlantic Treaty Organization (NATO).

Contemporary France

France is a country at the heart of European culture and politics but with a vivid and unique cultural tradition of its own. During the early 1990s, the socialist government was involved in a series of scandals, and the center-right government led by Jacques Chirac was elected in 1995. Chirac met with considerable resistance as he attempted to privatize many public companies and reduce spending on social services, and he lost his firm control over the government in the 1997 elections. In 1999, the common European currency was successfully launched, and the French continued to favor the integration of European states.

Since World War II, France has been home to many of the most important and influential intellectual figures in the world. Postmodern and cultural theorists, including Jacques Derrida, Jacques Lacan, and Michel Foucault, lived and worked in Paris, contributing to the city's unparalleled intellectual atmosphere. The French literary scene was also vibrant throughout the 1990s, a decade during which French literary efforts included a broad range of experimentalism.

Swedish Poetry after World War II

From the end of World War II until the mid-1960s, Swedish poetry was associated with high modernism and "formalism," or poetry that emphasizes structure and style over content. In the 1960s, however, a younger generation of poets began to emerge, with a tendency to focus on politics using a direct and engaging style. These writers (of Svenbro's generation) were inclined to disdain the distanced and measured tone that they associated with their predecessors, and their work was characterized by energetic and visceral, or nonintellectual and even earthy, language. The divide between the generations grew less urgent as the years passed, but the legacy of the poets of Svenbro's generation has continued.

Georg Stiernhielm and the Renaissance

Georg Stiernhielm, to whom Svenbro makes a key allusion in "Lepidopterology," was a poet, scholar, scientist, and civil servant who is known as the father of Swedish poetry. Stiernhielm's "Silkesmasken" ("The Silk-Worm") is considered the first sonnet in the Swedish language, the silkworm being, as John Matthias and Lars-Håkan Svensson write in their translator's notes to *Three-toed Gull*, a motif of the era that symbolized "spiritual regeneration or love's restorative power." As a prominent figure of the Northern European Renaissance, a period known for producing great innovations in the arts and sciences, Stiernhielm was influenced by the humanistic tradition that revived the classics of ancient Greece and Rome, cultivated an individualistic spirit, and departed from strictly religious subject matter. Stiernhielm's most famous work is the epic and philosophical poem *Hercules* (1658), in which the classical story of the demigod Hercules is applied to Swedish culture.

Critical Overview

In Sweden, Svenbro is considered one of the most prominent and popular poets of his generation, which included a group of writers who emerged in the 1960s and sought to move away from the formalism of their predecessors. Although Svenbro's first poetry collection was not widely successful, his second collection, published in 1979, earned him a reputation as an original and compelling poet, and he has since received numerous awards in Sweden for his poetry. Svenbro's work has also been translated into French, German, and Italian, and he has established himself as a leading scholar and poet on the European continent. However, Svenbro's first collection in English, *Three-toed Gull*, has received little critical attention since it was published by Northwestern University Press in 2003.

Criticism

Scott Trudell

Trudell is an independent scholar with a bachelor's degree in English literature. In the following essay, Trudell discusses Svenbro's commentary on literary aesthetics throughout the first two sections of Three-toed Gull *in order to analyze the poet's treatment of poetry and linguistics in "Lepidopterology."*

"Lepidopterology" is one of the more accessible poems of Svenbro's collection, with its clear narrative progression and its single extended metaphor in which a butterfly, in its various stages of development, is compared to the human psyche. Like many of the other poems in *Three-toed Gull*, however, it is also a subtle and challenging meditation on language and aesthetics, a branch of philosophy that studies the nature of beauty. Its dramatization of the "seemingly insoluble conflict between dream and reality" that locks itself into a closed cocoon is a reference to poetry, another type of cocoon that holds language in one place. The central question of "Lepidopterology" is how meaning and significance break out of this cocoon, bridging the gap between words and reality and creating a successful poem.

Svenbro is a classical scholar with an interest in the origins of language, and throughout his work, he is invested in the process of self-consciously approaching, interpreting, and interacting with words. The first two sections of *Three-toed Gull* focus overtly on the history and psychology of language, the various approaches to taking ownership of language and meaning, the connection between language and representation, and Svenbro's own relationship to the language of his poetry. In fact, because its themes are developed throughout the poems that surround it, the full resonance of "Lepidopterology" is unavailable to readers until they place it in the context of Svenbro's wider exploration of linguistics, or the study of speech and language. The goal of this essay, therefore, is to highlight the poet's theory of literary aesthetics and to apply this theory to "Lepidopterology."

The aesthetic vision of *Three-toed Gull* begins with the first poem, "A Critique of Pure Representation." Here, Svenbro establishes the idea that language is "not god, / not a position from which the world 'down there' can be gauged" but a physical and self-referential phenomenon. This is a somewhat difficult concept, since it is not necessarily clear, at first, what exactly Svenbro means when he describes language "attain[ing] weight" and "constitut[ing]," as opposed to describing, the real world. Unless readers are well acquainted with postmodern linguistic theory, they might be left wondering how and why a word could be a physical object, like a stone.

In the poem that follows "A Critique of Pure Representation," however, Svenbro provides a more specific explanation of what it means to consider language as a series of worldly objects as opposed to an abstract system of classification. The metaphor for the history of the Swedish language that is presented in "Material for a Geological Theory of Language" provides a groundwork for considering words both less and more than an objective format for describing reality. Although it is presented as a subtext—the underlying, implied meaning—surrounded by parentheses, the observation in lines 21–23 is extremely useful in understanding Svenbro's linguistic theory: "Language is disintegration, / but concurrent with disintegration there is construction / whereby crumbling material is given another meaning." Here, the idea that language is disintegration—that describing something in words makes it fall apart and lose its meaning—comments on the idea that language is capable of objective representation. Svenbro is suggesting that the traditional view of language, as an inflexible

What Do I Read Next?

- Svenbro's poem "Polyphony" (2003) uses an organ (the musical instrument) as a metaphor for the human body in order to dramatize the expression of love in the polyphonic human voice. It relates in many interesting ways (including its use of personification and conceit to explore the nature of the human psyche) to "Lepidopterology," which immediately precedes it in *Three-toed Gull*.

- Tomas Tranströmer's *New Collected Poems* (1997), edited and translated by Robin Fulton, includes this eminent Swedish poet's most influential work. From the elegant "17 Poems" to the challenging "The Sad Gondola," it offers an excellent introduction to a poet whose work has influenced Svenbro.

- *The Craft of Zeus: Myths of Weaving and Fabric* (1996), by Svenbro and John Scheid, is an analytical commentary on Greek and Roman myth and society, with a focus on weaving—a central concept in classical thought—and its significance in the literature and culture of the ancients.

- Anne Carson's *Autobiography of Red* (1998) is a brilliant novel in verse, in which a young man named Geryon falls in love with the fascinating but cruel Herakles. Incorporating classical mythology into contemporary life, Carson portrays Geryon as a red monster like the creature from Herakles's famous tenth labor, but a monster with a sweet and noble soul.

---

system of abstract concepts used to describe reality, is inadequate for pinning down the meaning of something as variable as the real world. In fact, humanity's attempts to describe reality have resulted in a "crumbling" of meaning; abstract words cannot correspond to their previous or original meanings because the world, language, and interpretations are constantly changing. Svenbro suggests, therefore, that it is better to view words as physical objects that have a time, a place, and an age. This limits the ability of words to describe reality of all times and cultures, but it also increases their power to represent specific and actual meanings.

"The Phonetics of Resistance" is a playful and perhaps ironic poem that addresses the idea of words as variable objects in another context. Describing an inflexible skeleton of language as a "reproducible paradigm" that people repeat forever, Svenbro suggests (probably ironically, since a skeleton is a dead body) that language can be both permanent and physical after all. Similarly, "Homage to T. S. Eliot" suggests that there used to be a permanent and objective "gold standard" in values as well as language, but Svenbro becomes ironic when he suggests a return to this system. Calling it "the despotism of fictive values," the speaker suggests that a fixed standard of abstract

language would result in a tyranny by which the meanings of words would not actually correspond to the real world.

It is important to note, however, that Svenbro's commentary about the variability of language does not tend to suggest that words and their meanings are completely displaced from their tradition. An accomplished classicist, Svenbro is always aware of how language relates to its sources. In "Hermes *Boukólos*," for example, Svenbro uses the topic of bucolic poetry, or pastoral poetry about rural themes, and the metaphor of cows (to stand for words or lines of a poem) to suggest that the significance of a poem is related to its linguistic tradition somewhat like a herd of cattle is related to its ancestors.

Svenbro expands on this intriguing metaphor of cattle for poetry, taking into account the phenomenon of interpretation. Claiming that "all poetry is bucolic and the interpreter a cattle thief / who before restoring the cows he has stolen / makes them calve in secret and keeps the calves for himself," the speaker implies that a reading of a poem produces a greater distance between the poetry and its significance. Nevertheless, readers have their own physical, real icons of interpretation. Furthermore, Svenbro

> *Since language is incapable of containing or classifying the full significance of the human psyche inside a poem, it must simply attempt to indicate the various paths toward which the reader can access the fuller resonance of the subject."*

highlights the idea that the process of interpretation occurs at night and that readers must trace the hoof marks of the cows in order to "close on [the] heels" of possessing their interpretations. Then, in a final twist, Svenbro suggests that these hoof marks are the same as those of traditional generations and that therefore the readers' lengthy process of interpretation can be traced back, albeit imperfectly, to the linguistic tradition behind the poems.

Numerous additional poems develop, explore, or test Svenbro's linguistic theory, whereby words are treated as physical objects instead of inflexible abstract codes. Like "Hermes *Boukólos*," they often involve a somewhat ambiguous and playful treatment of language, significance, and tradition. In "Classic Experiment," for example, the speaker imagines himself within a simile from Homer's *Iliad*, in a world/interpretation that seems to have broken free from the original significance of the epic poem. "Mont Blanc" then brings up the possibility of "a new language without syntax / . . . ris[ing] out of the dusky blue of existence," while "The Lake School Manifesto" presents a vision and interpretation of the *Iliad* that is incorporated into a local Swedish tradition and natural climate.

Svenbro presents a multifaceted and subtle theory of literary aesthetics, therefore, in which language and poetry are physical, malleable phenomena. Throughout Svenbro's metaphors and visions of linguistics, there is a refusal to accept the commonly held notion that words are abstract concepts used to describe the real world. Instead, to Svenbro, words are physically immediate objects, and interpretations

of words are fleeting processes that involve an interaction with these objects. Poetry, meanwhile, is a process of suggesting and indicating the tracks to take toward the meaning and significance of these words and interpretations.

"Lepidopterology" is a particularly interesting poem in this context because it can be read as a metaphor for the poetic process. Comparing the science of lepidopterology to the act of writing a poem, Svenbro emphasizes that the classification process is not enough to capture permanent and fixed meaning for all time. Taxonomy, which involves categorizing and classifying the pupa of the butterfly, is successful only in preserving the caterpillar's period of "total paralysis of the will," resulting in a lifeless exhibit in a "showcase in some windless museum." As Svenbro emphasizes in "A Critique of Pure Representation" and throughout the first two sections of *Three-toed Gull*, language is "not a position from which the world 'down there' can be gauged." If the butterfly across all of its stages of life is a metaphor for the human psyche, language that attempts to classify the world from the taxonomical standpoint of pure representation can capture nothing more than the dry, lifeless pupa stage.

Indeed, in order to find the language to depict the "high-soaring dreams" of the human psyche, represented by a fully developed butterfly, the poet must take Georg Stiernhielm's "great step forward." Since language is incapable of containing or classifying the full significance of the human psyche inside a poem, it must simply attempt to indicate the various paths toward which the reader can access the fuller resonance of the subject. A poem, to Svenbro, "is only the shroud left on the ground," like the caterpillar's cocoon, left behind in a "miserable crumpled heap" when the high-soaring dreams of the psyche fly "out of language." Physical and alterable, words are objects open to interpretation, and the poetic process is a method of organizing them as an inspiration and a guideline toward the true meaning of the work. Recognizing the limitations of language and the power of interpretation allows a poet to inspire readers to achieve the "victory announced by the butterfly's wings."

Source: Scott Trudell, Critical Essay on "Lepidopterology," in *Poetry for Students*, Thomson Gale, 2006.

David Kelly

Kelly is an instructor of creative writing and literature at two colleges in Illinois. In this essay, he considers whether Svenbro's use of dry, clinical language in his poem is justified.

Readers familiar with Svenbro's poetry are accustomed to finding in his work an open terrain, where art meets science on equal footing. Readers who are not accustomed to his work are sometimes surprised at the degree to which he tends to slip out of his poetic voice, adapting a scientific tone. In his poem "Lepidopterology," for instance, Svenbro examines the struggle of the caterpillar to grow into a butterfly, a natural progression that to this day provides poets with metaphors for aspiration, isolation, growth, and self-awareness. Many poets would find themselves content with simply focusing on one of nature's most poignant and fascinating events, but Svenbro goes beyond the butterfly's story to the story of the scientists who examine it and the poet Georg Stiernhielm, who gave science a new way of looking at it, which, Svenbro claims, opened the door for psychology several centuries before Sigmund Freud. If "Lepidopterology" were just a poem about a poem, it would stay in the familiar area of poetic language. It is a poem about scientific breakthrough, though, and so Svenbro uses a type of language, basically scientific in tone, that is unusual in poetry. With no clues in the poem's style to show his awareness of shifting tones, readers are left wondering if the inconsistency is a conscious poetic device or a sign of lack of control.

People are often thought to have different, exclusive abilities when it comes to different intellectual functions. Most people are categorized as predominantly "artistic" or "logical," "verbal" or "numeric." Schools divide areas of study into the broad categories of "sciences" and "humanities," as if the two types of thought are meant to compete with each other. There are, of course, people who overcome the common expectations by showing themselves able to cross the barrier: lawyers who publish novels, for instance, or dedicated musicians who are able to work at accounting jobs in order to support themselves when their true gift fails to pay the bills. Generally, though, the skills of even the most well-rounded individuals are not considered to be equally proportioned, so that they end up being considered good in science but great in art or greatly creative but superbly logical. Western thought might be able to accept the two modes of thought as equal, but it will always be dedicated to keeping them separate.

Modes of writing are similarly separated, falling on various places in a spectrum that divides at the halfway point into "creative writing" and "technical writing." Poetry hovers at one extreme, standing for creativity and implied rather than overt expression. Readers accept mystery from poetry, which frees it from the requirements of clarity that

> *Poetry hovers at one extreme, standing for creativity and implied rather than overt expression.*"

constrain expository writing: trying to understand all of a poem's mysteries is sometimes viewed as a hostile act, as if the inquisitor is looking to "analyze it to death." Poems are permitted "poetic license," which in general parlance means that they can use words that are not technically correct but that nonetheless capture the correct meaning on a different level. Writing that is intended primarily to instruct and to convey information is considered poetry's diametric opposite.

By these standards, Svenbro's poem "Lepidopterology" suffers from a personality disorder. Like a poem, it approaches its readers from the intuitive side of their brains, discussing abstract issues with words that hint at Svenbro's meaning without spelling it out. In other places, though, the poem presents information dryly, directly, using the tone of a textbook or lecture hall. Assuming that Svenbro was aware of the inconsistency, there are several ways to look at "Lepidopterology." It could be called an homage to Georg Stiernhielm, whose groundbreaking achievement in his poem "The Silk-Worm" Svenbro celebrates. It could be considered a case of form serving function, as Svenbro adapts a pedantic tone to drive home to readers the fact that his subject is an admittedly boring one, taking them through the back corridors of academic history. Or it could be seen as a hybrid, mixing poetic sensibilities with distinctly theoretical views while allowing neither to dominate.

Readers have no problem recognizing "Lepidopterology" as a poem. It has the shape of a poem. Though not relying on such formal elements as line breaks, stress patterns, or repetition in sounds, Svenbro's conscious decisions about where each line should end still tell readers that a poetic sensibility is in control of this work. Furthermore, the poem uses phrases throughout that engage the reader's imagination, as effective poetry ought to, by implying situations that are more complex than the words on the page overtly claim. Phrases like "its difficult sloughing," "the frustrated dreams of the caterpillar," "insoluble conflict between dream and reality," and "the right to believe in the impossible" all serve to raise the objective facts of the caterpillar's worldly situation above the obvious. Surface reality is taken to a new, less obvious level of awareness. This is the business of poetry.

For about half its length, the poem proceeds effectively as a poetic meditation on the broader consequences of this one insect's progression, from caterpillar to pupa to butterfly. Just past the halfway point, though, the time changes: instead of evoking the mysteries of the universe, Svenbro starts to talk like a professor, professing his ideas directly and clearly.

This new, businesslike approach starts in the seventeenth line, with the mention of Georg Stiernhielm. It is rare, but in no way strange, for a poem to pay homage to a respected writer within its lines, but Svenbro handles this homage in a way that is conspicuously formal and stiff. Using first and last name together, he suggests that his reader is not expected to be familiar with Stiernhielm's work, introducing him as his name might be found in a reference work. The poem abandons the verbal flexibility that is usually the mark of artistic freedom and instead turns stiff in its language. The way Svenbro carefully announces Stiernhielm's name and his most important work suggests that they might pop up on a quiz when the last line is over.

Svenbro follows this initial formality with one of the stiffest and most inelegant lines a poem could serve up: "and thus became the founder of lepidopterology on Swedish soil." There is nothing even vaguely poetic about the phrasing (other than the inherent music in the word "lepidopterology"), a fact that Svenbro was surely aware of. He follows that line with one that nearly matches it in terms of blunt functionality: "in his poem psychology took a great step forward." Both of these statements would be considered strong, clear, and succinct if they appeared in an essay, spelling out Svenbro's position without the slightest hesitation. But words like "thus," "founder," and even "psychology" are descriptive words, more commonly associated with academics than with art.

There is, of course, no rule that says poets should be limited to using only words that are musical or words that have multiple implications. Artists always work with what they have available to them, making sculptures from scrap iron, music from bells and whistles, and paintings that stare with open eyes at the drudgery of everyday life. The potential problem with Svenbro's shift in tone, from the lofty to the academic, is that such a shift seems to indicate the sort of inconsistency that can cause readers to abandon faith in a work. Each poem is limited to having its own identity, and a shift in tone can be taken as a pretty clear indicator of a split personality. This is not necessarily the case, though. The overriding rule must be that the poet's word choices should serve the poem's overall message. If this poem's message is one of inconsistency, then inconsistency in the tone would be entirely appropriate.

Just before Stiernhielm's name is introduced, the poem foretells its shift in tone with a long phrase telling the story of how the poetic understanding of the butterfly's genesis relates to the scientific understanding of it. Starting in line 11 with "But in the deepest winter," Svenbro sets up the background, giving readers the opportunity to put this natural event into the perspective of the history of the human intellect. Before Stiernhielm, both science and poetry had exhausted ways of looking at the butterfly—imagination itself was frozen, moribund. The poem claims that taxonomy was "dried-out," a static museum piece, until "something totally unforeseen occurred": Stiernhielm's poem "The Silk-Worm."

The complexity of Svenbro's style in "Lepidopterology" is not obvious, but it is undeniable. After using the first half of the poem to identify a malaise that had ground scientific thought to a halt, linking it to the spent imaginations of poets that were as "dry" as the pupa's cocoons, he turns the poem over to science, for a while at least. The point at which the poem becomes dry and academic is the point at which Svenbro lets science speak for itself. It is perfectly fitting that Svenbro should explain his recognition for the significance that "The Silk-Worm" has to psychology by discussing both it and its author with scientific terminology, using a scientist's voice.

There is a reason that this shift in tone is confusing: Stiernhielm is identified primarily as a poet. If this poem were concerned with the author of a treatise or a doctrine, rather than a poem, then Svenbro could more easily use words like "founder" and "full-fledged" without seeming to change styles, because the style would clearly be linked to the subject. Read as Svenbro's praise of Stiernhielm as a poet, though, this stiff language seems out of place. Read as Svenbro's description of a historic upheaval in scientific thought, it seems only natural that abstract language should be used.

"Lepidopterology" is a poem about how butterflies go through a growth process, from frustration to resignation, before they fulfill their full potential. Svenbro establishes that early in the poem and then dismisses it as obvious symbolism. He then draws a parallel to the process of human understanding, which grew from intellectual stagnation to the poem "The Silk-Worm." The poem corresponds with the butterfly's dormant pupa stage, and it leads to a sense of human psychology just as light and beautiful as the butterfly that emerges from a cocoon. Readers who insist that poetry be "beautiful" understand a poem about butterflies, but they do not know how to react when the butterfly represents science. If Georg Stiernhielm used poetry to bring about a new era of science, then it is only right that Svenbro's poem should go in the same direction, following poetic language with a boxy scientific tone. It may stray from the kind of language that poets usually work with, but Svenbro, as he does throughout his poetry, creates a common ground where the fruits of scientific exploration over the centuries are recognized as natural wonders that are just as worthy of poetic concentration as nature's own fruitful bounty.

Source: David Kelly, Critical Essay on "Lepidopterology," in *Poetry for Students*, Thomson Gale, 2006.

Pamela Steed Hill

Hill is the author of a poetry collection, has published widely in literary journals, and is an editor for a university publications department. In the following essay, she examines the "triangle" of metaphors that come together at the end of the poem to make a resounding statement about the nature of science, language, and renewed possibility.

In *Three-toed Gull*, Svenbro's first volume of poetry translated into English, the Swedish-born author dedicates much effort to examining things, people, and places in terms of the words that name them. That is, this is a book full of language about language, poetry about poetry. But it is also a book about science and history, philosophy and logic, and even love. Regardless of the translation, it is clear that Svenbro's focus is on words, names, titles, descriptors—essentially, anything that attempts to *identify*. In "Lepidopterology," much attention is given to butterflies, as the title of the poem suggests, but there is much more going on than fuzzy critters turning into colorful bugs and flying away. Here, the insects lend identity to both psychology and poetry as well as to themselves, creating a triangle of metaphors, with each "leg" bearing equal importance.

Metaphor is one of the most common literary devices, and poets put it to good use in much of

> *If ever a poem had a happy ending (and so many do not!), this is it. But Svenbro does a masterly job at keeping it from sliding into sentimental schmaltz."*

their work. Expressing ideas by invoking images of various dissimilar objects often leads to new ways of thinking about things. In this poem, caterpillars, butterflies, behavioral science, and a long-dead Swedish poet combine into a motley group of odd kin. But Svenbro manages to weave the language around the images so smoothly and to make connections so easily that what first appears strange and disparate ends up seeming perfectly natural.

The first two of the three central metaphors at work in "Lepidopterology" are introduced in the first line. The idea of the butterfly's holding "a prominent place in psychology" is an intriguing notion, and the manner in which Svenbro builds upon it incites curiosity. The biology of the lepidoptera's transformation from caterpillar to pupa to imago, or adult butterfly, is dealt with directly throughout the poem. Caterpillars *do* go through a period of "difficult sloughing," as they eat and grow very quickly and must shed their skin several times during this phase of metamorphosis. And when caterpillars become pupae, they experience a kind of "total paralysis," as they are unable to eat or even move during this stage. All the action, so to speak, takes place *inside* their bodies—a biological fact that Svenbro cleverly melds with the psychological fact of sleeping and dreaming.

As noted, the physical aspects of metamorphosis are overtly described in the poem, but facets of the second leg of the metaphor triangle—the field of psychology—are only alluded to. The depiction of the lepidoptera's "pupa stage" as "a period of total paralysis" turns into a reference to psychology with the addition of the words "of the will." While one can make an argument for the ability to use willpower or to possess a will at any level of the taxonomic chart, what is happening to the caterpillar/butterfly here is purely a function of biology. Human beings, on the other hand, may feel a "total paralysis *of the will*" (italics added).

Like the butterfly in its pupa stage, human beings also experience a stage of sleep—the "rapid eye movement," or REM, stage—in which skeletal muscles are essentially paralyzed. The body may twitch or jerk, but any controlled movement is effectively stopped. However, also like the pupa, there is much action going on inside, at least as far as the brain goes. REM is known in psychology as the period of sleep in which vivid dreams occur, and people awakened during this time often can report the action of the dream in graphic detail. But Svenbro goes a step further with the metaphor by bringing Freudian aspects of psychology into the picture.

Do caterpillars get frustrated? Do they dream? While these may be questions that modern science can never answer definitively, most members of the scientific community would say no. *People*, on the other hand, *do* get frustrated and do dream—so the two together may result in "frustrated dreams." Sigmund Freud and many other analytical psychologists assert that dreams hold the key to what is really going on inside a person's mind, because they are just mental manifestations of the subconscious doing what the conscious mind will not allow it to do. In other words, the "superego" loses its control when the body goes to sleep, and the brain throws an "id" party. Svenbro, however, does not become specific in naming Freud's noted three aspects of personality (id, ego, and superego). Instead, he lets his biology-turned-poetry make the connections for him.

The image of "high-soaring dreams" juxtaposed against an "ungainly earthbound body" conveys a very visual picture of frustration. It is an almost *tangible* look at the "insoluble conflict between dream and reality." In essence, the mind wants to fly, but the body is stuck on the ground. More than any other analogy in the poem, this comparison between the biology of the insect and the psychology of the person explains why the butterfly has "held a prominent place" in the study of humankind. Who has not had an unreachable dream but dreamed about it anyway? Who has not longed for something that seems impossible to obtain but still imagined what it would be like to have it? The caterpillar is simply going through a natural physical process, but a human being's "ungainly earthbound body," metaphorically speaking, implies not only impossible dreams but also the sense of despair and hopelessness that often accompanies such frustration. And in Svenbro's poem, it gets worse before it gets better.

As previously noted, pupae neither eat nor move during this stage of development, right before the final one when the butterfly emerges. In "Lepidopterology," the poet takes some license with what the pupa's mindset—as though it has one—might be at this time. It appears to be in a state of "total resignation." In fact, it is so dejected that it spins "a shroud around its body, / and prepare[s] to die." "Shroud," of course, is the perfect funereal descriptor to liken the creature's gauzy protective covering to a garment for a dead body. But once again, what the words actually describe is the biological process of the pupa; what they *imply* is the psychological process of an individual who is feeling despondent and hopeless.

The third leg of the metaphor triangle now comes into full play as an obscure Swedish poet, Georg Stiernhielm, is introduced as the savior of the pupa—as well as the savior of the human psyche. Svenbro plainly states that the emergence of the butterfly from the seemingly lifeless pupa "gives us the right to believe in the impossible." If there is one main theme in this poem, it is this: never give up; anything is possible.

With a few strokes of the pencil, Stiernhielm delivers the ugly bug from its desolate state to the winds on the wings of a beautiful butterfly. With the same strokes, he propels psychology forward as a "full-fledged science"—saved from its graceless place in the company of rogue theories and pseudosciences. And how does one humble scholar, scientist, and public official in seventeenth-century Sweden accomplish such an admirable feat? With his poetry, of course. With the sheer beauty of language itself—words that set both the butterfly and the study of the human mind free.

"Lepidopterology" ends on a remarkably positive note. The butterfly's "brilliant and dizzying love" is a far cry from its previous notion to lie down and die. Psychology has come a long way, too, rising "from its cocoon, its prehistory" to stand proudly among the respected fields of behavioral and natural sciences. It seems that nature owes a lot to poetry. But note that even Stiernhielm's work that sets all this in motion, "The Silk-Worm," becomes "only the shroud left on the ground," just like the butterfly's death wrap that it sheds in order to live. The poem, then, must be only a framework. Like the pupa's spun encasement, the poem provides a protective shell in which its fledgling occupant, language, can grow and change and develop. Once the words have ripened, once they have metamorphosed into mature, flourishing articulation, they will break free from the poem's walls and fly on their own. As Svenbro puts it, when the butterfly "finally flies out of language," the right to believe in the impossible is affirmed.

If poetry is the third leg of the metaphor triangle, it is also the triangle's glue. It holds the entire structure together. Dissimilar subjects such as lepidopterology and psychology need something to act as a connecter, and language—with its flexibility, playfulness, and downright beauty—does just that. But the overall hopefulness, rejuvenation, and "victory" that this work deems always possible are not limited to any one aspect of motivating factors. That is, even language itself must not be allowed to put any chains on possibility. *Definitions* must remain fluid and leave room for dynamic and creative meanings. Note that the butterfly flies *out* of language, as though it is indebted to the vehicle that helped it grow but now needs the freedom to do as it pleases on its own. Only complete independence assures the continuous unfolding of possibility.

That said, however, there is little doubt that language and words and their relationships with *things* are of paramount importance in Svenbro's work. This is evident in his poem "A Critique of Pure Representation," the first poem to appear in *Three-toed Gull* and a work that sets the stage for several subsequent poems in the collection, including "Lepidopterology." In "Critique," Svenbro notes: "In order to restore to the words their semantic roughness / I told myself that there was no difference / between the stone I held in my hand and the word 'stone' / clattering in language." Here, "stone" is both a word and a thing, and, while they have a congenial relationship, each one enjoys an identity independent of the other. "Stone" may represent the thing "stone" in some instances, but neither is limited by the connection. And it is no surprise that Svenbro uses a rock metaphor to make a point about something else—something human: "To each and every one the possibility of speaking on his own behalf / without being represented by somebody else / and to the words the possibility of representing themselves."

In "Lepidopterology," the butterfly, the field of psychology, and the art of poetry all strive for the possibility of speaking for themselves. One needs only to consider the image projected by the poem's final three lines to believe they all achieve it. The "victory announced" is nearly audible, and it is made even visible with phrases like "ablaze in

the sun" and "brilliant and dizzying love." If ever a poem had a happy ending (and so many do not!), this is it. But Svenbro does a masterly job at keeping it from sliding into sentimental schmaltz. Instead, he brings together his triangle of metaphors with skillful precision and uses it to make a profound statement about the nature of relationships among a variety of subjects—and the unlimited possibility that underlies them all.

Source: Pamela Steed Hill, Critical Essay on "Lepidopterology," in *Poetry for Students*, Thomson Gale, 2006.

Sources

Matthias, John, and Lars-Håkan Svensson, "Translators' Notes," in *Three-toed Gull*, by Jesper Svenbro, translated by John Matthias and Lars-Håkan Svensson, Northwestern University Press, 2003, p. 131.

Svenbro, Jesper, *Three-toed Gull*, translated by John Matthias and Lars-Håkan Svensson, Northwestern University Press, 2003, pp. 5–7, 10, 16–18, 23.

Further Reading

Fulton, Robin, ed. and trans., *Five Swedish Poets*, Norvik Press, 1998.

   In this compelling volume, the respected critic and translator Robin Fulton provides selections from the contemporary Swedish poets Kjell Espmark, Lennart Sjogren, Staffan Soderblom, Werner Aspenstrom, and Eva Strom, including a brief critical introduction to each.

Moffett, Judith, ed. and trans., *The North! To the North!: Five Swedish Poets of the Nineteenth Century*, Southern Illinois University Press, 2001.

   This collection of nineteenth-century Swedish poets provides useful background information about Svenbro and the post–World War II poetry scene in Sweden.

Smith, William Jay, and Leif Sjöberg, eds., *The Forest of Childhood: Poems from Sweden*, New Rivers Press, 1996.

   Smith and Sjöberg's collection of contemporary Swedish poems helps place Svenbro in his literary context.

Warme, Lars G., ed., *A History of Swedish Literature*, University of Nebraska Press, 1996.

   This useful and comprehensive reference work traces Swedish literature from its beginnings through the contemporary era, outlining the context of major Swedish literary figures, including Georg Stiernhielm, and discussing how literature has helped develop Swedish identity.

Lost in Translation

James Merrill
1974

"Lost in Translation" was first published in the *New Yorker* on April 6, 1974. It later became part of James Merrill's collection *Divine Comedies*, for which he won the Pulitzer Prize in 1976. This work, and the subsequent award, helped cement Merrill's reputation as one of the top young American poets.

The poem is a complex study of loss and the artistic rendering of experience. Merrill presents fragments of experience that become apt metaphors of loss and dislocation in a post-Vietnam, post-Watergate world. The poem's fragmented, yet ultimately unified form highlights the contradictory nature of the creation of art, as the artist strives to "translate" experience into the stylized structure of a poem.

Merrill focuses on the speaker's memories of his childhood at the point when his parents were separating and he was struggling to adapt to his newly disrupted world. The boy anxiously awaits the arrival of a puzzle, which he and his French nanny will put together. When the puzzle finally arrives, it comes alive to him, as it evolves into a metaphor for his own experience. As the pieces of the puzzle "translate" into a unified, meaningful whole, Merrill explores the tensions between art and reality and the problems inherent in establishing an absolute vision of human experience.

Author Biography

James Ingram Merrill was born in New York City on March 3, 1926, to Charles Merrill, a stockbroker and cofounder of the firm Merrill Lynch, and Helen Ingram, a newspaper publisher. Merrill developed an appreciation for languages at a young age, when he learned French and German from his governess, who appears in his poem "Lost in Translation." His parents encouraged his poetry writing during his adolescence. This was apparent when Merrill's father had a collection of Merrill's poetry, *Jim's Book*, published when his son was only sixteen.

Merrill attended Amherst College, where he first met Robert Frost, one of his major influences. He had to leave Amherst from 1944 to 1945 to serve in the U.S. Army at the end of World War II. After the war, he returned to college, had his first book of poems printed privately under the title *The Black Swan* (1946), and graduated from Amherst summa cum laude in 1947.

After college, Merrill moved back to New York City to write. However, he found the atmosphere of the city too distracting, so he decided instead to travel throughout Europe for the next two and a half years with his companion, David Jackson. Merrill's memoir, *A Different Person* (1993), describes this period in Europe.

In 1951, *First Poems*, his first trade book, was published and received favorable reviews. In 1955, he moved to Stonington, Connecticut, with Jackson. Merrill then founded the Ingram Merrill Foundation, an organization that awards grants to artists and writers. His first novel, *The Seraglio*, was published in 1957. Two years later, he and Jackson moved to Athens, Greece.

In the years following the move, Merrill's poetry gained acclaim, and he cemented his reputation as one of the top young American poets. In 1976, he won the Pulitzer Prize for *Divine Comedies*, which includes the poem "Lost in Translation." He received several other awards for his work, including the National Book Award in Poetry in 1967 for *Nights and Days*, the Bollingen Prize in 1973 for *Braving the Elements*, a second National Book Award for *Mirabell: Books of Number* in 1978, the National Book Critics Circle Award for his epic poem *The Changing Light at Sandover* in 1982, and the first Rebekah Johnson Bobbitt National Prize in poetry awarded by the Library of Congress for *The Inner Room* in 1990. He was also a finalist for the National Book Award in fiction for *The (Diblos) Notebook* in 1965. Merrill

James Merrill AP/Wide World Photos

served as a chancellor of the Academy of American Poets from 1979 until his death in 1995. He died in Tucson, Arizona, at age sixty-eight from a heart attack brought on by complications of AIDS.

Poem Summary

Stanzas 1–3

The opening quotation of "Lost in Translation" is from a translation by the German poet Rainer Maria Rilke (1875–1926) of lines 61–64 in the poem "Palme" by the French poet Paul Valéry (1871–1945). Rilke writes, as Merrill quotes:

Diese Tage, die leer dir scheinen
und wertlos für das All
haben Wurzeln zwischen den Steinen
und trinken dort überall.

These lines in English would be "These days, which seem empty / and entirely fruitless to you, / have roots between the stones / and drink from everywhere." This passage announces two of the subjects of the poem: translation and search for meaning. The first three lines of the poem itself then create an atmosphere of anticipation as a boy waits in "daylight" and "lamplight" for a "puzzle

Media Adaptations

- Random House Audio has published an audio-cassette of Merrill's poetry, read by the author, as part of "The Voice of the Poet" series (1999).

which keeps never coming." The juxtaposition of "tense" and "oasis" in the description of the table-top in line 4 suggests that the puzzle will provide pleasure for the boy, but pain if it never arrives. This juxtaposition is extended into the next two lines as life becomes either a rising "mirage" or something falling "into place."

In lines 8 through 11, the speaker lists the activities the boy engages in during his "summer without parents," cared for by his governess. The activities do not seem pleasurable to the boy, as he notes the "sour windfalls of the orchard" behind them. The speaker indicates the real cause of his unease when he notes that the boy's parents are absent, suggesting that this is a "puzzle" to the boy, "or should be." The stanza ends where it began, with the boy's impatience over the missing puzzle, which he notes in his diary ("Line-a-Day").

In the second stanza, the speaker notes that the boy is in love with his governess, whose husband died in Verdun, a World War I battle. The religious governess, "Mademoiselle," prays for him, as does a French priest, and helps him put on puppet shows. She talks with him at night about pre–World War II tensions in Europe and her "French hopes, German fears." Mademoiselle knows little more than the "grief and hardship" she has suffered.

The two continue to wait for the puzzle as even Mademoiselle's watch becomes impatient, "[throwing] up its hands." She tries to alleviate the boy's "steaming bitterness" with sweets, an act that translates as telling him to "have patience, my dear," which is expressed in French ("Patience, chéri") and in German ("Geduld, mein Schatz"), the two languages she has been teaching him.

The lines evoke a memory in the speaker, who digresses in a parenthetical passage to present time.

He notes that the other evening he remembered reading something by Valéry that triggered a memory of Rilke's translation of Valéry's "Palme," which appears at the beginning of the poem. He makes the connection between Valéry's poem and the boy's situation, admitting here that he is the boy. The thought of the tree in that poem, which has "roots between the stones and drink[s] from everywhere," becomes a "sunlit paradigm." It is a model for him of "patience in the blue," ("patience dans l'azur"), a characterization of the slow growth of the palm tree. He goes back to the past when he tries to translate the French words into their German equivalents, asking Mademoiselle hypothetically if he is correct.

In the third stanza, the promised puzzle appears from a New York City shop and has a thousand wooden pieces, smelling like sandalwood. Some pieces have shapes he has seen before in other puzzles, including a "branching palm" that the speaker insists was really there and not just imagined. Mademoiselle excitedly spreads out the pieces that initially look like "incoherent faces in a crowd," before a pattern can be discerned. Each piece will eventually be placed together by "law," the design of the puzzle maker. The "plot thickens" as the pieces interlock and become a story.

Stanza 4

In the first line of the fourth stanza, Mademoiselle attends to the puzzle's borders, but the speaker jumps immediately to the future, this time to an evening in London, the past December. People are gathered in "the library" for a demonstration by a psychic. The audience has seen an object hidden in a casket behind a panel before he arrived. The psychic shuts his eyes and tries to visualize the object. He sees something in the object's history that may involve the chopping down of trees, "groaning and cracking" as they approach a lumber mill.

What the psychic has been describing is the process of making a puzzle piece from plywood. He suggests that the process appears to be complex, but it is not complex compared with the "hazard and craft," the fate ("karma"), that made its original matter. This process of making a puzzle piece, along with arranging the pieces to form the puzzle, can be likened to the creative process of the poet. After the psychic identifies the piece, he opens his eyes and is applauded. The speaker, however, feels an unidentified sense of dread, perhaps a result of the contemplation of "karma," and immediately turns his attention once more to the past.

Stanzas 5–6

The next stanza continues the focus on creation as it opens with a repetition of part of the first line of the previous stanza, with Mademoiselle forming the borders of the puzzle. The speaker suggests that the pieces have their own artistic energy, as they are "align[ing] themselves" into a scene of the earth or sky, taking over the act of creation. He describes the straight-edged pieces as naïve scientists, studying the origins of the universe, "whose views clash." The others, "nomad inlanders," begin to arrange themselves into different shapes that in time become "sophisticated unit[s]."

Eventually, by suppertime, clear pictures have formed and come to life for Mademoiselle and the boy. In one cloud, they see a sheik with a "flashing sword hilt" and, in the other, a "backward-looking slave or page-boy," whose feet are not yet complete, helping a woman off a camel. Mademoiselle mistakenly thinks the boy is the woman's son. The speaker finds some crucial pieces just before bedtime, which help "orient" the images. He leaves the puzzle with a yellow section, which "promises" to be a "sumptuous tent."

The boy writes in his diary that he has begun the puzzle and peeks at Mademoiselle's letter to the priest, in which she has written "this innocent mother, this poor child, what will become of them?" ("cette innocente mère / Ce pauvre enfant, que deviendront-ils?"), referring, most likely, to the boy and his mother. In another parenthetical digression, the speaker notes that when he was a boy, he did not try to find out more about Mademoiselle, who was French only by marriage. A friend later reveals that the speaker's own French has a German accent ("Tu as l'accent allemand"), taught by Mademoiselle, who was of English and Prussian ancestry. The speaker does not find this out until years later, however. He recognizes how Mademoiselle must have suffered, being caught between the German and French worlds just as World War II was breaking out. The speaker returns to the past as Mademoiselle says goodnight to the boy, telling him to "sleep well" ("schlaf wohl") in German and calling him "darling" ("chéri") in French. She kisses him and makes the sign of the cross, a Catholic blessing, on his forehead.

Stanzas 7–14

In these stanzas, the speaker focuses on the world of the puzzle as "it assembles on the shrinking Green." He describes the "noblest" slaves ("avatars") with their plumes, scars, and vests trimmed with fur ("vair"). In another scene in the picture, "old wives" ease boredom with a narcotic made from hemp ("kef") and sweet drinks, insisting that if Allah wills ("Insh'Allah"), their straying husbands will tire of their mistresses or kill them.

The speaker digresses for a moment, suggesting that this is hardly a subject for "the Home," and notes that the puzzle is a recreation of a painting allegedly done by a follower ("a minor lion") of the French Orientalist artist Jean-Léon Gérôme (1824–1904). He asks "dear Richard" (most likely Richard Howard, to whom Merrill dedicated the poem) to investigate the true author.

In stanza 11, the speaker introduces Houri, one of the beautiful maidens living with the blessed in the Islamic paradise, and Afreet, an evil demon in Arabic mythology. In a play on the word *thieves*, he calls the two "thick as Thebes," referring to the ancient capital of Upper Egypt. Both try to claim the boy in the puzzle, who cannot decide "whom to serve" and has not yet found his feet. The suggestion here is that the boy in the puzzle represents the boy in the poem, who is torn between two divorcing parents. The speaker hopes the boy will find "that piece of Distance" from this troubled situation, the "Eternal Triangle": father, mother, child.

The puzzle is done, except for the sky; the blue pieces become fragments revolting against being placed into a pattern, not knowing how they will fit together. They have "quite a task" arranging the pieces of "Heaven," but they eventually do. And then the puzzle is complete. The boy's missing feet have been found under the table, and the last pieces have been put into place.

Stanzas 15–18

With the puzzle complete, Mademoiselle returns to her work on the puppet shows, and "all too soon" the puzzle is dismantled. When lifted, the puzzle stays together in some parts and separates in others. Each image in the puzzle eventually falls apart, including the tent, which appears as a creamy sauce ("mousseline"). Only the green top of the table, "on which the grown-ups gambled" remains as the day ends. The speaker sees analogies, since he is a poet, between the green table and the "green dusk"—a false coincidence, since he can construct his own memory of the event. He also notes his "mangy tiger safe on his bared hearth," analogous to the tiger in the puzzle. These analogies, or similarities between unlike things, reinforce the boy's connection to the puzzle.

The speaker explains that before the puzzle was boxed and sent back to the shop on New York

City's Upper East Side (the "mid-Sixties"), one piece "contrived," as if by its own intention, "to stay in the boy's pocket." Finding further analogies between the puzzle and life, the speaker admits that last puzzle pieces often went missing, like the high notes of Maggie Teyte, an English soprano (1888–1976) famous for her singing of French songs; the popularity of collies; a house; and bits of Mademoiselle's "truth."

Back in the present, the speaker notes that he has spent the last few days searching in Athens for Rilke's translation of Valéry's "Palme." He notes the difficulty that Rilke had, or any translator has, in the process of translation: how much of the original he had to sacrifice in order to portray "its underlying sense"; how much the "warm Romance" of the original "faded"; how the nouns were exaggerated and thus lonelier, cut off from the source. The German accent mark ("umlaut"), representative of Rilke's language, can only "peep" and "hoot," since it is like an "owlet," without maturity, becoming an echo ("reverberation") that nonetheless is "fill[ed] with stars."

The speaker ends with a series of contradictions, asking whether the original is lost or buried, "one more missing piece." But then he insists that "nothing's lost" or else all our experience with the world necessitates translation and that "every bit of us is lost in it. / (Or found-." In parenthesis, he reflects on the end of a relationship with a former lover ("S"), surprised at the resulting peacefulness. The final image is of the loss of that relationship, which becomes "a self-effacing tree," the context of a poem perhaps, "turn[ing] the waste," as does the tree, into "shade and fiber, milk and memory." Here the speaker reflects on the power of art to ease a sense of loss and "translate" sorrow into comforting images of shade and sustenance. This last image ties to the loss experienced by the boy in the first stanza, when he suffers the absence of his parents and turns to the construction of a puzzle to provide him with comfort.

Themes

Artistic Creation

Merrill suggests that the poet "translates" experience into the form and content of poetry. This process is not perfect, since the final work of art is never an exact translation of the original source material. He focuses much of "Lost in Translation" on this complex process. The poem begins with two contrasting images: the library, a place of study, and the card table, a place of play for the boy and the adults who gamble on it. This juxtaposition suggests that the work of a poet, which the speaker often refers to as he thinks about Rilke's translation of Valéry, necessitates both study and play. The poet must study the works of other poets, their forms and content, as he plays with words to discover a new artistic creation that will more closely express the poet's experience.

When the speaker studies Valéry's "Palme," he focuses on "That sunlit paradigm whereby the tree / Taps a sweet wellspring of authority." The tree in the poem becomes a paradigm that he can use to express himself through his own poem. When he thinks of the tree in "Palme," a characterization of the slow growth of the palm tree, it triggers his memory of the time he waited for the puzzle to arrive and Mademoiselle tried to calm his "steaming bitterness" with words of comfort: "Patience, chéri. Geduld, mein Schatz." The patient growth of the tree, "Patience dans l'azure," finds a correlation in Mademoiselle's words.

Many of the pieces of the puzzle, which becomes a metaphor for the boy's situation, "take / Shapes known already—the craftsman's repertoire." He finds one shaped like a palm, like the one in the poem that recalls Mademoiselle's comfort words. Yet the boy makes his own interpretation of the pictures in the puzzle, one that more closely correlates with his experience. He refuses ultimately, though, to identify himself with the boy in the puzzle when he insists that Mademoiselle is wrong when she decides that the page-boy is the woman's son, suggesting the difficulties inherent in artistic representation.

Power of Art

Merrill notes the power of art when the speaker's reading of "Palme" triggers a childhood memory. He invests the puzzle with a similar power when the pieces appear to arrange themselves as Mademoiselle and the boy withdraw into the background. The pieces "align themselves with earth or sky" and become "naïve cosmogonists / Whose views clash" or "nomad inlanders" who "Begin to cluster . . . /. . . on the straggler . . . / To form a more sophisticated unit." The figures in the picture come alive and gaze at each other across clouds.

The closing lines suggest the power of art to help us cope with loss. As the speaker thinks of a ruined past relationship, the loss becomes "a self-effacing tree," like the palm in the poem and in the

Topics For Further Study

- Read some representative poetry by W. H. Auden and compare themes and structures used in his poetry with those of "Lost in Translation." Three poems you might want to look at are "Musée des Beaux Arts," "Stop All the Clocks. . ."("Twelve Songs: IX," sometimes called "Funeral Blues"), and "The Unknown Citizen."

- Some scholars find elements of the confessional, an autobiographical verse form, in Merrill's poetry. Research this school of poetry and Merrill's life and determine whether there is any evidence for this claim.

- Research the effects of divorce on children. What effects do you see on the boy in the poem?

- Many poets have focused on childhood memories in their poetry, including "Piano" by D. H. Lawrence, "My Papa's Waltz," by Theodore Roethke, and "Those Winter Sundays" by Robert Hayden. In each of these poems, as in "Lost in Translation," the speaker describes a childhood memory that involves a parent. After reading these selections, write your own poem that focuses on a particular memory that you have of an experience with one or both of your parents.

puzzle, turning "the waste" into "shade and fiber, milk and memory."

Style

Iambic Pentameter and Blank Verse

The intricate five-part structure of the poem reinforces the link between the puzzle and the boy/poet. The first part, stanzas 1–3, focusing on the wait for the puzzle, is arranged in verse paragraphs that often contain iambic pentameter lines, ten-syllable lines with metrical units of one unstressed syllable followed by one stressed syllable. This section ends with the suggestion that all the parts of the poem come together to form an organic whole, much like the pieces of the puzzle: "The plot thickens / As all at once two pieces interlock."

In the second section, stanza 4, Merrill shifts from blank verse (unrhymed lines of iambic pentameter) to a more poetic form, as the lines get shorter and more rhythmic. The time and place move to a scene in the future when the speaker witnessed a psychic's performance. The link between the first and second sections is established by having both scenes set in a library and through the puzzle piece that the psychic "sees" hidden in the box.

The third section, stanzas 5 and 6, returns to the blank verse of the first section as the scene shifts back to the boy and Mademoiselle and to the picture in the puzzle emerging, along with certain details of Mademoiselle's background. The fourth section, stanzas 7–14, focuses on the completion of the puzzle, as it shifts to tightly controlled quatrains (stanzas of four lines each) until the final stanza, which breaks off into a closed couplet. A closed couplet is two lines of rhymed verse that comes to a strong conclusion, as here, where the two lines announce that the last piece has been found and the puzzle is complete. This section links to the subject of the final section, through the focus on artistic creation, after the puzzle is taken apart and shipped back to the shop. This fifth section, stanzas 15–18, returns to the initial verse paragraph form.

Historical Context

World War II

The world experienced a decade of aggression in the 1930s that would culminate in World War II. This war resulted from the rise of totalitarian regimes in Germany, Italy, and Japan. These militaristic regimes gained control as a result of the

Compare & Contrast

- **Early 1970s:** After fighting a brutal and unpopular war in Vietnam, the United States pulls out its troops. Soon after, Saigon falls to the Communists.

  Today: The United States is involved in another unpopular war, this time in Iraq. Even though elections have taken place, many believe that civil war will break out in that country.

- **Early 1970s:** Communist insurgents refuse to recognize elections in South Vietnam and continue fighting against the South Vietnamese and American troops.

  Today: Insurgents in Iraq, made up of Iraqi civilians and terrorist groups, carry out similar attacks against occupational forces.

- **Early 1970s:** The Watergate scandal exposes corrupt campaign practices, including break-ins at the Democratic National Committee headquarters and illegal wiretaps of American citizens.

  Today: Scandals emerge during the 2004 presidential election concerning smear campaigns like that conducted by the "Swift Boat Veterans" and alleged illegal voting procedures.

Great Depression experienced by most of the world in the early 1930s and from the conditions created by the peace settlements following World War I. The dictatorships established in each country encouraged expansion into neighboring countries. In Germany, Adolf Hitler strengthened the army during the 1930s. In 1936, Benito Mussolini's Italian troops overtook Ethiopia. From 1936 to 1939, Spain was engaged in civil war involving the fascist army of Francisco Franco, aided by Germany and Italy. In March 1938, Germany annexed Austria, and in March 1939, Germany occupied Czechoslovakia. Italy invaded Albania in April 1939.

One week after Nazi Germany and the USSR signed the Treaty of Nonaggression, on September 1, 1939, Germany invaded Poland, and World War II began. On September 3, 1939, Great Britain and France declared war on Germany after a U-boat sank the British ship *Athenia* off the coast of Ireland. Another British ship, *Courageous*, was sunk on September 19 that same year. All the members of the British Commonwealth, except Ireland, soon joined Britain and France in their declaration of war.

Vietnam War

The Vietnam War was a conflict fought in South Vietnam and the surrounding areas of Cambodia and Laos. Fighting on one side were the U.S.-backed South Vietnamese forces and an international coalition (including, among others, South Korea, Thailand, and Australia). The other side of the conflict was represented by North Vietnamese forces and a South Vietnamese guerrilla militia known as the Vietcong. The war started in 1954, soon after the provisions of the Geneva Conference divided Vietnam into the Democratic Republic of Vietnam (North Vietnam) and the Republic of Vietnam (South Vietnam). Conflict initially broke out as a civil war between North Vietnam and South Vietnam but escalated as the United States threw its support to South Vietnam, initially by sending money and advisers and later by sending troops as well.

After the Gulf of Tonkin Resolution was passed in August 1964, the United States increased its military aid to South Vietnam. By the end of the decade there were 550,000 American troops caught up in the conflict. North Vietnam gained armaments and technical support from the Soviet Union and other Communist countries. Despite massive bombing attacks, the United States and South Vietnam failed to push back the insurgency.

Progress was made with peace talks when President Lyndon B. Johnson decided not to seek reelection in 1968. After Richard Nixon was elected that year, he began troop withdrawals along with intensified bombing campaigns. In 1970, Nixon ordered the invasion of Communist strongholds in Cambodia.

Public opinion in the United States turned against the war as the number of casualties grew and reports of war crimes like the massacre of civilians at My Lai surfaced. Huge demonstrations took place in Washington, D.C., as well as in other cities and on college campuses. A peace agreement was finally reached in January 1973, but fighting between North Vietnam and South Vietnam did not abate. On April 30, 1975, South Vietnamese President Duong Van Minh surrendered to the Communists. Saigon fell as the last American troops left the country. More than 50,000 American soldiers died in the conflict, along with approximately 400,000 South Vietnamese and over 900,000 North Vietnamese.

Watergate

The Watergate affair refers to a series of scandals that eventually led to Richard Nixon's resignation of the presidency of the United States. It began with the burglarizing, on June 17, 1972, of the headquarters of the Democratic National Committee, located in the Watergate apartment complex in Washington, D.C. Police arrested five men who had attempted to break in to the party offices and plant wiretaps. Two of those involved in the break-in were employees of President Nixon's reelection committee.

One of the burglars, James McCord, sent a letter to the trial judge, John Sirica, claiming that a large-scale cover-up of the burglary was being conducted by the White House. His charges led to the ensuing political scandal. The media took an active role in covering the investigations. Bob Woodward and Carl Bernstein, both reporters for the *Washington Post*, broke many significant details concerning the break-in and subsequent cover-up, aided by their mysterious informant, "Deep Throat."

At a special Senate committee investigatory hearing of corrupt campaign practices, the former White House counsel John Dean testified that the former attorney general John Mitchell had approved the burglary and that two of the president's top aides had been involved in the cover-up. Special prosecutor Archibald Cox found through his investigations of the affair that the Nixon reelection committee had conducted widespread political espionage that included illegal wiretapping of American citizens.

Cox sued Nixon in order to get him to hand over tapes of his presidential conversations during the early 1970s. Nixon initially refused, but he was eventually forced to give them up. One of the tapes contained a significant gap, allegedly caused by Nixon's secretary. Another, however, contained conversations in which Nixon admitted that he had participated in the Watergate cover-up from the outset. This tape became known as the "smoking gun" tape.

By 1974, the majority of Americans believed that Nixon was involved in the cover-up, and confidence in his administration steadily eroded. The public began to call for Nixon to resign. On July 30, 1974, the House Judiciary Committee adopted three articles of impeachment against Nixon for obstruction of justice. Nixon later admitted that he had tried to halt the FBI's investigation into the break-in. At 9 p.m. on August 8, 1974, Richard Nixon appeared on national television and resigned the office of the presidency. The next morning, Nixon resigned formally; transferred the office to Gerald Ford, who became the new president; and left the White House.

By the end of the 1970s, Americans appeared to adopt a pervasive attitude of pessimism. The Vietnam War and the Watergate scandal had shaken their belief in government, and a distrust of human nature had grown after the assassinations of John Fitzgerald Kennedy, Robert Kennedy, and Dr. Martin Luther King, Jr.

Critical Overview

In an article for the *New York Times Book Review* on *Scripts for the Pageant*, Denis Donoghue determines that Merrill's "common style is a net of loose talk tightening to verse, a mode in which nearly anything can be said with grace." He finds a strong connection between W. H. Auden and Merrill, an association other scholars have noted as well, especially in his *Divine Comedies*.

Louis Simpson writes in his review of that collection, also in the *New York Times Book Review*: "Auden would have liked all this very much—he had small patience with simplicity, whether natural or assumed." Simpson likens the poems in *Divine Comedies* to "a kaleidoscope—a brightly colored pattern or scene twitching into another pattern." Deeming Merrill's writing "ingenious" and "witty," Simpson finds that "a society of cultivated readers might give [the poems] a high place" but acknowledges that Merrill would be too obscure for most. Still, he writes, "it is hardly the poet's fault that there are few readers of this kind of poetry."

Harold Bloom, in his review for the *New Republic*, claims, "James Merrill . . . has convinced many discerning readers of a greatness, or something like it, in his first six volumes of verse, but until this year I remained a stubborn holdout." Bloom insists that *Divine Comedies* "converts" him, "absolutely if belatedly, to Merrill. . . . The book's eight shorter poems surpass nearly all the earlier Merrill."

One of the eight shorter poems in the collection is the celebrated "Lost in Translation." The poem was apparently also important to Merrill, who moved it to the final position in *From the First Nine, 1946–1976*, the reissued edition of his first nine volumes of poetry. As any poet knows, the words at the end of a line or a poem, or in this case a book, are placed there for special emphasis.

Echoing many a scholar's view of the poem's theme, Robert B. Shaw, in his article in the *New York Times Book Review*, states that Merrill "makes his most profound impression on the reader . . . as a connoisseur of loneliness: the loneliness of a child grown up and still in search of his absent parents." Willard Spiegelman, in his article on Merrill for the *Dictionary of Literary Biography*, calls the poem "impressive" and argues that it "pinpoints, more succinctly than any of Merrill's other short poems, the issues of loss and possession." He cites a quote from Robert Frost, who claimed that poetry "is what is lost in translation," and concludes, "Merrill's poem proves the adage wrong, since loss through translation is the motive for the poem itself."

Donoghue writes that Merrill "has always been sensitive to 'the golden things that go without saying,' and the things, equally golden, that have gone without saying until he has said them." It is this poetic craftsmanship that has prompted others, like R. W. Flint in his article for the *New York Times Book Review*, to conclude that Merrill "has long since taken his place as one of the most accomplished satirists, wits and lyricists of the age."

Criticism

Wendy Perkins

Perkins is a professor of American and English literature and film. In the following essay, Perkins examines the exploration of the problematic process of gaining knowledge in Merrill's poem.

Prior to the twentieth century, authors structured their works to reflect their belief in the stability of character and the intelligibility of experience. Traditionally, literary works ended with a clear sense of closure, as conflicts were resolved and characters gained knowledge about themselves and their world. Poetic images coalesced into an organic whole that expressed the poet's view of the coherence of experience. Many writers during the twentieth century challenged these assumptions as they expanded literature's traditional form to accommodate their characters' and their own questions about the indeterminate nature of knowing in the modern age—a major thematic concern for these writers. The critic Allan Rodway, in an article on the problem of knowledge in Tom Stoppard's plays, explains this focus as a question: "How do we know we really *know* what we think we know?" James Merrill continues this inquiry in "Lost in Translation" as he examines the tentative nature of communication and its relationship to the difficulties inherent in the process of gaining absolute knowledge.

In an article in the *New York Times Book Review*, later reprinted as "Acoustical Chambers" in *Recitative: Prose*, Merrill discusses the autobiographical nature of "Lost in Translation" and the inability of words to convey truth. He notes that he had a governess named "Mademoiselle," who was neither French—which she had led him to believe—nor an unmarried woman (she was a widow). He remembers, "By the time I was eight I had learned from her enough French and German to understand that English was merely one of many ways to express things." He also discovered the difficulties of translation, since "the everyday sounds of English could mislead you by having more than one meaning." After thinking about how specific words could have alternate meanings in different contexts, he concludes, "Words weren't what they seemed. The mother tongue could inspire both fascination and distrust."

In "Lost in Translation," Merrill uses a puzzle as a metaphor for the problematic nature of acquiring knowledge, a process that depends on the arrangement of words and memory into a coherent pattern. He does this through the fragmented form of the poem, which shifts back and forth in time, and through its language, which juxtaposes contrasting images in four languages.

The poem's main focus is on the speaker, who, through memory, tries to piece together a concrete image of himself as a boy. This task, however, becomes impossible, owing to the fact that the poem contains so many gaps, as David Perkins notes in "The Achievement of James Merrill." Perkins writes that, when the speaker tries to interpret his experience, "too many interpretations come to mind" as he "moons and pores over events, memories, images, words, detecting always more possible meanings."

The speaker tries to focus on one main event in his past: a time when he and his French nanny put together an intricate puzzle sent by his absent parents. What the boy sees in the puzzle appears to express the problems he is experiencing at home. A male and a female figure in the puzzle become combatants, waging a battle over who will win a page-boy. The boy in the puzzle looks backward, much like the speaker who digs into the past to try to gain a true sense of self.

Perkins concludes that the scene depicted in the puzzle represents "family tensions at a time when [Merrill's] father was taking a new wife. The past— that summer, his parents, and what was going on between them—is similarly a puzzle . . . and solving it is impossible." The boy cannot understand why his parents are not with him: "a summer without parents is the puzzle." The piece that will provide the answer is missing, as is the last puzzle piece. Appropriately, the missing pieces are the boy's feet, which would "ground" him in the puzzle. The boy similarly lacks grounding without the knowledge of his place in his newly disrupted family.

Although the pieces that make the puzzle complete are eventually found, the puzzle must be dismantled and put away "all too soon." In this process, each image eventually falls apart. The boy holds on to one piece, which means that the puzzle will never again be complete. The speaker admits that last puzzle pieces often go missing, like bits of Mademoiselle's "truth." As he struggles to find all the missing pieces that will identify his place in his shifting familial triangle, the boy also, unknowingly, has been denied information about Mademoiselle's identity, since she has withheld facts about herself in an effort to hide her Prussian ancestry, a dangerous secret during the war years.

The poem suggests that memory is unreliable and therefore cannot provide absolute knowledge of the past. Perkins concludes that "to recall the past is inevitably to transform it creatively, as the painting both reflected and transformed the family crisis, or as Merrill does in writing the poem." Merrill employs metaphors of creation in his focus on the speaker's attempts to understand

What Do I Read Next?

- Several scholars see similarities between Merrill and W. H. Auden. Look at some of Auden's poems in *Collected Poems* (1991).

- *Divine Comedies* (1976) also contains *The Book of Ephraim*, another of Merrill's celebrated poems.

- Merrill's epic poem *The Changing Light at Sandover* (1982) has themes similar to those of "Lost in Translation."

- For a comparative study of American poetry, read Richard Howard's *Alone with America: Essays on the Art of Poetry in the United States since 1950* (1980).

his past. The dominant metaphor is of translation, which Perkins notes is "a process in which the original is both reconstituted and lost."

The speaker reveals that he is actively constructing his memory of his past in an attempt to understand it, when he compares images in the puzzle to objects in his home. He notes "the false eyes of (coincidence)" in his "mangy tiger safe on his bared hearth," similar to the boy's translating a "vibrant egg-yolk yellow" into a "pelt of what emerging animal / . . . To form a more sophisticated unit" in the puzzle.

The speaker attempts to translate Rilke's translation of Valéry's poem "Palme," as the boy tries to "translate" the images of the puzzle, suggesting that gaining complete understanding of each is impossible. The boy sees a sheik in one cloud (which is how he describes the pieces of the puzzle already fitted together) and a "dark-eyed woman veiled in mauve" in another. The two gaze at each other "with marked if undecipherable feeling." These two figures become Houri, one of the beautiful maidens living with the blessed in the Islamic paradise, and Afreet, an evil demon in Arabic mythology, who fight over the page-boy, in an analogous situation to that of the boy. Mademoiselle determines that the boy is the woman's son, but the speaker insists that

> *What the boy sees in the puzzle appears to express the problems he is experiencing at home.*

she is mistaken. Of course, Mademoiselle's reliability is in question after the speaker discovers the truths she has hidden about herself. The speaker points out the difficulties in translation here. If he is not the boy in the puzzle, then who is he and how will he come to understand his experience?

Evans Lansing Smith, in his article on the poem for *Explicator*, concludes that Mademoiselle's "genealogical puzzle implicates the historical and linguistic complexities of the modern world, because she speaks English, French, and German in the poem, sometimes simultaneously." She often uses different languages in the same sentence ("Schlaf wohl, chéri" and "Patience, chéri. Geduld, mein Schatz"). These three languages, as well as Arabic, are used in the poem, suggesting the inexactness of language. The speaker notes the difficulties of finding exact translations when he questions his German equivalent to "patience dans l'azure" ("Geduld im . . . Himmelblau?").

Merrill reinforces this view through his word choice in the poem. Perkins concludes that "his syntax extends horizontally, packing thought within thought. . . . He spreads metaphors like nets to see what they will catch." Merrill inserts clever juxtapositions that, in effect, construct and deconstruct reality and knowledge. For example, he includes oxymorons, that is, contradictory or seemingly incompatible words, in the phrases "keeps never coming," "Full of unfulfillment," and "Sour windfalls." In other lines he juxtaposes daylight with lamplight and "arisen" with "fallen," creating "a see-saw" of language and so of reality. Merrill ends the poem with a series of contradictions that reinforce the problematic nature of translation and of understanding, suggesting that "nothing's lost" and then "all is translation / And every bit of us is lost in it / (Or found."

Daniel Mendelsohn, in his review of *Collected Poems*, concludes that in his poetry, Merrill flips

"the world upside down for you, making you wonder about that stuff you thought was 'air'—and . . . about just where you stand in relation to everything and anything." The questions Merrill raises in "Lost in Translation" force us to recognize our inexact knowledge of ourselves and our world.

Source: Wendy Perkins, Critical Essay on "Lost in Translation," in *Poetry for Students*, Thomson Gale, 2006.

Evans Lansing Smith

In the following essay, Smith discusses the metaphor of the puzzle in "Lost in Translation" and how Merrill links the content of the poem to its form.

Putting broken pieces back together by the power of poetry is one of James Merrill's great themes. A good example is his wonderful poem "Lost in Translation," which uses the metaphor of the puzzle as an analogy for a traumatic childhood, marriage and divorce, the mysteries of reading and writing, and the creation and destruction of the world.

In the first stanza (a curtal sonnet), the boy and his governess, "Mademoiselle," wait for the jigsaw puzzle to arrive from a toyshop in Manhattan. The puzzle arrives; its pieces are spilled out upon the empty green card table (where the adults gamble). As it is gradually assembled, it becomes plain that the puzzle reflects the boy's situation in relation to his parents; "A summer without parents is the puzzle," the poet remarks, "Or should be." Like the page in the puzzle, the boy's "feet have not been found," nor his role in relation to his parents: is he a "son," a "slave or page boy"; will he be possessed by "Houri or Afreet," those forces of good and evil that "claim the Page"? His parents' divorce is equally bewildering, and it is mirrored by the picture that gradually emerges as Mademoiselle and the boy put its pieces together. A bearded Sheik on one cloud stares "eye to eye across the green abyss" at a "dark-eyed woman veiled in mauve" on another cloud. She is "being helped down from her camel" by a small boy, whom Mademoiselle significantly mistakes for "Her son."

As it turns out, "His French Mademoiselle" is herself a puzzle, the pieces of whose biography are slowly put together as the poem progresses, and over the years that follow its construction. She is only "French by marriage," having been "a widow since Verdun." She is the "Child of an English mother, a remote / Descendant of the great explorer Speke, / And Prussian father"—all of Europe, it seems, has gone into the making of Mademoiselle. Her genealogical puzzle implicates the historical and linguistic complexities of the modern world, because she speaks English, French, and German in the poem, sometimes simultaneously. She mixes up pieces of the language, saying "Schlaf wohl, cheri," before the boy goes to bed, and "Patience, cheri. Geduld mein Schatz" while he anxiously waits for the puzzle to arrive.

But the puzzle is more than a biographical, historical, and linguistic metaphor: it serves naturally as a symbol for the interlocking mysteries of hermeneutics and poeisis, of interpretation and composition. We as readers struggle to put the pieces of the poem (parents, Mademoiselle, the boy, the picture of the puzzle, the psychic parlor game in London, the poem by Rilke) together, pieces that the poet has assembled. From the start, the poem is connected to the dynamics of poeisis, of storytelling: Each item of the "craftsman's repertoire" can be "put aside, made stories of" until "The plot thickens / As all at once two pieces interlock."

Merrill uses two clever devices to link the content of the poem (puzzle as metaphor of poesis) with its form. The first involves four parenthetical digressions inserted between passages devoted to the puzzle, like the pieces between its parts. One parenthesis is devoted to Rilke's lost version of a poem by Valery. A second longer parenthesis (an entire stanza inserted, like the middle of a puzzle between its "Straight-edge pieces," between the repeated remark that "Mademoiselle does borders") is devoted to a psychic in London, who identifies an unseen object as "'Plywood. Piece of a puzzle.'" A third provides Mademoiselle's biography, and a fourth is addressed to Richard Howard, whom the poet asks to track down the French painting on which the puzzle is based.

The second device linking the form of the poem to the metaphor of the puzzle is one familiar to all readers of Merrill. In the central section of the poem, where all the pieces of the puzzle are finally put together, Merrill moves from the longer stanzas (mostly in blank verse, with a scattering of rhyme) to a sequence of seven carefully crafted and consistently rhymed quatrains (aaba) closed by a couplet when the last piece is found. That yields a double sonnet, composed of three quatrains preceding the parenthetical stanza addressed to Richard Howard, and three quatrains succeeding. All are devoted to the completion of the "World" represented by the puzzle's picture. All the syllables, stanzas, and rhymes fall into place, to generate a formal image of completion (of both poem and puzzle). Even so, the reader is not denied the

> *The puzzle is more than a biographical, historical, and linguistic metaphor: it serves naturally as a symbol for the interlocking mysteries of hermeneutics and poeisis, of interpretation and composition."*

pleasure of Mademoiselle and the boy, for what initially appears to be a series of an arbitrary number of quatrains, turns out to be a double sonnet, whose seven quatrains correspond to the seven days of the Creation.

For the creation and destruction of the world, the emergence of cosmos from chaos, turns out to be the final tenor of the metaphor of the puzzle—which has served equally well as a symbol for the complexities of biography, history, language, poeisis, and hermeneutics. Before the puzzle arrives from the shop, the card table prepared for it is empty, "a tense oasis of green felt," or "green abyss," analogous to the "void" on the "face of the deep" in Genesis 1:2. After the puzzle finally arrives, its "thousand hand-sawn / Sandal-scented pieces" are scattered over the green abyss in a profusion analogous to the "Chaos" of the beginning in Hesiod's Theogony. It is out of the emptiness of the abyss, and the chaotic sprawl of the puzzle pieces, that a cosmos will gradually be assembled—a "World" of earth and sky, with a city ("Thebes") inhabited by the archetypal characters of "the craftsman's repertoire" (witch, Sheik, veiled woman, page, retinue of vassals, demonic forces of "Houri" and "Afreet"). All in all, the poet acknowledges, it is "Quite a task, / Putting together Heaven, yet we do."

Merrill emphasizes the cosmic metaphor of the puzzle by calling it a "World that shifts like sand," and by calling the earth and sky "naive cosmogonists / Whose views clash," like the contestants in the divorce. The parenthesis devoted to the psychic's identification of an invisible object as a piece of a puzzle also brings the vast process of cosmogenesis into the metaphorical domain of the poem. It evokes the "fir forest" in which the "Trees tower" that will yield the wood for the puzzle, which forms a "a pattern" quite "superficial" in comparison to that "long term lamination / Of hazard and craft, the karma that has / Made it matter in the first place."

If the completion of the puzzle mirrors the creation of the world, so its return to the toyshop signifies a miniature apocalypse. When Mademoiselle and the boy lift the "two corners" of the puzzle, it hangs together for a moment, and then collapses: "a populace / Unstitched of its attachments, rattled down" onto the green surface of the table, and then the sky "crumbled, too," long after the city had fallen and the "tent [. . .] swept away." Then the pieces are "boxed and readdressed / To the puzzle shop in the mid-Sixties," leaving only "the green / On which the grown-ups gambled," and "A green dusk" illuminated by the "Last glow of west." The Creation—that puzzle whose mysteries we will never comprehend—has returned to the "abyss" of its beginning.

Source: Evans Lansing Smith, "Merrill's 'Lost in Translation'," in *Explicator*, Vol. 59, No. 3, Spring 2001, p. 156.

David Kalstone

In the following essay, Kalstone considers the verse of The Fire Screen, Braving the Elements, *and* Divine Comedies.

It would be interesting to know at what point Merrill saw a larger pattern emerging in his work—the point at which conscious shaping caught up with what unplanned or unconscious experience had thrown his way. In retrospect a reader can see that *Braving the Elements* (1972) gathers behind it the titles—with full metaphorical force—of Merrill's previous books. In *The Country of a Thousand Years of Peace, Water Street, Nights and Days* and *The Fire Screen,* he had referred to the four elements braved in the book which followed them. (*Divine Comedies* extends it one realm further.) The books do present experience under different aspects, almost as under different zodiacal signs. And *The Fire Screen* is, among other things—and preeminently—the book of love. It reads like a sonnet sequence following the curve of a love affair to its close. Like important sonnet sequences, the implied narrative calls into play a range of anxieties not strictly connected to love, in Merrill's case challenging some of the balanced views of *Nights and Days.*

"The Friend of the Fourth Decade" is the launching point for this book—the poet at forty, setting one part of himself in dialogue with another. What is being tested here is the whole commitment to memory, to personal history, to a house and settling down—the very material to which Merrill entrusted himself after *Water Street.* The "friend" is an alter ego who comes to visit—really to confront—his poet-host, after a long absence. In the opening scene, against the settled atmosphere of his host's house, the friend is shot through with the setting sun so that he appears to be "Any man with ears aglow, / . . . gazing inward, mute." The temptation the friend represents is crystallized in a dream at the close of the poem. "Behind a door marked danger . . ."

> Swaddlings of his whole civilization,
> Prayers, accounts, long priceless scroll,
> Whip, hawk, prow, queen, down to some last
> Lost comedy, all that fine writing
> Rigid with rains and suns,
> Are being gingerly unwound.
> There. Now the mirror. Feel the patient's heart
> Pounding—oh please, this once—
> Till nothing moves but to a drum.
> See his eyes darkening in bewilderment—
> No, in joy—and his lips part
> To greet the perfect stranger.

The friend has taught him a mesmerizing game in which saved-up postcards, a whole history of personal attachments, are soaked while the ink dissolves. The views remain, but the messages disappear, "rinsed of the word." When the poet tries it himself, watching his mother's "Dearest Son" unfurl in the water, the message remains legible. "The memories it stirred did not elude me."

"The Friend of the Fourth Decade" tests a dream of escape, a drama extended and detailed by the poems set in Greece which follow it in *The Fire Screen.* In some sense the book is like Elizabeth Bishop's *Questions of Travel,* a deepening encounter with another language and a more elemental culture, in which the speaker becomes, from poem to poem, more identified with his new world, cleansed of the assumptions of the old. In "To My Greek," the Greek language, encountered as if it were a demon lover, or a siren, becomes a radiant, concrete release from the subtleties of the "mother tongue" and the burden of "Latin's rusted treasure." A newcomer to Greek, he is forced to be simple, even silly. With Merrill the experience is characteristically amplified. He treats it as a temptation to become "rinsed of the word" and to humble himself speechless in the presence of "the perfect stranger." Both the transcendental and the self-destructive overtones of that phrase from "The Friend of the Fourth Decade," where the "perfect stranger" is also Death, haunt this book.

The initiation into Greece is inseparable from the exhilaration and the mystery of a love affair. It was anticipated in "Days of 1964," the wonderful Cavafid conclusion to *Nights and Days,* and is allowed to run its course in *The Fire Screen.* In "The Envoys" Merrill finds a series of emblems for the sense of adventure and risk experienced in the lover's presence. In three narrative panels, he introduces creatures the lover momentarily traps and tames, binds and then frees: a scurrying lizard, a frightened kitten and a beetle threaded and whirled around his head:

> You knotted the frail harness, spoke,
> Revolved. Eureka! Round your head
> Whirred a living emerald satellite.
> The experience is absorbed as a "modulation into a
> brighter key / Of terror we survive to play."
> Teach me, lizard, kitten, scarabee—
> Gemmed coffer opening on the dram
> Of everlasting life he represents,
> His brittle pharoahs in the vale of Hence
> Will hear who you are, who I am,
> And how you bound him close and set him free.

What he shares with the creatures is a moment at the gates of some other world, not insisted on, but imagined as if he were enjoying the danger. All the Greek poems, not only the love poems, benefit from that expansion of feeling. In a dramatic monologue whose tripping couplets are meant to suggest the energetic singsong of a simple Greek speaker, "Kostas Tympakianakis," Merrill seems almost literally to take up the speaker's invitation: "You'll see a different cosmos through the eyes of a Greek." He adopts the violence, the pride, the clear-eyed tone of the Greek. He accepts the welcome challenge, "Use my name," slips on the offered identity, but registers the gap between them in Kostas's final line: "Who could have imagined such a life as mine?" It is a small but telling rebuke of the poet's imagination always ticking away, its pressures momentarily relieved by taking on the voice of another. *The Fire Screen* contains several poems given over to the pleasures of evoking particular figures, humble like Kostas or sophisticated like Maria, the "muse of my off-days." It sees Greek peasant life through others' eyes ("David's Night at Veliès") or addresses itself to shared moments of happiness, as in "16.ix.65," with "evening's four and twenty candles" and the four friends who return from the beach "with honey on our drunken feet."

But at the core of the Greek section of this book are the love poems, some of them full of lyric intensity, others sharp and painful, like the dramatic

> *We must pay special attention to his puns and his settings; they open alternative perspectives against which to read the time-bound and random incidents of daily life."*

soliloquy or fragment "Part of the Vigil," which is, in a sense, the turning point of the affair, a surreal exploration of the images in the lover's heart:

> What
> If all you knew of me were down there, leaking
> Fluids at once abubble, pierced by fierce
> Impulsions of unfeeling, life, limb turning
> To burning cubes, to devil's dice, to ash—
> What if my effigy were down there? What,
> Dear god, if it were not!
> If it were nowhere in your heart!
> Here I turned back.

The lover's image is to "Blaze on" in the poet's own "saved skin." But the poems which follow register both the end of the affair and the folly of thinking of the Greek experience as an escape or oblivion. "Another August," "A Fever" and "Flying to Byzantium" are among the most powerful poems in the book. With "Mornings in a New House," as he imagines a dwelling half way back toward cooler American landscapes, the whole experience modulates into a new key, absorbed, retrospective, fading into myth.

It is appropriate in Merrill's work that recovery should be imagined in terms of a "new house" (or a repainted one in the more comic and detached version of "After the Fire"). "Mornings in a New House" has him, "a cold man" who "hardly cares," slowly brought to life by a fire laid at dawn. Once again the new house is the available image to set against exposure. "The worst is over," the fire a tamed recall of the shattered (or spent?) affair. Against its "tamed uprush. . . . Habit arranges the fire screen." The details of the screen, embroidered by his mother, place the entire lapsed passion into a withering perspective:

> Crewel-work. His mother as a child
> Stitched giant birds and flowery trees

To dwarf a house, her mother's—see the chimney's
Puff of dull yarn! Still vaguely chilled,

Guessing how even then her eight
Years had foreknown him, nursed him, all,
Sewn his first dress, sung to him, let him fall,
Howled when his face chipped like a plate,
He stands there wondering until red
Infraradiance, wave on wave,
So enters each plume-petal's crazy weave,
Each worsted brick of the homestead,
That once more, deep indoors, blood's drawn,
The tiny needlewoman cries,
And to some faintest creaking shut of eyes
His pleasure and the doll's are one.

It is hard to disentangle the impulses which contribute to this poem—harder even because the poet has added a footnote taking some of it back, imagining passion as itself a defense, not a danger, like the screen of fire that protects Brünnhilde in Wagner's opera. But, in the poem proper, the fire screen is devised against the damages of love. It bears, in a sense, the whole retrospective power of his writing, the ability of memory and art to absorb and rearrange experience. What marks this off from earlier moments in Merrill's poetry is the long perspective which the poem opens up, receding past his immediate pain, past his own childhood of "The Broken Home," to his mother who stitched the screen as a device involving *her* mother.

After all the carefully noted impulses in *The Fire Screen* to leave the mother behind—the attempts to rinse away her handwriting in "Friend of the Fourth Decade"; even the efforts to be free of Latin languages, the "mother tounge"—the poet returns to her in a new way. The "new house" of this poem is interwoven with the house his mother had sewn, *her* mother's house, dwarfed by giant birds and flowery trees. The discovery of these entwined destinies "deep indoors" draws blood. There is something like the remorse of "Childlessness" in what happens. The resources of art are seen as self-protective, even vengeful, a miniaturization of human powers, like the moment in the earlier poem when the annihilated village—teeming generations in dwarfed versions—is loaded aboard sampans and set adrift. But in "Mornings in a New House" the experience is without guilt and is shared in its brittle complexity. Waves of warmth and anger carry him inward to an identification with the "tiny needlewoman" mother, to share the childish pleasure and fear which even then would shape her feelings for the child *she* would one day have. With "some faintest creaking shut of eyes" they both become toys in a larger pattern, at once foreshortened and part of their shared, terrifying but ungrudging

humanity. I think what is most notable in this poem is that Merrill, however rueful and pained, has emerged from the erotic fire into a newly defined and felt natural perspective—one which becomes visible and palpable at length in many of the poems of his next book, *Braving the Elements.*

II

I have talked about the double action we must watch in Merrill's poems, the way he twins a witty surface with the poet's power to discover the veined patterns of his life. We must pay special attention to his puns and his settings; they open alternative perspectives against which to read the time-bound and random incidents of daily life. In *Braving the Elements* (1972) and *Divine Comedies* (1976), he has become a master of this idiosyncratic method, something one might call—with apologies—symbolic autobiography, Merrill's way of making apparently ordinary detail transparent to deeper configurations.

This is quite clear in "After the Fire" and "Log," which move us from the world of *The Fire Screen* to that of *Braving the Elements.* The brisk narrative of "After the Fire" brings back the Greek housekeeper Kyria Kleo, whom in "Days of 1964" he had seen wearing "the erotic mask / Worn the world over by illusion / To weddings of itself and simple need." Now, in the new key of "After the Fire," the Athens house has been repainted after a mysterious blaze. Under its "quiet sensible light gray," the house hides his old love affairs as it hides those of Kleo and her rumpled son Noti, their erotic escapades buried and part of the past. The mood of *Braving the Elements* is the mood of the opening invocation, "Log": banked flames of passion, burning and diminution, a life "consumed with that which it was nourished by." The muse discovered "After the Fire" is Kleo's mother, the half-crazed crone. In the yiayia's presence, the candles which gutter before old lovers' ghosts are replaced:

The snuffed-out candle-ends grow tall and shine,
Dead flames encircle us, which cannot harm,
The table's spread, she croons, and I
Am kneeling pressed to her old burning frame.

The comic crone turns before our eyes into a sybilline figure, mistress of the now harmless flames of passionate memory. She is, in a sense, the informing spirit of the book, for what is new about *Braving the Elements* is the way it opens to long—in some cases, geological—perspectives, the kind of prehistoric, penetrating wisdom which dwarfs and absorbs moments of intense present pain. The book contains, once again, love poems and poems involving the Oedipal trials of childhood. But these familiar sources of anxiety are in *Braving the Elements* transposed to a different key, resolved as by the all-embracing parenthesis of dream.

For example, family triangles make mysterious appearances in "18 West 11th Street," but as part of a poem in which several generations are run through a New York house, almost as in a strip of film. The house is one in which Merrill spent the first years of his childhood. With one of those attempts history makes to try and rival fiction, this was also the house accidentally destroyed in 1971 by Weathermen who were using it as a center for making bombs in the absence of the owners, parents of one of the revolutionaries. Richard Sáez, in a penetrating reading of the poem, points to the unlikely and eloquent connection it makes between "Cathy Wilkerson's destruction of her paternal home and James Merrill's pained elegies for his." The parallels, Sáez asserts, "are acts of fate as well as their active wills," as poet and radicals enact in their mutually incompatibile fashions, but with equal intensity, the conflict of generations. " '18 West 11th Street', like the House of Thebes, becomes an emblem for some unavoidable matrix of fate which involves both poet and revolutionary." Inexcapably linked to one another, the generations are themselves dissolved in the mirrors of the house and the long stretches of time, each generation finding its own means to suffer and to rebel. Sáez is right to single out the close of the poem as having a special new power in Merrill's work:

> Forty-odd years gone by,
> Toy blocks. Church bells. Original vacancy.
> O deepening spring.

Sáez points out—that "the 'Original vacancy' of the poem's conclusion is not merely the scene of departure from the poet's childhood. It is man's timeless exclusion from his unforgotten home." Yes, but the phrase also looks forward and seems to say "To Let." With the church bells and "toy blocks" the cityscape seems both distanced and renewed. Of course, the toy blocks are also the children's devices against their parents, whether as poems or explosives. And they are assumed into the ongoing beauty of the exclamation. "O deepening spring." Here Sáez is particularly acute: "In the concluding tercet nature itself is deflected from its amoral cyclical course to be glazed—not with the gilding, yellowing dust of earlier and lesser achieved poems but—with a patina of human destiny."

That same sense of unfolding destiny informs "Up and Down," a poem whose ingredients are familiar in Merrill's work, but never in so rich a combination. In an earlier book this might well have been two separate poems: one, "Snow King Chair Lift," reflecting the brief exhilarating rising arc of a love affair; the other, "The Emerald," an extraordinary and sympathetic encounter with his mother. But one thing Merrill does in his work is move toward larger and larger units of composition, not only long poems, but combinations of different forms, like the free juxtapositions of prose and more or less formal verse units in "The Thousand and Second Night" and "From the Cupola." The two sections of "Up and Down" limn out, together, an emotional landscape which neither of them could singly suggest.

On the surface it is a poem of contrasts: rising in a ski lift with a lover, descending into a bank vault with the mother; the ostensible freedom of one experience, while in the other, "palatial bronze gates shut like jaws." Yet the exhilaration of the ski lift—it begins in dramatic present tenses—is what is relegated finally to a cherished snapshot and to the past tense: "We gazed our little fills at boundlessness." The line almost bursts with its contradictions: unslaked appetite, or appetite only fulfilled and teased by "gazing our little fills." The lovers have not quite reached the condition of the Shakespearean "pitiful thrivers in their gazing spent"; they are more buoyant, but with a redirected and only momentary pleasure. "The Emerald," on the other hand, begins in brisk easy narrative pasts and moves toward a moment in the very present which the ski-lift section had forsaken. More important, whatever the surface contrasts between the two sections, there is an irresistible connection between the discoveries made by each. Or rather, the feelings of the opening poem enable the son to understand what happens to the mother in the closing poem. In the vault an unexpected secret jumps to light:

> Rustle of tissue, a sprung
> Lid. Her face gone queerly lit, fair, young,
> Like faces of our dear ones who have died.
> No rhinestone now, no dilute amethyst,
> But of the first water, linking star to pang,
> Teardrop to fire, my father's kisses hang
> In lipless concentration round her wrist.

The effect resembles the moment of thunder and lightning on the chair-lift in Part I, but here things are seen in a prolonged transforming light, the queer deathlike glow when the "mudbrown" coffin of a box is opened. It is as if the glimpse of "boundlessness" in Part I can only be extended and refined in the eternal light of underground. The poet and his mother are seen as part of a performance in the "green room" which the emerald suggests. Before his eyes she grows both youthful and like the dead. Surviving two husbands, she can still be transfixed by memory, transformed by the bracelet. "My father's kisses hang / In lipless concentration round her wrist." Contraries are reconciled: "star to pang, / Teardrop to fire." She is bride, widow and mother all at once, and something like the eternally preserved Mesopotamian consorts, "girl-bride jewelled in his grave."

Against this background mother and son have the unspoken reconciliation discussed earlier in this chapter. He slips onto her finger the emerald she had intended for his bride, the very ring his father gave her when the poet was born. All these elements compose an increasingly luminous frieze: "The world beneath the world is brightening." It is one of those moments assumed, as many are in *Braving the Elements,* into an ongoing process of time, and experienced not elegiacally but with a sense of promise. That deepening emotional landscape is most strongly suggested in the new physical surroundings of *Braving the Elements.* A series of difficult poems takes place in the Far West. Pieces like "Under Libra" and "In Nine Sleep Valley" are love poems played out against dwarfing panoramas and the geological erosions of a non-human world.

> Geode, the troll's melon
> Rind of crystals velvet smoke meat blue
> Formed far away under fantastic
> Pressures, then cloven in two
> By the taciturn rock shop man, twins now forever
> Will they hunger for each other
> When one goes north and one goes east?
> I expect minerals never do,
> Enough for them was a feast
> Of flaws, the molten start and glacial sleep,
> The parting kiss.
> Still face to face in halfmoonlight
> Sparkling comes easy to the Gemini.
> Centimeters deep yawns the abyss.

In "Under Libra" ancient stones are introduced into the poet's house ostensibly as doorstops and paperweights, but really as reminders of another scale of living. He goes "in the small hours from room to room / Stumbling onto their drugged stubborn sleep." These talismans overshadow desire; they place it in a perspective where past and future edge out the present. The solid human protagonists of the poem are dissolved before our eyes:

> . . . .Ten years from next morning, pen in hand,
> Looking through saltwater, through flames,
> Enkindlings of an absent *I* and *you.*
> Live, spitting pronouns, sparks that flew
> And were translated into windiest

> Esperanto, zero tongue of powers
> Diplomatic around 1 a.m.'s
> Undripping centerpiece, the Swan. . . .
> Days were coming when the real thing
> No longer shrugged a wing.

Some of the poems are pure ventriloquism. "The Black Mesa" speaks; so do "Banks of a Stream Where Creatures Bathe." They seem to embody a consensus of human voices, mythically inured to experience. History, the details of private lives—everything repeats itself in the long views these poems take. Hearing the poet take on these roles is like talking to survivors. "The Black Mesa," addressing the low flatland, musters for a moment the tone of an eager roue, but finally lapses back into a weary geological view of his experience, outwaiting all competitors and invaders: "I steal past him who next reclaims you, keep / Our hushed appointments, grain by grain. . . . / Dust of my dust, when will it all be plain?" The effect is to make expressions of human tenderness mere instances of the larger erosions and destinies which outlast them.

"Syrinx" is the most successful of such poems. She is, of course, an established mythological figure, brightly familiar from Marvell: "And Pan did after Syrinx speed / Not as a nymph, but for a reed." Merrill takes up her fragile link to the nature from which she was abstracted, "a thinking reed." Just who is she in this version? She addresses the poet as if she were his muse and his lover. She is sophisticated enough to know about slipware and to quote Pascal; also, to make puns about fashion and the Pan-pipe's traditional shape: "Among the wreckage, bent in Christian weeds, / Illiterate—X my mark—I tremble, still / A thinking reed."

"Bent in Christian weeds" makes it sound as if she were used to dresses by Chanel, and "Illiterate—X my mark" walks a tightrope of ingenuity and feeling. As unlikely as her witty denial of literacy may be, Syrinx keeps shucking off the claims of words as if they were merely garments. The most outrageous example is the incorporation of the musical scale: "Who puts his mouth to me / Draws out the scale of love and dread—/ O ramify, sole antidote!" The musician's breath or the lover's kiss, and then the high tragedienne's apostrophe, which, on a second glance, taking in the enjambment ("d—/ O"), we see disintegrate magically into the musical scale. This is precisely the action the poem repeats over and over: a human gesture, then the witty afflatus and effort of words which slip back before our eyes into analytic formulas, the do-re-mi of the scale, or the particles of a mathematical formula which expresses metastasis. Syrinx seems caught between human demands and ingenuity, which make her "tremble, still" and, on the other hand, her sense of being a worn part of a growing and disintegrating world:

> Foxglove
> Each year, cloud, hornet, fatal growths
> Proliferating by metastasis
> Rooted their total in the gliding stream.

Over and over the cleverness of the poem is matched by a hypnotic natural intonation, no more than in the astonishing close; as Syrinx slides back into her "scarred case,"

> Whose silvery breath-tarnished tones
> No longer rivet bone and star in place
> Or keep from shriveling, leather round a stone,
> The sunbather's precocious apricot
> Or stop the four winds racing overhead
> Nought
> Waste Eased
> Sought

Those last four words clothe the cardinal points in notions of human aspiration and loss, which we may understand in varying combinations and intensities, depending on the order in which we read them. But ultimately they slip back into the toneless ideogram of the ongoing winds. How odd human words and feelings seem, depicted in this particular way. The lozenge of four words is tinged by, but ultimately surpasses, individual feelings.

Source: David Kalstone, "Essay on Three Collections by James Merrill," in *Modern Critical Views: James Merrill*, edited by Harold Bloom, Chelsea House Publishers, 1985, pp. 57–67.

Sources

Bloom, Harold, "The Year's Books: Harold Bloom on Poetry, Part I," in *New Republic*, November 20, 1976, p. 21.

Donoghue, Denis, "What the Ouija Board Said," in *New York Times Book Review*, June 15, 1980, p. 3.

Flint, R. W., "Metamorphic Magician," in *New York Times Book Review*, March 13, 1983, p. 6.

Mendelsohn, Daniel, "A Poet of Love and Loss," in *New York Times Book Review*, March 4, 2001, p. 16.

Merrill, James, "Acoustical Chambers," in *Recitative: Prose*, edited by J. D. McClatchy, North Point Press, 1986, pp. 3–4.

———, "Lost in Translation," in *Collected Poems*, Knopf, 2001, pp. 362–67.

Perkins, David, "The Achievement of James Merrill," in *A History of Modern Poetry: Modernism and After*, Harvard University Press, 1987, pp. 644–45.

Rodway, Allan, "Stripping Off," in *London Magazine*, Vol. 16, No. 3, August–September 1976, pp. 66–73.

Shaw, Robert B., "James Merrill and the Ouija Board," in *New York Times Book Review*, April 29, 1979, p. 4.

Simpson, Louis, "Divine Comedies," in *New York Times Book Review*, March 21, 1976, p. 210.

Smith, Evans Lansing, "Merrill's 'Lost in Translation,'" in *Explicator*, Spring 2001, Vol. 59, No. 3, p. 156.

Spiegelman, Willard, "James Merrill," in *Dictionary of Literary Biography*, Volume 165: *American Poets since World War II*, edited by Joseph Conte, Gale Research, 1996, pp. 173–87.

Further Reading

Blasing, Mutlu Konuk, "Rethinking Models of Literary Change: The Case of James Merrill," in *American Literary History*, Vol. 2, No. 2, Summer 1990, pp. 299–317.

Blasing explores a postmodernist emphasis in Merrill's work.

Buckley, C. A., "Quantum Physics and the Ouija-Board: James Merrill's Holistic World View," in *Mosaic*, Vol. 26, No. 2, Spring 1993, pp. 39–61.

Buckley focuses on Merrill's interplay of science and poetry.

Vendler, Helen Hennessey, "James Merrill," in *Part of Nature, Part of Us: Modern American Poets*, Harvard University Press, 1980, pp. 205–32.

Vendler includes a comprehensive explication of the *Divine Comedies*.

White, Edmund, "On James Merrill," in *The Burning Library: Essays*, edited by David Bergman, Knopf, 1994, pp. 43–55.

White focuses on Merrill's "ambitious" *The Book of Ephraim*.

The Nerve

Glyn Maxwell

2002

Glyn Maxwell takes his readers to a very special place with his poem "The Nerve," a spot on the edge of everyday familiarity. It is a lively position to take, Maxwell writes in his poem, when a person finds himself standing "suddenly very far" from what he knows. It is the excitement that comes from facing the unknown that this poem attempts to identify and encourages its readers to find.

Maxwell knows about standing outside his known parameters. He is a British citizen living in New England, facing a new culture and a new, though similar, language of expression. With this poem, he shares his feelings about what happens when a person "cross[es] a line" and sees life from a different, unexpected perspective. The experience can have several different consequences: some might be positive; others might not. "But you ought to recognise it," says the poem.

"The Nerve" was published in a collection of the same title. In 2002, that collection was chosen by the *New York Times* as a Notable Book of the Year. The title poem reflects certain aspects of Maxwell's life in suburban New England, but the poem is not just about him. It could be about a man; it could be about a woman. It is about life, anywhere.

Author Biography

Glyn Maxwell, author of the poem "The Nerve," is a multitalented writer well known for his plays, novels, and opera librettos. He is also a teacher and an editor. Of all his abilities, this award-winning author is most recognized as a gifted poet.

Maxwell was born in Hertfordshire, England, in 1962. He received his bachelor's degree from Oxford University. Shortly after graduation, Maxwell won a scholarship to Boston University and came to the United States to study poetry and theater under Derek Walcott. After returning to England, Maxwell worked as a literary reviewer and later as a visiting writer at Warwick University. Then, in 1996, he returned to the United States, after being offered a position at Amherst College in Massachusetts. Since then, he has taught writing at Princeton, Columbia University, and the New School in New York City. Since 2001, he has also been the poetry editor at the *New Republic*.

Tale of the Mayor's Son, Maxwell's first book of poetry, was published in 1990. Two years later, with the publication of his second collection, *Out of the Rain* (1992), Maxwell's works began to be recognized with honors. *Out of the Rain* won the Somerset Maugham Award, while *Rest for the Wicked* (1995) was short-listed for the T. S. Eliot Prize and the Whitbread Poetry Award. In 1998, Maxwell's collection *The Breakage* was also short-listed for the T. S. Eliot Prize as well as for the Forward Poetry Prize for best poetry of the year. Three of his books, *Boys at Twilight* (2000), *Time's Fool* (2000), and *The Nerve* (2002) have, at various times, all been chosen as Notable Book of the Year by the *New York Times*. *The Nerve* also won the Geoffrey Faber Memorial Prize, in 2004. In *The Sugar Mile* (2005), Maxwell imagines (in a long series of poems) a conversation that might have taken place between two expatriates from Britain who meet in a city bar.

Besides his poetry collections, Maxwell has also published two novels, *Blue Burneau* (1994), which was short-listed for the Whitbread First Novel Award, and *Moon Country* (1996). He has also had seven of his plays professionally dramatized and is working on his second opera libretto. Maxwell lives in the United States with his wife and daughter.

Glyn Maxwell   © Nina Subin

Poem Summary

Stanzas 1–3

Maxwell's poem "The Nerve" begins with a reference to some ambiguous "rough shape," which is not explained fully. The reader is engaged by the intrigue of not knowing what the speaker is talking about, but there is no full engagement. The speaker could be talking about anything at this point. It is not until the second line that this "rough shape" is given a little more detail. The meaning of this shape does not become too much clearer, but in attaching the phrase "your life," the speaker draws the reader immediately into the poem. The speaker is talking directly to the reader, making the reader feel as if he or she had better pay attention. The speaker continues with words such as "your town" and "a dusty shop you pause in," constantly tugging at the reader to participate in this poem.

It is also obvious that it is not just the reader who is involved here. By the tone of the words, it is apparent that the speaker is talking about something that he himself has experienced. He understands the feeling of someone being "suddenly very far" from what is known. He could not have stated this phenomenon unless he, too, had gone through it. Now not only is the speaker talking directly to the reader, he is also sharing something extraordinary with him or her. He knows what it feels like and tries to stir that memory in the reader by referring to childhood. "You found it as a child," the speaker states. This is as if he is asking: Don't you remember? Then the speaker gives an example from his own experience, one that could easily correspond to the reader's experience—playing around one's house and knowing the boundaries of safety, sensing that beyond those parameters lies the great unknown or, as the speaker states in the fourth stanza, "the world's end."

Stanzas 4–6

Once the speaker rouses that memory of the unknown, that "breeze of being gone," he takes the reader more directly to the theme of the poem by mentioning "a single nerve." The speaker is not concrete in describing it, but rather comes to it obliquely. First it is "low down." In stanza 5, the speaker continues to throw out hints. The nerve "sags." That is all that the speaker is willing to give away. The rest of the definition is left to the reader. However, in the next few phrases, the speaker empathizes with the reader. He is sure that when the reader finds that nerve, he or she will be thrown off guard, be "chilled" to have found it so suddenly. Then there is a slight admonishment. After all, the speaker relates, "you ought to recognize it." Since it was there when you were a child, you knew it once, the speaker implies. And now, the awareness of that nerve has returned, but it cannot be depended on. It may well "fail" you "utterly." The speaker appears to be saying that if a person is suddenly awakened to the unknown, to a side of oneself that one was not aware of, it will possibly be a shock. This will change a person. That change, however, may not be for the best. It may all "go wrong."

Stanzas 7–9

The speaker begins stanza 7 with the thought that the change, which a person explores in oneself because this nerve has been touched, may even betray, that is, "be Judas," the man who betrayed Christ. That is a serious affair. And some "others," whether they are family, friends, or strangers, will offer no support. They will be "mute," unaware of "your pain." Ironically, they will "assume they're safe with you." These others, who remain untouched, will think "you" remain the same as they are. Because they have not changed, they do not see the change in "you." They do not know that because of that nerve, the person being addressed is wandering in uncharted waters, exploring new fields beyond the usual boundaries.

Rather than panicking about this situation, which sounds rather unstable, the speaker turns the reader around. "Treasure the nerve," he tells readers. Despite the challenges and possible disorientation, "treasure its dis- / belief." Do not dwell in

the land of safety, where everyone else lives. Strain to see through the known; reach for places that are "inhospitable." A place that has different rules might even be "unfair." The speaker is encouraging the reader to be strong, to go where others are afraid to venture.

Stanzas 10–12

Going toward the unknown, beyond the ordinary boundaries, past the safety nets of experience and well-worn belief, will have its challenges, the speaker warns. It will be a place of no set rules, "arbitrary." The reader may well have to endure pain and suffering, something that one will see coming and will think about before continuing on the journey. Choices will not be made for one. These are uncharted waters. The reader will have grave decisions to make. "You will face the choices that the nerve / has suffered." Those choices made, there are two possible consequences: "to be plucked" and "to have brought the soldiers running" or "to lie low" and "have perished years / ago." One is the consequence of love. The other is the consequence of fear.

Themes

Passion

When Maxwell urges his readers in his poem "The Nerve" to "cross a line" into the unknown, he might well be referring to coming alive with passion. Although there is also the sense of death in the poem, with such phrases as "a breeze of being gone," there is a stronger pull that suggests one should use that realization of death to live life to its fullest, in other words, to live with passion. If people get caught in believing that they will live forever, they may find that they are not really living at all. Life can become very boring, the speaker suggests, if one does not seize every moment as if it were the last. Through the poem, readers are encouraged to push themselves to the edge. That is where passion is found. Excitement flows through one's veins when everything feels new. To find the passion in life, one must clear the vision he or she has of life and must live in the present moment, where everything is fresh and new. The world of passion is one that the reader may have thought of as a child, when passion ran high and dreams were unlimited by social conditioning. Passion demands that one forgo the road that ineffectually promises safety. "For that act / of love," the poem states, one

Topics For Further Study

- Maxwell has often stated that he is influenced by the British poet W. H. Auden. Read several of Auden's poems and find one that is very similar to Maxwell's poem "The Nerve" in style, tone, theme, or all three. Analyze both poems. How are they similar? How do they differ? Write a poem of your own in a similar style. Here are three suggestions for a poem by Auden you might pick: "Let History Be My Judge," "Stop All the Clocks . . ." ("Twelve Songs: IX," sometimes called "Funeral Blues"), and "The Novelist."

- Complete a study of the circumstances of the life and times of the poet W. H. Auden compared with those that Maxwell must face today. In what environment did Auden live? Since both poets write of ordinary life, how were their lives similar? What were the social concerns in Auden's time while he lived in the United States? What are they today? Also look at the politics of the two different eras. How might politics have influenced the societies of both men?

- Read Henry David Thoreau's *Walden*. Focus on Thoreau's encouragement to his readers not to worry about keeping pace with those around them. Then write a paper pretending that Thoreau and Maxwell are having a conversation. On which topics do you think they would agree? On which would they disagree? Be as inventive as you want to be, without worrying about whether you are representing either of these authors accurately.

- Take a survey in your neighborhood. Ask each adult to tell you about one incident in his or her life that they would define as unusual. Or ask them what was the most exciting experience of their life so far. Then visit a third-grade class and ask for the teacher's permission to question the students. Get the children to tell you what they think would be the most exciting thing to do as an adult. Compare the two surveys and write up your study.

should be willing to endure whatever this path of passion might bring, despite its illogical rules and "inhospitable" circumstances. One should push beyond self-imposed or socially induced boundaries and wander to places "very far from what you know." These are all the ingredients of a passionate life, of someone who is willing to witness new and unfamiliar surroundings and experiences, despite the unexpected challenges that one may be forced to face. It is all worth it, according to the poem. One should "treasure the nerve" of passion.

Going against the Grain

Most people, the speaker of this poem suggests, live in a world of set rules and practiced patterns. They live, like children, in a fenced-in, small world. Although they may see the "next field," they are afraid to cross over the boundaries. They feel safe in this enclosed, familiar world, where experiences are predictable and sane. But that is not the world that the speaker lives in, and through this poem, the speaker urges his readers to go against that grain, to push themselves away from the masses of people who "are mute." By going against the grain and not following the crowd, the speaker does not promise an easy life but suggests that it will be better than living half-dead. Going against the grain is not a popular practice. Group psychology dictates that everyone huddle together for protection. This might work in some instances, but for an overall philosophy of life, the speaker of this poem believes that it is more stimulating and more promising to strike out on one's own, "where you will face the choices that the nerve / has suffered." The nerve is what keeps you alive, and that nerve can be found only by striking out on one's own path and not succumbing to the urge to do what everyone else is doing.

The Unknown

Many people have a great fear of the unknown, the speaker of this poem suggests. As children, many thought that by going past the boundaries that were set by their parents, they would come to harm. In childhood, the unknown may have been simply the neighbor's yard or a great wood behind the house. If children went beyond these boundaries into unfamiliar territory, they might have been punished with tighter restrictions, or they might have been told that they would be stolen away by a stranger. Some people still carry those fears with them as they adjust to adult life. Many people, the poem suggests, find a completely safe environment—or at least one that they think is completely safe—and they stay within parameters that they set for themselves. Their boundaries are reminiscent of those set by their parents or suggested by social standards, or at least what some people perceive to be socially correct. Because of their fears, they very seldom wander across those boundaries into the field of the unknown. Everything outside the familiar is frightening. But the speaker paints a very different picture of the unknown. Although he suggests that there is no promised safety and even talks of pain, he encourages his readers not to be afraid of the unknown. It might bring a world of new, "unfair" rules and "inhospitable" environments to those who wander too far, but pushing oneself into unfamiliar places and unknown experiences is the only worthwhile exploration that one can make in this life.

Style

Cadence

Maxwell's poem "The Nerve" is written in iambic feet, each foot containing first an unstressed syllable and then a stressed syllable. Note the word "perhaps" in the first stanza. The first syllable (per-) is unstressed, with the second syllable (-haps) receiving the stress. For people who speak English, iambic meter in poetry is the most natural rhythm. It is a rhythm most similar to the spoken language.

"The Nerve" is composed of twelve stanzas. Each stanza is a quatrain; that is, it contains four lines. The pattern of the rhythm is (with some exceptions) basically a first line of five iambic feet (a pentameter), a second line of three iambic feet (a trimeter), a third line of two iambic feet (a dimeter), and a last line of one iambic foot (a monometer). The use of iambic meter, because it most closely reflects natural speech, could have been chosen by Maxwell to project the overall conversational tone of his poem.

Tone

The tone of a poem is the perceived attitude that the author has toward his audience. With "The Nerve," at times the tone is that of a friend, as if the speaker were talking to someone he cared about. He offers a personal experience to back up his beliefs of how one should confront life. There is no sense of his knowing more than the reader knows but rather that he would like to share something he has learned with a peer. He uses down-to-earth language and images, even to the point of explaining his ideas as those that a child naturally encounters. He also speaks of dusty stores, fields, and bars—commonplace environments.

The speaker's tone is also at times that of a teacher, encouraging and nurturing. This is evident in the phrases such as "you ought to recognize it" and "treasure the nerve." The shortness of the stanzas is easily digested in a relaxed manner, as if the speaker were talking in a quiet, but reassuring voice. The vocabulary is simple, and there is only one allusion—to Judas—which is almost universally understood.

Enjambment

Enjambment is the continuation of the sense of a particular line (that is, the grammatical sense) beyond the end of the line. This might be done for a variety of reasons. One is for dramatic effect, creating a pause for the reader to reflect for a few seconds before continuing. Sometimes enjambment merely breaks the monotony of continually reading the same patterned meters of each stanza. In the first stanza of "The Nerve," a slight enjambment occurs at the end of the first line. "Somewhere at the side of the rough shape" reads as if that were a complete thought. However, as readers go on to the second line, they realize that it is not just some random "rough shape" that the speaker is discussing but rather the rough shape that "your life makes in your town." Then, at the end of the first stanza, there is another, more dramatic enjambment that causes a fairly abrupt change in perspective. The last two lines of stanza 1 are these: "you cross a line, / perhaps." That leaves the impression that the reader may or may not cross a line. That is one interpretation of what the speaker is saying. But continuing to the second stanza, the reader realizes that the speaker is really referring to the idea that the reader might cross this line, perhaps "in a dusty shop." That changes the sense of where the speaker is going. Rather than questioning whether the reader is going to cross the line at all, the speaker emphasizes, in the second stanza, more or less that the reader will eventually cross that line and the only question is where this will occur.

A second dramatic enjambment occurs in the eighth stanza, between the third and fourth lines. Here the poet hyphenates the word *disbelief*. Although readers may never be certain why an author does one thing or another, one can make intelligent or intuitive guesses. Here, the reason might be that Maxwell wanted to stress the word *belief* rather than its opposite, *disbelief*. Of course, one can argue that the metric beat of the poem demanded this hyphenation, but someone else can argue that Maxwell could have chosen another word. It is easier to assume that he hyphenated this one on purpose. He used the hyphen to cause a brief stop, to throw the reader off just a little, to make an emphatic point.

Shape

The shape of Maxwell's poem is not based on grammatical construction. The first two stanzas, plus the first line in stanza 3, complete the first sentence. The second sentence ends in the middle of line 1 of stanza 8. And the third sentence continues to the end of the poem. The shape is determined by the cadence, that is, the rhythm of the stressed and unstressed syllables, and the poet's choice of how many metered feet will be contained in each line. By ignoring grammatical construction—in other words, not allowing a period at the end of a sentence to dictate the end of a line—the author has created a sense of flow, like a small creek making its way downstream around boulders and fallen trees. The shape reflects, in some way, the theme of the poem, as it provides a sense of pattern but takes the reader outside that pattern at the same time. The definitive shape is the quatrain, with its patterned lines. Still, the meaning of the poem lies past the quatrains, as it pushes through the empty spaces between the stanzas and continues beyond the normal boundaries.

Historical Context

Brief History of British Poetry

Maxwell comes from a very long line of British poets, who have influenced his writing. British poetry is traceable as far back as the seventh century. It was then that a monk known as Caedmon wrote a hymn in verse, the first known British poem. Although the date is still in dispute, one of the next surviving verses is the well-known epic poem *Beowulf*, written perhaps in the eighth century but possibly as late as the tenth.

Poetry continued to flourish in later centuries, as witnessed by the several surviving texts composed during the Anglo-Norman period of British history. Poems from this period include Layaman's twelfth-century poem *Brut*, written in a dialect of Middle English, as well as the Gawain poet's *Sir Gawain and the Green Knight* and William Langland's *Piers Plowman*, both dating to the fourteenth century. Poetry would change after this point in British history, as the language of the country went through a massive mutation, evolving into what would become the genesis of modern English. Geoffrey Chaucer, who would become the major poet of the Middle Ages, lived at this time. His central work was *The Canterbury Tales*, a story of thirty pilgrims who pass the time of their long journey by telling one another stories. Chaucer was a great influence on British poetry into the following centuries.

The next great period for British poetry was the era of Queen Elizabeth I, who ruled from 1558 to 1603. This was a period famous for lyrical songs. It was also a time that saw the development of meters in poetry as well as an emphasis on courtly poems. William Shakespeare wrote his sonnets in the late sixteenth century. Other poets of the Elizabethan era include Sir Walter Raleigh, Christopher Marlowe, and Ben Jonson. This literary period also saw the development of the metaphysical poets, who appealed to the intellect rather than to the emotions. Often associated with these poets were John Donne and John Milton. Alexander Pope followed, with his emphasis on satire.

The Romantic period coalesced at the end of the eighteenth century under the influence of the great poets William Blake, William Wordsworth, Percy Bysshe Shelley, George Gordon Byron, and John Keats, to name just a few. The Romantics moved away from the metaphysical emphasis and focused on emotions and the individual.

Alfred Tennyson, Robert Browning, and Elizabeth Barrett Browning are Victorian-era poets, writing during the mid- to late nineteenth century. One of Tennyson's major works was *Ulysses*, which was published in 1842. While Robert Browning became rich after publishing *The Ring and the Book*, a long blank verse (a poem with no rhyming) in 1868, his wife, Elizabeth Barrett Browning, became famous for her *Sonnets from the Portuguese*.

The most well-known of twentieth-century British poets include William Butler Yeats, D. H. Lawrence, Rudyard Kipling, and T. S. Eliot. During World War II and shortly afterward, Romanticism was revisited and revised, and poets once again moved away from the rational and emphasized emotional reactions to life. This movement was best exemplified by one of Britain's greatest poets, Dylan Thomas. The latter part of the twentieth century saw an increased interest in poetry by women and by immigrants, especially from the West Indies. But general lack of publishing opportunities for poets has seen an overall decline in the publishing of books of poetry in the last decade, with poets having to turn to small presses and dealing with a less-than-enthusiastic public audience than poets of earlier centuries enjoyed.

W. H. Auden

Almost every time that Maxwell's poetry is discussed, a comparison is made to the British poet W. H. Auden. Maxwell himself has stated that Auden has a great influence on his writing.

Auden was born Wystan Hugh Auden in 1907. When his poetry collection simply called *Poems* was published in 1930, Auden was deemed one of the leading voices of his generation. He was often praised for his poetic technical precision and for his ability to write verse in a great variety of forms. He also was known for the way he was capable of bringing everyday events and vernacular, or everyday, language, into his poetry. His subjects also enjoyed a wide range, covering topics as different as social issues, science, and politics.

Auden was a great traveler, and his experiences in other countries provided him with a wealth of material upon which to draw. He explored areas throughout Europe, visited China and Iceland, and eventually settled in the United States. Like Maxwell, Auden wrote not only poetry but also plays, opera librettos, and essays; he also worked as an editor.

In 1996, Maxwell published, with his fellow poet Simon Armitage, the book *Moon Country: Further Reports from Iceland*, which covers a trip that the author made to Iceland, mimicking a similar trip that Auden had previously made. Maxwell's book covers the politics and geography of this country and is written in poetry and in prose. The trip was made in honor of W. H. Auden.

World Affairs at the Turn of the Twenty-First Century

Maxwell's poem "The Nerve" might be interpreted in many different ways; still, one cannot help but wonder if the underlying tone of exploring the unknown was stimulated by the great sense of uncertainty that enveloped the world after the terrorist attacks on the World Trade Center in New York City and on the Pentagon in Washington, D.C., in September 2001. Maxwell was living in Massachusetts at the time and often traveled to New York City to teach. The sense of fear and the mention of soldiers in his poem, as well as the statements that urge his readers to explore new beliefs and new rules, may have been an outcome of these horrific affairs that caught the world so totally off guard.

Before the attacks, awareness of international affairs among most American citizens was in decline. With the demise of a threat from the Soviet Union, many people in the United States enjoyed an undefined sense of security. There seemed to be no need to worry about attacks from any other country. The U.S. military represented the most significant force on the planet.

Then, on September 11, 2001, two planes flew into the twin towers of the World Trade Center. One other plane, several hundred miles south, plowed into the Pentagon. A fourth plane, which some believe was headed for the White House or the U.S. Capitol, had its mission thwarted by a group of brave airline passengers; this plane crashed in a field in Pennsylvania. Thousands of deaths occurred. And the world outlook changed.

The sense of security in the United States was shattered. Citizens realized that their country was not as isolated as many had previously thought. Their country was just as vulnerable as any other. Terrorists could strike anywhere. This realization brought with it a new fear. The familiar had been shattered, much as in Maxwell's poem. People had to change their beliefs and restructure their lives. The terrorists' attacks altered more than the skyline of one of the largest and most powerful cities in the world. They changed the world itself.

Critical Overview

"The Nerve" was published in a collection that bears the same title, and that book was chosen by the *New York Times* as Notable Book of the Year for 2002. In his review of the book, the *New York Times* writer David Orr finds that "Maxwell writes smart, formal lyrics that pay conscious tribute to the English verse tradition" and then goes on to describe this collection with words such as "low-key," "specific," and "decent." To explain this last adjective, Orr states that he is not giving Maxwell merely "faint praise." Quite the contrary, Orr says that the way that Maxwell writes poetry makes it appear that Maxwell "grew up talking in sonnets."

Orr comments directly about the poem "The Nerve," relating the theme of the piece to Maxwell's possible sense of feeling a bit out of step with his new surroundings in the United States. "The Nerve," Orr states, is a philosophical poem "in which Maxwell's silvery intelligence gets free rein." Orr concludes that "Maxwell is an intelligent and sensitive writer, and *The Nerve* is one of the most enjoyable books of this year."

Writing for *Publishers Weekly*, Michael Scharf refers, in general, to Maxwell's poetry as being "deft arrangements of ordinary (often suburban) experience into elaborate (often Audenesque) stanzas." More specifically, when discussing Maxwell's collection *The Nerve*, Scharf expects that "readers who seek variety in formal choices will be pleased."

"Maxwell is a substantial writer," states David Mason for Washington's *Weekly Standard*. He is a cross between W. H. Auden and Robert Frost, Mason goes on to say. In addition, Maxwell knows "how to face his generation's largely suburban experience" as a poet, and he articulates this experience, according to Mason, "with mature precision." As Mason says, "our nerves are lines of sensitive impulse, connecting brain and body," and that is why Maxwell's poetry is indeed "a nervy business."

Maxwell is also compared to W. H. Auden in a review by Daniel L. Guillory for the *Library Journal*. Guillory writes that this is because Maxwell, like Auden, "is a wry social commentator, fascinated by American phenomena." Later in the review, Guillory adds that Maxwell "is able to bring an effortless moral and aesthetic compression to his work" and states that Maxwell is a poet to be watched.

Criticism

Joyce Hart

Hart is a published author and freelance writer. In the following essay, Hart looks for the story in Maxwell's poem and analyzes why Maxwell left out certain details.

Hidden within a poem often lies a fuller story. Maxwell's poem "The Nerve" is a good example of this. This poem, as with many other verses, can be

> *He sets the reader in a comfortable position, bringing to mind an environment that is at once familiar and nonthreatening."*

read in many different ways. In large part, that is what makes poetry so fascinating. Some people may read poetry for the sheer beauty of its construction, with the poet's meticulous attention to rhyme and meter kept foremost in mind. Others might read poetry for the beautiful and succinct images that such writing can produce. But some readers pay special attention to the story of a poem, searching behind the short, clipped lines in each crisp stanza, trying to conceive a fuller picture of the material the poet left out. Such readers could be of any age, but in *Mortification: Writers' Stories of Their Public Shame* (2004), written by Robin Robertson and quoted in Dinitia Smith's review of that book in the *New York Times*, Maxwell offered the views of a specific thirteen-year-old girl, who, after hearing Maxwell read one of his poems, wanted a more detailed story. This young girl asked Maxwell what the poem was really about. The poet stammered a little as he explained his poem, retelling it in a fuller, more comprehensible story format. After hearing the poem's more detailed version in prose, the girl's response was "Why didn't you just write that then?"

Those who are used to reading fiction may ask the same question. Oh, they may enjoy the beauty of the careful attention a poet pays to words and the position of those words on paper. They also might like the ease with which they read the poem: the way the syllables roll so easily off the tongue and how the sounds of the words feel as if they were born to be together. But sometimes it is just plain hard trying to figure out what the poet is actually trying to say. Of course, that is one of the pleasures of poetry—like putting a puzzle together. A good piece of fiction should also have a few holes, so the reader does not sit back passively, like viewers watching a not-so-enticing television show. Still, poetry can have so many holes, sometimes quite big. As the young girl suggested, Why not tell it all?

What Do I Read Next?

- Maxwell's writing is often compared quite favorably to W. H. Auden's work. To make this comparison, read Auden's *Collected Poems* (1991). This is an extensive collection of Auden's poems, which capture, at times, his emotional responses as he reflects on such topics as the political, philosophical, and religious sentiments of his time.

- *Other: British and Irish Poetry since 1970* (1999), edited by Richard Caddel and Peter Quartermain, is a good place to start for an introduction to other contemporary British poets. Included in this collection are works from Caribbean-influenced poets as well as more traditional lyric poetry. Observations from several different ethnicities are represented, most with unconventional outlooks.

- In an attempt to help bridge the cultural gap between the United States and Great Britain, Dana Gioia has put together a book of British poems and offers his own interpretations. The book is called *Barrier of a Common Language: An American Looks at Contemporary British Poetry* (2003).

- Maxwell has been publishing collections of his poetry for more than twenty years. For a taste of some of his best poetry written in story form, read *Time's Fool* (2000). This book relates a tale in verse, focusing on a young man who is cursed to remain seventeen forever while the world around him ages.

- Maxwell's *Rest for the Wicked* (1995) reexamines some of his feelings as he matured into an adult. His use of British slang, polished by his great sense of lyricism, makes this collection fun to read.

- Don Paterson and Charles Simic have put together a book of poems written by young British authors who have yet to receive much literary acclaim. This does not mean that their poetry is not worth reading; these young poets just have not yet been discovered. The collection is simply called *New British Poetry* (2004) and was published by Graywolf Press. The book offers readers a good chance to get ahead of the crowd.

What is the story behind "The Nerve?" First, the poem is attempting to communicate a philosophy. The poet has learned a significant lesson about life, which has helped him understand his experiences in a new light. This has more than likely taught him something valuable, because he obviously wants to share it. He wants to pass on his discoveries, believing that they might help someone else. The poet tells his story not by using the pronouns *I* and *me*, however; instead, he pulls the reader into his story by using *you*. In this way, he is telling his readers, through an unstated undercurrent, that this is what has happened to him, and now he wants the reader to try it. Then he embarks on the journey.

He sets the reader in a comfortable position, bringing to mind an environment that is at once familiar and nonthreatening. "Somewhere," he begins, meaning that it could be anywhere. It could be in a heat-damp southern swamp or in a glacier-cold northwestern mountaintop. He is not specific, because this is not his story (he is subtly proclaiming); it is the reader's. He is also not specific about the details of the life he is describing. He merely portrays it as a "rough shape." This allows his readers the opportunity of trying this poem on without worrying that it will not fit. Everyone can identify with "somewhere" as well as with a roughly shaped life.

So far then, there is a person, walking along through his or her town in some unspecified location. The person is not thinking about much, just walking, when all of a sudden, the speaker announces: "you cross a line, / perhaps." This image is similar to one that may have occurred in anyone's childhood. Remember the bully who dared you to cross a line that had been drawn in the dirt?

Whether you did or did not do it, you knew that the minute you did cross that line, something different would happen. That is the tension the poet creates in using this phrase. You are just walking along, minding your own ordinary business, when you cross into another world. You could be anywhere, the speaker reminds you—"in a dusty shop" or "a bar." Again, these are common places; there is nothing unusual about them. They could exist in any big city, like New York, or in any small town, like Sisters, Oregon. Every town has old shops and bars. What is unusual is the experience of crossing that line. This situation could be compared to a story from the old television series *The Twilight Zone.* You—an ordinary person, in an ordinary town, in an ordinary place of business—abruptly find yourself "very far from what you know." You can almost hear the violins and cellos playing in the background as the drama of the story increases to a frenzied pitch.

As in any good story, the poet does not want to strain his readers too much, so he releases the tension. He brings the reader back to a familiar scene—childhood. This strange place the speaker has introduced, so distant from what the reader knows, is no different from what he or she felt as a child, or so the speaker tries to convince the reader. Remember staring across the fence of your backyard into the "next field?" Remember how you wondered what lay out there beyond those safe boundaries? Remember how your imagination swirled with the possibilities? That is where the speaker is trying to take the reader. Yes, it was perhaps a little scary, but the thought of it was also very exciting. It could have been "the world's end, / a breeze of being gone." What would that feel like—to be gone?

That part of the poem is probably the easiest from which to make a story. After the first three stanzas, the poem becomes more abstract, less specific. It is here that the speaker begins his discussion of the nerve, and it is here that the holes begin to develop. What is this nerve? What does the speaker mean when he states that "it begins to give, / a single nerve, / low down"? There seems to be some kind of awakening taking place. To recapitulate, the reader is standing there, and something changes. You have crossed some kind of line, and you begin to feel things (a nerve implies feeling things) that you never felt before. It is low down and sagging, maybe because it has been unused for so many years. It once was higher, when you were a child. But now it has "felt the gravity." Instead of thinking of sagging as falling toward the ground,

the reader might want to think of it as sagging in consciousness. You are in the dusty shop, and you suddenly remember the feeling. It is buried beneath a lot of memories and experiences, so it feels slightly familiar, but at the time it seems new and strange. And "you are chilled / to have been told / that way—." It rose into your conscious mind too suddenly. It is at this point in the poem that the speaker offers a warning and an admonishment of sorts. "You ought to recognize it," the speaker says. You should never have lost track of it. It was there when you were a child, and you let it go. Then he adds that if you do not watch out, you might lose it entirely. It might, "one day, / fail utterly."

Readers still do not know what "it" is. The poet invited everyone into his poem by being vague about the town, the "rough shape," and the "dusty shop," and now he is not telling his readers what the nerve is. Like the thirteen-year-old girl in Maxwell's audience, everyone would probably like to know in more depth what he is talking about. After all, whatever the speaker refers to, it sounds as if it is something that has changed his life, and there are moments in everyone's life when they crave something different. If the speaker is, in fact, warning his readers that if they do not recognize this "it," something could "go wrong," why does he not just spit it out? Perhaps, by leaving this hole, this lack of definition, the poet makes the reader work. Maybe the poet cannot take the reader directly to this feeling, whatever it is, because the reader has to find it for himself or herself. The speaker has stated, after all, that it is something that the "you" in this poem knew as a child, and "you" are the only one who knows what that is.

Throughout the second half of this poem, the speaker continues to provide his reader with hints or clues about this nerve. He offers more warnings, too, telling the reader that friends may not understand what he or she is going through when this nerve has awakened. He also counsels the reader that once a person acknowledges this new world, he or she will encounter a whole new set of rules that, unlike the ordinary world, does not provide a sense of safety. The person may find the environment to be "inhospitable" and "unfair." Here, the poem is reminiscent of the telling of a typical myth—a story in which a hero or heroine is called upon to complete a dangerous task. The journey might prove to be exciting and rewarding, but it will not be without its risks. Despite the warnings, the speaker encourages the reader by insinuating that no matter what the risks, the reader will be compelled to go forward; as he puts it in the poem, the reader will "start for."

As the speaker briefly describes some of the events that readers might encounter on this journey, readers can continue to compare this poem with a mythic tale. One may be "plucked," the speaker warns, and may suffer. Then he adds, if one acts out of love, one may be saved. If, however, one acts out of fear, one may perish. Here, one can imagine J. R. R. Tolkien's story *The Lord of the Rings* or any such story told in a mythlike manner, a tale in which the hero sets forth on a quest to save his village and finds that the journey is filled with danger. The challenges are all but insurmountable, but if the hero's heart is pure, he will survive. According to Joseph Campbell, one of the greatest scholars of mythology, myths have been told throughout the history of humankind to provide clues by which people can better envision their lives. Campbell also was a strong proponent of following one's passion in life in order to live more fully. The clues and hints provided in Maxwell's philosophical poem appear to be telling us the same thing. The poem, despite the fact that it consists of a mere forty-eight short lines, does tell a complete story. Yes, the poem has many holes, but you can fill them with your imagination.

Source: Joyce Hart, Critical Essay on "The Nerve," in *Poetry for Students*, Thomson Gale, 2006.

Sandra M. Gilbert

In the following review of Maxwell's The Boys at Twilight *and the work of five other male poets, Gilbert praises the collection as "a good introduction to the kind of high-spirited rhyme-&-chime" that Maxwell "does best."*

No doubt because I've spent so much of my working life musing on the measures of the female literary tradition, I'm not usually asked to review a same-sex set of male-authored books. Yet as feminist theorists were the first (but are now not the only ones) to note, the intricate and subtle relationships between gender and genre that often shape the cadences of women's writing just as surely and often inform men's work. Taken together, for instance, the six poets under scrutiny here begin to seem eerily representative of contemporary modes of masculinity—seem, that is, like a fairly typical bunch of twentieth/twenty-first century guys—whose recent collections fit into a jig-saw puzzle that might help us figure out, in the words of the old movie, where the boys are.

In a sense, of course, it's reductive to imagine these artists—all serious and accomplished writers—as a kind of pobiz platoon, but I have to confess that now such a fancy has come to mind it's hard to dismiss. For even the titles of some of their books—e.g., Heroin, Atomic Field, The Boys at Twilight—seem to insist on a sometimes tormented, sometimes rueful male sensibility. Indeed, just as women now and then feel the need to write about such supposedly "feminine" topics as, say, grandmothers, kitchens, birthing and nursing, most of these guys evidently feel a need to write about stereotypical "guy" subjects: rootless wanderings, brutal addictions, cosmic speculations, and even more specifically, as the jacket copy of Glyn Maxwell's *The Boys at Twilight* declares, "men at war, boys at play, boys grown up, men overreaching and reverting." And if women writers can now and then be understood through stereotypes willingly adopted or willfully imposed (female female impersonations like "femme fatale," "innocent virgin," "rebellious feminist," "earth mother"), their masculine contemporaries can also be grasped through analyses of male male impersonations like "tough guy," "sensitive young/middle-aged man," "son of famous father," "recovering druggie/alcoholic," "boy genius," etc. Like most of us, to be sure, these writers adopt different roles at different times, yet it's interesting how well suited each is in a costume of masculinity that's sometimes as aware of its own artifice as it is artfully tailored to fit the demands of the page.

The rather ostentatiously youthful Glyn Maxwell, for instance, who peers cherubically out of a slick flap photo, comes off as both a bravura "boy genius" and a bravura commentator on boys and boyhood. His dauntingly massive *Time's Fool: A Tale in Verse* is a 396-page record, in Dantesque terza rima, of the travails of a single seventeen-year old, who has been condemned to the hell of riding a "Ghost Train" around and through suburban England—a fate that may seem infernal indeed to those who've suffered the vagaries of the British rail system. Like Wagner's Flying Dutchman, to whom the text helpfully refers us, Maxwell's doomed teenager circles the world in search of love or perhaps some more au courant redemption, and like the speaker of the *Divine Comedy,* he is accompanied by a "Poet" (capitalized) who raffishly plays Virgil to his Dante. But Edmund Lea, whose name allusively invokes the very Edward Lear who wrote such charming nonsense verse at the last fin de siecle, is a nonsensical creation indeed—perhaps deliberately so—compared to his great literary precursors. Unfortunately, he's also a tedious figure, often puerile in his preoccupations with his old girlfriend Clare and the geography of Hartisle, his allegorically named hometown.

"This place is Chadwick Grove," Edmund explains to the Poet (whose own name, "Glen," allusively invokes the authorial "Glyn"),

> the outskirts of, though that's a place that's all
> outskirt. No one ever says what of.
>
> You'll see a hill come up. Behind the hill
> some lights I think are Stortwood, or, who knows,
> Chadwick proper. Then there'll come a tunnel
>
> we used to say was haunted with the souls
> of a crash in 1930. You'll excuse me
> if I don't believe this anymore. Those tales
>
> are little winding relics.

And within a few more lines a monologue that has already begun to seem like something of a "winding relic" frankly acknowledges its own tedium:

> Soon the tunnel, home in a bare mile.
> I'll know the names of streets by then, I'm afraid,
>
> and tire you like a tour guide.

To be fair, Maxwell tries to help his hapless readers rather more than his self-pitying "Passenger from Hell" aids the unfortunate Glen. As if writing program notes for a post-romantic redaction of Der Fliegende Hollander, he supplies glosses to each chapter. Chapter one ("The Chance in Hell"), for instance, opens with the following portentous announcement:

> CHRISTMAS EVE, 1984. Edmund Lea has ridden a Ghost Train for fourteen years and believes he is in Hell. . . . He tells the Poet how seven years earlier, the Train arrived back at his home town, Hartisle, on Christmas Eve 1977 . . . [where he discovered that] He has not aged, but the world had not waited. Only Clare, the girl he loved, recognized him, but she was now a wife and mother. His family were not at home.

And with comparable solemnity, chapter three ("My First Poem"), summarizes what we will soon learn is the tale's originatory moment:

> AUTUMN 1970. Edmund falls in love with Clare, a classmate, and believes his love is returned. He is the envy of all his friends, but on Christmas Eve a stranger, Cole, arrives at the Oak pub and seduces Clare.

Alas, though, if it is a or the Dantesque (or Wagnerian) moment that the author of this tome implicitly defines as a Turning Point, the Scene in the Pub leaves something to be desired:

> In my seat
> was Clare when I got back, and on her stool
> the NAVY man who had arrived that night,
> who wore all dark and wasn't from our school,
> who lit his cigarette and was engaged
> in deep talk with another listening gift,
>
> I noticed, on his other side. I reached
> our table and knelt down alongside Clare,
> the other side from him. Gently I touched

> *The rather ostentatiously youthful Glyn Maxwell, for instance, who peers cherubically out of a slick flap photo, comes off as both a bravura 'boy genius' and a bravura commentator on boys and boyhood."*

> her hand and she looked down. She said, 'He's here,
> he's coming through the rye' and carried on,
> quarreling with Nick about some war
>
> he said was not 'true war.' The NAVY man
> was scrutinizing him. The atmosphere
> was purest smoke through which I led my hand
>
> towards her thigh, gold-colored and so near,
> and let it rest and and have her move away
> as if earth had itself marooned me here
>
> by quickening. The stranger had his say
> about all kinds of things I couldn't follow,
> and "Time!" was called to a great choral cry
>
> of disappointment.

O well, Edmund, better luck next time might be a more appropriate response to the disappointment about to ensue than the 200-odd pages that actually follow this moment. For although many who have been seventeen (and which readers of *POETRY* have not?) remember the age as a year that sometimes seemed both perpetual and painful—as durable as unendurable—whether one is time's wise man or "time's fool," one usually and usefully discovers that seventeen, along with sixteen and fifteen, passes like a train in the night. And that's an especially Good Thing if it entails the kind of Sturm und Drang Edmund Lea, and Glyn Maxwell, might do better to have journeyed beyond.

Time's Fool seems like a particularly misbegotten enterprise because Maxwell is in fact a poet of unusual facility and (at times) felicity. *The Boys at Twilight,* a collection of poems drawn from his first three volumes, is a good introduction to the kind of high-spirited rhyme-&-chime—a sort of darkly postmodern vers de société—that he does best. Certainly its title poem offers a more balanced and distanced view of male youth ("the boy with you as the sun goes red / . . . Has remembered words you forgot you said") than the wretched Edmund's plodding, or do I mean chugging, tale. Better still, the unpretentiously sardonic and charming "Tale of a Chocolate Egg," which appeared in Maxwell's first book, *Tale of the Mayor's Son,* constitutes a salutary antithesis to the overinflated saga of the Teen on the Train. For one thing, this quest-romance, comically meditating on the desires elicited by a giant billboard advertising a single piece of candy, takes up a little more than fourteen pages, compared to the later work's 396. For another, its tone is chatty and colloquial, insouciantly concluding "What else? The bloke (my hero, I admit) / Scoffed the thing and didn't die of it." ("Scoffed" here looks to me like a typo for "scarfed" but perhaps British spelling for "scarfed" [i.e., gobbled] is "scoffed"?)

Similarly high-spirited though with a serious core, "Sulk" is an astutely observant elegy for the kind of sci-fi, futuristically glamorous "future" Stanley Kubrick and others promised for the millennial year 2001 but at which we (naturally) haven't yet arrived:

> What we are at is pining for our lost
> Future. How we are doing that is simple:
> Slouching beside our low glass tables dressed
> In shimmering precious suit from nape to ankle.
>
> That's how it was to have been. The walls of silver,
> The doors that slish behind, the ultramarine
> Drink, the apotheosis of the letter
> Z in Christian names and the light this clean.
>
> Instead it's a sulk we'll have. We're the spoiled child
> With centuries for uncles, and those uncles
> Leaning along the shelves, disabused and old
> And letting us learn or not from the foul troubles
>
> They dumped on us. . . .

In a strenuously witty poem entitled "Don't Waste Your Breath," Maxwell makes it quite clear that he knows his strengths and weaknesses, defining the latter at one point as including at least a few of the following:

> Reading verse to lesser mammals,
> Tailing cats or humping camels,
> Hectoring sheep.
> Pleading with a traffic warden,
> Writing things that sound like Auden
> In his sleep.

At his worst (as in *Time's Fool*), Maxwell does sound like someone preachily "hectoring sheep," so

it's a whole lot better when he writes "things that sound like Auden / In his sleep." In any case, to do just that is no mean feat, as many of the glossy and shapely verses in *The Boys at Twilight* tend to prove.

If at his best Maxwell has the boyish pizzazz of, say, a slightly somnolent early Auden, he's a shoo-in for the role of "the Kid" in this platoon, and a kid who radiates exuberant innocence when compared to embittered tough guys like Franz Wright, "the Recovering Alcoholic Son of a Famous (Dead) Dad," and Charlie Smith, "the Former Heroin Addict." Wright's work, for instance, is phlegmy with the kind of regret that the Marlboro Man must have felt after too many packs. Though the jacket copy on *The Beforelife,* his thirteenth collection, describes him as a "lyric visionary" who is the "son of the beloved postwar poet James Wright," the weighty sufferings he records in this volume seem for the most part anything but "lyric" and "visionary," nor does the "Famous (Dead) Dad" come off as particularly "beloved." On the contrary, unlike the parent to whom he often seems to want to insist on comparison, this Wright all too often appears hellbent on an out-of-the-side-of-the-mouth sneering cynicism, as in "Translation," where we're jokily assured that "Death is nature's way / of telling you to be quiet," or in the one-line "Body Bag," which triumphantly reveals that "Like the condom in a pinch one size fits all."

Presumably "The Dead Dads" is intended to excavate the anguish that shaped these often all too banal ironies, but as psychoanalytic exposition it falls short of the mark, even though as an effort at grown-up poetry it does conclude with a nice neat twist of the knife:

> It's easier to get a rope
> through the eye of a needle than
> the drunk son of a drunk
>
> into stopping
> into waking—oh no, not
> this guy, he's intent on
>
> finding out and finding out
> exactly
> what the poor old f—er felt like
>
> and hell,
> all he has asked
> is one good cold responsible
>
> look at the corpse
> when it meets him, living,
> at the door—. . . .

Especially if the reader resists the "look" at father/son similarities and dissimilarities that this piece, like a number of others, so bleakly invites, it's plain that Wright junior has some talent for clear, spare versifying of the raw-and-nitty-gritty. But when even his spare lines are unsparing in self-indulgence—as in "Empty Stage," which begins with a parody of the standard twelve-step confessional opener ("My name is Franz, and I'm a recovering a—hole")—more than a purely formal discipline may be in order. Maybe this gloomy ironist needs to be a bit more ironic about his irony?

At the same time, to be fair to Wright, his poems hardly lack self-knowledge. "Memoir," one of the more successful pieces in The Beforelife, limns a sepulchrally comic self-portrait:

> Just hope he forgot the address
> and don't answer the phone
>
> for a week:
> put out all the lights
>
> in the house—
> behave like you aren't there
>
> if some night when
> it's blizzarding, you see
>
> Franz Wright arrive
> on your street with his suitcase
>
> of codeine pills,
> lugging that heavy
>
> black manuscript
> of blank texts.

Yet still: even here one wants to say, Hey, hang on a minute, man, these texts aren't exactly blank no matter what color you want to call your manuscript.

Where Franz Wright suffers in taut short lines, Charlie Smith aches in long limber ones; where Wright is tersely glum, Smith is extravagantly grim. Alcohol versus heroin? Both these tormented tough guy poets hint at such a range of addictions and depressions that, apart from the sheer chutzpah it would take to theorize the question, it would be empirically foolish to speculate. What's sure, though, is that Smith's poems have a sprezzatura, an almost Byronic crackle and verve, that's in itself kind of addictive. The title poem of *Heroin,* for example, begins, improbably,

> I left a message for my editor to send copies of the contracts
> to my new agent,
> and then I read a passage about how no one talks
> about heroin anymore, and the old life came back to
> me. . . .

and then, arrow to terrible target, zeroes in on a Surprise Ending that really works:

> I loved the graciousness of heroin, the way everything

externalized
and obvious in the daylight opened its shirt and
revealed its soft pale breasts.
The world slept curled in its own foolhardiness.
And my wife came carefully over the blankets to me
and seemed
not to mind who I was. We inserted words
into spaces in the rain. For years I remembered the words
and whispered them to myself, half thinking I might
conjure her back into the world. They never caught us.
We missed them on the way to Mexico, to Puebla,
where eventually the line gave out. We slept on a
bench outside a church.
It was two days before she died without regaining consciousness,
as I say in the memoir they are paying me so
handsomely for.

To be sure, the right-on quality of that last line locates its author in a docudrama of hell not all that different from Edmund Lea's Ghost Train through suburban England or Franz Wright's boozy redaction of Hamlet. Things "as they are," as Smith notes in a poem appropriately called "Honesty," include "modernity hamming it up" on and off the page or the screen, and getting paid "handsomely" for its confessional melodrama. But there's a fine line between the wry consciousness that what Sylvia Plath called "the peanut-crunching crowd" will fork over good money to watch the po-mo poet's "big striptease" and the impulse to really let it rip and capitalize on every last drop of marketable angst. "Lady Lazarus" is only one of countless poems in which Plath lunged along that line like a master tightrope walker, but not many can follow in such perilous footsteps. Certainly Smith teeters toward the sawdust pretty often, as in "Of This I Speak to No One," where a versified public tantrum ("stoned & crying, saying impossible impossible") isn't much mitigated by the carefully ironic way the hullabaloo of the text contradicts the caution of the title:

> I have been screaming all day in my head
> and then I hit the dog across the back
> attempting to train it to love me,
> the dog that is now scared of mc and can't stay
> away from the garbage, who lives at the neighbors'
> and stands on their front porch looking impassively at
> me,
> like a friend who believes the baseless charges.
> Of this I can speak to no one, as you
> can't speak of the crows and the terrible thoughts
> coming out of the woods like old men in gray suits.
> Each night we are exchanged
> for something much worse than we imagined,

which is why late in the day
I go out to the woods where the poplars are greasy
and the oaks are against me
and lie down across the grain of the mountain curs-
ing,
trying to tear the itch off my hands.

A little more than halfway through this passage I, at least, am inclined to decide that the poet
can "speak to no one" of all this because he should
speak to no one. His dog story is great, yes, but the
"terrible thoughts / coming out of the woods like
old men in gray suits" are just a little too reminiscent of Seventies surrealism at its more simplistic,
and as for getting "exchanged" each night "for
something much worse," well, exactly what's that
"something much worse" to a guy who already has
such theatrically "terrible thoughts"?

Nonetheless, the impatience Smith here and
there evokes is probably a measure of the admirable
invention and brilliance he exhibits in so many
other places. The magical "Beds," for instance, has
something of the incantatory charisma of Kenneth
Koch's "Sleeping with Women"—and deploys a
comparable male braggadoccio as it conjures up

drunken beds, sopping watery beds, pissed-in beds,
. . . .all I have slept in,
beds I have knelt beside and dreamed of,
bench one foot wide for a bed in Saipan,
hay barn in Turkey bed, dawn like sherbet
naked men stood up out of, trickling weedy beds,
greetings and goodbyes from beds,
sullen, imperious beds . . . [sic] there was always a
bed,
place to lie down, if only for a pause, in jail
or in the aisle of a bus. . . .

Maybe because (unlike Wright, who is a
poet/translator) Smith is a poet/novelist, the best of
his poems are fortified against self-pity by a narrative precision that gives rich texture to tales of
Rootless Wanderings that might otherwise be
stereotypical or banal. Maybe Franz Wright, and
for that matter Glyn Maxwell, should try prose for
a while.

Like Charlie Smith, Nicholas Christopher is a
poet/novelist, and like both Smith and Wright, he's
something of a tough guy, or anyway a guy given
to tough—or perhaps, more accurately, guarded—
understatement. He neither reveals nor revels in
past addictions, however, and those peccadilloes to
which he does confess appear to be the usual features of a well-spent hip youth. In fact, *Atomic
Field,* his sixth collection, consists of two autobiographical sequences that are essentially snapshots
of the author, first at eleven, then at twenty-one.
And here's where understatement becomes as much

a formal strategy as a mode of dramatic self-
presentation. For throughout this volume Christopher seems, for better or worse, bent on recording
those "spots of time" out of which Wordsworth
thought everyone's past was constituted with a kind
of "objective" (well, pseudo objective) photorealism rather than with the feelingful intensity for
which the author of *The Prelude* strove. Thus one
of the book's earlier poems begins

A four-story building.
Gray brick with brown trim.
A brown door lighted by a yellow bulb that repels
insects.
Eight identical apartments.
Flowerpots in some of the windows.
A fire escape which I climb
to the roof at night.

And another opens

The old woman upstairs with the canary that does-
n't
sing
bleaches her shell collection once a year
in her claw-foot tub
while listening to the records she and her husband
used to play at the beach cottage they rented
every summer for thirty years, until he died.

The apparent flatness of affect here—almost a
kind of zombie tone—is clearly deliberate, and in-
termittently effective at capturing the bewildered,
sometimes pained, sometimes simply acquiescent
sensibility of an eleven year old, as in number 14
of the 1962 sequence:

There is always someone on crutches in this
luncheonette.
Or so it seems.
A former GI.
A bus driver who was hit by a truck.
A nurse who never recovered from polio.
And behind the counter, the bald man
with the hook for a hand,
who can twirl his moustache with it.

Too often, though, such a stance of documentary dispassion leads to just plain prosiness. The
verse beginning "A four-story building," for instance, ends with its protagonist on his apartment
house roof, watching "jets with flashing pinpoint
lights" as they "arc in and out of the airport." The
(presumably hard-won) minimalist ending, though,
inflates a small, childhood apercu into a point that
hardly bears Wordsworthian emphasis:

Later I concentrate on the stars,
which constantly change position
while appearing never to move.

By labeling his two sequences with simply
the years—"1962," "1972"—in which the individual poems are set, Christopher signals a further

documentary ambition: to contextualize the texts of his protagonist's individual history with the social history of two decades crucial to his growing up. And *Atomic Field,* the title he bestows on the whole collection, further implies that he wants to break down experience into, as it were, atomic particles—constructing each poem out of dots (rather than spots) of time like a literary pointillist—while also conjuring up the threat of: nuclear disaster that children were particularly taught to fear in those years. But again, the social history of the period emerges as both obvious and anti-climactic in, say, the characterizations of culture heroes or heroines. The death of Marilyn Monroe, for instance, elicits the not very inspired comment that she will

> never again . . . blow a kiss
> laughing from an open window,
> never with a careless gesture throw off
> the blanket of white roses that covers her now.

And James Bond is tamely described as "Connoisseur of fast cars, crack shot . . . a man of strong appetites and silences . . . whose adversary—a mad scientist / extravagant as Caligula—goes by the name of No."

Christopher's observations of 1972 are just a bit keener, though these too tend to belabor the obvious (i.e., the tie-dyes, groovy pads, backpacking journeys, and psychedelic voyages of a hippie youth). Here and there, a way station on one of his farther-out trips flickers momentarily to life:

> On the southern coast of Crete
> where even the shadows of the palms smolder
> and tumblers of raki waft smoke
> and steam pours from bursting melons,
> naked girls are lolling, burnt-orange, in the boiling
> surf.
> They live in the black caves along the beach,
> and for a week I'm one of their guests,
> drinking wine mixed with honey,
> making love between handwoven blankets,
> gazing cross-legged at the thin line
> that is Africa shimmering on the horizon.

So far, so good, as a witty journey back in time. And it's amusing, too, to learn that

> Some Americans in loincloths have founded
> a school of Pythagoras in a hut beneath the cliffs.
> They eat only figs, olives and barley cakes
> and at nightfall play lutes and timbrels. . . .

But like so many other components of these two ambitious sequences, this one grinds to a disappointing halt, as we discover that while the hip Pythagoreans "play lutes and timbrels" they

> watch stars across the galaxy conjoin into circles
> which mesh like the gears of a clock,
> measuring—to the last second—every man's life.

Are we meant to regard this final epiphany as the narrator's youthful insight—or as the middleaged poet's backward glance at travell'd roads? Either way, it seems curiously meager, even (or perhaps especially) as a self-conscious allusion to the eleven-year-old's rooftop vision—in poem 12 of "1962"—of the stars "which constantly change position / while appearing never to move."

If in my fantasy platoon Wright and Smith are suffering tough guys, and Christopher is a guarded, low-key guy, Paul Breslin is a sensitive guy, the Alan Alda of the bunch. Perhaps for obvious reasons, this means he's written some of the most interesting and successful of the poems I read for this review: as a "Sensitive Man," he's willing to take the risk of feeling but unwilling to subject his readers to self-indulgent theatrics. *You Are Here* doesn't have a very prepossessing tide (*Heroin* and *Atomic Field*—even *The Beforelife*—rank higher as grabbers) and it doesn't have the kind of crackling ferocity that marks Smith's verse or the kind of virtuoso sheen that characterizes Maxwell's work. Yet despite an apparent modesty of presentation this fine first book is full of soundly crafted, tightly controlled, often very moving poetry. Like Christopher, Breslin writes about meticulously dated boyhood memories (to which the second half of his collection is devoted), and like most of the other poets considered here he meditates on civilization and its discontents. But his continual interest in moving from his own individual docudrama toward larger issues suggests not just what I'm stereotyping as "sensitivity" but also notable generosity.

Thus in—among other pieces—"The Question," "Book Club," and "White Wound/Black Scar," Breslin transforms recollections of personal encounters with public trauma into incisive looks at identity politics unmarred by preachiness or special pleading. And in the impressive "Three Poems of Elijah," he offers a revision of Biblical narrative that perhaps inevitably concludes with a reference to the Holocaust but, again, a reference that's remarkably fresh and free of sermonizing. In "His Unease in Heaven," the third poem in the series, the ancient prophet, ostensible speaker of the whole sequence, watches "a line of souls ascending, veiled in smoke, / through chimneys of the buildings far below," and in the enigmatic silence with which God responds to the questions of the suffering dead he muses on the hopes with which he himself traditionally haunts the ceremony of the Passover seder:

> Each spring at Passover, I walk the earth
> until I find a likely looking house,
> and watch the family seder through the window.

They pour the wine, though casually, as if
I'll never come for it. Only the children
quicken with the old anticipation,
hearing their father sing, Elijah, come. . . .
He rises, and he sets the door ajar.
O when will He Who Is That Which He Is
unlock the storehouse of the folded rainbow,
and bid me come to sit with them this night
that will not be like any other night,
drinking the heavy wine the living drink?

Breslin's memoiristic poems are often as eloquent and almost always as straightforward as this
passage, for as an autobiographer in verse he is both
unpretentious and unsententious, avoiding, on the
one hand, the temptation of literary "photorealism"
and on the other hand the lure of confessional melodrama. Evidently, like Wright, he had an alcoholic
father, and in "Scenes from Childhood" he remembers the horror induced by parental quarrels:

Don't they know
the house is alive?

How can they call me
out of the sunlight

into its mouth?
At night it threatens

to grind me apart—
I will live on as pieces.

But though his own sufferings must surely
have been as "grinding" as he says they were, he
plainly struggles to transcend his own pain in order
to articulate sympathy for what he makes clear was
his father's torment. Perhaps a male parent's alcoholic angst—in Franz Wright's overheated phrase,
"what the poor old f—er felt like"—seems less
infamous if the dead dad is less famous?

In any case, Breslin's "Keepsake," subtitled
"1962" (no doubt out of an impulse, like Christopher's, to investigate and recreate the chronology of
childhood) is impressively charitable in its portrait
of a hopeless, hapless, lost father. Beginning with a
recollection of personal trauma ("It seemed impossible to move my face / which hung there numb"),
this poignantly elegiac piece expands into a vision
of someone else's trauma that's moving precisely
because it's both clinical and compassionate:

There is no picture of my father leaving
our house on Crandon. Scarcely on his feet,
each arm draped on the shoulders of a friend,
he mumbled an inaudible good-bye
and nodded, meaning he was ready, as
their dark suits filled the doorway, then descended
into the bright spring day, and down the walk.
I must have watched him go: I have this picture.

Similar to "Keepsake" in scrupulousness of observation as well as moral scrupulousness—which

is to say, willingness to take seriously the risk of
feeling with and for another—is "My Father's Father Before Him." Subtitled "1951," this poem is
addressed to the dead dad whose misdoings caused
such pain while also eliciting impressive empathy.
I quote the work in its entirety because it seems to
me one of the most representative as well as one of
the most successful selections in *You Are Here:*

Had he snapped like a dried moth
when I hugged him, I'd have said,
"Of course."
His three-piece suits had pinstripes
so fine they disappeared in the black cloth.
Only the gold chain of his pocketwatch
had light or color, the face
too pale to have blood in it.
Something had gone out
in the eyes. They were done
with looking.
Absently
he gave out presents,
denying us
nothing. It was Mother
who told him to stop
while you said nothing.

He came from Toronto. How polar,
how sunless, must that city be
to make such skin and such eyes!
I still mistype it
"Toronot"—abode of nonbeing,
your birthplace and secret home.

Those hot summer evenings, the grill
smoking with meat, your friends
stood around in shorts and short sleeves.
You laughed too much and too loudly,
sprung from Toronot till they went home.

Of the six poets considered here, the late Larry
Levis would have been the most likely candidate
for the part of the "guy who's been around." He
could hardly, of course, have been a candidate for
the "old man" of the group: his early death—in
1996 at the age of forty-nine—came as a shock to
the poetry community, and I'd guess that at least
Breslin and Smith are his contemporaries. But with
seven collections of poetry to his credit, two, including the one under review here, published
posthumously, Levis was an experienced and mas-
terful artist, and more specifically a writer whose
work constitutes a kind of microhistory of American
verse from the early Seventies to the present. As I
roam through the poems David St. John, the editor
of *The Selected Levis,* has chosen from the poet's
early volumes—*Wrecking Crew* (1972) and *The Afterlife* (1977)—I seem to be rereading things I first
encountered in journals like *Kayak* and *Crazy
Horse* that were popular in the "deep-image" Seventies. And as I move on to the poems from Levis's

later volumes—*The Dollmaker's Ghost* (1981), *Winter Stars* (1985), and *The Widening Spell of the Leaves* (1991)—I sense a strengthening of American poetry's ambition, an outward urge of verse itself, not unlike what Levis so magically calls "the widening spell of the leaves."

I certainly don't went to be teleological here, don't want to imply in some mock Tennysonian way that "all creation [of poetry] moves" to a single "far-off, divine event," nor do I mean to idealize the dead. Even in the carefully winnowed volume St. John offers us, Levis's work is uneven. Some of the early poems, in particular, are mannered and derivative. "For the Country" (from *Wrecking Crew*), for instance, offers a brand of cynical political generalization that usually emerged more effectively in the productions of Seventies rock musicians and moviemakers, with section 4 of the sequence merely a tissue of easy paradoxes:

> You are the sweet, pregnant,
> teen-age blonde thrown from the speeding car.
>
> You are a dead, clean-shaven astronaut
> orbiting perfectly forever.
>
> You are America.
> You are nobody.
> I made you up.
> I take pills and drive a flammable truck
> until I drop.
>
> I am the nicest guy in the world,
> closing his switchblade and whistling.

And a piece called "Matinee," section 8 of the ambitious and frequently comic "Linnets" (from *The Afterlife*), proposes a surrealistic dream-scene in which one wonders whether substitutions of one simile or metaphor for another would make much difference. The opening line—"Your family stands over your bed / like Auks of estrangement"—seems especially arbitrary: why not, for example, Owls or Gulls "of estrangement?" And the final triplet—

> They [the family] lift higher and higher
> over the snow on the Great Plains.
> Goodbye, tender blimps

—sounds dated and silly.

But as his command of the poetic line widened, Levis's poetry became almost literally breathtaking, a kind of verse that spelled itself out and cast its spell in such sinewy inventive cadences that the leaves to which he referred in "the widening spell of the leaves" might well have been those most powerfully American bits of foliage, *Leaves of Grass.* And imagine having the nerve to ventriloquize Whitman! Yet this is what Levis did in a poem (from *Winter Stars*) simply—and daringly—entitled "Whitman":

> On Long Island, they moved my clapboard house
> Across a turnpike, & then felt so guilty they
> Named a shopping center after me!
>
> Now that I'm required reading in your high schools,
> Teenagers call me a fool.
> Now what I sang stops breathing.
>
> And yet
> It was only when everyone stopped believing in me
> That I began to live again—
> First in the thin whine of Montana fence wire,
> Then in the transparent, cast-off garments hung
> In the windows of the poorest families,
> Then in the glad music of Charlie Parker.
> At times now,
> I even come back to watch you
> From the eyes of a taciturn boy at Malibu.
> Across the counter at the beach concession stand,
> I sell you hot dogs, Pepsis, cigarettes—
> My blond hair long, greasy, & swept back
> In a vain old ducktail, deliciously
> Out of style.
> And no one notices.
> Once, I even came back as me,
> An aging homosexual who ran the Tilt-a-Whiff
> At country fairs, the chilled paint on each gondola
> Changing color as it picked up speed,
> And a Mardi Gras tattoo on my left shoulder.
> A few of you must have seen my photographs,
> For when you looked back,
> I thought you caught the meaning of my stare:
>
> Still water,
> merciless.
>
> A Kosmos. One of the roughs.
>
> And Charlie Parker's grave outside Kansas City
> Covered with weeds.
>
> Leave me alone.
> A father who's outlived his only child.
>
> To find me now will cost you everything.

Not only do I not want to idealize Larry Levis by assuming him into some kind of definitive Dead Poet's Society, I don't want to sentimentalize or fictionalize him. And yet one can't help wondering what the risks he took did "cost" him. Not "everything," perhaps, but quite a lot, given the gravity of his achievement. The *Selected Levis* doesn't include any work from his extraordinarily inventive, posthumously published and presciently titled volume *Elegy;* yet as David St. John comments in a fine editorial afterward, even the last three books Levis produced during his lifetime seem to reflect "a complex midlife reckoning with death's allure and power," a reckoning that may well have been expensive to an artist so wholeheartedly committed to his craft.

Certainly the final piece in this collection is suggestive in the deep and dangerous game it plays with the meaning of nothingness, "the blank wave sprawl of fact" that indifferently engulfs the "small crowd of roughnecks at Poe's funeral" and "Lincoln & Whitman, joining hands one overcast spring afternoon" and the assassins Bakunin and Oswald.

As a kind of coda to this meditation on "where the boys are," I'd like to give the last two sections of this poem, entitled "At the Grave of My Guardian Angel: St. Louis Cemetery, New Orleans." For though the text is too long to reproduce here in its entirety, even part of it can serve as a sort of Whitmanic guide to the rich and risky place a poet, male or female, can get to if s/he eschews mannerism, self-pity, toughness, bombast.

> But it's all or nothing in this life; it's smallpox,
> quicklime, & fire.
> It's the extinct whistling of an infantry; it is all the
> faded rosettes of blood
> Turning into this amnesia of billboards & the
> ceaseless
> hunh? of traffic.
> It goes on & I go with it; it spreads into the sun &
> air
> & throws out a fast shade
> That will never sleep, and I go with it; it breaks
> Lincoln & Poe into small drops of oil spreading
> Into endless swirls on the water, & I recognize the
> pattern.
>
> There there now, Nothing.
> Stop your sniveling. Stop sifting dirt through your
> fingers into your glass of milk,
> A milk still white as stone; whiter even. Why don't
> you finish it?
> We'd better be getting on our way soon, sweet
> Nothing.
> I'll buy you something pretty from the store.
> I'll let you wear the flower in your hair even
> though
> you can only vanish entirely underneath its brown,
> implacable petals.
> Stop your sniveling. I can almost see the all night
> diner looming
> Up ahead, with its lights & its flashing sign a
> testimony to failure.
> I can almost see our little apartment under the free-
> way
> overpass, the cups on the mantle rattling
> continually—
> The Mojave one way; the Pacific the other.
> At least we'll have each other's company.
> And it's not as if you held your one wing, tattered
> as
> it was, in contempt
> For being only one. It's not as if you were frivo-
> lous.
> It's not like that. It's not like that at all.
> Riding beside me, your seat belt around your invis-
> ible
> waist. Sweet nothing.
> Sweet, sweet Nothing.

In the face of angst—political, personal, metaphysical, whatever—this poem says, even nothing is something, if only an ironically "sweet" something. Whitman, the granddaddy of at least five out of six of these guys, knew that too, as Levis reminds us. And speaking of the Dead Poet's Society, that guy Walt, never tough though always "one of the roughs," may be dust under our American boot-soles but he is good health to us nevertheless and he still stops somewhere, waiting for us.

Source: Sandra M. Gilbert, Review of *The Boys at Twilight: Poems 1990–1995*, in *Poetry*, Vol. 178, No. 4, July 2001, pp. 216–30.

Sources

Guillory, Daniel L., Review of *The Nerve*, in *Library Journal*, Vol. 127, No. 13, August 2002, p. 101.

Mason, David, "A Nervy Business," in *Weekly Standard*, Vol. 9, No. 31, April 26, 2004, pp. 35–36.

Maxwell, Glyn, *The Nerve*, Houghton Mifflin Company, 2002, pp. 2–3.

Orr, David, "So Long at the Fair," in *New York Times*, November 17, 2002, p. 7.

Scharf, Michael, Review of *The Nerve*, in *Publishers Weekly*, Vol. 249, No. 29, July 22, 2002, p. 170.

Smith, Dinitia, "You're Published. Now the Fun Begins? Think Again," in *New York Times*, April 14, 2004, p. E3.

Further Reading

DiYanni, Robert, *Literature: Reading Fiction, Poetry, and Drama*, McGraw-Hill, 2001.
    DiYanni takes examples of literary work from the classics through contemporary works and presents the formal tools of literary analysis. In understanding these basic elements, students can more deeply appreciate the meaning of a particular piece of literature and better understand how creative pieces are put together.

Johnston, Dileri Borunda, *Speak American: A Survival Guide to the Language and Culture of the U.S.A.*, Random House, 2000.
    Want to know what it might be like to have come to the United States from another country? Look through the eyes of someone from England or India or Africa and see the challenges they must face in learning not only the basic language but also all the idioms and slang Americans take for granted. This

book offers a view from the outside, giving American-born students a different glimpse of their own language and culture.

Koch, Kenneth, and Kate Farrell, *Sleeping on the Wing: An Anthology of Modern Poetry with Essays on Reading and Writing*, Vintage, 1982.

Although this book is more than twenty years old, creative writing teachers still find it applicable. Koch and Farrell have put together a large sampling of poems and essays about the poems, and then they guide students through a series of writing exercises. This book is useful for the student who wants to do more than just read poetry.

Pinsky, Robert, *The Sounds of Poetry: A Brief Guide*, Farrar, Straus and Giroux, 1999.

The poet laureate Robert Pinsky has a very personal relationship with poetry, and in this book he shares

some of the reasons why he enjoys the art so much. His discussions, as he breaks down some of the best poems into their syllables, are not only accessible but enlightening as well.

Ryden, Kent C., and Wayne Franklin, *Landscape with Figures: Nature and Culture in New England*, University of Iowa Press, 2001.

In Maxwell's poem, the poet offers a look at one man's life amid contemporary New England culture. Maxwell stresses the importance of taking a step back and trying to see life through different lenses. Ryden and Franklin do the same, giving their readers a different way to look at New England—through nature. The land and the history of New England are linked, according to these authors, and they provide another way of understanding how the New England culture has been formed.

Pine

Kimiko Hahn
1999

"Pine" is a beautiful example of the work of the award-winning poet Kimiko Hahn and reflects her mixed cultural Japanese American background. The poem is as delicate and subtle as a Japanese painting. It is as sensual as Hahn's own favorite literature, the poetry of Japanese women of the Heian era court, and it is as accessible as any modern American narrative poem. With just the right number of allusions and images, Hahn gently taps her audience on their shoulders and encourages them (as well as her fictitious student audience) to work harder, to dig deeper into their souls in order to tap a creative source that not only will help them understand their emotions but also will assist them in creating a piece of work that will move their future as readers. It is a poem about writing poetry as well as a poem of sensual delights.

Hahn's poem was published in 1999 in her collection *Mosquito and Ant*. The title of this book refers to a form of writing used long ago by Asian women. Hahn's writing is also influenced by the traditional Japanese poetry called *tanka*—a system used by Japanese women in ancient times to relate their emotions to one another, usually following an evening encounter with their lovers.

In "Pine," Hahn uses the title word in two ways. In indicating a pine tree, a popular symbol in Japanese literature, culture, and lore, Hahn makes reference to strength and endurance, encouraging her audience to suffer through the hardships they may encounter as they struggle to write poetry and to draw on those challenges to bring their inner feelings to full light. But she also uses "pine" in another way, a more American manner. In the English language, "pine" can be a verb. To pine for something is to long for it, to sulk, to brood. In other words, the subject of this poem is the emotions. The speaker of the poem wants to feel emotions, and she encourages young poets in the poem's last line: "So prick my skin."

Author Biography

Kimiko Hahn, an award-winning poet, was born in 1955 in Mount Kisco, New York. Her mother, of Japanese ancestry and born in Hawaii, and her father, of German ancestry and born in Wisconsin, were both artists. When Hahn was ready for college, she enrolled at the University of Iowa, where she decided upon a double major in English and East Asian studies. Upon graduation, she was accepted at Columbia University and eventually received a master's degree in Japanese literature.

Hahn's first book, written in collaboration with her fellow poets Gale Jackson and Susan Sherman, was published in 1988 as *We Stand Our Ground.* In this work, Hahn and her coauthors explore the challenges of finding a common ground among people with differing ethnic backgrounds. Hahn states that she leans more toward her mother's Japanese background and has spent most of her adult life exploring Japanese culture, language, and literature. Her mother's heritage is not the only thing that influences Hahn's writing. Her mother suffered an accidental death, and Hahn often explores this circumstance in her poetry.

Besides reflecting on the loss of her mother and the effect it has had on her own children, Hahn also takes up other themes, including the relationships between men and women and topics that deal with the body and desire and with the use of language. Of particular interest to Hahn are the lives of women, which are common subjects of her writing. She is also especially fond of women writers of ancient Japanese times.

Hahn has written six collections of poetry: *Air Pocket* (1989); *Earshot* (1992), which won the Theodore Roethke Memorial Poetry Prize and the Association of Asian America Studies Literature Award; *The Unbearable Heart* (1995), which received an American Book Award; *Volatile* (1999); *Mosquito and Ant* (1999), in which "Pine" appears; and *The Artist's Daughter* (2002). Besides winning

Kimiko Hahn   Colleen McKay

specific awards for particular publications, Hahn has also received awards for her work in general. Such prizes include the Lila Wallace–Reader's Digest Writer's Award and fellowships from the New York Foundation for the Arts and the National Endowment for the Arts. Included in her list of credits is a television script, *Ain't Nuthin' but a She-Thing*, written in 1995 for a special two-hour presentation for HBO. The television production included brief portraits of ten women.

Hahn has been an associate professor in the English department at Queens College (CUNY). Previously, she was an editor for the magazine *Bridge: Asian-American Perspectives.*

Poem Text

i.
I thought wearing an evergreen dress
might be enough to express the longing
of the pine
though it or because it retains its scent
throughout the snowfall   5
and above the tree line. That's what I thought.

ii.
I needle my students

and a few write inflamed poems
to my ideological bent and my ankle bracelet.
I lay awake in the neighbor's light   10
through the curtain of flurries
we find in the real morning—
the one with real light.
And the only way to guide them
through their own compost   15
is to needle them harder—
to make them work not for me
but for the spruce
scraping at their windows. Still
X sends terrifying love letters   20
that send so much blood to the chest
the fingers are cold.

iii.

You say it's from *a crush*.

iv.

You say quit using these *he* and *hims*
when the specificity of *John*   25
is more engaging.
I needle: make me feel.

v.

Next time I make a C-note
from a poem
I will send you a red dress   30
I have tried on myself first.
The silk, light as the lotion
on the nape of your neck.

vi.

silk, rayon, chiffon,

vii.

You say it's the *he* in *heat*.   35

viii.

I see pine and I see
what I know is feeling.
I imagine stepping barefoot
under those trees
onto a bed of their   40
brown needles.
So prick my skin.

Poem Summary

Stanza 1

In "Pine," the first word of the first stanza is the pronoun *I*. Each stanza thereafter starts with either *I* or *you*. In setting up this pattern of address, Hahn develops the sense of writing a letter, one of the characteristics of the Japanese poetic form called tanka. This brings a certain intimacy to the poem, and thus Hahn draws her readers into her poetry. Whether readers consider themselves the third party witness to the communication or, even more intimately, see themselves, by the use of the pronoun *you*, as the person intended, Hahn

accomplishes her mission of connecting with her audience.

In the second line of the first stanza, Hahn brings out another element of the tanka—emotion. The second line ends with "longing." By placing "longing" at the end of this line, Hahn emphasizes the emotion. Then, in the third line, she connects "longing" with "of the pine." Is there longing in a pine tree? Or is the poet using the pine tree to represent something else? One possible interpretation an American audience might make stems from the double meaning of "pine." Thus, the alternate meaning of "pine" further accentuates "longing." "Pine" refers to a Japanese motif. The pine tree, often used in Japanese writing and also in Japanese painting, stands for endurance. Thus the longing that Hahn has introduced, which is later emphasized with the pine, could signify either that the speaker is enduring the longing or possibly that the longing itself is enduring, or everlasting. It is not clear whether the poet wants to focus on the depth of the longing or rather the continuing effect of it, but the next couple of lines add more detail to this concept. Here, the speaker introduces the pronoun *it*. She does not explain what "it" refers to. Is it the longing or the pine tree or the dress? Whatever it is, it "retains its scent," but the scent of what? The obvious answer would be the scent of the pine. So the reader must ask what the scent of the pine represents in this poem. And the only possible answer is "the longing." In this way the first stanza comes back to where it began. To emphasize this circular motion, Hahn adds, at the very end of the stanza, "That's what I thought," repeating a similar phrase that appeared in the first line of the poem.

These last words of the first stanza are complex, though they at first appear simplistic. Even though the last phrase of this stanza is similar to the first phrase, the feeling of each is very different. In the beginning, it seems as if Hahn is stating a fact. At the end, however, we are not so sure. The speaker is no longer confident that what she "thought" was correct. The difference between the beginning and the ending is that in the middle something has happened. The speaker originally thought the wearing of the green dress "might be enough," but after wearing the dress, perhaps she discovered it was not enough. With this thought, Hahn leads her readers into the next stanza.

Stanza 2

If the speaker is questioning her own ability to express her longing in the first stanza, she definitely is questioning her students' ability in the second stanza. She has concern for their writing. She wants her students to express their longing, their emotions. Instead, she is seeing in their poems anything but their true feelings. They misread her prodding of them to open up to their emotions, and they produce instead "inflamed poems." But these poems are not about their real selves. Rather they are poems written to please her.

After the first three lines of this second stanza, the poet changes direction abruptly. From her concerns about her students, she turns to a personal image. This change appears to be detached from the previous lines. However, if the reader takes into account that the teacher/speaker is searching for a way to get her students to write more eloquently about themselves, it could be that she is trying to demonstrate how to do this. She provides a very vivid image through which the reader not only sees the picture the speaker is painting but also can feel the emotion behind it. "I lay awake," the speaker states. Readers should question what is keeping her awake. She also lies "in the neighbor's light," from which could be inferred that she has gone to bed early, at least before her neighbors have gone to bed. There is something going on inside the speaker, which Hahn expresses very simply. But the emotions she is putting across are not so simple. In not blurting out the details exactly, the speaker again draws in her reader, forcing them to come to their own conclusions. This is exactly the kind of writing the speaker wants her students to compose.

Stanzas 3–7

In the next five stanzas, some of them only one phrase long, the poem is dominated by comments directed not at the speaker's students but at the anonymous "you," who appears to be a person who is critiquing the speaker, helping her look at her own work in the same way that she looks at her students' writing. The message to be more specific is one of the directives that comes through in the fourth stanza. This is something that almost all writing teachers tell their students.

At the end of the fourth stanza, the poet brings her readers back to the opening premise, mentioning the "needle," which is reminiscent of both the pine tree and the prodding of her students. "Make me feel," the speaker states. It is not clear if this statement is directed to the lover, the "*John*" in the previous lines, or if the speaker is still enticing her students to create poems that move her; perhaps it is the speaker talking to herself about her own writing. Nonetheless, with this line, the speaker also returns to the way in which she creates feeling in a

poem. In the fifth stanza, she demonstrates how to use words so profoundly and yet so simply that her readers feel what she wants them to feel. First she reminds the reader of the beginning of the poem. She does this by mentioning a dress again; this time, however, the dress is not a cool green but a more blazing red. The emotions are getting hotter. She then describes materials that most readers can relate to for their softness, silkiness, and smoothness—all sensual textures. In case readers are not familiar with silk, rayon, and chiffon, she provides yet another sensual image—that of a smooth lotion, light "on the nape of your neck." Finally, in stanza 7, she adds the word "*heat*," to make sure everyone understands where she is going.

Stanza 8

Hahn ends her poem by discussing her knowledge of feelings. She is getting closer to identifying them, but she still only sees them. She is not feeling them. With her closing line, she addresses someone, but the person's identity is not clear. It may be the person to whom she is writing the poem. It may be her lover. It may be her students. Or it may be that she is writing to her muse. What is clear is that she is waiting for someone or something to make her feel an emotion. And she has no problem vividly requesting it with her last words: "So prick my skin."

Themes

Longing

The speaker of this poem mentions several ways in which she experiences longing. Although it is not always clear what she is longing for, woven throughout this poem, including in its title, is a sense that something is missing in her life. In the beginning, she dresses in a manner that she hopes will express her longing. In the following section, she longs for her students to write poems that communicate their deep-seated needs. At the same time, she is also brooding over the fact that she is having trouble teaching her students how to bring out their emotions in a satisfying way through their writing. Also, in the second stanza, the speaker mentions a letter she has received from some unnamed lover, who is also filled with a strong sense of yearning.

While the speaker as teacher tries to find a way to bring out the best writing in her students, she also longs to improve her own writing. Someone in her audience (she may be writing to another poet,

Topics For Further Study

- The Heian period in Japanese history is rich with literary accomplishments. Research this topic, and choose two female authors who you think might be included in Hahn's reference to the Immortal Sisters—female poets of that period to whom Hahn often addresses her own poetry. In comparing the writing of the Heian writers to Hahn's, look for similar subjects, style, tone, and themes. How is Hahn's poetry like that of the women of the Heian period? How do her poems differ?

- Compose a series of tanka poems. In the first set, describe a beautiful scene you have experienced in nature. In the second, focus on your relationship with someone close to you. For the third set, write as if you were corresponding with other women (or men), discussing particular details of what it is like to be a woman (or man) living in the United States. Be as strict as you can with the tanka format, counting the syllables and putting as much emotion as you can into the short form.

- Men wrote poetry in the Heian period also, and poems in the tanka style are still written by men.

Research this topic. How do these poems differ from women's, if they do at all? Are the subjects the same? Are the emotions expressed differently?

- Japanese literature is known for its use of symbols, such as the pine tree. However, writers of American poetry and prose also use symbols. One such symbol is the oak tree, which is used to express strength. Research this topic. List typical American symbols and what they represent. Then reread one of your favorite poems or works of fiction to see if any of these symbols are used.

- Write a poem (in any format), a short story, or a short essay in which you focus on the five senses: sight, touch, smell, taste, and hearing. The purpose of this exercise is to describe a scene, a person, an encounter, or an experience using all five senses to bring that experience alive for your readers. Reread Hahn's poem "Pine" to remind yourself how she used the five senses and to give yourself hints on how you might do the same. Use metaphors to enhance your writing.

---

but this is not clear) is needling her to improve her style of writing, to express her longing in a more specific way. By the end of the poem, the speaker states that she can see the feeling. Although this is not the actual longing in and of itself, at least the speaker has acknowledged it. It is not obvious, however, whether she is referring to her own longing or that of her students. This is not ultimately important, as the theme of longing is present throughout the poem no matter whose longing it is.

Teaching Poetry

Whether the speaker is talking to herself or to her students, winding through this poem is the theme of teaching someone to write better poetry. The speaker mentions that she needles her students to prod them to reach down into their feelings and to express those feelings in their work. At the

same time, she appears also to be teaching or reminding herself to do the same. She wants to needle her students, but she also wants someone to needle her. She wants to find ways of bringing out the emotion of an event without overwhelming the reader. She also wants her students to find the things in their lives that matter to them and not write what they think she wants them to write. The more she talks about her desire that the students learn how to write poetry, the more it seems apparent that the speaker also wants, or needs, someone to teach her how to write better poetry. At some points in the poem, it appears that the speaker has decided that instead of telling the students how to write better poems, she (and thus the teacher inside her) might demonstrate what a good poem sounds like by teaching herself how to write one as well.

Emotions

Longing is one of the main emotions expressed in this poem, but Hahn conveys several other emotions. There are the emotions that are retained in memory, as the speaker refers to the scent of the pine in a snowfall. Emotions are felt, the speaker states, not only in the moment but also in memory, when something like a snowfall reminds you of an earlier snowfall and all the feelings that are associated with it. In the same stanza, the speaker reflects on the emotions that arise with self-doubt, when she repeats the phrase "That's what I thought." This is a fearful emotion. What if what she had thought previously was not true? What if what she had done was for naught?

There is another somewhat fearful emotion in the second stanza, or at least a feeling of frustration. The speaker refers to herself as a teacher, but she is having trouble getting through to her students. This raises the issue of how good a teacher she is if she cannot teach them how to write better poetry. Next, Hahn looks at the issue of judging her own poetry. Maybe her writing is not that good. She prods the students, she states, but she also questions whether that is working. Maybe she should be prodding herself, too.

The speaker wants to feel emotions, and she wants her students to feel them, but she also wants her students' poetry to make her feel her students' emotions. The poem is one big cycle of emotions. The speaker goes on to engage emotions other than longing. She wants to earn money from her poetry so that she can buy gifts for her unnamed friend. She wants to give her friend enjoyment. She wants her friend to feel good about herself, to pamper herself, to bring herself alive with sensual pleasures. In other words, she wants her friend to feel more emotion.

In the seventh stanza, there is a curious statement that could be read as loneliness: "You say it's the *he* in *heat*," the line reads. Does this mean that a woman needs a man in order to find emotion? The line could also be read as another type of frustration. Or it could be an admonishment of some kind—one woman reminding another that a person alone is not limited to an unemotional life, that emotion can be found without having a man in one's life. Whichever way the line is read, "*heat*" is a reference to passion, another word for emotion. In the final stanza, the speaker seems to be confirming the idea that a woman, or any person alone, can experience feelings. The speaker steps out into the forest barefoot and is no longer just looking at feelings; she is experiencing them herself.

Style

Tanka in English

Translating the tanka form of poetry into English can be very challenging because of the difference not only in the shape of the two different languages (English, which is based on individual letters and emphasized syllables, and Japanese, which is based on syllables and no stress) but also in the way both languages express images. Japanese poets are very subtle when creating metaphors. In Japanese, for example, metaphors are placed in a poem, and the reader, accustomed to their meaning, assumes the correct interpretation. Because of these and other differences in language, writing tanka-inspired poems in English results in the rules being eased. So in the Hahn poem "Pine," there is no strict adherence to the shape of the poem. Hahn's poem is short, and the language is rather simple, but the form is free. There is no strict counting of syllables, for example, as there is in the Japanese form. However, Hahn does demonstrate the influence of the Japanese tanka in other ways.

One facet of tanka that can be adapted to English is the Japanese love of wordplay. In Hahn's poem, the author uses "pine" to mean two different things. "Pine" can describe a tree or it can be a verb meaning "to long for." Although the Japanese language allows for much more complexity of wordplay than English, poets of the English language can find ways to enjoy this game as well. Hahn also often refers to a "needle" in this poem. This word harkens back to the pine tree, but it is also used in its verbal form, meaning "to pester or to provoke."

Another aspect of tanka poetry that is easily translated into English is the expression of emotion. Many tanka poems reveal a sadness, one of the stronger emotions used in poetry. Although the poetic form is brief, tanka, in its simplicity, is a good vehicle for expressing strong emotions. This is the whole premise of Hahn's poem. She knows that a reader must feel something while reading the poem. For the reader to feel, the poem must be infused with emotion. This does not mean that one must write melodramatically, but rather that one must select one's words carefully and simply, as the tanka form requires, and also choose the deepest feelings beneath these words.

Hahn also employs the tanka technique of using the last line of a stanza to reflect the first line. In the first stanza, Hahn begins with "I thought." Then, at the end of the stanza, the last words are the same: "I thought." Not only does this technique emphasize a circular closure, it also brings forth a deeper understanding. In the beginning, this phrase appears as a reflection, but at the end, it calls up a questioning attitude. The speaker is second-guessing herself. Hahn also repeats the concept of being needled or of needling someone throughout her poem. This ties the various stanzas together and keeps the idea of the pine alive from beginning to end.

Entwining Subjects

Hahn's poem covers two subjects at once. These subjects are related on some levels but on the surface they appear very different. The speaker begins with a generalized statement about feelings, as if she were talking about a personal affair. In the second stanza, she refers to her students, whom she is prompting to infuse their writing with more emotion. It is the emotions that are apparent in both stanzas. But the audience in the first stanza seems to be more personal, while the audience in the second is the speaker's classroom filled with students. The rest of the poem is also more personal. The speaker attempts to explain how she deals with her emotions, as if she is writing to a friend about a love affair. By writing in this way, rather than telling her students how to write about emotions, the speaker is showing her students through the example of her own writing. Thus, the topic of emotions is elucidated in two different ways.

Sensuality

A key element in this poem is sensuality. In the first stanza, the speaker refers to the scent of the pine, a scent that every reader will know. It is the perfume of a freshly cut Christmas tree. After calling up the sense of smell, the speaker brings in the sense of touch. She mentions the pine needles, another familiar tactile memory. Who has not been pricked by pointed evergreen needles? So now the speaker has brought two strong, sensually charged images into her poem. To enhance the poem visually, she adds a flurry of snowflakes. Snowstorms are magical images and spark the imagination and the senses. Then the speaker arouses hearing in the second stanza: "the spruce / scraping at their windows." More tactile images appear, including "fingers" that "are cold" and the soft touch of "lotion / on the nape of your neck." She also adds the slithery feel of "silk, rayon, chiffon," all very smooth materials that most women will relate to. Finally, the speaker takes the reader outside and walks barefoot on a blanket of pine needles, a tickly situation that connects the body to the earth and joins the reader to the poem.

Historical Context

Japanese Tanka Poetry

Hahn has stated that her own writing is heavily influenced by the ancient Japanese poetic form called tanka. This form is more than one thousand years old and became very popular, especially with women who lived courtly lives during the Heian period (794–1185). Tanka has a set pattern (that is often revised) of syllables per line. The pattern follows a 5-7-5-7-7 scheme and has often been credited as the forerunner of the more popular poetic form haiku. The Japanese language is syllabic (as opposed to English, which is broken down into individual, single letters) and more easily fits the simple pattern of tanka. However, in recent years, tanka has become a very attractive style of writing English-language poems.

Tanka poems were popular with courtly women, who often were kept in solitude. It was through tanka that they expressed deep emotions, giving them psychological outlets for the aftereffects of love affairs, failed as well as romanticized. At one point, writing tanka was even turned into a game, with one person writing the first three lines of the poem and someone else completing the form. Tanka was not restricted to love affairs, however. Any topic that elicited strong emotions was used, including a love of nature, of one's family, or of an especially beautiful place. Unlike English poetry, rhyming and meter are not aspects of tanka, owing to the fact that all but a minimum of Japanese syllables end in vowels, thus giving the language a natural rhyming sound no matter what words are used. Also, because of a lack of accented syllables in the Japanese language, there is no sense of rhythm inherent in Japanese poetry. The basic premise for Japanese poetry, therefore, is conveying images. Poems offer a simple and often beautiful scene or, in the case of many tanka poems, a strong emotion.

Since tanka was a poetic form used by women in the Japanese court, the subject matter was elevated, reflecting higher ideals and concepts than the base or mundane topics of daily life. The language used was often simple, however, thus not becoming a distraction from the simple and pure beauty of the image that the poem presented. One would not discuss vulgar topics, for instance, or use vulgar language.

Ono no Komachi is one of the more famous and legendary female tanka poetesses of the Heian court. Several of her tanka poems have been preserved, and elements of her life have been immortalized in many Japanese Noh plays. According to legend, Komachi was unbelievably beautiful and was capable of casting romantic spells on men. As the story goes, one such lover was admonished by Komachi to wait outside her quarters for one hundred days before she would see him. However, this young man died on the one-hundredth day, and afterward Komachi was cursed. She lost her beauty and lived the rest of her days as a wretchedly poor old woman. Another Noh play, however, releases her from this curse; her powers return, and she bewitches yet another young man with her romantic spell.

Tanka Poetry in the United States

Many poets in the United States have turned to the study and appreciation of tanka poetry, both in translation and as a creative style through which to write poems. In attempts to create tanka in English during the early 1960s, a strict adherence to the basic form of 5-7-5-7-7 syllables per poem was followed. But since then, a freer form, often called free verse, has been used, with twelve to more than thirty syllables; sometimes these syllables are arranged in five lines. Even these parameters are often ignored. Today, English-language tanka continues to find its own shape. The major emphasis that remains intact from the original Japanese format is that the poems are short and continue to provide emotionally charged images.

Many magazines feature tanka, as do online groups, college courses, and annual contests dedicated to this type of poetic writing. For example, the Mirrors International Tanka Award contest first began collecting entries and providing prizes in 1990. One of the prominent judges of this contest is Jane Reichhold, a scholar and translator of Japanese tanka verse. The online publication *American Tanka* has been produced since 1996, showcasing some of the best English versions of this type of poetry. Online, one can also find several sites created by elementary and high school classes that discuss and demonstrate the writing of English-style tanka. The International Tanka Contest, first held in 1999, judges the best tanka in Japanese and in English. The originator of this contest, Mutsuo Shukuya, has stated that he was inspired to create this contest after hearing Japan's prime minister express a need for Japanese people to reach out to the rest of the world and share a mutual understanding of cultures. The Tanka Society of America, formed in 2000, is a nonprofit organization with the goal of promoting the understanding and appreciation of tanka poetry, in all its various forms.

Teaching Creative Writing

It was not always believed that creative writing was something that could be taught. Critics insisted that either a person was born with the talent or not. Although there were classes that focused on the teaching of writing, they were concentrated on more practical genres, not on fiction or poetry.

About seventy years ago, however, college administrators decided that writing classes in poetry and fiction might have a beneficial effect on students, so published authors of poetry and fiction were invited to various schools, where they offered lectures. Amherst, for instance, asked Robert Frost to take on the role of poet in residence, one of the first schools to do so. In 1931, the New School in New York City initiated a writing program, led by the famed Manhattan editor Gorham Munson. In 1938, the University of Iowa began what today has evolved into one of the country's most famous creative writing programs. The idea was similar to Amherst's: invite published writers to teach courses to budding writers. Some of the more famous of the first teachers to do so at the University of Iowa included the poet Robert Penn Warren and the short-story writer Flannery O'Conner.

The concept of a master of fine arts degree in writing took longer to develop, but by 1975 there were more than a dozen schools offering this degree, which focuses on writing fiction and poetry. According to a recent report, that number has increased by almost nine times, and programs include the writing of creative nonfiction. Although the idea that creative writing cannot be taught continues to persist today and there is a rising level of criticism against such programs as master of fine arts programs, both creative writing in colleges and writing workshops for the general public keep growing in popularity across the United States.

Critical Overview

Hahn's "Pine" has not yet been singled out for specific critical appraisal, but her collections of poetry have attracted the attention of reviewers. Overall, her poetry, which has been published in many literary magazines in addition to being collected in her own publications, has moved her readers to the point at which they find they must use words such as "powerful," "beautiful," "emotional," and "breathtaking" to describe her work.

In a *Publishers Weekly* review of the collection *Mosquito and Ant*, in which the poem "Pine" appears, the critic begins the article with the sentence: "Bold, brave and sharp, Hahn's fourth and fifth books . . . are large in the range of their concerns and the intensity of their passions." This reviewer comments on the influence of Japanese poetry on Hahn's work and compliments the sharpness and tightness of her writing. The subject matter of Hahn's work, this reviewer finds, is the concern of women, and this does not exclude topics considered political. In further remarks, this critic writes that Hahn's poetry uses "visceral sexuality" to help ground the poetic abstractions encountered in her writing in "concerns" that are "concrete." Comparing Hahn's work to another ancient type of Japanese writing, a form referred to as *zuihitsu*, the critic adds that Hahn brings her writing alive and creates a "tighter, more fully realized work" and thus creates a place "where women write to each other in charged, clandestine code."

Reviewing an earlier collection of Hahn's work, *The Unbearable Heart*, in *Booklist*, the critic Elizabeth Millard finds this book, whose poetry focuses on the death of the author's mother, not to be morbid or melodramatic but rather filled with "dark beauty." Hahn has a way of taking her readers to very sensitive places, this reviewer stated, without making them feel overwhelmed with misery. "Virtually every line," Millard writes, "contains a breathtaking disclosure." Although Millard refers to the poems in this collection as "raw," she adds such praiseworthy adjectives to her description as "powerful" and "utterly radiant." In conclusion, Millard tells her readers that this Hahn collection "should not be missed."

Hahn's collection *The Artist's Daughter* likewise has received praise from critics. The *Library Journal's* Ellen Kaufman writes that, despite the gruesome subject matter of several of the poems in this collection, topics that include cannibalism and cadavers, Hahn has a talent that is able to produce "music" in her writing and does so through what Kaufman refers to as "the shapely statement." Although Kaufman faults the poetess for some "choppy, fragmented lines" and relationships that appear "forced," overall, she recommends this collection to her readers.

Finally, there is Laura Rosenthal's review for the *Minneapolis Star Tribune*. She also read Hahn's *Mosquito and Ant* and opens her critical analysis by discussing other reviewers' comments concerning the topics of Hahn's more recent poetry. Many of these reviewers have referred to Hahn's poems as placing an emphasis on subjects that pertain to people who are middle aged. Rosenthal finds no problem with this, since it reflects Hahn's life experiences and does not otherwise negatively influence her writing. Rosenthal enjoys Hahn's insights, which could have been gained only from an older person's perspective. Rosenthal also points out Hahn's connection to the Heian poetesses of Japan, whose practice of writing in poetic form to other women Hahn emulates. Many of the poems in this collection, Rosenthal discovers, are very similar to those of this ancient poetic tradition. In this way, Hahn demonstrates her investment in her mother's culture, through which the poet explores her role as an artist and reflects on her experiences as a wife, a mother, and a daughter.

Criticism

Joyce Hart

Hart is a published author and freelance writer. In the following essay, Hart explores Hahn's poem to see if the poet practices what she preaches by infusing her writing with a sensual texture that Hahn's audience can not only see but also feel.

In her poem "Pine," Hahn starts right at the title to provide her readers with a few hints not only as to what this poem is about but also how it was put together. The title demonstrates that there will be a mention of nature, for instance, but looked at more closely, there will also be double meanings applied throughout. If just the surface of the poem is skimmed, readers might make quick judgments about the subject matter. Words like "pine," "evergreen," and "tree line," all mentioned in the first few lines, make this poem appear to be about nature. In part, this is true. This poem is not just about the nature of the earth, however; it is about human nature, too. Even more than that, it is about how nature and human nature can come together in a poem. Hahn's poem "Pine" is about many things, including poetry itself, and that is why this short piece of literature becomes more and more intriguing with every new reading.

On one level, the speaker of this poem appears to have one clear goal—to teach her students how to write poems that are steeped in emotion. The speaker, as teacher, seeks subtle expressions, and she seems frustrated when her students turn in work that does not meet her goals. She cannot get her students to dig into their own psyches and from

What Do I Read Next?

- Joseph Bruchac's *Breaking Silence: An Anthology of Contemporary Asian American Poets* (1983) provides an introduction to poetry written by a wide range of Asian American authors. Included in this collection are several poems by Hahn, such as "When You Leave," "Dance Instructions for a Young Girl," and "A Girl Combs Her Hair." Other writers represented in this book are some of the most well-known Asian American poets in contemporary literature: Garrett Kaoru Hongo, Joy Kogawa, Diana Chang, Marilyn Chin, Gail N. Harada, Alex Kuo, Deborah Lee, Jim Mitsui, David Mura, and Traise Yamamoto.

- Akiko Baba is one of modern Japan's most famous writers of tanka. In *Heavenly Maiden Tanka* (1999), one hundred of Baba's tanka poems have been translated. For a better understanding of where Hahn is coming from, read and enjoy Baba's poetry.

- The poetry of Cathy Song, a well-known Asian American poet, was collected in *Frameless Windows, Squares of Light: Poems* (1988; reissued in 2003). In this book, Song again captures small moments in life and expands their beauty, a hallmark of her poetry. Many of these poems reflect Song's joy of motherhood as she explores her emotions watching her children grow up. The lessons she learns are not restricted only to those who have given birth and raised children, however. Song's writing goes beyond these narrow definitions and offers every reader insights into life no matter what the circumstances.

- For an examination of the times before Asian American literature enjoyed the popularity and recognition it benefits from today, readers might be interested in Helen Zia's *Asian American Dreams: The Emergence of an American People* (2001). Zia was raised in New Jersey in the 1950s, before the great literary movement that pushed Asian American literature into the forefront of study on most American college campuses. Zia

reflects on the challenges that she faced, unaware of her own cultural differences as well as any camaraderie she might have experienced in knowing other Asian Americans who shared her interests and background. As she becomes more involved in her own awakening, she builds a community around her of other people who are living on the fringes of society.

- There is a new generation of Asian American poets, and Victoria M. Chang and Marilyn Chin have collected these young poets' works in *Asian American Poetry: The Next Generation* (2004). Readers will find in this anthology a sampling of works of such new poets as Lisa Asagi, Rick Barot, Jennifer Chang, Linh Dinh, Suji Kwock Kim, Srikanth Reddy, and Adrienne Su.

- Li-Young Lee is one of the first Asian American poets to receive critical attention and helped clear the path for the current generation. In his *Book of My Nights: Poems* (2001), Lee looks back at his childhood and explores his relationship with his father, a man who was a personal doctor for Mao Zedong.

- Another path maker in the quest to bring Asian American poetry to the forefront of university study is Garrett Hongo, born in Hawaii and professor at the University of Oregon. Hongo's writing is often compared to that of Walt Whitman. Readers can come up with their own comparisons while reading Hongo's *The River of Heaven: Poems* (1988), a collection of poems about what it is like to live in a society that pushes nonwhite citizens to the margins.

- In *The Unbearable Heart* (1995), Hahn focuses on the effects of her mother's death not only on herself but also on her children.

- In 2002, *The Artist's Daughter: Poems* was published. Here Hahn explores her various roles in life as mother, lover, wife, and poet as well as her mixed heritage.

> *Strip yourselves of the garbage you carry around with you and see your lives for what they really are, the speaker is saying."*

there allow words to rise naturally from their own experience, words that are rich in intriguing and compelling drama. Instead, her students want to please her. They try to guess what she wants, or they try to emulate her by digesting her beliefs and then spitting them back at her. In this way, they end up writing poems that are focused on frivolous things like the speaker's ankle bracelet. She needles them, pushes them, maybe even screams and hollers at them: Wake up! Find your own feelings! Don't try to borrow mine!

It appears that in her yelling at them, the speaker herself is stirred. The form of this poem resembles a letter to a friend, similar to the traditional Japanese poetic standard, the tanka. In ancient times, women wrote tanka poems to one another. Even though Hahn's poem appears to be a letter to someone else, often people write to friends in order to expose their thoughts to themselves. Sometimes in telling someone else what one is thinking, one gains insight into one's own life. Hahn could have created this poem in an attempt to overcome a blockage in her own writing. She might be asking herself the same question that she has asked her students: Am I also staying on the surface of things? In writing about wearing a green dress, she realizes that it might not have been a very succinct way of expressing her emotions, even though she had hoped it would be enough. Yes, the dress might be as green as a pine, but the jump across the chasm between her emotions and the wearing of a green dress is quite a wide distance. The speaker probably senses this, because she questions the significance of the dress by the end of the first stanza. She is pining, she tells her readers, but perhaps no one has been able to read her signals. Surely the wearing of green is interesting, but the symbol of the dress is on her—on the surface of

things. In other words, the speaker, in wearing the dress, has not opened up fully enough for her emotions to be completely understood, to be laid out in a clear and undeniable exposure. Rather than revealing her true emotions, her wearing of the dress is only a hint at what lies underneath. The speaker could be hiding her emotions and therefore is as guilty as her students are in writing on the surface.

When the speaker realizes that the dress does not properly express her feelings, she goes deeper. Just as she needles her students, poking them with something sharp and penetrating to awaken them, she also needles herself. She dives into her inner thoughts and discovers the source of her emotions. It is possible that the evergreen dress was the first hint that she needed to express her feelings. The evergreen color reminded her of the pine tree, and the pine tree reminded her that she was longing/ pining for something. So she tries again. With each succeeding line and stanza, she comes closer not only to understanding the exact emotion that she is feeling but also to writing a better poem.

To take their attention from her ankle bracelet and turn it back onto their own inner lives, the speaker exposes something more personal about herself. She offers them an example, by confessing that she has been unable to sleep. She does this with some of the most simple and beautiful lyrics in the entire poem. Who cannot relate to the wonder of a "curtain" of snow flurries? What child has not pressed his or her nose to the cold windowpane and stared at the transformation that a snowstorm can invoke? The speaker reverts to this childlike state to rediscover the "real morning— / the one with real light." As adults, people tend to cover over their emotions with superficial things. They have learned to hide their feelings. They have been told that it is not right to express oneself with such honesty. But young children have no such fears or barriers; they tend to see things for what they are. They have not yet collected the "compost" that the speaker refers to in the next lines. They have no garbage building up around their emotions; their emotions are raw and true. That is what the speaker/teacher/poet is looking for in her writing as well as in that of her students. Strip yourselves of the garbage you carry around with you and see your lives for what they really are, the speaker is saying. Listen not to my words and try to repeat them; listen not to my beliefs and try to replicate them. She tells her students to listen instead to "the spruce / scraping at their windows." In other words, she says, listen to the sounds and watch the events that are occurring all around you. Listen to your own inner voice, and write about the things that make you cry, make you laugh, make you feel good about your life.

The lines at the end of the second stanza are a little difficult to understand. "Still / X sends terrifying love letters / that send so much blood to the chest / the fingers are cold." The speaker appears to be addressing the friend to whom she is writing. The word "terrifying" makes this statement a little frightening. It is possible that in her effort to awaken emotion in one of her students, she has aroused a beast, and maybe she must now tame that beast. After all, too much emotion can be just as bad as too little. Then, in the next short stanza, it appears that the speaker's friend, the one to whom she is writing, has tempered the speaker's fears, telling her that the student the speaker refers to as "X" just has a crush on her. This is possibly the consequence of the speaker's having exposed her emotions to the class. The warning here seems to be that there is a price to be paid by letting others know one's inner thoughts, but this does not inhibit the speaker's expression. In fact, the "terrifying love letter" seems to encourage her. "I needle: make me feel," she writes. She cannot encourage her students to open up and then turn around and suppress her own feelings. If she is brave enough to face the consequences, maybe her students will follow suit. So she demonstrates that she is practicing what she preaches.

In the final stanza, the speaker continues on her journey. She is gaining on her emotions; rather than just guessing about them and expecting others to guess too, she can now almost see them. She is not quite on top of them, not truly feeling the real emotion yet, but she is close enough to "imagine." Then she closes her poem with another beautiful and telling scene. She offers this stanza to her students, showing them through her writing what poetry is all about, at least for her. She demonstrates how to make others understand what she is trying to say. She gives them the picture of her standing barefoot, exposed to the elements. Instead of wearing a green dress to symbolize the pine tree (and her longing), she now walks out and stands under real pine trees. Rather than needling her students to write better, she walks barefoot on the needles and invites the needles to prick her skin. She wants to do more than think about her emotions, see her emotions, or even write about her emotions. She wants to feel them. With this image, she encourages her students to do the same.

Source: Joyce Hart, Critical Essay on "Pine," in *Poetry for Students*, Thomson Gale, 2006.

Anthony Martinelli

Martinelli is a Seattle-based freelance writer and editor. In this essay, Martinelli examines how Hahn uses homonyms in her poem to examine the pleasures and pains of love and relationships.

The poem "Pine" appears in Hahn's collection *Mosquito and Ant* (1999). The work takes on a strange form, with the poem broken into eight parts, separated by roman numerals. Although the poetic form is of great interest, it is the use of homonyms that is the most intriguing with regard to the exploration of the poem's subject matter: love. In "Pine," Hahn looks at the ups and downs of relationships, love, and the inevitable risks that ensue when two individuals engage one another. The poem relies heavily upon trees to establish a metaphor about love and the personal struggle that accompanies the pursuit of love. In beautiful language, Hahn uses homonyms related to evergreen trees to deliver a powerful, emotive description of the pleasure, pain, and timelessness associated with love.

The poem is written in the first person, making the emotions all the more personal, touching, and heart-wrenching. In the opening stanza, Hahn talks of her attempts to divulge her feelings for another. She writes,

> I thought wearing an evergreen dress
> might be enough to express the longing
> of the pine
> though it or because it retains its scent
> throughout the snowfall
> and above the tree line. That's what I thought.

In the first line of the first stanza, Hahn begins to develop the tree metaphor with reference to her dress. The scent of the tree permeates all, even reaching far beyond the tree line, into the wasteland that exists at higher elevations, plagued with permafrost and little to no vegetation. The distant scent of the pine creates a longing for the tree, and Hahn hopes that her unrequited lover will feel for her what a hiker might feel for a pine tree far above the tree line as the lonely soul marches through a lifeless wasteland. Hahn hopes to deliver all of this feeling and emotion by wearing her evergreen dress. With this emotional outpouring Hahn begins developing her first homonym: *pine*.

A *pine* is defined as any of several types of evergreen trees that have needlelike leaves and bear cones. Their sap produces turpentine and tar. Essentially, this is a strict definition of the large, wonderfully scented trees that Hahn uses to draw comparisons to her dress. It is, of course, a tree with which many North Americans are familiar, whether

> *With this final line, Hahn concludes that it is far better to risk needling than to live on forever pining."*

they grow outside their homes or are cut down and used as Christmas trees. But for Hahn, they represent something beyond big, beautiful, scented ornamentals. The scent and the longing for the scent is a metaphor for her unrequited longing for her lover—the man for whom she has donned her dress. Intrinsic to the first stanza is Hahn's emotional outpouring of her longing, her *pining*. As a verb, *pine* means "to suffer intense longing." The connection of these two homonyms paints a rich picture of unrequited love and the deep, personal yearning one feels for another. The pine scent metaphor supports this idea, because it is easy to imagine the longing a hiker must feel for trees, for example, when he smells the rich scent of the pine as he walks through the desolate, lonely permafrost above the tree line. This *pining for pine* mirrors Hahn's longing for her lover.

In the second stanza, Hahn shifts gears and turns away from longing to discuss her life as a professor. She writes, "I needle my students / and a few write inflamed poems / to my ideological bent and my ankle bracelet." Here, Hahn expresses herself as a tough, inciting professor who delivers her message with fervor, via her "ideological bent," and she says she understands that some of her students pine over her and write poems to her ankle bracelet. The most important line of this stanza, however, is the first, in which she introduces another tree-linked homonym: needle. The verb *needle* means "to goad or taunt." Hahn prods her students, stirring their emotions to extract a response in the form of poetry. She writes, "And the only way to guide them / through their own compost / is to needle them harder—," meaning that she must provoke her students to help them escape from the clutches of their *compost*, that is, their *bulls*——. Hahn is describing the pain—the needling—that her students must endure in order to unearth the pleasures of poetry they so eagerly pine for in her classroom. This correlation between

the students' enduring Hahn's needling to fulfill their pining for poetry is the setting for Hahn's own exploration of her longing for her lover.

As a noun, a *needle* is a rigid and narrow leaf. With this definition, Hahn is poised to return to the examination of her personal, emotional struggle for her lover. The end of the second stanza rushes into the feelings of her heart, as she states, "Still / X sends terrifying love letters / that send so much blood to the chest / the fingers are cold." Here, Hahn switches from her students back to herself and her relationship and focuses on this topic until the end of the poem. The third stanza is short, and with it Hahn begins addressing another person. She writes in the one-line third stanza, "You say it's from *a crush*" and, into the fourth stanza, "You say quit using *he* and *hims* / when the specificity of *John* / is more engaging. / I needle: make me feel." These stanzas are an exchange between Hahn and a trusted other person, possibly a student, given the directive "You say." In any case, these stanzas are important because the role of needling in Hahn's relationship to her "*John*" begins to surface. In the final line of the fourth stanza, Hahn seems to recognize that pain is feeling and that she must risk needling to reach what she pines for—her lover, her *John*.

The three stanzas that follow, two of which consist of only one line, address Hahn's lust, something yet unexplored in her examination of love. In the fifth stanza, Hahn professes to her lover, "Next time I make a C-note / from a poem / I will send you a red dress / I have tried on myself first." Two lustful images emerge from these lines: first, that Hahn intends to send her lover a dress that has touched her skin and, second, that the dress will come from the sale of a poem. The idea of a dress that has touched the skin of another is a clear symbol of physical desire, but to tie the dress to her poetry is to link her physical desire to her deep, emotional pining for her lover's heart.

In the end, Hahn returns to the role of homonyms and her exploration of love through the tree metaphor. The final stanza reads,

> I see pine and I see
> what I know is feeling.
> I imagine stepping barefoot
> under those trees
> onto a bed of their
> brown needles.
> So prick my skin.

There is a deep clarity and sadness in this stanza; Hahn sees the forest of love for the trees. In seeing an individual pine, she sees what she knows is feeling. Her emotions for her "*John*" are clear—she pines for him. The pine trees represent something unparalleled and ancient, that is, the philosophical *being* of love, which has been explored, examined, and left unanswered for eternity. However, Hahn, in seeing the forest, still understands that her pine tree is her subjective interaction with the overarching concept of love and that these risky, subjective encounters are her only opportunities to explore and feel love.

This revelation is startling, because with it undeniably comes the pain—the needling—of uncertainty. Hahn pines for her lover. She spots him from afar and thinks of him when he may not be near (like the hiker and the scent of the tree). But in order to reach her lover, she must make herself vulnerable, "stepping barefoot / under those trees / onto a bed of their / brown needles." These lines present a clear understanding: to get close to that which you pine for, you must make yourself vulnerable to needling. Falling in love is risky business, because to be left without a reciprocated emotion is to be pricked deeply. With this infliction, the brown needles are no longer green and fragrant, giving off a scent for which Hahn pines. In fact, they take on the opposite role; the needles actually *needle*.

Hahn does not reveal whether she is successful with her lover. For Hahn, love is always and forever a double-edged sword, and her use of homonyms and the metaphor of the trees support how she defines love. The homonyms build the foundation, because the tree is a representation of her lover. The needles are green and everlasting, giving off a scent that travels far and wide, permeating everything. The pine is tall, ancient, and strong, living through snowfall, sunshine, seasons, and epochs. Then, on the flip side, the homonyms of these glorious representations of love are verbs that are weak or uncomfortable. To pine is to long for something that is forever unrequited, and to needle is to tease; neither action is comfortable. Thus, in every beautiful pine full of fragrant needles resides the possibility of unrequited longing and emotional distress from goading.

This is Hahn's commentary about love. If a person does not approach someone he or she loves, that person will live forever pining over unrequited love. But if a person approaches the loved one, that person becomes vulnerable to painful needling and may live forever with rejection. Of course, without the risk, there is no hope for reward. Thus, in the last line of her poem, Hahn expresses what undoubtedly is her true feeling about love. She writes,

"So prick my skin" and takes a step toward the pine, willing to risk the physical and emotional pain associated with rejection. With this final line, Hahn concludes that it is far better to risk needling than to live on forever pining.

Source: Anthony Martinelli, Critical Essay on "Pine," in *Poetry for Students*, Thomson Gale, 2006.

Scott Trudell

Trudell is an independent scholar with a bachelor's degree in English literature. In the following essay, he discusses the theme of sexual desire, particularly fervent, middle-aged female desire, in "Pine" and throughout Mosquito and Ant.

"Pine" is a poem about frustration, longing, and desire and their consequences. The speaker aches for her lover, John, but he is unavailable to her, and his letters leave her fingers "cold" and insensible—without feeling—despite the fact that they send "so much blood to the chest." Because she cannot have him, and because she has a desperate desire to feel something, she finds ways to procure secondary, or indirect, feelings instead. The speaker compares herself to a pine tree, for example, going so far as attempting to dress in the color of a pine in order to express the other meaning of the word: longing and languishing from that longing.

One of the most interesting aspects of the speaker's pining for John is the fact that her desire transforms, adjusts, and transfers to other people and other situations as she attempts to satisfy it. These attempts range from "prick[ing]" pine needles on her skin to refocusing her desire on her students and her companion, to whom the poem is addressed. Many of these actions relate to other poems in *Mosquito and Ant*, a collection that continually revisits the complex theme of desire, particularly female sexual desire.

In order to analyze a poem or theme in *Mosquito and Ant*, it is first important to recognize that the collection functions as a whole and actually concentrates on a single main character. Such clues as the main character's repeated references to her lover, husband, daughters, and job as a poetry teacher are the most straightforward suggestions that one woman is the subject of all of the poems in the collection. Also, because the collection refers to an ancient Chinese tradition by which women communicated with each other, it soon becomes clear that each poem is actually addressed by one speaker, or narrator, to her friend "L."

As this main character expresses her state of being to "L," she soon begins to let on that she is

In fact, Hahn is implying that John is not the solitary object of the speaker's desire but instead a target for a much more diverse sexual appetite: a sort of general target, as his name 'X' suggests."

having a midlife crisis of sorts. For example, in the speaker's initial correspondence to "L," labeled as such in the subtitle to "Wax," she presents a forceful poem about her desire to "stay a woman," as though she is in danger of losing her womanhood. Hahn makes it perfectly clear that female identity is inextricably connected to sexual desire, and she even goes so far as to imply that inexhaustible sexual desire constitutes, or defines, womanhood. Here, as in a great many of the poems of *Mosquito and Ant*, the speaker's vitality, and her spark for life, are centered on her sexual encounters and fantasies, whether they be with her husband, her lover, or "L." Sex seems to be her most important inspiration, and the speaker's most passionate, energetic, and meaningful moments tend to be connected with sexual desire.

The speaker's constant allusions to her sexual fantasies and desires in her correspondence to "L" suggest that sexuality, namely, sexual dissatisfaction, is the key to her midlife crisis. When in "Morning Light" the central female character feels "buried: that there is no feeling left in her body only the idea of feelings," this seems to be mainly from the lack of sexual passion in her marriage and her dejected feelings of worth as a sexual being. The poem spends much of its time either musing back to the time when the woman's husband was thrilling and she was sexually alluring or lamenting the fact that life is no longer this way. The most significant moment of the poem comes when the woman remembers climbing onto her husband's lap to arouse him, when, instead, he "kissed her lightly and urged her off." This rejection fuels the insecurity and dissatisfaction that grow and fester in the woman's memories and in her present morning routine.

In the poems that follow, whether they focus on the speaker's intriguing relationship with "L," the nature of language and correspondence, or her day-to-day existence with her husband and daughters, Hahn insistently harkens back to sexuality as the one thing that consistently brings feeling back into the speaker's body. Other important aspects of the speaker's life cannot be divided or separated from sexual desire. This is an important reason why, in poems such as "Croissant," the speaker is able to shift swiftly but seamlessly from her thoughts about her lover "X," to her description of sex to her eldest daughter, to the observation that she and her daughters "fall in love" with a female photographer.

Indeed, sex is not taboo or foreign to the speaker's relationship with her daughters; it is extremely important to the mother-daughter bond, as evidenced in the poem "Tissue." Discussing her longing for her mother, the speaker describes how a baby puts its fist in its mouth: "The fist feels good, tastes vaguely *like mother*. / The nipple. The Other." She then extends this idea to apply to her own daughter, noting that she listens to her heartbeat the way the mother listens to the baby inside her body. Because "The Other" can refer to the sexual other, or the object of sexual desire, and because the mother-daughter relationship is characterized as a passageway back into the womb, Hahn is suggesting that sex and sexual reproduction permeate all manners of existence. There is no strict dividing line between different forms of love and desire, particularly in the speaker's earnest and occasionally even desperate middle-aged search for meaning.

The concept of transference, in which sexual desire permeates many other aspects of the speaker's life, is particularly important in "Pine." When the speaker "needle[s]" her students and offers to send "L" a dress that she has tried on herself, it is as though she believes that she will be able to feel vicariously through others—as though she will satisfy her own desires based on what "L" and the students feel. In fact, one of the most interesting aspects of this poem is that it never allows the speaker to actually feel anything, however much she desires this. She is continually feeling and experiencing through a medium, beginning with the evergreen dress worn to attempt (unsuccessfully) to express the longing of the pine tree, which communicates the speaker's longing for John. The "inflamed" poems of her students are merely surrogates for the speaker's own flame for John, and the speaker cannot experience "real" light (which is the neighbor's, not hers), since it is blocked by a curtain.

This building tension and refusal to release it continue into the next lines about guiding the students "through their own compost" and "needl[ing] them harder." These lines are somewhat confusing, since "them" grammatically seems to refer to the "flurries" but must actually refer to the students, because the speaker is discussing how to encourage them to work through their discarded poetry. Then the speaker switches subjects again, to say that "X" sends her "terrifying love letters" that make her lose feeling in her fingers. Not only does this stanza describe desires and longings that are distanced from feelings, it also confuses and melds the speaker's sexual desire for John with many other desires. In fact, Hahn is implying that John is not the solitary object of the speaker's desire but instead a target for a much more diverse sexual appetite: a sort of general target, as his name "X" suggests.

"The Tumbler," which comes immediately before "Pine" in *Mosquito and Ant*, is an example of a poem that demonstrates this idea particularly clearly, since it is focused on the speaker's homoerotic desire for "L." In the first stanza of "The Tumbler," the speaker says she calls "L" "to hear you / tell me you love me," and by the end of the poem there is little doubt that this is very much an erotic and sexual love. In the fifth stanza, as usual, Hahn makes an abrupt segue from her fantasies about "X" to address "L," which, as usual, mixes and melds the reader's ideas about who is actually her object of desire. This time, however, the speaker is directly sexual in her comments to "L," telling her, "You think morning glories open / because you open / in that light," which implies that "L" is opening sexually for the speaker. The final stanza emphasizes this point even more overtly, because the speaker describes herself as "ripped open / to the moon's movements" and the moon is a classic archetype of femininity and love.

A variety of additional poems are steeped in homoerotic female sexuality, including the collection's final four poems, which focus on mothers and daughters. "Responding to Light," for example, stems from the speaker's insatiable sexual appetite as she imagines the sexual development of her daughters. The lines "squeezes her nipple or flicks her vulva— / if she tastes her taste / she is tasting her mother and daughter" demonstrate that the speaker's relationship with her daughters does not just maintain a level of comfort with sexual content but actually revels in sexuality. The mother-daughter relationship is one of the most personal, and uniquely feminine, motifs in the collection; the speaker draws attention to it by placing it as a particularly important aspect of her multifaceted sexual desire.

It is "L," however, who is the most frequent female object of desire for the speaker; this should come as no surprise, given that Hahn's collection of erotic poems about love and desire are all directed at one principal audience: "L." The speaker refers frequently to John and her husband, but she has a tendency to drift, in her many abrupt changes of subject, to "L" and to their communal female sexual desire. By the fourth stanza of "Pine," for example, the speaker is mixing up pronouns as she demands either John or "L" to "make me feel," and then she moves to a specific and erotic description of giving "L" a dress that she has tried on herself. Then, in the seventh stanza, the line "You say it's the *he* in *heat*" implies that John or "X" is only a part of the concept of sexual heat, which takes its biological meaning of a female animal ready to copulate.

The speaker's sexual desire is therefore particularly telling when it is focused, as it very often is, on other females; it demonstrates the importance of female communal desire and female sexuality in Hahn's collection. In fact, female sexuality, which extends to nearly every aspect of the speaker's life, is the key to unlocking the meaning of Hahn's collection. Sexual desire is not merely a by-product of menopause or middle-aged feelings of insecurity or inadequacy but a defining aspect of the meaning that the speaker and Hahn find in life. Constantly moving from one object of erotic desire to the next, female sexuality provides the collection with its purpose, direction, and vitality.

Source: Scott Trudell, Critical Essay on "Pine," in *Poetry for Students*, Thomson Gale, 2006.

Sources

Hahn, Kimiko, *Mosquito and Ant*, W. W. Norton, 1999, pp. 17–21, 33–36, 67–68, 72, and 77–80.

Kaufman, Ellen, Review of *The Artist's Daughter*, in *Library Journal*, Vol. 127, No. 14, September 1, 2002, p. 181.

Millard, Elizabeth, Review of *The Unbearable Heart*, in *Booklist*, Vol. 92, No. 9–10, January 1, 1996, p. 778.

Review of *Mosquito and Ant*, in *Publishers Weekly*, Vol. 246, No. 17, April 26, 1999, p. 76.

Rosenthal, Laura, "Escaping the Pigeonhole," Review of *Mosquito and Ant*, in *Minneapolis Star Tribune*, August 15, 1999.

Further Reading

Baird, Merrily C., *Symbols of Japan: Thematic Motifs in Art and Design*, Rizzoli, 2001.

Japanese literature and art are full of symbols, and one of the most common symbols is that of the pine tree. To better understand a piece of Japanese art or a work of literature, it is helpful to be aware of the symbolic language. This great reference book offers its readers an insider's point of view.

Hirshfield, Jane, *The Ink Dark Moon: Love Poems by Ono no Komachi and Izumi Shikibu, Women of the Ancient Court of Japan*, Vintage, 1999.

Komachi and Shikibu were women poets of the Heian period. They, along with other poets from that time, have greatly influenced Hahn's writing. This book offers the reader a taste of the sensual love poems from that era.

Huang, Guiyou, ed., *Asian American Poets: A Bio-Bibliographical Critical Sourcebook*, Greenwood Press, 2002.

Huang has collected brief biographies on a wide selection of Asian American poets. Also included in this book is a wealth of information not only on the works of these writers but also on their critical reception. Forty-eight poets are included, with a focus on such writers as Cathy Song, Meena Alexander, and Virginia R. Cerenio.

Keene, Donald, *Anthology of Japanese Literature: From the Earliest Era to the Mid-Nineteenth Century*, Grove Press, 1955.

Donald Keene is one of the United States' most renowned translators of Japanese literature. In this anthology, Keene guides the reader on a great journey through some of the best Japanese work ever written. Included is a large section of literature from the Heian period.

Yamamoto, Traise, *Masking Selves, Making Subjects: Japanese American Women, Identity, and the Body*, University of California, 1999.

In this study, Yamamoto looks at different relationships, such as that between language and the body as well as nationalism and identity, in the writing of Asian American poetry, fiction, and autobiography. Yamamoto believes that many Asian American women mask themselves for protection and that they take on some of the stereotypical definitions imposed upon them by the dominant culture; she uses their writing to prove her hypothesis.

Practice

Ellen Bryant Voigt
2002

"Practice" appears in Ellen Bryant Voigt's 2002 poetry collection *Shadow of Heaven*. The title *Shadow of Heaven* is derived from these lines of John Milton's *Paradise Lost*, quoted by David Baker in his review of Voigt's book: "What if Earth / Be but the shadow of Heaven, and things therein / Each to other like, more than on Earth is thought?" Critics have noted that, as Voigt's sixth volume of published poetry, this book reflects her maturation as a woman and as a poet while preserving the themes and stylistic tendencies that have marked her past work. The accomplishment of this collection was recognized in its designation as a National Book Award finalist.

"Practice" slowly unfolds an expression of deep emotional pain that ultimately reveals itself as grief. As the speaker considers the passage of time and its effect—or lack thereof—on heartache, she interjects a telling natural image. "Practice" is not a lengthy poem, but it is dense and challenging, inviting the reader to uncover its layers of meaning. This poem is a fitting example of Voigt's work, especially her mature work, because it offers her characteristic clear voice; use of themes and images from nature; emotional subject matter; and sensitive, honest expression. Because it introduces the idea of an afterlife, it relates to the title of the book, making it a suitable representative of the volume as a whole.

Author Biography

Ellen Bryant Voigt's poetry is known for its regionalism, its reflective character, and its everyday subject matter. She draws from her experiences as mother, wife, daughter, teacher, writer, and mentor. Her particular strain of feminism is not harsh or demanding, but instead seeks to demonstrate the inherent value of a woman's experience and the unique perspective it offers. She accomplishes this by being sensitive and honest and by writing in a way that is both accessible and thought provoking. Voigt's poems are often used to illustrate the existence and balance of opposing forces, such as good and evil or separation and connection. Her work has earned her a loyal following of readers and students as well as a number of awards, including fellowships from the National Endowment for the Arts and the Guggenheim Foundation, the 1983 Alice Fay di Castagnola Award from the Poetry Society of America, the 1983 Sara Teasdale Award, 1983 and 1991 Pushcart prizes, the 1986 Gretchen Warren Poetry Award, the 1987 Emily Clark Balch Award, the 1999 Hanes Poetry Award, and Lila Wallace–Reader's Digest awards in 1999 through 2002. From 1999 to 2003, Voigt was Vermont's state poet. In 2002, she was inducted into the Fellowship of Southern Writers.

Voigt was born May 9, 1943, in Danville, Virginia, to Lloyd Gilmore Bryant (a farmer) and Missouri Eleanor Bryant (an elementary school teacher). She describes her early years as having unfolded in a now-extinct culture, in which extended family gathered for Sunday dinner, her father sang in a barbershop quartet, and she played the piano at church. Her years of piano practice eventually evolved into a career as a concert pianist, and her musical background, in turn, has influenced her poetry. She cites Bach and Brahms as poetic influences.

Voigt earned a bachelor's degree from Converse College in South Carolina, graduating in 1964. Although she was initially drawn to the school for its music conservatory, she ultimately gravitated toward literature and began to seriously study poetry. She went on to complete a master of fine arts degree from the University of Iowa in 1966.

Voigt married Francis George Wilhelm Voigt, a college dean, on September 5, 1965. The couple had two children, Julia and William. In 1966, Voigt began teaching at Iowa Wesleyan College. In 1970, the family moved to Vermont, where Voigt accepted a position teaching in, and later overseeing, a new writing program at Goddard College. From 1979 to 1982, she was an associate professor of creative writing at the Massachusetts Institute of Technology. Since 1981, Voigt has been on the faculty of the master of fine arts program for writers at Warren Wilson College in North Carolina. In addition, she has served as a visiting writer at numerous universities and has worked on staff at writers conferences all over the United States.

Voigt's first published poetry collection, *Claiming Kin*, was released in 1976, thanks to a grant from the Vermont Council on the Arts. This volume was embraced by critics as promising and was praised for its union of subject matter and style. The publication of *Claiming Kin* and its subsequent critical attention opened new opportunities for Voigt. In 1983, her much-anticipated second volume of poetry was published; *The Forces of Plenty* conveys the experiences of a woman in her midlife years who is dealing with domestic ups and downs, changes in family dynamics, and the inevitable deepening of wisdom about life. In 1987, *The Lotus Flowers* was released. As in her previous work, regionalism plays a role in this book, alongside themes of nature, death, and home. In the 1990s, Voigt saw the publication of her next two collections, *Two Trees* (1992) and *Kyrie* (1995), the latter of which was a finalist for a National Book Critics Circle Award. Voigt released *Shadow of Heaven* in 2002 to rave reviews; it includes the poem "Practice" and holds the honor of being a National Book Award finalist.

Poem Text

To weep unbidden, to wake
at night in order to weep, to wait
for the whisker on the face of the clock
to twitch again, moving
the dumb day forward—   5

is this merely practice?
Some believe in heaven,
some in rest. *We'll float,*
you said. *Afterward*
we'll float between two worlds—   10

five bronze beetles
stacked like spoons in one
peony blossom, drugged by lust:
if I came back as a bird
I'd remember that—   15

Until everyone we love
is safe is what you said.

Poem Summary

Lines 1–6

The speaker in "Practice" opens by describing seemingly unprovoked weeping. She mentions watching a clock, waiting to see it move as evidence that time is passing. Her attitude toward time, toward the thought of having to get through another day, is revealed in the phrase "dumb day," which seems to mean that the day is both ignorant and unknowing and also mute. The day, in other words, offers her no emotional support or comfort. She then asks if this experience of weeping and waiting for time to pass is "merely practice."

Voigt sets up this first section as a single thought by waiting until the end of the sixth line to provide ending punctuation, in this case an inconclusive question mark. This choice expresses the speaker's uncertainty and vulnerability. Voigt also unifies the first six lines by structuring them with several infinitives ("to weep," "to wake," and "to wait"). This approach reflects the speaker's uncertainty, because the infinitives seem to lack an anchor. For example, the statement "I need to weep" is more defined than the phrase "to weep." By using a series of infinitives, Voigt subtly illustrates the speaker's lack of direction in the midst of her emotional turmoil.

Lines 7–10

The next statement the speaker makes is very short: "Some believe in heaven, / some in rest." The speaker is pondering what happens after death, but she does not seem to have a strong belief of her own. She makes this statement casually and then turns her attention to someone to whom she is now speaking. At this point, she repeats what this other person has told her: *"We'll float, / you said. Afterward / we'll float between two worlds—."* She is somehow taken with the idea that after death, people retain a connection to this world.

Lines 11–15

The speaker is then distracted by her own thoughts. Voigt introduces an image—it is unclear whether the image is real or imagined—of five beetles in a peony blossom. The beetles are helpless, "drugged by lust," and the speaker remarks that if she came back as a bird, she would remember that image. This comment is telling in two ways. First, it reveals that the speaker considers the idea that after death, souls return to earth in another form. Second, it reveals that she sees the world as dangerous and opportunistic. If she were a bird, she would look for bugs to eat in peony blossoms, where they are apparently defenseless.

Lines 16–17

In the last two lines of the poem, Voigt brings the speaker back to her conversation with the unseen other person. The digression about the beetles is contained within dashes, so the reader should be aware that the thought in the last two lines completes the thought in lines 9 and 10. To clarify, Voigt puts the unseen person's comments in italics. An important revelation in the last two lines of the poem is that the source of the speaker's pain—alluded to by the references to life after death—is grief at the loss of a loved one. The speaker says, *"until everyone we love / is safe* is what you said." This remark indicates that the speaker is pained at not being able to keep everyone she loves safe. Ending with "is what you said" suggests that the speaker is not entirely sure that she agrees with what the other person has told her, because she does not adopt the belief as her own. This sentiment is rooted in the same uncertainty and vulnerability that the speaker describes at the beginning of the poem. Voigt, therefore, gives us a snapshot of deep pain and grief, rather than portraying someone's growing and moving through a painful experience.

Themes

Grief

In the first three words of "Practice," Voigt establishes that this is a poem about emotional pain. "To weep unbidden" are words that describe pain from within, and as the poem unfolds and discusses death and then ends with a reference to loved ones, the reader understands that the speaker is pained by the loss of someone she loved. The speaker considers different views on what happens when someone dies. Perhaps they go to heaven, perhaps they merely rest, perhaps they somehow drift between the two worlds, or perhaps they return to earth in another form. These thoughts come so easily to the speaker that the reader cannot help but believe that the speaker has given these notions some thought, yet the tone of the poem indicates that she is still unsure of what she personally believes. It is a struggle for her to find peace in something, but uncertainty about the afterlife does not provide it.

The speaker's grief is not mild, as indicated by her uncontrollable weeping. It wakes her at night, and it makes time pass too slowly. She watches the clock as if seeing time pass will ease her pain, but it does not. Her question "is this merely practice?" seems to reflect a pessimistic and fatalistic view of what it means to live in the world. According to the speaker, enduring such pain might be practice for enduring future loss. In any case, by the end of

Topics For Further Study

- Read "Practice" and try to imagine that you are the speaker. Consider each line as if it expresses your feelings. To whom are you speaking, and what is the nature of your relationship with that person? How long have you been grieving, and were you prepared for the loss? Once you have emotional insight into the speaker, compose a companion poem written by the speaker a year later. How have your feelings and perspectives changed? How have they stayed the same? Although you may choose to write the poem longer or shorter, more or less abstractly, or in a slightly different form, keep in mind that you are writing in the voice of the same speaker, so there should be cohesiveness between the two works.

- Choose an art medium and style that appeals to you, and create an art piece that represents the image of the beetles and the peony. Try to make your artwork reflect the speaker's feelings about the image. Provide a title or a caption for your finished work.

- Find two other poems (by other poets) that express or comment on grief. Create a lesson plan using these poems along with "Practice" to teach about the theme of grief and its many expressions in poetry. Be sure to point out the differences and similarities between the selections.

- The speaker initially turns her attention to a clock. What are the psychological relationships between time and strong emotions? Find out what psychologists or therapists have to say on the subject and write a short report. When you are done, discuss the new insights you have gained into the poem and the speaker.

- Voigt often uses images from nature to teach a lesson or to express a feeling in her poetry. Choose a poem from either *Claiming Kin* or *The Forces of Plenty* (her first two books) in which Voigt uses an image from nature. Compare and contrast the way she uses nature in your chosen poem with her method in "Practice" to see how a single poet can use nature in similar and different ways. Take what you learn and prepare a brief lecture and a writing exercise to help teach high school students about poetry.

- The speaker refers to differing beliefs concerning the afterlife and its relationship to this world (lines 8–11 and line 15). Research four different religions or philosophies to see what they say about the afterlife and whether those who have died interact with the mortal world. Present your findings in a display that includes Voigt's poem, with the relevant lines from the poem highlighted. Prepare a presentation discussing these differing beliefs on the afterlife, noting which of the four religions or philosophies you studied most closely matches, in your opinion, what is professed in Voigt's poem.

---

the poem, the speaker has not found any real meaning in her pain or her loss.

Life after Death

The second half of the poem is concerned with various explanations for what happens after a person dies. The speaker comments that some people believe in heaven, while others believe that death is a state of perpetual rest. The latter may refer to the belief that there actually is no afterlife and that once the body dies, it is the end of the person's life

entirely. In contrast, the idea of heaven is that when the body dies, the person's soul goes on to an eternity of peace and joy.

The speaker then considers the explanation offered by an unseen other, who states that after death, people float between the mortal world and the immortal world. This idea seems to open up the possibility of having the best of both realities, with the dead being able to keep a connection to loved ones left behind. In the speaker's tangent about five beetles in a peony, she remarks offhandedly that she would remember the image of the beetles if she came back as a bird. This introduces the idea of reincarnation and of returning to earth in a different form after death.

Mortality

Faced with the experience of grief, the speaker cannot help but consider mortality and the circle of life. Voigt introduces the theme of mortality in several different ways. First, the speaker describes waiting for the clock to advance the day forward, even though time's passage brings no relief. Mortality is closely tied to time because only the mortal world is subject to the limits and challenges of time. Further, a being that is mortal will eventually run out of time. The presentation of the clock as an enemy supports this theme.

Another way Voigt approaches the theme of mortality is by exploring the speaker's uncertainty about immortality. The speaker is sure only of what she knows, which in this case is the inevitable pain of living in the world and facing her own mortality and the mortality of her loved ones. On the subject of immortality in the afterlife, she is unable to reach a conclusion, which sets up tension between the speaker's pain at the mortality that is central to this life and uncertainty about whether there is such a thing as immortality. The result is a feeling of hopelessness and despair.

The third way the speaker illustrates the theme of mortality is through her depiction of the beetles and the bird. Here, she describes the circle of life; some creatures must perish so that others may live. The five helpless beetles are at the mercy of a hungry bird, which will not likely dispense mercy. Much more subtle is the fact that the beetles may be in the peony because they are looking for something to eat. So, just as the bird would eat the beetles, the beetles would eat from the peony. Together, these elements depict the circle of life in nature, as it takes place every day.

Style

Imagery

"Practice" is written in only seventeen short lines. Voigt makes the most of her brevity by introducing strong, compelling imagery that serves multiple purposes. The first image is that of the clock with its "whisker" (hand) twitching. The use of the word "whisker" brings the clock to life, as if it were an animal with the power to make time

progress. The image is believable because the reader can immediately understand that a clock resembles an animal's face, but the image also reveals the speaker's feelings about time. In her grief-stricken state, the speaker feels that time is not on her side. She wishes that it would pass more quickly, perhaps by being subject to the will of a living thing. Although she knows that time passes at its own pace, regardless of her wants, she indulges the idea that time can be manipulated. Mourning can be a very lonely experience, so the speaker may also long to see the face of another living thing, like a cat, to save her from her solitude.

The next image is that of floating between two worlds after death. This is a vague image, which is fitting for something otherworldly and ambiguous. Still, the image is a peaceful one, in which the souls of the dead float effortlessly and seemingly of their own will from the earthly world to the world of the afterlife. The image of floating contrasts with the heaviness of the pain and the struggle the speaker feels.

The last image is of "five bronze beetles" who are "drugged by lust" in a peony blossom. The image is beautiful, bright, and sensual. Peonies are very lush flowers with numerous fluttering petals, and the image of five shining beetles crowded inside one is breathtaking. Added to the visual picture is the idea that the scent of the peony (which is similar to a rose) is so strong that it has rendered the beetles helpless and blissful. While Voigt creates this stunning scene from nature, she chooses to show the speaker's dark side through it. The speaker does not marvel at the image or take comfort in the beauty of nature; instead, she tells herself that if she comes back as a bird, she will remember those defenseless beetles in that peony. The implication is that five beetles make a very satisfying meal for a bird.

Alliteration

Throughout "Practice," Voigt emphasizes certain words or images by using alliteration—the repetition of consonant sounds in neighboring words. This is an efficient and noninvasive way to give special attention to certain words in such a brief poem. The first three lines include the following words: weep, wake, weep (again), wait, and whisker. Voigt's use of alliteration in these lines gives them unity and a subtle distinction from the next part of the poem. When she then writes "dumb day," she gives the term auditory punch. Reading the poem aloud, a listener would hear the alliterative words very clearly because of the hard, thumping sound they create. Similarly, in Voigt's image of the beetles and the peony, she describes the bugs as "five bronze beetles / stacked like spoons." By using alliteration, Voigt brings a very specific image into sharp focus without having to go into extraneous detail.

Historical Context

America after September 11

When the World Trade Center towers in New York City and the Pentagon in Washington, D.C., were hit by hijacked passenger planes, daily life for Americans in every region and walk of life was affected to some degree. While feelings and attitudes were much more intense in the months immediately following the terrorist attacks, Americans still cite the attack as a part of the fabric of their communities and their everyday lives. Perhaps the most enduring effects of the attacks are that Americans feel less "bulletproof" than they did before, and they regard their loved ones as even more precious. Witnessing the desperation and grief of the families who lost loved ones in the attacks, including rescue workers, was a life-altering experience for many people. Americans did not have to be directly affected by the attacks or the devastating aftermath to feel the weight of the tragedy.

Pew Research Center for the People & the Press, based in Washington, D.C., prepared a survey on post–September 11 attitudes. Their findings were based on Gallup polls, independent research, and surveys conducted in November 2001. They found that since September 11 religion has become more important to Americans but acceptance of diversity in religious life has not suffered. Americans are better educated about and more tolerant of Muslim Americans, despite the fact that the terrorists were Muslim. The Pew Research Center found that although Americans cited religion as increasingly important in their lives, participation in worship services and attendance at other religious events has not increased. On the other hand, Pew researchers also found that while people may not be participating more in organized worship, they do claim to have more active prayer lives. In fact, 44 percent of the people surveyed in November 2001 answered that they pray more than they did in March 2001. This figure is down, however, from the 69 percent who, in a survey conducted September 13–17, 2001, said they prayed more. Examining the answers very closely, Pew researchers found that most of the increased religious activity was from "highly religious" Americans already attending church, whose church activity subsequently increased after the terrorist attacks.

The Pew Research Center reported that Americans gave higher priority to their family lives as of November 2001 (when the study was conducted). Almost 40 percent said they tried to spend more time with their families over the holidays, and over half of the parents surveyed said they were setting aside more time to spend with their children. Women were especially motivated to connect with family members; while 41 percent of women sought extra time with family, 33 percent of men reported the same. Similarly, 59 percent of mothers were making a stronger effort to spend time with their children, as opposed to 47 percent of men.

Religious Diversity

In modern-day America, there is great effort to promote religious tolerance so that everyone may enjoy freedom of religion. Although surveys still show that Judeo-Christian denominations are the largest religious population, other religions have growing communities of believers. According to the American Religious Identity Survey conducted in 2001, 76.5 percent of Americans are Christian, 1.3 percent are Jewish, and 13.2 percent consider themselves nonreligious. In addition, 0.5 percent of the population are Muslim, another 0.5 percent are Buddhist, and 0.4 percent are Hindu; while these numbers make up a small percentage of the population, they represent increased numbers over a decade ago. The number of Muslims between 1990 and 2001 more than doubled, the number of Buddhists rose 170 percent, and the number of Hindus grew 237 percent. In contrast, the number of agnostics dropped 16 percent, now accounting for 0.5 percent of the population.

The growing diversity in the religious life of Americans is significant to the culture. Americans are more likely to discuss religious views with people of other faiths, and they are more likely to consider new beliefs. They are also, in many cases, better educated or at least more aware of the beliefs that other religions espouse. Communities and schools are making more efforts to raise awareness of and sensitivity to differing belief systems.

Critical Overview

Voigt's standing in American poetry has brought comparisons to great poets of the past and present. When Voigt served as Vermont's poet laureate,

Rebecca Dinan Schneider of *Writer* generously praised her, writing, "Following in the footsteps of such luminaries as Robert Frost, Galway Kinnell and Louise Gluck might be challenging, but Vermont's fourth state poet, Ellen Bryant Voigt, is up to the task." Critics often discuss Voigt's work in the context of modern southern poetry, again drawing comparisons to numerous respected poets. She is regarded not just as an important female voice but also as a poet with a particular perspective, purpose, and sensitivity. In their book *Teaching the Art of Poetry*, David Cappella and Baron Wormser observe:

> Urged forward by social changes in recent decades, poets such as Betty Adcock, Carol Cox, Kate Daniels, Lola Haskins, Elizabeth Morgan, Martha McFerren, Dara Wier, Margaret Gibson, and Ellen Bryant Voigt have published already a body of work as visibly a part of southern culture as it is astringent, feminist, and formally challenging.

The essayist J. D. McClatchy (quoted in *Teaching the Art of Poetry: The Moves*) considers Voigt to be among the best of the modern women poets. In his essay "Twenty Questions," which appears in his book by the same title, McClatchy remarks:

> It is interesting—from a purely sociological point of view—to note that these younger generations have many more strong women poets than earlier generations did. It may be merely coincidental—certainly no woman in the past was kept from writing poetry by any malign political conspiracy. It's just that the good women writers tended to be novelists rather than poets. Not today. Louise Gluck, Sandra McPherson, Marilyn Hacker, the late Amy Clampitt, Jorie Graham, Rachel Hadas, Rita Dove, Gjertrud Schnackenberg, Mary Jo Salter, Ellen Bryant Voigt, Debora Greger, Thylias Moss, Heather McHugh, Alice Fulton—it's a crowded field.

Critics embraced *Shadow of Heaven*, in which "Practice" appears, and they have praised its clarity, subject matter, and craftsmanship. In a review of *Shadow of Heaven* for *Booklist*, Donna Seaman describes the poems in this collection as "exact in their forms, and calm in tone, refined distillations of deep feelings and long meditations on nature and life." Seaman is impressed by the discipline apparent in Voigt's work, in which the poems are thoughtfully written with attention to form and word choice. "Practice" is a good example of Voigt's precise use of language.

A few critics point to the influence of the Romantic poets on Voigt's work. Judith Harris in the *Women's Review of Books* observes that Voigt's poems are "perfectly realized, rare in their formal variety and textured innovations on the lyric." She says that *Shadow of Heaven* is "Keatsian in its themes" but that "Voigt's poems reach into abstraction only when the literal has been exhausted." In his *Poetry* review of *Shadow of Heaven*, David Baker sees a surprising relationship between Voigt's poetry and that of traditional Romantic poets. He explains:

> It's fascinating to see a belated romanticism like Voigt's. . . . I am constantly struck by the fine particulars of her work, her faith in the extended, storied detail, when many earlier romantics made their mature and later lyrics increasingly abstract or obtuse.

Voigt's poetry often reflects the relationship between people and nature, a relationship that can be instructive, moving, comforting, or tumultuous. Her work also is generally characterized by emotional honesty. In *Publishers Weekly*, Michael Scharf and Jeff Zaleski find *Shadow of Heaven* to be "dominated by mourning and memory" and place it among Voigt's best work. Comparing the "more casual work" that appears later in the book to the poems at the beginning of the book (where "Practice" appears), Scharf and Zaleski conclude, "Readers will return more often . . . to the clear voice in the first sections."

Criticism

Jennifer Bussey

Bussey holds a master's degree in interdisciplinary studies and a bachelor's degree in English literature. She is an independent writer specializing in literature. In the following essay, she provides a close reading of Ellen Bryant Voigt's poem to reveal how the grief expressed is a specific kind of grief. It is newly inflicted and is also the speaker's first experience with grief.

Voigt's carefully wrought poem "Practice" is featured in her sixth volume of poetry, *Shadow of Heaven*. In it, the speaker expresses the deep, penetrating pain of grief at having lost a loved one. The reader is challenged to read the poem closely to understand the speaker's feelings, because the speaker is too pained to be able to explain herself in a clear and organized way. Even though the speaker in "Practice" is not chaotic in her expression, there are definite signals throughout the poem that the grief is over a recent loss and that this is the speaker's first experience with such pain. This poem is one that is easily skimmed, given a cursory reading, but to do so robs the reader of the

What Do I Read Next?

- The November 24, 1999, issue of *Atlantic Unbound* contains "Song and Story: An Interview with Ellen Bryant Voigt." In this interview, Voigt answers Steven Kramer's questions about her work in general and speaks at length about her book *Kyrie* and the orchestral piece "Voices of 1918," which was based on the book. Voigt's experiences as a concert pianist and as a poet bring to light her views on art in general.

- Voigt's *Claiming Kin* (1976) is her first collection of poetry. Praised by readers and critics, this collection established Voigt as a promising new poet and opened doors to new opportunities for her.

- In *The Flexible Lyric (The Life of Poetry)* (1999), Voigt shares her insights and views on the craft of poetry. Voigt wrote these essays based on her involvement in writing programs for new writers and following her publication of five volumes of poetry.

- *Poems of Mourning* (1998), edited by Peter Washington and part of the Everyman's Library, is a collection of poems that consider the experience of grief. The poetry included is by such well-known writers as Emily Dickinson, Wallace Stevens, A. E. Housman, and Gerard Manley Hopkins. While there is no commentary provided for individual poems, readers will come away with a strong sense of the expression of grief in poetry, across time and literary movements.

---

subtle emotional underpinnings of the speaker's expression. Voigt brings her talent and experience as a poet to this poem to give it rich layers of meaning and emotional honesty.

In human experience and in its poetic expression, there are many kinds of grief. The one felt by the speaker in "Practice" has a specific character, but readers who have endured grief can relate to the speaker's heartache. Right from the beginning, the speaker begins giving clues that the grief she feels is from a very recent loss. The first two lines of the poem read, "To weep unbidden, to wake / at night in order to weep." These words reveal that the pain is so deeply felt that when she weeps, her sobbing seems to be completely unprovoked. The pain is also very disruptive, actually waking her from much-needed rest to weep even more. This need for almost constant emotional release is common when a person is struggling with the shock of an unexpected loss. At first, there is little else than the pain, and the person has no choice but to endure the suffering until the experience is better internalized and his or her life begins to make sense again. That the weeping wakes the speaker from sleeping indicates that the person has not yet absorbed the loss and that the shock of the loss is ever present.

The speaker describes watching the face of the clock, waiting for it "to twitch" the day away. At this point, time is the speaker's enemy, and it is something she wishes would pass quickly. Not much time has elapsed between the news of the loss and the moment of the poem. Until the speaker has the benefit of the passing of more time, the loss will continue to feel very near. The saying that time heals all wounds is meaningless to her because healing has not yet begun. Her referring to "the dumb day" offers a double meaning. Not only is the day unknowing and uncaring, it is also mute and offers no words of reassurance. The speaker is alone in a room with just a clock that offers no relief.

A friend suggests that after death *"we'll float between two worlds."* The speaker considers that perspective, presumably because she wants to cling to the idea that the one she loved and lost is not so far away after all. If her loved one is floating between the two worlds, then there is a possibility that he or she is present, maybe even in the very room where the speaker is sitting and weeping. This helps her feel that the relationship with the lost loved one is not lost but has just taken on a new form. She longs to reestablish a connection and feel close again.

Without transition, the speaker veers off into describing a scene from nature. The disjointed and distracted nature of this sudden aside demonstrates the speaker's inability to focus at this early stage of grief. The sudden departure occurs during a discussion of the afterlife, indicating her need to think about something else. In the digression, the speaker describes five bronze beetles crowded in a single peony, revealing a very angry and vengeful side of her grief. This is also an indicator that the loss is recent. Psychologists generally agree that there are five stages of grief through which people pass on their way to accepting loss. The first is denial, which clearly does not apply to the speaker, and the next is anger. She describes a beautiful, contented scene of five beetles "stacked like spoons" and "drugged by lust" in the intensely fragrant peony, yet she does not find in this image a soothing promise of peacefulness in nature; instead, she sees an opportunity for the vicious cycle of nature to unfold. She states that if she came back to earth as a bird, she would remember that image. The reader can assume that since birds eat bugs, the speaker is drawn to the idea of participating in the circle of life as the taker of life. She is tired of feeling like a victim to the cycle of life and death and takes some pleasure in imagining being the instigator. Her willingness to take advantage of the beetles in their helpless state ("drugged") may be an important clue to the speaker's devastation. She may be hinting that the one she lost was helpless at the moment of death and that the event was unexpected.

The poem also provides clues that the speaker is experiencing grief for the first time. Her question "is this merely practice?" suggests that she is lost, victimized, and confused by her grief. It also expresses a fatalistic and cynical response to her loss and the emotional pain she cannot escape. She wonders if enduring the grieving process is something that will be a recurring theme for the rest of her life and if this first time is practice for the next time and the next. The thought that such loss might be reduced to "merely practice" is devastating, and it is no wonder that the speaker feels cynicism toward the world.

Faced with loss, many people seek comfort and answers in their beliefs about the afterlife. The speaker in "Practice" seems to be confronting these ideas in earnest for the first time. She casually reviews that some people believe in heaven, while

> *Even though the speaker in 'Practice' is not chaotic in her expression, there are definite signals throughout the poem that the grief is over a recent loss and that this is the speaker's first experience with such pain."*

others believe in rest. She talks to a friend, repeating what he or she has offered as a possible explanation, and, in her beetle tangent, she introduces the possibility of reincarnation. What is very significant is that she does not adopt any of these views as her own. She restates what others believe, but she does not seem to have an opinion or perspective of her own. She remarks, "Some believe in heaven, / some in rest. *We'll float*, / you said." These are the beliefs of other people ("some" and "you") but not of the speaker. This is a strong indication that her current experience is the first time that she has really considered these ideas in the context of a personal loss. It also indicates that she is having an especially hard time finding any comfort. While she longs to reconnect with the one she has lost, she is not even sure where he or she is.

Finally, in the last two lines, the speaker's tone is forlorn and cynical. She is reminding her friend that he or she claimed that in the afterlife, people float between the two worlds "*until everyone we love / is safe* is what you said." The speaker does not claim this sentiment as her own but instead feels as if her friend has made a promise, and she intends to hold him or her to that promise. She is unconvinced, however, and the lines seem to express uncertain desperation, as if she is afraid of being misled. At the same time, this concluding statement carries a touch of cynicism in its tone. Her cynical response indicates that she is trying to work through her first experience with grief. She lacks any previous experience or wisdom of her own. She does not yet embrace the belief in the safety of her loved ones in the afterlife. By putting the idea back on her friend, the speaker shows that she is still un-convinced. Unfortunately, this means that she has not found any real source of peace or comfort. As the poem draws to a close, the speaker is no closer to accepting the death of her loved one. She is not ready to heal, and the poem has come full circle. The insecurity of the last lines surely means that she will continue to "weep unbidden, to wake / at night in order to weep," as she described in the first lines of the poem.

Source: Jennifer Bussey, Critical Essay on "Practice," in *Poetry for Students*, Thomson Gale, 2006.

Lois Kerschen

Kerschen is a public school administrator and freelance writer. In this essay, she discusses how the poem "Practice" fits into the tradition of lyric poetry and the poetic practices of Voigt.

Voigt is best known as a writer of lyric poetry, although she is also a teacher and critic of poetry. She has written numerous articles and essays on the subject of the structure of poetry in which she has strongly defended the value of lyric poetry. Voigt's poem "Practice," published in her 2002 collection entitled *Shadow of Heaven*, is a good example of the classic elements of lyric poetry and her poetic works in general.

The most important characteristic of lyric poetry is its musical quality. In ancient Greek times, poets accompanied their works with music played on a lyre; thus the name *lyric* is applied to poetry that relies on the sound of words to create music from language. Not surprisingly, Voigt started out at college as a music major but became more cap-tivated by the poetic music of language than by the instrumental music of her piano. Still, her connec-tion to music remains strong. Tony Hoagland, writ-ing in *Ploughshares*, reports that Voigt has said her poetic influences were "Bach and, later, Brahms." Further, Voigt has been quoted in *Writer* as saying that her "formula" for poetry is "precision about this world, mystery about the other world—and music." She added, "I hear a piece of music in the poem: a line, sentence, something working, which in turn establishes the tone."

"Practice," a poem that ponders the relationship of life on earth with that in heaven, fits this formula. The precision comes in the description of the "whisker on the face of the clock" to convey the ag-onizingly slow passage of time, one "twitch" at a time, when one is in mourning. The mystery comes from the subject, one of the greatest mysteries of hu-man life: the question of the relationship of this life to the afterlife. The music comes from the poetic de-vices of language that make a poem musical and a song memorable, such as internal forms of repetition.

The alliteration of the first stanza in "Practice" repeats the consonant *w* in "weep," "wake" (first line), "weep," "wait" (second line), and "whisker" (third line). "Wake" and "wait" even add a moment of rhyme. There is also repetition in the construc-tion of phrases: "Some believe in heaven, / some in rest" and "*We'll float*" (line 8) and, again, "*we'll float*" (line 10). Alliteration is used once more in the third stanza, with the *b* sound of "bronze," "bee-tles," "blossom," "back," and "bird." An *s* sound is used in line 12, "stacked like spoons," and in the last line, "*is safe* is what you said."

Lyric poetry is characterized by a short length, a commonplace subject, and an intensity of feel-ings. "Practice" fits all these characteristics. It is only seventeen lines long. Its dual subject is two experiences that virtually every human goes through: grief over the loss of a loved one and won-dering about the afterlife. Since these two experi-ences are highly charged with emotion, there is an automatic intensity of feeling, both on the part of the poet and in the reaction of the reader. Emotions invoked include grief over the loss of a loved one, loneliness resulting from the separation, the feel-ing that time has gone into slow motion to drag out one's pain, anxiety over the future both in this life and the next, and curiosity about the next life, if it exists. The grief and loneliness are expressed through the depiction of weeping, sleeplessness, and the slow passage of time. There is also a hint of despair in the poem: "moving / the dumb day forward" indicates that the narrator does not see the point in going on without the lost love. Days are no longer new opportunities, just a dumb idea. The narrator is asking "What's the point?" when the second stanza opens with "is this merely practice?"

Voigt's poetry is noted for having an element of opposition, juxtaposition, and that is definitely found in "Practice" with the questions of how and why concerning life on earth versus life in heaven. The title of the collection that contains this poem, *Shadow of Heaven*, is a phrase taken from John Milton's *Paradise Lost*: "what if Earth / Be but the shadow of Heaven, and things therein / Each to other like, more than on Earth is thought?" In a re-view of Voigt's book for *Poetry*, David Baker, who quotes Milton's line, says that "Voigt delights in such ironic pleasures" and has, throughout her ca-reer, "pitted dialectical forces against each other." Baker finds that in *Shadow of Heaven*, "Voigt's powers of opposition are stronger and more vivid than ever."

This opposition also involves an opposition to narrative, as evidenced by the title of another of Voigt's articles: "Narrative and Lyric: Structural Corruption." Although she admits that the two can be used together effectively in a poem, she defines the "pure" lyric as one in which "the reader is divorced from narrative context, and even narrative speculation." The plotline of lyric poetry, she says, is built from sounds and feelings, and progression is achieved thorough repeated sounds. The alliteration and repeated phrase structures of "Practice" give the lines of the poem a pull from one to another, but this is not a "and then, and then" structure. The subject from the first stanza about weeping and waiting on time is changed to the subject of what is involved in the afterlife in the second stanza, thus moving from one emotion to another with the connecting line "is this merely practice?" The first line of the second stanza is a natural mental transition from contemplating one's lost love to wondering if one will ever see that person again in another life; that is, it is a plotline of feelings.

The third stanza is a further break from narrative. In a list of recommendations on how to avoid the narrative in poetry, Voigt continues, in her article, to advise that the reader should be distracted from narrative by deactivating time. In "Practice" this technique is accomplished with the use of the third stanza to break into the narrator's remembrance of the description the lost love had given about the afterlife. In real life, our thoughts often jump around as one thought leads us to suddenly think of something else. Trying to envision floating between two worlds, heaven and earth, the narrator imagines coming back to earth as a bird who remembers where the beetles, absorbed in a feeding frenzy on the peony, are easy prey.

In an article for the *Southern Review*, "In Defense of Lyric," Voigt opines that "emotional life is finally all that connects us, one to another, in what used to be called the human condition." This "old-fashioned view," Voigt says, "stands at the heart of the lyric project." She explains that great poems do not have to deal with "extraordinary life circumstances" but instead "a relentless 'striving to be accurate' and, sometimes, a certain ruthlessness toward the very sensibility that produces the poem." In "Practice," the third stanza is not a ruthless interruption necessarily, but it is a break from the original feelings of grief—a time-out, so to speak, for a more lighthearted emotion. Nonetheless, the

> *The poem may be about grief and the afterlife, but Voigt's poetic talent manipulates the structure to make room for a nature scene and to make use of that scene for dramatic impact."*

connection between the living person and the dead person is, of course, strictly emotional at this point, but nonetheless real.

In *Writer*, Rebecca Dinan Schneider quotes Voigt on Robert Frost, as she explains

'A poem begins in delight and ends in wisdom.' Poetry is made of delight: delight at the sounds of words, delight in a formal arrangement, delight in a precise image or in something inexplicable you see in the world. . . . But in the end, it needs to uncover something.

Apparently, Betty Adcock, in a review of *Shadow of Heaven* for the *Southern Review*, finds Voigt successful in applying this principle to her work. Adcock concludes that Voigt's work rewards close reading because "small beauties of the line, echoes of metaphor, carry the poem toward true lyric closure, the surprise that does not simply close but continues the possibilities." In "Practice," the two-line last stanza does indeed continue the possibilities. What is meant by *"until everyone we love / is safe"*? Does she mean safe from damnation, safe from the pains of the world? If we will float between two worlds until everyone we love is safe, what happens when your loved ones are all present? Do we make the transition to heaven together? Are we freed to go back to earth as birds? Voigt leaves the reader to speculate on the possibilities.

Voigt is often described as a classical poet in that she is loyal to the traditions of lyric poetry. One of the traditions for which Voigt is particularly noted is the inclusion of nature in a poem, a device in which she excels, according to the critics. Ken Tucker, in a review of *Shadow of Heaven* for the *New York Times Book Review*, says that her descriptions of nature are rich and that "every tree, bird or insect resonates with symbolism for the life of a relative or a complex emotion." When this critique is applied to "Practice," the third stanza takes on even more meaning. Do the five bronze beetles represent the lost love that the narrator would pursue as a bird? Would the bird approach with the same lustful yearning that the beetles are experiencing for the peony? Whatever the possibilities for interpretation, it remains that the description of the beetles on the peony achieves the goal of a lyric poet: to leave a memorable image for the reader.

Donna Seaman, reviewing *Shadow of Heaven* for *Booklist*, remarks on the "meditations on nature and life as seen flourishing in wondrous manifestations right in her own backyard" that Voigt brings to her poems. Certainly, "Practice" provides a scene from that backyard with the third stanza's beetles, peony blossom, and bird. The poem may be about grief and the afterlife, but Voigt's poetic talent manipulates the structure to make room for a nature scene and to make use of that scene for dramatic impact. Critics also often comment on the tension and balance usually found in Voigt's poems. In "Practice," there is a tension established and a balance of subject achieved between life on earth and life in the afterworld. Similarly, there is a tension in the remark from the departed person that is split by an intervening stanza and the balance established between contemplation of the spiritual set against contemplation of the beetles "stacked like spoons" on the peony blossom.

Voigt wrote a lengthy article on syntax, "Syntax: Rhythm of Thought, Rhythm of Song," for *Kenyon Review* in 2003. In it she explains that syntax identifies the order of language, that is, how the words are put together. Obviously, for a poet, syntax is critical when it comes to pattern and variation, balance and asymmetry, repetition and surprise. However, Voigt adds that poetry likewise makes use of another rhythmic system besides that of syntax, and that is the rhythm of the line. She asserts that "uneven stanza and sentence length allow energy and variation into a poem." A good poem orchestrates these two rhythmic systems of syntax and line. "Practice," then, qualifies as a good poem because even though the line and stanza lengths are basically the same throughout, the sentence length is carefully controlled for effect. The opening sentence runs the length of the first stanza and into the first line of the second stanza. The next sentence runs one and a half lines, or seven words, and the next sentence is just four words. The sentence after that is the one interrupted by the third

stanza. This variation keeps the reader awake and on the hook.

Another element of the classic tradition in lyric poetry is homelike familiarity and a clarity of verse that makes the poem seem simple even as it carries a profound reflection on issues of importance. Once again, Voigt epitomizes the lyric poet with "Practice" because of its simple structure, encompassing the complex issues of love, grief, life, death, and the afterlife, all built around a moment of natural beauty as beetles savor a garden blossom. If lyric poetry is the emotional expression of deep feelings that have sprung up from the poet's heart to touch others with their musical language and thoughtful insights, then Voigt has succeeded in offering "Practice" as a lyric poem.

Source: Lois Kerschen, Critical Essay on "Practice," in *Poetry for Students*, Thomson Gale, 2006.

Joyce Hart

Hart is a published author and freelance writer. In the following essay, Hart explores the hints that Voigt offers to suggest the underlying meaning in her poem.

How can anyone interpret the meaning of a poem—a collection of abbreviated phrases, words placed just so and chosen for rhythm and sound as well as to express an emotion—such as Voigt's "Practice?" How can readers be expected to find significance in this type of writing when so much information is left out? Some poets claim that despite the fact that they consciously chose the words and phrases, even they are not completely sure of some of their poems' deeper intentions. Other poets read their own poems to learn more about themselves, as if the poems were as much messages to the writers as they might be to those who read them. How, then, does one unscramble these poetic puzzles? One way is to search for hints that the poet, consciously or unconsciously, has left behind.

Voight's poem is full of such clues. One of the first clues signals that the subject of this poem is sad or, even more dramatic, tragic. Evidence for this conclusion can be derived from the first two words. "To weep," the poet begins. And readers must then wonder what it is that is making the speaker of the poem cry. But before that can be accomplished, readers must listen to the speaker, who takes the time to first emphasize her sorrow. In doing so, the speaker makes readers aware that this sorrow of hers is not a passing emotion. She is not merely crying; her tears fall even though she does not consciously ask for them. They appear "unbidden"; it is as if they come of their own accord, appearing without her being able to control them. Moreover, the speaker's weeping is so strong it awakens her from her sleep. From these first clues, readers can already deduce that this poem is meant to relay no ordinary grief. This poem is not about a momentary depression. The tears that are flowing are rooted in some event that has caused a dramatic change in the speaker's life, something more aligned with tragedy. Because the poem has begun with such gravity, one cannot help but consider that it might be about death.

If this is true, readers may wonder at this point, who has died? And what kind of relationship did this unnamed person have with the speaker of this poem? Even though there are no direct references to anyone—no name is provided, not even a gender-specific pronoun like *he* or *she*—there is a somewhat oblique mention of masculinity. The speaker uses the word "whisker," which may or may not have been meant to indicate gender. In other words, this small detail of a whisker might not have any association whatsoever with the person the speaker of this poem is addressing. But then why did the poet choose this particular image? And although the whisker is used to denote the slow passing of time, it is curious how the mind works. For instance, at the mention of a whisker, some readers might immediately get a masculine impression. Men have whiskers on their faces, especially at night. Could the speaker, who has been awakened by her tears, be thinking of a male lover who once slept in her bed? Could she be mourning the death of a male friend? Although readers may never know for sure either the reason for the poet's choice of this word or the true importance of this image of a whisker, it still lends a hint of masculinity to the poem. Of course, the reason behind the poet's selection of this word could have absolutely nothing to do with a man and provides only an image of how slowly time is passing.

As readers continue through the poem, it becomes evident that it offers no more clues to certain answers of these questions. Rather, the speaker moves away from any further reference to the person about whom she is writing and returns to describing her feelings. She focuses on the burden of her sorrow, which she demonstrates by suggesting that it makes time go by so slowly. The speaker watches the hands on the "face of the clock," waiting for them to move, a habit to which many readers will relate. When one feels anxious about the present moment and wishes to be taken out of one's current emotional state, time seems to drag endlessly.

> *Thus, the poem provides not merely a window into the soul of the poet but also insight into the reader's mind, the reader's beliefs, and the reader's emotional stance on the poem's themes and images."*

Watching the hands on a clock only worsens the situation. But even when time does inevitably pass, the speaker suggests that this has little worthwhile purpose. The inevitable new day that is dawning, as the speaker describes it, is "dumb." The day, in other words, holds no significance for her, since the death of her friend has stripped life of its meaning. The speaker has no reason to go on, or at least this is what is implied.

Moving on to the second stanza, the speaker asks the question "Is this merely practice?" This, in turn, requires readers to ask more questions of their own. What is the speaker talking about here? To what kind of practice is she referring? If this poem is about death, is the speaker relating the awful emotional hollowness that she is experiencing to the pain of death? Is she saying that she believes that the sorrow that she is currently feeling might be comparable to what she will feel when she dies? Does she think that her own death will feel like the emptiness of her present sorrow? The fact that the speaker is asking these questions suggests that she is not sure of what she believes in. Although death is an unknown, most people speculate at some time in their lives what death is like and may even wonder what, if anything, exists as an afterlife. Is this what the poet is doing? To gain further insight in order to unravel the meaning, readers have to push forward from this point, hoping that the poet will offer more information to help answer these questions.

The next thing that happens in this poem is that the speaker lists a few philosophical ideas that she might hold about an afterlife. "Some believe in heaven, / some in rest." The word "heaven" confirms that the speaker is definitely concentrating on the possibility of an afterlife and also suggests a religious connotation. Readers cannot be sure if this is the speaker's belief, but the guesswork about whether or not this is a poem whose subject is death is laid to the side. At this point in the poem, the theme of death is not just hinted at; it is, in fact, made concrete. Readers have gathered enough information now to confirm this. The clues that follow will help illuminate the speaker's intent, helping readers decide if the poet is writing about the death of a friend or if she is writing because she is concerned about her own death. First, the speaker provides further hints as to whom this poem is directed.

Although no further details are given about the specific person who has died, the speaker does give a clue about her relationship to this person. She uses the pronoun "we," for example, which implies a connection between the speaker and the unnamed person. Whoever this person was, he or she thought of himself or herself as being part of a couple with the speaker of the poem. "*We'll float,*" this unnamed person had said at one point before his or her death. Then the speaker continues the phrase with the word "*Afterward*"—another allusion to death and afterlife. "*We'll float between two words,*" the phrase continues. What is going on here? These words suggest not only that the two of them will be together as a couple but also that they, after death, will be neither here nor there. Does this mean that they will be neither alive nor dead? Or does it imply that they believe in some kind of an after-death journey that would take them from one world of the living to another world of the dead? The poem indicates that they believe in a kind of netherworld, that they will float between these two places—the beginning of their journey and the final resting place. With this in mind, the image conjures up a sort of way station. Although they might no longer maintain a physical presence on earth, neither will they be able to continue on their way. It sounds as if the speaker and the person who has died believe that they will wait before finding out their final destination, or at least this is what the speaker and this unnamed person had, at one time, discussed.

With this information in hand, readers can go back to the earlier mention of waiting, as in waiting for time to pass: "to wait / for the whisker on the face of the clock / to twitch again." Maybe this is the clue that was meant to shed light on the concept of "practice." Could the practice the poet has mentioned refer to waiting? The speaker waits for time to pass after the death of her friend, just as

this friend had told her that they would wait ("*float between two worlds*") until everyone they loved was safe. Could the poet be trying to find solace in her enforced period of waiting by thinking of what this friend had told her? In reflecting on her present, heavy emotional state, is she attempting to rise above her situation by considering her need to discipline her sorrow as practice for the unavoidable time of her own death?

At this point in the poem, the speaker takes a distinct break not only in her thoughts but also in the poem, using dashes in the writing to break the flow, much as she might have broken the flow of her tears, temporarily forgetting her mourning. She appears to be drawn out of her sorrow, at least momentarily, by an image she sees. The "five bronze beetles" that she notices impress her. She remembers the words of her friend—that they would float together; it is possible that the speaker is briefly filled with hope of their reunion. Maybe her eyes are momentarily cleared so that she is not focused on her loss or on her longing, and she sees something that in some way amuses her. There is a chance that she suddenly remembers another belief, one that restores her hope. The poem suggests that the speaker believes in reincarnation, that death is not a final destination but rather a way station. She might one day return after death, embodied as a bird. This belief appears to lift her spirits so that she makes a mental note of the beetles "drugged by lust." The beetles are feasting in a peony, and if the speaker returns after death as a bird, she wants to remember this image because the beetles will make a tasty meal. This seems to provide her with a more pleasant view of death. Perhaps death is not the end of everything. Maybe she will be reunited with her friend who had passed away and with those she has loved in this lifetime; perhaps she will come back once again to enjoy a new life on earth.

None of the clues in this poem are definite. After all, poetry is not akin to science. In reading poetry, speculation is required on the part of the reader. But, then, that is one element that makes reading poetry not only enjoyable but also enlightening. As readers contemplate the words and phrases of this poem, they measure the meaning, or the hints of meaning, against their own beliefs. Thus, the poem provides not merely a window into the soul of the poet but also insight into the reader's mind, the reader's beliefs, and the reader's emotional stance on the poem's themes and images.

Source: Joyce Hart, Critical Essay on "Practice," in *Poetry for Students*, Thomson Gale, 2006.

Ned Balbo

In the following review of Shadow of Heaven, *Balbo says Voight evokes Walt Whitman and praises her "restraint, her common sense, amid the splendor."*

One of our essential poets, Ellen Bryant Voigt has long looked to the natural world for signs of mortality and renewal, and yet her restraint, her common sense, amid the splendor, is extraordinary. In *Shadow of Heaven,* her sixth collection, Voight contemplates flowers rooted to soil yet reaching for sky, "even that late-to-arrive pastel, all stalk / with a few staggered blossoms" ("Autumn in the Yard We Planted"). Grief, in part, drives this necessity, as when the speaker of "Last Letter" imagines the gap left by her death, her husband's need to fill that gap "the harder task, / it's true." Elsewhere, Voigt envisions the dead in order to better understand the living: "they descend . . . frantic" for thousands more "vast blue cloud-blemished skies" ("High Winds Flare Up and the Old House Shudders"). The tension of earth and sky, opposing forces kept in balance, is central to the book, and Voigt shifts her gaze repeatedly so as not to neglect either. In "The Garden, Spring, The Hawk," a sequence of vivid twelve-line poems, "the country of one's origin / is always she," the poet asserts, "the ground beneath the plow," while in "The Art of Distance," focused on memory and aesthetics, a grieving father requires his children to cook a turtle's carcass, quintessential earth-born creature "two feet wide, / a rock from the creek," their ritual "deflecting sorrow and terror into a steady fierceness." Voigt's sympathy and skill extend to the literary world: "What I Remember of Larry's Dream of Yeats" offers a roomful of poets as, "pleated around a straight-backed chair . . . his face above the mustache open, Larry Levis holds the floor, leading Voigt to conclude, "So weren't the dream / and the telling of the dream, more lanky shrewd inclusive / Levis poems . . . ?" Human company and friendship defy the threat of nonexistence, as "Dooryard Flower" further confirms, in its evocation of Walt Whitman: "Because you're sick I want to bring you flowers." Here, the shadow of heaven is also the fatal shadow "on your lungs, your liver, / and elsewhere," the speaker's gift of daffodils, "the only glorious thing" in bloom, carried for the friend who won't survive. Like Whitman in "When Lilacs Last in the Dooryard Bloom'd," Voight, too, writes with the knowledge of death walking on either side; and, once again, we can be thankful to receive the poems she bears: "a sun, a children's choir, host / of

transient voices, first bright / splash in the gray exhausted, world" ("Dooryard Flower").

Source: Ned Balbo, Review of *Shadow of Heaven*, in *Antioch Review*, Vol. 61, No. 1, Winter 2003, pp. 183–84.

Betty Adcock

In the following excerpted review of Shadow of Heaven, *Adcock praises Voight's poetry for its "strongly muscular lyrics" and for having "an honesty and music heaven might envy."*

Shadow of Heaven, Ellen Bryant Voigt's sixth book of poems, takes its title from Milton's lines, " . . .what if Earth be / but the shadow of Heaven, and things therein, / Each to other like, more than on Earth be thought?" Voigt's strongly muscular lyrics, poems of earth indeed, celebrate and mourn that realm, and us in it, with an honesty and music heaven might envy. In what may be her finest book, she steps closer to her own life even as she practices the necessary lyric distance that takes in field and forest, garden and season, our shared mortality as well as personal loss and conundrum.

The book opens with "Largesse," its setting Provence, its tone dark. House and landscape here are both beautiful and threatening, blue shutters "banging," the night rain opening "a deep gash in the yard." The speaker questions her reasons for the sadness she has felt in the market, where a perfect bounty overflows. She finds herself caught in that nameless sadness that can overcome us in even the best times, the loveliest places. Describing the market's open stalls rich with olives, herbs, tomatoes, she ends the second of four stanzas with

hanging there beside the garlic braid,
meek as the sausage, plucked fowl with feet.

The internal rhyme creates emphasis, implying emblem, but of what? What we are? Mortality? Death as a thing with . . . feet? A small moment but an important one, this kind of spiked subtlety marks Voigt's work generally and this book particularly. The last stanza moves the lyric action from the remembered market to observation in a dream, a nightmare revisited, in which the speaker is blind and carrying a baby whose head, as if made of china, bears a crack. We are not given antecedents of this dream nor reason for it, any more than there is graspable explanation for the earlier sadness. The dangerous ledge on which the speaker stands in the dream becomes a bridge "like a tongue." And then we are back at the poet's desk, the place from which poets must always speak, perhaps in the tongue of nightmare. Here she may look

> *She steps closer to her own life even as she practices the necessary lyric distance that takes in field and forest, garden and season, our shared mortality as well as personal loss and conundrum."*

down on the "'rain-ruined nest the sangliers / had scrabbled in the thyme." Or, from that vantage point, she can look up toward the mountain that's "in all the paintings"—toward earth or heaven, reflections. The last line intrigues precisely because it points heavenward, toward mystery, and to the direction of the rest of the book, implying dream and reality, journeys and choices:

. . . . I looked up.
That's where one looks in the grip of a dream.

I have spent more time than would seem needful on the opening poem. This is at least partly because Voigt's work so rewards close reading. Small beauties of the line, echoes of metaphor, carry the poem toward true lyric closure, the surprise that does not simply close but continues the possibilities.

The book is divided into four sections. The second is a lyric sequence addressed to the poet's sister, written from Baton Rouge, a place not home (home would be the poet's native Virginia) but a deeper South, a "clearer paradigm" of home, the place that is always "she, the ground beneath the plow." Again throughout this sequence, we have the speaker looking out onto present and imagined (or remembered) landscapes from a room, a desk where the tongue, the language, is our only bridge, no matter where we stand. She's speaking to her sister, the one who took the path southern girls were destined to take, took it early:

Like an unsheathed falcon to the falconer
you flew, at eighteen, to his outstretched arm.
Restricted, active plural:
and with it, your one
vocation. Why so eager for received idea?

"I can't even imagine a different life," the sister has told her, spading plants into the expected garden. The speaker, the clever one, the one who hated the kitchen conversation of women, the one who went away and chose, it seems, differently, finds in her meditations her own daughter's dream, in which the speaker becomes accomplice in the "hunt and run / purse and title at the finish line." The daughter has dreamed her poet-mother planting a garden of hugely outsized vegetables and flowers leading the girl toward a field planted full of lace, "web of froth and steel / a wedding gown." The poem's motion, like that of the book's opening poem, is from plenty to nightmare.

The linked lives of women in a family, and linked lives of women in a wider tribe, are glimpsed in bright patches, the hawk in a tree "who mates for life / all that's vivid kept to the underside." The choices women make, those that are forced and those that are chosen, the ones they know they've made and the ones they keep from themselves—all are called forth here. The poems touch also on regional identity and denial as well as the "hunt and run" that is not only about women and marriage but the world and its beautiful hungers, the world full to bursting of "fluent azaleas . . . fruited peppers . . . courting and throbbing songbirds . . . slutty blossoming"—all so palpable in Louisiana's air of the deepest South, paradigm of an inheritance loved and fought back, and of love itself, hunger and fruit, as well as received ideal that clips all wings. The aggressive feeding cardinals, the mockingbird like the "emperor's toy," and the recurring cat, perhaps real and half-blind, perhaps itself a toy of science— these animate the Louisiana scene on which the speaker meditates in the final poem. A college student doing research with a cat is measuring the time between birds' sighting of the hungry animal and their flight. Asked if he has named his cat, he says "Oh no, this is science."

. . . . Intending, perhaps, like the exile,
to keep a little distance from what we are.

The poems are letters to a sister, ruminations on women's lives, and held in the sticky thicket of southern landscape, memory, and inheritance— however disinherited. The place from which these poems are written is both exile and home.

The book might be called a travelogue of sorts, picturing, assessing places elsewhere, and the speaker in them: Louisiana, Provence, Florida among the elderly, as well as that one place containing, and perhaps explaining, the one self, that place most difficult to explore, most difficult to find.

Explore she does, and Voigt's lyrics, built from the ground up solid as towers, continue throughout the book in praise and despair, sometimes in the space of one line, of "what we are" and our need for distance. The poems reach up, because that's where you look "in the grip of a dream." And because this brilliant lyric poet cannot help it.

Section four contains the harsh and wonderful "Plaza del Sol," a poem describing aged tourists in Florida, an unflinching portrait of the ugly, the truth of what years do to the body, and in its very detail a celebration of "the crushed grape of the birthmark," "the brother with breasts, his wife with none," the "set of toes shingled with horn." They have been raised from the dead here, brought in from the cold. They are ourselves, if not now, soon. The poet's unflinching look at us has the care and music of love because it does not flinch. This section contains also the fine "Marriage," "Autumn in the Yard We Planted," and "Last Letter," all dealing with long marriage, mixed blessings, and mortality. This section also contains an ambitious longer poem, "What I Remember of Larry's Dream of Yeats." Though I usually dislike poems in which a clubby group of poets possessing a shared past is presented to us with the expectation that all readers should know them by their first names, this elegy for the poet Larry Levis, which invokes a circle of his friends, is both moving and instructive. Voigt's gift for the tight dramatic moment comes to her rescue throughout, and the poem's powerful ending sends the reader back to the beginning to read the whole again, and then to the bookshelf to revisit Levis's haunting work.

The final section's title poem, the last in the book, is "Dooryard Flower." The tellingly homegrown blossom is the daffodil, Wordsworth's flower, the one that blooms earliest and that will outstay generations of return. These are the antique, ruffled ones our ancestors cultivated in cottage gardens, not the classically proportioned narcissus or jonquil but a scrambled ruff of yellow like a child's drawing of a flower. Given to a dying neighbor, and to the reader, they are "the first bright / splash in the grey, exhausted world, a feast / of the dooryard flower we call butter and-eggs." So when the poet brings her gaze from distant sky and mountain to near ground, from exile to home, she does so in the task of picking flowers for a neighbor who is dying. It is a celebration, the shadow of heaven as close as the backyard. *Shadow of Heaven,* like that dooryard flower, is a feast.

Source: Betty Adcock, "Getting Serious," in *Southern Review*, Vol. 39, No. 3, Summer 2003, pp. 650–70.

Sources

Adcock, Betty, "Getting Serious," in *Southern Review*, Vol. 39, No. 3, Summer 2003, pp. 650–71.

Baker, David, Review of *Shadow of Heaven*, in *Poetry*, Vol. 181, No. 4, February 2003, pp. 285–97.

Cappella, David, and Baron Wormser, *Teaching the Art of Poetry: The Moves*, Lawrence Erlbaum Associates, 2000, p. 149, 266.

Harris, Judith, "Death and Transfiguration," in *Women's Review of Books*, Vol. 20, No. 4, January 2003, pp. 17–18.

Hoagland, Tony, "About Ellen Bryant Voigt," in *Ploughshares*, Vol. 22, No. 4, Winter 1996/1997, pp. 222–25.

Scharf, Michael, and Jeff Zaleski, Review of *Shadow of Heaven*, in *Publishers Weekly*, Vol. 248, No. 47, November 19, 2001, pp. 63–64.

Schneider, Rebecca Dinan, "Bringing Poetry to the People," in *Writer*, Vol. 114, No. 4, April 2001, pp. 34–39.

Seaman, Donna, Review of *Shadow of Heaven*, in *Booklist*, Vol. 98, No. 11, February 1, 2002, p. 918.

Tucker, Ken, Review of *Shadow of Heaven*, in the *New York Times Book Review*, April 14, 2002, p. 20.

Voigt, Ellen Bryant, "Practice," in *Shadow of Heaven: Poems*, W. W. Norton, 2002, p. 24.

———, "In Defense of Lyric: Point of View," in *Southern Review*, Vol. 29, No. 2, Spring 1993, pp. 239–58.

———, "Narrative and Lyric," in *Southern Review*, Vol. 30, No. 4, Autumn 1994, pp. 725–41.

———, "Syntax: Rhythm of Thought, Rhythm of Song," in *Kenyon Review*, Vol. 25, No. 1, Winter 2003, pp. 144–63.

Further Reading

Barge, Laura, "Changing Forms of Pastoral Poetry in Southern Poetry," in *Southern Literary Journal*, Vol. 26, No. 1, Fall 1993, pp. 30–42.

Barge reviews the work of past and contemporary southern writers and their presentation of pastoral themes and images. In addition to discussing one of Voigt's poems, Barge looks at the work of John Crowe Ransom, Alice Walker, and other poets.

Farrell, Kate, ed., *Art and Nature: An Illustrated Anthology of Nature Poetry*, Bulfinch, 1992.

The use of nature in poetry is a longstanding tradition, and this book brings another dimension to that tradition by pairing 186 poems with artwork from the Metropolitan Museum of Art. Although this book does not contain Voigt's work, it is a good visual tool for understanding the richness of nature in poetry.

Orr, Gregory, and Ellen Bryant Voigt, eds., *Poets Teaching Poets: Self and the World*, University of Michigan Press, 1996.

This book contains essays written by lecturers at the respected Warren Wilson Master of Fine Arts program in writing, which was established by Voigt. These essays draw heavily on the history and traditions of poetry and on the great poets of the past to offer guidance for poets seeking to hone their craft.

Yeatts, Todd McGregor, *Danville*, Arcadia Publishing, 2005.

More than 200 photographs complement this book, which relates the history and charms of Danville, Virginia—Voigt's hometown—and explains how it has changed over the years. Yeatts also considers what the future may hold for this town, whose popularity is growing.

September

Joanne Kyger
1975

"September," by the American poet Joanne Kyger, was first published in Kyger's collection *All This Every Day* in 1975. It has since been reprinted in *Going on: Selected Poems, 1958–1980* (1983) and *As Ever: Selected Poems* (2002). All three volumes are currently in print.

Kyger began her long poetic career as a young woman who moved to San Francisco in 1957 at the time of the literary movement known as the San Francisco Renaissance. There she was influenced by such poets as Jack Spicer and Robert Duncan and made friends with the "Beat" poets, including Gary Snyder and Allen Ginsberg. Kyger has continued to publish her poems in a career that spans more than forty-five years.

"September" is an oblique poem; it hints at meanings rather than stating them outright. Kyger is interested in the way the mind connects one thing after another, and she does not feel that all the connections should be spelled out. Like many of her poems, "September" moves from outer to inner realities. It is primarily about spiritual revelation, the moment when perception is lifted above the ordinary, everyday world into some new dimension of life.

Author Biography

Joanne (Elizabeth) Kyger was born on November 19, 1934, in Vallejo, California, the daughter of Jacob Holmes (a career navy officer) and Anne

Joanne Kyger © Chris Felver

(Lamont) Kyger. When Kyger was young, the family moved around frequently because of her father's naval career, but when she was fourteen, the family settled permanently in Santa Barbara, California. Kyger attended high school in Santa Barbara and Santa Barbara College (now University of California, Santa Barbara) from 1952 to 1956, although she left college one course short of a degree. Introduced to the poetry of William Butler Yeats, Ezra Pound, and T. S. Eliot at college, she soon discovered that she wanted to be a writer. Moving to the North Beach district of San Francisco and working at a bookstore by day, she would write poetry in the evenings and take it to The Place, a bar in North Beach where the bohemian poets of the San Francisco Renaissance gathered. Kyger's mentors were Jack Spicer and Robert Duncan, and she also made friends with the poets Philip Whalen, Gary Snyder, and, later, Robert Creeley and Allen Ginsberg.

Many of the San Francisco poets of the day made trips to Japan, and in February 1960, Kyger embarked for that country. Shortly after her arrival, she and Snyder were married. Kyger recorded their life in Kyoto and their trip to India (January to May 1962) in her *Japan and India Journals 1960–1964* (1981; reprinted as *Strange Big Moon*, 2000).

Kyger and Snyder were divorced in 1964, and Kyger returned to America feeling freer to chart her own poetic course. Her first collection, which included work dating back to 1958, was *The Tapestry and the Web* (1965). The book was illustrated by the painter Jack Boyce, whom Kyger married in 1966.

In the next few years, Kyger traveled to Spain, France, Italy, and England, returning to San Francisco, by way of New York, in 1967. In San Francisco, she worked for a year on the KQED Artists in Television series. In 1969, Kyger and Boyce moved to Bolinas in Marin County, California, which became a center of literary activity during the 1970s, with Kyger as a leading voice. Kyger's marriage broke down in 1970, and Boyce died in 1972.

Kyger's poetry collections during this period were *Joanne* (1970), *Places to Go* (1970), and *Desecheo Notebook* (1971). The last named was the result of a trip to the island of Desecheo, near Puerto Rico, in 1971. *Trip out and Fall Back* followed in 1974. Later collections include *All This Every Day* (1975), which contains the poem "September"; *The Wonderful Focus of You* (1980); and *Up My Coast* (1981). *Mexico Blondé* (1981) was inspired by trips to Chiapas, Mexico, in 1972, 1976, and 1981.

Two selections of Kyger's poems have appeared, bringing her work for the first time to a larger readership: *Going on: Selected Poems, 1958–1980* (1983) and *As Ever: Selected Poems* (2002). Both volumes include "September." Kyger's collection *God Never Dies: Poems from Oaxaca* (2004) was published by Blue Press of Santa Cruz, California, in an edition of three hundred copies. It was inspired by a visit Kyger made to Oaxaca, Mexico.

Poem Text

The grasses are light brown
and ocean comes in
long shimmering lines
under the fleet from last night
which dozes now in the early morning   5

Here and there horses graze
on somebody's acreage

Stangely, it was not my desire

that bade me speak in church to be released
but memory of the way it used to be in   10
careless and exotic play

when characters were promises
then recognitions. The world of transformation
is real and not real but trusting.

Enough of these lessons? I mean   15
didactic phrases to take you in and out of
love's mysterious bonds?

    Well I myself am not myself.

    and which power of survival I speak
for is not made of houses.   20

    It is inner luxury, of golden figures
that breathe like mountains do
    and whose skin is made dusky by stars.

Poem Summary

Lines 1–7

"September" begins with the poet's early morning observations of the late summer or autumn landscape. Although no specific location is mentioned, it is probably in California, perhaps in Bolinas, north of San Francisco, where Kyger was living when she wrote this poem. The descriptions are simple: the grass is light brown, the ocean shimmers, and horses graze. A motionless fleet of ships can be seen, tranquil in the morning light.

Lines 8–14

This straightforward scene prompts the poet to reflect on her thoughts. It appears that some time in the recent past she spoke in church, although she does not disclose what she spoke about. She says that it was not because of a desire to be released that she spoke, although she is silent on what she might have wanted to be released from. From burdens? From worries? From her existence in time? She does not say. What prompted her to speak appears to be a memory of childhood, perhaps, or an earlier time in her life: "memory of the way it used to be in / careless and exotic play." This suggests that she is looking back to a freer, happier time. The next line, which offers some kind of description about that careless play, is cryptic: "when characters were promises / then recognitions." This could perhaps refer to a time as a child, when she was just learning to read. Each "character" (that is, letter of the alphabet) seemed to hold a promise to the child, which blossomed into recognition when she learned to put characters together to create or to read words. The poet seems to use that memory as a springboard to hint perhaps at a free-flowing way of being in which the solidity or fixedness of external things is not absolute.

This hint is carried into the line that follows, in which the poet states the first of the two paradoxes around which the poem appears to revolve: "The

world of transformation / is real and not real but trusting." The first phrase establishes that the world is not fixed; it is in transformation. At one level, the statement is obvious, since in nature everything is in flux, in process of transformation (which may be particularly noticeable in the autumn, with its sense of the things of nature passing away). At another level, however, the phrase indicates the power of the human mind to transform the world it perceives. This is suggested by the sentence "The world of transformation / is real and not real." In other words, the "real" world that humans perceive is, in a sense, created by the fluid consciousness of the perceiver, and it is therefore not "real" in the sense of permanently existing outside the perceiving self. The poet must trust in the validity of her own perceptions, which create the world anew in each moment. She will return to this idea at the end of the poem.

Lines 15–17

Next, the poet addresses the reader directly, in the form of a question, "Enough of these lessons?" This suggests that she has suddenly become aware that she may have been burdening the reader with her speculations, her reflections. As she continues, she asks another question, not of the reader this time but of herself: "I mean / didactic phrases to take you in and out of / love's mysterious bonds?" The question mark implies that the answer to the question is not wholly known to her. It is as if she is watching the process of her own mind, observing the thoughts that arise, and then thinking aloud about their significance. The hint at "love's mysterious bonds" is not elaborated on, but it indicates perhaps that the poet's metaphysical musings cannot be divorced from the binding and unifying power of love.

Line 18

The second paradox of the poem follows, and it is given a line all to itself: "Well I myself am not myself." The poet seems to say that there may be more than one self. Perhaps she means that there is a surface self that belongs to the ego, one that gives a person his or her sense of individuality separate from other people, and another, deeper self that possesses a more universal awareness and is not attached to the individual ego. The paradox is important because it seems to be the second self, the self that is not the usual self, that provides the poet with her final, visionary insight in the last lines of the poem.

Lines 19–23

The poet then speaks of a "power of survival" that is "not made of houses." She seems to be

Topics For Further Study

- Why were the poets of the San Francisco Renaissance attracted to Zen Buddhism? What does Zen offer that is not found in the Judeo-Christian tradition?

- What is poetry for? What is the role of poetry in America today? Does poetry fulfill any useful function in society?

- Write a poem with varying line lengths and varying placement of the lines on the page; that is, do not use straight left-hand margins. Try to

ensure that line breaks and line placements are not arbitrary but are necessary for the effectiveness of the poem. In what ways would your poem differ if it had straight left-hand margins?

- Write a poem that starts with a description of a landscape, moves on to your own thoughts as they arise, and ends with an unexpected perception or realization. Try not to force it, just let the thoughts flow out spontaneously.

---

saying that the usual way in which people try to ensure their survival and security, by building or buying a house and establishing themselves in society, is not the power she is talking about. Houses relate to the external world, and the use of the word here may have a particular irony for California residents, since California is a region affected by earthquakes, which can destroy a house in a few moments. The power of survival the poet refers to is something within, an "inner luxury," the vision of which is described in the last three lines. It appears that it can be defined only by poetic images, of golden figures with dusky skin, who perhaps exist in some other-realm accessible only to the person who is awake inside.

Themes

The Power of the Mind

The themes of the poem are presented obliquely, but there is a strong suggestion of the power of the alert, open human mind to penetrate beyond the mundane reality that the senses perceive. The poem therefore moves from outer to inner realities. It starts with the poet's observations of the external scene, a pleasant landscape in September, but then quickly moves beyond that as the poet gives her attention to the processes of her own mind. Her

attitude is open and nonrestrictive. She appears to be ready to play with concepts, ideas, and memories as they come up and allow them to take her to new perceptions. There is a hint halfway through the poem about the "world of transformation," which suggests an inner process that will happen if the poet (or reader) has the ability to trust, which means not trying to force the outcome but allowing the process to happen naturally. The process culminates in the kind of visionary perception conveyed in the last three lines:

> It is inner luxury, of golden figures
> that breathe like mountains do
> and whose skin is made dusky by stars.

This is an expansive inner landscape, in contrast to the unremarkable outer landscape described in the first seven lines of the poem. These final images cannot be logically explained; they are suggestive of some vast, precious, perhaps almost godlike reality ("golden figures") that is as solid as mountains and as infinite as the stars and which is imbued with life and breath. In that sense, they are metaphors for an expanded, transformed state of inner being that feels spacious and unbounded, free of the normal petty contents of the ego-bound mind. From the mundane sight of grass and ocean, the poet has opened herself to a cosmic reality that can be described only in transcendent images. The suggestion is that the inner eye that can perceive such realities is altogether superior to the limited outer eyes with which the poet began.

The Paradox of Being

The paradox "I myself am not myself" suggests that the everyday self, that sense of "I" that humans carry around with them at all times, is not the ultimate reality. Indeed, it may have no reality at all. Kyger has been a longtime practitioner of Buddhism, and there is a hint in this paradoxical line of the Buddhist belief that the concept of an independent, continuously existing self is merely an illusion perpetrated by the individual ego. In reality, there is no permanent self, only a kind of void, or emptiness, lying behind the constant stream of shifting thoughts and perceptions. It is this moment of realization, when the ego disappears, that opens the way for the startling, transforming images with which the poem concludes. For a Buddhist, the way the world and the self are perceived in the state of nirvana (a state of being beyond the confusions of the ego) is very different from the way they are perceived in the state of samsara (ignorance), in which the ego seems real.

A similar paradox occurs earlier in the poem: "The world of transformation / is real and not real," which suggests the Hindu concept of maya. Maya is the belief that the world as normally perceived is an illusion, since only Brahman, the eternal omnipresent reality, is real. Everything else is impermanent and therefore unreal.

These two paradoxes of being suggest the reversal of values on which the poem turns, from the material to the nonmaterial worlds. The reversal is implied by the phrase "inner luxury," which seems to refer back to the allusion to "houses" in the previous line. The poet rejects all material realities as providing no "power of survival." Only spiritual realities are true, however mysterious and indefinable they may be. They have a power to meet the real needs of human life, in contrast to the materialism with which most humans try to ensure their security.

Style

Varying Lines and Margins

The poem does not have a formal structure of rhyme and meter. Punctuation is sparse, particularly in the first fourteen lines, and conventions of typography are not always observed. (For example, not all the sentences begin with a capital letter or end with a period.) However, that does not mean the poem lacks structure, and it is a structure that appeals to the eye as much as the ear, through the way the poem is laid out on the page. The lines are artfully arranged to reflect the thematic movement of the poem from outer to inner realities. The first five lines, which record the placid autumnal scene, appear as a single block of text, with the first words of each line having the same left-hand margins. This arrangement corresponds to a fixed landscape—one that is what it is and cannot be altered. But in the remainder of the poem, as it moves from outer world to inner world, the placement of the lines varies considerably. The variety reflects the loose, unstructured, free-flowing quality of the poet's mind, as it leaps or glides unpredictably from thought to thought. The process even begins with the arrangement on the page of the last two lines of the initial landscape ("Here and there horses graze / on somebody's acreage"), which suggests that the poet's thoughts are already starting to move away from the landscape into her fluid inner world.

Another effect of using varying margins is to vary the amount and the position of white space on the page. The splitting up of the poem into nine short verse units, ranging in length from one to five lines, also creates expanses of white space on the page that give the printed appearance of the poem a "roomy" or airy quality. Such spaces suggest metaphorically the initially unapparent activity of the mind as it moves around within itself and then emerges with new perceptions and thoughts. When the poem is read aloud, the white spaces, as well as the varied placement of the lines, should be conveyed by the pauses of the speaking voice. Such pauses point to the processes of the working mind as well as the rhythm of the poet's breath, as silence gives way to the bubbling up of thoughts from within.

Historical Context

San Francisco Renaissance

The San Francisco Renaissance is the name given to the explosion of a new kind of poetic activity that began in San Francisco in the mid-1950s. It marked a reaction against the dominance of formal, academic poetry in favor of freer, more experimental forms. Poets associated with the new movement included Allen Ginsberg, Gary Snyder, Philip Whalen, Robert Duncan, and Jack Spicer. On October 7, 1955, several of these poets participated in a famous poetry reading at Six Gallery. It was the first public reading of Allen Ginsberg's poem *Howl*, which was published the following year by City Lights Books. City Lights was a bookstore and small publishing house set up by another San Francisco poet, Lawrence Ferlinghetti, who

Compare *&* *Contrast*

- **1970s:** The Watergate scandal leads to the resignation of President Richard M. Nixon in 1974. Along with American failure in the Vietnam War, this leads to a mood of cynicism and pessimism in the nation. People tend to mistrust government.

  Today: Republicans and Democrats alike decry the "big government" programs of the 1960s and 1970s. However, reducing the size of the federal government proves to be no easy task.

- **1970s:** Throughout the decade, there is a heightened concern for preserving the environment. The first Earth Day is celebrated in 1970, and

Congress passes legislation to ensure preservation of clean air and water.

Today: The Bush administration loosens many federal environmental regulations. Environmentalists claim that the administration favors the interests of big business and that the result will be an increase in pollution.

- **1970s:** Abortion rights are guaranteed in the landmark Supreme Court decision *Roe vs. Wade* in 1973.

  Today: In a highly conservative political climate, anti-abortion activists step up their campaign to have *Roe vs. Wade* overturned.

---

would go on to publish many of the "Beat" poets, as Ginsberg, Snyder, and others became known. *Howl* called attention to the side of American life that did not fit in with the prosperous conformism of the 1950s ("I saw the best minds of my generation destroyed by madness, starving, hysterical naked"). The poem created a wave of excitement throughout the American literary scene, as did the novel *On the Road* (1957), by Jack Kerouac, who had been present at the famous Six Gallery reading. *On the Road* was an account of Kerouac's travels in California and Mexico. Its rebellion against middle-class norms made it synonymous in the public mind with what became known as the "Beat generation." The Beats were the forerunners of the "hippie" generation of the 1960s. According to Bill Berkson, in his article on Kyger in *Dictionary of Literary Biography*, "The San Francisco art-and-poetry world in the late 1950s and early 1960s was a charged mixture of excitement, fun, pills, alcohol, highly principled criticism, megalomania, insularity, and sophistication."

Often meeting at The Place, a bar in North Beach, the Beats and other poets of the San Francisco Renaissance not only championed freer lifestyles but also sought out new ways of transcending mundane, day-to-day reality, often through

drugs but also through Eastern forms of spirituality, such as Zen Buddhism. Snyder was particularly known for his serious interest in Zen, an inclination that was shared by Kyger. Kyger was one of the few women associated with the San Francisco Renaissance, although she was younger than the others and in 1957, when she arrived in San Francisco, had not yet established herself as a mature poetic voice. Her mentors were Duncan and Spicer. Spicer was an eccentric, but influential poet who taught a workshop entitled "Poetry as Magic" at the San Francisco Public Library in 1957. He also published *J*, a mimeographed poetry magazine, which printed the work of poets who were not well known. Kyger's first poems appeared in *J*. Spicer did not consider himself a Beat poet, believing that Ferlinghetti and others had become too commercial. He published his own uncopyrighted work in very small editions and did not allow them to be sold outside San Francisco. Sometimes he would simply give them away at readings.

Public readings were a major feature of San Francisco's literary culture during this period, many notable ones being organized by the Poetry Center at San Francisco State. The poets believed in the importance of spoken poetry as a way of connecting poet to audience in a more direct, visceral way than through the printed word. Kyger's first public reading took place at the Beer and Wine Mission on March 7, 1959. Spicer helped her to arrange the reading, and she later looked back on it as a significant moment in her poetic career.

The Bolinas Poets

In the early 1970s, many California poets, including Kyger, lived in Bolinas, a small town north of San Francisco. These poets, who included Robert Creeley, Bill Berkson, David Meltzer, Philip Whalen, Anne Waldman, and many others, gave rise to what was called the Bolinas group or, even more grandly, the Bolinas Renaissance. They did not form a school in the sense that they shared the same poetic philosophy. Some were Beats from San Francisco, while others had been part of the Black Mountain School, associated with North Carolina; there were also some poets of the New York School. In Bolinas, many of them became involved in local environmental issues. In 1970, City Lights published an anthology of Bolinas poets titled *On the Mesa*. A few years later, Berkson, who was a friend of Kyger's, founded the magazine *Big Sky* as a forum for Bolinas poets. He also published books under the Big Sky imprint. These books included Kyger's *All This Every Day* (1975). The Bolinas group lost momentum in the late 1970s, when many of the poets left. Kyger, however, remained and still lives in Bolinas.

Critical Overview

"September" was first published by a small poetry press in 1975, and it was not until it was reprinted in Kyger's *As Ever: Selected Poems*, published in 2002 by Penguin, that it became available for a larger readership. *As Ever: Selected Poems* was Kyger's most significant publication to date and brought her achievements as a poet over a period of more than forty years into clear view. The collection was received enthusiastically by the reviewer for *Publishers Weekly*, who hailed Kyger's "belated, ecstatic debut on the national stage." The reviewer remarked on Kyger's capacity for "hippie dizziness" but also "level-headed surprises," as well as her "genius for moment-by-moment description." Referring to a quality of her verse that has perhaps restricted a greater appreciation of her achievement in academic poetry circles, the reviewer commented: "Though formalists may object to her apparent artlessness, Kyger's obsession for detail draws on a passionate intelligence that is seldom trivial."

Kyger is perhaps most appreciated by other poets. David Meltzer, who has known Kyger for more than forty years and was himself a member of the San Francisco Renaissance, wrote the introduction to *As Ever: Selected Poems*. Although he does not comment directly on "September," the following observation might be applied directly to it: "Her work demands and awakens attention to the extraordinary, the so-called 'everyday'; daybook moments written by a highly selective eye / I selectively and attentively annotating what's before and beyond her eyes."

Criticism

Bryan Aubrey

Aubrey holds a PhD in English and has published many articles on contemporary poetry. In this essay, he shows how Kyger's study and practice of Zen Buddhism influences the spiritual search that is at the heart of her poetry.

Kyger's poetic stance is one of openness to the momentary fluctuations of perception and thought. She is ready, should the moment strike, to be opened up to a different, fuller way of experiencing herself and the world, but she prefers not to force such experiences. Although her manner can sometimes be playful and lighthearted, she is, in fact, a serious and uncompromising seeker of truth in the momentary here and now. The results of her quest are often tentative and fleeting; they are never dogmatic. Her poetry hovers on the brink of spiritual revelation, of a sudden breakthrough in consciousness, but it can just as readily fall back into the mundane and the everyday. Her poems have an air of spontaneity about them that is not illusory. Kyger does not like to revise her work much, as she told the interviewer Dale Smith in the online literary magazine *Jacket*:

> When you "get going" in the process of writing, there's a breath and rhythm that starts to build up inside; the song starts singing, the vowels fall into place with the breathing and rhythm. When you try and re-stress and re-do the words and lines, it's very hard to re-create the original brightness. That's why it's nice to get it close, as close as you can the first time.

Like many of the poets of the San Francisco Renaissance, Kyger was strongly influenced in the 1950s and 1960s by Zen Buddhism, and her poems offer occasional glimpses or hints of the condition Zen describes as satori. D. T. Suzuki, who in the 1950s was the foremost expert on Zen in the West

What Do I Read Next?

- Kyger's *Strange Big Moon: The Japan and India Journals: 1960–1964* (2000) is a journal of her stay in Japan as well as her four-month visit to India in early 1962, when she was a young poet married to Gary Snyder. In these years, Kyger was developing her poetic sensibility and her Buddhist practice, which would become central to her life.

- Philip Whalen, who wrote *Overtime: Selected Poems* (1999), was a leading member of the San Francisco Renaissance and a friend and mentor of Kyger's, as well as friend of Snyder, Ginsberg, and Kerouac. He later became a Buddhist monk and was appointed dharma sangha (head monk) in Santa Fe, New Mexico, in 1984. Whalen belonged to no poetic school, and his work differed from those of the Beats. It is known for its reverence for the mundane world, sense of humor often turned on Whalen himself, and apolitical stance. This collection is organized chronologically and covers all periods of his work.

- Brenda Knight's compilation *Women of the Beat Generation: The Writers, Artists and Muses at the Heart of Revolution* (1996) is an anthology of the life, times, and writings of forty women

from the Beat era. This volume includes a bibliography for each woman, anecdotal information, and rare archival photographs. It also features commentary by Anne Waldman and Allen Ginsberg.

- Richard Peabody's *A Different Beat: Writings by Women of the Beat Generation* (1998) also examines the role of women during the Beat era. Although some of the writers Peabody covers are the same as those selected by Knight, there is little overlap because the works selected are different. This anthology includes work by lesser-known writers like Bonnie Bremser and Fran Landesman and excerpts from unpublished memoirs by two of Jack Kerouac's former wives, Frankie "Edie" Parker and Joan Haverty.

- *The Gary Snyder Reader: Prose, Poetry, and Translations, 1952–1998* (2000), by Gary Snyder, is a large volume that covers forty-six years of his writing, including some unpublished material. It contains poetry, essays, letters, journals from his travels, meditations, and notes that reflect the development over the years of his philosophical and cultural ideas. There is also a chronology of Snyder's life.

---

and whose writings first introduced this spiritual tradition to the San Francisco poets, describes satori as "an intuitive looking into the nature of things." It is "the unfolding of a new world hitherto unperceived in the confusion of a dualistically trained mind." In the moment of satori, or enlightenment, "our entire surroundings are viewed from quite an unexpected angle of perception."

This mode of experience illuminates not only Kyger's poem "September" but also a number of other poems that she wrote at about the same time, during the 1970s, and published in her volume *All This Every Day* (1975). Like "September," "A small field of tall golden headed grass" begins with an observation of the outer landscape but then

quickly moves inward, into the poet's mind. The mood is more somber than "September," and the poet reproaches herself for not being more open to life. But then, at the end of the poem, as in "September," there is a moment of transformed perception. The outer world is suddenly seen in a completely different light, and this also represents the expanded inner world of the poet:

> But then in the sun, looking out to sea,
> center upon center unfold, lotus pearls,
> the boundless waves of bliss

This passage well illustrates another of Suzuki's descriptions of satori, as a "turning of the mental hinge to a wider and deeper world." The imagery in the poem is explicitly Buddhist, since in Buddhist symbolism the opened lotus signifies full enlightenment and mental purity. The lack of a period at the end of the poem suggests that the waves of bliss are indeed boundless and without end. According to many spiritual traditions, this is the true nature of the mind when it is no longer attached to the individual ego. It has become free of the endless cycle of desire that produces only suffering.

Like "September" and "A small field of tall golden headed grass," "April 4 1975 Time of wonder" begins with the contemplation of a landscape and then moves to the poet's own thoughts. This time the poet waits for a moment of revelation that, unlike in the other poems, does not happen:

> The same landscape only changed
> by progression of time. Waiting to be moved
> by the impulses of heaven. To have the chance
> funnel
> descend. Into the grassy bird lit day.

Just as the lack of punctuation in the earlier poem indicates the boundless nature of the mind, here the unexpected period after "descend" emphasizes that the "chance funnel" (the moment of altered or enlightened perception) is for some reason blocked. The mind will not flow freely. The day is "bird lit" but not illumined by any light from another dimension of life. The remainder of the poem emphasizes the heavy entanglements of human life that make spiritual vision nearly impossible.

The frustrations and disappointments of seeking authenticity in life, of trying to see herself and the world truly, are often apparent in Kyger's poems of this period. Spiritual discipline, in the form of Zen meditation, is not easy. "It is true, there is power within us. But I am so / improperly trained," she laments ("It is true, there is power within us"). Sometimes she questions the nature of the ego that seems to provide a sense of security but blocks spiritual vision: "What is this self / I think I will lose if I leave what I know" ("It's a great day"). Frustration with the spiritual path is also the theme of "The far off pine whose branches turn yellow," which is yet another poem that begins with a landscape in a particular month (in this case, June) and then moves inward, to the poet's mind. But as in "April 4 1975 Time of wonder," there is no moment of epiphany or breakthrough at the end of the poem, only fruitless effort:

> Oh I am so tired, in this little room,
> trying to open the path of rhythm with rhythm,
> positively
> breathing

But the last line well expresses the main thrust of Kyger's spiritual quest, which is to be aware, in fleeting moments that may come without warning and apparently without cause, of the clear light of truth."

Kyger refers at once to the practice of Zen meditation, which involves putting attention on the breath, and to the practice of writing, in which she attempts to put what is known as the "breath line" on the page. This term derives from the poet and critic Charles Olson, who was an early influence on Kyger. Olson argued in his influential pamphlet "Projective Verse" that the unit of poetry was not the traditional metrical foot but the breath of the poet, which conveys his or her particular voice. The way the words are arranged on the page should reflect the rhythms of breathing and of thinking. It was Olson who taught Kyger to discard straight left-hand margins in favor of varied placement of the poetic line, a method Olson called "field composition." (Kyger remarked in her interview with Smith, "It's so boring to pick up a book of poetry and see that left-handed margin going evenly up and down the page like a little platoon of soldiers.") When the poem is seen as a field, it becomes akin to a musical score, in which the varying line lengths and placements indicate the entire aural structure of the poem, with its varying pauses and degrees of emphasis.

This attention to the placement of lines is apparent in another of Kyger's Zen-like poems that probes the nature of the self, "Is this the Buddha?"

> Is this the Buddha?
> That individual will die
> that day dream
> Individual.

The short lines seem almost to float in an expansive free space. Since they are short, they should be read slowly, with plenty of pauses for breath. Pausing will allow for the contemplation of the idea that the individual self is an illusion, no more than a daydream, to sink in and allow the possibility of

> *She shares with the Beats their proverbial wanderlust—mental, psychological, spiritual. Her politics are environmental. She locates the world in tangibles. She is very much a poet of place.*"

deeper understanding to emerge in the second part of the poem. This deeper understanding involves the revelation that there are two selves, one temporary and illusory and the other permanent and real. It is the same implication that is contained in "September," when the poet states, "I myself am not myself."

This frequent exploration of the paradox of the self in Kyger's poetry also informs the witty "No one was watching the tortillas." The poem well illustrates Suzuki's comment that "The Zen masters . . . are always found trying to avail themselves of every apparently trivial incident of life in order to make the disciples' minds flow into a channel hitherto altogether unperceived." The poet is engaged in the thoroughly mundane activity of watching tortillas as they cook, when it appears that a moment of satori comes, as if from nowhere. The ordinary day-to-day self disappears for a moment:

No one was watching the tortillas.
You were.
That's my new name. No one.

In this "tiny pause"—a suspension of time in a moment of eternity—illumination comes: "I am Beautiful." The poem, which must be read aloud for its full effect, concludes

See I am It. I am getting It.
I am the big rolling breathing, sliding
sighing, lifting,
Ground!

As will be clear from this discussion, it is no easy thing to convey through words the nature of satori. Kyger is not limited by the concepts and symbols of Zen Buddhism, and she also draws on Native American and shamanistic imagery. During

this period in her poetry, she is fond of using the word "golden" to express a kind of perfection beyond the everyday world. There are the mysterious "golden figures" in "September," for example, which puts one in mind of the well-known story of the Han emperor Mingdi, who in A.D. 68 had a vision in a dream of a golden figure. Told by his ministers the next morning that he had seen the Buddha, Mingdi dispatched an official to India to find out more about Buddhism, which eventually led to the establishment of Buddhism in China.

Continuing with Kyger's use of the word "golden," in "Who even said I was a poet" are the lines "And the sky who is my father / opens the world of the golden kingdom." In "When I used to focus on the worries," another moment of self-forgetting produces a flurry of visionary images culminating in "The streets become golden." In "Often I try so hard with stimulants," "golden" is associated with truth: "Whereas the real state is called golden / where things are exactly what they are." There may be a joke lurking here, since California, where Kyger lives, is known as the "Golden State." But the last line well expresses the main thrust of Kyger's spiritual quest, which is to be aware, in fleeting moments that may come without warning and apparently without cause, of the clear light of truth.

Source: Bryan Aubrey, Critical Essay on "September," in *Poetry for Students*, Thomson Gale, 2006.

Anne Waldman

In the following foreword to Kyger's Strange Big Moon, *Waldman describes Kyger and the work at the time of her travels.*

Where does Kyger, poet, fit? Then and now, one might ask. Twenty-six years old when the *Journals* open she has already been at the center of a literary life in San Francisco, been close to Robert Duncan, and one of the young writers included in Jack Spicer's exacting gnostic circle. She is bosom pal to Philip Whalen. She fits awkwardly alongside the confessionalism and publicized indulgences of The Beats. In the highly competitive gossipy community around The Place, a bar in North Beach, she is known as "Miss Kids." Her poetic alignments are with myth with memory with dream. There's a distinctly feminine strength and humility both to the tone and the look of her poems on the page. She already has a singular style in the grace of her line and breath, and she is a master of arrangement. She follows mind's restless patternings. She has yet to publish her first book of poems, *The Tapestry and the Web,* hints and murmurs of which resonate through the poetry and thinking of the *Journals.* Her writing is not at all like the hipness and frankness of Diane diPrima, her nearest female contemporary. When the *Journals* moves to India, Kyger is horrified by Allen Ginsberg's ego as perceived first hand (he wants to read *Howl* to everyone he meets, including the Dalai Lama.) These India travels provide the source of her campiest wit, as she writes to her friend Nemi Frost in a letter that has been famously quoted from the book: "The thing is, I am sounding rather bitter because its been years since I've been able to get any wild martini attention. All I do is stand around in this black drip dry dress in India." Joanne Kyger the Writer forms both a public and private identity here. Taking the measure of her male poet-companions, she is most definitively in a different "space." Perhaps the initial publication of this book in 1981 and the enthusiastic response to it gave Kyger permission to write her own poetry in a way that was closer to this original looseness and bravado.

Joanne Kyger is commonly linked to both the San Francisco Renaissance through her association to Duncan and Spicer, and the Beat literary movement through her marriage and friendships. Yet she never seems to get her due on either front. She shares with the Beats their proverbial wanderlust—mental, psychological, spiritual. Her politics are environmental. She locates the world in tangibles. She is very much a poet of place. Through friendships in the late 60s and early 70s with Ted Berrigan, Joe Brainard, Bill Berkson and others, she also shares an affinity with the New York School. She has been a major figure in the Bolinas literary Renaissance. Yet she remains in a category of her own design and making. Absent from many of the current anthologies of contemporary poets, Kyger's work also suffers from being outside the ken of the critical attention given Language-centered writing. I would argue that it is now time for her work to be given the close reading it deserves. She has been an active, consistently engaged, engaging poet for over forty years. Her public readings are legendary. She is a brilliant and generous teacher. May the republication of the *Journals* spark some serious consideration to her life and work.

Her story reminds us that in the 1960s there was still the bohemian possibility of a serious writer living on very little money. That was before "experimental" poetry became an academic pursuit and was funded primarily by grants and university positions. Those years also were a time when some poets were deeply immersed in non-Western spiritual traditions

and looked to Asia instead of Europe to expand their sensibilities.

The Japan and India Journals has an honorable place in the annals of the New American Poetry. It is one of the most salient and valuable documents of a writer's life and mind, written during a decisive and exciting time for American poetry. The perspicacity, honesty, struggles and charms of its heroine survive in its pages. It is a happy occasion that this marvelous book finally be brought back to print.

Source: Anne Waldman, "Foreword," in *Strange Big Moon: The Japan and India Journals: 1960–1964*, North Atlantic Books, 2000, pp. viii–x.

Sources

Berkson, Bill, "Joanne Kyger," in *Dictionary of Literary Biography*, Vol. 16: *The Beats: Literary Bohemians in Postwar America*, edited by Ann Charters, Gale Research, 1983, pp. 324–28.

Ginsberg, Allen, "Howl," in *The Norton Anthology of American Literature*, Vol. 2, W. W. Norton, 1979, p. 2410.

Kyger, Joanne, *As Ever: Selected Poems*, Penguin, 2002, pp. 132, 133, 145, 146, 150, 165, 167.

Meltzer, David, "Introduction," in *As Ever: Selected Poems*, by Joanne Kyger, Penguin, 2002, pp. xvii–xx.

Nahem, Lawrence, "A Conversation with Joanne Kyger," *Occident*, Vol. 8, Spring 1974, pp. 142–57.

Olson, Charles, "Projective Verse," in *Collected Prose*, edited by Donald Allen and Benjamin Friedlander, University of California Press, 1997, pp. 239–49.

Opstedal, Kevin, "A Literary History of the San Andreas Fault: Bolinas Section," in *JACK*, Vol. 1, No. 3, available online at www.jackmagazine.com/issue3/renhist.html

Review of *As Ever: Selected Poems*, in *Publishers Weekly*, Vol. 249, No. 24, June 17, 2002, p. 57.

Smith, Dale, "Energy on the Page: Joanne Kyger in Conversation with Dale Smith," in *Jacket*, No. 11, April 2000, available online at www.jacketmagazine.com/11/kyger-iv-dale-smith.html

Suzuki, D. T., *Zen Buddhism: Selected Writings of D. T. Suzuki*, edited by William Barrett, Doubleday Anchor Books, 1956, pp. 83–108.

Further Reading

Davidson, Michael, *The San Francisco Renaissance: Poetics and Community at Mid-century*, Cambridge University Press, 1991.
  Davidson points out that even though the term San Francisco Renaissance is usually associated with the

Beat movement, it was, in fact, a collage of different communities, often at odds with one another, whose agendas were social and political as much as aesthetic. These various communities provided important contexts for subsequent counterculture developments, such as gay liberation, feminism, and the New Left.

Friedman, Amy L., "Joanne Kyger, Beat Generation Poet: 'A Porcupine Traveling at the Speed of Light,'" in *Reconstructing the Beats*, edited with an introduction by Jennie Skerl, Palgrave Macmillan, 2004, pp. 73–88.

This is an overview of Kyger's career that emphasizes the difficulties she has encountered as a woman poet in a competitive male environment and the lasting influence on her work of Beat poetics and relationships with Beat poets.

Notley, Alice, "Joanne Kyger's Poetry," in *Arshile: A Magazine of the Arts*, No. 5, 1996, pp. 95–110.

Notley discusses a wide range of Kyger's poetry and some of the influences on her work. Drawing on her experience of having heard Kyger read her poetry aloud on several occasions, Notley argues that Kyger is a poet of the voice rather than the printed word. Notley also has praise for Kyger's commitment to truth.

Russo, Linda, "To Deal with Parts and Particulars: Joanne Kyger's Early Epic Poetics," in *Girls Who Wore Black: Women Writing the Beat Generation*, edited by Ronna C. Johnson and Nancy M. Grace, Rutgers University Press, 2002, pp. 178–204.

Russo discusses Kyger's work as a woman poet; in particular, she examines Kyger's first work, *The Tapestry and the Web* (1965), which was inspired in part by Homer's *Odyssey*. Russo argues that Kyger explores and challenges received notions of gender and poetic authority.

Song: To Celia

Ben Jonson

1616

Although Ben Jonson is best known for his plays, his poetry had a significant impact on seventeenth-century poets and has come to be as highly regarded as that of his contemporary William Shakespeare. Edmund Gosse, in *The Jacobean Poets*, concludes that Jonson was "rewarded by the passionate devotion of a tribe of wits and scholars . . . and he enjoys the perennial respect of all close students of poetry." Jonson's lyric ballad "Song: To Celia" is his most beloved and anthologized poem. Soon after its publication, it was put to music by an anonymous composer, after which it became a popular song in public houses. "Song: To Celia" was included in the book *The Forest*, published in 1616. It appears in the sixth edition of *The Norton Anthology of English Literature* (1993).

Jonson's "Song: To Celia" is a short monologue in which a lover addresses his lady in an effort to encourage her to express her love for him. Jonson includes conventional imagery, such as eyes, roses, and wine, but employs them in inventive ways. As a result, the poem becomes a lively, expressive song extolling the immortality of love. John Addington Symonds, in his 1886 study of Jonson, calls the poem a masterpiece in its "purely lyric composition" and individuality. He concludes that Jonson's lyrics "struck the key-note of the seventeenth century."

Author Biography

Ben Jonson was born in London during the reign of Queen Elizabeth, sometime between May 1572

Ben Jonson © Bettmann/Corbis

and January 1573. His father, a clergyman, died one month before he was born. Two years after his birth, his mother married a bricklayer. Jonson attended Saint Martin's parish school and, later, Westminster School, where he was influenced by a teacher named William Camden, who taught him the classics. In 1589, Jonson left Westminster to work as a bricklayer with his stepfather, but his bricklaying career was short-lived. Jonson entered the army briefly and then joined a theater company run by Philip Henslowe, a theatrical entrepreneur. In 1594, he married Anne Lewis, with whom he had at least two children.

Jonson was able to support himself and his growing family through his dual career as an actor and a writer. His work, however, would frequently cause him problems. He was first arrested for co-authoring and acting in a satire called *The Isle of Dogs* in 1597. The Privy Council considered it to be lewd, seditious, and slanderous and ordered London theaters to ban the play. It was subsequently destroyed.

In 1598, Jonson killed Gabriel Spencer, an actor, in a duel and was arrested for the murder. Jonson escaped hanging by proving that he could read and write; this allowed him to be tried in a more lenient court, which sentenced him to imprisonment. During his incarceration, he asserted his independence in the predominantly Protestant era by converting to Catholicism, influenced by a priest who used to visit him in prison. Soon after his release that year, Jonson saw his first play performed at the Globe Theatre. *Every Man in His Humour* included William Shakespeare in its cast and was responsible for making Jonson a celebrity. His next plays were satirical comedies: *Every Man out of His Humour* (1599) and *Cynthia's Revels* (1600). He soon followed with the comedy *The Poetaster*, which satirized the works of his fellow playwrights Thomas Dekker and John Marston. They reciprocated with a play called *Satiromastix* that attacked Jonson and his work.

Jonson again came under attack, this time for his plays *Sejanus, His Fall* (1603) and *Eastward Ho!* (1605), which the Privy Council deemed treasonous. Ironically, in 1605, Jonson was appointed Court Poet. During this time he wrote *The Alchemist* (1610) and *Bartholomew Fair* (1614), two of his most successful comedies. Jonson then became the nation's unofficial poet laureate in 1616. That same year, *The Forest*, a book of his poems including "Song: To Celia" and "To Heaven," was published. His esteem and influence at court were reinforced when he received an honorary master's degree from Oxford University in 1620. Jonson was considered for a knighthood and was nominated to become the Master of the Revels, which would have made him supervisor of dramatists and their manuscripts, but he died in 1637, before he could assume the post. He was buried at Westminster Abbey. The tombstone slab reads, "O rare Ben Jonson," an appropriate epigraph for one of the major dramatists and poets of the seventeenth century.

Poem Text

> Drink to me only with thine eyes,
> And I will pledge with mine:
> Or leave a kiss but in the cup,
> And I'll not look for wine.
> The thirst that from the soul doth rise   5
> Doth ask a drink divine
> But might I of Jove's nectar sup,
> I would not change for thine.
> I sent thee late a rosy wreath,
> Not so much honoring thee,   10
> As giving hope that there
> It could not withered be
> But thou thereto didst only breathe

And sent it back to me;
Since when it grows and smells, I swear,   15
Not of itself, but thee.

Poem Summary

Lines 1–4

The speaker in "Song: To Celia" opens with a plea for his lady to express her love by gazing upon him. His plea is assertive, in the form of a command to drink to him with her eyes. He wants more than an expression of her love, however; he wants a pledge. He notes this in the second line when he declares that he will return the pledge with his own eyes. The reference to the cup that is commonly filled with wine becomes an apt metaphor for what he is asking from his lady. One usually makes a toast, a pledge of some sort, when first sipping a cup of wine. The speaker wants his lady to make a pledge to him with her eyes rather than while drinking from a cup of wine. This pledge would be more personal and so more meaningful to him.

By suggesting that his lady could convey such a pledge through her gaze, he pays tribute to her expressive eyes. He suggests that their connection is so intimate that they do not need the words of a speech to communicate their feelings for each other. This act reflects medieval love conventions, which propose that love is received through the eyes.

When the speaker gives his lady an alternative way to express her love, he suggests that she may be reluctant to do so. Leaving a kiss in the cup would allow her to respond to him in a more modest manner. This alternative, he states, would be just as pleasing to him. When he insists that he will "not look for wine," he implies that her kiss will intoxicate him more than any alcohol could. Wine would be an inadequate replacement for her love.

Jonson smoothly integrates the images of eyes, drinking, and wine in these first lines, which reinforces and heightens his speaker's expression of love and longing. Initially, the metaphor of drinking with one's eyes seems too forced, yet eyes produce liquid and can "brim over" with tears of sadness or joy. This liquidity, rather than that of wine, becomes the speaker's preferred method of demonstration. The image of the kiss also integrates smoothly with the others. "Kisses sweeter than wine" has become a standard expression of love.

Lines 5–8

The next four lines extend the metaphor set up in the first four lines. The speaker insists that if his lady would leave a kiss for him in the cup, he would prize it more than nectar from the gods. He claims that his soul "thirsts" for love and that only "a drink divine" that transcends even Jove's nectar can quench it. "Jove" refers to the god Jupiter, lord of the classical gods and a recurrent symbol of divinity in secular poetry. The gods drank a heavenly nectar far finer than any wine mortals drank.

According to Marshall Van Deusen, writing in "Criticism and Ben Jonson's 'To Celia,'" in the book *Essays in Criticism* and citing the *Oxford English Dictionary* definition, the word "change" in line 8 means "to make an exchange." Here the speaker is saying that he would not take Jove's nectar in exchange for that of his lady. By insisting that he values his lady's kiss more than the nectar of the gods, he elevates her to, or higher than, the status of a goddess. This type of extreme compliment is defined as "hyperbole."

There has been some disagreement on the meaning of lines 7 and 8. The popular interpretation is the one provided in the previous paragraph. Some scholars, however, insist that a literal interpretation of the lines is that the speaker would not give up Jove's nectar for his lady's kiss.

Van Deusen also notes in his essay that one of the two quotations given as illustration of the definition of "change" in the *Oxford English Dictionary* could suggest by analogy that the lines mean "if I were to have the chance offered me to sup of Jove's nectar, and if your wine were also available, I would not change for . . . yours." Van Deusen points out that defenders of this interpretation cite Jonson's "antipathy to hyperbole" and argue that the lines are complimentary "precisely because they set the exact limits of legitimate praise and avoid irresponsible exaggeration." Van Deusen comments, however, that Jonson has elsewhere used hyperbole. He also cites the source of the poem, letters from the philosopher Philostratos, in support of the popular interpretation, translating the corresponding passage from Philostratos to "when I am thirsty, I refuse the cup, and take thee."

Lines 9–12

In line 9, the speaker notes that he recently ("late") sent his lady a wreath of roses, a flower traditionally associated with beauty. Jonson uses the rosy wreath, however, in an unconventional way. The speaker admits that his primary motive

Topics For Further Study

- Read one of Shakespeare's sonnets. Compare the sonnet's theme and structure to those of "Song: To Celia."

- Investigate the development of the ballad. How does the poem "Song: To Celia" follow the conventions of the ballad form?

- Read Jonson's *Volpone*, focusing on the character of Celia. Do you see parallels between the Celia in the play and the Celia in the poem? What are the similarities or differences in the two characters named Celia?

- Many poems of the Elizabethan era have a clear rhythm that would make them easy to set to music. How do you think Jonson's poem would sound put to music? Do you think it would be fast or slow? Try reciting Jonson's poem to music you hear on the radio, such as pop, rock, jazz, or hip-hop. What musical category do you think best suits this poem? Explain why. What instruments were popular during the Elizabethan era? Which Elizabethan instruments do you think would work best to accompany Jonson's poem if it were set to music?

for sending it was not to honor her beauty, as any lover would with red roses, but for another purpose, which reflects her more intense charms. He does not discount her beauty, noting that he is sending the wreath "not so much" for her honor, but insists that he has a greater purpose. When he claims that the wreath would not wither in his lady's presence, he suggests her power over it.

Lines 13–16

The last four lines of the poem focus on this power and his lady's active connection with nature. Traditionally in love lyrics, the lady's breath is always perfumed. When the speaker swears that his lady's breath transformed the wreath, he claims that her perfume transcended the perfume of the rose. Her power does not stop there. She also gives the gift of immortality to the wreath, which continues to grow and produce a pleasing scent.

The imagery here not only illustrates the endurance of love but also suggests the fertility of the lady. If readers combine the images of the first stanza with the second, they see the speaker's lady become a fertility goddess, whose divine charms convey immortality as she affects and becomes a part of the objects around her.

By continuing undaunted toward his goal, the speaker cleverly sidesteps the suggestion that his lady is rejecting his offers of love when she returns the wreath. Even if he does not have her physical presence, he has her essence, which has been transferred to the wreath.

Themes

Courtly Love

Jonson borrowed the conventions of courtly love for the poem but manipulated them to create his unique voice. Traditionally, the lover in these poems is stricken by his lady's beauty, which causes him to idealize her. Ever obedient to her wishes, the humble lover strives to be worthy of her. His feelings of love ennoble him and lead him on the path to moral excellence.

Jonson expresses the cult of the beloved in his poem through his vision of the lady whose kisses are sweeter than the nectar of the gods and whose breath can grant immortality. Yet this speaker does not humble himself to his mistress. He has a calm assurance not found in conventional courtly love poems. In the first stanza, he subtly acknowledges that his lady might be reluctant to express her love for him when he suggests that she leave a kiss in the cup. Traditional lovers would prostrate themselves at their lady's feet, but Jonson's speaker calmly provides an alternative to drinking to him with her eyes.

In the second stanza the speaker alludes to the lady's rejection of his tokens of love when he notes that she sent the rosy wreath back to him. Traditionally, the ladies in courtly love lyrics appear immune to their lovers' terms of endearment. Jonson uses the traditional hyperbolic Petrarchan conceit—an elaborate, especially clever metaphor used to idolize a lady while lamenting her cruelty or indifference—in an innovative way. (Petrarch was a prominent Italian poet of the fourteenth century whose sonnet, with its distinctive construction and themes, became an important poetic model.) Jonson's speaker refuses to recognize the lady's indifference as he offers her signs of his love.

Power

This refusal alters the balance of power in the poem. In courtly love poems, the lady retains power over the speaker, who succumbs to her great beauty. He continually pays tribute to this beauty through the use of hyperbole. Jonson's speaker also uses this device as he praises his lady, but he does not flatter her physical attributes. He finds instead a potent essence within her that transfers kisses into wine and transfers immortality to a rosy wreath. The last four lines of the poem focus on this power and the lady's active connection with nature.

While the speaker acknowledges this force within his lady, he refuses to grant her complete control over him. He admits that his thirst for her would be quenched by drinking her kisses, but he will not openly acknowledge her seeming indifference to him. He maintains his calm composure when she returns the wreath to him and cleverly turns her action into a compliment, noting that the wreath continues to grow and that he can smell her essence on it. Jonson's speaker shows no signs that he considers himself to be her inferior as he tries to find alternate ways for her to express her love for him.

Style

Sound

Repetition of sounds in a poem can emphasize key words and images and so create poetic structure. In addition, sounds can provide pleasure. Jonson uses alliteration, the repetition of initial consonant sounds, in line 6 in the words "drink" and "divine" to emphasize the value the speaker places on his mistress's kiss. He repeats this technique in line 9 with the words "rosy" and "wreath," which highlights her connection with nature. Jonson makes a clever connection

between the speaker and his mistress through examples of consonance, the repetition of final consonant sounds, as well as word placement. He ends lines 2, 4, 6, and 8 with the words "mine," "wine," "divine," and "thine," respectively, suggesting that the union of the two would be more divine than wine. The placement of these rhyming words at the ends of the lines reinforces his point.

Language

The poem's popularity is most likely due to its use of simple, direct language that is not difficult for the reader to understand. Robert C. Evans, in his article on Jonson for the *Dictionary of Literary Biography*, concludes that Jonson's "'plain style' was neither artless nor utterly clear" and that it avoids the extremes of "sublimity and vulgarity." Evans argues that Jonson's style was "meant to communicate, to have an effect, and it gives his poetry a directness, practicality, seriousness, and force that loftier, lower, or more complicated phrasing would obscure."

These qualities are clearly displayed in "Song: To Celia" in that the lyrics appear more like rhymed prose than poetry. The speaker focuses on actions rather than elaborate metaphors as he describes his love for his lady. He does not effusively describe any distinguishing characteristics about his lady's eyes, for example, or her kisses or her breath. He concentrates instead on what his response would be to her pledges to him. This plain language of love contrasts to the elaborate conceits of John Donne's poetry as in his poem "A Valediction: Forbidding Mourning." Here, the speaker describes himself and his love's souls as "stiff twin compasses": "Thy soul, the fixed foot, makes no show / To move, but doth, if th' other do."

Historical Context

The Seventeenth-Century Court

The dominant forms of literature during the Elizabethan age and under James I and Charles I, the first two Stuart kings, were courtly. The literature read by the courtiers—members of the court and those who frequented it—were the sonnet sequence (a lyric poem of fourteen rhyming lines of equal length), as illustrated in Shakespeare's sonnets; the pastoral romance (which celebrates an idolized vision of love), as in Sir Philip Sidney's *Arcadia*; the chivalric epic (a long poem presenting an idealized code of behavior), as in Edmund

Compare & Contrast

- **1600s:** Men who wanted to gain the affection of their lovers would sing them lyrics written by poets like Jonson and Campion.

  Today: Valentine's Day has made fortunes for companies like Hallmark, since the preferred token of affection has become a card, often containing a verse that expresses an artificial sentiment.

- **1600s:** Love sonnets and songs had distinctive styles and forms that employed measured rhythm and rhyme schemes.

  Today: Modern poetry is often characterized by its free verse and unregulated style.

- **1600s:** While the Church of England was the dominant religious body in Britain, poets often evoked Greek and Roman gods in their poetry, as Jonson does when his speaker compares his lady's kisses to Jove's nectar.

  Today: Most modern poetry is secular, or worldly, reflecting the gradual decline of the influence of religion on the arts. Religious groups, however, are becoming more politically active as the country is split between conservative and liberal sensibilities.

Spenser's *Faerie Queene*; the sermon; and the masque (a spectacular performance that combines drama, music, and dance), as in Jonson's "Pleasure Reconciled to Vertue." Authors like Jonson wrote almost exclusively for the court, since that is where they received their patronage and acclaim.

The literature of the age reflected the distinctive values of court society. Literary works centered on the promotion of a hierarchical order, which necessitated allegiance to the Church of England and the monarch. Robert M. Adams, in his overview of the age, notes that the Elizabethan monarchy and the Church gained such elevated and powerful status owing to the firm belief in "the inevitable structure of things, the natural pattern of the world." This hierarchical form focused on the great chain of being, Adams concludes, where "every creature had his place in the great order of divine appointments; and the different families of being were bound together by a chain of universal analogy."

These values, which were carried over into the reign of James I, promoted literature that was intricate, ornate, and allusive (making reference to important events, literature, or people). Favored subjects included the heroic passions: love, which may or may not be accompanied by marriage; aggression, which often led to a war that lacked a specific political

context; and a yearning for a closer relationship with God, expressed as devotional piety. Honor became the paramount principle that governed the works.

Seventeenth-Century Poetry

One of the most significant events of the seventeenth century was the Puritan Revolution of 1640–1660. The Puritans criticized literary works that did not address religious themes and that expressed too much emotion. None of the literature of the age, with the exception of works by John Milton, expressed evident sympathy with Puritan doctrine, which began to emerge in the decades before the revolution. Yet a challenge to tradition and a desire for social and political change began to appear, reflecting the revolutionary spirit of the age. Two distinct poetic groups formed during this period: the metaphysical poets led by Donne, including George Herbert, Richard Crashaw, Henry Vaughan, Abraham Cowley, and John Cleveland, and Jonson and "Ben's Sons," the Cavalier poets Thomas Carew, Robert Herrick, Sir John Suckling, Edmund Waller, and Sir William Davenant. Although some crossover occurred, these two school were defined by distinct characteristics.

According to J. A. Cuddon in his *Dictionary of Literary Terms and Literary Theory*, the metaphysical poets, who wrote deeply intellectual and philosophical poems, incorporated striking and "original images and conceits . . ., wit, ingenuity, dexterous use of colloquial speech, [and] considerable flexibility of rhythm and meter." Their "complex themes (both sacred and profane)" were conveyed through "a liking for paradox [contradictions] . . . a direct manner, a caustic [biting] humour, a keenly felt awareness of mortality . . . and . . . compact expression."

In contrast, Jonson and the Cavalier poets altered the traditional sonnet form, creating works that employed direct, often colloquial, or everyday, language. The term "Cavalier" comes from these poets' rejection of earnestness or intensity. These poets continued to promote the ideal of the Renaissance man—lover, wit, soldier, poet—but ignored traditional religious themes. Robert C. Evans, in his article on Jonson for the *Dictionary of Literary Biography*, writes of Jonson's influence on this school of poetry. Evans notes that Jonson's "'plain style' made him a crucial figure in a central tradition, but his deceptively complex works reward close reading." Evans deems Jonson's work to be "sophisticated, self-conscious, and strongly influenced by the Greek and Roman classics," yet it "nonetheless rarely seems foreign or artificial. His vigorous and colloquial style exemplifies both wide reading and a deep interest in 'reality.'"

The sonnet, the most popular poetic form at the close of the Elizabethan age and the beginning of the Jacobean age (early 1600s), faded from view in the latter half of the seventeenth century. Blank verse (unrhymed verse) was replaced by the couplet (a pair of rhyming verse lines), which provided a skillful meter for the expression of alternate points of view, a popular technique in John Dryden's work. By the end of the century, satiric poetry, which ridicules vices, follies, and abuses, came into vogue. The poetic satirist's favorite form was the closed or heroic couplet, a verse couplet that comes to a strong conclusion. The latter form was developed by Sir John Denham and Edmund Waller and perfected by Andrew Marvell, Dryden, and Alexander Pope. Dryden emerged as the reigning satirist of the age with the publication of *Absalom and Achitophel* in 1681, *The Medal* in 1682, *Mac Flecknoe* in 1682, and *The Hind and the Panther* in 1687.

Seventeenth-Century Song

Some poems, such as William Blake's *Songs of Innocence*, are called songs even though they are not set to music; the term usually refers to a poem that is intended to be sung or chanted, with or without musical accompaniment. The form became popular in the sixteenth and seventeenth centuries, along with its two most famous composers, Thomas Campion ("There is a Garden in Her Face") and John Dowland ("Weep you no more, sad fountains"). In the seventeenth century, the poets Herrick, Richard Lovelace, Jonson, Milton, and Dryden wrote highly acclaimed songs in plays and masques and as nondramatic verse.

Jonson focused more than his predecessors on the value of rhyme in his lyric verses, highlighting a sense of proportion and structural beauty. His songs showed classical restraint and conciseness of style in their rejection of extravagance and mannerism (the excessive use of a distinctive style). Jonson's "sons" carried on the style of his songs, as seen in the lyrics of Herrick and Carew, as well as in those by William Cartwright, Thomas Randolph, and Waller. The orderly structure and grace of their lyrics were reinforced by their substitution of the language of courtly gallantry for the Petrarchan language of prostrate adoration.

Critical Overview

When *The Forest*, containing "Song: To Celia," was published in 1616, it affirmed Jonson's position as one of the court's most distinguished poets. That same year, Jonson was appointed poet laureate of England. In addition, his nearly two decades of celebrated writing were capped that year with the appearance of his massive folio *Workes*, a fitting testimony to his illustrious reputation and his marked influence on other poets of the age.

"Song: To Celia," Jonson's favorite of all of his lyrics, quickly became his most admired poem. It was put to music later in the century by an anonymous composer, after which it became a popular song in public houses. The poem has continued to enjoy a reputation as one of Jonson's finest lyrics.

John Addington Symonds, in his 1886 study of Jonson, argues that the poem, one of five by Jonson that he names, is a masterpiece "in purely lyric composition" and has "a quality which is definite and individual. No one before him wrote pieces of the sort so terse, so marked by dominant intelligence, so aptly fitted for their purpose." He concludes that, along with those of Shakespeare, Jonson's lyrics "struck the key-note of the seventeenth century."

Claude J. Summers, in his *Classic and Cavalier: Celebrating Jonson and the Sons of Ben*, addresses current opinion when he writes that the "recent quickening of critical interest in Jonson's nondramatic poetry has led to a new appreciation of his 'subtle sport' and to a new willingness to read him on his own terms." This appreciation is echoed by Marchette Chute in *Ben Jonson of Westminster*, who writes, "Song: To Celia "is an almost perfect example of a classical poem, achieving the balanced Greek harmony and the lucid singing line in which each word fulfills its purpose and there is not one too many."

Criticism

Wendy Perkins

Perkins is a professor of American and English literature and film. In this essay, she examines Jonson's craftsmanship and the way he reworked borrowed material in the poem.

In "Jonson's Poetry, Prose and Criticism," J. B. Bamborough writes that while Jonson placed a high value on poetry, he regarded it as "essentially an Art, rather than as the expression of personality or a way of conveying a unique perception of Truth. Skill was the quality most inescapably demanded of the poet." Bamborough says that Jonson makes this point when he writes "For to Nature, Exercise. Imitation, and Studie, *Art* must be added, to make all these perfect." Jonson's neoclassical position states that writing well necessitates first mastering the subject and then examining how other writers have expressed it. Thus, according to Bamborough, "Originality and Inspiration, as the Romantics understood them, do not, or need not, enter into this."

Jonson's policy of studying other writers' work led him to incorporate some of that work into his own. G. A. E. Parfitt, in "The Nature of Translation in Ben Jonson's Poetry," notes that Jonson's practice of borrowing material from other sources and incorporating it into his own work was "not theoretically a departure from ordinary renaissance principles: it conformed to standard educational doctrine and, viewed broadly, it is an activity similar to that of many other authors of the period." Parfitt states that "only in Jonson does the use of classical material seem a natural and essential aspect of the poet's creativity." He adds that this use appears "to have become a central habit of his mind when that mind was at its most creative." Jonson's creative reworking of

borrowed materials is well illustrated in the evolution of his poem "Song: To Celia."

In his study of Jonson, John Addington Symonds comments that Jonson's "wholesale and indiscriminate translation[s]" of other writers' work was "managed with admirable freedom" as Jonson made the work his own. Symonds notes, "This kind of looting from classical treasuries of wit and wisdom was accounted no robbery in that age" and was, in fact, praised by Jonson's contemporaries. Symonds quotes John Dryden, who, while admitting that there were "few serious thoughts which are new" in Jonson's poetry, praises the poet's willingness "to give place to the classics in all things." Dryden claims that Jonson "invades authors like a monarch; and what would be theft in other poets is only victory in him."

Bamborough quotes Jonson's comments on the assimilation process: those who study "the best authors" will discover "somewhat of them in themselves, and in the expression of their minds, even when they feele it not, be able to utter something like theirs, which hath an Authoritie above their owne." Parfitt concludes that Jonson's "familiarity with 'the best authors' made the dividing line between original and borrowed material disappear stylistically." In "Song: To Celia," Jonson crafts a poem that "utter[s] something" from one of these authors, but he makes it uniquely his own.

Scholars have agreed that Jonson used certain letters of Philostratos, a philosopher of the third century A.D., as the source material for "Song: To Celia." Parfitt argues that in the poem, Jonson "takes over the bantering tone of the original and something of Philostratos's ingenuity but shows no sign of subservience to his material." Jonson retains but fine-tunes the classical style of the original, as expressed in the poem's economy, carefully structured statement, and sense of harmony.

J. Gwyn Griffiths, in her article on Philostratos's letters, cites translations from the excerpts that Jonson borrowed for "Song: To Celia." The first stanza of the poem is a reworking of two letters, numbered XXXII and XXXIII. In the first letter, Philostratos writes "I, as soon as I see thee, am thirsty, and stand unwilling to drink, though holding the cup; I do not lift the cup to my lips, but I know that I am drinking thee." In the second letter, he writes

> Drink to me only with thine eyes, which even Zeus tasted, and then procured for himself a handsome cup-bearer. Or if thou wilt, do not rashly use up the wine, but pour in some water only, and putting the cup to thy lips, fill it with kisses, and so give it to

the needy. For no one is so unloving as to desire the gift of Dionysos after the vines of Aphrodite.

Jonson takes the first phrase of the second letter, along with some of the ideas of both, and crafts a self-contained unit in the first stanza of his poem. Here Jonson presents a much clearer and more lyrical depiction of the situation: the speaker's request to his lady that she give him an expression of her love. In the letter, the speaker dilutes his main focus by including the figures of Zeus, a "handsome" cup bearer, Dionysos, and Aphrodite. Jonson instead keeps our attention on the speaker's request, which expresses his own feelings for his lady. He evokes the name of only one god and only in a passing reference to the god's nectar, employing it as a clever expression of his lady's charms.

Jonson also establishes a clear structure that is absent in the letters. Marshall Van Deusen, in his article on the poem for *Essays in Criticism*, points out the logical connection between the statements in the first stanza. He notes that "as the lady's kiss in the cup satisfied physical thirst better than wine, so her nectar should satisfy the thirst of the soul better than Jove's drink could."

The relationship between the speaker and thirst is not made clear in the first letter, when he declares that he becomes thirsty when he sees his lady. It is also not evident how the essence of the lady appears in the cup. The second letter adds some clarification, but together the two pieces are disjointed. Jonson elucidates the connection between lady and cup in the first four lines of the poem and extends the image into the next four, where the speaker uses it to offer a high compliment to his lady.

Jonson's speaker asserts a calm assurance in his monologue to his lady through his sparse, precise imagery and avoidance of elevated language. Bamborough places Jonson alongside Sidney and other writers who insisted on "'dignifying the vernacular' [everyday speech] by 'purifying' it, freeing it from obscurity, rusticity, clumsiness and affectation, whether this last took the form of . . . importation from ancient or modern languages." Jonson, Bamborough insists, believed that English should be "transformed into an expressive and worthy literary language by revealing its true genius, not by divorcing it from the actual speech of men."

The poem moves between the abstract and the concrete, smoothly integrating in the first stanza the dominant images of eyes, wine, kisses, and the act of drinking into an expression of the speaker's love for his lady. The harmonious interplay of the imagery is reinforced with the musicality of the lyric

> *The second stanza complements the first with its extension of the focus on the lady's extraordinary powers."*

in its alliteration and structured rhyme scheme. Energy is generated through the rhythm of the lines as well as the exactness of the imagery, aided by Jonson's use of active verbs like "drink," "rise," "sup," and "breathe."

The poem's short length and tight structure provide an appropriate venue for intimate thoughts; single, simple ideas; and extended metaphors. The second stanza complements the first with its extension of the focus on the lady's extraordinary powers. In the first, she transforms kisses into nectar, and, in the second, she transfers her essence to a rosy wreath, granting it immortality.

In the second stanza, Jonson translates Philostratos's Letters II and XLVI. In the first letter, the speaker writes, "I have sent thee a wreath of roses, not so much honouring thee, though that too was my intent, as bestowing a favour upon the roses themselves, that they might not be withered." In the second, he writes, "If thou wouldst gratify thy lover, send back the remnants of the roses, no longer smelling of themselves only, but also of thee."

The speaker includes a clumsy contradiction in the last line of the second letter when he insists that the roses no longer smell of themselves alone but "also" of thee. "Also" should have been "only" if the intention was to declare that the lady transformed the roses. Jonson makes that intention clear in his last stanza and reveals how the transformation is made. The second stanza focuses on the lady's power over nature, much in the same way that the first suggested her power over her lover. In the first, she quenches her lover's "thirst"; in the second, she grants immortality to the wreath through her breath, which is not identified in the letter. This more active connection between lady and wreath suggests a heightening of her power; it also adds to the harmonious structure of the lyric.

An examination of the development of "Song: To Celia" centers on the poet as craftsman, providing evidence to support Jonson's reputation as a master of his art. In this carefully designed lyric, Jonson has wedded a classical sensibility with his unique voice, producing one of the finest love poems of the age.

Source: Wendy Perkins, Critical Essay on "Song: To Celia," in *Poetry for Students*, Thomson Gale, 2006.

G. A. E. Parfitt

In the following essay, Parfitt interprets Jonson's poems in light of the chief features of his best verse—"energy, assuredness, and rhythmical alertness"—and contrasts their tendency to simplify and exaggerate.

Although there is enough of it to occupy the bulk of a volume of the Oxford edition of his works, Ben Jonson's poetry does not receive much primarily critical attention. Part of this neglect comes from the fact that the plays are Jonson's main achievement (and even these live in the deep shadow of Shakespeare) but one must also take account of the doubts critics have expressed concerning the intrinsic merits of the poetry. These doubts usually take the form of equating Jonson's 'classicism'—that most protean of qualities—with dulness and alienation from any English tradition of language and thought, or of the belief that he lacked inspiration and was, in Coleridge's sense, a poet of fancy. The first of these reservations has had some recent attention and I cannot now take the discussion further, except to remark in passing that there is little in Jonson's thought or use of language which lacks English antecedents and that where he is distinctively classical (mainly in the lack of supernatural emphasis in his ethical thought and in the non-resonance and unusual directness of his use of language) it is in a way which does not make him an isolated figure. The second point is, however, the one I wish to take up here.

The suggestion that Jonson lacked inspiration is clear in Gregory Smith's remark that his poetry is without 'that spiritual suggestion which in master-verse lies behind the magic of phrase and rhythm' and again in Swinburne's comment that we can expect 'no casual inspiration, no fortuitous impulse' [*Ben Jonson,* 1919]. The Romantic background is clear enough—Arnold gone to seed—but, although outdated, these remarks have not really been displaced, as anyone who has read J. B. Bamborough's British Council booklet will appreciate. Dr. Leavis speaks well of Jonson's poetry and Yvor Winters sees his verse as the culmination of 16th century plain-style poetry. In addition one or two recent anthologies have included a larger and more intelligent selection of his work, but there is still little evidence that Jonson is being read more widely or more wisely than he was 40 years ago; mainly, I think, because he does not fit very well into the framework of metaphysical poetry, lacking the more striking qualities of that mode. Jonson, in fact, loses two ways: if we are critics or critically-influenced readers of poetry we are likely to look for, and most appreciate, density of texture displayed in such forms as irony, paradox and ambiguity; if we are more occasional readers of poetry or reactionaries we are liable to be close to the Romantic critical tradition. In neither case will Jonson be an obvious poet for us to read—and, yet, if we will read him, as we should, with as much attention and as few preconceptions as possible, we can see that he offers a great deal. An attempt to demonstrate this will need to take further account of the possible objections to Jonson, but it will be best to begin by asking what qualities Jonson's poetry has and whether they amount to anything very much.

It is important, first of all, to be aware of what acts as the basic impulse in Jonson's poetry. Part of Shakespeare's fascination is that the particular area of experience he is examining seems to suggest and define the moral values relevant to it. There is a remarkable lack of preconception in Shakespeare which makes him perhaps the most non-didactic poet in English, but it is a quality which appears in most great poetry and is, I think, almost part of any adequate definition of the term. Jonson, on the other hand, works largely from values to experience, for his *a priori* belief in certain ethical tenets governs his selection, analysis and expression of material. This is strength, in the consistency, weight and conviction it lends to his poetry, but also potential weakness in that it can lead to inflexibility and one-sidedness. But this feature of Jonson's poems does not make him that near-contradiction in terms, a purely cerebral poet. His intellect is usually less obtrusive than Donne's, acting mainly to keep the development of his poems clear and to focus them on the topic in hand, and the wrongheadedness of seeing him as a mainly intellectual writer can be demonstrated in most of his major poems (which, apart from 'To Penshurst', are not those most widely known). 'An Epistle to a Friend, to persuade him to the Warres' [*The Under-wood* XV] contains a mass of satirical detail which has obviously been selected to give a peculiar emotional slant to the poem: very little attempt is made to convince us by discursive reasoning of the alleged decadence of the society being examined, and instead Jonson overwhelms us with the sheer emotional weight of detail. In 'To Sir Robert Worth' [*The Forrest* III] there is a clear antithesis between town and country life and our intellectual reaction must be that the matter is more complex than Jonson pretends. If we give assent to the poem's vision it may partly be because our minds suggest an element of truth in Jonson's simplification, but it is mainly because his belief in this vision is made emotionally convincing by the pressure of the chosen details and by the impact of the confident rhythms. Although frigidity is a reasonable charge against some of the lyrics, a general reputation for intellectual pedantry is not justified in Jonson's poems and is an unnecessary blockage to appreciation.

But if Jonson's basic impulse is didactic in the way just suggested, what are the chief features of his best verse? The qualities I should stress are energy, assurance and rhythmical alertness, all of which can be found in the 'Epistle to a Friend' already mentioned:

> Wake, friend, from forth thy Lethargie; the Drum
> Beates brave, and loude in Europe, and bids come
> All that dare rowse: or are not loth to quit
> Their vitious ease, and be o'erwhelm'd with it.
> It is a call to keepe the spirits alive
> That gaspe for action, and would yet revive
> Mans buried honour, in his sleepie life:
> Quickening dead Nature, to her noblest strife.

Energy here is present in the clarity and immediate impact of the basic conception, and also in the concentrated power of such words as 'dare', 'vitious', 'o'erwhelm'd', 'gaspe' and 'sleepie', while assurance is the conviction that this (to our eyes) unusual attitude is reasonable in this context and the weight with which this conviction is pressed home. The rhythmical alertness is the way in which the stresses and sense-units are varied so that a strong emotional appeal and an impression of reasoned argument can co-exist with a kind of idiomatic directness appropriate to the topic.

It would be misleading, however, to expect from Jonson energy in an obviously striking form: he is not normally a coiner of instantly memorable phrases, but he has a remarkable fundamental strength which makes itself felt in almost any extended passage, and, as we become familiar with his poems, we sense also the unobtrusive local energy. The opening lines of 'To Heaven' [*The Forrest* XV] make their first impact because of their poise rather than of anything striking in the language:

> Good, and great God, can I not thinke of thee,
> But it must straight, my melancholy bee?

The words are self-effacing, passing one through to the overall meaning without asking to be examined minutely."

> Is it interpreted in me disease,
> That, laden with my sinnes, I seeke for ease?
> O, be thou witnesse, that the reynes dost know,
> And hearts of all, if I be sad for show,
> And judge me after. . . .

The words are self-effacing, passing one through to the overall meaning without asking to be examined minutely. But—and here another Jonsonian quality, precision of word-choice, needs emphasis—they can stand up to such examination, for while it will reveal few deep-seated associations and fewer ambiguities, it increases respect for the essential rightness of 'reynes' and 'interpreted' and understanding of how the conventional adjectives 'good' and 'great', and the standard image in 'laden', gain weight and point from the confident rhythms, from careful placing, and ultimately from the wider context of Jonson's thought.

The same process, whereby we slowly come to feel the strength of detail in Jonson's poetry, is evident in 'An Epistle Mendicant' [*The Underwood* LXXI] where, rarely, there is a single formative image. The poem begins:

> Poore wretched states, prest by extremities,
> Are faine to seeke for succours, and supplies
> Of Princes aides, or good mens Charities.
> Disease, the Enemie, and his Ingineeres,
> Wants, with the rest of his conceal'd compeeres,
> Have cast a trench about mee, now five yeares.

The immediate appeal is emotional (sympathy for the bedridden old poet and admiration for the dignity of his request for help) but what is particularly impressive is how Jonson controls and defines his situation, almost objectively and without self-pity.

This is achieved by the use of a single image with no immediately obvious conceptual or emotional contact with his plight, and by the careful description of this 'external' image rather than of the plight. It is applied to himself in 'cast a trench about

What Do I Read Next?

- Shakespeare's songs from his plays illustrate the Elizabethan forms of the song. Spanning the late sixteenth and early seventeenth centuries, these songs include "When Daises Pied" from *Love's Labour's Lost* (1598).

- In his famous poem "To Penthurst" (1616), Jonson celebrates the values of serenity and good humor in a setting reminiscent of the Garden of Eden.

- Jonson's classic satire *Volpone* (1606) focuses on the consequences of greed.

- For a comparative study of the love poetry of the age, read Anne Ferry's *All in War with Time: Love Poetry of Shakespeare, Donne, Jonson, Marvell* (1975).

me' and 'block'd up, and straightened, narrow'd in, Fix'd to the bed, and boords. . . .', and the application is an imaginative one, but Jonson makes no attempt to strike logical sparks from it and there is nothing startling in the choice of descriptive language. Yet its exactness is clear, perhaps most in the simple adjectives of the very first phrase: poverty and misery are the two aspects of a besieged town which most demand humane attention, and they apply with equal force to Jonson himself. Again, the poem's assurance is marked by the easy movement between abstract and concrete: 'Disease' and 'Wants' 'cast a trench', and the image continues the description of siege while applying metaphorically to the poet's isolation and incapacitation. 'An Epistle Mendicant' is a small-scale achievement but it is still impressive and the reasons why this is so provide a more general summary of Jonson's qualities as a poet. The technical achievement is one of economy, energy and exactness, together with control and rhythmical alertness. Behind this lie an ability to see the relevant experience in a wider context, and an ability to place it and to give it just the amount of emphasis and development it will bear, and no more. The

achievement is a real one partly because it is small: Jonson will not inflate himself.

This discussion of Jonson's characteristics as a poet may have suggested how well his style is fitted to the demands made on it by the nature of his interest in the communication of an ethical attitude. A suitable style for this purpose must convince us of the validity of his ethical analysis, both by allowing direct and forceful comment upon the society being analysed and equally impressive description of that society. It must also seem serious without becoming so elevated that, in relation to the very ordinary people and activities under examination, it seems absurd. The style of Jonson's best poetry fits such a prescription well. It has the range for satirical detail:

> Some alderman has power
> Or cos'ning farmer of the customes so,
> T'advance his doubtful issue, and ore-flow
> A Princes fortune. . . .
> [*The Forrest XIII*]

and for impressive statement of what is praiseworthy:

> Where comes no guest, but is allowed to eate,
> Without his feare, and of the lordes owne meate:
> Where the same beere, and bread, and selfe-same wine,
> That is his Lordships, shall be also mine.
> [*The Forrest II*]

It can condemn directly with conviction:

> 'Tis growne almost a danger to speake true
> Of any good minde now: There are so few,
> The bad, by number, are so fortified,
> As what th'have lost t'expect, they dare deride.
> [*The Forrest XIII*]

and can give advice with equal assurance:

> Thy morning's and thy evening's vow
> Be thankes to him, and earnest prayer, to finde
> A body sound, with sounder minde;
> To doe thy countrey service, thy selfe right;
> [*The Forrest XIII*]

The style and what it communicates should not too easily be set aside as trivial because, on the one hand, it shows little sign of inspired insights, or, on the other, because it yields little of the density of texture which we tend to admire so much. Not only is the style a fit vehicle for the content (I am aware of the oversimplification) but it often makes the sort of imaginative demand that we seek in poetry. Here is a passage of natural description from 'To Sir Robert Wroth':

> The mowed meddowes, with the fleeced sheepe,
> And feasts, that either shearers keepe;
> The ripened eares, yet humble in their height,

And furrowes laden with their weight,
The apple-harvest, that doth longer last;
The hogs return'd home fat from mast;
The trees cut out in log; and those boughs made
A fire now, that lent a shade!

The corn, although ripe and high, is humble because its weight makes it bow and because it functions to feed Man, while the trees provide him with first shade and later heat. Jonson is trying to convey a sense of a satisfying Man-Nature relationship and he does this through smooth and balanced rhythms. The sensuousness of the passage from which this extract is taken is as apt here as it would be inapt in most of Jonson's work and is far more important than any intellectual perception we may have about the relationship in question. We are made to feel, as well as to perceive, that the relationship exists and matters. Later in the same poem there is another kind of imaginative demand:

Goe enter breaches, meet the cannons rage,
That they may sleepe with scarres in age.
And shew their feathers shot, and cullors torne,
And brag, that they were therefore borne.
Let this man sweat, and wrangle at the barre,
For every price, in every jarre,
And change possessions, oftner with his breath,
Then either money, warre, or death. . . .

More by the rhythms than by direct statement Jonson reinvokes the folly and confusion of the life described at the beginning of the poem, and the even movement of the nature-passage just mentioned is replaced by a more disjointed motion, which brings out strongly the erratic nature of this kind of life and the contrast between energy expended and result obtained. Here again, the verse is embodying the imagined experience.

What does all this amount to? As already hinted it amounts to an attempt at the convincing communication of an ethical viewpoint, one which is not original but nevertheless coherent and consistently held and which has validity. The validity springs from its humanity and emphasis upon man as a social creature with social responsibilities: the fact that the strands which make up Jonson's ethical viewpoint are largely derivative, commonplaces of English, Roman or Greek thought, increases the validity because they represent centuries of thought and experience. We have seen that the ethical viewpoint is communicated less by discursive reasoning than by exactness of description and accumulation of detail, to which we must add restriction of the associative potential of words. The result is a kind of verse which is active and concrete, with a life which comes from simplification and restricted resonance. It is verse which makes no attempt to embody the fully variety and uncertainty of experience, and hence has little use for such devices as irony, paradox and ambiguity. Eliot rightly argued that Jonson's is a genuine created world, but L. C. Knights's remark that 'Exclusion was the condition of Jonson's achievement' [*A Guide to English Literature,* ed. B. Ford, II, 1956] makes the vital point—to create an imagined world Jonson had to simplify. I am inclined to see the reason for this less in some deficiency in Jonson than as an inevitable consequence of having an ethical system regulating his selection and treatment of material. Simplification is a condition of his achievement, and in case too much should be made of this it may be as well to remember that Jonson's simplification is only an extreme form of any artistic attempt.

In the satirical poems this simplification is obvious enough, for selection and exaggeration is basic in satire, where all things must be black or white, with the black stressed, for if satire admitted the moral complexity of life it would cease to shock. But Jonson is not only a satirist, for he pays considerable attention to what he considers morally good, using similar simplification to describe this:

And such a force the faire example had,
As they that saw
The good, and durst not practise it, were glad
That such a Law
Was left yet to Mankind:
[*The Under-wood LXX*]

What Jonson speaks of in his poetry constitutes a created world because of the consistency and coherence already mentioned. Considering the bulk of his verse this is a remarkable fact, but it is more important to realise that the creation and sustaining of this world depends largely upon the restriction of the emotive and associational power of words. Such power leads naturally to complexity and this would introduce doubts and questions to a world which only exists by their exclusion. This in turn means that, almost by definition, Jonson is involved in a kind of poetry which must severely restrict the use of some of the poetic attributes most emphasized by modern critics. What is lost is the complexity and ambiguity of Shakespeare's world, and even of Donne's, where more of the full range of human experience is present (both in total and at any given moment) than in Jonson's world. But it is tempting to draw an obvious conclusion too readily, because the Jonsonian world illuminates certain areas of the real one more intensely because of the narrow focus and more emphatically because of the distortions.

The best illustration is from the plays. Of course Volpone is inhuman, but his inhumanity depends upon the exaggeration of some human traits and the omission of others. A comparison of Volpone and Shylock which concludes that the latter is the greater creation because more human would be both correct and beside the point, because if Shylock is more human it is also true that Volpone shows us more of Man's capacity to exploit Man and is the more striking example of what happens when the humane virtues are ignored. If Volpone ever made the appeal to our sympathy which Shylock does in the trial scene of *The Merchant of Venice* the impact of Jonson's play would be diminished at once. It is only because the greed of Voltore, Corvino and Corbacchio is so absolute, and Volpone and Mosca are so faithless, selfish and ruthless, that the play is such a terrifying parable.

But the poems also illustrate that the simplification in Jonson serves a purpose. At its simplest this is evident in the brutality of the epigram 'On Spies':

Spies, you are lights in State, but of base stuffe,
Who, when you have burnt yourselves down to snuffe,
Stinke, and are throwne away. End faire enough.
[*Epigrammes LIX*]

We have heard enough about the modern spy to imagine that his Elizabethan counterpart was probably the same sad mixture of twisted idealism and greed, but Jonson allows us to see only the sordidness and expendability. The candle-image is made brutally one-sided but it illustrates certain aspects of the Spy's business with a degree of force which springs directly from the suppression of other aspects. We might also consider whether the impact of 'Stinke' (depending so much on placing), the contempt of 'End faire enough' (depending so much on the rhyme), the compressed irony of 'lights in state', and the manner in which the potential associations of the candle-image are restricted (for candles give a pleasing light and rich shadows) do not constitute a real poetic achievement.

In a more complex way the selection and compression of detail in the satirical epistles evokes with great power, the frenzied futility of a life lived only on the surface:

As if a Brize were gotten i' their tayle,
And firke, and jerke, and for the Coach-man raile,
And jealous each of other, yet thinke long
To be abroad chanting some baudie song,
And laugh, and measure thighes, then squeake, spring, itch,
Do all the tricks of a saut Lady B—. . . .
[*The Under-wood XV*]

Although this is a far from fair picture of humanity, or of any individual, the unfairness—mainly through accumulation of active belittling verbs—makes it a very effective expression of how crudely mechanical and inhuman our life can be. The poem, as a whole, extends our experience of ourselves in the manner of Juvenal or Breughel, or as Gillary does with the brutality of his cartoons.

I have suggested that there is a similar kind of valid simplification in Jonson's description of what he sees as morally good. This description often occurs in his complimentary poems, a *genre* in which we do not expect measured criticism, but Jonson is unusual in that the qualities he celebrates are always those which belong to his own ethical position: he never praises one man for qualities condemned in another and never praises actions or attributes which, on other evidence, he would normally condemn. This consistency, together with the deep personal feeling for a set of ethical beliefs, gives Jonson's complimentary verse a sense of conviction which it would otherwise lack. Nevertheless, the convention of the *genre* whereby only the good is mentioned, and the fact that the good celebrated refers outside the individual concerned to an ethical code which is by definition generalised, means that human material is simplified and idealised, so that morally good qualities stand out, like caricature in reverse:

Jephson, thou man of men, to whose lov'd name
All gentrie, yet, owe part of their best flame!
So did thy vertue enforme, thy wit sustaine
That age, when thou stood'st up the master-braine:
Thou wert the first, mad'st merit know her strength,
And those that lack'd it, to suspect at length,
'Twas not entayl'd on title.
[*Epigrammes CXVI*]

This is very ordinary Jonson, and in praise of an almost-forgotten man: it would be easy to leave it at that, except that the exaggerations contribute to a statement of one of Jonson's firmest beliefs (that merit and title are not synonymous) and that the assurance of the rhythms and weight of the language (entail, inform, sustain) communicate a seriousness which goes beyond mere flattery.

In a more ambitious poem like 'To Penshurst' simplification operates in a less obvious way. The poem is Jonson's most successful attempt to create in verse his belief in moral good attained and sustained in society, but he makes no effort to convey a total impression of life at Penshurst. Instead he idealizes it. There is, of course, a firm grasp of physical detail, but the result is a firmly realized ideal, for Jonson presents no reservations and the only hints of anything non-ideal are there for contrast. There is exaggeration (especially in the description of the fish), while the attitude of the country people to the great house and the account of the Sidneys' hospitality are both clearly simplified. In the same way, the descriptions of the family-life at Penshurst and of the children's education are miniatures of Elizabethan ideals. It could be demonstrated that each of the aspects of Penshurst which Jonson emphasizes relates to a contemporary belief or problem: the poem's greatness is largely in the way in which Jonson has presented the ideal in active and precise detail. We see the ideal in operation and are almost convinced of its practicability, but the achievement is, of necessity perhaps, one of exclusion.

If my discussion of the qualities of Jonson's poetry, and of how these are used, is accepted, it follows that to demand a different kind of poetry, and to censure Jonson for not providing it, involves rejection of what his poetry, with its characteristic features of simplification and exaggeration, achieves. We cannot—as I hope I have made clear—distinguish between Jonson's style and his concerns, for the former is a condition of the latter. To say that Jonson's verse is poor poetry because it lacks 'inspiration', or because it is without that particular density of texture which we indicate by such words as 'ambiguity' and 'association' is to say that what is achieved as a result of these limitations is not sufficient to compensate for them.

At this point I begin to think of babies and bathwater, but let us put the 'inspiration' and 'ambiguity *et al.*' views as strongly as possible, before setting Jonson's achievement against them. For present purposes we may, I think, link them. Both point to a type of language which can and does communicate insights which impress us as true, but which are incapable of scientific proof, by a subtle, supremely delicate, use of words and rhythm. This use of language is able to give some degree of expression to the ineffable by exploiting facets of language (ambiguity, irony, paradox, association, rhythmical linking) which are usually seen as weaknesses in discursive usage. The theory of inspiration stresses the actual apprehension of non-scientific truth, while the modern critic of poetic texture emphasizes the embodying of such apprehension in word and rhythm. In neither case is Jonson an obvious poet to illustrate the relevant activity: he makes few apparent attempts to raid the unconscious or to achieve the startling but convincing insight, and the texture of his verse does not respond very much to searches for paradox, association, etc. The latter fact, in particular, suggests that Jonson is not after the sudden break-through or the moment of vision. Instead he makes a constant effort to embody in verse a coherent view of life based on ethical distinctions, and the result is a created world, simplified from the actual, but seldom untrue to aspects of it and therefore always relevant to it. The relevance is of a valuable kind because the simplification and exaggeration of Jonson's poetic world highlights and probes aspects of the actual, leading to insights which spring directly from the application of a firmly-held ethical view to the society in which Jonson lived. Again, these insights are only possible because of the simplification: they do not occur in spite of it. Much of Shakespeare's appeal may lie in his extraordinary ability to set ethical values against individuals and situations, but this does not alter Man's need to accept some standards as conditionally true, and to guide his life by the analysis of it in accordance with these standards, Jonson's achievement is to show this process in action, by embodying the standards in concrete terms and by evoking a sense of their absence.

The achievement is an important one, but it may not be clearly poetic, and our view of this point will depend on how we define that word. I should prefer to put the matter negatively. If the type of textual density of which I have spoken is an essential criterion of the poetic Jonson is only a poet occasionally, and the same is true if the poetic must include the faculty of the starting insight. But the inspiration theory is notoriously difficult to be exact about and textual density is too exclusive a standard. I am happier with the remarks of T. E. Hulme:

> There are two things to distinguish, first the particular faculty of mind to see things as they really are, and apart from the conventional ways in which you have been trained to see them. . . . Second, the concentrated state of mind, the grip over oneself which is necessary in the actual expression of what one sees. To prevent one falling into the conventional curves of ingrained technique, to hold on through infinite detail and trouble to the exact curve you want. Wherever you get this sincerity, you get the fundamental quality of good art [*Speculations,* 1949].

Jonson certainly has this 'fundamental quality': his integrity to the experience he is trying to communicate, the honesty of the matter-and-manner relationship in his verse, and his notable sense of linguistic appropriateness make him an important poet, more so than is commonly realised and more so than some more fashionable writers.

Source: G. A. E. Parfitt, "The Poetry of Ben Jonson," in *Essays in Criticism*, Vol. 18, No. 1, January 1968, pp. 18–31.

J. Gwyn Griffiths

In the following essay excerpt, Griffiths discusses how Jonson borrowed wholesale from "the Letters of Philostratos, a sophist of the third century A.D."

It is not generally known that a striking parallel to the second verse of Ben Jonson's "To Celia" ('I sent thee late a rosy wreath . . .') occurs in the *Greek Anthology*. An epigram there by an anonymous poet is briefer than Jonson's verse, but the thought is precisely the same:

'I send thee sweet perfume, granting a favour to the perfume, not to thee; for thou thyself canst perfume even the perfume.'

It is known, however, that the actual source of the whole song is to be found in the *Letters* of Philostratos, a sophist of the third century A.D. It seems that Bentley was the first to discover that, for Jonson had not dreamt of acknowledging his debt. Writing in *The Observer*, Bentley expressed his disgust at the fact that 'our learned poet Ben Jonson had been poaching in an obscure collection of love letters . . . more calculated to disgust a man of Jonson's classical taste, than to put him upon the humble task of copying them'. He adds that 'the little poem he has taken from this despicable sophist is now become a very popular song'.

The following are the passages from Philostratos to which the song is traced.

Letter XXXII. . . .

'I, as soon as I see thee, am thirsty, and stand unwilling to drink, though holding the cup; I do not lift the cup to my lips, but I know that I am drinking thee.'

Letter XXXIII. . . .

'Drink to me only with thine eyes, which even Zeus tasted, and then procured for himself a handsome cup-bearer. Or if thou wilt, do not rashly use up the wine, but pour in some water only, and putting the cup to thy lips, fill it with kisses, and so give it to the needy. For no one is so unloving as to desire the gift of Dionysos after the vines of Aphrodite.'

Letter II. . . .

'I have sent thee a wreath of roses, not so much honouring thee, though that too was my intent, as bestowing a favour upon the roses themselves, that they might not be withered.'

Letter XLVI. . . .

'If thou wouldst gratify thy lover, send back the remnants of the roses, no longer smelling of themselves only, but also of thee.'

It will be seen that sometimes Jonson follows the original very closely. At the same time he has transformed it and fashioned a dainty lyric.

Source: J. Gwyn Griffiths, "A Song from Philostratos," in *Greece & Rome*, Vol. 11, No. 33, May 1942, pp. 135–36.

Sources

Adams, Robert M, "The Seventeenth Century (1603–1660)," in *The Norton Anthology of English Literature*, Vol. 1, edited by M. H. Abrams, W. W. Norton, 1979, pp. 1049–58.

Bamborough, J. B., "Jonson's Poetry, Prose and Criticism," in *Ben Jonson*, Hutchinson, 1970, pp. 151–76.

Chute, Marchette, *Ben Jonson of Westminster*, E. P. Dutton, 1965, p. 237.

Cuddon, J. A., "Metaphysical," in *A Dictionary of Literary Terms and Literary Theory*, 3d ed., Blackwell Reference, 1991, pp. 543–45.

Donne, John, "A Valediction: Forbidding Mourning," in *The Norton Anthology of English Literature*, 6th ed., edited by M. H. Abrams, W. W. Norton, 1993, pp. 1069–70.

Evans, Robert C., "Ben Jonson," in *Dictionary of Literary Biography*, Vol. 121: *Seventeenth-Century British Nondramatic Poets, First Series*, edited by M. Thomas Hester, Gale Research, 1992, pp. 186–212.

Gosse, Edmund, "Ben Jonson—Chapman," in *The Jacobean Poets*, Charles Scribner's Sons, 1894, pp. 23–46.

Griffiths, J. Gwyn, "A Song from Philostratos," in *Greece and Rome*, Vol. 11, No. 23, May 1942, pp. 135–36.

Jonson, Ben, "Song: To Celia," in *The Norton Anthology of English Literature*, 6th ed., edited by M. H. Abrams, W. W. Norton, 1993, pp. 1225–26.

Parfitt, G. A. E., "The Nature of Translation in Ben Jonson's Poetry," in *Studies in English Literature, 1500–1900*, Vol. 13, No. 2, Spring 1973, pp. 344–59.

Summers, Claude J., *Classic and Cavalier: Celebrating Jonson and the Sons of Ben*, University of Pittsburgh Press, 1982, pp. xi–xvii.

Symonds, John Addington, *Ben Jonson*, D. Appleton, 1886.

Van Deusen, Marshall, "Criticism and Ben Jonson's 'To Celia,'" in *Essays in Criticism*, Vol. 7, 1957, pp. 95–103.

Further Reading

Bentley, Gerald Eades, *Shakespeare and Jonson. Their Reputations in the Seventeenth Century Compared*, 2 vols., University of Chicago Press, 1945.

In this comparative study, Bentley focuses on the poetic skills of the two masters.

Eckhard, Auberlen, *The Commonwealth of Wit: The Writer's Image and His Strategies of Self-Representation in Elizabethan Literature*, Gunter Narr Verlag, 1984.

This work explores Jonson's expression of self in his works within the context of Elizabethan literature.

Levin, Harry, "An Introduction to Ben Jonson," in *Ben Jonson: A Collection of Critical Essays*, edited by Jonas A. Barish, Prentice Hall, 1963, pp. 40–59.

Levin's introduction exposes some of the notable misunderstandings surrounding Jonson's work.

Riggs, David, *Ben Jonson: A Life*, Harvard University Press, 1989.

Riggs offers a comprehensive look at Jonson and the age in which he wrote.

Glossary of Literary Terms

A

Abstract: Used as a noun, the term refers to a short summary or outline of a longer work. As an adjective applied to writing or literary works, abstract refers to words or phrases that name things not knowable through the five senses.

Accent: The emphasis or stress placed on a syllable in poetry. Traditional poetry commonly uses patterns of accented and unaccented syllables (known as feet) that create distinct rhythms. Much modern poetry uses less formal arrangements that create a sense of freedom and spontaneity.

Aestheticism: A literary and artistic movement of the nineteenth century. Followers of the movement believed that art should not be mixed with social, political, or moral teaching. The statement "art for art's sake" is a good summary of aestheticism. The movement had its roots in France, but it gained widespread importance in England in the last half of the nineteenth century, where it helped change the Victorian practice of including moral lessons in literature.

Affective Fallacy: An error in judging the merits or faults of a work of literature. The "error" results from stressing the importance of the work's effect upon the reader—that is, how it makes a reader "feel" emotionally, what it does as a literary work—instead of stressing its inner qualities as a created object, or what it "is."

Age of Johnson: The period in English literature between 1750 and 1798, named after the most prominent literary figure of the age, Samuel Johnson. Works written during this time are noted for their emphasis on "sensibility," or emotional quality. These works formed a transition between the rational works of the Age of Reason, or Neoclassical period, and the emphasis on individual feelings and responses of the Romantic period.

Age of Reason: See *Neoclassicism*

Age of Sensibility: See *Age of Johnson*

Agrarians: A group of Southern American writers of the 1930s and 1940s who fostered an economic and cultural program for the South based on agriculture, in opposition to the industrial society of the North. The term can refer to any group that promotes the value of farm life and agricultural society.

Alexandrine Meter: See *Meter*

Allegory: A narrative technique in which characters representing things or abstract ideas are used to convey a message or teach a lesson. Allegory is typically used to teach moral, ethical, or religious lessons but is sometimes used for satiric or political purposes.

Alliteration: A poetic device where the first consonant sounds or any vowel sounds in words or syllables are repeated.

Allusion: A reference to a familiar literary or historical person or event, used to make an idea more easily understood.

Amerind Literature: The writing and oral traditions of Native Americans. Native American literature was originally passed on by word of mouth, so it consisted largely of stories and events that were easily memorized. Amerind prose is often rhythmic like poetry because it was recited to the beat of a ceremonial drum.

Analogy: A comparison of two things made to explain something unfamiliar through its similarities to something familiar, or to prove one point based on the acceptedness of another. Similes and metaphors are types of analogies.

Anapest: See *Foot*

Angry Young Men: A group of British writers of the 1950s whose work expressed bitterness and disillusionment with society. Common to their work is an antihero who rebels against a corrupt social order and strives for personal integrity.

Anthropomorphism: The presentation of animals or objects in human shape or with human characteristics. The term is derived from the Greek word for "human form."

Antimasque: See *Masque*

Antithesis: The antithesis of something is its direct opposite. In literature, the use of antithesis as a figure of speech results in two statements that show a contrast through the balancing of two opposite ideas. Technically, it is the second portion of the statement that is defined as the "antithesis"; the first portion is the "thesis."

Apocrypha: Writings tentatively attributed to an author but not proven or universally accepted to be their works. The term was originally applied to certain books of the Bible that were not considered inspired and so were not included in the "sacred canon."

Apollonian and Dionysian: The two impulses believed to guide authors of dramatic tragedy. The Apollonian impulse is named after Apollo, the Greek god of light and beauty and the symbol of intellectual order. The Dionysian impulse is named after Dionysus, the Greek god of wine and the symbol of the unrestrained forces of nature. The Apollonian impulse is to create a rational, harmonious world, while the Dionysian is to express the irrational forces of personality.

Apostrophe: A statement, question, or request addressed to an inanimate object or concept or to a nonexistent or absent person.

Archetype: The word archetype is commonly used to describe an original pattern or model from which all other things of the same kind are made. This term was introduced to literary criticism from the psychology of Carl Jung. It expresses Jung's theory that behind every person's "unconscious," or repressed memories of the past, lies the "collective unconscious" of the human race: memories of the countless typical experiences of our ancestors. These memories are said to prompt illogical associations that trigger powerful emotions in the reader. Often, the emotional process is primitive, even primordial. Archetypes are the literary images that grow out of the "collective unconscious." They appear in literature as incidents and plots that repeat basic patterns of life. They may also appear as stereotyped characters.

Argument: The argument of a work is the author's subject matter or principal idea.

Art for Art's Sake: See *Aestheticism*

Assonance: The repetition of similar vowel sounds in poetry.

Audience: The people for whom a piece of literature is written. Authors usually write with a certain audience in mind, for example, children, members of a religious or ethnic group, or colleagues in a professional field. The term "audience" also applies to the people who gather to see or hear any performance, including plays, poetry readings, speeches, and concerts.

Automatic Writing: Writing carried out without a preconceived plan in an effort to capture every random thought. Authors who engage in automatic writing typically do not revise their work, preferring instead to preserve the revealed truth and beauty of spontaneous expression.

Avant-garde: A French term meaning "vanguard." It is used in literary criticism to describe new writing that rejects traditional approaches to literature in favor of innovations in style or content.

B

Ballad: A short poem that tells a simple story and has a repeated refrain. Ballads were originally intended to be sung. Early ballads, known as folk ballads, were passed down through generations, so their authors are often unknown. Later ballads composed by known authors are called literary ballads.

Baroque: A term used in literary criticism to describe literature that is complex or ornate in style or diction. Baroque works typically express tension, anxiety, and violent emotion. The term "Baroque Age" designates a period in Western European literature beginning in the late sixteenth century and ending about one hundred years later.

Works of this period often mirror the qualities of works more generally associated with the label "baroque" and sometimes feature elaborate conceits.

Baroque Age: See *Baroque*

Baroque Period: See *Baroque*

Beat Generation: See *Beat Movement*

Beat Movement: A period featuring a group of American poets and novelists of the 1950s and 1960s—including Jack Kerouac, Allen Ginsberg, Gregory Corso, William S. Burroughs, and Lawrence Ferlinghetti—who rejected established social and literary values. Using such techniques as stream-of-consciousness writing and jazz-influenced free verse and focusing on unusual or abnormal states of mind—generated by religious ecstasy or the use of drugs—the Beat writers aimed to create works that were unconventional in both form and subject matter.

Beat Poets: See *Beat Movement*

Beats, The: See *Beat Movement*

Belles-lettres: A French term meaning "fine letters" or "beautiful writing." It is often used as a synonym for literature, typically referring to imaginative and artistic rather than scientific or expository writing. Current usage sometimes restricts the meaning to light or humorous writing and appreciative essays about literature.

Black Aesthetic Movement: A period of artistic and literary development among African Americans in the 1960s and early 1970s. This was the first major African American artistic movement since the Harlem Renaissance and was closely paralleled by the civil rights and black power movements. The black aesthetic writers attempted to produce works of art that would be meaningful to the black masses. Key figures in black aesthetics included one of its founders, poet and playwright Amiri Baraka, formerly known as LeRoi Jones; poet and essayist Haki R. Madhubuti, formerly Don L. Lee; poet and playwright Sonia Sanchez; and dramatist Ed Bullins.

Black Arts Movement: See *Black Aesthetic Movement*

Black Comedy: See *Black Humor*

Black Humor: Writing that places grotesque elements side by side with humorous ones in an attempt to shock the reader, forcing him or her to laugh at the horrifying reality of a disordered world.

Black Mountain School: Black Mountain College and three of its instructors—Robert Creeley, Robert Duncan, and Charles Olson—were all influential in projective verse. Today poets working in projective verse are referred to as members of the Black Mountain school.

Blank Verse: Loosely, any unrhymed poetry, but more generally, unrhymed iambic pentameter verse (composed of lines of five two-syllable feet with the first syllable accented, the second unaccented). Blank verse has been used by poets since the Renaissance for its flexibility and its graceful, dignified tone.

Bloomsbury Group: A group of English writers, artists, and intellectuals who held informal artistic and philosophical discussions in Bloomsbury, a district of London, from around 1907 to the early 1930s. The Bloomsbury Group held no uniform philosophical beliefs but did commonly express an aversion to moral prudery and a desire for greater social tolerance.

Bon Mot: A French term meaning "good word." A *bon mot* is a witty remark or clever observation.

Breath Verse: See *Projective Verse*

Burlesque: Any literary work that uses exaggeration to make its subject appear ridiculous, either by treating a trivial subject with profound seriousness or by treating a dignified subject frivolously. The word "burlesque" may also be used as an adjective, as in "burlesque show," to mean "striptease act."

C

Cadence: The natural rhythm of language caused by the alternation of accented and unaccented syllables. Much modern poetry—notably free verse—deliberately manipulates cadence to create complex rhythmic effects.

Caesura: A pause in a line of poetry, usually occurring near the middle. It typically corresponds to a break in the natural rhythm or sense of the line but is sometimes shifted to create special meanings or rhythmic effects.

Canzone: A short Italian or Provencal lyric poem, commonly about love and often set to music. The *canzone* has no set form but typically contains five or six stanzas made up of seven to twenty lines of eleven syllables each. A shorter, five- to ten-line "envoy," or concluding stanza, completes the poem.

Carpe Diem: A Latin term meaning "seize the day." This is a traditional theme of poetry, especially lyrics. A *carpe diem* poem advises the reader or the person it addresses to live for today and enjoy the pleasures of the moment.

Catharsis: The release or purging of unwanted emotions—specifically fear and pity—brought about by exposure to art. The term was first used by the Greek philosopher Aristotle in his *Poetics* to refer to the desired effect of tragedy on spectators.

Celtic Renaissance: A period of Irish literary and cultural history at the end of the nineteenth century. Followers of the movement aimed to create a romantic vision of Celtic myth and legend. The most significant works of the Celtic Renaissance typically present a dreamy, unreal world, usually in reaction against the reality of contemporary problems.

Celtic Twilight: See *Celtic Renaissance*

Character: Broadly speaking, a person in a literary work. The actions of characters are what constitute the plot of a story, novel, or poem. There are numerous types of characters, ranging from simple, stereotypical figures to intricate, multifaceted ones. In the techniques of anthropomorphism and personification, animals—and even places or things—can assume aspects of character. "Characterization" is the process by which an author creates vivid, believable characters in a work of art. This may be done in a variety of ways, including (1) direct description of the character by the narrator; (2) the direct presentation of the speech, thoughts, or actions of the character; and (3) the responses of other characters to the character. The term "character" also refers to a form originated by the ancient Greek writer Theophrastus that later became popular in the seventeenth and eighteenth centuries. It is a short essay or sketch of a person who prominently displays a specific attribute or quality, such as miserliness or ambition.

Characterization: See *Character*

Classical: In its strictest definition in literary criticism, classicism refers to works of ancient Greek or Roman literature. The term may also be used to describe a literary work of recognized importance (a "classic") from any time period or literature that exhibits the traits of classicism.

Classicism: A term used in literary criticism to describe critical doctrines that have their roots in ancient Greek and Roman literature, philosophy, and art. Works associated with classicism typically exhibit restraint on the part of the author, unity of design and purpose, clarity, simplicity, logical organization, and respect for tradition.

Colloquialism: A word, phrase, or form of pronunciation that is acceptable in casual conversation but not in formal, written communication. It is considered more acceptable than slang.

Complaint: A lyric poem, popular in the Renaissance, in which the speaker expresses sorrow about his or her condition. Typically, the speaker's sadness is caused by an unresponsive lover, but some complaints cite other sources of unhappiness, such as poverty or fate.

Conceit: A clever and fanciful metaphor, usually expressed through elaborate and extended comparison, that presents a striking parallel between two seemingly dissimilar things—for example, elaborately comparing a beautiful woman to an object like a garden or the sun. The conceit was a popular device throughout the Elizabethan Age and Baroque Age and was the principal technique of the seventeenth-century English metaphysical poets. This usage of the word conceit is unrelated to the best-known definition of conceit as an arrogant attitude or behavior.

Concrete: Concrete is the opposite of abstract, and refers to a thing that actually exists or a description that allows the reader to experience an object or concept with the senses.

Concrete Poetry: Poetry in which visual elements play a large part in the poetic effect. Punctuation marks, letters, or words are arranged on a page to form a visual design: a cross, for example, or a bumblebee.

Confessional Poetry: A form of poetry in which the poet reveals very personal, intimate, sometimes shocking information about himself or herself.

Connotation: The impression that a word gives beyond its defined meaning. Connotations may be universally understood or may be significant only to a certain group.

Consonance: Consonance occurs in poetry when words appearing at the ends of two or more verses have similar final consonant sounds but have final vowel sounds that differ, as with "stuff" and "off."

Convention: Any widely accepted literary device, style, or form.

Corrido: A Mexican ballad.

Couplet: Two lines of poetry with the same rhyme and meter, often expressing a complete and self-contained thought.

Criticism: The systematic study and evaluation of literary works, usually based on a specific method or set of principles. An important part of literary studies since ancient times, the practice of criticism has given rise to numerous theories, methods, and "schools," sometimes producing conflicting, even contradictory, interpretations of literature in general as well as of individual works. Even such basic issues as what constitutes a poem or a novel have been the subject of much criticism over the centuries.

D

Dactyl: See *Foot*

Dadaism: A protest movement in art and literature founded by Tristan Tzara in 1916. Followers of the movement expressed their outrage at the destruction brought about by World War I by revolting against numerous forms of social convention. The Dadaists presented works marked by calculated madness and flamboyant nonsense. They stressed total freedom of expression, commonly through primitive displays of emotion and illogical, often senseless, poetry. The movement ended shortly after the war, when it was replaced by surrealism.

Decadent: See *Decadents*

Decadents: The followers of a nineteenth-century literary movement that had its beginnings in French aestheticism. Decadent literature displays a fascination with perverse and morbid states; a search for novelty and sensation—the "new thrill"; a preoccupation with mysticism; and a belief in the senselessness of human existence. The movement is closely associated with the doctrine Art for Art's Sake. The term "decadence" is sometimes used to denote a decline in the quality of art or literature following a period of greatness.

Deconstruction: A method of literary criticism developed by Jacques Derrida and characterized by multiple conflicting interpretations of a given work. Deconstructionists consider the impact of the language of a work and suggest that the true meaning of the work is not necessarily the meaning that the author intended.

Deduction: The process of reaching a conclusion through reasoning from general premises to a specific premise.

Denotation: The definition of a word, apart from the impressions or feelings it creates in the reader.

Diction: The selection and arrangement of words in a literary work. Either or both may vary depending on the desired effect. There are four general types of diction: "formal," used in scholarly or lofty writing; "informal," used in relaxed but educated conversation; "colloquial," used in everyday speech; and "slang," containing newly coined words and other terms not accepted in formal usage.

Didactic: A term used to describe works of literature that aim to teach some moral, religious, political, or practical lesson. Although didactic elements are often found in artistically pleasing works, the term "didactic" usually refers to literature in which the message is more important than the form. The term may also be used to criticize a work that the critic finds "overly didactic," that is, heavy-handed in its delivery of a lesson.

Dimeter: See *Meter*

Dionysian: See *Apollonian and Dionysian*

Discordia concours: A Latin phrase meaning "discord in harmony." The term was coined by the eighteenth-century English writer Samuel Johnson to describe "a combination of dissimilar images or discovery of occult resemblances in things apparently unlike." Johnson created the expression by reversing a phrase by the Latin poet Horace.

Dissonance: A combination of harsh or jarring sounds, especially in poetry. Although such combinations may be accidental, poets sometimes intentionally make them to achieve particular effects. Dissonance is also sometimes used to refer to close but not identical rhymes. When this is the case, the word functions as a synonym for consonance.

Double Entendre: A corruption of a French phrase meaning "double meaning." The term is used to indicate a word or phrase that is deliberately ambiguous, especially when one of the meanings is risque or improper.

Draft: Any preliminary version of a written work. An author may write dozens of drafts which are revised to form the final work, or he or she may write only one, with few or no revisions.

Dramatic Monologue: See *Monologue*

Dramatic Poetry: Any lyric work that employs elements of drama such as dialogue, conflict, or characterization, but excluding works that are intended for stage presentation.

Dream Allegory: See *Dream Vision*

Dream Vision: A literary convention, chiefly of the Middle Ages. In a dream vision a story is presented as a literal dream of the narrator. This device was commonly used to teach moral and religious lessons.

E

Eclogue: In classical literature, a poem featuring rural themes and structured as a dialogue among shepherds. Eclogues often took specific poetic forms, such as elegies or love poems. Some were written as the soliloquy of a shepherd. In later centuries, "eclogue" came to refer to any poem that was in the pastoral tradition or that had a dialogue or monologue structure.

Edwardian: Describes cultural conventions identified with the period of the reign of Edward VII of England (1901–1910). Writers of the Edwardian Age typically displayed a strong reaction against the propriety and conservatism of the Victorian Age. Their work often exhibits distrust of authority in religion, politics, and art and expresses strong doubts about the soundness of conventional values.

Edwardian Age: See *Edwardian*

Electra Complex: A daughter's amorous obsession with her father.

Elegy: A lyric poem that laments the death of a person or the eventual death of all people. In a conventional elegy, set in a classical world, the poet and subject are spoken of as shepherds. In modern criticism, the word elegy is often used to refer to a poem that is melancholy or mournfully contemplative.

Elizabethan Age: A period of great economic growth, religious controversy, and nationalism closely associated with the reign of Elizabeth I of England (1558–1603). The Elizabethan Age is considered a part of the general renaissance—that is, the flowering of arts and literature—that took place in Europe during the fourteenth through sixteenth centuries. The era is considered the golden age of English literature. The most important dramas in English and a great deal of lyric poetry were produced during this period, and modern English criticism began around this time.

Empathy: A sense of shared experience, including emotional and physical feelings, with someone or something other than oneself. Empathy is often used to describe the response of a reader to a literary character.

English Sonnet: See *Sonnet*

Enjambment: The running over of the sense and structure of a line of verse or a couplet into the following verse or couplet.

Enlightenment, The: An eighteenth-century philosophical movement. It began in France but had a wide impact throughout Europe and America. Thinkers of the Enlightenment valued reason and believed that both the individual and society could achieve a state of perfection. Corresponding to this essentially humanist vision was a resistance to religious authority.

Epic: A long narrative poem about the adventures of a hero of great historic or legendary importance. The setting is vast and the action is often given cosmic significance through the intervention of supernatural forces such as gods, angels, or demons. Epics are typically written in a classical style of grand simplicity with elaborate metaphors and allusions that enhance the symbolic importance of a hero's adventures.

Epic Simile: See *Homeric Simile*

Epigram: A saying that makes the speaker's point quickly and concisely.

Epilogue: A concluding statement or section of a literary work. In dramas, particularly those of the seventeenth and eighteenth centuries, the epilogue is a closing speech, often in verse, delivered by an actor at the end of a play and spoken directly to the audience.

Epiphany: A sudden revelation of truth inspired by a seemingly trivial incident.

Epitaph: An inscription on a tomb or tombstone, or a verse written on the occasion of a person's death. Epitaphs may be serious or humorous.

Epithalamion: A song or poem written to honor and commemorate a marriage ceremony.

Epithalamium: See *Epithalamion*

Epithet: A word or phrase, often disparaging or abusive, that expresses a character trait of someone or something.

Erziehungsroman: See *Bildungsroman*

Essay: A prose composition with a focused subject of discussion. The term was coined by Michel de Montaigne to describe his 1580 collection of brief, informal reflections on himself and on various topics relating to human nature. An essay can also be a long, systematic discourse.

Existentialism: A predominantly twentieth-century philosophy concerned with the nature and perception of human existence. There are two major strains of existentialist thought: atheistic and Christian. Followers of atheistic existentialism believe that the individual is alone in a godless universe and that the basic human condition is one of suffering and loneliness. Nevertheless, because there are no fixed values, individuals can create their own characters—indeed, they can shape themselves—through the exercise of free will. The atheistic strain culminates in and is popularly associated with the works of Jean-Paul Sartre. The Christian existentialists, on the other hand, believe that only in God may people find freedom from life's anguish. The two strains hold certain beliefs in common: that existence cannot be fully understood or described through empirical effort; that anguish is a universal element of life; that individuals must bear responsibility for their actions; and that there is no common standard of behavior or perception for religious and ethical matters.

Expatriates: See *Expatriatism*

Expatriatism: The practice of leaving one's country to live for an extended period in another country.

Exposition: Writing intended to explain the nature of an idea, thing, or theme. Expository writing is often combined with description, narration, or argument. In dramatic writing, the exposition is the introductory material which presents the characters, setting, and tone of the play.

Expressionism: An indistinct literary term, originally used to describe an early twentieth-century school of German painting. The term applies to almost any mode of unconventional, highly subjective writing that distorts reality in some way.

Extended Monologue: See *Monologue*

F

Feet: See *Foot*

Feminine Rhyme: See *Rhyme*

Fiction: Any story that is the product of imagination rather than a documentation of fact. Characters and events in such narratives may be based in real life but their ultimate form and configuration is a creation of the author.

Figurative Language: A technique in writing in which the author temporarily interrupts the order, construction, or meaning of the writing for a particular effect. This interruption takes the form of one or more figures of speech such as hyperbole, irony, or simile. Figurative language is the opposite of literal language, in which every word is truthful, accurate, and free of exaggeration or embellishment.

Figures of Speech: Writing that differs from customary conventions for construction, meaning, order, or significance for the purpose of a special meaning or effect. There are two major types of figures of speech: rhetorical figures, which do not make changes in the meaning of the words; and tropes, which do.

Fin de siecle: A French term meaning "end of the century." The term is used to denote the last decade of the nineteenth century, a transition period when writers and other artists abandoned old conventions and looked for new techniques and objectives.

First Person: See *Point of View*

Folk Ballad: See *Ballad*

Folklore: Traditions and myths preserved in a culture or group of people. Typically, these are passed on by word of mouth in various forms—such as legends, songs, and proverbs—or preserved in customs and ceremonies. This term was first used by W. J. Thoms in 1846.

Folktale: A story originating in oral tradition. Folktales fall into a variety of categories, including legends, ghost stories, fairy tales, fables, and anecdotes based on historical figures and events.

Foot: The smallest unit of rhythm in a line of poetry. In English-language poetry, a foot is typically one accented syllable combined with one or two unaccented syllables.

Form: The pattern or construction of a work which identifies its genre and distinguishes it from other genres.

Formalism: In literary criticism, the belief that literature should follow prescribed rules of construction, such as those that govern the sonnet form.

Fourteener Meter: See *Meter*

Free Verse: Poetry that lacks regular metrical and rhyme patterns but that tries to capture the cadences of everyday speech. The form allows a poet to exploit a variety of rhythmical effects within a single poem.

Futurism: A flamboyant literary and artistic movement that developed in France, Italy, and Russia from 1908 through the 1920s. Futurist theater and poetry abandoned traditional literary forms. In their place, followers of the movement attempted to achieve total freedom of expression through bizarre imagery and deformed or newly invented words. The Futurists were self-consciously modern artists who attempted to incorporate the appearances and sounds of modern life into their work.

G

Genre: A category of literary work. In critical theory, genre may refer to both the content of a given work—tragedy, comedy, pastoral—and to its form, such as poetry, novel, or drama.

Genteel Tradition: A term coined by critic George Santayana to describe the literary practice of certain late nineteenth-century American writers, especially New Englanders. Followers of the Genteel

Tradition emphasized conventionality in social, religious, moral, and literary standards.

Georgian Age: See *Georgian Poets*

Georgian Period: See *Georgian Poets*

Georgian Poets: A loose grouping of English poets during the years 1912–1922. The Georgians reacted against certain literary schools and practices, especially Victorian wordiness, turn-of-the-century aestheticism, and contemporary urban realism. In their place, the Georgians embraced the nineteenth-century poetic practices of William Wordsworth and the other Lake Poets.

Georgic: A poem about farming and the farmer's way of life, named from Virgil's *Georgics.*

Gilded Age: A period in American history during the 1870s characterized by political corruption and materialism. A number of important novels of social and political criticism were written during this time.

Gothic: See *Gothicism*

Gothicism: In literary criticism, works characterized by a taste for the medieval or morbidly attractive. A gothic novel prominently features elements of horror, the supernatural, gloom, and violence: clanking chains, terror, charnel houses, ghosts, medieval castles, and mysteriously slamming doors. The term "gothic novel" is also applied to novels that lack elements of the traditional Gothic setting but that create a similar atmosphere of terror or dread.

Graveyard School: A group of eighteenth-century English poets who wrote long, picturesque meditations on death. Their works were designed to cause the reader to ponder immortality.

Great Chain of Being: The belief that all things and creatures in nature are organized in a hierarchy from inanimate objects at the bottom to God at the top. This system of belief was popular in the seventeenth and eighteenth centuries.

Grotesque: In literary criticism, the subject matter of a work or a style of expression characterized by exaggeration, deformity, freakishness, and disorder. The grotesque often includes an element of comic absurdity.

H

Haiku: The shortest form of Japanese poetry, constructed in three lines of five, seven, and five syllables respectively. The message of a *haiku* poem usually centers on some aspect of spirituality and provokes an emotional response in the reader.

Half Rhyme: See *Consonance*

Harlem Renaissance: The Harlem Renaissance of the 1920s is generally considered the first significant movement of black writers and artists in the United States. During this period, new and established black writers published more fiction and poetry than ever before, the first influential black literary journals were established, and black authors and artists received their first widespread recognition and serious critical appraisal. Among the major writers associated with this period are Claude McKay, Jean Toomer, Countee Cullen, Langston Hughes, Arna Bontemps, Nella Larsen, and Zora Neale Hurston.

Hellenism: Imitation of ancient Greek thought or styles. Also, an approach to life that focuses on the growth and development of the intellect. "Hellenism" is sometimes used to refer to the belief that reason can be applied to examine all human experience.

Heptameter: See *Meter*

Hero/Heroine: The principal sympathetic character (male or female) in a literary work. Heroes and heroines typically exhibit admirable traits: idealism, courage, and integrity, for example.

Heroic Couplet: A rhyming couplet written in iambic pentameter (a verse with five iambic feet).

Heroic Line: The meter and length of a line of verse in epic or heroic poetry. This varies by language and time period.

Heroine: See *Hero/Heroine*

Hexameter: See *Meter*

Historical Criticism: The study of a work based on its impact on the world of the time period in which it was written.

Hokku: See *Haiku*

Holocaust: See *Holocaust Literature*

Holocaust Literature: Literature influenced by or written about the Holocaust of World War II. Such literature includes true stories of survival in concentration camps, escape, and life after the war, as well as fictional works and poetry.

Homeric Simile: An elaborate, detailed comparison written as a simile many lines in length.

Horatian Satire: See *Satire*

Humanism: A philosophy that places faith in the dignity of humankind and rejects the medieval perception of the individual as a weak, fallen creature. "Humanists" typically believe in the perfectibility of human nature and view reason and education as the means to that end.

Humors: Mentions of the humors refer to the ancient Greek theory that a person's health and personality were determined by the balance of four basic fluids in the body: blood, phlegm, yellow bile, and black bile. A dominance of any fluid would cause extremes in behavior. An excess of blood created a sanguine person who was joyful, aggressive, and passionate; a phlegmatic person was shy, fearful, and sluggish; too much yellow bile led to a choleric temperament characterized by impatience, anger, bitterness, and stubbornness; and excessive black bile created melancholy, a state of laziness, gluttony, and lack of motivation.

Humours: See *Humors*

Hyperbole: In literary criticism, deliberate exaggeration used to achieve an effect.

I

Iamb: See *Foot*

Idiom: A word construction or verbal expression closely associated with a given language.

Image: A concrete representation of an object or sensory experience. Typically, such a representation helps evoke the feelings associated with the object or experience itself. Images are either "literal" or "figurative." Literal images are especially concrete and involve little or no extension of the obvious meaning of the words used to express them. Figurative images do not follow the literal meaning of the words exactly. Images in literature are usually visual, but the term "image" can also refer to the representation of any sensory experience.

Imagery: The array of images in a literary work. Also, figurative language.

Imagism: An English and American poetry movement that flourished between 1908 and 1917. The Imagists used precise, clearly presented images in their works. They also used common, everyday speech and aimed for conciseness, concrete imagery, and the creation of new rhythms.

In medias res: A Latin term meaning "in the middle of things." It refers to the technique of beginning a story at its midpoint and then using various flashback devices to reveal previous action.

Induction: The process of reaching a conclusion by reasoning from specific premises to form a general premise. Also, an introductory portion of a work of literature, especially a play.

Intentional Fallacy: The belief that judgments of a literary work based solely on an author's stated or implied intentions are false and misleading. Critics who believe in the concept of the intentional fallacy typically argue that the work itself is sufficient matter for interpretation, even though they may concede that an author's statement of purpose can be useful.

Interior Monologue: A narrative technique in which characters' thoughts are revealed in a way that appears to be uncontrolled by the author. The interior monologue typically aims to reveal the inner self of a character. It portrays emotional experiences as they occur at both a conscious and unconscious level. Images are often used to represent sensations or emotions.

Internal Rhyme: Rhyme that occurs within a single line of verse.

Irish Literary Renaissance: A late nineteenth- and early twentieth-century movement in Irish literature. Members of the movement aimed to reduce the influence of British culture in Ireland and create an Irish national literature.

Irony: In literary criticism, the effect of language in which the intended meaning is the opposite of what is stated.

Italian Sonnet: See *Sonnet*

J

Jacobean Age: The period of the reign of James I of England (1603–1625). The early literature of this period reflected the worldview of the Elizabethan Age, but a darker, more cynical attitude steadily grew in the art and literature of the Jacobean Age. This was an important time for English drama and poetry.

Jargon: Language that is used or understood only by a select group of people. Jargon may refer to terminology used in a certain profession, such as computer jargon, or it may refer to any nonsensical language that is not understood by most people.

Journalism: Writing intended for publication in a newspaper or magazine, or for broadcast on a radio or television program featuring news, sports, entertainment, or other timely material.

K

Knickerbocker Group: A somewhat indistinct group of New York writers of the first half of the nineteenth century. Members of the group were linked only by location and a common theme: New York life.

Kunstlerroman: See *Bildungsroman*

L

Lais: See *Lay*

Lake Poets: See *Lake School*

Lake School: These poets all lived in the Lake District of England at the turn of the nineteenth century. As a group, they followed no single "school" of thought or literary practice, although their works were uniformly disparaged by the *Edinburgh Review.*

Lay: A song or simple narrative poem. The form originated in medieval France. Early French *lais* were often based on the Celtic legends and other tales sung by Breton minstrels—thus the name of the "Breton lay." In fourteenth-century England, the term "lay" was used to describe short narratives written in imitation of the Breton lays.

Leitmotiv: See *Motif*

Literal Language: An author uses literal language when he or she writes without exaggerating or embellishing the subject matter and without any tools of figurative language.

Literary Ballad: See *Ballad*

Literature: Literature is broadly defined as any written or spoken material, but the term most often refers to creative works.

Lost Generation: A term first used by Gertrude Stein to describe the post-World War I generation of American writers: men and women haunted by a sense of betrayal and emptiness brought about by the destructiveness of the war.

Lyric Poetry: A poem expressing the subjective feelings and personal emotions of the poet. Such poetry is melodic, since it was originally accompanied by a lyre in recitals. Most Western poetry in the twentieth century may be classified as lyrical.

M

Mannerism: Exaggerated, artificial adherence to a literary manner or style. Also, a popular style of the visual arts of late sixteenth-century Europe that was marked by elongation of the human form and by intentional spatial distortion. Literary works that are self-consciously high-toned and artistic are often said to be "mannered."

Masculine Rhyme: See *Rhyme*

Measure: The foot, verse, or time sequence used in a literary work, especially a poem. Measure is often used somewhat incorrectly as a synonym for meter.

Metaphor: A figure of speech that expresses an idea through the image of another object. Metaphors suggest the essence of the first object by identifying it with certain qualities of the second object.

Metaphysical Conceit: See *Conceit*

Metaphysical Poetry: The body of poetry produced by a group of seventeenth-century English writers called the "Metaphysical Poets." The group includes John Donne and Andrew Marvell. The Metaphysical Poets made use of everyday speech, intellectual analysis, and unique imagery. They aimed to portray the ordinary conflicts and contradictions of life. Their poems often took the form of an argument, and many of them emphasize physical and religious love as well as the fleeting nature of life. Elaborate conceits are typical in metaphysical poetry.

Metaphysical Poets: See *Metaphysical Poetry*

Meter: In literary criticism, the repetition of sound patterns that creates a rhythm in poetry. The patterns are based on the number of syllables and the presence and absence of accents. The unit of rhythm in a line is called a foot. Types of meter are classified according to the number of feet in a line. These are the standard English lines: Monometer, one foot; Dimeter, two feet; Trimeter, three feet; Tetrameter, four feet; Pentameter, five feet; Hexameter, six feet (also called the Alexandrine); Heptameter, seven feet (also called the "Fourteener" when the feet are iambic).

Modernism: Modern literary practices. Also, the principles of a literary school that lasted from roughly the beginning of the twentieth century until the end of World War II. Modernism is defined by its rejection of the literary conventions of the nineteenth century and by its opposition to conventional morality, taste, traditions, and economic values.

Monologue: A composition, written or oral, by a single individual. More specifically, a speech given by a single individual in a drama or other public entertainment. It has no set length, although it is usually several or more lines long.

Monometer: See *Meter*

Mood: The prevailing emotions of a work or of the author in his or her creation of the work. The mood of a work is not always what might be expected based on its subject matter.

Motif: A theme, character type, image, metaphor, or other verbal element that recurs throughout a single work of literature or occurs in a number of different works over a period of time.

Motiv: See *Motif*

Muckrakers: An early twentieth-century group of American writers. Typically, their works exposed the wrongdoings of big business and government in the United States.

Muses: Nine Greek mythological goddesses, the daughters of Zeus and Mnemosyne (Memory). Each muse patronized a specific area of the liberal arts and sciences. Calliope presided over epic poetry, Clio over history, Erato over love poetry, Euterpe over music or lyric poetry, Melpomene over tragedy, Polyhymnia over hymns to the gods, Terpsichore over dance, Thalia over comedy, and Urania over astronomy. Poets and writers traditionally made appeals to the Muses for inspiration in their work.

Myth: An anonymous tale emerging from the traditional beliefs of a culture or social unit. Myths use supernatural explanations for natural phenomena. They may also explain cosmic issues like creation and death. Collections of myths, known as mythologies, are common to all cultures and nations, but the best-known myths belong to the Norse, Roman, and Greek mythologies.

N

Narration: The telling of a series of events, real or invented. A narration may be either a simple narrative, in which the events are recounted chronologically, or a narrative with a plot, in which the account is given in a style reflecting the author's artistic concept of the story. Narration is sometimes used as a synonym for "storyline."

Narrative: A verse or prose accounting of an event or sequence of events, real or invented. The term is also used as an adjective in the sense "method of narration." For example, in literary criticism, the expression "narrative technique" usually refers to the way the author structures and presents his or her story.

Narrative Poetry: A nondramatic poem in which the author tells a story. Such poems may be of any length or level of complexity.

Narrator: The teller of a story. The narrator may be the author or a character in the story through whom the author speaks.

Naturalism: A literary movement of the late nineteenth and early twentieth centuries. The movement's major theorist, French novelist Emile Zola, envisioned a type of fiction that would examine human life with the objectivity of scientific inquiry. The Naturalists typically viewed human beings as either the products of "biological determinism," ruled by hereditary instincts and engaged in an endless struggle for survival, or as the products of "socioeconomic determinism," ruled by social and economic forces beyond their control. In their works, the Naturalists generally ignored the highest levels of society and focused on degradation: poverty, alcoholism, prostitution, insanity, and disease.

Negritude: A literary movement based on the concept of a shared cultural bond on the part of black Africans, wherever they may be in the world. It traces its origins to the former French colonies of Africa and the Caribbean. Negritude poets, novelists, and essayists generally stress four points in their writings: One, black alienation from traditional African culture can lead to feelings of inferiority. Two, European colonialism and Western education should be resisted. Three, black Africans should seek to affirm and define their own identity. Four, African culture can and should be reclaimed. Many Negritude writers also claim that blacks can make unique contributions to the world, based on a heightened appreciation of nature, rhythm, and human emotions—aspects of life they say are not so highly valued in the materialistic and rationalistic West.

Negro Renaissance: See *Harlem Renaissance*

Neoclassical Period: See *Neoclassicism*

Neoclassicism: In literary criticism, this term refers to the revival of the attitudes and styles of expression of classical literature. It is generally used to describe a period in European history beginning in the late seventeenth century and lasting until about 1800. In its purest form, Neoclassicism marked a return to order, proportion, restraint, logic, accuracy, and decorum. In England, where Neoclassicism perhaps was most popular, it reflected the influence of seventeenth-century French writers, especially dramatists. Neoclassical writers typically reacted against the intensity and enthusiasm of the Renaissance period. They wrote works that appealed to the intellect, using elevated language and classical literary forms such as satire and the ode. Neoclassical works were often governed by the classical goal of instruction.

Neoclassicists: See *Neoclassicism*

New Criticism: A movement in literary criticism, dating from the late 1920s, that stressed close textual analysis in the interpretation of works of literature. The New Critics saw little merit in historical and biographical analysis. Rather, they aimed to examine the text alone, free from the question of how external events—biographical or otherwise—may have helped shape it.

New Journalism: A type of writing in which the journalist presents factual information in a form usually used in fiction. New journalism emphasizes description, narration, and character development to bring readers closer to the human element of the story, and is often used in personality profiles and in-depth feature articles. It is not compatible with "straight" or "hard" newswriting, which is generally composed in a brief, fact-based style.

New Journalists: See *New Journalism*

New Negro Movement: See *Harlem Renaissance*

Noble Savage: The idea that primitive man is noble and good but becomes evil and corrupted as he becomes civilized. The concept of the noble savage originated in the Renaissance period but is more closely identified with such later writers as Jean-Jacques Rousseau and Aphra Behn.

O

Objective Correlative: An outward set of objects, a situation, or a chain of events corresponding to an inward experience and evoking this experience in the reader. The term frequently appears in modern criticism in discussions of authors' intended effects on the emotional responses of readers.

Objectivity: A quality in writing characterized by the absence of the author's opinion or feeling about the subject matter. Objectivity is an important factor in criticism.

Occasional Verse: Poetry written on the occasion of a significant historical or personal event. *Vers de societe* is sometimes called occasional verse although it is of a less serious nature.

Octave: A poem or stanza composed of eight lines. The term octave most often represents the first eight lines of a Petrarchan sonnet.

Ode: Name given to an extended lyric poem characterized by exalted emotion and dignified style. An ode usually concerns a single, serious theme. Most odes, but not all, are addressed to an object or individual. Odes are distinguished from other lyric poetic forms by their complex rhythmic and stanzaic patterns.

Oedipus Complex: A son's amorous obsession with his mother. The phrase is derived from the story of the ancient Theban hero Oedipus, who unknowingly killed his father and married his mother.

Omniscience: See *Point of View*

Onomatopoeia: The use of words whose sounds express or suggest their meaning. In its simplest sense, onomatopoeia may be represented by words that mimic the sounds they denote such as "hiss" or "meow." At a more subtle level, the pattern and rhythm of sounds and rhymes of a line or poem may be onomatopoeic.

Oral Tradition: See *Oral Transmission*

Oral Transmission: A process by which songs, ballads, folklore, and other material are transmitted by word of mouth. The tradition of oral transmission predates the written record systems of literate society. Oral transmission preserves material sometimes over generations, although often with variations. Memory plays a large part in the recitation and preservation of orally transmitted material.

Ottava Rima: An eight-line stanza of poetry composed in iambic pentameter (a five-foot line in which each foot consists of an unaccented syllable followed by an accented syllable), following the *abababcc* rhyme scheme.

Oxymoron: A phrase combining two contradictory terms. Oxymorons may be intentional or unintentional.

P

Pantheism: The idea that all things are both a manifestation or revelation of God and a part of God at the same time. Pantheism was a common attitude in the early societies of Egypt, India, and Greece—the term derives from the Greek *pan* meaning "all" and *theos* meaning "deity." It later became a significant part of the Christian faith.

Parable: A story intended to teach a moral lesson or answer an ethical question.

Paradox: A statement that appears illogical or contradictory at first, but may actually point to an underlying truth.

Parallelism: A method of comparison of two ideas in which each is developed in the same grammatical structure.

Parnassianism: A mid nineteenth-century movement in French literature. Followers of the movement stressed adherence to well-defined artistic forms as a reaction against the often chaotic expression of the artist's ego that dominated the work of the Romantics. The Parnassians also rejected the moral, ethical, and social themes exhibited in the works of French Romantics such as Victor Hugo. The aesthetic doctrines of the Parnassians strongly influenced the later symbolist and decadent movements.

Parody: In literary criticism, this term refers to an imitation of a serious literary work or the signature style of a particular author in a ridiculous manner. A typical parody adopts the style of the original and applies it to an inappropriate subject for humorous effect. Parody is a form of satire and could be considered the literary equivalent of a caricature or cartoon.

Pastoral: A term derived from the Latin word "pastor," meaning shepherd. A pastoral is a literary composition on a rural theme. The conventions of the pastoral were originated by the third-century Greek poet Theocritus, who wrote about the experiences, love affairs, and pastimes of Sicilian shepherds. In a pastoral, characters and language of a courtly nature are often placed in a simple setting. The term pastoral is also used to classify dramas, elegies, and lyrics that exhibit the use of country settings and shepherd characters.

Pathetic Fallacy: A term coined by English critic John Ruskin to identify writing that falsely endows nonhuman things with human intentions and feelings, such as "angry clouds" and "sad trees."

Pen Name: See *Pseudonym*

Pentameter: See *Meter*

Persona: A Latin term meaning "mask." *Personae* are the characters in a fictional work of literature. The *persona* generally functions as a mask through which the author tells a story in a voice other than his or her own. A *persona* is usually either a character in a story who acts as a narrator or an "implied author," a voice created by the author to act as the narrator for himself or herself.

Personae: See *Persona*

Personal Point of View: See *Point of View*

Personification: A figure of speech that gives human qualities to abstract ideas, animals, and inanimate objects.

Petrarchan Sonnet: See *Sonnet*

Phenomenology: A method of literary criticism based on the belief that things have no existence outside of human consciousness or awareness. Proponents of this theory believe that art is a process that takes place in the mind of the observer as he or she contemplates an object rather than a quality of the object itself.

Plagiarism: Claiming another person's written material as one's own. Plagiarism can take the form of direct, word-for-word copying or the theft of the substance or idea of the work.

Platonic Criticism: A form of criticism that stresses an artistic work's usefulness as an agent of social engineering rather than any quality or value of the work itself.

Platonism: The embracing of the doctrines of the philosopher Plato, popular among the poets of the Renaissance and the Romantic period. Platonism is more flexible than Aristotelian Criticism and places more emphasis on the supernatural and unknown aspects of life.

Plot: In literary criticism, this term refers to the pattern of events in a narrative or drama. In its simplest sense, the plot guides the author in composing the work and helps the reader follow the work. Typically, plots exhibit causality and unity and have a beginning, a middle, and an end. Sometimes, however, a plot may consist of a series of disconnected events, in which case it is known as an "episodic plot."

Poem: In its broadest sense, a composition utilizing rhyme, meter, concrete detail, and expressive language to create a literary experience with emotional and aesthetic appeal.

Poet: An author who writes poetry or verse. The term is also used to refer to an artist or writer who has an exceptional gift for expression, imagination, and energy in the making of art in any form.

Poete maudit: A term derived from Paul Verlaine's *Les poetes maudits* (*The Accursed Poets*), a collection of essays on the French symbolist writers Stephane Mallarme, Arthur Rimbaud, and Tristan Corbiere. In the sense intended by Verlaine, the poet is "accursed" for choosing to explore extremes of human experience outside of middle-class society.

Poetic Fallacy: See *Pathetic Fallacy*

Poetic Justice: An outcome in a literary work, not necessarily a poem, in which the good are rewarded and the evil are punished, especially in ways that particularly fit their virtues or crimes.

Poetic License: Distortions of fact and literary convention made by a writer—not always a poet—for the sake of the effect gained. Poetic license is closely related to the concept of "artistic freedom."

Poetics: This term has two closely related meanings. It denotes (1) an aesthetic theory in literary criticism about the essence of poetry or (2) rules prescribing the proper methods, content, style, or diction of poetry. The term poetics may also refer to theories about literature in general, not just poetry.

Poetry: In its broadest sense, writing that aims to present ideas and evoke an emotional experience in the reader through the use of meter, imagery, connotative and concrete words, and a carefully constructed structure based on rhythmic patterns. Poetry typically relies on words and expressions that have several layers of meaning. It also makes use of the effects of regular rhythm on the ear and may make a strong appeal to the senses through the use of imagery.

Point of View: The narrative perspective from which a literary work is presented to the reader. There are four traditional points of view. The "third person omniscient" gives the reader a "godlike" perspective, unrestricted by time or place, from which to see actions and look into the minds of characters. This allows the author to comment openly on characters and events in the work. The "third-person" point of view presents the events of the story from outside of any single character's perception, much like the omniscient point of view, but the reader must understand the action as it takes place and without any special insight into characters' minds or motivations. The "first person" or "personal" point of view relates events as they are perceived by a single character. The main character "tells" the story and may offer opinions about the action and characters which differ from those of the author. Much less common than omniscient, third person, and first person is the "second-person" point of view, wherein the author tells the story as if it is happening to the reader.

Polemic: A work in which the author takes a stand on a controversial subject, such as abortion or religion. Such works are often extremely argumentative or provocative.

Pornography: Writing intended to provoke feelings of lust in the reader. Such works are often condemned by critics and teachers, but those which can be shown to have literary value are viewed less harshly.

Post-Aesthetic Movement: An artistic response made by African Americans to the black aesthetic movement of the 1960s and early 1970s. Writers since that time have adopted a somewhat different tone in their work, with less emphasis placed on the disparity between black and white in the United States. In the words of post-aesthetic authors such as Toni Morrison, John Edgar Wideman, and Kristin Hunter, African Americans are portrayed as looking inward for answers to their own questions, rather than always looking to the outside world.

Postmodernism: Writing from the 1960s forward characterized by experimentation and continuing to apply some of the fundamentals of modernism, which included existentialism and alienation. Postmodernists have gone a step further in the rejection of tradition begun with the modernists by also rejecting traditional forms, preferring the antinovel over the novel and the antihero over the hero.

Pre-Raphaelites: A circle of writers and artists in mid nineteenth-century England. Valuing the pre-Renaissance artistic qualities of religious symbolism, lavish pictorialism, and natural sensuousness, the Pre-Raphaelites cultivated a sense of mystery and melancholy that influenced later writers associated with the Symbolist and Decadent movements.

Primitivism: The belief that primitive peoples were nobler and less flawed than civilized peoples because they had not been subjected to the corrupt influence of society.

Projective Verse: A form of free verse in which the poet's breathing pattern determines the lines of the poem. Poets who advocate projective verse are against all formal structures in writing, including meter and form.

Prologue: An introductory section of a literary work. It often contains information establishing the situation of the characters or presents information about the setting, time period, or action. In drama, the prologue is spoken by a chorus or by one of the principal characters.

Prose: A literary medium that attempts to mirror the language of everyday speech. It is distinguished from poetry by its use of unmetered, unrhymed language consisting of logically related sentences. Prose is usually grouped into paragraphs that form a cohesive whole such as an essay or a novel.

Prosopopoeia: See *Personification*

Protagonist: The central character of a story who serves as a focus for its themes and incidents and as the principal rationale for its development. The protagonist is sometimes referred to in discussions of modern literature as the hero or antihero.

Proverb: A brief, sage saying that expresses a truth about life in a striking manner.

Pseudonym: A name assumed by a writer, most often intended to prevent his or her identification as the author of a work. Two or more authors may work together under one pseudonym, or an author may use a different name for each genre he or she publishes in. Some publishing companies maintain "house pseudonyms," under which any number of authors may write installations in a series. Some authors also choose a pseudonym over their real names the way an actor may use a stage name.

Pun: A play on words that have similar sounds but different meanings.

Pure Poetry: poetry written without instructional intent or moral purpose that aims only to please a reader by its imagery or musical flow. The term pure poetry is used as the antonym of the term "didacticism."

Q

Quatrain: A four-line stanza of a poem or an entire poem consisting of four lines.

R

Realism: A nineteenth-century European literary movement that sought to portray familiar characters, situations, and settings in a realistic manner. This was done primarily by using an objective narrative point of view and through the buildup of accurate detail. The standard for success of any realistic work depends on how faithfully it transfers common experience into fictional forms. The realistic method may be altered or extended, as in stream of consciousness writing, to record highly subjective experience.

Refrain: A phrase repeated at intervals throughout a poem. A refrain may appear at the end of each stanza or at less regular intervals. It may be altered slightly at each appearance.

Renaissance: The period in European history that marked the end of the Middle Ages. It began in Italy in the late fourteenth century. In broad terms, it is usually seen as spanning the fourteenth, fifteenth, and sixteenth centuries, although it did not reach Great Britain, for example, until the 1480s or so. The Renaissance saw an awakening in almost every sphere of human activity, especially science, philosophy, and the arts. The period is best defined by the emergence of a general philosophy that emphasized the importance of the intellect, the individual, and world affairs. It contrasts strongly with the medieval worldview, characterized by the dominant concerns of faith, the social collective, and spiritual salvation.

Repartee: Conversation featuring snappy retorts and witticisms.

Restoration: See *Restoration Age*

Restoration Age: A period in English literature beginning with the crowning of Charles II in 1660 and running to about 1700. The era, which was characterized by a reaction against Puritanism, was the first great age of the comedy of manners. The finest literature of the era is typically witty and urbane, and often lewd.

Rhetoric: In literary criticism, this term denotes the art of ethical persuasion. In its strictest sense, rhetoric adheres to various principles developed since classical times for arranging facts and ideas in a clear, persuasive, appealing manner. The term is also used to refer to effective prose in general and theories of or methods for composing effective prose.

Rhetorical Question: A question intended to provoke thought, but not an expressed answer, in the reader. It is most commonly used in oratory and other persuasive genres.

Rhyme: When used as a noun in literary criticism, this term generally refers to a poem in which words sound identical or very similar and appear in parallel positions in two or more lines. Rhymes are classified into different types according to where they fall in a line or stanza or according to the degree of similarity they exhibit in their spellings and sounds. Some major types of rhyme are "masculine" rhyme, "feminine" rhyme, and "triple" rhyme. In a masculine rhyme, the rhyming sound falls in a single accented syllable, as with "heat" and "eat." Feminine rhyme is a rhyme of two syllables, one stressed and one unstressed, as with "merry" and "tarry." Triple rhyme matches the sound of the accented syllable and the two unaccented syllables that follow: "narrative" and "declarative."

Rhyme Royal: A stanza of seven lines composed in iambic pentameter and rhymed *ababbcc*. The name is said to be a tribute to King James I of Scotland, who made much use of the form in his poetry.

Rhyme Scheme: See *Rhyme*

Rhythm: A regular pattern of sound, time intervals, or events occurring in writing, most often and most discernably in poetry. Regular, reliable rhythm is known to be soothing to humans, while interrupted, unpredictable, or rapidly changing rhythm is disturbing. These effects are known to authors, who use them to produce a desired reaction in the reader.

Rococo: A style of European architecture that flourished in the eighteenth century, especially in

France. The most notable features of *rococo* are its extensive use of ornamentation and its themes of lightness, gaiety, and intimacy. In literary criticism, the term is often used disparagingly to refer to a decadent or overly ornamental style.

Romance:

Romantic Age: See *Romanticism*

Romanticism: This term has two widely accepted meanings. In historical criticism, it refers to a European intellectual and artistic movement of the late eighteenth and early nineteenth centuries that sought greater freedom of personal expression than that allowed by the strict rules of literary form and logic of the eighteenth-century Neoclassicists. The Romantics preferred emotional and imaginative expression to rational analysis. They considered the individual to be at the center of all experience and so placed him or her at the center of their art. The Romantics believed that the creative imagination reveals nobler truths—unique feelings and attitudes—than those that could be discovered by logic or by scientific examination. Both the natural world and the state of childhood were important sources for revelations of "eternal truths." "Romanticism" is also used as a general term to refer to a type of sensibility found in all periods of literary history and usually considered to be in opposition to the principles of classicism. In this sense, Romanticism signifies any work or philosophy in which the exotic or dreamlike figure strongly, or that is devoted to individualistic expression, self-analysis, or a pursuit of a higher realm of knowledge than can be discovered by human reason.

Romantics: See *Romanticism*

Russian Symbolism: A Russian poetic movement, derived from French symbolism, that flourished between 1894 and 1910. While some Russian Symbolists continued in the French tradition, stressing aestheticism and the importance of suggestion above didactic intent, others saw their craft as a form of mystical worship, and themselves as mediators between the supernatural and the mundane.

S

Satire: A work that uses ridicule, humor, and wit to criticize and provoke change in human nature and institutions. There are two major types of satire: "formal" or "direct" satire speaks directly to the reader or to a character in the work; "indirect" satire relies upon the ridiculous behavior of its characters to make its point. Formal satire is further divided into two manners: the "Horatian," which

ridicules gently, and the "Juvenalian," which derides its subjects harshly and bitterly.

Scansion: The analysis or "scanning" of a poem to determine its meter and often its rhyme scheme. The most common system of scansion uses accents (slanted lines drawn above syllables) to show stressed syllables, breves (curved lines drawn above syllables) to show unstressed syllables, and vertical lines to separate each foot.

Second Person: See *Point of View*

Semiotics: The study of how literary forms and conventions affect the meaning of language.

Sestet: Any six-line poem or stanza.

Setting: The time, place, and culture in which the action of a narrative takes place. The elements of setting may include geographic location, characters' physical and mental environments, prevailing cultural attitudes, or the historical time in which the action takes place.

Shakespearean Sonnet: See *Sonnet*

Signifying Monkey: A popular trickster figure in black folklore, with hundreds of tales about this character documented since the nineteenth century.

Simile: A comparison, usually using "like" or "as," of two essentially dissimilar things, as in "coffee as cold as ice" or "He sounded like a broken record."

Slang: A type of informal verbal communication that is generally unacceptable for formal writing. Slang words and phrases are often colorful exaggerations used to emphasize the speaker's point; they may also be shortened versions of an often-used word or phrase.

Slant Rhyme: See *Consonance*

Slave Narrative: Autobiographical accounts of American slave life as told by escaped slaves. These works first appeared during the abolition movement of the 1830s through the 1850s.

Social Realism: See *Socialist Realism*

Socialist Realism: The Socialist Realism school of literary theory was proposed by Maxim Gorky and established as a dogma by the first Soviet Congress of Writers. It demanded adherence to a communist worldview in works of literature. Its doctrines required an objective viewpoint comprehensible to the working classes and themes of social struggle featuring strong proletarian heroes.

Soliloquy: A monologue in a drama used to give the audience information and to develop the speaker's character. It is typically a projection of the speaker's innermost thoughts. Usually delivered while the speaker is alone on stage, a soliloquy is intended to present an illusion of unspoken reflection.

Sonnet: A fourteen-line poem, usually composed in iambic pentameter, employing one of several rhyme schemes. There are three major types of sonnets, upon which all other variations of the form are based: the "Petrarchan" or "Italian" sonnet, the "Shakespearean" or "English" sonnet, and the "Spenserian" sonnet. A Petrarchan sonnet consists of an octave rhymed *abbaabba* and a "sestet" rhymed either *cdecde, cdccdc,* or *cdedce.* The octave poses a question or problem, relates a narrative, or puts forth a proposition; the sestet presents a solution to the problem, comments upon the narrative, or applies the proposition put forth in the octave. The Shakespearean sonnet is divided into three quatrains and a couplet rhymed *abab cdcd efef gg.* The couplet provides an epigrammatic comment on the narrative or problem put forth in the quatrains. The Spenserian sonnet uses three quatrains and a couplet like the Shakespearean, but links their three rhyme schemes in this way: *abab bcbc cdcd ee.* The Spenserian sonnet develops its theme in two parts like the Petrarchan, its final six lines resolving a problem, analyzing a narrative, or applying a proposition put forth in its first eight lines.

Spenserian Sonnet: See *Sonnet*

Spenserian Stanza: A nine-line stanza having eight verses in iambic pentameter, its ninth verse in iambic hexameter, and the rhyme scheme *ababbcbcc.*

Spondee: In poetry meter, a foot consisting of two long or stressed syllables occurring together. This form is quite rare in English verse, and is usually composed of two monosyllabic words.

Sprung Rhythm: Versification using a specific number of accented syllables per line but disregarding the number of unaccented syllables that fall in each line, producing an irregular rhythm in the poem.

Stanza: A subdivision of a poem consisting of lines grouped together, often in recurring patterns of rhyme, line length, and meter. Stanzas may also serve as units of thought in a poem much like paragraphs in prose.

Stereotype: A stereotype was originally the name for a duplication made during the printing process; this led to its modern definition as a person or thing that is (or is assumed to be) the same as all others of its type.

Stream of Consciousness: A narrative technique for rendering the inward experience of a character. This technique is designed to give the impression of an ever-changing series of thoughts, emotions, images, and memories in the spontaneous and seemingly illogical order that they occur in life.

Structuralism: A twentieth-century movement in literary criticism that examines how literary texts arrive at their meanings, rather than the meanings themselves. There are two major types of structuralist analysis: one examines the way patterns of linguistic structures unify a specific text and emphasize certain elements of that text, and the other interprets the way literary forms and conventions affect the meaning of language itself.

Structure: The form taken by a piece of literature. The structure may be made obvious for ease of understanding, as in nonfiction works, or may be obscured for artistic purposes, as in some poetry or seemingly "unstructured" prose.

Sturm und Drang: A German term meaning "storm and stress." It refers to a German literary movement of the 1770s and 1780s that reacted against the order and rationalism of the enlightenment, focusing instead on the intense experience of extraordinary individuals.

Style: A writer's distinctive manner of arranging words to suit his or her ideas and purpose in writing. The unique imprint of the author's personality upon his or her writing, style is the product of an author's way of arranging ideas and his or her use of diction, different sentence structures, rhythm, figures of speech, rhetorical principles, and other elements of composition.

Subject: The person, event, or theme at the center of a work of literature. A work may have one or more subjects of each type, with shorter works tending to have fewer and longer works tending to have more.

Subjectivity: Writing that expresses the author's personal feelings about his subject, and which may or may not include factual information about the subject.

Surrealism: A term introduced to criticism by Guillaume Apollinaire and later adopted by Andre Breton. It refers to a French literary and artistic movement founded in the 1920s. The Surrealists sought to express unconscious thoughts and feelings in their works. The best-known technique used for achieving this aim was automatic writing—transcriptions of spontaneous outpourings from the unconscious. The Surrealists proposed to unify the contrary levels of conscious and unconscious, dream and reality, objectivity and subjectivity into a new level of "super-realism."

Suspense: A literary device in which the author maintains the audience's attention through the buildup of events, the outcome of which will soon be revealed.

Syllogism: A method of presenting a logical argument. In its most basic form, the syllogism consists of a major premise, a minor premise, and a conclusion.

Symbol: Something that suggests or stands for something else without losing its original identity. In literature, symbols combine their literal meaning with the suggestion of an abstract concept. Literary symbols are of two types: those that carry complex associations of meaning no matter what their contexts, and those that derive their suggestive meaning from their functions in specific literary works.

Symbolism: This term has two widely accepted meanings. In historical criticism, it denotes an early modernist literary movement initiated in France during the nineteenth century that reacted against the prevailing standards of realism. Writers in this movement aimed to evoke, indirectly and symbolically, an order of being beyond the material world of the five senses. Poetic expression of personal emotion figured strongly in the movement, typically by means of a private set of symbols uniquely identifiable with the individual poet. The principal aim of the Symbolists was to express in words the highly complex feelings that grew out of everyday contact with the world. In a broader sense, the term "symbolism" refers to the use of one object to represent another.

Symbolist: See *Symbolism*

Symbolist Movement: See *Symbolism*

Sympathetic Fallacy: See *Affective Fallacy*

T

Tanka: A form of Japanese poetry similar to *haiku*. A *tanka* is five lines long, with the lines containing five, seven, five, seven, and seven syllables respectively.

Terza Rima: A three-line stanza form in poetry in which the rhymes are made on the last word of each line in the following manner: the first and third lines of the first stanza, then the second line of the first stanza and the first and third lines of the second stanza, and so on with the middle line of any

stanza rhyming with the first and third lines of the following stanza.

Tetrameter: See *Meter*

Textual Criticism: A branch of literary criticism that seeks to establish the authoritative text of a literary work. Textual critics typically compare all known manuscripts or printings of a single work in order to assess the meanings of differences and revisions. This procedure allows them to arrive at a definitive version that (supposedly) corresponds to the author's original intention.

Theme: The main point of a work of literature. The term is used interchangeably with thesis.

Thesis: A thesis is both an essay and the point argued in the essay. Thesis novels and thesis plays share the quality of containing a thesis which is supported through the action of the story.

Third Person: See *Point of View*

Tone: The author's attitude toward his or her audience may be deduced from the tone of the work. A formal tone may create distance or convey politeness, while an informal tone may encourage a friendly, intimate, or intrusive feeling in the reader. The author's attitude toward his or her subject matter may also be deduced from the tone of the words he or she uses in discussing it.

Tragedy: A drama in prose or poetry about a noble, courageous hero of excellent character who, because of some tragic character flaw or *hamartia*, brings ruin upon him- or herself. Tragedy treats its subjects in a dignified and serious manner, using poetic language to help evoke pity and fear and bring about catharsis, a purging of these emotions. The tragic form was practiced extensively by the ancient Greeks. In the Middle Ages, when classical works were virtually unknown, tragedy came to denote any works about the fall of persons from exalted to low conditions due to any reason: fate, vice, weakness, etc. According to the classical definition of tragedy, such works present the "pathetic"—that which evokes pity—rather than the tragic. The classical form of tragedy was revived in the sixteenth century; it flourished especially on the Elizabethan stage. In modern times, dramatists have attempted to adapt the form to the needs of modern society by drawing their heroes from the ranks of ordinary men and women and defining the nobility of these heroes in terms of spirit rather than exalted social standing.

Tragic Flaw: In a tragedy, the quality within the hero or heroine which leads to his or her downfall.

Transcendentalism: An American philosophical and religious movement, based in New England from around 1835 until the Civil War. Transcendentalism was a form of American romanticism that had its roots abroad in the works of Thomas Carlyle, Samuel Coleridge, and Johann Wolfgang von Goethe. The Transcendentalists stressed the importance of intuition and subjective experience in communication with God. They rejected religious dogma and texts in favor of mysticism and scientific naturalism. They pursued truths that lie beyond the "colorless" realms perceived by reason and the senses and were active social reformers in public education, women's rights, and the abolition of slavery.

Trickster: A character or figure common in Native American and African literature who uses his ingenuity to defeat enemies and escape difficult situations. Tricksters are most often animals, such as the spider, hare, or coyote, although they may take the form of humans as well.

Trimeter: See *Meter*

Triple Rhyme: See *Rhyme*

Trochee: See *Foot*

U

Understatement: See *Irony*

Unities: Strict rules of dramatic structure, formulated by Italian and French critics of the Renaissance and based loosely on the principles of drama discussed by Aristotle in his *Poetics*. Foremost among these rules were the three unities of action, time, and place that compelled a dramatist to: (1) construct a single plot with a beginning, middle, and end that details the causal relationships of action and character; (2) restrict the action to the events of a single day; and (3) limit the scene to a single place or city. The unities were observed faithfully by continental European writers until the Romantic Age, but they were never regularly observed in English drama. Modern dramatists are typically more concerned with a unity of impression or emotional effect than with any of the classical unities.

Urban Realism: A branch of realist writing that attempts to accurately reflect the often harsh facts of modern urban existence.

Utopia: A fictional perfect place, such as "paradise" or "heaven."

Utopian: See *Utopia*

Utopianism: See *Utopia*

V

Verisimilitude: Literally, the appearance of truth. In literary criticism, the term refers to aspects of a work of literature that seem true to the reader.

Vers de societe: See *Occasional Verse*

Vers libre: See *Free Verse*

Verse: A line of metered language, a line of a poem, or any work written in verse.

Versification: The writing of verse. Versification may also refer to the meter, rhyme, and other mechanical components of a poem.

Victorian: Refers broadly to the reign of Queen Victoria of England (1837–1901) and to anything with qualities typical of that era. For example, the qualities of smug narrowmindedness, bourgeois materialism, faith in social progress, and priggish morality are often considered Victorian. This stereotype is contradicted by such dramatic intellectual developments as the theories of Charles Darwin, Karl Marx, and Sigmund Freud (which stirred strong debates in England) and the critical attitudes of serious Victorian writers like Charles Dickens and George Eliot. In literature, the Victorian Period was the great age of the English novel, and the latter part of the era saw the rise of movements such as decadence and symbolism.

Victorian Age: See *Victorian*

Victorian Period: See *Victorian*

W

Weltanschauung: A German term referring to a person's worldview or philosophy.

Weltschmerz: A German term meaning "world pain." It describes a sense of anguish about the nature of existence, usually associated with a melancholy, pessimistic attitude.

Z

Zarzuela: A type of Spanish operetta.

Zeitgeist: A German term meaning "spirit of the time." It refers to the moral and intellectual trends of a given era.

Cumulative Author/Title Index

A

Accounting (Alegría): V21
Ackerman, Diane
  On Location in the Loire Valley:
  V19
Acosta, Teresa Palomo
  My Mother Pieced Quilts: V12
Address to the Angels (Kumin):
  V18
The Afterlife (Collins): V18
An African Elegy (Duncan): V13
Ah, Are You Digging on My Grave?
  (Hardy): V4
Ai
  Reunions with a Ghost: V16
Air for Mercury (Hillman): V20
Akhmatova, Anna
  Midnight Verses: V18
Alabama Centennial (Madgett): V10
The Alchemy of Day (Hébert): V20
Alegría, Claribel
  Accounting: V21
Alexander, Elizabeth
  The Toni Morrison Dreams: V22
All It Takes (Phillips): V23
Allegory (Bang): V23
American Poetry (Simpson): V7
Ammons, A. R.
  The City Limits: V19
An Arundel Tomb (Larkin): V12
Anasazi (Snyder): V9
And What If I Spoke of Despair
  (Bass): V19
Angelou, Maya
  Harlem Hopscotch: V2
  On the Pulse of Morning: V3
Angle of Geese (Momaday): V2

Annabel Lee (Poe): V9
Anniversary (Harjo): V15
Anonymous
  Barbara Allan: V7
  Go Down, Moses: V11
  Lord Randal: V6
  The Seafarer: V8
  Sir Patrick Spens: V4
  Swing Low Sweet Chariot: V1
Anorexic (Boland): V12
Answers to Letters (Tranströmer):
  V21
Any Human to Another (Cullen): V3
A Pièd (McElroy): V3
Apple sauce for Eve (Piercy): V22
Arnold, Matthew
  Dover Beach: V2
Ars Poetica (MacLeish): V5
The Arsenal at Springfield
  (Longfellow): V17
The Art of the Novel (Sajé): V23
Arvio, Sarah
  Memory: V21
As I Walked Out One Evening
  (Auden): V4
Ashbery, John
  Paradoxes and Oxymorons: V11
Astonishment (Szymborska): V15
At the Bomb Testing Site (Stafford):
  V8
Atwood, Margaret
  Siren Song: V7
Auden, W. H.
  As I Walked Out One Evening:
  V4
  Funeral Blues: V10
  Musée des Beaux Arts: V1
  The Unknown Citizen: V3

Aurora Leigh (Browning): V23
Auto Wreck (Shapiro): V3
Autumn Begins in Martins Ferry,
  Ohio (Wright): V8

B

Ballad of Orange and Grape
  (Rukeyser): V10
Baraka, Amiri
  In Memory of Radio: V9
Barbara Allan (Anonymous): V7
Barbie Doll (Piercy): V9
Ballad of Birmingham (Randall): V5
Bang, Mary Jo
  Allegory: V23
Barrett, Elizabeth
  Sonnet 43: V2
The Base Stealer (Francis): V12
Bashō, Matsuo
  Falling Upon Earth: V2
  The Moon Glows the Same: V7
  Temple Bells Die Out: V18
Bass, Ellen
  And What If I Spoke of Despair:
  V19
Baudelaire, Charles
  Hymn to Beauty: V21
The Bean Eaters (Brooks): V2
Because I Could Not Stop for Death
  (Dickinson): V2
Bedtime Story (MacBeth): V8
Behn, Robin
  Ten Years after Your Deliberate
  Drowning: V21
La Belle Dame sans Merci (Keats):
  V17

The Bells (Poe): V3
Beowulf (Wilbur): V11
Beware: Do Not Read This Poem
    (Reed): V6
Beware of Ruins (Hope): V8
Bialosky, Jill
    Seven Seeds: V19
Bidwell Ghost (Erdrich): V14
Biele, Joelle
    Rapture: V21
Birch Canoe (Revard): V5
Birches (Frost): V13
Birney, Earle
    Vancouver Lights: V8
A Birthday (Rossetti): V10
Bishop, Elizabeth
    Brazil, January 1, 1502: V6
    Filling Station: V12
Blackberrying (Plath): V15
Black Zodiac (Wright): V10
Blake, William
    The Lamb: V12
    The Tyger: V2
A Blessing (Wright): V7
Blood Oranges (Mueller): V13
The Blue Rim of Memory (Levertov):
    V17
Blumenthal, Michael
    Inventors: V7
Bly, Robert
    Come with Me: V6
    Driving to Town Late to Mail a
        Letter: V17
Bogan, Louise
    Words for Departure: V21
Boland, Eavan
    Anorexic: V12
    It's a Woman's World: V22
The Boy (Hacker): V19
Bradstreet, Anne
    To My Dear and Loving
        Husband: V6
Brazil, January 1, 1502 (Bishop): V6
Bright Star! Would I Were Steadfast
    as Thou Art (Keats): V9
Brooke, Rupert
    The Soldier: V7
Brooks, Gwendolyn
    The Bean Eaters: V2
    The Sonnet-Ballad: V1
    Strong Men, Riding Horses: V4
    We Real Cool: V6
Brouwer, Joel
    Last Request: V14
Browning, Elizabeth Barrett
    Aurora Leigh: V23
    Sonnet 43: V2
    Sonnet XXIX: V16
Browning, Robert
    My Last Duchess: V1
    Porphyria's Lover: V15
Burns, Robert
    A Red, Red Rose: V8

Business (Cruz): V16
The Bustle in a House (Dickinson):
    V10
But Perhaps God Needs the Longing
    (Sachs): V20
Butcher Shop (Simic): V7
Byrne, Elena Karina
    In Particular: V20
Byron, Lord
    The Destruction of Sennacherib:
        V1
    She Walks in Beauty: V14

C

The Canterbury Tales (Chaucer): V14
Cargoes (Masefield): V5
Carroll, Lewis
    Jabberwocky: V11
Carson, Anne
    New Rule: V18
Carver, Raymond
    The Cobweb: V17
Casey at the Bat (Thayer): V5
Castillo, Ana
    While I Was Gone a War Began:
        V21
Cavafy, C. P.
    Ithaka: V19
Cavalry Crossing a Ford (Whitman):
    V13
Celan, Paul
    Late and Deep: V21
The Charge of the Light Brigade
    (Tennyson): V1
Chaucer, Geoffrey
    The Canterbury Tales: V14
Chicago (Sandburg): V3
Childhood (Rilke): V19
Chocolates (Simpson): V11
The Cinnamon Peeler (Ondaatje):
    V19
Cisneros, Sandra
    Once Again I Prove the Theory of
        Relativity: V19
The City Limits (Ammons): V19
Clifton, Lucille
    Climbing: V14
    Miss Rosie: V1
Climbing (Clifton): V14
The Cobweb (Carver): V17
Coleridge, Samuel Taylor
    Kubla Khan: V5
    The Rime of the Ancient Mariner:
        V4
Colibrí (Espada): V16
Collins, Billy
    The Afterlife: V18
Come with Me (Bly): V6
The Constellation Orion (Kooser):
    V8
Concord Hymn (Emerson): V4
The Conquerors (McGinley): V13

The Continuous Life (Strand): V18
Cool Tombs (Sandburg): V6
The Country Without a Post Office
    (Shahid Ali): V18
Courage (Sexton): V14
The Courage That My Mother Had
    (Millay): V3
Crane, Stephen
    War Is Kind: V9
The Creation (Johnson): V1
Creeley, Robert
    Fading Light: V21
The Cremation of Sam McGee
    (Service): V10
The Crime Was in Granada
    (Machado): V23
Cruz, Victor Hernandez
    Business: V16
Cullen, Countee
    Any Human to Another: V3
cummings, e. e.
    i was sitting in mcsorley's: V13
    l(a: V1
    maggie and milly and molly and
        may: V12
    old age sticks: V3
    somewhere i have never
        travelled,gladly beyond: V19
The Czar's Last Christmas Letter. A
    Barn in the Urals (Dubie):
    V12

D

The Darkling Thrush (Hardy): V18
Darwin in 1881 (Schnackenberg):
    V13
Dawe, Bruce
    Drifters: V10
Daylights (Warren): V13
Dear Reader (Tate): V10
The Death of the Ball Turret Gunner
    (Jarrell): V2
The Death of the Hired Man (Frost):
    V4
Death Sentences (Lazić): V22
Deep Woods (Nemerov): V14
Dennis, Carl
    The God Who Loves You: V20
The Destruction of Sennacherib
    (Byron): V1
Dickey, James
    The Heaven of Animals: V6
    The Hospital Window: V11
Dickinson, Emily
    Because I Could Not Stop for
        Death: V2
    The Bustle in a House: V10
    "Hope" Is the Thing with
        Feathers: V3
    I felt a Funeral, in my Brain: V13
    I Heard a Fly Buzz—When I
        Died—: V5

Much Madness Is Divinest Sense:
V16
My Life Closed Twice Before Its
Close: V8
A Narrow Fellow in the Grass:
V11
The Soul Selects Her Own
Society: V1
There's a Certain Slant of Light:
V6
This Is My Letter to the World:
V4
Digging (Heaney): V5
Dobyns, Stephen
It's like This: V23
Do Not Go Gentle into that Good
Night (Thomas): V1
Donne, John
Holy Sonnet 10: V2
A Valediction: Forbidding
Mourning: V11
Dove, Rita
Geometry: V15
This Life: V1
Dover Beach (Arnold): V2
Dream Variations (Hughes): V15
Drifters (Dawe): V10
A Drink of Water (Heaney): V8
Drinking Alone Beneath the Moon
(Po): V20
Driving to Town Late to Mail a
Letter (Bly): V17
Drought Year (Wright): V8
Dubie, Norman
The Czar's Last Christmas Letter.
A Barn in the Urals: V12
Du Bois, W. E. B.
The Song of the Smoke: V13
Duncan, Robert
An African Elegy: V13
Dugan, Alan
How We Heard the Name: V10
Dulce et Decorum Est (Owen): V10
Dunn, Stephen
The Reverse Side: V21
Duration (Paz): V18

E

The Eagle (Tennyson): V11
Early in the Morning (Lee): V17
Easter 1916 (Yeats): V5
Eating Poetry (Strand): V9
Elegy for My Father, Who is Not
Dead (Hudgins): V14
Elegy Written in a Country
Churchyard (Gray): V9
An Elementary School Classroom in
a Slum (Spender): V23
Eliot, T. S.
Journey of the Magi: V7
The Love Song of J. Alfred
Prufrock: V1

The Waste Land: V20
Emerson, Ralph Waldo
Concord Hymn: V4
The Rhodora: V17
Erdrich, Louise
Bidwell Ghost: V14
Espada, Martín
Colibrí: V16
We Live by What We See at
Night: V13
Ethics (Pastan): V8
The Exhibit (Mueller): V9

F

Facing It (Komunyakaa): V5
Fading Light (Creeley): V21
Falling Upon Earth (Bashō): V2
A Far Cry from Africa (Walcott): V6
A Farewell to English (Hartnett):
V10
Farrokhzaad, Faroogh
A Rebirth: V21
Fenton, James
The Milkfish Gatherers: V11
Fern Hill (Thomas): V3
Fiddler Crab (Jacobsen): V23
Fifteen (Stafford): V2
Filling Station (Bishop): V12
Fire and Ice (Frost): V7
The Fish (Moore): V14
For a New Citizen of These United
States (Lee): V15
For An Assyrian Frieze (Viereck):
V9
For Jean Vincent D'abbadie, Baron
St.-Castin (Nowlan): V12
For Jennifer, 6, on the Teton (Hugo):
V17
For the Union Dead (Lowell): V7
For the White poets who would be
Indian (Rose): V13
The Force That Through the Green
Fuse Drives the Flower
(Thomas): V8
Forché, Carolyn
The Garden Shukkei-en: V18
The Forest (Stewart): V22
Four Mountain Wolves (Silko): V9
Francis, Robert
The Base Stealer: V12
Frost, Robert
Birches: V13
The Death of the Hired Man: V4
Fire and Ice: V7
Mending Wall: V5
Nothing Gold Can Stay: V3
Out, Out—: V10
The Road Not Taken: V2
Stopping by Woods on a Snowy
Evening: V1
The Wood-Pile: V6
Funeral Blues (Auden): V10

G

Gacela of the Dark Death (García
Lorca): V20
Gallagher, Tess
I Stop Writing the Poem: V16
García Lorca, Federico
Gacela of the Dark Death: V20
The Garden Shukkei-en (Forché):
V18
Geometry (Dove): V15
Ghazal (Spires): V21
Ginsberg, Allen
A Supermarket in California: V5
Giovanni, Nikki
Knoxville, Tennessee: V17
Glück, Louise
The Gold Lily: V5
The Mystery: V15
Go Down, Moses (Anonymous): V11
The God Who Loves You (Dennis):
V20
The Gold Lily (Glück): V5
A Grafted Tongue (Montague): V12
Graham, Jorie
The Hiding Place: V10
Mind: V17
Gray, Thomas
Elegy Written in a Country
Churchyard: V9
The Greatest Grandeur (Rogers):
V18
Gregg, Linda
A Thirst Against: V20
Grennan, Eamon
Station: V21
Gunn, Thom
The Missing: V9

H

H.D.
Helen: V6
Hacker, Marilyn
The Boy: V19
Hahn, Kimiko
Pine: V23
Hall, Donald
Names of Horses: V8
Hardy, Thomas
Ah, Are You Digging on My
Grave?: V4
The Darkling Thrush: V18
The Man He Killed: V3
Harjo, Joy
Anniversary: V15
Harlem (Hughes): V1
Harlem Hopscotch (Angelou): V2
Hartnett, Michael
A Farewell to English: V10
Hashimoto, Sharon
What I Would Ask My Husband's
Dead Father: V22

Having a Coke with You (O'Hara):
    V12
Having it Out with Melancholy
    (Kenyon): V17
Hawk Roosting (Hughes): V4
Hayden, Robert
    Those Winter Sundays: V1
Heaney, Seamus
    Digging: V5
    A Drink of Water: V8
    Midnight: V2
    The Singer's House: V17
Hébert, Anne
    The Alchemy of Day: V20
Hecht, Anthony
    "More Light! More Light!": V6
The Heaven of Animals (Dickey): V6
Helen (H.D.): V6
Herbert, Zbigniew
    Why The Classics: V22
Herrick, Robert
    *To the Virgins, to Make Much of
    Time:* V13
The Hiding Place (Graham): V10
High Windows (Larkin): V3
The Highwayman (Noyes): V4
Hillman, Brenda
    Air for Mercury: V20
Hirsch, Edward
    Omen: V22
Hirshfield, Jane
    *Three Times My Life Has
    Opened:* V16
His Speed and Strength (Ostriker): V19
Hoagland, Tony
    Social Life: V19
Holmes, Oliver Wendell
    Old Ironsides: V9
Holy Sonnet 10 (Donne): V2
Hope, A. D.
    Beware of Ruins: V8
Hope Is a Tattered Flag (Sandburg):
    V12
"Hope" Is the Thing with Feathers
    (Dickinson): V3
The Horizons of Rooms (Merwin): V15
The Hospital Window (Dickey): V11
Housman, A. E.
    To an Athlete Dying Young: V7
    When I Was One-and-Twenty: V4
How We Heard the Name (Dugan):
    V10
Howe, Marie
    What Belongs to Us: V15
Hudgins, Andrew
    *Elegy for My Father, Who is Not
    Dead:* V14
Hugh Selwyn Mauberley (Pound): V16
Hughes, Langston
    Dream Variations: V15
    Harlem: V1
    Mother to Son: V3
    The Negro Speaks of Rivers: V10
    Theme for English B: V6

Hughes, Ted
    Hawk Roosting: V4
    Perfect Light: V19
Hugo, Richard
    For Jennifer, 6, on the Teton: V17
Hunger in New York City (Ortiz): V4
Huong, Ho Xuan
    Spring-Watching Pavilion: V18
Hurt Hawks (Jeffers): V3
Hymn to Aphrodite (Sappho): V20
Hymn to Beauty (Baudelaire): V21

I

I felt a Funeral, in my Brain
    (Dickinson): V13
I Go Back to May 1937 (Olds): V17
I Hear America Singing (Whitman):
    V3
I Heard a Fly Buzz—When I Died—
    (Dickinson): V5
I Stop Writing the Poem (Gallagher):
    V16
i was sitting in mcsorley's
    (cummings): V13
The Idea of Order at Key West
    (Stevens): V13
If (Kipling): V22
In a Station of the Metro (Pound): V2
In Flanders Fields (McCrae): V5
In Memory of Radio (Baraka): V9
In Particular (Byrne): V20
In the Land of Shinar (Levertov): V7
In the Suburbs (Simpson): V14
Incident in a Rose Garden (Justice):
    V14
Inventors (Blumentha): V7
An Irish Airman Foresees His Death
    (Yeats): V1
Island of the Three Marias (Ríos):
    V11
Ithaka (Cavafy): V19
It's a Woman's World (Boland): V22
It's like This (Dobyns): V23

J

Jabberwocky (Carroll): V11
Jacobsen, Josephine
    Fiddler Crab: V23
Jarrell, Randall
    *The Death of the Ball Turret
    Gunner:* V2
Jeffers, Robinson
    Hurt Hawks: V3
    Shine Perishing Republic: V4
Johnson, James Weldon
    The Creation: V1
Jonson, Ben
    Song: To Celia: V23
Journey of the Magi (Eliot): V7
Justice, Donald
    Incident in a Rose Garden: V14

K

Keats, John
    La Belle Dame sans Merci: V17
    *Bright Star! Would I Were
    Steadfast as Thou Art:* V9
    Ode on a Grecian Urn: V1
    Ode to a Nightingale: V3
    *When I Have Fears that I May
    Cease to Be:* V2
Kelly, Brigit Pegeen
    The Satyr's Heart: V22
Kenyon, Jane
    Having it Out with Melancholy:
    V17
    *"Trouble with Math in a One-
    Room Country School":* V9
Kilroy (Viereck): V14
King James Bible
    Psalm 8: V9
    Psalm 23: V4
Kinnell, Galway
    Saint Francis and the Sow: V9
Kipling, Rudyard
    If: V22
Kizer, Carolyn
    To an Unknown Poet: V18
Knoxville, Tennessee (Giovanni): V17
Koch, Kenneth
    Paradiso: V20
Komunyakaa, Yusef
    Ode to a Drum: V20
Kooser, Ted
    The Constellation Orion: V8
Komunyakaa, Yusef
    Facing It: V5
Kubla Khan (Coleridge): V5
Kumin, Maxine
    Address to the Angels: V18
Kunitz, Stanley
    The War Against the Trees: V11
Kyger, Joanne
    September: V23

L

l(a (cummings): V1
The Lady of Shalott (Tennyson): V15
Lake (Warren): V23
The Lake Isle of Innisfree (Yeats):
    V15
The Lamb (Blake): V12
Lament for the Dorsets (Purdy): V5
Landscape with Tractor (Taylor):
    V10
Lanier, Sidney
    Song of the Chattahoochee: V14
Larkin, Philip
    An Arundel Tomb: V12
    High Windows: V3
    Toads: V4
The Last Question (Parker): V18
Last Request (Brouwer): V14

Late and Deep (Celan): V21
Lawrence, D. H.
    Piano: V6
Layton, Irving
    A Tall Man Executes a Jig: V12
Lazić, Radmila
    Death Sentences: V22
Leda and the Swan (Yeats): V13
Lee, Li-Young
    Early in the Morning: V17
    *For a New Citizen of These
        United States:* V15
    The Weight of Sweetness: V11
Lepidopterology (Svenbro): V23
Levertov, Denise
    The Blue Rim of Memory: V17
    In the Land of Shinar: V7
Leviathan (Merwin): V5
Levine, Philip
    Starlight: V8
Longfellow, Henry Wadsworth
    The Arsenal at Springfield: V17
    Paul Revere's Ride: V2
    A Psalm of Life: V7
Lord Randal (Anonymous): V6
Lorde, Audre
    What My Child Learns of the Sea:
        V16
Lost in Translation (Merrill): V23
Lost Sister (Song): V5
The Love Song of J. Alfred Prufrock
    (Eliot): V1
Lowell, Robert
    For the Union Dead: V7
    *The Quaker Graveyard in
        Nantucket:* V6
Loy, Mina
    Moreover, the Moon: V20

M

MacBeth, George
    Bedtime Story: V8
Machado, Antonio
    The Crime Was in Granada: V23
MacLeish, Archibald
    Ars Poetica: V5
Madgett, Naomi Long
    Alabama Centennial: V10
maggie and milly and molly and may
    (cummings): V12
Malroux, Claire
    Morning Walk: V21
The Man He Killed (Hardy): V3
Marlowe, Christopher
    *The Passionate Shepherd to His
        Love:* V22
A Martian Sends a Postcard Home
    (Raine): V7
Marvell, Andrew
    To His Coy Mistress: V5
Masefield, John
    Cargoes: V5

Maternity (Swir): V21
Matsuo Bashō
    Falling Upon Earth: V2
    The Moon Glows the Same: V7
    Temple Bells Die Out: V18
Maxwell, Glyn
    The Nerve: V23
McCrae, John
    In Flanders Fields: V5
McElroy, Colleen
    A Pièd: V3
McGinley, Phyllis
    The Conquerors: V13
    *Reactionary Essay on Applied
        Science:* V9
McKay, Claude
    The Tropics in New York: V4
Meeting the British (Muldoon): V7
Memoir (Van Duyn): V20
Memory (Arvio): V21
Mending Wall (Frost): V5
Merlin Enthralled (Wilbur): V16
Merriam, Eve
    Onomatopoeia: V6
Merrill, James
    Lost in Translation: V23
Merwin, W. S.
    The Horizons of Rooms: V15
    Leviathan: V5
Metamorphoses (Ovid): V22
Midnight (Heaney): V2
Midnight Verses (Akhmatova): V18
The Milkfish Gatherers (Fenton): V11
Millay, Edna St. Vincent
    *The Courage That My Mother
        Had:* V3
    Wild Swans: V17
Milosz, Czeslaw
    Song of a Citizen: V16
Milton, John
    [On His Blindness] Sonnet 16: V3
    *On His Having Arrived at the Age
        of Twenty-Three:* V17
Mind (Graham): V17
Mirror (Plath): V1
Miss Rosie (Clifton): V1
The Missing (Gunn): V9
Momaday, N. Scott
    Angle of Geese: V2
    *To a Child Running With
        Outstretched Arms in Canyon
        de Chelly:* V11
Montague, John
    A Grafted Tongue: V12
Montale, Eugenio
    On the Threshold: V22
The Moon Glows the Same (Bashō):
    V7
Moore, Marianne
    The Fish: V14
    Poetry: V17
"More Light! More Light!" (Hecht):
    V6

Moreover, the Moon (Loy): V20
Morning Walk (Malroux): V21
Mother to Son (Hughes): V3
Much Madness Is Divinest Sense
    (Dickinson): V16
Muldoon, Paul
    Meeting the British: V7
    Pineapples and Pomegranates:
        V22
Mueller, Lisel
    Blood Oranges: V13
    The Exhibit: V9
Musée des Beaux Arts (Auden): V1
Music Lessons (Oliver): V8
My Father's Song (Ortiz): V16
My Last Duchess (Browning): V1
*My Life Closed Twice Before Its
    Close* (Dickinson): V8
My Mother Pieced Quilts (Acosta):
    V12
My Papa's Waltz (Roethke): V3
The Mystery (Glück): V15

N

Names of Horses (Hall): V8
A Narrow Fellow in the Grass
    (Dickinson): V11
The Negro Speaks of Rivers
    (Hughes): V10
Nemerov, Howard
    Deep Woods: V14
    The Phoenix: V10
Neruda, Pablo
    Tonight I Can Write: V11
The Nerve (Maxwell): V23
New Rule (Carson): V18
Not Waving but Drowning (Smith):
    V3
Nothing Gold Can Stay (Frost): V3
Nowlan, Alden
    *For Jean Vincent D'abbadie,
        Baron St.-Castin:* V12
Noyes, Alfred
    The Highwayman: V4
The Nymph's Reply to the Shepherd
    (Raleigh): V14

O

O Captain! My Captain! (Whitman):
    V2
Ode on a Grecian Urn (Keats): V1
Ode to a Drum (Komunyakaa): V20
Ode to a Nightingale (Keats): V3
Ode to the West Wind (Shelley): V2
O'Hara, Frank
    Having a Coke with You: V12
    Why I Am Not a Painter: V8
old age sticks (cummings): V3
Old Ironsides (Holmes): V9
Olds, Sharon
    I Go Back to May 1937: V17

Oliver, Mary
    Music Lessons: V8
    Wild Geese: V15
Omen (Hirsch): V22
On Freedom's Ground (Wilbur): V12
[On His Blindness] Sonnet 16
    (Milton): V3
On His Having Arrived at the Age of
    Twenty-Three (Milton): V17
On Location in the Loire Valley
    (Ackerman): V19
On the Pulse of Morning (Angelou):
    V3
On the Threshold (Montale): V22
Once Again I Prove the Theory of
    Relativity (Cisneros): V19
Ondaatje, Michael
    The Cinnamon Peeler: V19
    To a Sad Daughter: V8
Onomatopoeia (Merriam): V6
Ordinary Words (Stone): V19
Ortiz, Simon
    Hunger in New York City: V4
    My Father's Song: V16
Ostriker, Alicia
    His Speed and Strength: V19
Out, Out— (Frost): V10
Overture to a Dance of Locomotives
    (Williams): V11
Ovid, (Naso, Publius Ovidius)
    Metamorphoses: V22
Owen, Wilfred
    Dulce et Decorum Est: V10
Oysters (Sexton): V4

P

Paradiso (Koch): V20
Paradoxes and Oxymorons
    (Ashbery): V11
Parker, Dorothy
    The Last Question: V18
The Passionate Shepherd to His Love
    (Marlowe): V22
Pastan, Linda
    Ethics: V8
Paul Revere's Ride (Longfellow): V2
Pavese, Cesare
    Two Poems for T.: V20
Paz, Octavio
    Duration: V18
Perfect Light (Hughes): V19
Phillips, Carl
    All It Takes: V23
The Phoenix (Nemerov): V10
Piano (Lawrence): V6
Piercy, Marge
    Apple sauce for Eve: V22
    Barbie Doll: V9
Pine (Hahn): V23
Pineapples and Pomegranates
    (Muldoon): V22

Pinsky, Robert
    Song of Reasons: V18
Plath, Sylvia
    Blackberrying: V15
    Mirror: V1
A Psalm of Life (Longfellow): V7
Po, Li
    Drinking Alone Beneath the
      Moon: V20
Poe, Edgar Allan
    Annabel Lee: V9
    The Bells: V3
    The Raven: V1
Poetry (Moore): V17
Pope, Alexander
    The Rape of the Lock: V12
Porphyria's Lover (Browning): V15
Pound, Ezra
    Hugh Selwyn Mauberley: V16
    In a Station of the Metro: V2
    The River-Merchant's Wife: A
      Letter: V8
Practice (Voigt): V23
Proem (Tennyson): V19
Psalm 8 (King James Bible): V9
Psalm 23 (King James Bible): V4
Purdy, Al
    Lament for the Dorsets: V5
    Wilderness Gothic: V12

Q

The Quaker Graveyard in Nantucket
    (Lowell): V6
Queen-Ann's-Lace (Williams): V6

R

Raine, Craig
    A Martian Sends a Postcard
      Home: V7
Raleigh, Walter, Sir
    The Nymph's Reply to the
      Shepherd: V14
Randall, Dudley
    Ballad of Birmingham: V5
The Rape of the Lock (Pope): V12
Rapture (Biele): V21
The Raven (Poe): V1
Reactionary Essay on Applied
    Science (McGinley): V9
A Rebirth (Farrokhzaad): V21
A Red, Red Rose (Burns): V8
The Red Wheelbarrow (Williams):
    V1
Reed, Ishmael
    Beware: Do Not Read This Poem:
      V6
Remember (Rossetti): V14
Reunions with a Ghost (Ai): V16
Revard, Carter
    Birch Canoe: V5
The Reverse Side (Dunn): V21

The Rhodora (Emerson): V17
Rich, Adrienne
    Rusted Legacy: V15
Richard Cory (Robinson): V4
Rilke, Rainer Maria
    Childhood: V19
The Rime of the Ancient Mariner
    (Coleridge): V4
Ríos, Alberto
    Island of the Three Marias: V11
The River-Merchant's Wife: A Letter
    (Pound): V8
The Road Not Taken (Frost): V2
Robinson, E. A.
    Richard Cory: V4
Roethke, Theodore
    My Papa's Waltz: V3
Rogers, Pattiann
    The Greatest Grandeur: V18
Rose, Wendy
    For the White poets who would be
      Indian: V13
Rossetti, Christina
    A Birthday: V10
    Remember: V14
Rukeyser, Muriel
    Ballad of Orange and Grape: V10
Rusted Legacy (Rich): V15

S

Sachs, Nelly
    But Perhaps God Needs the
      Longing: V20
Sailing to Byzantium (Yeats): V2
Saint Francis and the Sow (Kinnell):
    V9
Sajé, Natasha
    The Art of the Novel: V23
Salter, Mary Jo
    Trompe l'Oeil: V22
Sandburg, Carl
    Chicago: V3
    Cool Tombs: V6
    Hope Is a Tattered Flag: V12
Sappho
    Hymn to Aphrodite: V20
The Satyr's Heart (Kelly): V22
Schnackenberg, Gjertrud
    Darwin in 1881: V13
The Seafarer (Anonymous): V8
The Second Coming (Yeats): V7
September (Kyger): V23
Service, Robert W.
    The Cremation of Sam McGee:
      V10
Seven Seeds (Bialosky): V19
Sexton, Anne
    Courage: V14
    Oysters: V4
Shahid Ali, Agha
    The Country Without a Post
      Office: V18

Shakespeare, William
  Sonnet 18: V2
  Sonnet 19: V9
  Sonnet 29: V8
  Sonnet 30: V4
  Sonnet 55: V5
  Sonnet 116: V3
  Sonnet 130: V1
Shapiro, Karl
  Auto Wreck: V3
She Walks in Beauty (Byron): V14
Shelley, Percy Bysshe
  Ode to the West Wind: V2
Shine, Perishing Republic (Jeffers):
  V4
Silko, Leslie Marmon
  Four Mountain Wolves: V9
  Story from Bear Country: V16
Simic, Charles
  Butcher Shop: V7
Simpson, Louis
  American Poetry: V7
  Chocolates: V11
  In the Suburbs: V14
The Singer's House (Heaney): V17
Sir Patrick Spens (Anonymous): V4
Siren Song (Atwood): V7
60 (Tagore): V18
Small Town with One Road (Soto):
  V7
Smart and Final Iris (Tate): V15
Smith, Stevie
  Not Waving but Drowning: V3
Snyder, Gary
  Anasazi: V9
  True Night: V19
Social Life (Hoagland): V19
The Soldier (Brooke): V7
*somewhere i have never
  travelled,gladly beyond*
  (cummings): V19
Song, Cathy
  Lost Sister: V5
Song of a Citizen (Milosz): V16
Song of Reasons (Pinsky): V18
Song of the Chattahoochee (Lanier):
  V14
The Song of the Smoke (Du Bois):
  V13
Song: To Celia (Jonson): V23
Sonnet 16 [On His Blindness]
  (Milton): V3
Sonnet 18 (Shakespeare): V2
Sonnet 19 (Shakespeare): V9
Sonnet 30 (Shakespeare): V4
Sonnet 29 (Shakespeare): V8
Sonnet XXIX (Browning): V16
Sonnet 43 (Browning): V2
Sonnet 55 (Shakespeare): V5
Sonnet 116 (Shakespeare): V3
Sonnet 130 (Shakespeare): V1
The Sonnet-Ballad (Brooks): V1
Soto, Gary
  Small Town with One Road: V7

The Soul Selects Her Own Society
  (Dickinson): V1
Southbound on the Freeway
  (Swenson): V16
Spender, Stephen
  An Elementary School Classroom
    in a Slum: V23
Spires, Elizabeth
  Ghazal: V21
Spring-Watching Pavilion (Huong):
  V18
Stafford, William
  At the Bomb Testing Site: V8
  Fifteen: V2
  Ways to Live: V16
Starlight (Levine): V8
Station (Grennan): V21
Stevens, Wallace
  The Idea of Order at Key West:
    V13
  Sunday Morning: V16
Stewart, Susan
  The Forest: V22
Stone, Ruth
  Ordinary Words: V19
*Stopping by Woods on a Snowy
  Evening* (Frost): V1
Story from Bear Country (Silko):
  V16
Strand, Mark
  The Continuous Life: V18
  Eating Poetry: V9
Strong Men, Riding Horses (Brooks):
  V4
Sunday Morning (Stevens): V16
A Supermarket in California
  (Ginsberg): V5
Svenbro, Jesper
  Lepidopterology: V23
Swenson, May
  Southbound on the Freeway: V16
Swing Low Sweet Chariot
  (Anonymous): V1
Swir, Anna
  Maternity: V21
Szymborska, Wislawa
  Astonishment: V15

T

Tagore, Rabindranath
  60: V18
A Tall Man Executes a Jig (Layton):
  V12
Tate, James
  Dear Reader: V10
  Smart and Final Iris: V15
Taylor, Henry
  Landscape with Tractor: V10
Tears, Idle Tears (Tennyson): V4
Teasdale, Sara
  There Will Come Soft Rains: V14
Temple Bells Die Out (Bashō): V18

*Ten Years after Your Deliberate
  Drowning* (Behn): V21
Tennyson, Alfred, Lord
  The Charge of the Light Brigade:
    V1
  The Eagle: V11
  The Lady of Shalott: V15
  Proem: V19
  Tears, Idle Tears: V4
  Ulysses: V2
Thayer, Ernest Lawrence
  Casey at the Bat: V5
Theme for English B (Hughes): V6
There's a Certain Slant of Light
  (Dickinson): V6
There Will Come Soft Rains
  (Teasdale): V14
A Thirst Against (Gregg): V20
This Life (Dove): V1
Thomas, Dylan
  Do Not Go Gentle into that Good
    Night: V1
  Fern Hill: V3
  The Force That Through the
    Green Fuse Drives the
    Flower: V8
Those Winter Sundays (Hayden): V1
Three Times My Life Has Opened
  (Hirshfield): V16
Tintern Abbey (Wordsworth): V2
*To a Child Running With
  Outstretched Arms in Canyon
  de Chelly* (Momaday): V11
To a Sad Daughter (Ondaatje): V8
To an Athlete Dying Young
  (Housman): V7
To an Unknown Poet (Kizer): V18
To His Coy Mistress (Marvell): V5
*To His Excellency General
  Washington* (Wheatley): V13
To My Dear and Loving Husband
  (Bradstreet): V6
*To the Virgins, to Make Much of
  Time* (Herrick): V13
Toads (Larkin): V4
Tonight I Can Write (Neruda): V11
The Toni Morrison Dreams
  (Alexander): V22
Tranströmer, Tomas
  Answers to Letters: V21
Trompe l'Oeil (Salter): V22
The Tropics in New York (McKay):
  V4
True Night (Snyder): V19
Two Poems for T. (Pavese): V20
The Tyger (Blake): V2

U

Ulysses (Tennyson): V2
Ungaretti, Giuseppe
  Variations on Nothing: V20
The Unknown Citizen (Auden): V3

V

A Valediction: Forbidding Mourning
(Donne): V11
Van Duyn, Mona
Memoir: V20
Vancouver Lights (Birney): V8
Variations on Nothing (Ungaretti):
V20
Viereck, Peter
For An Assyrian Frieze: V9
Kilroy: V14
Voigt, Ellen Bryant
Practice: V23

W

Walcott, Derek
A Far Cry from Africa: V6
The War Against the Trees (Kunitz):
V11
War Is Kind (Crane): V9
Warren, Rosanna
Daylights: V13
Lake: V23
The Waste Land (Eliot): V20
Ways to Live (Stafford): V16
We Live by What We See at Night
(Espada): V13
We Real Cool (Brooks): V6
The Weight of Sweetness (Lee): V11

What Belongs to Us (Howe): V15
*What I Would Ask My Husband's
Dead Father* (Hashimoto):
V22
What My Child Learns of the Sea
(Lorde): V16
Wheatley, Phillis
*To His Excellency General
Washington:* V13
*When I Have Fears That I May
Cease to Be* (Keats): V2
*When I Heard the Learn'd
Astronomer* (Whitman): V22
When I Was One-and-Twenty
(Housman): V4
While I Was Gone a War Began
(Castillo): V21
Whitman, Walt
Cavalry Crossing a Ford: V13
I Hear America Singing: V3
O Captain! My Captain!: V2
*When I Heard the Learn'd
Astronomer:* V22
Why I Am Not a Painter (O'Hara):
V8
Why The Classics (Herbert): V22
Wilbur, Richard
Beowulf: V11
Merlin Enthralled: V16
On Freedom's Ground: V12
Wild Geese (Oliver): V15

Wild Swans (Millay): V17
Wilderness Gothic (Purdy): V12
Williams, William Carlos
*Overture to a Dance of
Locomotives:* V11
Queen-Ann's-Lace: V6
The Red Wheelbarrow: V1
The Wood-Pile (Frost): V6
Words for Departure (Bogan): V21
Wordsworth, William
*Lines Composed a Few Miles
above Tintern Abbey:* V2
Wright, Charles
Black Zodiac: V10
Wright, James
A Blessing: V7
*Autumn Begins in Martins Ferry,
Ohio:* V8
Wright, Judith
Drought Year: V8

Y

Yeats, William Butler
Easter 1916: V5
*An Irish Airman Foresees His
Death:* V1
The Lake Isle of Innisfree: V15
Leda and the Swan: V13
Sailing to Byzantium: V2
The Second Coming: V7

Cumulative Nationality/Ethnicity Index

Acoma Pueblo

Ortiz, Simon
  Hunger in New York City: V4
  My Father's Song: V16

African American

Ai
  Reunions with a Ghost: V16
Angelou, Maya
  Harlem Hopscotch: V2
  On the Pulse of Morning: V3
Baraka, Amiri
  In Memory of Radio: V9
Brooks, Gwendolyn
  The Bean Eaters: V2
  The Sonnet-Ballad: V1
  Strong Men, Riding Horses: V4
  We Real Cool: V6
Clifton, Lucille
  Climbing: V14
  Miss Rosie: V1
Cullen, Countee
  Any Human to Another: V3
Dove, Rita
  Geometry: V15
  This Life: V1
Giovanni, Nikki
  Knoxville, Tennessee: V17
Hayden, Robert
  Those Winter Sundays: V1
Hughes, Langston
  Dream Variations: V15
  Harlem: V1
  Mother to Son: V3
  The Negro Speaks of Rivers: V10
  Theme for English B: V6

Johnson, James Weldon
  The Creation: V1
Komunyakaa, Yusef
  Facing It: V5
  Ode to a Drum: V20
Lorde, Audre
  What My Child Learns of the Sea:
    V16
Madgett, Naomi Long
  Alabama Centennial: V10
McElroy, Colleen
  A Pièd: V3
Phillips, Carl
  All It Takes: V23
Randall, Dudley
  Ballad of Birmingham: V5
Reed, Ishmael
  Beware: Do Not Read This Poem:
    V6

American

Ackerman, Diane
  On Location in the Loire Valley:
    V19
Acosta, Teresa Palomo
  My Mother Pieced Quilts: V12
Ai
  Reunions with a Ghost: V16
Alegría, Claribel
  Accounting: V21
Alexander, Elizabeth
  The Toni Morrison Dreams: V22
Ammons, A. R.
  The City Limits: V19
Angelou, Maya
  Harlem Hopscotch: V2
  On the Pulse of Morning: V3

Ashbery, John
  Paradoxes and Oxymorons: V11
Arvio, Sarah
  Memory: V21
Auden, W. H.
  As I Walked Out One Evening: V4
  Musée des Beaux Arts: V1
  The Unknown Citizen: V3
Bang, Mary Jo
  Allegory: V23
Bass, Ellen
  And What If I Spoke of Despair:
    V19
Behn, Robin
  Ten Years after Your Deliberate
    Drowning: V21
Bialosky, Jill
  Seven Seeds: V19
Biele, Joelle
  Rapture: V21
Bishop, Elizabeth
  Brazil, January 1, 1502: V6
  Filling Station: V12
Blumenthal, Michael
  Inventors: V7
Bly, Robert
  Come with Me: V6
  Driving to Town Late to Mail a
    Letter: V17
Bogan, Louise
  Words for Departure: V21
Bradstreet, Anne
  To My Dear and Loving
    Husband: V6
Brooks, Gwendolyn
  The Bean Eaters: V2
  The Sonnet-Ballad: V1
  Strong Men, Riding Horses: V4
  We Real Cool: V6

Brouwer, Joel
  Last Request: V14
Byrne, Elena Karina
  In Particular: V20
Carver, Raymond
  The Cobweb: V17
Castillo, Ana
  While I Was Gone a War Began:
    V21
Cisneros, Sandra
  *Once Again I Prove the Theory of
    Relativity:* V19
Clifton, Lucille
  Climbing: V14
  Miss Rosie: V1
Collins, Billy
  The Afterlife: V18
Crane, Stephen
  War Is Kind: V9
Creeley, Robert
  Fading Light: V21
Cruz, Victor Hernandez
  Business: V16
Cullen, Countee
  Any Human to Another: V3
cummings, e. e.
  i was sitting in mcsorley's: V13
  l(a: V1
  *maggie and milly and molly and
    may:* V12
  old age sticks: V3
  *somewhere i have never
    travelled,gladly beyond:* V19
Dennis, Carl
  The God Who Loves You: V20
Dickey, James
  The Heaven of Animals: V6
  The Hospital Window: V11
Dickinson, Emily
  *Because I Could Not Stop for
    Death:* V2
  The Bustle in a House: V10
  *"Hope" Is the Thing with
    Feathers:* V3
  I felt a Funeral, in my Brain: V13
  *I Heard a Fly Buzz—When I
    Died—:* V5
  Much Madness Is Divinest Sense:
    V16
  *My Life Closed Twice Before Its
    Close:* V8
  A Narrow Fellow in the Grass:
    V11
  *The Soul Selects Her Own
    Society:* V1
  There's a Certain Slant of Light:
    V6
  This Is My Letter to the World: V4
Dobyns, Stephen
  It's like This: V23
Dove, Rita
  Geometry: V15
  This Life: V1

Dubie, Norman
  *The Czar's Last Christmas Letter.
    A Barn in the Urals:* V12
Du Bois, W. E. B.
  The Song of the Smoke: V13
Dugan, Alan
  How We Heard the Name: V10
Duncan, Robert
  An African Elegy: V13
Dunn, Stephen
  The Reverse Side: V21
Eliot, T. S.
  Journey of the Magi: V7
  *The Love Song of J. Alfred
    Prufrock:* V1
Emerson, Ralph Waldo
  Concord Hymn: V4
  The Rhodora: V17
Erdrich, Louise
  Bidwell Ghost: V14
Espada, Martín
  Colibrí: V16
  *We Live by What We See at
    Night:* V13
Forché, Carolyn
  The Garden Shukkei-En: V18
Francis, Robert
  The Base Stealer: V12
Frost, Robert
  Birches: V13
  The Death of the Hired Man: V4
  Fire and Ice: V7
  Mending Wall: V5
  Nothing Gold Can Stay: V3
  Out, Out—: V10
  The Road Not Taken: V2
  *Stopping by Woods on a Snowy
    Evening:* V1
  The Wood-Pile: V6
Gallagher, Tess
  I Stop Writing the Poem: V16
Ginsberg, Allen
  A Supermarket in California: V5
Giovanni, Nikki
  Knoxville, Tennessee: V17
Glück, Louise
  The Gold Lily: V5
  The Mystery: V15
Graham, Jorie
  The Hiding Place: V10
  Mind: V17
Gregg, Linda
  A Thirst Against: V20
Gunn, Thom
  The Missing: V9
H.D.
  Helen: V6
Hacker, Marilyn
  The Boy: V19
Hahn, Kimiko
  Pine: V23
Hall, Donald
  Names of Horses: V8

Harjo, Joy
  Anniversary: V15
Hashimoto, Sharon
  *What I Would Ask My Husband's
    Dead Father:* V22
Hayden, Robert
  Those Winter Sundays: V1
Hecht, Anthony
  "More Light! More Light!": V6
Hillman, Brenda
  Air for Mercury: V20
Hirsch, Edward
  Omen: V22
Hirshfield, Jane
  *Three Times My Life Has
    Opened:* V16
Hoagland, Tony
  Social Life: V19
Holmes, Oliver Wendell
  Old Ironsides: V9
Howe, Marie
  What Belongs to Us: V15
Hudgins, Andrew
  *Elegy for My Father, Who is Not
    Dead:* V14
Hughes, Langston
  Dream Variations: V15
  Harlem: V1
  Mother to Son: V3
  The Negro Speaks of Rivers: V10
  Theme for English B: V6
Hugo, Richard
  For Jennifer, 6, on the Teton:
    V17
Jarrell, Randall
  *The Death of the Ball Turret
    Gunner:* V2
Jeffers, Robinson
  Hurt Hawks: V3
  Shine, Perishing Republic: V4
Johnson, James Weldon
  The Creation: V1
Justice, Donald
  Incident in a Rose Garden: V14
Kelly, Brigit Pegeen
  The Satyr's Heart: V22
Kenyon, Jane
  Having it Out with Melancholy:
    V17
  *"Trouble with Math in a One-
    Room Country School":* V9
Kinnell, Galway
  Saint Francis and the Sow: V9
Kizer, Carolyn
  To An Unknown Poet: V18
Koch, Kenneth
  Paradiso: V20
Komunyakaa, Yusef
  Facing It: V5
  Ode to a Drum: V20
Kooser, Ted
  The Constellation Orion: V8
Kumin, Maxine
  Address to the Angels: V18

Kunitz, Stanley
    The War Against the Trees: V11
Kyger, Joanne
    September: V23
Lanier, Sidney
    Song of the Chattahoochee: V14
Lee, Li-Young
    Early in the Morning: V17
    *For a New Citizen of These
        United States:* V15
    The Weight of Sweetness: V11
Levertov, Denise
    The Blue Rim of Memory: V17
    In the Land of Shinar: V7
Levine, Philip
    Starlight: V8
Longfellow, Henry Wadsworth
    The Arsenal at Springfield: V17
    Paul Revere's Ride: V2
    A Psalm of Life: V7
Lorde, Audre
    What My Child Learns of the Sea:
        V16
Lowell, Robert
    For the Union Dead: V7
    *The Quaker Graveyard in
        Nantucket:* V6
Loy, Mina
    Moreover, the Moon: V20
MacLeish, Archibald
    Ars Poetica: V5
Madgett, Naomi Long
    Alabama Centennial: V10
McElroy, Colleen
    A Pièd: V3
McGinley, Phyllis
    The Conquerors: V13
    *Reactionary Essay on Applied
        Science:* V9
McKay, Claude
    The Tropics in New York: V4
Merriam, Eve
    Onomatopoeia: V6
Merrill, James
    Lost in Translation: V23
Merwin, W. S.
    The Horizons of Rooms: V15
    Leviathan: V5
Millay, Edna St. Vincent
    *The Courage that My Mother
        Had:* V3
    Wild Swans: V17
Momaday, N. Scott
    Angle of Geese: V2
    *To a Child Running With
        Outstretched Arms in Canyon
        de Chelly:* V11
Montague, John
    A Grafted Tongue: V12
Moore, Marianne
    The Fish: V14
    Poetry: V17
Mueller, Lisel
    The Exhibit: V9

Nemerov, Howard
    Deep Woods: V14
    The Phoenix: V10
O'Hara, Frank
    Having a Coke with You: V12
    Why I Am Not a Painter: V8
Olds, Sharon
    I Go Back to May 1937: V17
Oliver, Mary
    Music Lessons: V8
    Wild Geese: V15
Ortiz, Simon
    Hunger in New York City: V4
    My Father's Song: V16
Ostriker, Alicia
    His Speed and Strength: V19
Parker, Dorothy
    The Last Question: V18
Pastan, Linda
    Ethics: V8
Phillips, Carl
    All It Takes: V23
Piercy, Marge
    Apple sauce for Eve: V22
    Barbie Doll: V9
Pinsky, Robert
    Song of Reasons: V18
Plath, Sylvia
    Blackberrying: V15
    Mirror: V1
Poe, Edgar Allan
    Annabel Lee: V9
    The Bells: V3
    The Raven: V1
Pound, Ezra
    Hugh Selwyn Mauberley: V16
    In a Station of the Metro: V2
    *The River-Merchant's Wife: A
        Letter:* V8
Randall, Dudley
    Ballad of Birmingham: V5
Reed, Ishmael
    Beware: Do Not Read This Poem:
        V6
Revard, Carter
    Birch Canoe: V5
Rich, Adrienne
    Rusted Legacy: V15
Ríos, Alberto
    Island of the Three Marias: V11
Robinson, E. A.
    Richard Cory: V4
Roethke, Theodore
    My Papa's Waltz: V3
Rogers, Pattiann
    The Greatest Grandeur: V18
Rose, Wendy
    *For the White poets who would be
        Indian:* V13
Rukeyser, Muriel
    Ballad of Orange and Grape:
        V10
Salter, Mary Jo
    Trompe l'Oeil: V22

Sandburg, Carl
    Chicago: V3
    Cool Tombs: V6
    Hope Is a Tattered Flag: V12
Schnackenberg, Gjertrud
    Darwin in 1881: V13
Sexton, Anne
    Courage: V14
    Oysters: V4
Shapiro, Karl
    Auto Wreck: V3
Silko, Leslie Marmon
    Four Mountain Wolves: V9
    Story from Bear Country: V16
Simic, Charles
    Butcher Shop: V7
Simpson, Louis
    American Poetry: V7
    Chocolates: V11
    In the Suburbs: V14
Snyder, Gary
    Anasazi: V9
    True Night: V19
Song, Cathy
    Lost Sister: V5
Soto, Gary
    Small Town with One Road: V7
Spires, Elizabeth
    Ghazal: V21
Stafford, William
    At the Bomb Testing Site: V8
    Fifteen: V2
    Ways to Live: V16
Stevens, Wallace
    The Idea of Order at Key West:
        V13
    Sunday Morning: V16
Stewart, Susan
    The Forest: V22
Stone, Ruth
    Ordinary Words: V19
Strand, Mark
    The Continuous Life: V18
Swenson, May
    Southbound on the Freeway: V16
Tate, James
    Dear Reader: V10
    Smart and Final Iris: V15
Taylor, Henry
    Landscape with Tractor: V10
Teasdale, Sara
    There Will Come Soft Rains: V14
Thayer, Ernest Lawrence
    Casey at the Bat: V5
Van Duyn, Mona
    Memoir: V20
Viereck, Peter
    For An Assyrian Frieze: V9
    Kilroy: V14
Voigt, Ellen Bryant
    Practice: V23
Warren, Rosanna
    Daylights: V13
    Lake: V23

Wheatley, Phillis
  To His Excellency General
    Washington: V13
Whitman, Walt
  Cavalry Crossing a Ford: V13
  I Hear America Singing: V3
  O Captain! My Captain!: V2
  When I Heard the Learn'd
    Astronomer: V22
Wilbur, Richard
  Beowulf: V11
  Merlin Enthralled: V16
  On Freedom's Ground: V12
Williams, William Carlos
  Overture to a Dance of
    Locomotives: V11
  Queen-Ann's-Lace: V6
  The Red Wheelbarrow: V1
Wright, Charles
  Black Zodiac: V10
Wright, James
  A Blessing: V7
  Autumn Begins in Martins Ferry,
    Ohio: V8

Asian American

Hahn, Kimiko
  Pine: V23
Hashimoto, Sharon
  What I Would Ask My Husband's
    Dead Father: V22

Australian

Dawe, Bruce
  Drifters: V10
Hope, A. D.
  Beware of Ruins: V8
Wright, Judith
  Drought Year: V8

Canadian

Atwood, Margaret
  Siren Song: V7
Birney, Earle
  Vancouver Lights: V8
Carson, Anne
  New Rule: V18
Hébert, Anne
  The Alchemy of Day: V20
Jacobsen, Josephine
  Fiddler Crab: V23
Layton, Irving
  A Tall Man Executes a Jig: V12
McCrae, John
  In Flanders Fields: V5
Nowlan, Alden
  For Jean Vincent D'abbadie,
    Baron St.-Castin: V12
Purdy, Al
  Lament for the Dorsets: V5
  Wilderness Gothic: V12

Strand, Mark
  Eating Poetry: V9

Canadian, Sri Lankan

Ondaatje, Michael
  The Cinnamon Peeler: V19
  To a Sad Daughter: V8

Chilean

Neruda, Pablo
  Tonight I Can Write: V11

Chinese

Po, Li
  Drinking Alone Beneath the
    Moon: V20

Egyptian, Greek

Cavafy, C. P.
  Ithaka: V19

English

Alleyn, Ellen
  A Birthday: V10
Arnold, Matthew
  Dover Beach: V2
Auden, W. H.
  As I Walked Out One Evening:
    V4
  Funeral Blues: V10
  Musée des Beaux Arts: V1
  The Unknown Citizen: V3
Blake, William
  The Lamb: V12
  The Tyger: V2
Bradstreet, Anne
  To My Dear and Loving
    Husband: V6
Brooke, Rupert
  The Soldier: V7
Browning, Elizabeth Barrett
  Aurora Leigh: V23
  Sonnet XXIX: V16
  Sonnet 43: V2
Browning, Robert
  My Last Duchess: V1
  Porphyria's Lover: V15
Byron, Lord
  The Destruction of Sennacherib:
    V1
  She Walks in Beauty: V14
Carroll, Lewis
  Jabberwocky: V11
Chaucer, Geoffrey
  The Canterbury Tales: V14

Coleridge, Samuel Taylor
  Kubla Khan: V5
  The Rime of the Ancient Mariner:
    V4
Donne, John
  Holy Sonnet 10: V2
  A Valediction: Forbidding
    Mourning: V11
Eliot, T. S.
  Journey of the Magi: V7
  The Love Song of J. Alfred
    Prufrock: V1
  The Waste Land: V20
Fenton, James
  The Milkfish Gatherers: V11
Gray, Thomas
  Elegy Written in a Country
    Churchyard: V9
Gunn, Thom
  The Missing: V9
Hardy, Thomas
  Ah, Are You Digging on My
    Grave?: V4
  The Darkling Thrush: V18
  The Man He Killed: V3
Herrick, Robert
  To the Virgins, to Make Much of
    Time: V13
Housman, A. E.
  To an Athlete Dying Young: V7
  When I Was One-and-Twenty: V4
Hughes, Ted
  Hawk Roosting: V4
  Perfect Light: V19
Jonson, Ben
  Song: To Celia: V23
Keats, John
  La Belle Dame sans Merci: V17
  Bright Star! Would I Were
    Steadfast as Thou Art: V9
  Ode on a Grecian Urn: V1
  Ode to a Nightingale: V3
  When I Have Fears that I May
    Cease to Be: V2
Kipling, Rudyard
  If: V22
Larkin, Philip
  An Arundel Tomb: V12
  High Windows: V3
  Toads: V4
Lawrence, D. H.
  Piano: V6
Levertov, Denise
  The Blue Rim of Memory: V17
Loy, Mina
  Moreover, the Moon: V20
Marlowe, Christopher
  The Passionate Shepherd to His
    Love: V22
Marvell, Andrew
  To His Coy Mistress: V5
Masefield, John
  Cargoes: V5
Maxwell, Glyn
  The Nerve: V23

Milton, John
[On His Blindness] Sonnet 16: V3
*On His Having Arrived at the Age
of Twenty-Three:* V17
Noyes, Alfred
The Highwayman: V4
Owen, Wilfred
Dulce et Decorum Est: V10
Pope, Alexander
The Rape of the Lock: V12
Raine, Craig
*A Martian Sends a Postcard
Home:* V7
Raleigh, Walter, Sir
*The Nymph's Reply to the
Shepherd:* V14
Rossetti, Christina
A Birthday: V10
Remember: V14
Service, Robert W.
The Cremation of Sam McGee: V10
Shakespeare, William
Sonnet 18: V2
Sonnet 19: V9
Sonnet 30: V4
Sonnet 29: V8
Sonnet 55: V5
Sonnet 116: V3
Sonnet 130: V1
Shelley, Percy Bysshe
Ode to the West Wind: V2
Smith, Stevie
Not Waving but Drowning: V3
Spender, Stephen
*An Elementary School Classroom
in a Slum:* V23
Tennyson, Alfred, Lord
The Charge of the Light Brigade:
V1
The Eagle: V11
The Lady of Shalott: V15
Proem: V19
Tears, Idle Tears: V4
Ulysses: V2
Williams, William Carlos
Queen-Ann's-Lace: V6
The Red Wheelbarrow: V1
Wordsworth, William
*Lines Composed a Few Miles
above Tintern Abbey:* V2
Yeats, W. B.
Easter 1916: V5
*An Irish Airman Forsees His
Death:* V1
The Lake Isle of Innisfree: V15
Leda and the Swan: V13
Sailing to Byzantium: V2
The Second Coming: V7

French

Baudelaire, Charles
Hymn to Beauty: V21

Malroux, Claire
Morning Walk: V21

German

Blumenthal, Michael
Inventors: V7
Erdrich, Louise
Bidwell Ghost: V14
Mueller, Lisel
Blood Oranges: V13
The Exhibit: V9
Rilke, Rainer Maria
Childhood: V19
Roethke, Theodore
My Papa's Waltz: V3
Sachs, Nelly
*But Perhaps God Needs the
Longing:* V20
Sajé, Natasha
The Art of the Novel: V23

Ghanaian

Du Bois, W. E. B.
The Song of the Smoke: V13

Greek

Sappho
Hymn to Aphrodite: V20

Hispanic

Castillo, Ana
While I Was Gone a War Began:
V21
Cruz, Victor Hernandez
Business: V16
Espada, Martín
Colibrí: V16

Indian

Shahid Ali, Agha
Country Without a Post Office:
V18
Tagore, Rabindranath
60: V18

Indonesian

Lee, Li-Young
Early in the Morning: V17
*For a New Citizen of These
United States:* V15
The Weight of Sweetness: V11

Iranian

Farrokhzaad, Faroogh
A Rebirth: V21

Irish

Boland, Eavan
Anorexic: V12
It's a Woman's World: V22
Grennan, Eamon
Station: V21
Hartnett, Michael
A Farewell to English: V10
Heaney, Seamus
Digging: V5
A Drink of Water: V8
Midnight: V2
The Singer's House: V17
Muldoon, Paul
Meeting the British: V7
Pineapples and Pomegranates:
V22
Yeats, William Butler
Easter 1916: V5
*An Irish Airman Foresees His
Death:* V1
The Lake Isle of Innisfree: V15
Leda and the Swan: V13
Sailing to Byzantium: V2
The Second Coming: V7

Italian

Montale, Eugenio
On the Threshold: V22
Pavese, Cesare
Two Poems for T.: V20
Ungaretti, Giuseppe
Variations on Nothing: V20

Jamaican

McKay, Claude
The Tropics in New York: V4
Simpson, Louis
In the Suburbs: V14

Japanese

Ai
Reunions with a Ghost: V16
Bashō, Matsuo
Falling Upon Earth: V2
The Moon Glows the Same: V7
Temple Bells Die Out: V18

Jewish

Blumenthal, Michael
Inventors: V7
Espada, Martín
Colibrí: V16
*We Live by What We See at
Night:* V13
Hirsch, Edward
Omen: V22

Piercy, Marge
    Apple sauce for Eve: V22
    Barbie Doll: V9
Sachs, Nelly
    *But Perhaps God Needs the
        Longing:* V20
Shapiro, Karl
    Auto Wreck: V3

Kiowa

Momaday, N. Scott
    Angle of Geese: V2
    *To a Child Running With
        Outstretched Arms in Canyon
        de Chelly:* V11

Lithuanian

Milosz, Czeslaw
    Song of a Citizen: V16

Mexican

Paz, Octavio
    Duration: V18
Soto, Gary
    Small Town with One Road: V7

Native American

Ai
    Reunions with a Ghost: V16
Erdrich, Louise
    Bidwell Ghost: V14
Harjo, Joy
    Anniversary: V15
Momaday, N. Scott
    Angle of Geese: V2
    *To a Child Running With
        Outstretched Arms in Canyon
        de Chelly:* V11
Ortiz, Simon
    Hunger in New York City: V4
    My Father's Song: V16
Revard, Carter
    Birch Canoe: V5
Rose, Wendy
    *For the White poets who would be
        Indian:* V13
Silko, Leslie Marmon
    Four Mountain Wolves: V9

Story from Bear Country: V16

Osage

Revard, Carter
    Birch Canoe: V5

Polish

Herbert, Zbigniew
    Why The Classics: V22
Milosz, Czeslaw
    Song of a Citizen: V16
Swir, Anna
    Maternity: V21
Szymborska, Wislawa
    Astonishment: V15

Roman

Ovid (Naso, Publius Ovidius)
    Metamorphoses: V22

Romanian

Celan, Paul
    Late and Deep: V21

Russian

Akhmatova, Anna
    Midnight Verses: V18
Levertov, Denise
    In the Land of Shinar: V7
Merriam, Eve
    Onomatopoeia: V6
Shapiro, Karl
    Auto Wreck: V3

St. Lucian

Walcott, Derek
    A Far Cry from Africa: V6

Scottish

Burns, Robert
    A Red, Red Rose: V8
Byron, Lord
    The Destruction of Sennacherib: V1
MacBeth, George
    Bedtime Story: V8

Senegalese

Wheatley, Phillis
    *To His Excellency General
        Washington:* V13

Serbian

Lazić, Radmila
    Death Sentences: V22

Spanish

García Lorca, Federico
    Gacela of the Dark Death:
        V20
Machado, Antonio
    The Crime Was in Granada:
        V23
Williams, William Carlos
    The Red Wheelbarrow: V1

Swedish

Sandburg, Carl
    Chicago: V3
Svenbro, Jesper
    Lepidopterology: V23
Tranströmer, Tomas
    Answers to Letters: V21

Vietnamese

Huong, Ho Xuan
    Spring-Watching Pavilion: V18

Welsh

Levertov, Denise
    In the Land of Shinar: V7
Thomas, Dylan
    *Do Not Go Gentle into that Good
        Night:* V1
    Fern Hill: V3
    *The Force That Through the
        Green Fuse Drives the
        Flower:* V8

Yugoslavian

Lazić, Radmila
    Death Sentences: V22

Subject/Theme Index

A

Abandonment
An Elementary School Classroom in a Slum: 101, 103, 107
Adulthood
An Elementary School Classroom in a Slum: 102–106
Pine: 236–237
Adventure and Exploration
Fiddler Crab: 110, 116–118
Alcoholism, Drugs, and Drug Addiction
The Nerve: 212, 214–215, 217–218
Alienation
An Elementary School Classroom in a Slum: 100–101, 103, 108
Allegory
Allegory: 4–5
An Elementary School Classroom in a Slum: 92
Alliteration
It's like This: 142
Practice: 243–244, 248–249
Ambiguity
An Elementary School Classroom in a Slum: 101, 103–104
Song: To Celia: 278, 281, 283
American Northeast
The Nerve: 202, 208
American South
Practice: 254–255
American West
September: 259–260, 262–263
Anger
It's like This: 139–140, 143
Art and the Artist
Allegory: 4

Artistic Creation
Lost in Translation: 188
Asia
Lost in Translation: 184, 187, 189–191
Authoritarianism
The Crime Was in Granada: 57, 59–60
Autobiography
An Elementary School Classroom in a Slum: 100–109

B

Beauty
Fiddler Crab: 125–130, 132–136
Pine: 222, 228–230
Song: To Celia: 271–273, 275
Betrayal
The Crime Was in Granada: 54, 57
Bildungsroman
Aurora Leigh: 45
Brutality
The Crime Was in Granada: 58
Buddhism
September: 263–266

C

Capitalism
An Elementary School Classroom in a Slum: 87, 90, 92–94
Childhood
The Crime Was in Granada: 69, 72, 75–76
An Elementary School Classroom in a Slum: 100–102, 104–107, 109

The Nerve: 212–213, 216–218
Civil Rights
An Elementary School Classroom in a Slum: 87, 90, 93–94
Class Conflict
An Elementary School Classroom in a Slum: 95
Classicism
Allegory: 3–5, 7
An Elementary School Classroom in a Slum: 105, 106, 109
Lepidopterology: 170, 176
Song: To Celia: 271, 275–276, 278
The Commonality of God
Fiddler Crab: 115
Communism
An Elementary School Classroom in a Slum: 91–97
Lost in Translation: 190–191
Communism and Education
An Elementary School Classroom in a Slum: 91
Contradiction
All It Takes: 18
Couplet
The Art of the Novel: 28, 32
Courage
The Art of the Novel: 33
Aurora Leigh: 50–52
The Crime Was in Granada: 80
Courtly Love
Song: To Celia: 272
Creativity
Lepidopterology: 179
Pine: 222, 229
Crime and Criminals
The Crime Was in Granada: 56–59

*An Elementary School Classroom
in a Slum:* 90, 92–93
Lost in Translation: 191
Cruelty
The Crime Was in Granada: 56–60
*An Elementary School Classroom
in a Slum:* 100
Lake: 158, 160–162
Curiosity
Fiddler Crab: 127
Cynicism
*An Elementary School Classroom
in a Slum:* 90
Practice: 247

D

Dance
The Crime Was in Granada: 62
Death
All It Takes: 14, 17–18, 21–22
The Crime Was in Granada: 54,
56–59, 61–62, 64, 68–71,
74–76, 80–83, 85
Fiddler Crab: 113–116, 121–122,
124, 127–129
It's like This: 140, 142, 144–145,
148–150
Lake: 156, 158, 160, 162–165
The Nerve: 214–220
Practice: 241–243, 251–252
Depression and Melancholy
The Crime Was in Granada:
70–71, 73, 75
It's like This: 143–145
Description
The Crime Was in Granada: 56,
59, 62
*An Elementary School Classroom
in a Slum:* 104, 106, 108
Lake: 158, 160, 162
Lepidopterology: 172–174
Practice: 248—250
Song: To Celia: 279–283
Despair
Allegory: 1, 4, 6
Dialogue
The Crime Was in Granada:
70–71, 73, 76
Disease
Lake: 160–162
Disease and Human Perspective
Lake: 160
Divorce
Lost in Translation: 194–195
Dreams and Reality
Lepidopterology: 174
Dreams and Visions
The Crime Was in Granada: 76–85
Fiddler Crab: 131–133, 135–136
Lepidopterology: 170, 172–175,
181–182
Practice: 253–255

E

Elegy
The Crime Was in Granada:
58–59
Emotions
All It Takes: 16–19, 24
Allegory: 7
The Art of the Novel: 30–32, 38
Aurora Leigh: 42
The Crime Was in Granada: 59,
75–77
*An Elementary School Classroom
in a Slum:* 89, 91, 104, 109
Fiddler Crab: 125, 136
It's like This: 139–140, 144, 147,
151, 154
Lake: 160–162, 164–165
Lost in Translation: 199–200
The Nerve: 207–208
Pine: 222–230, 232–235
Practice: 239, 241, 245–252
Song: To Celia: 274, 278–279
Eternity
The Crime Was in Granada:
69–71, 73
Lost in Translation: 199–200
Pine: 233–235
Practice: 242
Europe
Aurora Leigh: 41–43, 45–48,
50–52
The Crime Was in Granada: 54,
57–64, 80–82, 85
Lepidopterology: 170, 175–176
Lost in Translation: 186, 188–190
The Nerve: 208
Evil
*An Elementary School Classroom
in a Slum:* 90, 94, 106
Exile
*An Elementary School Classroom
in a Slum:* 101, 103, 106, 109
Practice: 254–255
Existence
It's like This: 142
Existentialism
It's like This: 137, 144–145
Exploitation
*An Elementary School Classroom
in a Slum:* 95–97
Expressionism
Allegory: 7–9

F

The Fallen Woman
Aurora Leigh: 44
Fate and Chance
Allegory: 1, 4–5, 11
The Art of the Novel: 37–38
The Crime Was in Granada:
68–71, 74–75

Fiddler Crab: 132–135
The Nerve: 212–214, 217, 219
Practice: 241, 243
Fear and Terror
The Crime Was in Granada: 78–81
*An Elementary School Classroom
in a Slum:* 101, 104, 106, 108
Fiddler Crab: 123–124
The Nerve: 204–206, 208
Fiction Versus Real Life
The Art of the Novel: 30
Folklore
*An Elementary School Classroom
in a Slum:* 104
Forgiveness
*An Elementary School Classroom
in a Slum:* 101, 106, 109

G

Gender Roles
*An Elementary School Classroom
in a Slum:* 105, 107
Generosity
All It Takes: 16–18
Ghost
The Nerve: 212–213, 215
God
All It Takes: 17–18, 20
The Crime Was in Granada: 68,
73–76
Fiddler Crab: 110, 113–120, 126,
128–129
Lake: 163–165
Going Against the Grain
The Nerve: 205
Gratitude
All It Takes: 17–18
Grief
Practice: 241
Grief and Sorrow
The Art of the Novel: 30, 32
The Crime Was in Granada:
56–57, 59, 69–71, 75, 77, 79,
81–83, 85
Lake: 156, 160–161, 163–165
Practice: 239, 241, 243–252
Guilt
*An Elementary School Classroom
in a Slum:* 101–103, 106–107

H

Happiness and Gaiety
The Art of the Novel: 34, 36
The Crime Was in Granada:
70–72, 81–82
Fiddler Crab: 124–126, 129
Hatred
*An Elementary School Classroom
in a Slum:* 104, 106–107
Heaven
Practice: 239, 241–243, 247–255

Hell
  The Nerve: 212–215
Heroism
  The Art of the Novel: 28, 30,
    32–38
  Aurora Leigh: 51–52
  The Crime Was in Granada: 80,
    84
  The Nerve: 211–212, 214, 217
History
  Allegory: 7
  Aurora Leigh: 51–53
  *An Elementary School Classroom
    in a Slum:* 91–94
  Lepidopterology: 173, 175
  Lost in Translation: 186
Homosexuality
  *An Elementary School Classroom
    in a Slum:* 101–104, 106–109
Honor
  Song: To Celia: 272, 274
Hope
  The Crime Was in Granada: 68,
    70, 74–76, 81–83
  *An Elementary School Classroom
    in a Slum:* 87, 89–90, 92–93,
    95–97
  Fiddler Crab: 122–123, 125
Hopelessness
  It's like This: 140
Human Traits
  Song: To Celia: 282
Humiliation and Degradation
  The Crime Was in Granada: 54,
    56–57
Humor
  *An Elementary School Classroom
    in a Slum:* 105, 108–109
  Lost in Translation: 197–198, 200

I

Identity
  Allegory: 5
Ignorance
  The Crime Was in Granada:
    78–80
  The Nerve: 202, 204, 206, 208
Imagery and Symbolism
  All It Takes: 14, 16
  Allegory: 1, 3, 6–9
  The Art of the Novel: 30, 32
  The Crime Was in Granada:
    65–69, 71, 73–74, 76, 79–84
  It's like This: 143, 151
  Lake: 156, 158, 160–162,
    164–165
  Lepidopterology: 170, 172–173,
    175–178, 181–183
  Lost in Translation: 184, 188,
    192–196
  Pine: 227, 233–235
  Song: To Celia: 269, 271–273, 277

Imagination
  The Crime Was in Granada: 76,
    78, 83–85
  Lepidopterology: 179–180
  Pine: 228
Insanity
  Lake: 156, 162
Invisibility
  All It Takes: 17
Irony
  All It Takes: 21, 23
  Allegory: 3–4, 6, 8
  The Crime Was in Granada: 73,
    75–76
  The Nerve: 214–215
  Song: To Celia: 278, 281–283
Islamism
  The Crime Was in Granada:
    69–70, 73–74
Isolation
  It's like This: 141

K

Killers and Killing
  The Crime Was in Granada: 54,
    56–59
Knowledge
  Aurora Leigh: 41, 45–46
  *An Elementary School Classroom
    in a Slum:* 92
  Lepidopterology: 175, 181
  Lost in Translation: 192–194
Knowledge and Revolution
  *An Elementary School Classroom
    in a Slum:* 92

L

Landscape
  All It Takes: 16–18
  Allegory: 11–12
  The Crime Was in Granada:
    68–70, 75
  Fiddler Crab: 110, 112–116,
    121–122, 124–125
  Lake: 156, 158–163, 166–168
  The Nerve: 212–213, 215–217, 219
  Practice: 253–255
  September: 259–265
Law and Order
  The Crime Was in Granada: 59
  *An Elementary School Classroom
    in a Slum:* 93–94
  Lost in Translation: 186, 190–191
The Levels of Time
  Fiddler Crab: 113
Life After Death
  Practice: 242
Life As Survival
  Fiddler Crab: 115
Literary Aesthetics and Science
  Lepidopterology: 173

Literary Criticism
  The Art of the Novel: 28, 30
  Aurora Leigh: 46–47
  It's like This: 137, 145
Literary Terms
  Allegory: 6
Loneliness
  The Crime Was in Granada: 76
  *An Elementary School Classroom
    in a Slum:* 104
  It's like This: 150, 154
Longing
  Pine: 225
Love
  All It Takes: 18
Love and Passion
  All It Takes: 17–19
  The Art of the Novel: 28–34,
    36–38
  Aurora Leigh: 40–45, 47–49
  The Crime Was in Granada: 69,
    71–72, 74, 79–82, 84–85
  *An Elementary School Classroom
    in a Slum:* 102–108
  Fiddler Crab: 121, 123–129,
    131–134, 136
  It's like This: 139–141, 143, 145
  Lake: 156, 160–161, 163,
    166–167
  Lepidopterology: 173–175
  Lost in Translation: 196–200
  The Nerve: 204–205, 212–215,
    217
  Pine: 222, 225, 227–230, 233–237
  Practice: 248–250
  Song: To Celia: 269, 271–275,
    277–278
Love Or Art
  Aurora Leigh: 44
Lower Class
  *An Elementary School Classroom
    in a Slum:* 87, 89–90, 92–93,
    95–97
Loyalty
  *An Elementary School Classroom
    in a Slum:* 101, 108
  Lost in Translation: 195
  Song: To Celia: 269, 274
Lyric Poetry
  Practice: 248–250

M

Marriage
  All It Takes: 19–20
  Aurora Leigh: 41–45
  Lost in Translation: 194
Memory and Reminiscence
  The Crime Was in Granada:
    69–72, 76–78, 80–83, 85
  Lost in Translation: 184, 186–189
Mental Instability
  Lake: 156

Subject/Theme Index

Middle Class
  *An Elementary School Classroom
    in a Slum:* 89–90, 92, 95–97
Middle East
  It's like This: 144
Modernism
  It's like This: 143–144
Money and Economics
  *An Elementary School Classroom
    in a Slum:* 87, 89–93
Morals and Morality
  Aurora Leigh: 40, 42, 44–46
  *An Elementary School Classroom
    in a Slum:* 95, 106
  Fiddler Crab: 110, 112, 115, 117
  Song: To Celia: 278, 280–283
Mortality
  Practice: 243
Motherhood
  The Crime Was in Granada: 69,
    71–72, 76
Murder
  The Crime Was in Granada: 54,
    56–59
Music
  Allegory: 3–4, 6, 11
  Aurora Leigh: 46
  The Crime Was in Granada: 56,
    58, 62–64, 68, 70, 73, 75, 83,
    84–85
  It's like This: 143, 151, 153
  Lost in Translation: 196, 198, 200
  Practice: 248, 250
  Song: To Celia: 269, 274–276
Mystery and Intrigue
  The Crime Was in Granada: 76,
    78–81, 83, 85
  Fiddler Crab: 114, 117–118, 125,
    127, 130
  Lost in Translation: 191
Myth, Fate, and Allegory
  Allegory: 4
Myths and Legends
  All It Takes: 14, 17
  Allegory: 1, 3–5, 7, 10–12
  The Crime Was in Granada: 80–84
  *An Elementary School Classroom
    in a Slum:* 102–104, 108–109
  It's like This: 143–145
  Lake: 163–165
  Lost in Translation: 197, 200

N

Narration
  Allegory: 1, 4
  Aurora Leigh: 41, 45, 47
  The Crime Was in Granada:
    70–72, 76
  *An Elementary School Classroom
    in a Slum:* 93, 107–108
  Fiddler Crab: 110, 113, 115–116,
    118–120, 123–124, 132, 134

  Lost in Translation: 196–199
  The Nerve: 216–217
  Practice: 248–250
Nature
  All It Takes: 14, 16–17
  The Crime Was in Granada: 69,
    76, 78, 79–82, 84–85
  *An Elementary School Classroom
    in a Slum:* 101–104, 107–109
  Fiddler Crab: 116, 122, 128
  Lake: 160–161, 166
  Lost in Translation: 184, 191,
    199–200
  The Nerve: 214
  Practice: 239, 243, 245, 249–250
  September: 259, 264–266
North America
  *An Elementary School Classroom
    in a Slum:* 87, 90–91, 94
  Lost in Translation: 190–191
  The Nerve: 208–209
Nurturance
  The Crime Was in Granada: 69,
    71, 76

P

Painting
  Allegory: 1, 3–10
  The Crime Was in Granada: 58,
    60, 77, 84
  It's like This: 153
The Paradox of Being
  September: 261
Passion
  The Nerve: 204
Patience
  Lost in Translation: 186, 188, 191
Perception
  The Crime Was in Granada: 76,
    78, 80, 83–84
  *An Elementary School Classroom
    in a Slum:* 101, 103, 105–107,
    109
  September: 257, 259–261, 263–266
  Song: To Celia: 278, 280–281, 283
Permanence
  The Crime Was in Granada:
    68–69, 75
  Lepidopterology: 177–178
  Pine: 224
  Practice: 241–242, 244
Persecution
  *An Elementary School Classroom
    in a Slum:* 89–90
Personal Identity
  Allegory: 1, 3, 5
  *An Elementary School Classroom
    in a Slum:* 100–106, 108–109
Personification
  The Crime Was in Granada:
    56–57, 59
  Lepidopterology: 172, 174–175

  Song: To Celia: 281, 283
Philosophical Ideas
  Allegory: 1, 5–6, 8
  The Crime Was in Granada: 69,
    71, 74–75
  It's like This: 137, 140, 143–144
Plants
  All It Takes: 16–18
  Pine: 233–235
Poetry
  All It Takes: 14–26
  Allegory: 1, 3–12
  The Art of the Novel: 28, 30–38
  Aurora Leigh: 40–53
  The Crime Was in Granada: 54,
    56–59, 61–62, 64–85
  *An Elementary School Classroom
    in a Slum:* 87, 90–95, 97–100
  Fiddler Crab: 110–126, 128–136
  It's like This: 137–154
  Lake: 156–169
  Lepidopterology: 170, 172–183
  Lost in Translation: 184–189,
    191–201
  The Nerve: 202–220
  Pine: 222–230, 232–237
  Practice: 239, 241–255
  September: 257, 259–267
  Song: To Celia: 269, 271–283
Politicians
  Lost in Translation: 190–191
Politics
  All It Takes: 19–20
  Aurora Leigh: 46–47
  The Crime Was in Granada: 54,
    57, 59–61, 65–68, 79, 81–85
  *An Elementary School Classroom
    in a Slum:* 87, 91, 93–97
  Lepidopterology: 170, 175
  Lost in Translation: 190–191
  September: 262
Postmodernism
  Allegory: 6
Poverty
  *An Elementary School Classroom
    in a Slum:* 90–94
Power
  Song: To Celia: 273
Power of Art
  Lost in Translation: 188
The Power of the Mind
  September: 260
Pride
  Lepidopterology: 173, 175
**The Proper Subject Matter of
Poetry**
  Aurora Leigh: 43
Prostitution
  Aurora Leigh: 40, 43–44, 50
Psychology
  Lepidopterology: 173
Psychology and the Human Mind
  Allegory: 6

The Crime Was in Granada: 69,
76–81, 83–85
*An Elementary School Classroom
in a Slum:* 100–107, 109
Lake: 159–160, 162
Lepidopterology: 170, 172–175,
181–183

R

Race
*An Elementary School Classroom
in a Slum:* 87, 90–91, 93–94,
100–101, 105
Racism and Prejudice
*An Elementary School Classroom
in a Slum:* 93–94
Religion and Religious Thought
All It Takes: 17–18
The Crime Was in Granada: 73–74
*An Elementary School Classroom
in a Slum:* 100, 102, 104–105
Fiddler Crab: 110, 115–117, 120,
122–123, 129
It's like This: 143–144
Practice: 244
Song: To Celia: 271–272, 274–275
Role of Women
The Art of the Novel: 31
Roman Catholicism
Fiddler Crab: 110, 115–117

S

Satire
Song: To Celia: 275, 278,
280–282
Science and Technology
Lepidopterology: 170, 172–175,
179–182
Search for Knowledge
Aurora Leigh: 41, 43, 45–47
*An Elementary School Classroom
in a Slum:* 87, 90–94, 97
Self-Realization
The Crime Was in Granada:
77–80, 83, 85
Sentimentality
The Crime Was in Granada:
68–71, 75, 80–81
Setting
Fiddler Crab: 134–135
Lost in Translation: 196–198

Sex and Sexuality
All It Takes: 19–20
*An Elementary School Classroom
in a Slum:* 100–109
Pine: 235–237
Shame
The Crime Was in Granada: 57
Sickness
Lake: 158–162
Sin
*An Elementary School Classroom
in a Slum:* 87, 90–91, 93–94
Social Order
*An Elementary School Classroom
in a Slum:* 93, 95, 97
Socialism
*An Elementary School Classroom
in a Slum:* 87, 91–94
Solitude
The Crime Was in Granada: 68,
71, 76
Sonnet
The Crime Was in Granada:
64–68
Song: To Celia: 273–275
Soothsayer
The Crime Was in Granada:
77–78, 83
Lost in Translation: 186, 189, 195
Soul
The Crime Was in Granada:
79–81, 83, 85
Spirituality
Fiddler Crab: 110, 115–117
Storms and Weather Conditions
All It Takes: 16–19
Fiddler Crab: 122–125
Structure
The Crime Was in Granada: 64
Practice: 248–250
September: 261
Song: To Celia: 273–275, 277
Surrealism
The Crime Was in Granada: 61
Survival
Fiddler Crab: 113–120

T

Teaching Poetry
Pine: 226
Terminal Illness
Lake: 160

Time and Change
The Crime Was in Granada: 56,
72, 74, 76
Lake: 166–167
September: 259–261
Tone
All It Takes: 21–22
The Crime Was in Granada: 58–59
Lake: 158–160, 163, 165
Lepidopterology: 179–181
The Nerve: 203, 206, 208
Trust
All It Takes: 17–19, 22

U

Understanding
The Crime Was in Granada: 71,
75–79, 81
*An Elementary School Classroom
in a Slum:* 105, 107
Fiddler Crab: 110, 113–115, 118
September: 266
Song: To Celia: 279
The Unknown
The Nerve: 206

W

War, the Military, and Soldier Life
Aurora Leigh: 46
The Crime Was in Granada: 54,
57–60, 64–68
*An Elementary School Classroom
in a Slum:* 94
Lost in Translation: 186, 189–191
The Nerve: 204, 208, 212–214,
217, 220
Watergate
Lost in Translation: 184, 190–191
Wildlife
Fiddler Crab: 126–128
Practice: 241, 243, 248–250
Woman As Artist
Aurora Leigh: 43
World War II
Lost in Translation: 186–187,
189–190

Y

Yearning
Pine: 224–227, 233–236

Cumulative Index of First Lines

A

A brackish reach of shoal off Madaket,— (The Quaker Graveyard in Nantucket) V6:158

"A cold coming we had of it (Journey of the Magi) V7:110

A few minutes ago, I stepped onto the deck (The Cobweb) V17:50

A gentle spring evening arrives (Spring-Watching Pavilion) V18:198

A line in long array where they wind betwixt green islands, (Cavalry Crossing a Ford) V13:50

A narrow Fellow in the grass (A Narrow Fellow in the Grass) V11:127

A pine box for me. I mean it. (Last Request) V14: 231

A poem should be palpable and mute (Ars Poetica) V5:2

A stone from the depths that has witnessed the seas drying up (Song of a Citizen) V16:125

A tourist came in from Orbitville, (Southbound on the Freeway) V16:158

A wind is ruffling the tawny pelt (A Far Cry from Africa) V6:60

a woman precedes me up the long rope, (Climbing) V14:113

About me the night moonless wimples the mountains (Vancouver Lights) V8:245

About suffering they were never wrong (Musée des Beaux Arts) V1:148

Across Roblin Lake, two shores away, (Wilderness Gothic) V12:241

After the double party (Air for Mercury) V20:2–3

After the party ends another party begins (Social Life) V19:251

After you finish your work (Ballad of Orange and Grape) V10:17

Again I've returned to this country (The Country Without a Post Office) V18:64

"Ah, are you digging on my grave (Ah, Are You Digging on My Grave?) V4:2

All Greece hates (Helen) V6:92

All my existence is a dark sign a dark (A Rebirth) V21:193–194

All night long the hockey pictures (To a Sad Daughter) V8:230

All over Genoa (Trompe l'Oeil) V22:216

All winter your brute shoulders strained against collars, padding (Names of Horses) V8:141

Also Ulysses once—that other war. (Kilroy) V14:213

Among the blossoms, a single jar of wine. (Drinking Alone Beneath the Moon) V20:59–60

Anasazi (Anasazi) V9:2

"And do we remember our living lives?" (Memory) V21:156

And God stepped out on space (The Creation) V1:19

And what if I spoke of despair—who doesn't (And What If I Spoke of Despair) V19:2

Animal bones and some mossy tent rings (Lament for the Dorsets) V5:190

Any force— (All It Takes) V23:15

April is the cruellest month, breeding (The Waste Land) V20:248–252

As I perceive (The Gold Lily) V5:127

As I walked out one evening (As I Walked Out One Evening) V4:15

As virtuous men pass mildly away (A Valediction: Forbidding Mourning) V11:201

As you set out for Ithaka (Ithaka) V19:114

At noon in the desert a panting lizard (At the Bomb Testing Site) V8:2

Ay, tear her tattered ensign down! (Old Ironsides) V9:172

B

Back then, before we came (On Freedom's Ground) V12:186

Bananas ripe and green, and ginger-root (The Tropics in New York) V4:255

Because I could not stop for Death— (Because I Could Not Stop for Death) V2:27

Before the indifferent beak could let her drop? (Leda and the Swan) V13:182

Be happy if the wind inside the orchard (On the Threshold) V22:128

Bent double, like old beggars under slacks, (Dulce et Decorum Est) V10:109

Between my finger and my thumb (Digging) V5:70

Beware of ruins: they have a treacherous charm (Beware of Ruins) V8:43

Bright star! would I were steadfast as thou art— (Bright Star! Would I Were Steadfast as Thou Art) V9:44

But perhaps God needs the longing, wherever else should it dwell, (But Perhaps God Needs the Longing) V20:41

By the rude bridge that arched the flood (Concord Hymn) V4:30

By way of a vanished bridge we cross this river (The Garden Shukkei-en) V18:107

C

Celestial choir! enthron'd in realms of light, (To His Excellency General Washington V13:212

Come with me into those things that have felt his despair for so long— (Come with Me) V6:31

Complacencies of the peignoir, and late (Sunday Morning) V16:189

Composed in the Tower, before his execution ("More Light! More Light!") V6:119

D

Darkened by time, the masters, like our memories, mix (Black Zodiac) V10:46

Death, be not proud, though some have called thee (Holy Sonnet 10) V2:103

Devouring Time, blunt thou the lion's paws (Sonnet 19) V9:210

Do not go gentle into that good night (Do Not Go Gentle into that Good Night) V1:51

Do not weep, maiden, for war is kind (War Is Kind) V9:252

Don Arturo says: (Business) V16:2

Drink to me only with thine eyes, (Song: To Celia) V23:270–271

(Dumb, (A Grafted Tongue) V12:92

E

Each day the shadow swings (In the Land of Shinar) V7:83

Each morning the man rises from bed because the invisible (It's like This) V23:138–139

Each night she waits by the road (Bidwell Ghost) V14:2

F

Face of the skies (Moreover, the Moon) V20:153

Falling upon earth (Falling Upon Earth) V2:64

Far far from gusty waves these children's faces. (An Elementary School Classroom in a Slum) V23:88–89

Five years have past; five summers, with the length (Tintern Abbey) V2:249

Flesh is heretic. (Anorexic) V12:2

For a long time the butterfly held a prominent place in psychology (Lepidopterology) V23:171–172

For three years, out of key with his time, (Hugh Selwyn Mauberley) V16:26

Forgive me for thinking I saw (For a New Citizen of These United States) V15:55

From my mother's sleep I fell into the State (The Death of the Ball Turret Gunner) V2:41

G

Gardener: Sir, I encountered Death (Incident in a Rose Garden) V14:190

Gather ye Rose-buds while ye may, (To the Virgins, to Make Much of Time) V13:226

Gazelle, I killed you (Ode to a Drum) V20:172–173

Go down, Moses (Go Down, Moses) V11:42

Gray mist wolf (Four Mountain Wolves) V9:131

H

"Had he and I but met (The Man He Killed) V3:167

Had we but world enough, and time (To His Coy Mistress) V5:276

Half a league, half a league (The Charge of the Light Brigade) V1:2

Having a Coke with You (Having a Coke with You) V12:105

He clasps the crag with crooked hands (The Eagle) V11:30

He was found by the Bureau of Statistics to be (The Unknown Citizen) V3:302

He was seen, surrounded by rifles, (The Crime Was in Granada) V23:55–56

Hear the sledges with the bells— (The Bells) V3:46

Her body is not so white as (Queen-Ann's-Lace) V6:179

Her eyes were coins of porter and her West (A Farewell to English) V10:126

Here they are. The soft eyes open (The Heaven of Animals) V6:75

His speed and strength, which is the strength of ten (His Speed and Strength) V19:96

Hog Butcher for the World (Chicago) V3:61

Hold fast to dreams (Dream Variations) V15:42

Hope is a tattered flag and a dream out of time. (Hope is a Tattered Flag) V12:120

"Hope" is the thing with feathers— (Hope Is the Thing with Feathers) V3:123

How do I love thee? Let me count the ways (Sonnet 43) V2:236

How shall we adorn (Angle of Geese) V2:2

How soon hath Time, the subtle thief of youth, (On His Having Arrived at the Age of Twenty-Three) V17:159

How would it be if you took yourself off (Landscape with Tractor) V10:182

Hunger crawls into you (Hunger in New York City) V4:79

I

I am not a painter, I am a poet (Why I Am Not a Painter) V8:258

I am the Smoke King (The Song of the Smoke) V13:196

I am silver and exact. I have no preconceptions (Mirror) V1:116

I am trying to pry open your casket (Dear Reader) V10:85

I became a creature of light (The Mystery) V15:137

I cannot love the Brothers Wright (Reactionary Essay on Applied Science) V9:199

I felt a Funeral, in my Brain, (I felt a Funeral in my Brain) V13:137

I gave birth to life. (Maternity) V21:142–143

I have just come down from my father (The Hospital Window) V11:58

I have met them at close of day (Easter 1916) V5:91

I haven't the heart to say (To an Unknown Poet) V18:221

I hear America singing, the varied carols I hear (I Hear America Singing) V3:152

I heard a Fly buzz—when I died— (I Heard a Fly Buzz—When I Died—) V5:140

I know that I shall meet my fate (An Irish Airman Foresees His Death) V1:76

I leant upon a coppice gate (The Darkling Thrush) V18:74

I lie down on my side in the moist grass (Omen) v22:107

I looked in my heart while the wild swans went over. (Wild Swans) V17:221

I prove a theorem and the house expands: (Geometry) V15:68

I see them standing at the formal gates of their colleges, (I go Back to May 1937) V17:112

I sit in the top of the wood, my eyes closed (Hawk Roosting) V4:55

I thought wearing an evergreen dress (Pine) V23:223–224

I'm delighted to see you (The Constellation Orion) V8:53

I've known rivers; (The Negro Speaks of Rivers) V10:197

I was born too late and I am much too old, (Death Sentences) V22:23

I was sitting in mcsorley's. outside it was New York and beautifully snowing. (i was sitting in mcsorley's) V13:151

I will arise and go now, and go to Innisfree, (The Lake Isle of Innisfree) V15:121

If all the world and love were young, (The Nymph's Reply to the Shepard) V14:241

If ever two were one, then surely we (To My Dear and Loving Husband) V6:228

If I should die, think only this of me (The Soldier) V7:218

If you can keep your head when all about you (If) V22:54–55

"Imagine being the first to say: *surveillance*," (Inventors) V7:97

In 1790 a woman could die by falling (The Art of the Novel) V23:29

In 1936, a child (Blood Oranges) V13:34

In a while they rose and went out aimlessly riding, (Merlin Enthralled) V16:72

In China (Lost Sister) V5:216

In ethics class so many years ago (Ethics) V8:88

In Flanders fields the poppies blow (In Flanders Fields) V5:155

In India in their lives they happen (Ways to Live) V16:228

In May, when sea-winds pierced our solitudes, (The Rhodora) V17:191

In the bottom drawer of my desk . . . (Answers to Letters) V21:30–31

In the groves of Africa from their natural wonder (An African Elegy) V13:3

In the Shreve High football stadium (Autumn Begins in Martins Ferry, Ohio) V8:17

In the sixty-eight years (Accounting) V21:2–3

In Xanadu did Kubla Khan (Kubla Khan) V5:172

Ink runs from the corners of my mouth (Eating Poetry) V9:60

Is it the boy in me who's looking out (The Boy) V19:14

It is a cold and snowy night. The main street is deserted. (Driving to Town Late to Mail a Letter) V17:63

It is an ancient Mariner (The Rime of the Ancient Mariner) V4:127

It is in the small things we see it. (Courage) V14:125

It little profits that an idle king (Ulysses) V2:278

It looked extremely rocky for the Mudville nine that day (Casey at the Bat) V5:57

It must be troubling for the god who loves you (The God Who Loves You) V20:88

It seems vainglorious and proud (The Conquerors) V13:67

It starts with a low rumbling, white static, (Rapture) V21:181

It was in and about the Martinmas time (Barbara Allan) V7:10

It was many and many a year ago (Annabel Lee) V9:14

Its quick soft silver bell beating, beating (Auto Wreck) V3:31

J

Januaries, Nature greets our eyes (Brazil, January 1, 1502) V6:15

Just off the highway to Rochester, Minnesota (A Blessing) V7:24

just once (For the White poets who would be Indian) V13:112

L

l(a (l(a) V1:85

Let me not to the marriage of true minds (Sonnet 116) V3:288

Let us console you. (Allegory) V23:2–3

Listen, my children, and you shall hear (Paul Revere's Ride) V2:178

Little Lamb, who made thee? (The Lamb) V12:134

Long long ago when the world was a wild place (Bedtime Story) V8:32

M

maggie and milly and molly and may (maggie & milly & molly & may) V12:149

Mary sat musing on the lamp-flame at the table (The Death of the Hired Man) V4:42

Men with picked voices chant the names (Overture to a Dance of Locomotives) V11:143

"Mother dear, may I go downtown (Ballad of Birmingham) V5:17

Cumulative Index of First Lines

Much Madness is divinest Sense— (Much Madness is Divinest Sense) V16:86

My black face fades (Facing It) V5:109

My father stands in the warm evening (Starlight) V8:213

My heart aches, and a drowsy numbness pains (Ode to a Nightingale) V3:228

My heart is like a singing bird (A Birthday) V10:33

My life closed twice before its close— (My Life Closed Twice Before Its Close) V8:127

My mistress' eyes are nothing like the sun (Sonnet 130) V1:247

My uncle in East Germany (The Exhibit) V9:107

N

Nature's first green is gold (Nothing Gold Can Stay) V3:203

No easy thing to bear, the weight of sweetness (The Weight of Sweetness) V11:230

Nobody heard him, the dead man (Not Waving but Drowning) V3:216

Not marble nor the gilded monuments (Sonnet 55) V5:246

Not the memorized phone numbers. (What Belongs to Us) V15:196

Now as I was young and easy under the apple boughs (Fern Hill) V3:92

Now as I watch the progress of the plague (The Missing) V9:158

Now I rest my head on the satyr's carved chest, (The Satyr's Heart) V22:187

Now one might catch it see it (Fading Light) V21:49

O

O Captain! my Captain, our fearful trip is done (O Captain! My Captain!) V2:146

O Lord our Lord, how excellent is thy name in all the earth! who hast set thy glory above the heavens (Psalm 8) V9:182

O my Luve's like a red, red rose (A Red, Red Rose) V8:152

O what can ail thee, knight-at-arms, (La Belle Dame sans Merci) V17:18

"O where ha' you been, Lord Randal, my son? (Lord Randal) V6:105

O wild West Wind, thou breath of Autumn's being (Ode to the West Wind) V2:163

Oh, but it is dirty! (Filling Station) V12:57

old age sticks (old age sticks) V3:246

On either side the river lie (The Lady of Shalott) V15:95

On the seashore of endless worlds children meet. The infinite (60) V18:3

Once upon a midnight dreary, while I pondered, weak and weary (The Raven) V1:200

Once some people were visiting Chekhov (Chocolates) V11:17

One day I'll lift the telephone (Elegy for My Father, Who Is Not Dead) V14:154

One foot down, then hop! It's hot (Harlem Hopscotch) V2:93

one shoe on the roadway presents (A Piéd) V3:16

Out of the hills of Habersham, (Song of the Chattahoochee) V14:283

Out walking in the frozen swamp one gray day (The Wood-Pile) V6:251

Oysters we ate (Oysters) V4:91

P

Pentagon code (Smart and Final Iris) V15:183

Poised between going on and back, pulled (The Base Stealer) V12:30

Q

Quinquireme of Nineveh from distant Ophir (Cargoes) V5:44

R

Recognition in the body (In Particular) V20:125

Red men embraced my body's whiteness (Birch Canoe) V5:31

Remember me when I am gone away (Remember) V14:255

S

Shall I compare thee to a Summer's day? (Sonnet 18) V2:222

She came every morning to draw water (A Drink of Water) V8:66

She sang beyond the genius of the sea. (The Idea of Order at Key West) V13:164

She walks in beauty, like the night (She Walks in Beauty) V14:268

Side by side, their faces blurred, (An Arundel Tomb) V12:17

Since the professional wars— (Midnight) V2:130

Since then, I work at night. (Ten Years after Your Deliberate Drowning) V21:240

S'io credesse che mia risposta fosse (The Love Song of J. Alfred Prufrock) V1:97

Sky black (Duration) V18:93

Sleepless as Prospero back in his bedroom (Darwin in 1881) V13:83

so much depends (The Red Wheelbarrow) V1:219

So the man spread his blanket on the field (A Tall Man Executes a Jig) V12:228

So the sky wounded you, jagged at the heart, (Daylights) V13:101

Softly, in the dark, a woman is singing to me (Piano) V6:145

Some say it's in the reptilian dance (The Greatest Grandeur) V18:119

Some say the world will end in fire (Fire and Ice) V7:57

Something there is that doesn't love a wall (Mending Wall) V5:231

Sometimes walking late at night (Butcher Shop) V7:43

Sometimes, a lion with a prophet's beard (For An Assyrian Frieze) V9:120

Sometimes, in the middle of the lesson (Music Lessons) V8:117

somewhere i have never travelled,gladly beyond (somewhere i have never travelled,gladly beyond) V19:265

South of the bridge on Seventeenth (Fifteen) V2:78

Stop all the clocks, cut off the telephone, (Funeral Blues) V10:139

Strong Men, riding horses. In the West (Strong Men, Riding Horses) V4:209

Such places are too still for history, (Deep Woods) V14:138

Sundays too my father got up early (Those Winter Sundays) V1:300

Swing low sweet chariot (Swing Low Sweet Chariot) V1:283

T

Take heart, monsieur, four-fifths of this province (For Jean Vincent D'abbadie, Baron St.-Castin) V12:78

Tears, idle tears, I know not what they mean (Tears, Idle Tears) V4:220

Tell me not, in mournful numbers (A Psalm of Life) V7:165

Temple bells die out. (Temple Bells Die Out) V18:210

That is no country for old men. The young (Sailing to Byzantium) V2:207

That negligible bit of sand which slides (Variations on Nothing) V20:234

That time of drought the embered air (Drought Year) V8:78

That's my last Duchess painted on the wall (My Last Duchess) V1:165

The apparition of these faces in the crowd (In a Station of the Metro) V2:116

The Assyrian came down like the wolf on the fold (The Destruction of Sennacherib) V1:38

The broken pillar of the wing jags from the clotted shoulder (Hurt Hawks) V3:138

The bud (Saint Francis and the Sow) V9:222

The Bustle in a House (The Bustle in a House) V10:62

The buzz saw snarled and rattled in the yard (Out, Out—) V10:212

The courage that my mother had (The Courage that My Mother Had) V3:79

The Curfew tolls the knell of parting day (Elegy Written in a Country Churchyard) V9:73

The fiddler crab fiddles, glides and dithers, (Fiddler Crab) V23:111–112

The force that through the green fuse drives the flower (The Force That Through the Green Fuse Drives the Flower) V8:101

The grasses are light brown (September) V23:258–259

The green lamp flares on the table (This Life) V1:293

The ills I sorrow at (Any Human to Another) V3:2

The instructor said (Theme for English B) V6:194

The king sits in Dumferling toune (Sir Patrick Spens) V4:177

The land was overmuch like scenery (Beowulf) V11:2

The last time I saw it was 1968. (The Hiding Place) V10:152

The Lord is my shepherd; I shall not want (Psalm 23) V4:103

The man who sold his lawn to standard oil (The War Against the Trees) V11:215

The moon glows the same (The Moon Glows the Same) V7:152

The old South Boston Aquarium stands (For the Union Dead) V7:67

The others bent their heads and started in ("Trouble with Math in a One-Room Country School") V9:238

The pale nuns of St. Joseph are here (Island of Three Marias) V11:79

The Phoenix comes of flame and dust (The Phoenix) V10:226

The plants of the lake (Two Poems for T.) V20:218

The rain set early in to-night: (Porphyria's Lover) V15:151

The river brought down (How We Heard the Name) V10:167

The rusty spigot (Onomatopoeia) V6:133

The sea is calm tonight (Dover Beach) V2:52

The sea sounds insincere (The Milkfish Gatherers) V11:111

The slow overture of rain, (Mind) V17:145

The Soul selects her own Society—(The Soul Selects Her Own Society) V1:259

The time you won your town the race (To an Athlete Dying Young) V7:230

The way sorrow enters the bone (The Blue Rim of Memory) V17:38

The whiskey on your breath (My Papa's Waltz) V3:191

The white ocean in which birds swim (Morning Walk) V21:167

The wind was a torrent of darkness among the gusty trees (The Highwayman) V4:66

There are strange things done in the midnight sun (The Cremation of Sam McGee) V10:75

There have been rooms for such a short time (The Horizons of Rooms) V15:79

There is a hunger for order, (A Thirst Against) V20:205

There is no way not to be excited (Paradiso) V20:190–191

There is the one song everyone (Siren Song) V7:196

There's a Certain Slant of Light (There's a Certain Slant of Light) V6:211

There's no way out. (In the Suburbs) V14:201

There will come soft rains and the smell of the ground, (There Will Come Soft Rains) V14:301

There you are, in all your innocence, (Perfect Light) V19:187

These open years, the river (For Jennifer, 6, on the Teton) V17:86

They eat beans mostly, this old yellow pair (The Bean Eaters) V2:16

they were just meant as covers (My Mother Pieced Quilts) V12:169

They said, "Wait." Well, I waited. (Alabama Centennial) V10:2

This girlchild was: born as usual (Barbie Doll) V9:33

This is my letter to the World (This Is My Letter to the World) V4:233

This is the Arsenal. From floor to ceiling, (The Arsenal at Springfield) V17:2

This is the black sea-brute bulling through wave-wrack (Leviathan) V5:203

This poem is concerned with language on a very plain level (Paradoxes and Oxymorons) V11:162

This tale is true, and mine. It tells (The Seafarer) V8:177

Thou still unravish'd bride of quietness (Ode on a Grecian Urn) V1:179

Three times my life has opened. (Three Times My Life Has Opened) V16:213

Time in school drags along with so much worry, (Childhood) V19:29

to fold the clothes. No matter who lives (I Stop Writimg the Poem) V16:58

To weep unbidden, to wake (Practice) V23:240

Tonight I can write the saddest lines (Tonight I Can Write) V11:187

Toni Morrison despises (The Toni Morrison Dreams) V22:202–203

tonite, *thriller* was (Beware: Do Not Read This Poem) V6:3

Turning and turning in the widening gyre (The Second Coming) V7:179

'Twas brillig, and the slithy toves (Jabberwocky) V11:91

Two roads diverged in a yellow wood (The Road Not Taken) V2:195

Tyger! Tyger! burning bright (The Tyger) V2:263

W

wade (The Fish) V14:171

Wanting to say things, (My Father's Song) V16:102

We are saying goodbye (Station) V21:226–227

We could be here. This is the valley (Small Town with One Road) V7:207

We met the British in the dead of winter (Meeting the British) V7:138

We real cool. We (We Real Cool) V6:242

Well, son, I'll tell you (Mother to Son) V3:178

What dire offense from amorous causes springs, (The Rape of the Lock) V12:202

What happens to a dream deferred? (Harlem) V1:63

What of the neighborhood homes awash (The Continuous Life) V18:51

What thoughts I have of you tonight, Walt Whitman, for I walked down the sidestreets under the trees with a headache self-conscious looking at the full moon (A Supermarket in California) V5:261

Whatever it is, it must have (American Poetry) V7:2

When Abraham Lincoln was shoveled into the tombs, he forgot the copperheads, and the assassin . . . in the dust, in the cool tombs (Cool Tombs) V6:45

When I consider how my light is spent ([On His Blindness] Sonnet 16) V3:262

When I have fears that I may cease to be (When I Have Fears that I May Cease to Be) V2:295

When I heard the learn'd astronomer, (When I Heard the Learn'd Astronomer) V22:244

When I see a couple of kids (High Windows) V3:108

When I see birches bend to left and right (Birches) V13:14

When I was born, you waited (Having it Out with Melancholy) V17:98

When I was one-and-twenty (When I Was One-and-Twenty) V4:268

When I watch you (Miss Rosie) V1:133

When, in disgrace with Fortune and men's eyes (Sonnet 29) V8:198

When the mountains of Puerto Rico (We Live by What We See at Night) V13:240

When the world was created wasn't it like this? (Anniversary) V15:2

When they said *Carrickfergus* I could hear (The Singer's House) V17:205

When you consider the radiance, that it does not withhold (The City Limits) V19:78

Whenever Richard Cory went down town (Richard Cory) V4:116

While I was gone a war began. (While I Was Gone a War Began) V21:253–254

While my hair was still cut straight across my forehead (The River-Merchant's Wife: A Letter) V8:164

While the long grain is softening (Early in the Morning) V17:75

While this America settles in the mould of its vulgarity, heavily thickening to empire (Shine, Perishing Republic) V4:161

While you are preparing for sleep, brushing your teeth, (The Afterlife) V18:39

Who has ever stopped to think of the divinity of Lamont Cranston? (In Memory of Radio) V9:144

Whose woods these are I think I know (Stopping by Woods on a Snowy Evening) V1:272

Why should I let the toad *work* (Toads) V4:244

Y

You are small and intense (To a Child Running With Out-stretched Arms in Canyon de Chelly) V11:173

You do not have to be good. (Wild Geese) V15:207

You should lie down now and remember the forest, (The Forest) V22:36–37

You stood thigh-deep in water and green light glanced (Lake) V23:158

You were never told, Mother, how old Illya was drunk (The Czar's Last Christmas Letter) V12:44

Cumulative Index of
Last Lines

A

. . . a capital T in the endless mass of the text. (Answers to Letters) V21:30–31

a fleck of foam. (Accounting) V21:2–3

A heart whose love is innocent! (She Walks in Beauty) V14:268

a man then suddenly stops running (Island of Three Marias) V11:80

A perfect evening! (Temple Bells Die Out) V18:210

a space in the lives of their friends (Beware: Do Not Read This Poem) V6:3

A sudden blow: the great wings beating still (Leda and the Swan) V13:181

A terrible beauty is born (Easter 1916) V5:91

About my big, new, automatically defrosting refrigerator with the built-in electric eye (Reactionary Essay on Applied Science) V9:199

about the tall mounds of termites. (Song of a Citizen) V16:126

Across the expedient and wicked stones (Auto Wreck) V3:31

affirming its brilliant and dizzying love. (Lepidopterology) V23:171

Ah, dear father, graybeard, lonely old courage-teacher, what America did you have when Charon quit poling his ferry and you got out on a smoking bank and stood watching the boat disappear on the black waters of Lethe? (A Supermarket in California) V5:261

All losses are restored and sorrows end (Sonnet 30) V4:192

Amen. Amen (The Creation) V1:20

Anasazi (Anasazi) V9:3

and all beyond saving by children (Ethics) V8:88

and all the richer for it. (Mind) V17:146

And all we need of hell (My Life Closed Twice Before Its Close) V8:127

And, being heard, doesn't vanish in the dark. (Variations on Nothing) V20:234

and changed, back to the class ("Trouble with Math in a One-Room Country School") V9:238

And Death shall be no more: Death, thou shalt die (Holy Sonnet 10) V2:103

and destruction. (Allegory) V23:2–3

And drunk the milk of Paradise (Kubla Khan) V5:172

and fear lit by the breadth of such calmly turns to praise. (The City Limits) V19:78

And Finished knowing—then— (I Felt a Funeral in My Brain) V13:137

And gallop terribly against each other's bodies (Autumn Begins in Martins Ferry, Ohio) V8:17

and go back. (For the White poets who would be Indian) V13:112

And handled with a Chain—(Much Madness is Divinest Sense) V16:86

And has not begun to grow a manly smile. (Deep Woods) V14:139

And his own Word (The Phoenix) V10:226

And I am Nicholas. (The Czar's Last Christmas Letter) V12:45

And I was unaware. (The Darkling Thrush) V18:74

And in the suburbs Can't sat down and cried. (Kilroy) V14:213

And it's been years. (Anniversary) V15:3

and leaving essence to the inner eye. (Memory) V21:156

And life for me ain't been no crystal stair (Mother to Son) V3:179

And like a thunderbolt he falls (The Eagle) V11:30

And makes me end where I begun (A Valediction: Forbidding Mourning) V11:202

And 'midst the stars inscribe Belinda's name. (The Rape of the Lock) V12:209

And miles to go before I sleep (Stopping by Woods on a Snowy Evening) V1:272

and my father saying things. (My Father's Song) V16:102

And no birds sing. (La Belle Dame sans Merci) V17:18

And not waving but drowning (Not Waving but Drowning) V3:216

And oh, 'tis true, 'tis true (When I Was One-and-Twenty) V4:268

And reach for your scalping knife. (For Jean Vincent D'abbadie, Baron St.-Castin) V12:78

and retreating, always retreating, behind it (Brazil, January 1, 1502) V6:16

And settled upon his eyes in a black soot ("More Light! More Light!") V6:120

And shuts his eyes. (Darwin in 1881) V13: 84

And so live ever—or else swoon to death (Bright Star! Would I Were Steadfast as Thou Art) V9:44

and strange and loud was the dingoes' cry (Drought Year) V8:78

and stride out. (Courage) V14:126

and sweat and fat and greed. (Anorexic) V12:3

And that has made all the difference (The Road Not Taken) V2:195

And the deep river ran on (As I Walked Out One Evening) V4:16

And the midnight message of Paul Revere (Paul Revere's Ride) V2:180

And the mome raths outgrabe (Jabberwocky) V11:91

And the Salvation Army singing God loves us. . . . (Hope is a Tattered Flag) V12:120

and these the last verses that I write for her (Tonight I Can Write) V11:187

and thickly wooded country; the moon. (The Art of the Novel) V23:29

And those roads in South Dakota that feel around in the darkness . . . (Come with Me) V6:31

and to know she will stay in the field till you die? (Landscape with Tractor) V10:183

and two blankets embroidered with smallpox (Meeting the British) V7:138

and waving, shouting, *Welcome back.* (Elegy for My Father, Who Is Not Dead) V14:154

And—which is more—you'll be a Man, my son! (If) V22:54–55

and whose skin is made dusky by stars. (September) V23:258–259

And would suffice (Fire and Ice) V7:57

And yet God has not said a word! (Porphyria's Lover) V15:151

and you spread un the thin halo of night mist. (Ways to Live) V16:229

And Zero at the Bone— (A Narrow Fellow in the Grass) V11:127

(answer with a tower of birds) (Duration) V18:93

Around us already perhaps future moons, suns and stars blaze in a fiery wreath. (But Perhaps God Needs the Longing) V20:41

As any She belied with false compare (Sonnet 130) V1:248

As ever in my great Task-Master's eye. (On His Having Arrived at the Age of Twenty-Three) V17:160

As far as Cho-fu-Sa (The River-Merchant's Wife: A Letter) V8:165

As the contagion of those molten eyes (For An Assyrian Frieze) V9:120

As they lean over the beans in their rented back room that is full of beads and receipts and dolls and clothes, tobacco crumbs, vases and fringes (The Bean Eaters) V2:16

aspired to become lighter than air (Blood Oranges) V13:34

at home in the fish's fallen heaven (Birch Canoe) V5:31

away, pedaling hard, rocket and pilot. (His Speed and Strength) V19:96

B

Back to the play of constant give and change (The Missing) V9:158

Before it was quite unsheathed from reality (Hurt Hawks) V3:138

before we're even able to name them. (Station) V21:226–227

Black like me. (Dream Variations) V15:42

Bless me (Hunger in New York City) V4:79

bombs scandalizing the sanctity of night. (While I Was Gone a War Began) V21:253–254

But, baby, where are you?" (Ballad of Birmingham) V5:17

But be (Ars Poetica) V5:3

but it works every time (Siren Song) V7:196

but the truth is, it is, lost to us now. (The Forest) V22:36–37

But there is no joy in Mudville—mighty Casey has "Struck Out." (Casey at the Bat) V5:58

But we hold our course, and the wind is with us. (On Freedom's Ground) V12:187

by good fortune (The Horizons of Rooms) V15:80

C

Calls through the valleys of Hall. (Song of the Chattahoochee) V14:284

chickens (The Red Wheelbarrow) V1:219

clear water dashes (Onomatopoeia) V6:133

come to life and burn? (Bidwell Ghost) V14:2

Comin' for to carry me home (Swing Low Sweet Chariot) V1:284

crossed the water. (All It Takes) V23:15

D

Dare frame thy fearful symmetry? (The Tyger) V2:263

"Dead," was all he answered (The Death of the Hired Man) V4:44

deep in the deepest one, tributaries burn. (For Jennifer, 6, on the Teton) V17:86

Delicate, delicate, delicate, delicate—now! (The Base Stealer) V12:30

Die soon (We Real Cool) V6:242

Do what you are going to do, I will tell about it. (I go Back to May 1937) V17:113

Down in the flood of remembrance, I weep like a child for the past (Piano) V6:145

Downward to darkness, on extended wings. (Sunday Morning) V16:190

Driving around, I will waste more time. (Driving to Town Late to Mail a Letter) V17:63

dry wells that fill so easily now (The Exhibit) V9:107

E

endless worlds is the great meeting of children. (60) V18:3

Eternal, unchanging creator of earth. Amen (The Seafarer)
V8:178

Eternity of your arms around my neck. (Death Sentences)
V22:23

every branch traced with the ghost writing of snow. (The
Afterlife) V18:39

F

fall upon us, the dwellers in shadow (In the Land of
Shinar) V7:84

Fallen cold and dead (O Captain! My Captain!) V2:147

filled, never. (The Greatest Grandeur) V18:119

Firewood, iron-ware, and cheap tin trays (Cargoes) V5:44

Fled is that music:—Do I wake or sleep? (Ode to a
Nightingale) V3:229

For I'm sick at the heart, and I fain wad lie down." (Lord
Randal) V6:105

For nothing now can ever come to any good. (Funeral
Blues) V10:139

forget me as fast as you can. (Last Request) V14:231

from one kiss (A Rebirth) V21:193–194

G

going where? Where? (Childhood) V19:29

H

Had anything been wrong, we should certainly have heard
(The Unknown Citizen) V3:303

Had somewhere to get to and sailed calmly on (Mus,e des
Beaux Arts) V1:148

half eaten by the moon. (Dear Reader) V10:85

hand over hungry hand. (Climbing) V14:113

Happen on a red tongue (Small Town with One Road)
V7:207

Has no more need of, and I have (The Courage that My
Mother Had) V3:80

Hath melted like snow in the glance of the Lord! (The
Destruction of Sennacherib) V1:39

He rose the morrow morn (The Rime of the Ancient
Mariner) V4:132

He says again, "Good fences make good neighbors."
(Mending Wall) V5:232

He writes down something that he crosses out. (The Boy)
V19:14

here; passion will save you. (Air for Mercury) V20:2–3

Has set me softly down beside you. The Poem is you
(Paradoxes and Oxymorons) V11:162

History theirs whose languages is the sun. (An Elementary
School Classroom in a Slum) V23:88–89

How at my sheet goes the same crooked worm (The Force
That Through the Green Fuse Drives the
Flower) V8:101

How can I turn from Africa and live? (A Far Cry from
Africa) V6:61

How sad then is even the marvelous! (An Africian Elegy)
V13:4

I

I am black. (The Song of the Smoke) V13:197

I am going to keep things like this (Hawk Roosting) V4:55

I am not brave at all (Strong Men, Riding Horses) V4:209

I could not see to see— (I Heard a Fly Buzz—When I
Died—) V5:140

I didn't want to put them down. (And What If I Spoke of
Despair) V19:2

I have just come down from my father (The Hospital
Window) V11:58

I cremated Sam McGee (The Cremation of Sam McGee)
V10:76

I hear it in the deep heart's core. (The Lake Isle of
Innisfree) V15:121

I never writ, nor no man ever loved (Sonnet 116) V3:288

I romp with joy in the bookish dark (Eating Poetry) V9:61

I see Mike's painting, called SARDINES (Why I Am Not
a Painter) V8:259

I shall but love thee better after death (Sonnet 43) V2:236

I should be glad of another death (Journey of the Magi)
V7:110

I stand up (Miss Rosie) V1:133

I stood there, fifteen (Fifteen) V2:78

I take it you are he? (Incident in a Rose Garden) V14:191

I turned aside and bowed my head and wept (The Tropics
in New York) V4:255

I'll be gone from here. (The Cobweb) V17:51

I'll dig with it (Digging) V5:71

If Winter comes, can Spring be far behind? (Ode to the
West Wind) V2:163

In a convulsive misery (The Milkfish Gatherers) V11:112

In balance with this life, this death (An Irish Airman
Foresees His Death) V1:76

in earth's gasp, ocean's yawn. (Lake) V23:158

In Flanders fields (In Flanders Fields) V5:155

In ghostlier demarcations, keener sounds. (The Idea of
Order at Key West) V13:164

In hearts at peace, under an English heaven (The Soldier)
V7:218

In her tomb by the side of the sea (Annabel Lee) V9:14

in the family of things. (Wild Geese) V15:208

in the grit gray light of day. (Daylights) V13:102

In the rear-view mirrors of the passing cars (The War
Against the Trees) V11:216

In these Chicago avenues. (A Thirst Against) V20:205

in this bastion of culture. (To an Unknown Poet) V18:221

iness (l(a) V1:85

Into blossom (A Blessing) V7:24

Is Come, my love is come to me. (A Birthday) V10:34

is love—that's all. (Two Poems for T.) V20:218

is safe is what you said. (Practice) V23:240

is still warm (Lament for the Dorsets) V5:191

It asked a crumb—of Me (Hope Is the Thing with
Feathers) V3:123

It is our god. (Fiddler Crab) V23:111–112

it is the bell to awaken God that we've heard ringing.
(The Garden Shukkei-en) V18:107

It rains as I write this. Mad heart, be brave. (The Country
Without a Post Office) V18:64

It was your resting place." (Ah, Are You Digging on My
Grave?) V4:2

it's always ourselves we find in the sea (maggie & milly
& molly & may) V12:150

its bright, unequivocal eye. (Having it Out with
Melancholy) V17:99

It's the fall through wind lifting white leaves. (Rapture)
V21:181

its youth. The sea grows old in it. (The Fish) V14:172

J

Judge tenderly—of Me (This Is My Letter to the World)
V4:233

Just imagine it (Inventors) V7:97

L

Laughing the stormy, husky, brawling laughter of Youth,
half-naked, sweating, proud to be Hog Butcher,
Tool Maker, Stacker of Wheat, Player with
Railroads and Freight Handler to the Nation
(Chicago) V3:61

Learn to labor and to wait (A Psalm of Life) V7:165

Leashed in my throat (Midnight) V2:131

Let my people go (Go Down, Moses) V11:43

life, our life and its forgetting. (For a New Citizen of
These United States) V15:55

Like Stone— (The Soul Selects Her Own Society) V1:259

Little Lamb, God bless thee. (The Lamb) V12:135

Look'd up in perfect silence at the stars. (When I Heard
the Learn'd Astronomer) V22:244

love (The Toni Morrison Dreams) V22:202–203

M

'Make a wish, Tom, make a wish.' (Drifters) V10: 98

make it seem to change (The Moon Glows the Same)
V7:152

midnight-oiled in the metric laws? (A Farewell to English)
V10:126

Monkey business (Business) V16:2

More dear, both for themselves and for thy sake! (Tintern
Abbey) V2:250

My love shall in my verse ever live young (Sonnet 19)
V9:211

My soul has grown deep like the rivers. (The Negro
Speaks of Rivers) V10:198

N

never to waken in that world again (Starlight) V8:213

Nirvana is here, nine times out of ten. (Spring-Watching
Pavilion) V18:198

No, she's brushing a boy's hair (Facing It) V5:110

no—tell them *no*— (The Hiding Place) V10:153

Noble six hundred! (The Charge of the Light Brigade)
V1:3

nobody,not even the rain,has such small hands
(somewhere i have never travelled,gladly
beyond) V19:265

Not even the blisters. Look. (What Belongs to Us) V15:196

Not of itself, but thee. (Song: To Celia) V23:270–271

Nothing gold can stay (Nothing Gold Can Stay) V3:203

Nothing, and is nowhere, and is endless (High Windows)
V3:108

Now! (Alabama Centennial) V10:2

nursing the tough skin of figs (This Life) V1:293

O

O Death in Life, the days that are no more! (Tears, Idle
Tears) V4:220

O Lord our Lord, how excellent is thy name in all the
earth! (Psalm 8) V9:182

O Roger, Mackerel, Riley, Ned, Nellie, Chester, Lady
Ghost (Names of Horses) V8:142

Of all our joys, this must be the deepest. (Drinking Alone
Beneath the Moon) V20:59–60

of gentleness (To a Sad Daughter) V8:231

of love's austere and lonely offices? (Those Winter
Sundays) V1:300

of peaches (The Weight of Sweetness) V11:230

Of the camellia (Falling Upon Earth) V2:64

Of the Creator. And he waits for the world to begin
(Leviathan) V5:204

Of what is past, or passing, or to come (Sailing to
Byzantium) V2:207

Old Ryan, not yours (The Constellation Orion) V8:53

On the dark distant flurry (Angle of Geese) V2:2

On the look of Death— (There's a Certain Slant of Light)
V6:212

On your head like a crown (Any Human to Another) V3:2

One could do worse that be a swinger of birches.
(Birches) V13:15

Or does it explode? (Harlem) V1:63

Or help to half-a-crown." (The Man He Killed) V3:167

or last time, we look. (In Particular) V20:125

or nothing (Queen-Ann's-Lace) V6:179

or the one red leaf the snow releases in March. (Three
Times My Life Has Opened) V16:213

ORANGE forever. (Ballad of Orange and Grape) V10:18

our every corpuscle become an elf. (Moreover, the Moon)
V20:153

outside. (it was New York and beautifully, snowing . . .
(i was sitting in mcsorley's) V13:152

owing old (old age sticks) V3:246

P

patient in mind remembers the time. (Fading Light)
V21:49

Perhaps he will fall. (Wilderness Gothic) V12:242

Petals on a wet, black bough (In a Station of the Metro)
V2:116

Plaiting a dark red love-knot into her long black hair
(The Highwayman) V4:68

Powerless, I drown. (Maternity) V21:142–143

Pro patria mori. (Dulce et Decorum Est) V10:110

R

Rage, rage against the dying of the light (Do Not Go
Gentle into that Good Night) V1:51

Raise it again, man. We still believe what we hear. (The
Singer's House) V17:206

Remember the Giver fading off the lip (A Drink of Water)
V8:66

rise & walk away like a panther. (Ode to a Drum)
V20:172–173

Rises toward her day after day, like a terrible fish (Mirror)
V1:116

S

Shall be lifted—nevermore! (The Raven) V1:202

Shantih shantih shantih (The Waste Land) V20:248–252

Shuddering with rain, coming down around me. (Omen) v22:107

Simply melted into the perfect light. (Perfect Light) V19:187

Singing of him what they could understand (Beowulf) V11:3

Singing with open mouths their strong melodious songs (I Hear America Singing) V3:152

slides by on grease (For the Union Dead) V7:67

Slouches towards Bethlehem to be born? (The Second Coming) V7:179

So long lives this, and this gives life to thee (Sonnet 18) V2:222

So prick my skin. (Pine) V23:223–224

Somebody loves us all. (Filling Station) V12:57

spill darker kissmarks on that dark. (Ten Years after Your Deliberate Drowning) V21:240

Stand still, yet we will make him run (To His Coy Mistress) V5:277

startled into eternity (Four Mountain Wolves) V9:132

Still clinging to your shirt (My Papa's Waltz) V3:192

Stood up, coiled above his head, transforming all. (A Tall Man Executes a Jig) V12:229

Surely goodness and mercy shall follow me all the days of my life: and I will dwell in the house of the Lord for ever (Psalm 23) V4:103

syllables of an old order. (A Grafted Tongue) V12:93

T

Take any streetful of people buying clothes and groceries, cheering a hero or throwing confetti and blowing tin horns . . . tell me if the lovers are losers . . . tell me if any get more than the lovers . . . in the dust . . . in the cool tombs (Cool Tombs) V6:46

Than from everything else life promised that you could do? (Paradiso) V20:190–191

Than that you should remember and be sad. (Remember) V14:255

That then I scorn to change my state with Kings (Sonnet 29) V8:198

That when we live no more, we may live ever (To My Dear and Loving Husband) V6:228

That's the word. (Black Zodiac) V10:47

the bigger it gets. (Smart and Final Iris) V15:183

The bosom of his Father and his God (Elegy Written in a Country Churchyard) V9:74

The crime was in Granada, his Granada. (The Crime Was in Granada) V23:55–56

The dance is sure (Overture to a Dance of Locomotives) V11:143

The eyes turn topaz. (Hugh Selwyn Mauberley) V16:30

The garland briefer than a girl's (To an Athlete Dying Young) V7:230

The guidon flags flutter gayly in the wind. (Cavalry Crossing a Ford) V13:50

The hands gripped hard on the desert (At the Bomb Testing Site) V8:3

The holy melodies of love arise. (The Arsenal at Springfield) V17:3

the knife at the throat, the death in the metronome (Music Lessons) V8:117

The Lady of Shalott." (The Lady of Shalott) V15:97

The lightning and the gale! (Old Ironsides) V9:172

the long, perfect loveliness of sow (Saint Francis and the Sow) V9:222

The Lord survives the rainbow of His will (The Quaker Graveyard in Nantucket) V6:159

The man I was when I was part of it (Beware of Ruins) V8:43

the quilts sing on (My Mother Pieced Quilts) V12:169

The red rose and the brier (Barbara Allan) V7:11

The self-same Power that brought me there brought you. (The Rhodora) V17:191

The shaft we raise to them and thee (Concord Hymn) V4:30

The sky became a still and woven blue. (Merlin Enthralled) V16:73

The spirit of this place (To a Child Running With Out-stretched Arms in Canyon de Chelly) V11:173

The town again, trailing your legs and crying! (Wild Swans) V17:221

the unremitting space of your rebellion (Lost Sister) V5:217

The woman won (Oysters) V4:91

their guts or their brains? (Southbound on the Freeway) V16:158

There is the trap that catches noblest spiritts, that caught—they say—God, when he walked on earth (Shine, Perishing Republic) V4:162

there was light (Vancouver Lights) V8:246

They also serve who only stand and wait." ([On His Blindness] Sonnet 16) V3:262

They are going to some point true and unproven. (Geometry) V15:68

They rise, they walk again (The Heaven of Animals) V6:76

They think I lost. I think I won (Harlem Hopscotch) V2:93

This is my page for English B (Theme for English B) V6:194

This Love (In Memory of Radio) V9:145

Tho' it were ten thousand mile! (A Red, Red Rose) V8:152

Though I sang in my chains like the sea (Fern Hill) V3:92

Till human voices wake us, and we drown (The Love Song of J. Alfred Prufrock) V1:99

Till Love and Fame to nothingness do sink (When I Have Fears that I May Cease to Be) V2:295

To every woman a happy ending (Barbie Doll) V9:33

to glow at midnight. (The Blue Rim of Memory) V17:39

to its owner or what horror has befallen the other shoe (A Pied) V3:16

To live with thee and be thy love. (The Nymph's Reply to the Shepherd) V14:241

To strive, to seek, to find, and not to yield (Ulysses) V2:279

To the moaning and the groaning of the bells (The Bells) V3:47

To the temple, singing. (In the Suburbs) V14:201

U

Undeniable selves, into your days, and beyond. (The Continuous Life) V18:51

until at last I lift you up and wrap you within me. (It's like This) V23:138–139

Until Eternity. (The Bustle in a House) V10:62

unusual conservation (Chocolates) V11:17

Uttering cries that are almost human (American Poetry)
        V7:2

W

War is kind (War Is Kind) V9:253

watching to see how it's done. (I Stop Writing the Poem)
        V16:58

Went home and put a bullet through his head (Richard
        Cory) V4:117

Were not the one dead, turned to their affairs. (Out,
        Out—) V10:213

Were toward Eternity— (Because I Could Not Stop for
        Death) V2:27

What will survive of us is love. (An Arundel Tomb)
        V12:18

When I died they washed me out of the turret with a
        hose (The Death of the Ball Turret Gunner)
        V2:41

when they untie them in the evening. (Early in the
        Morning) V17:75

when you are at a party. (Social Life) V19:251

When you have both (Toads) V4:244

Where deep in the night I hear a voice (Butcher Shop)
        V7:43

Where ignorant armies clash by night (Dover Beach)
        V2:52

Which Claus of Innsbruck cast in bronze for me! (My
        Last Duchess) V1:166

Which for all you know is the life you've chosen. (The
        God Who Loves You) V20:88

which is not going to go wasted on me which is why I'm
        telling you about it (Having a Coke with You)
        V12:106

which only looks like an *l*, and is silent. (Trompe l'Oeil)
        V22:216

white ash amid funereal cypresses (Helen) V6:92

Who are you and what is your purpose? (The Mystery)
        V15:138

Wi' the Scots lords at his feit (Sir Patrick Spens) V4:177

Will always be ready to bless the day (Morning Walk)
        V21:167

will be easy, my rancor less bitter . . . (On the Threshold)
        V22:128

Will hear of as a god." (How we Heard the Name)
        V10:167

Wind, like the dodo's (Bedtime Story) V8:33

With gold unfading, WASHINGTON! be thine. (To His
        Excellency General Washington) V13:213

with my eyes closed. (We Live by What We See at Night)
        V13:240

With the slow smokeless burning of decay (The Wood-
        Pile) V6:252

With what they had to go on. (The Conquerors) V13:67

Without cease or doubt sew the sweet sad earth. (The
        Satyr's Heart) V22:187

Would scarcely know that we were gone. (There Will
        Come Soft Rains) V14:301

Y

Ye know on earth, and all ye need to know (Ode on a
        Grecian Urn) V1:180

You live in this, and dwell in lovers' eyes (Sonnet 55)
        V5:246

You may for ever tarry. (To the Virgins, to Make Much
        of Time) V13:226

you who raised me? (The Gold Lily) V5:127

you'll have understood by then what these Ithakas mean.
        (Ithaka) V19:114